ILLINOIS CENTRAL COLLEGE
PN6112.R47 1962
STACKS
Modern drama, nine plays.

A12900 305319

W9-BYQ-284

15101

PN
6112   REINERT
.R47   Modern drama
1962

Illinois Central College
Learning Resource Center

MODERN DRAMA

Nine Plays

Edited by

OTTO REINERT
University of Oslo

BOSTON
Little, Brown and Company
TORONTO

Illinois Central College
Learning Resouce Center

15101

COPYRIGHT © 1961, 1962, LITTLE, BROWN AND COMPANY (INC.)

ALL RIGHTS RESERVED. NO PART OF THIS BOOK
MAY BE REPRODUCED IN ANY FORM WITHOUT
PERMISSION IN WRITING FROM THE PUBLISHER.

LIBRARY OF CONGRESS CATALOG CARD NO. 62-12334

PN
6112
.R47
1962

SIXTH PRINTING

Published simultaneously in Canada
by Little, Brown & Company (Canada) Limited

PRINTED IN THE UNITED STATES OF AMERICA

PREFACE

MY AIM has been to provide a reasonably small, balanced volume that samples the main modes of modern drama without sacrificing literary excellence to representativeness. The general introduction sketches a theory of drama, discusses some features of *modern* drama, and defines some technical terms. The comments that appear with the individual plays are meant to stimulate, not to close minds. Certainly, all the plays are big enough to exercise more than one critic and reward more than one approach.

Seven of these plays appeared in my earlier volume, *Drama: An Introductory Anthology*; in fact, the present collection was largely suggested by reader reactions to that work. The introduction, the comments appended to each play, and the appendix containing biographical notes and suggestions for further reading follow the same pattern as that of the earlier collection. I again hope that this approach will provide the kind of guidance teachers want, and in the right amount.

O.R.
Oslo

CONTENTS

INTRODUCTION

A Definition of Drama

Drama, like poetry and fiction, is an art of words — mainly words of dialogue. People talking is the basic dramatic situation. The talk may be interrupted by wordless activity — sword-play, love-making — but such activity will derive its significance from its context of dialogue. If not, we are dealing with pantomime and not with drama.

A performance of drama is more than just an art of words, of course. It is the joint product of many arts, such as acting, directing, and stage designing. But the performance is no more the drama than the concert is the symphony. A play is a potential but never-to-be-realized performance, inherent in the configuration of the playwright's words, independent of the artists of the theater whom it keeps challenging to produce performed drama.

Drama is distinguished from the other forms of literature by performability and by the objectivity that performability implies. The statement "She is a woman without hope" is, as stage direction, undramatic. It could become a speech by one of the characters, or it could inspire an actress to perform an electrifying gesture of fluttering futility. But as stage direction it is novelistic rather than dramatic. It does not denote anything actable, and it violates the objectivity that is a condition for the playwright's craft: the tacit agreement between him and us that for the duration of the make-believe he does not exist at all, that the characters can be known only by what they reveal of themselves in speech and action. The play must tell itself; the characters must speak for themselves. Even the play that by design expresses the playwright's inmost self can reach us only as a piece of objective, external reality, a dynamic spectacle of speakers, among whom a self-projection of the playwright's has no separate esthetic status.

Plays and movies based on novels prove there is much that is performable in the other genres of literature as well. But the art of poet and novelist extends beyond dialogue and description of stageables. A novelist can suspend action indefinitely and discourse abstractly on any subject. He can judge and analyze human souls and, omniscient, enter into them at will. He can address his reader directly. And if he never makes use of these novelistic freedoms, he is, in effect, a dramatist, whether he calls his work a play or not.

Actually, this is a stricter definition of drama than many plays allow. Bernard Shaw, for example, often violates dramatic objectivity in stage directions that interpret his characters. The most flagrant example is perhaps the ending of *Candida*. When the heroine has sent her would-be lover, a young poet, "into the night" and turns to her husband, Shaw tells us, "They embrace. But they do not know the secret in the poet's heart." No amount of theatrical ingenuity can stage that last sentence. The point is not that Shaw's plays sometimes include bits of novels; we are concerned here with determining the quality that all plays have in common — the quality that makes them, distinctly, *drama*. Performability is that quality. The spectator is in the theater to watch and listen. Shaw's comments do not exist for him, except insofar as they may have been translated into the language of the theater: sights and sounds the audience can perceive, directly through the senses in the physical theater, imaginatively in the theater in the mind.

This is not to exclude from the genre of drama works that cannot, for technical reasons, be staged in any existing theater or which, if staged, would overtax the patience and subtlety of an audience. Not only are such pragmatic criteria obviously relative, there is also a sense in which dramatic poems like *Samson Agonistes* and *Prometheus Unbound*, though not intended for the stage and in some respects unperformable (if only by being bad box-office), are superbly dramatic. That is, their form is a system of speaking parts developing a coherent and complete action. Whatever abstracts they entail are expressed in speech, and speech is performable by impersonators of the fictitious speakers.

The mode of drama is the objectivity of the performable. Movement, directness, concreteness are its characteristics. The dramatic experience, whether in the theater or over a printed play, is one of urgent immediacy, of watching and listening to human destinies in the making, here and now, which the novelist or poet can duplicate only by being, precisely, dramatic.

Drama and the Reader

From such a definition it follows that the skillful reader of plays supplies vivid and relevant images to the dialogue, whether such images are suggested to him directly by speeches and stage directions or he translates what is unstageable in the printed play into concretes that participate in the total, complex image — words, movement, scene — of the drama being enacted in his mind.

Basic to any kind of meaningful response to literature is understanding of the author's words in context and of the underlying conditions for action in the imagined world. "Understanding" depends on more than conscientious use of footnotes and dictionary; it entails a total response: intellectual, emotional, sensory. And though all readers cannot respond equally well, they can all make the effort to engage more than the top of their minds and the shallows of their souls. Generally, in the case of plays from ages and cultures different from our own, *some* awareness of cultural background will be imperative, and *more* desirable, but the line between some and more is hard to draw in given cases. For some readers, at least, certain plays will create their own climate of understanding.

Perhaps the ideal performance of the play, the standard by which both a theatrical production and a reading of it should be judged, will be thought of as the performance the playwright himself envisioned for his play. But this is neither a practicable nor even a really reasonable formula. There are playwrights who have left no record as to how they thought their plays should be produced, or whose ideas are too vague or incomplete to be of much help, or who refuse to answer when asked. And even if we assume that the original staging realized the playwright's ideal, for most older plays we can reconstruct it only by means of more or less inferential evidence, either within the play itself or supplied by research. Nor are the playwright's views, when available, necessarily more valid than someone else's — just as composers are not necessarily the best performers of their own works or even the best critics of the performance of their works by others. Intention is not accomplishment.

There is more force to the argument that a meaningful reading of a play requires knowledge of the kind of theater for which it was written. To read Sophocles or Shakespeare, the argument goes, we must know something about Greek and Elizabethan stagecraft, see productions that try to reproduce the contemporary performance, see models or pictures or diagrams of the playhouses, or at the very least read descriptions of them.

It is certainly true that the more knowledge the reader has of the culture — including the theatrical culture — reflected in what he reads, the more significant and enjoyable his reading will be. And the impossibility of ever knowing everything about a play and the fact that knowledge alone is insufficient for recreating the sense impressions, the beliefs, attitudes, and moods of a bygone audience cannot invalidate the efforts of historians of drama and theater to know as much as possible. Though each culture, each age, each reader, even the same reader at different times, reads a literary work differently, knowledge of what can be factually known about it and its times is a protection against an anarchic subjectivity of interpretation that could eventually destroy its continuum of identity. This is part of the justification of scholarship.

But though knowledge of theatrical conditions, past or present, can discipline and enrich one's experience of a play, and though such knowledge is valuable for its own sake, it is still not a precondition for the dramatic imagination itself. The images that arise in the mind during the reading of drama can be translated into stage actualities, but they are not images of such actualities. The reader does not ordinarily imagine a staged scene but its real life counterpart — not a stage castle, crypt, or kitchen, but the real thing. The exceptions are the director, designer, or actor who read with a projected performance in mind and — and he is the one who concerns us — the reader who comes to his reading of the play fresh from an impressive performance of it. His reading experience will no doubt be more vivid than it otherwise would have been, but it will also be more limited. His imagination will be channeled by his memory of the hundreds of big and little details of voice and mimicry, movement and set, costume and light, that together make up any particular actualization of the ideal abstract the play is. Any one performance, however brilliant, is bound to be different from — both more and less than — the literary work that occasioned it, forever detached as the latter is from the impermanent particulars of the real. A good production may help a reader imagine what he found unimaginable as he read the play, or it may cool and contain an imagination that catches fire too easily, but a reader to whom a play is nothing but a blueprint for an evening in the theater has abdicated his rights as reader. It is only because most people *can* stage a play in their imagination, alive with the sights and sounds of reality, that drama is literature at all — that is, capable of being experienced through reading. The theater is the home of drama, and drama may be the occasion for theater, but all theater is not drama, nor is the drama lost without the theater.

Dramatic Conventions

Understanding the underlying conditions for action in the imagined world involves understanding dramatic conventions — the conditions which playwright and audience between them have implicitly (whether they are conscious of it or not) agreed to accept as reality in the play. In the sense that what is called for is a willingness to take the world of imagination as reality for the time being, acceptance of conventions enters into any kind of successful artistic experience. But because the theater makes tangible the forms of the make-believe, conventions operate with particular force in the experience of drama — most insistently in the theater, but also in reading.

Chorus, soliloquy, and aside are examples of conventions, mainly of older drama. They were no more everyday realities then than they are now, but as artistic devices they were given status as reality because they satisfied needs for dramatic expression without going beyond what the contemporary public was willing to tolerate as make-believe. Some conventions may have been means to achieve certain kinds of communication under the technically limiting conditions of older theater. For example, such "facts" of the imagined world as location and time of day, which in the modern theater can be established by sets and electric lights, were on the Elizabethan stage communicated by the dialogue itself. Hence the rather remarkable number of Shakespearean characters who mention time and place in their speeches, particularly in the opening of scenes. To the extent that such information is for the benefit of the audience rather than for the listeners on stage, the device is conventional: a breach of reality for the sake of establishing, economically and often beautifully, "reality" within the play.

Conventions vary with time and place. Yesterday's conventions are today's absurdities and tomorrow's brilliant innovations. No play is without them. If a modern reader finds older drama "quaint" and "unrealistic," it may be because he takes the conventions of realism too much for granted, automatically regards them as authentically life-like, since most of the drama he meets in today's mass media is realistic. Or if he is sophisticated enough to recognize the conventions of realism and the necessity for them, he may still feel they are the only "natural" conventions. But if he objects to the artificiality of the neoclassical convention of the three unities (which demanded that the action of the play be confined to a single plot, a single place, and a single day), he ought also to object to the convention of today's film and television that presents human beings as disembodied heads in facial close-ups and to the three-walled rooms of most post-Renaissance theater. And there is no reason to believe that playgoers of the past would have found a modern theater, with its artificially lighted box peeked into by a supposedly nonexistent audience, any less unnatural than we presume to find the choric rituals and public unburdenings of soul in soliloquy in their plays. If the naïve or stubbornly literal-minded is bothered by the hero's apparent deafness to the villain's stage whisper, by the scarcity of actors on stage during Shakespeare's battle scenes,

or by the free and flexible treatment of time and place in a contemporary play like *The Glass Menagerie*, he simply fails to understand
or accept dramatic convention.

Action, Plot, Conflict

Like most serious writing, drama represents man's use of words to
make sense out of the myriad perplexities that befall him. The dramatist sees the world not primarily as shapes and colors and feelings, or as
an object for religious or philosophical or scientific contemplation, or
as a market, or as a reluctant machine that challenges his skill and ingenuity to make it run better. He sees it rather as an arena for human
action manifested in speech.

The newcomer to the reading of drama may at first find confusing
the conversations of unknowns, surprised in the embroilments with a
life of which he knows nothing. He may miss preliminary explanations,
the novelist's guiding hand. And if he has had experience with performed drama, he may also miss the aid to understanding provided by
the presences and the voices of actors and by the physical spectacle in
which they appear. That he can be guided by stage directions and
ponder the dialogue at his leisure he may feel to be poor compensation
for the absence of the sights and sounds of performance.

What the characters say and do begins to make sense only as we
learn more about them, but we learn more about them only by what
they say and do. Gradually they become more than a list of names.
They reveal their antecedents and their present situations, their motives and purposes, they assume plot identity and "character." We
learn to respond to the revealing remark or gesture, to listen to the
eloquence of their silence, to sense their continuous pressure on the
plot. Among them, they define and develop the dramatic action.

Dramatic action is neither physical activity nor simply the sum of
everything that happens on stage: conversation, eating, people running
up and down staircases, laughter, doors closing, lights going on. These
are part of the action, but in the traditional (mainly Aristotelian)
definition action itself is a more comprehensive concept. A set of defini-
tions may be useful at this point.

A play is a patterning of language, character, event, and spectacle,
each element a function of the other three. Its plot is the particular
sequence of events that gives it the coherence and movement toward a
given end that could not inhere in a random aggregate of happenings.
Plot is the way the playwright has chosen to tell his story, the detailed
arrangement of incidents for maximum meaning, beauty, and suspense.
The action of the play is both the summation of the plot and the ab-

straction of its meaning, the distillation of the play's totality, the answer, in a single phrase, to the question, "What happens?" We call tragic the action that ends by exacting suffering or death from the protagonist as the price at which we (and perhaps he) are brought to new or heightened awareness of man's being and his relation to the ultimate moral or metaphysical issues in life. We call comic the action that concerns man in his mundane or social relationships, exposes vice and folly for contempt and laughter, and ends by vindicating reason, moderation, good-will, love, virtue, or other sane and normal human values. Tragedy's domain is the infinite, its characteristic subject matter the mystery of evil and suffering. Comedy's domain is the finite, its characteristic subject matter man's triumphs and tribulations as gregarious animal.

Formally, most plots are divisible into four parts. (1) The exposition, which gives essential information about the characters' backgrounds and sets the plot in motion. (2) The complication, usually the bulk of the play, interweaving the characters' shifting fortunes and including the climax, a point of high tension and the critical juncture at which a decision or an event irretrievably determines the result of the action. (3) The reversal, or peripety, the point at which the complication culminates in the resolution of the plot: the protagonist's fortune changing from good to bad (tragedy) or from bad to good (comedy). (4) The dénouement or unraveling, which presents the consequences of the reversal, ties up loose ends, and allows the audience to regain emotional equilibrium. The plays in which the four parts of the plot are neatly distinct and laid end to end are few and not likely to be of the highest order. Much more commonly, plot is a complex, organic structure, whose parts blend into one another and overlap or alternate. To use the terms mechanically in dramatic analysis will almost certainly end in critical disaster. It is also true that this whole paradigm of formal analysis applies only partly, or insignificantly, or even not at all, to some modern plays. *The Ghost Sonata* hardly lends itself to this kind of traditional analysis, and though *The Lesson* is a more coherent play than Strindberg's it would be difficult to isolate its exposition or sharply distinguish its climax from its peripety. Nevertheless, the apparatus of formal analysis is still sufficiently relevant to a sufficient number of modern plays and modes of plays to make it worthwhile to try to apply our terms, by way of illustration, to *The Wild Duck*.

The *story* of the play is the entire chronicle of the interlocking fortunes of the Ekdal and Werle families, beginning with Hjalmar's and Gregers' boyhood and youth (only glimpsed and hinted at in the play), Werle's philandering, his wife's jealousy and drinking, and the shady forest deal that eventually ruined Old Ekdal. The *plot* is the causally connected sequence of events that gradually reveals the significance of the past. The *action* is the enlightenment of Hjalmar, for that enlightenment is what motivates Gregers' moves, and the action is over when the enlightenment is complete — ironically so — the moment Hedvig's suicide proves to Hjalmar her love for him. In most plays the *exposition* is over early, but though in *The Wild Duck* it begins in the very first speech in Act I, it may be said to continue, intermittently, to the point near the end of Act IV when Hjalmar realizes (or *thinks* he realizes, for the possibility that he is Hedvig's real father after all is never categorically ruled out and thus constitutes another one of the play's many ironies) that Hedvig is not his child. It follows that the exposition and the *complication* overlap — in fact, the complication may be defined as the conflict between Gregers' efforts to further the revelation of the past (*i.e.*, the exposition) and Relling's and Gina's efforts to prevent it. Act I is almost all exposition — the gossip between the two servants, the conversations between Gregers and Hjalmar and between Gregers and Werle — but its conclusion, Gregers' announcement that he has a "mission" to fulfill, looks forward to the complication, which begins in Act II with Gregers' arrival at the Ekdals'. Henceforth, the Ekdal household is both troubled and divided, as the exposition-complication continues. The play's *climax* is the moment at the end of Act III when Hjalmar accepts Gregers's invitation to go for a walk and thus dooms himself to learn "the truth." The *reversal* is double. There is first the scene in which Gregers interprets the shot in the attic for Hjalmar and the latter as a result decides once again to give Hedvig his love. Then there is his discovery a few moments later that the proof of her deserving his love is her suicide. Within seconds Hjalmar moves from disillusionment and cynicism through joy to sorrow. The *dénouement* is what follows Relling's pronouncement that Hedvig is dead: Molvik's drunken and fragmentary burial service, Hjalmar's and Gina's reactions, and Gregers's and Relling's final comments.

Plot generates and releases suspense — the feeling in the audience that keeps it wondering what happens next. One charactristic of great drama is that its suspense survives knowledge of "how things come out," because our absorbed wait for what is going to happen concerns the outcome less than it concerns the happenings themselves. We may know exactly what happens in *The Wild Duck* and still attend, fascinated, half moved, half amused, to every small step in the developing tragicomedy. In fact, superior plays have a way of seeming better in later readings. What we lose in mere thrill we gain in understanding and enjoyment through our intimacy with the characters and our knowledge of events to come. Familiarity also increases our appreciation and enjoyment of dramaturgy: the exercise of the playwright's craft, the manipulation of plot and character in the integrated structure of successful dramatic action. As the football fan goes to the game not just to learn who wins but to enjoy the game being played, so the lover of drama seeks vicarious experience of significant action in artistic form — not just information about a result.

Conflict is the element in plot that creates suspense; it is what the plot is about. In *The Wild Duck* the conflict may be variously defined — perhaps most simply as idealism (Gregers) against realism (Relling) with Hjalmar as the bone of contention between them. Or we may sense the conflict chiefly as irony: the distance between what Gregers *thinks* his purpose — to re-establish the Ekdal marriage on a foundation of truth — will accomplish both for the Ekdals (true happiness) and for himself (a degree of expiation of his father's guilt) and what it actually *does* accomplish: bereavement for the Ekdals (ironically involving new lies for Hjalmar to live on) and complete futility for himself. Or the conflict may be felt to inhere in the bitter or cynical wisdom that contrasts the saving lie with the destructive truth.

Double or multiple conflict need not be a symptom of structural weakness. The several conflicts — or even, as in some of Shakespeare's plays, the different plots — may appear as different facets of a many-sided subject, each presenting it in a new view. A wider definition of the play's issue may subsume them all. For example, in Chekhov's *Three Sisters* most of the characters are kept from achieving happiness and self-fulfillment by some obstacle or other — some quality in themselves, other people, circumstances. These various conflicts cohere in a complex but single image of the passion of frustration, of the clash of aspiration with reality.

Conflict is opposition of forces, of whatever kind: man versus mountain, man versus God, man versus himself. It may be as simple as that of a fairy tale (bad queen versus good princess, bad guy versus good sheriff). It may be as elemental as that of *The Ghost Sonata*, as preposterous as that of *The Lesson*, as commonplace and tenuous as that of *The Glass Menagerie*, as dialectical and ambiguous as that of *The Wild Duck*, as grimly ethical as that of *Purgatory*, as nearly farcical as that of *Arms and the Man*, as metaphysical as that of two such different plays as *Six Characters in Search of an Author* and *The Good Woman of Setzuan*. Drama without conflict is unthinkable. For the essence of the dramatic experience is the fascination with the progress of clashing forces toward resolution: the hero's death or triumph, the villain's defeat, the wedding, the re-establishment of order in a private, a communal, or a universal cosmos.

The spoken word is the medium of drama, the objectivity of the performable its mode or manner of being, the surrender of our imagination to that of the playwright the condition for its existence for us, but the drama itself is the action of human conflict. This action we witness partly as safe and superior deities, enjoying the pleasure of dramatic irony at the expense of people who do not know what is happening to them; partly as sympathetic observers, commiserating with the good, relishing the downfall of the bad; and partly as fellow fools and sufferers: there but for the grace of God go we.

Some Notes on the History of Modern Drama

The reasons why certain periods excel in certain forms of literature rather than in others involve too many incalculables of individual talent and experience and of collective temper of the times to be confidently set down. A brief account of modern drama can only record the fact that during most of the eighteenth and nineteenth centuries in the Western world literary imagination of high order tended to express itself in lyrics and novels rather than in actable plays. There were exceptions — the comedies of Holberg and Goldsmith and Sheridan, Goethe's and Schiller's romantic dramas of storm and stress — but the exceptions only set off the surrounding gloom. The period was one of great performers, from Garrick to Bernhardt; of smaller, more numerous theaters and growing audiences; and of the introduction of footlights, box sets, and historical accuracy in costume and setting. It is important in the history of the theater. But original, serious playmaking was largely limited to closet plays in verse (among them Goethe's *Faust*, Byron's *Manfred*, Shelley's *Prometheus Unbound*, perhaps Ibsen's *Brand* and *Peer Gynt*, and a series of turgid imitations of Shakespeare), Gothic melodrama of rant and spectacle, and craftsmanlike but empty intriguery.

Ibsen's European success (or notoriety) with naturalistic[1] plays

1 As few writers on modern drama fail to point out, "naturalism" and "realism" are troublesome terms. "Naturalism" commonly connotes philosophical determinism and, as a literary term, a program, based on determinism, of depicting human life, with as much scientific objectivity and accuracy as possible, as conditioned by heredity and environment. "Realism" is usually a more general term, denoting representationalism in any art. As a literary term it is independent of genres and periods. Both terms have occasionally been appropriated for that branch of late nineteenth-century literature that dealt primarily with the sordid and the vicious in lower-class life. I use "naturalism" for the Ibsen-Chekhov tradition in modern drama. For my purposes "naturalism" and "realism" are roughly synonymous, but except in a few cases where I think the usage justifies itself I have preferred the more specific term in order not to divorce my key term altogether from the idea of determinism that is implicit in Ibsen as well as in Zola — though, of course, in a far less extreme and dogmatic form.

about 1880 is usually taken to mark the beginning of modern drama. Like all such divisions this too involves a degree of arbitrariness. For if naturalism is defined as the faithful representation in action, dialogue, and setting of the social, psychological, and moral conditions of ordinary life, then there were naturalistic plays before 1880: Büchner's *Woyzeck* (1836), Hebbel's *Maria Magdalena* (1844), Turgenev's *A Month in the Country* (1850) — and non-naturalistic plays not very long after: Rostand's *Cyrano de Bergerac* (1897), Yeats' *Kathleen ni Houlihan* (1902), Maeterlinck's *Pelléas and Mélisande* (1903). Ibsen is "the father of modern drama" in the sense that he was the first to bring dramatic genius to bear upon realistic material and form at a time when the public was ready at least to go to see naturalism in the theater, if not yet to be very comfortable with it as art or ideology. But Ibsen did not invent naturalism either in theory or in practice. He was not even a consistent practitioner of naturalism. Many of his plots are constructed on the model of Eugene Scribe's well-made carpentry of coincidence and intrigue, and not all his plays, even after the 1880's, can be called naturalistic except in externals. Nevertheless, the triumph of naturalism and the subsequent modifications of it, departures from it, and reactions against it, both literary and theatrical, are in essence the story of drama during the last eighty years. And only in this view does an apparently chaotic development assume a semblance of order.

What has by now become a commonplace in histories of modern drama is perfectly true: *it is not any one thing.* One can make certain valid generalizations about different plays and playwrights within the major eras of earlier drama: Marlowe, Shakespeare, and Webster (say) all seem to share certain basic assumptions about life, language, and the theater. But what formula or definition, philosophical or esthetic, will link Ibsen and Yeats, Chekhov and Pirandello, Shaw and Ionesco? The old distinctions between tragedy and comedy, melodrama and farce, have largely lost their meaning in today's generic confusion. A sense of revolt has superseded a sense of tradition. It may be that we are still too close to modern drama to see it in proper perspective, but it is difficult to imagine a future generation of literary historians to whom our variety of style and purpose will appear as sameness. Beside the general democratization of subject matter the only safe generalization about modern drama is an assertion of its heterogeneity. And the variety is evident not only in a chronological view but in cross-sections of modern drama at any time. This is hardly surprising. Wars, depressions, revolutions, social change, technological advance, new concepts in science and philosophy — in this welter of phenomena, drama, traditionally of all the arts the most sensitive to the cultural matrix, has naturally been various. So restless is our time, so doubt-ridden, so rapid

and cosmopolitan the spread of our culture — Ionesco and Ibsen are
both hits in Tokyo — that it would be strange if our drama did *not*
appear protean in its quest for expressive form.

The success of stage realism — that is, approximation, usually within
but sometimes deliberately outside artistic form, to photographic and
stenographic replicas of actuality — about 1880 was only a belated mani-
festation of a revolution which had already taken place in poetry and
fiction and which was itself the natural result of a series of industrial,
political, and scientific revolutions that profoundly altered Western
man's material life, institutions, and ideas from about 1750 on. Some
one hundred years later the new society was, however imperfectly and
disastrously, industrialized, urbanized, democratized, and probably also
secularized to a degree beyond that of any earlier known society. The
uneasy peace of the Victorian age was presided over by a prosperous
and proper middle class. The representation of this new bourgeois culture on the stage was an obvious task for drama, but it rose to the challenge only decades after the contemporary novel had done so, partly
because of official censorship in different forms (the almost-two-
hundred-year monopoly of the two patented playhouses in London
ended only in 1843, when London was a city of about a million and
a half), partly because of long-established middle-class attitudes to
plays as sinful or at least frivolous, and partly because no playwright
succeeded in creating an audience for a new kind of play. It was not
that models were lacking or the need not felt. In English drama, for
example, the tradition of the middle-class play goes back to the anony-
mous *Arden of Feversham* and to Thomas Heywood's *A Woman Killed
with Kindness*, both Renaissance plays contemporary with a dominant
aristocratic blank verse tragedy. The common man was again the hero
of a serious play in George Lillo's *London Merchant* (1731), although
Lillo's sententious moralizing and his occasional use of blank verse remove the play from consideration as a genuine precursor of nineteenth-
century stage naturalism. In 1758 the French encyclopedist Diderot
deplored the non-existence of middle-class drama. His sentiment was
repeated, in different forms, by Friedrich Hebbel (himself the author
of the pre-naturalistic *Maria Magdalena*), Otto Ludwig, and Hermann
Hettner in Germany, by the brothers Goncourt in France, and by
George Brandes in Denmark. By his call, in 1872, for a drama that
would "submit problems to debate," Brandes influenced Ibsen, who in
the early seventies had come to a crossroads in his dramatic career.
Thus Brandes became the godfather of the problem play and, more
indirectly, of its propagandistic cousin, the thesis play. In 1873 Émile
Zola dramatized his naturalistic novel *Thérèse Raquin* in order to provide a specimen of naturalistic drama in the narrow, philosophical

sense of the term, *i.e.*, meticulous and artless slice-of-life writing on the deterministic premise that only a clinical description of man's conditioning circumstances will yield the objective truth about him. Thus was the ground prepared for a playwright who could shape the ideology of naturalism to the demands of art. Clearly, the new drama was not going to be of men and gods, of aristocratic scapegoats for cosmic ills, of titanic poetic utterance, but of common words and common lives, fit for democratic audiences.

Ibsen pioneered in naturalism with plays that disclosed the death of the spirit behind the outward decencies of the bourgeois family. Despite their objective surface the liberal implications of *A Doll's House* (1879), *Ghosts* (1881), and *An Enemy of the People* (1882) are so obvious that Ibsen in the popular mind ever since has been identified with liberal iconoclasm. This was the Ibsen that was acted in the new theaters, all bearing names denoting "freedom," that opened in the great European capitals as fora for new ideas and battlegrounds for attacks on bigotry, prudery, and reaction: André Antoine's Théâtre Libre in Paris (1887), Otto Brahm's Freie Bühne in Berlin (1889), and J. T. Grein's Independent Theater in London (1891). These are the theaters of ideological Ibsenism, as Shaw explained it in his *Quintessence of Ibsenism* in 1891. There are good historical reasons why much subsequent naturalistic drama was written in the service of liberalism and radicalism, both political and non-political.

But the crusading spirit of the champions of the naturalistic movement has to some extent obscured the nature of the achievement of the playwrights they championed. Irrelevant to their argument were the symbolism and near-mysticism, akin almost to the contemporary neo-romanticism in France, of Ibsen's last phase and the delicate patterns of Chekhov's action. We see more than message and verisimilitude (if we see them at all) in Ibsen's multi-leveled interiors, Strindberg's cataclysmic sexual battles, Shaw's gay butchery of sacred and profane cows, and Chekhov's records of moral and psychological paralysis in the landed gentry in pre-revolutionary Russia. We no longer rank thesis playwrights such as Galsworthy and Brieux with the four classic writers of naturalistic theater. With all their sincere liberalism and all their technical competence the disciples lacked what their masters had: command of action, believable on its own terms, so patterned and so submitted to imaginative pressure as to glow and heat, the art of dialogue that vibrates with more than lifelikeness, psychological wisdom not subservient to thesis. Much of the liberalism in the name of Marx and Freud that went into the making of naturalistic plays in the twenties and thirties is forgotten today, not because it argued corrupt theses but because it failed to raise topical indictment and espousal to the level of universal art. The names likely to endure from among the second generation of naturalists are those of playwrights who did not allow their compassion or indignation or enthusiasm to make their vision of life simple — Gorky (*The Lower Depths*), Hauptmann (*The Weavers*), Schnitzler (*The Lonely Way*). More objective, more impassioned, and more talented than the thesis playwrights, Eugene O'Neill almost staggered under a burden of schematic Freudianism in his two most ambitious naturalistic plays, the neo-tragedies *Mourning Becomes Electra* and *Strange Interlude*. The less intellectualized and less theme-conscious *Desire Under the Elms* came closer to realizing his ambition: to elevate the destiny of the common man in his socio-economic setting to the dignity of classical tragedy. But dogmatism is risky when speaking of modern drama. There is, on the other hand, Bertolt Brecht's epic theater, which, though a more spacious and flexible scenic world than that of strict naturalism, is still not so far removed from it as not to be evidence in support of the argument that thesis — in this case social thesis of Marxist bias — can serve as the basis for excellent drama.

Beside major plays the naturalistic tradition has also engendered one of the main influences on modern acting (and, one assumes, though the case would be hard to prove, on modern playwriting): the Stanislavsky method. Deliberate emphasis on realistic ensemble acting rather than on brilliant elocution and posturing by individual star performers characterized the productions of the Duke of Meiningen's company that toured Europe between 1874 and 1890. But in his rehearsals at the Moscow Art Theater beginning in 1898 Konstantin Stanislavsky broadened and systematized the Meiningen manner. The main points of his method are: repertory system of production and long rehearsal periods in order to turn a company of individual actors into a true ensemble, the cultivation of the actor's "magical if" that enables him to believe in the reality of what he is doing, his use of his private memories and imagination to further that conscious and intense concentration of his whole being by which alone he can hope to achieve complete identification with his part (the actor should "be," not "act"), and his creation of "the fourth-wall illusion" in the audience by acting as if the audience were not there. Despite challenges from stylized acting and Brechtian theories of *Verfremdung* (esthetic distancing), the Stanislavsky method continues to dominate our theater. Today the revolution it effected is so much an accomplished fact that we must make an effort to remember that Stanislavskyism has not always been axiomatic.

Non-naturalism in modern drama has (to make the complex simple) assumed four major forms. Needless to say, there are plays that defy such rigorous classification, just as there are some that straddle the whole fissure between naturalism and non-naturalism. Nevertheless, for the rather desperate purposes of a survey the distinctions are useful as long as they are not taken to represent a temporal sequence and as long as the existence of exceptions is kept in mind.

Two of the four forms are literary: neo-romanticism and verse drama. One is both literary and theatrical: expressionism. One is theatrical: the new stagecraft.[2] In various ways and degrees the original impetus behind them all has been reaction against what has been felt to be the inhibiting factuality, dogmatic thesis-mongering, and generally arid prosaism of naturalistic writing and staging. In the case of expressionism and the new stagecraft another important influence has been the whole complex of supra-rational, relativistic concepts of reality that have influenced all the arts and have manifested themselves in forms of surrealism, abstractionism, and non-representationalism in general. Psychology gives us man as primarily an irrational creature, chained to his subconscious. Modern science threatens to reduce empirical reality to one vast illusion, a meaningless flux of lawless force. The emphasis on subjective, inner reality, fragmentary and inchoate, in some characteristic forms of both expressionism and the new stagecraft reflects the philosophical nihilism and the despair that appear to be modern man's birthright. If man is nothing but a discoherent sequence of states of consciousness, a record of his reality ought to reflect that fact and be kaleidoscopic, illusory, and abstract. And if his language is inadequate for communication, words are of no consequence.

Of the four, neo-romanticism has been the least important. It culminated around the turn of the century in Rostand's exuberant poetic melodrama *Cyrano de Bergerac*, in the dreamily symbolic medievalism of Maeterlinck (in one of his phases), and in the poeticized Irish legends of the early Yeats. Today it survives mainly outside of serious drama altogether, as sweetmeats for Broadway sophisticates in the form of spectacular musicals of fantasy, pathos, whimsy, and sentimentality — *Peter Pans*, *Brigadoons*, *Camelots*. Verse drama, on the other hand, has enjoyed a kind of intermittent renaissance so far in this century. In Yeats the two movements fuse. It was very largely thanks to his efforts to create a center for Irish poetic drama based on national romanticism that the Abbey Theater came into being — interestingly enough, just about the same time as its naturalistic counterpart, the Moscow Art Theater. Thought Yeats' own verse plays were produced there, the Abbey is better known as the theater of Synge and O'Casey, realists of Irish peasant life (Synge's *Riders to the Sea* and *Playboy of the West-*

---

[2] I use this term rather than "theatricalism" in order to distinguish certain styles of staging and design from the playwright's flaunting of illusionism by way of deliberate acknowledgment and use of his theatrical medium in the written play — as in some of the plays by Pirandello, Wilder, and Brecht. The former I call "new stagecraft," the latter "theatricalism."

ern World) and urban slum life (O'Casey's *Juno and the Paycock* and *The Plough and the Star*), but both gifted with a lusty lyricism that transmutes the sordid and the drab into loveliness and which in Synge's case found expression also in plays in verse. Other major figures in twentieth-century poetic drama are T. S. Eliot and the Spanish peasant poet Garcia Lorca, while Maxwell Anderson in a series of blank verse tragedies and historical plays and Christopher Fry in image-studded comedies seem less original contributors to the genre. Eliot, like Yeats, has been a subtle and forceful champion-critic of verse drama, arguing that in committing himself to record the surface appearance of ordinary life the naturalistic playwright has cut himself off from the richest, most beautiful resources of language: rhythm, precision, intensity, grandeur. His own best play, *Murder in the Cathedral*, is an impressive piece of evidence for the viability of dramatic verse in other than the Elizabethan idiom, though in theme and setting it hardly represents *modern* drama.

Expressionism is both an elusive and an inclusive term. It is used here for drama that does not purport to be a record of objective actuality and which departs from the conventions of illusionistic staging and coherent action. The definition covers plays that used to be called "experimental" or "avant-garde." Any play in which the mind's interior is represented — by means of dream-like sequences, stylization of language, movement, and action, by various forms of scenic abstractionism and montage, or by several or all of such devices — is, to that extent, expressionistic. It follows that the category is a large and miscellaneous one. It includes Strindberg's chamber plays (such as *The Dream Play* and *The Ghost Sonata*) and O'Neill's dramatizations of atavism (*Emperor Jones, The Hairy Ape*) and his plays for masks and chorus (*The Great God Brown, Lazarus Laughed*). It includes the left-wing allegories of mass scenes, abstract sets, and nameless (or rather generically named) heroes and heroines in Kaiser's and Toller's German expressionism of the twenties (*e.g.*, Kaiser's *Man and the Masses*). It includes Andreyev's (*He Who Gets Slapped*) and Pirandello's somber-ironic probings of reality, Wilder's theatricalism (*Our Town, The Skin of Our Teeth*), Cocteau's sardonic reworking of old legend (*The Infernal Machine, Orpheus*), Beckett's (*Waiting for Godot, Endgame*) and Ionesco's quaintly moving images of surrealist futility. These plays are not all similar — most of them are quite dissimilar — but they are all part of a many-faceted revolt against the naturalistic proposition that representationalism is the means to the end of discovering truth about man. It follows also that expressionism, though often based on psychoanalysis (the stage is the subconscious; action is by free association) and often radical in its moral or political fervor, is not the exclusive property of any one school of thought. Such filmic elements as brief scenes, varied setting, visual symbols, abrupt movement, and large casts are among its formal characteristics.

The free and flexible staging called for by many expressionistic plays takes us, finally, to a consideration of the new stagecraft. What has just been said about expressionism explains why and in what manner these two forms of anti-naturalism so frequently are found together in script and production, why it could be argued, in fact, that the new stagecraft is simply an aspect of expressionism. Playwrights have always written with the physical conditions of their theater in mind, and the enormous technical resources available to the modern director and designer allow a range of experimentation and innovation that was hardly open to earlier playwrights. True, the unencumbered Elizabethan stage gave freedom to a Shakespeare's dramatic imagination, but it was the freedom offered by a void to be filled, not the freedom of a craftsman choosing among a multitude of tools.

Richard Wagner may be considered the father of the new stagecraft, because of his theory of the *Gesamtkunstwerk*, the work of all arts, in which poetry, musical composition, choreography, painting, acting, singing, lighting, directing all co-operated. Wagner's operas hardly belong to the history of modern drama, but it is relevant here to note the important influence of his theory on modern workers in the theater. Not even Stanislavsky's ideal of ensemble acting has contributed as much as Wagner's grand synthesis of all the theatrical arts to the apotheosis of the director as the co-ordinator of them all at the expense of both playwright and actor, which is one of the most distinctive phenomena in what may be called the sociology of the modern theater.

Despite their differences the various theories and practices of the new stagecraft all share an ambition to free the theatrical medium from the written word, particularly from the convention that actors are real people engaged in real conversations in real rooms. The new stagecraft is, essentially, the use of non-verbal means to the end of a more adaptable, comprehensive, and expressive medium of the theater. The ideal entails the obvious danger of dethroning the word for mere spectacle and mechanical ingenuity, but no one denies that it has enriched modern drama. Its development and diversification have been aided by innovations in the physical theater which at first seemed mainly to further the illusionism of naturalism. Chief among these were the revolving stage (brought to Europe from Japan in 1896 and used by Ibsen in *John Gabriel Borkman* that same year) and, above all, electric lighting. There are modern departures from conventional staging that appear to have been made for their own sake — because of the stager's understandable delight in his medium.

The Swiss Adolphe Appia and the Englishman Gordon Craig were influential theorists of the new stagecraft during the early decades of this century. Appia anatomized stage production into four plastic elements: vertical scenery, horizontal floor, moving actor, and lighted space. The playwright's words were to be subordinated to the total scenic spectacle of line, light, color, and movement, all focused on the actor's dramatic presence. Craig went even farther in visualizing a wordless theater of super-marionettes performing before vast and abstract designs. Neither Appia nor Craig gained enough of a hearing to be important practitioners of their own theories, but they were influential as writers and designers. Early Soviet theater (before the dreary triumph of social realism), represented by a "constructivist" like Meyerhold (later condemned and perhaps executed for "formalism"), was indebted to them. So was the productive and versatile German Max Reinhardt, perhaps the most eclectic worker in the modern theater, producing plays of all times and kinds in colossal and intimate theaters alike, re-introducing the Elizabethan apron stage, experimenting with theater-in-the-round. The fluid stylization of platform and staircase staging in Jacques Copeau's Vieux-Colombier (opened in 1913) and the use of transparencies and light to free stage realism from the solidities of the older naturalistic manner, as in some of Elia Kazan's recent productions of plays by Tennessee Williams and Arthur Miller, are other proofs of the versatility and adaptability of the new stagecraft.

These notes come to no conclusion — as perhaps it is impossible for notes on such a subject as modern drama to do. The diversity of that drama is obvious — in origin, content, literary and theatrical form and style, and present trends. To forecast its future seems foolish, to establish its rank among the great ages of drama premature. But the example of a single play may serve to support the belief that there is artistic vitality in the very heterogeneity of our drama. The dialogue of *The Glass Menagerie* is the naturalistic prose of ordinary people, but the many, short, and disjunctive scenes are a characteristic of new stagecraft, while the whole "memory play" apparatus is expressionistic. Like Ibsen's stage families, the Wingfields are trapped by their past: Amanda's image of herself as popular belle, the photograph of the absconded father, the return of Laura's high-school hero. The near-plotlessness and the repertory of modal counterpoint echo Chekhov. And in Tom's speeches and situation in the memory play (as distinct from the theatricalist present) there is a note of left-wing protest against constricting and degrading socioeconomic conditions. The wonder is that such a mixture of styles and motifs can be an artistic whole at all, but it is.

MODERN DRAMA

Nine Plays

Henrik Ibsen

THE WILD DUCK

A New Translation by Otto Reinert

Characters

WERLE, *a manufacturer and merchant*
GREGERS WERLE, *his son*
OLD EKDAL
HJALMAR EKDAL, *his son, a photographer*
GINA EKDAL, *Hjalmar's wife*
HEDVIG, *their daughter, fourteen years old*
MRS. SØRBY, *Werle's housekeeper*
RELLING, *a physician*
MOLVIK, *a former student of theology*
GRÅBERG, *a bookkeeper in Werle's office*
PETTERSEN, *Werle's servant*
JENSEN, *a hired waiter*
A FLABBY GENTLEMAN
A THIN-HAIRED GENTLEMAN
A NEARSIGHTED GENTLEMAN
SIX OTHER GENTLEMEN, *Werle's dinner guests*
OTHER HIRED WAITERS

SCENE: *The first act takes place at* WERLE'S; *the other four, in* HJALMAR EKDAL'S *studio.*

ACT I

An expensive-looking and comfortable study in WERLE'S *house; bookcases and upholstered furniture; in the middle of the room a desk with papers and ledgers; lamps with green shades give the room a soft, subdued light. In the rear, open double doors with*

1

*portieres pulled apart reveal a large, elegant drawing room, brightly
illuminated by lamps and candles. Front right, a small door to the
office wing. Front left, a fireplace with glowing coals in it. Farther
back on the left wall, double doors to the dining room.*

PETTERSEN, WERLE'S *servant, in livery, and the hired waiter*
JENSEN, *in black, are setting the study in order for the guests. In
the drawing room, two or three other hired waiters are lighting
candles, moving chairs, etc. Sounds of conversation and laughter
of many people come from the dining room. Someone signals he
wishes to make a speech by touching his glass with his knife. Silence follows, a short speech is made, there are noises of approval,
then again conversation.*

PETTERSEN (*lights a lamp by the fireplace and puts a shade on it*): Just
listen to that, Jensen. There's the old man now, proposing a long
toast to Mrs. Sørby.

JENSEN (*moving an armchair*): Do you think it's true what people say,
that the two of 'em — y'know — ?

PETTERSEN: Couldn't say.

JENSEN: I bet he used to be quite a goat in the old days.

PETTERSEN: Maybe so.

JENSEN: They say this dinner is for his son.

PETTERSEN: That's right. He came home yesterday.

JENSEN: It's the first I've heard Werle has a son.

PETTERSEN: He has a son, all right. But he's up at the works at Høydal
all the time. He hasn't been home as long as I've been here.

A HIRED WAITER (*in the drawing room doorway*): Pst, Pettersen,
there's an old fellow here, says he —

PETTERSEN (*under his breath*): Dammit! Can't have anybody in here
now!

(OLD EKDAL *appears from the right in the drawing room. He is
dressed in a shabby old coat with a high collar. Wool mittens. He
carries a walking stick and a fur cap in his hand. Under his arm a
parcel in thick paper. Dirty, reddish brown wig. Small, gray mustache.*)

PETTERSEN (*going towards him*): Good Lord! What are *you* doing
here?

EKDAL (*in the doorway*): Got to get into the office, Pettersen.

PETTERSEN: The office closed an hour ago, and —

EKDAL: They told me that downstairs. But Gråberg is still in there. Be
a good boy, Pettersen; let me in this way. (*Points to the small office
door.*) Been through here before.

PETTERSEN: Oh well, all right. (*Opens the door.*) But see you go out the other way. We're having guests tonight.

EKDAL: I know, I know — h'm! Thanks a lot, Pettersen, old boy. Good old friend. Thanks. (*Mutters.*) Ass!

(*He enters the office.* PETTERSEN *closes the door behind him.*)

JENSEN: Is he one of them office people, too?

PETTERSEN: Oh no. He just does some extra copying for them, when they need it. But he's been a fine enough fellow in his day, old Ekdal has.

JENSEN: You know, he sort of looked like that.

PETTERSEN: Oh yes. He used to be a lieutenant.

JENSEN: I'll be damned! A lieutenant!

PETTERSEN: Yessir: Then he got mixed up in some forest deal or something. They say he pretty near ruined Werle once. The two of 'em were partners — owned the Høydal works together. Oh yes, Ekdal and I are good friends. We've had many a drink together at Madam Eriksen's place, we have.

JENSEN: Didn't look to me like he'd have much to buy people drinks with.

PETTERSEN: Good Lord, Jensen. It's my treat, of course. I always say one should be nice to people who've seen better days.

JENSEN: So he went bankrupt?

PETTERSEN: Worse than that. He went to prison.

JENSEN: Prison!

PETTERSEN: Or something. — (*Listens.*) Shhh. They are getting up from the table.

(*Servants open the doors to the dining room.* MRS. SØRBY *appears, in conversation with a couple of the dinner guests. The rest of the company follows in small groups.* WERLE *is among them. The last to appear are* HJALMAR EKDAL *and* GREGERS WERLE.)

MRS. SØRBY (*to the servant, in passing*): Pettersen, tell them to serve the coffee in the music room, will you?

PETTERSEN: Very well, Mrs. Sørby.

(*She and the two guests go into the drawing room and disappear, right.* PETTERSEN *and* JENSEN *follow them out.*)

A FLABBY GENTLEMAN (*to* A THIN-HAIRED *one*): Phew! That dinner — It was almost too much for me.

THE THIN-HAIRED GENTLEMAN: Oh, I don't know. With a little bit of good will, it's amazing what one can accomplish in three hours.

THE FLABBY GENTLEMAN: Yes, but afterwards, afterwards, my dear
chamberlain!

A THIRD GENTLEMAN: I am told the coffee and liqueurs will be served
in the music room.

THE FLABBY GENTLEMAN: Wonderful! Then maybe Mrs. Sørby will
play something for us.

THE THIN-HAIRED GENTLEMAN (*in a low voice*): If only she doesn't play
us a different tune one of these days.

THE FLABBY GENTLEMAN: Don't worry. Bertha isn't one to let old
friends down.

(*They laugh and enter the drawing room.*)

WERLE (*in a low and troubled voice*): I don't think anybody noticed,
Gregers.

GREGERS (*looks at him*): Noticed what?

WERLE: You didn't either?

GREGERS: What?

WERLE: We were thirteen at the table.

GREGERS: Really? Were we thirteen?

WERLE (*with a glance at* HJALMAR EKDAL): Usually we are only twelve.
(*To the other guests:*) Gentlemen!

(*He and the remaining guests, except* HJALMAR *and* GREGERS,
leave through the drawing room, rear right.)

HJALMAR (*who has overheard the conversation*): You shouldn't have
invited me, Gregers.

GREGERS: Nonsense! This is supposed to be a party for *me*. Shouldn't
I invite my one and only friend?

HJALMAR: But I don't think your father approves. I never come to this
house.

GREGERS: So I hear. But I wanted to see you and talk to you. — Well,
well, we two old school fellows have certainly drifted apart. It must
be sixteen — seventeen years since we saw each other.

HJALMAR: Is it really that long?

GREGERS: It is indeed. And how are you? You look fine. You're almost
stout.

HJALMAR: Stout is hardly the word, but I suppose I look a little more
manly than I used to.

GREGERS: Yes, you do. Your appearance hasn't suffered any all these
years.

HJALMAR (*gloomily*): But the inner man — ! Believe me, that's a different story. You know, of course, how utterly everything has collapsed for me and mine since we last met.

GREGERS (*in a lower voice*): How is your father these days?

HJALMAR: I'd just as soon not talk about him. My poor, unfortunate father lives with me, of course. He has no one else in the whole world to turn to. But it is so terribly difficult for me to talk about these things. Tell me rather how you have been — up there at the works.

GREGERS: Lonely — blissfully lonely. I've had all the time in the world to think over all sorts of things. — Here. Let's make ourselves comfortable.

(*He sits down in an armchair near the fireplace and gets* HJALMAR *to take another chair beside him.*)

HJALMAR (*softly*): All the same, I do want to thank you, Gregers, for inviting me to your father's table. It proves to me you no longer bear me a grudge.

GREGERS (*surprised*): Grudge? What makes you think I ever did?

HJALMAR: You did at first, you know.

GREGERS: When?

HJALMAR: Right after the tragedy. Of course, that was only natural. After all, your own father only escaped by the skin of his teeth. Oh, that terrible old business!

GREGERS: And so I bore you a grudge? Who told you that?

HJALMAR: I know you did, Gregers. Your father said so himself.

GREGERS (*startled*): Father! Really? H'm. So that's why you've never written — not a single word.

HJALMAR: Yes.

GREGERS: Not even when you decided to become a photographer?

HJALMAR: Your father thought it would be better if I didn't write about anything at all.

GREGERS (*looking straight ahead*): Oh well, maybe he was right, at that. — But tell me, Hjalmar — do you feel you have adjusted pretty well to your situation?

HJALMAR (*with a small sigh*): Oh yes, I think I have. Can't say I haven't, anyway. At first, of course, things seemed very strange. My circumstances were so completely different. But then, everything had changed. Father's great, ruinous tragedy — The shame — The disgrace —

GREGERS (*feelingly*): Yes, yes. I see.

HJALMAR: Of course there was no way in which I could pursue my studies. There wasn't a penny left. Rather the opposite; there was debt. Mainly to your father, I think.

GREGERS: H'm —

HJALMAR: Well — then I thought it best to take the bull by the horns and make a clean break with the past — you know, all at once. Your father thought so, too, and since he had been so helpful, and —

GREGERS: Father helped you?

HJALMAR: Yes, surely you know that? Where do you think I got the money to learn photography and to set up my own studio? Things like that are expensive, I can tell you.

GREGERS: And father paid for all that?

HJALMAR: Yes, didn't you know? I understood him to say he had written to you about it.

GREGERS: Not a word that it was *he*. He must have forgotten. We only write business letters. So it was father — !

HJALMAR: It certainly was. But he has never wanted people to know that. It was he who made it possible for me to get married, too. Or maybe — maybe you didn't know that, either?

GREGERS: No! How could I? (*Shakes* HJALMAR'S *arm*.) My dear Hjalmar, I can't tell you how happy all this makes me — and pains me, too. Perhaps I have been unfair to father. In some respects, anyway. For this shows he has a heart, you know. A kind of conscience —

HJALMAR: Conscience?

GREGERS: Or whatever you want to call it. No, really, I can't tell you how glad I am to hear this about father. — So you are married, Hjalmar. That's more than I ever will be. I trust you find yourself happy as a married man?

HJALMAR: Yes, I certainly do. She is as good and competent a wife as any man could ask for. And she is by no means without culture.

GREGERS (*a little taken aback*): No, of course not.

HJALMAR: Life itself is an education, you see. Being with me every day — And then there are a couple of remarkable men we see quite a lot of. I assure you, you'd hardly recognize Gina.

GREGERS: Gina?

HJALMAR: Yes. Surely you remember her name was Gina?

GREGERS: Whose name? I haven't the slightest idea —

HJALMAR: But don't you remember she was here in the house for a while?

GREGERS (*looks at him*): Is it Gina Hansen — ?

HJALMAR: Of course it is Gina Hansen.

GREGERS: — who kept house for us the last year of mother's illness?

HJALMAR: That's it. But my dear friend, I know for a fact that your father wrote you about my marriage.

GREGERS (*who has risen*): Yes, so he did, that's true, but not that — (*paces the floor*). Wait a minute — Yes, he did — now when I think back. But father always writes such short letters. (*Sits down on the arm of the chair.*) Listen, Hjalmar — this interests me — how did you make Gina's acquaintance — your wife, I mean?

HJALMAR: Quite simply. You remember she didn't stay here very long. Everything was so unsettled during your mother's illness. Gina couldn't take that, so she gave notice and moved out. That was the year before your mother died. Or maybe it was the same year.

GREGERS: It was the same year. I was up at Høydal at the time. Then what happened?

HJALMAR: Well, Gina moved in with her mother, Madam Hansen, an excellent, hardworking woman, who ran a small eating place. And she had a room for rent, too. A nice, comfortable room.

GREGERS: Which you were lucky enough to get?

HJALMAR: Yes. Through your father, in fact. And it was there I really learned to know Gina.

GREGERS: And then you got engaged?

HJALMAR: Yes. It's easy for young people to fall in love, you know. H'm —

GREGERS (*gets up, walks up and down*): Tell me — after you'd become engaged, was that when father — I mean, was that when you took up photography?

HJALMAR: That's right. Naturally, I wanted to get married and have a place of my own, the sooner the better. And both your father and I agreed that photography was the best thing I could get into. Gina thought so, too. Oh yes, that was another reason. It so happened that Gina had learned how to retouch.

GREGERS: What a wonderful coincidence.

HJALMAR (*smiling contentedly*): Yes, wasn't it? Don't you think it worked out very well?

GREGERS: Remarkably well, I should say. So father has really been a kind of Providence for you, Hjalmar; hasn't he?

HJALMAR (*moved*): He did not abandon his old friend's son in his days of need. That's one thing about your father: he does have a heart.

MRS. SØRBY (*enters on* WERLE'S *arm*): I don't want to hear another word, my dear sir. You are not to stay in there staring at all those bright lights. It isn't good for you.

WERLE (*letting go of her arm and moving his hand across his eyes*): I almost think you are right.

(PETTERSEN *and* JENSEN *enter carrying trays with glasses of punch.*)

MRS. SØRBY (*to the guests in the drawing room*): Gentlemen, if you want a glass of punch, you'll have to take the trouble to come in here.

THE FLABBY GENTLEMAN (*to* MRS. SØRBY): Dear Mrs. Sørby, please tell me it isn't so. You have not withdrawn your cherished permission to smoke?

MRS. SØRBY: Yes, Chamberlain. No smoking here in Mr. Werle's own sanctum.

THE THIN-HAIRED GENTLEMAN: And when did you append these harsh paragraphs to the tobacco regulations, Mrs. Sørby?

MRS. SØRBY: After the last dinner, Chamberlain, when certain persons abused their liberties.

THE THIN-HAIRED GENTLEMAN: And will not even the smallest infraction be tolerated, Mrs. Sørby? Really none at all?

MRS. SØRBY: None whatsoever, Chamberlain.

(*Most of the guests are gathered in the study. The servants are serving punch.*)

WERLE (*to* HJALMAR, *over by a table*): Well, Ekdal, what is that you are looking at?

HJALMAR: Oh, just an album, sir.

THE THIN-HAIRED GENTLEMAN (*moving about*): Ah yes! Photographs! That's your line, of course.

THE FLABBY GENTLEMAN (*seated*): Haven't you brought some of your own along?

HJALMAR: No, I haven't.

THE FLABBY GENTLEMAN: Too bad. Looking at pictures is good for the digestion, you know.

THE THIN-HAIRED GENTLEMAN: And then it would have contributed a mite to the general entertainment.

A NEARSIGHTED GENTLEMAN: And all contributions are gratefully received.

MRS. SØRBY: The chamberlains think that when one has been invited to dinner, one ought to work for one's food, Mr. Ekdal.

THE FLABBY GENTLEMAN: With a cuisine like this that's only a pleasure.

THE THIN-HAIRED GENTLEMAN: Oh well, if it's a question of the struggle for existence —

MRS. SØRBY: You are so right!

(*They continue their conversation, laughing and joking.*)

GREGERS (*in a low voice*): You must join in, Hjalmar.

HJALMAR (*with a twist of his body*): What am I to say?

THE FLABBY GENTLEMAN: Don't you believe, sir, that Tokay may be considered relatively beneficial to the stomach?

WERLE (*by the fireplace*): I'll guarantee the Tokay you were served to-night, at any rate. It is one of the very best years. I am sure you noticed that yourself.

THE FLABBY GENTLEMAN: Yes, it really was unusually delicate-tasting.

HJALMAR (*hesitantly*): Do the years differ?

THE FLABBY GENTLEMAN (*laughs*): Ah, Mr. Ekdal! Splendid!

WERLE (*with a smile*): I see it is hardly worth while to serve you fine wine.

THE THIN-HAIRED GENTLEMAN: Tokay is like photographs, Mr. Ekdal. Both need sunshine. Or isn't that so?

HJALMAR: Yes, sunshine has something to do with it.

MRS. SØRBY: Just the same with chamberlains. They need sunshine, too — royal sunshine, as the saying goes.

THE THIN-HAIRED GENTLEMAN: Ouch! That's a tired old joke, Mrs. Sørby.

THE NEARSIGHTED GENTLEMAN: The lady will have her fun —

THE FLABBY GENTLEMAN: — and at our expense. (*Wagging his finger.*) Madam Bertha! Madam Bertha!

MRS. SØRBY: But it is true that vintages differ widely sometimes. The older the better.

THE NEARSIGHTED GENTLEMAN: Do you count me among the older vintages?

MRS. SØRBY: Far from it.

THE THIN-HAIRED GENTLEMAN: Well, well! But what about me, Mrs. Sørby?

THE FLABBY GENTLEMAN: And me? What vintages do we belong to?

MRS. SØRBY: I reckon you among the sweet vintages, gentlemen.

(*She sips a glass of punch. The chamberlains laugh and flirt with her.*)

WERLE: Mrs. Sørby always finds a way out — when she wants to. But gentlemen, you aren't drinking! Pettersen, please see to it that — ! Gregers, let's have a glass together.

(GREGERS *does not move.*)

Won't you join us, Ekdal? I had no opportunity at the table —

(GRÅBERG *comes in through the office door.*)

GRÅBERG: Beg your pardon, Mr. Werle, but I can't get out.

WERLE: They've locked you in again, eh?

GRÅBERG: Yes, they have, sir. And Flakstad has left with the keys.

WERLE: That's all right. You just come through here.

GRÅBERG: But there is somebody else —

WERLE: Doesn't matter. Come on, both of you.

(GRÅBERG *and* OLD EKDAL *enter from the office.*)

WERLE (*involuntarily*): Damn!

(*Laughter and talk among the guests cease.* HJALMAR *gives a start when he sees his father, puts down his glass, and turns away toward the fireplace.*)

EKDAL (*does not look up but makes quick little bows to both sides, as he mutters*): Beg pardon. Came the wrong way. Gate's locked. Gate's locked. Beg pardon. (*He and* GRÅBERG *go out, rear right.*)

WERLE (*between his teeth*): That idiot Gråberg!

GREGERS (*staring, his mouth hanging open, to* HJALMAR): Don't tell me that was — !

THE FLABBY GENTLEMAN: What is it? Who was that?

GREGERS: Nothing. Just the bookkeeper and somebody else.

THE NEARSIGHTED GENTLEMAN (*to* HJALMAR): Did *you* know that man?

HJALMAR: I don't know — I didn't notice —

THE FLABBY GENTLEMAN (*getting up*): What the devil has gotten into everybody? (*He walks over to some other guests, who are talking in low voices.*)

MRS. SØRBY (*whispers to the servant*): Give him something from the kitchen to take home. Something good.

PETTERSEN (*nods his head*): I'll do that, ma'am. (*Goes out.*)

GREGERS (*shocked, in a low voice to* HJALMAR): Then it really was he?

HJALMAR: Yes.

GREGERS: And you stood there and denied him!

HJALMAR (*in a fierce whisper*): But how could I — ?

GREGERS: — acknowledge your own father?

HJALMAR (*pained*): Oh, if you had been in my place, maybe —

(*The low conversation among the guests changes to forced gaiety.*)

THE THIN-HAIRED GENTLEMAN (*approaching* HJALMAR *and* GREGERS, *in a friendly mood*): Aha! Reminiscing about university days, gentlemen? — Don't you smoke, Mr. Ekdal? Can I give you a light? Oh that's right. We are not allowed —

HJALMAR: Thanks, I don't smoke.

THE FLABBY GENTLEMAN: Don't you have a nice little poem you could recite for us, Mr. Ekdal? You used to do that so beautifully.

HJALMAR: I am sorry. I don't remember any.

THE FLABBY GENTLEMAN: That's a shame. Well, in that case, Balle, what do we do?

(*They both walk into the drawing room.*)

HJALMAR (*gloomily*): Gregers — I am leaving! You see, when a man has felt Fate's crushing blow — Say goodbye to your father for me.

GREGERS: Yes, of course. Are you going straight home?

HJALMAR: Yes. Why?

GREGERS: I thought I might come up and see you a little later.

HJALMAR: No, don't do that. Not to my home. My home is a gloomy one, Gregers, particularly after a brilliant banquet such as this. We can meet somewhere in town.

MRS. SØRBY (*has come up to them; in a low voice*): Are you leaving, Ekdal?

HJALMAR: Yes.

MRS. SØRBY: Say hello to Gina.

HJALMAR: Thank you. I'll do that.

MRS. SØRBY: Tell her I'll be up to see her one of these days.

HJALMAR: Fine. (*To* GREGERS) You stay here. I'll slip out without anybody noticing. (*Drifts off. A little later he goes into the drawing room and out right.*)

MRS. SØRBY (*in a low voice to the servant who has returned*): Well, did you give the old man something?

PETTERSEN: Oh yes. A bottle of brandy.

MRS. SØRBY: Oh dear. Couldn't you have found something better?

PETTERSEN: But Mrs. Sørby, there's nothing he likes better than brandy.

THE FLABBY GENTLEMAN (*in the doorway to the drawing room, with a sheet of music in his hand*): Will you play a duet, Mrs. Sørby?

MRS. SØRBY: Yes, gladly.

THE GUESTS: Good! Good!

(*She and all the guests go out rear right.* GREGERS *remains standing by the fireplace.* WERLE *is looking for something on the desk and appears to wish to be left alone. Since* GREGERS *does not leave,* WERLE *walks towards the drawing room door.*)

GREGERS: Father, do you have a moment?

WERLE (*stops*): What is it?

GREGERS: I'd like a word with you.

WERLE: Couldn't it wait till we're alone?

GREGERS: No, it can't, for maybe we'll never be alone again.

WERLE (*coming closer*): What does that mean?

(*During the following scene, the sound of a piano is faintly heard from the music room.*)

GREGERS: How is it that that family has been allowed to go to ruin so miserably?

WERLE: I suppose you refer to the Ekdals?

GREGERS: Yes, I do mean the Ekdals. Lieutenant Ekdal was once your close friend.

WERLE: Yes, unfortunately. Too close. I have felt that keenly enough for many years. It was his fault that my good name and reputation, too, were — somewhat tarnished.

GREGERS (*in a low voice*): Was he the only one who was guilty?

WERLE: Who else, do you mean?

GREGERS: The two of you were together on that big purchase of forest land, weren't you?

WERLE: But it was Ekdal who surveyed the area — surveyed it fraudulently. It was he who felled all that timber on state property. He was responsible for everything that went on up there. I didn't know what he was doing.

GREGERS: I doubt that Lieutenant Ekdal himself knew what he was doing.

WERLE: That may well be. The fact remains that he was convicted and I was not.

GREGERS: Yes, I know there were no proofs.

WERLE: Acquittal is acquittal. Why do you want to bring back that miserable old business that gave me gray hairs before my time? Is that what has been on your mind all these years up there? I can assure you, Gregers, here in town that whole story has been forgotten long ago, as far as *I* am concerned.

GREGERS: But what about that unfortunate family?

WERLE: Well, now, exactly what do you want me to do for those people? When Ekdal got out, he was a broken man, beyond help altogether. Some people go to the bottom as soon as they've got some buckshot in them and never come up again. Believe me, Gregers, I've done all I possibly could do, if I didn't want to put myself in a false light and give people occasion for all sorts of talk and suspicion —

GREGERS: Suspicion? I see.

WERLE: I have given Ekdal copying work to do for the office, and I pay him far, far more than he is worth.

GREGERS (*without looking at him*): H'm. I don't doubt that.

WERLE: You are laughing? Don't you think I am telling you the truth?

Oh, to be sure, you won't find it in my books. I never enter expenses like that.

GREGERS (*with a cold smile*): No, I suppose there are certain expenses that are better not entered.

WERLE (*puzzled*): What do you mean?

GREGERS (*being brave*): Have you entered what it cost you to let Hjalmar Ekdal learn photography?

WERLE: I? What do you mean — entered?

GREGERS: I know now it was you who paid for it. And I also know it was you who set him up in business — quite comfortably, too.

WERLE: All right! And you still say I have done nothing for the Ekdals! I assure you, Gregers, those people have cost me a pretty penny!

GREGERS: Have you entered those expenses?

WERLE: Why do you ask?

GREGERS: I have my reasons. Listen — at the time you were providing so kindly for your old friend's son, wasn't that just when he was getting married?

WERLE: Damn it, Gregers! How can I remember — ! After so many years — !

GREGERS: You wrote me a letter at the time. A business letter, of course. And in a postscript you mentioned very briefly that Hjalmar Ekdal had married one Miss Hansen.

WERLE: That's right. That was her name.

GREGERS: But you did not say anything about Miss Hansen being Gina Hansen, our ex-housekeeper.

WERLE (*with scornful but forced laughter*): No, to tell the truth, it didn't occur to me that you were particularly interested in our ex-housekeeper.

GREGERS: I wasn't. But — (*Lowers his voice.*) somebody else in this house was.

WERLE: What do you mean? (*Flaring up.*) Don't tell me you're referring to me!

GREGERS (*in a low but firm voice*): Yes, I am referring to you.

WERLE: And you dare — ! You have the audacity — ! How can that ingrate, that — that photographer fellow — how dare he make accusations like that!

GREGERS: Hjalmar hasn't said a word. I don't think he has the faintest suspicion of anything like this.

WERLE: Then where do you get it from? Who could have said a thing like that!

GREGERS: My poor, unfortunate mother. The last time I saw her.

WERLE: Your mother! I might have thought so! You and she — you always stood together. It was she who first turned you against me.

GREGERS: No, it was all she had to go through, till things became too much for her and she died in sheer misery.

WERLE: Oh, nonsense! She didn't have to go through anything! No more than what others have had to, anyway. There's just no way of getting on with morbid, hysterical people — that's something *I* have had to learn! And here you are, with a suspicion like that — dabbling in old rumors and gossip against your own father. Listen here, Gregers. It really seems to me that at your age you might find something more useful to do.

GREGERS: Yes, it is about time.

WERLE: Then maybe your mind would be more at ease than it seems to be now. What is the point of working away, year in and year out, as just an ordinary clerk up there at Høydal, with not so much as a penny beyond regular wages? It's plain silly!

GREGERS: I wish I could believe that.

WERLE: Not that I don't understand, mind you. You want to be independent, don't want to be obliged to me for anything. But right now there is a chance for you to become independent, to be on your own in everything.

GREGERS: Oh? How so?

WERLE: When I wrote you that I needed you here in town right away — h'm —

GREGERS: Yes, what is it you want of me? I've been waiting to hear all day.

WERLE: I am offering you a partnership in the firm.

GREGERS: I! In your firm? As a partner?

WERLE: Yes. That doesn't mean we have to be together all the time. You could take over the business here in town and I could go up to Høydal.

GREGERS: You would want to do that?

WERLE: Well, you see, Gregers. I can't work as well as I used to. I'll have to save my eyes. They are getting weaker.

GREGERS: You have always had weak eyes.

WERLE: Not as bad as now. Besides — there are other things, too, that may make it advisable for me to live up there — for a while, anyway.

GREGERS: Nothing like this has ever even occurred to me.

WERLE: Look here, Gregers. I know there are many things that stand between us. But after all, we are father and son. It seems to me we ought to be able to come to some sort of understanding.

GREGERS: For appearance's sake, I suppose you mean.

WERLE: Well, that would be something, anyway. Think it over, Gregers. Wouldn't that be possible? What do you say?

GREGERS (*looks at him coldly*): There is something behind this.

WERLE: I don't understand.

GREGERS: You want to use me for something.

WERLE: In a relationship as close as ours I suppose one person can always be of use to the other.

GREGERS: Yes. So they say.

WERLE: I want to have you at home with me for a while. I am a lonely man, Gregers. I have always been lonely, but mostly now, when I am getting older. I need somebody around me.

GREGERS: You have Mrs. Sørby.

WERLE: So I do, and she has become almost indispensable to me. She is bright, she has an even temper, she brings life into the house — and I badly need that.

GREGERS: Well, then, everything is just as you want it.

WERLE: Yes, but I am afraid it won't last. A woman in her circumstances can easily have her position misconstrued in the eyes of the world. I'll almost go so far as to say it does a man no good either.

GREGERS: Oh, I don't know. When a man gives the kind of dinner parties you do he can take quite a few liberties.

WERLE: Yes, but what about *her*, Gregers? I am afraid she will not put up with it much longer. And even if she did, even if she ignored what people are saying and all that sort of thing, out of devotion to me — Do you really think, Gregers, you with your strong sense of justice, do you feel it would be —

GREGERS (*interrupting*): Just tell me this: are you going to marry her?

WERLE: What if I did? What then?

GREGERS: That's what I am asking. What then?

WERLE: Would it displease you very much?

GREGERS: No, not at all.

WERLE: Well, you see, I didn't know — I thought perhaps out of regard for your mother —

GREGERS: I am not given to melodramatics.

WERLE: Well, whether you are or not, you have lifted a stone from my heart. I can't tell you how pleased I am that I can count on your support in this matter.

GREGERS (*looks intently at him*): Now I see what you want to use me for.

WERLE: Use you for? What an expression!

GREGERS: Let's not be particular in our choice of words — not as long as we're by ourselves, at any rate. (*Laughs.*) So that's it. That's why I had to come to town at all costs. Because of Mrs. Sørby, there are arrangements being made for family life in this house. Touching scene between father and son! That would indeed be something new!

WERLE: I won't have you use that tone!

GREGERS: When were we ever a family here? Never in my memory. But now, of course, there is need for a display of domestic affection. It will look very well to have the son hastening home on wings of filial feeling to attend the aging father's marriage feast. What happens then to all the talk of what the poor, deceased mother had to suffer? It evaporates. Her son takes care of that.

WERLE: Gregers, I don't believe there is anyone you detest as much as me.

GREGERS (*in a low voice*): I have seen too much of you.

WERLE: You've seen me with your mother's eyes. (*Lowers his voice a little.*) But don't forget that those eyes were — clouded at times.

GREGERS (*his voice trembles*): I know what you have in mind. But who's to blame for mother's tragic weakness? You and all those — ! The last one was that female you palmed off on Hjalmar Ekdal, when you yourself no longer — !

WERLE (*shrugs his shoulders*): Word for word as if I were hearing your mother.

GREGERS (*paying no attention*): — and there he is now, with his great, trusting child's soul in the middle of all this deceit — sharing his roof with a woman like that, unaware that what he calls his home is based on a lie! (*Steps closer to* WERLE.) When I look back upon all you have done, I seem to see a battlefield strewn with mangled human destinies.

WERLE: I almost think the gap between us is too wide.

GREGERS (*with a formal bow*): So I have observed. That is why I take my hat and leave.

WERLE: You're leaving? The house?

GREGERS: Yes. For now at last I see a mission to live for.

WERLE: What mission is that?

GREGERS: You'd only laugh if I told you.

WERLE: A lonely man doesn't laugh so easily, Gregers.

GREGERS (*pointing to the rear*): Look, father. The chamberlains are playing blindman's buff with Mrs. Sørby. — Goodnight and good-bye.

(*He goes out rear right. The sound of people talking, laughing, and playing games can be heard from the drawing room, where the guests are now coming into view.*)

WERLE (*mutters scornfully*): Hah — ! The fool! And he says he is not melodramatic!

ACT II

(HJALMAR EKDAL's *studio, a large attic room. To the right, a slant-ing roof with skylights, half covered by blue cloth. The entrance door from the hallway is in the far right corner; the door to the living room farther forward on the same wall. There are two doors to the left, as well, with an iron stove between them. In the rear, wide, sliding, double doors. The studio is unpretentious but cozy. Between the two doors on the right and a little out from the wall is a sofa with a table and some chairs in front of it. On the table is a lighted lamp with a shade. Near the wall by the stove is an old armchair. Various pieces of photographic equipment here and there in the room. In the rear, to the left of the sliding doors, a shelf with a few books, bottles with chemical solutions, tools, and some other objects. Photographs, brushes, paper, etc., are lying on the table.*)

GINA EKDAL *sits by the table, sewing.* HEDVIG *sits on the sofa, read-ing, her hands shading her eyes, her thumbs in her ears.*)

GINA (*glances at* HEDVIG *a few times, as if secretly anxious*): Hedvig!

HEDVIG (*does not hear.*)

GINA (*louder*): Hedvig!

HEDVIG (*takes away her hands and looks up*): Yes, mother?

GINA: Hedvig, be a good girl. Don't read any more tonight.

HEDVIG: Please, mother, just a little bit longer? Can't I?

GINA: No. I want you to put that book away. Your father doesn't like you to read so much. He never reads at night.

HEDVIG (*closing her book*): Well, father doesn't care much for reading, anyway.

GINA (*puts her sewing aside and picks up a pencil and a small notebook from the table*): Do you remember how much we spent for the butter today?

HEDVIG: One crown and sixty-five øre.

GINA: That's right. (*Writes it down.*) We're using an awful lot of butter in this family. Then there was the sausage and the cheese — let me see — (*writing*) — and the ham — (*mumbles figures while adding up*). Goodness! it does add up —

HEDVIG: And the beer.

GINA: Right. (*Writes.*) It gets terrible expensive, but it can't be helped.

HEDVIG: And you and I didn't need anything hot for supper since father was out.

GINA: No, that's right. That helps some. And I did get eight crowns and fifty øre for the pictures.

HEDVIG: Was it that much?

GINA: Eight-fifty, exactly.

(*Silence.* GINA *picks up her sewing.* HEDVIG *takes paper and pencil and starts drawing, her left hand shading her eyes.*)

HEDVIG: Isn't it nice to think that father is at that big dinner party at Mr. Werle's?

GINA: Can't rightly say he's *his* guest. It was the son who invited him. (*After a pause.*) We have nothing to do with the old man.

HEDVIG: I can't wait till father comes home. He promised to ask Mrs. Sørby if he could take home something good for me.

GINA: Why yes, you can be sure there are plenty of good things in *that* house.

HEDVIG (*still drawing*): Besides, I think I am a little bit hungry, too.

(OLD EKDAL *enters right rear, the brown paper parcel under his arm, another parcel in his coat pocket.*)

GINA: So late you are today, Grandpa.

EKDAL: They'd locked the office. Had to wait for Gråberg. And then I had to go through — h'm —

HEDVIG: Did they give you any more copying to do, Grandpa?

EKDAL: This whole parcel. Look.

GINA: That's nice.

HEDVIG: And you've got another one in your pocket.

EKDAL: What? Oh never mind. That's nothing. (*Puts his walking stick away in the corner.*) This will keep me busy a long time, Gina. (*Slides one of the double doors half open.*) Shhh! (*Peeks into the attic for a while, then he cautiously slides the door shut. Chuckling.*) They're sound asleep the whole lot of 'em. And she herself's in the basket.

HEDVIG: Are you sure she won't be cold in that basket, Grandpa?

EKDAL: Cold? With all that straw? Don't you worry about *that*. (*Goes towards the door left rear.*) There are matches, aren't there?

GINA: On the dresser.

(EKDAL *goes into his room.*)

HEDVIG: It's nice that he got all that new work to do.

GINA: Yes, poor old thing. It will give him a little spending money.

HEDVIG: And he won't be able to stay down at that awful Madam Eriksen's all morning.

GINA: No; there's that, too.

HEDVIG: Do you think they're still at the table?

GINA: Lord knows. Could be.

HEDVIG: Just think of all that delicious food. I'm sure he'll be in a good mood when he comes home. Don't you think so, mother?

GINA: Yes, but what if we could tell him we'd rented the room. Wouldn't that be nice?

HEDVIG: But we don't need that tonight.

GINA: Oh yes we do. We could always use the money. The room is no good to us as it is.

HEDVIG: No, I mean that father will be in a good mood tonight, anyway. It's better to have the room for some other time.

GINA (*looking at her*): You like it when you have something nice to tell father when he comes home nights, don't you?

HEDVIG: It makes things more pleasant.

GINA (*reflectively*): Yes, I guess you're right about that.

(OLD EKDAL *enters from his room, heads for the kitchen door, left front.*)

GINA (*turning half around in her chair*): Do you need anything in the kitchen, Grandpa?

EKDAL: Yes. But don't you get up. (*Goes out.*)

GINA: I hope he isn't fooling around with the fire out there. (*After a while.*) Hedvig, go out and see what he's doing.

(OLD EKDAL *enters with a pitcher of hot water.*)

HEDVIG: Getting hot water, Grandpa?

EKDAL: That's right. Got some writing to do, but the ink's as thick as gruel. H'm —

GINA: But hadn't you better have supper first? It's all ready for you in your room.

EKDAL: Never mind supper, Gina. I tell you I'm busy. I don't want anybody coming in to me. Not anybody. H'm.

(*He goes into his room.* GINA *and* HEDVIG *look at each other.*)

GINA (*in a low voice*): I can't think where he got the money from. Can you?

HEDVIG: From Gråberg, maybe.

GINA: No, it wouldn't be that. Gråberg always gives me the money.

HEDVIG: Maybe he got a bottle on credit.

GINA: Him! Who'd give him credit?

(HJALMAR EKDAL, *in overcoat and gray hat, enters right.*)

GINA (*throws down her sewing, gets up*): Heavens, Ekdal! Home already?

HEDVIG (*getting up at the same time*): Father? So soon!

HJALMAR (*lays down his hat*): Most of them seemed to be leaving now.

HEDVIG: Already?

HJALMAR: Well, it was a dinner party, you know. (*Takes his coat off.*)

GINA: Let me help you.

HEDVIG: Me too. (*They help him off with his coat.* GINA *hangs it up in the rear.*) Were there many there, father?

HJALMAR: Not too many. About twelve or fourteen at the table.

GINA: Did you get to talk to all of them?

HJALMAR: Oh yes, a little. Though Gregers kept me engaged most of the evening.

GINA: Is he as ugly as he used to be?

HJALMAR: Well — I suppose nobody would call him handsome. Is father back?

HEDVIG: Yes, he is in there writing.

HJALMAR: Did he say anything?

GINA: No. About what?

HJALMAR: He didn't mention — ? I thought I heard he'd been with Gråberg. I think I'll go in to him for a moment.

GINA: No, you'd better not.

HJALMAR: Why not? Did he say he didn't want to see me?

GINA: He doesn't want to see anybody.

HEDVIG (*making signs to her*): Ahem!

GINA (*doesn't notice*): He's gotten himself some hot water.

HJALMAR: Ah! So he is —

GINA: Looks that way.

HJALMAR: Ah yes — my poor old white-haired father. Let him enjoy his little pleasures as best he can.

(OLD EKDAL, *a lighted pipe in his mouth, enters in an old smoking jacket.*)

EKDAL: Home again? Thought it was you I heard talking.

HJALMAR: Yes. I just came back.

EKDAL: Guess you didn't see me, did you?

HJALMAR: No, but they told me you'd gone through, so I thought I'd catch up with you.

EKDAL: H'm. That's good of you, Hjalmar. Who were they — all those people?

HJALMAR: Oh — all sorts. Chamberlain Flor and Chamberlain Balle and Chamberlain Kaspersen and chamberlain this and that. I don't know —

EKDAL (*nodding his head*): Hear that, Gina? He's been with nothing but chamberlains all evening.

GINA: Yes, I hear as they've become quite fancy in that house now.

HEDVIG: Did the chamberlains sing, father? Or recite poetry?

HJALMAR: No. They just talked nonsense. They wanted *me* to recite, though, but I didn't want to.

EKDAL: They couldn't get you to, eh?

GINA: Seems to me you might have done that.

HJALMAR: No. I don't see any reason why one has to oblige every Tom, Dick, and Harry all the time. (*Walks up and down.*) At any rate, I won't.

EKDAL: No point in being too obliging, you know. That's Hjalmar for you.

HJALMAR: I don't see why *I* always have to be the one who provides entertainment on the rare occasions when I am out for dinner. Let the others exert themselves for a change. Those fellows go from one big meal to the next, stuffing themselves day in and day out. Let *them* do something for all the food they are getting!

GINA: You didn't tell them that though, did you?

HJALMAR (*humming a little*): Well, I don't know about that. They were told a thing or two.

EKDAL: The chamberlains?

HJALMAR: Mmm — (*Casually.*) Then we had a little controversy over Tokay wine.

EKDAL: Tokay, no less! Say, that's a fine wine!

HJALMAR (*stops his walking*): It *may* be a fine wine. But let me tell you: not all the vintages are equally fine. It depends on how much sunshine the grapes get.

GINA: If you don't know everything — !

EKDAL: And they quarreled with that?

HJALMAR: They tried to, but then it was pointed out to them that it was the same way with chamberlains. Not all vintages are equally fine among chamberlains, either — so they were told.

GINA: Goodness! What you don't think of!

EKDAL: Heh-heh! So they got that to put in their pipe.

HJALMAR: Right to their face. That's how they got it.

EKDAL: Gina, d'ye hear that? He gave it to them right to their face!

GINA: Right to their face! Imagine!

HJALMAR: Yes, but I don't want you to talk about it. One doesn't talk about such things. Of course, the whole thing was done in the friendliest possible way. They are all of them pleasant, easy-going people. Why should I hurt them? No!

EKDAL: Right to their face, though —

HEDVIG (*ingratiatingly*): It's so nice to see you all dressed up, father. You look very well in tails.

HJALMAR: Yes, don't you think so? And it really fits me perfectly. As if it were tailor-made. Possibly a trifle tight in the armpits, that's all. Help me, Hedvig. (*Takes his dinner jacket off.*) I'd rather wear my own coat. Where is it, Gina?

GINA: Here it is. (*Helps him on with it.*)

HJALMAR: There now! Be sure to have Molvik get his suit back first thing in the morning.

GINA (*putting the clothes away*): I'll take care of it.

HJALMAR (*stretching*): Aaahh. This feels cozier after all. And this kind of loose-fitting, casual wear is really more in keeping with my whole appearance; don't you think so, Hedvig?

HEDVIG: Oh yes, father!

HJALMAR: Especially when I tie my neckcloth with loose, flying ends — like this? What do you think?

HEDVIG: Yes, it goes extremely well with your mustache. And with your curls, too.

HJALMAR: I'd hardly call my hair curly. Wavy, rather.

HEDVIG: Yes, for the curls are so large.

HJALMAR: Waves, really.

HEDVIG (*after a moment, pulling his sleeve*): Father?

HJALMAR: What is it?

HEDVIG: Oh, you know very well what it is!

HJALMAR: I certainly don't.

HEDVIG (*laughing and pleading*): Oh come on, father! Don't tease me!

HJALMAR: But what is it?

HEDVIG (*shaking him*): Father! Give it to me! You know, you promised me. Something good to eat.

HJALMAR: Oh, dear! I completely forgot!

HEDVIG: You are only teasing, father. Shame on you! Where is it?

HJALMAR: No, honest, I really did forget. But wait a moment. I have something else for you, Hedvig. (*Goes and searches his coat pockets.*)

HEDVIG (*jumps up and down, clapping her hands*): Oh mother, mother!

GINA: See what I mean? If you just give him time —

HJALMAR (*with a piece of paper*): Here it is.

HEDVIG: That? But that's just a piece of paper.

HJALMAR: It's the menu, Hedvig, the entire menu. Look here. It says "Menu." That means what you get to eat.

HEDVIG: Haven't you anything else for me?

HJALMAR: I tell you, I forgot all about it. But take my word for it: it's not such a great treat, all that rich food. You just sit down and read the menu, now, and I'll tell you later what the things taste like. Here you are, Hedvig.

HEDVIG (*swallowing her tears*): Thank you.

(*She sits down but doesn't read.* GINA *signals to her.* HJALMAR *notices.*)

HJALMAR (*pacing the floor*): It is really unbelievable all the things a father is supposed to keep in mind. And if he forgets the smallest item — ! Long faces right away. Oh well. One gets used to that, too. (*Stops by the stove where* OLD EKDAL *is sitting.*) Have you looked at them tonight, father?

EKDAL: I certainly have! She's in the basket!

HJALMAR: No! Really? In the basket? She is getting used to it then, I guess.

EKDAL: Didn't I tell you she would? But look, Hjalmar, there are still a few things —

HJALMAR: — improvements, yes, I know.

EKDAL: They've got to be done.

HJALMAR: Right. Let's talk about it now, father. Come over here to the sofa.

EKDAL: All right. H'm. Guess I want to fill my pipe first, though. Need to clean it, too — h'm — (*Goes into his room.*)

GINA (*with a smile, to* HJALMAR): Cleaning his pipe —

HJALMAR: Oh well, Gina — let him. The poor shipwrecked old man. — About those improvements — We'd better get to them tomorrow.

GINA: You won't have time tomorrow, Ekdal.

HEDVIG (*interrupting*): Oh, yes, mother.

GINA: For remember those prints you were going to retouch? They came for 'em again today.

HJALMAR: I see. It's those prints again, is it? Well, they'll get done. You can be sure of that. Perhaps there are some new orders come in, too?

GINA: Not a thing, worse luck. Tomorrow I've got only those two portraits I told you about.

HJALMAR: Is that all? Well, if one doesn't exert oneself, what can you expect?

GINA: But what can I do? I advertise in the papers all I can, seems to me.

HJALMAR: The papers, the papers — you see yourself how far that gets us. I suppose there hasn't been anyone to look at the room, either?

GINA: No, not yet.

HJALMAR: Just as I thought. Well, no — if one doesn't *do* anything — One has to make a real effort, Gina!

HEDVIG (*going to him*): Shall I get your flute, father?

HJALMAR: No, not the flute. *I* need no pleasures. (*Paces up and down.*) You'll see if I don't work tomorrow! You don't need to worry about *that!* You can be sure I shall work as long as my strength holds out —

GINA: But Ekdal, dear — I didn't mean it that way.

HEDVIG: How about a bottle of beer, father?

HJALMAR: Not at all. I don't need anything — (*Stops.*) Beer? Did you say beer?

HEDVIG (*brightly*): Yes, father; lovely, cool beer.

HJALMAR: Oh well — all right — since you insist, I suppose you may bring me a bottle.

GINA: Yes, do that. That'll be nice and cozy.

(HEDVIG *runs towards the kitchen door.*)

HJALMAR (*by the stove, stops her, looks at her, takes her by the head and presses her to him*): Hedvig! Hedvig!

HEDVIG (*happy, in tears*): Oh father! You are so sweet and good!

HJALMAR: No, no, don't say that. There I was — seated at the rich man's table — gorging myself on his ample fare — and I couldn't even remember —

GINA (*seated by the table*): Nonsense, Ekdal.

HJALMAR: It is not nonsense. But you must not reckon too strictly. You know I love you, regardless.

HEDVIG (*throwing her arms around him*): And we love you, father, so much, so much!

HJALMAR: And if I am unreasonable at times, remember — God forgive me — remember I am a man beset by a host of sorrows. Well, well! (*Drying his eyes.*) No beer at such a moment. Give me my flute.

(HEDVIG *runs to the shelf and fetches it.*)

HJALMAR: Thank you. There now. With my flute in my hand and you two around me — ah!

(HEDVIG *sits down by the table next to* GINA. HJALMAR *walks back and forth, playing a Bohemian folk dance. He plays loudly but in slow tempo and with pronounced sentiment.*)

HJALMAR (*interrupts his playing, gives his left hand to* GINA, *and says with strong emotion*): Our home may be mean and humble, Gina. But it is our home. And I say to you both: here dwells contentment!

(*He resumes his playing. Presently there is a knock on the door.*)

GINA (*getting up*): Shh, Ekdal. I think somebody's coming.

HJALMAR (*putting the flute back on the shelf*): Yes, yes of course. Somebody would —

(GINA *goes to open the door.*)

GREGERS WERLE (*out in the hall*): I beg your pardon —

GINA (*taking a step back*): Oh!

GREGERS: — isn't this where Mr. Ekdal lives, the photographer?

GINA: Yes, it is.

HJALMAR (*going to the door*): Gregers! So you did come, after all. Come in.

GREGERS (*entering*): I told you I wanted to see you.

HJALMAR: But tonight — ? Have you left the party?

GREGERS: Both party and home. Good evening, Mrs. Ekdal. I don't know if you recognize me.

GINA: Oh yes. Young Mr. Werle isn't hard to recognize.

GREGERS: No, for I look like my mother, and you remember her, I am sure.

HJALMAR: You have left your home?

GREGERS: Yes. I have taken a room at a hotel.

HJALMAR: Really? — Well, since you're here, take off your coat and sit down.

GREGERS: Thanks. (*Removes his overcoat. He has changed clothes and is now dressed in a plain, gray suit, of somewhat unfashionable cut.*)

HJALMAR: Here on the sofa. Make yourself comfortable.

(GREGERS *sits down on the sofa,* HJALMAR *on a chair by the table.*)

GREGERS (*looking around*): So this is your residence, Hjalmar. This is where you live.

HJALMAR: This is the studio, as you can see.

GINA: It's roomier in here, so this is where we mostly keep ourselves.

HJALMAR: The apartment we had before was really nicer than this, but there is one big advantage here: we have plenty of space.

GINA: And we have a room across the hallway that we're renting out.

GREGERS (*to* HJALMAR): You have lodgers, too?

HJALMAR: No, not yet. These things take time, you see. One has to be on the lookout. (*To* HEDVIG.) What about that beer?

(HEDVIG *nods her head and goes out into the kitchen.*)

•GREGERS: So that's your daughter.

HJALMAR: Yes, that's Hedvig.

GREGERS: Your only child, isn't she?

HJALMAR: Our only one. Our greatest joy in the world, and (*lowers his voice*) our greatest sorrow, as well.

GREGERS: What are you saying!

HJALMAR: Yes, Gregers, for there is every probability that she'll lose her sight.

GREGERS: Becoming blind!

HJALMAR: Yes. So far, there are only early symptoms, and things may be well with her for some time yet. But the doctor has warned us. It is coming, irresistibly.

GREGERS: But this is nothing less than a tragedy! How do you account for it?

HJALMAR (*with a sigh*): Heredity, most likely.

GREGERS (*struck*): Heredity?

GINA: Ekdal's mother had weak eyes.

HJALMAR: That's what father says. I of course don't remember her.

GREGERS: Poor child. How does she take it?

HJALMAR: Oh, we can't bring ourselves to tell her — I'm sure you can understand that. She suspects nothing. Joyous and carefree, chirping like a little bird, she'll flutter into life's endless night. (*Overcome by emotion.*) Oh Gregers, this is such a terrible burden for me.

(HEDVIG *enters with a tray with beer and glasses. She puts it down on the table.*)

HJALMAR (*stroking her hair*): Thanks. Thank you, Hedvig.

HEDVIG (*puts her arms around his neck and whispers something in his ear.*)

HJALMAR: No. No sandwiches now. (*Looks off.*) That is — unless Gregers wants some?

GREGERS (*with a gesture of refusal*): No. No thanks.

HJALMAR (*still in a melancholic mood*): Oh well, you might as well bring in some, all the same. A crust, if you have one. And plenty of butter, please.

GREGERS (*who has followed her with his eyes*): Otherwise she seems healthy enough.

HJALMAR: Yes, thank God, there is nothing else wrong with her.

GREGERS: I think she is going to look like you, Mrs. Ekdal. How old is she?

GINA: Hedvig is just about fourteen. Her birthday is day after tomorrow.

GREGERS: Quite big for her age, isn't she?

GINA: Yes, she has grown a lot lately.

GREGERS: It's by the children we tell we're growing older ourselves. How long have you two been married now?

GINA: We've been married for — let's see — fifteen years, pretty near.

GREGERS: Just imagine! Has it really been that long?

GINA (*taking notice, looks at him*): It certainly has.

HJALMAR: That's right. Fifteen years, less a few months. (*Changing topic.*) Those must have been long years for you up there at the works, Gregers.

GREGERS: They were long while they lasted. Now afterwards I hardly know where they went.

(OLD EKDAL *enters from his room, without his pipe, but with his old-fashioned lieutenant's cap on his head. His walk is a trifle unsteady.*)

EKDAL: I'm ready for you now, Hjalmar. Let's talk about this — h'm — What was it again?

HJALMAR (*going towards him*): Father, there's someone here. Gregers Werle. I don't know if you remember him?

EKDAL (*looks at* GREGERS, *who has stood up*): Werle? That's the son, isn't it? What does he want from me?

HJALMAR: Nothing. He has come to see me.

EKDAL: Then there's nothing wrong?

HJALMAR: Of course not.

EKDAL (*swinging one arm back and forth*): Not that I am scared, mind you, but —

GREGERS (*goes up to him*): I just wanted to bring you greetings from your old hunting grounds, Lieutenant Ekdal.

EKDAL: Hunting grounds?

GREGERS: Yes, the woods up around the Høydal works.

EKDAL: Oh yes, up there. Yes, I used to know that country quite well in the old days.

GREGERS: You were quite a hunter then, weren't you?

EKDAL: Could be. Maybe I was. You're looking at my get-up. I don't ask anybody's permission to wear it in the house. Just as long as I don't go outside —

(HEDVIG *brings a plate with open-faced sandwiches, which she puts down on the table.*)

HJALMAR: You sit down, father, and have a glass of beer. Help yourself, Gregers.

(EKDAL *mutters something and shuffles over to the sofa.* GREGERS *sits down on a chair next to him;* HJALMAR *is on the other side of* GREGERS. GINA *sits some distance from the table, sewing.* HEDVIG *is standing by her father.*)

GREGERS: Do you remember, Lieutenant Ekdal, when Hjalmar and I used to come up and visit you summers and Christmas?

EKDAL: You did? No; can't say as I do. But it's true I used to be a good hunter, if I do say so myself. I've killed bears, too. Nine of 'em.

GREGERS (*looks at him with compassion*): And now your hunting days are over.

EKDAL: Oh — I wouldn't say that. I still go hunting once in a while. Well, yes, not in the old way, of course. For you see, the woods — the woods — the woods —! (*Drinks.*) Nice-looking woods up there now?

GREGERS: Not as in your time. They have cut a great deal.

EKDAL: Cut? (*In a lower voice and as if afraid.*) That's risky business, that is. It has consequences. The woods are vengeful.

HJALMAR (*filling his glass*): Here, father. Have some more.

GREGERS: How can a man like you — such an outdoors man as you used to be — how can you stand living here in the middle of a musty city, within four walls?

EKDAL (*chuckles, glancing at* HJALMAR): Oh, it's not so bad here. Not bad at all.

GREGERS: But surely — all the things your soul grew used to up there —? The cool, invigorating breezes? The free life in woods and mountains, among beasts and birds —?

EKDAL (*smiling*): Hjalmar, shall we show it to him?

HJALMAR (*quickly, a little embarrassed*): Oh no, father. Not tonight.

GREGERS: What is it he wants to show me?

HJALMAR: Oh, it's just — something. You can see it some other time.

GREGERS (*continues addressing* OLD EKDAL): You see, this is what I had in mind, Lieutenant. Why don't you come up to Høydal with me? I'll probably be going back shortly. I'm sure you could get some copying work to do up there as well. For down here you can't have a thing to cheer you up and keep you occupied.

EKDAL (*looks at him in astonishment*): Don't I have —!

GREGERS: Yes, of course, you have Hjalmar. But then he has his own family. And a man like you, who have always loved the outdoors —

EKDAL (*striking the table*): Hjalmar, he *shall* see it!

HJALMAR: But father, do you really think so? It's dark and —

EKDAL: Nonsense. There's a moon. (*Getting up.*) I say he's got to see it. Let me out. Come and help me, Hjalmar!

HEDVIG: Oh yes, father! Do!

HJALMAR (*getting up*): Oh well, all right.

GREGERS (*to* GINA): What is it?

GINA: Oh, don't expect anything much.

(EKDAL *and* HJALMAR *have gone to the rear of the room. Each of them slides one of the double doors back.* HEDVIG *is helping the old man.* GREGERS *remains standing by the sofa.* GINA *keeps on sewing, paying no attention. Through the opened doors can be seen a big, elongated, irregular-shaped attic, with nooks and corners and a couple of chimneys standing free from the wall. Moonlight falls through several skylights, illuminating some parts of the room, while others are in deep shadow.*)

EKDAL (*to* GREGERS): You are welcome to come closer, sir.

GREGERS (*goes up to them*): What is this really?

EKDAL: See for yourself. H'm.

HJALMAR (*somewhat embarrassed*): This is all father's, you understand.

GREGERS (*at the door, peering into the attic*): Do you keep chickens, Lieutenant?

EKDAL: Should say we do. They're roosting now. But you ought to see those chickens in daylight!

HEDVIG: And there is —

EKDAL: Hush, don't say anything yet.

GREGERS: And I see you've got pigeons, too.

EKDAL: Could be we have. We've got pigeons, all right! The roosts are up on the rafters, for pigeons like to be up high, you know.

HJALMAR: They aren't all of them just ordinary pigeons.

EKDAL: Ordinary! I should say not! We've got tumblers and even a couple of pouters. But come over here. Do you see that pen over by the wall?

GREGERS: Yes. What do you use that for?

EKDAL: That's where the rabbits are at night.

GREGERS: Oh? You have rabbits, too, do you?

EKDAL: Damn right we have rabbits! He asks if we have rabbits, Hjalmar! H'm. But now we're coming to the *real* thing. Here we are. Move, Hedvig. You stand here and look down — there; that's right. Now, do you see a basket with straw in it?

GREGERS: Yes, I do. And I see a bird.

EKDAL: H'm — A "bird."

GREGERS: Isn't it a duck?

EKDAL (*offended*): I'd say it's a duck!

HJALMAR: But what kind of duck, do you think?

HEDVIG: It's not just an ordinary duck.

EKDAL: Hush!

GREGERS: And it's not a muscovy duck, either.

EKDAL: No, Mr. — Werle; it's not a muscovy, for it's a wild duck!

GREGERS: Is it really? A wild duck?

EKDAL: That's what it is. The — "bird," as you called it. A wild duck. It's our wild duck.

HEDVIG: *My* wild duck. For it belongs to me.

GREGERS: And it lives here in the attic? It's thriving?

EKDAL: What's so odd about that? She's got a big pail of water to splash around in.

HJALMAR: Fresh water every other day.

GINA (*turning to* HJALMAR): Ekdal, please. I'm freezing.

EKDAL: H'm. All right; let's close up. Just as well not to disturb their night's rest, anyway. Help me Hedvig.

(HJALMAR *and* HEDVIG *slide the double doors shut.*)

EKDAL: You can have a good look at her some other time. (*Sits down in the armchair by the stove.*) I'm telling you, they are strange birds, those wild ducks.

GREGERS: But how did you ever catch it, Lieutenant?

EKDAL: I didn't. There's a certain man in this town we can thank for her.

GREGERS (*struck by a thought*): Would that man be my father?

EKDAL: Indeed it is. It's your father, sure enough. H'm.

HJALMAR: Funny you'd guess that, Gregers.

GREGERS: You told me before that you owed a great deal to my father, so I thought that perhaps —

GINA: But we didn't get the duck from Werle himself.

EKDAL: It's Håkon Werle we have to thank for her all the same, Gina. (*To* GREGERS.) He was out in a boat, see, and took a shot at her. But he doesn't see so well, your father doesn't. H'm. Anyway, she was only wounded.

GREGERS: I see. She got some buckshot in her.

HJALMAR: Yes. A little.

HEDVIG: Right under the wing, so she couldn't fly.

GREGERS: Then she went to the bottom, I suppose.

EKDAL (*sleepily, his voice muffled*): So it did. Always do that, wild ducks. Dive straight to the bottom — far as they can, sir. Bite themselves fast in the grasses and roots and weeds and all the other damn stuff down there. And never come up again.

GREGERS: But, Lieutenant, *your* wild duck did.

EKDAL: He had such a wonderfully clever dog, your father. And that dog — it went down and got the duck up.

GREGERS (*to* HJALMAR): And so it came to you?

HJALMAR: Not right away. First your father took it home with him, but it didn't seem to get on too well there, and then he told Pettersen to get rid of it.

EKDAL (*half asleep*): H'm — Pettersen — Ass —

HJALMAR: That's how we got it, for father knows Pettersen a little, and when he heard about the wild duck, he asked Pettersen to give it to him.

GREGERS: And now it seems perfectly contented in there in the attic.

HJALMAR: Yes, you would hardly believe how well it gets on. It's becoming fat. I think perhaps it's been in there so long that it has forgotten what wild life is like. And that makes all the difference.

GREGERS: I am sure you are right, Hjalmar. The thing to do is never to let it look at sea and sky again. — But I don't think I should stay any longer. I believe your father is asleep.

HJALMAR: Oh, as far as that is concerned —

GREGERS: Oh yes, one thing more. You said you had a room for rent? A vacant room?

HJALMAR: We do. What of it? Do you know anyone who — ?

GREGERS: Could I get it?

HJALMAR: You?

GINA: Oh, Mr. Werle, I'm sure *you* don't want to —

GREGERS: Couldn't I have it? If I can, I'll move in first thing in the morning.

HJALMAR: Yes, indeed, with the greatest pleasure.

GINA: No, but Mr. Werle, that's not a room for you.

HJALMAR: Gina! How can you say that?

GINA: It's not large enough or light enough, and —

GREGERS: That doesn't matter, Mrs. Ekdal.

HJALMAR: I think it's quite a nice room myself, and decently furnished, too.

GINA: But remember those two downstairs.

GREGERS: Who are they?

GINA: There's one who used to be a private tutor.

HJALMAR: Molvik is his name. He studied to be a minister once.

GINA: And then there's a doctor, name of Relling.

GREGERS: Relling? I know him slightly. He used to practice up at Høydal.

GINA: They are a couple of real wild characters those two. Out all hours of the night, and when they come home they aren't always — y'know —

GREGERS: One gets used to that sort of thing. I hope I'll be like the wild duck.

GINA: H'm. Well, I think you ought to sleep on it first.

GREGERS: I take it you don't really want me in the house, Mrs. Ekdal.

GINA: Good Lord! How can you say a thing like that?

HJALMAR: Yes, Gina. It really does seem very odd of you. (*To* GREGERS.) Does this mean you'll be staying in town for a while?

GREGERS (*putting on his overcoat*): Yes, I think I'll stay.

HJALMAR: But not with your father? What do you intend to do?

GREGERS: If I knew that, Hjalmar, I'd be much better off. But when you're cursed with a name like "Gregers" — and then "Werle" after that — Did you ever hear of an uglier name?

HJALMAR: I don't think it's ugly at all.

GREGERS: Ugh! I feel like spitting in the face of anybody with a name like that. But since it's my cross in life to be Gregers Werle, such as I am —

HJALMAR: Ha-ha! If you weren't Gregers Werle, what would you like to be?

GREGERS: If I could choose, I'd like to be a really clever dog.

GINA: A dog!

HEDVIG (*involuntarily*): Oh no!

GREGERS: Yes, an exceptionally skillful dog — the kind that goes down to the bottom after wild ducks when they've dived down among the weeds and the grass down there in the mud.

HJALMAR: Honestly, Gregers. This makes no sense whatever.

GREGERS: I suppose it doesn't. But tomorrow morning, then, I'll be moving in. (*To* GINA.) You won't have any trouble with me; I'll do everything myself. (*To* HJALMAR.) The other things we can talk about tomorrow. — Goodnight, Mrs. Ekdal. (*Nods to* HEDVIG.) Goodnight!

GINA: Goodnight, Mr. Werle.

HEDVIG: Goodnight.

HJALMAR (*who has lighted a candle*): Wait a moment. I'll see you down. I'm sure it's all dark on the stairs.

(GREGERS *and* HJALMAR *go out through the entrance door, right rear.*)

GINA (*staring ahead, her sewing lowered in her lap*): Wasn't it funny all that talk about wanting to be a dog?

HEDVIG: Do you know, mother — I think he really meant something else.

GINA: What would that be?

HEDVIG: No, I couldn't say, but it was just like he had something else in mind all the time.

GINA: You think so? It sure was funny, though.

HJALMAR (*returning*): The lamp was still burning. (*Blows out the candle and sits down.*) Ah, at last it's possible to get a bite to eat. (*Starts on the sandwiches.*) Now do you see what I mean, Gina — about seizing the opportunity?

GINA: What opportunity?

HJALMAR: Well — it was lucky, wasn't it, that we got the room rented? And then to somebody like Gregers, a dear old friend.

GINA: Well, I don't know what to say to that.

HEDVIG: Oh mother, you'll see it will be fun.

HJALMAR: I must say you are strange. First you wanted nothing more than to get a lodger; then when we do, you don't like it.

GINA: I know, Ekdal. If only it had been somebody else. What do you think old Werle will say?

HJALMAR: He? It's none of his business.

GINA: But don't you see that something's bound to be wrong between the two of 'em, since the young one is moving out. Sure you know how those two are.

HJALMAR: That may be so, but —

GINA: And maybe Werle will think you are behind it!

HJALMAR: All right! Let him think that. Oh, by all means, Werle has done a great deal for me — I'm the first to admit it. But that doesn't mean I everlastingly have to let him run my life.

GINA: But Ekdal, dear, it could hurt Grandpa. Perhaps he'll lose what little he's making from working for Gråberg.

HJALMAR: I almost wish he would! Is it not humiliating for a man like me to see his gray-haired father treated like dirt? Ah, but soon now the time will be ripe. I feel it. (*Takes another sandwich.*) As sure as I have a mission in life, it shall be accomplished!

HEDVIG: Oh yes, father!

GINA: Shhh! Don't wake him up.

HJALMAR (*in a lower voice*): I say it again: I *will* accomplish it! The day will come, when — That's why it's such a good thing we got the room rented out, for that makes me more independent. And that's necessary for a man with a mission in life. (*Over by the armchair, with feeling.*) Poor old white-haired father. Trust your Hjalmar. He has broad enough shoulders — powerful shoulders, at any rate. Some day you'll wake up, and — (*to* GINA.) Or don't you believe that?

GINA (*getting up*): Sure I do, but let's first get him to bed.
HJALMAR: Yes, let us.

(*They tenderly lift the old man.*)

ACT III

(*The studio. It is morning. Daylight comes in through the sky-light, the blue cloth having been pulled aside.*

HJALMAR *sits at the table, retouching a photograph. Several other photographs are lying in front of him. After a while,* GINA, *in coat and hat, enters from outside. She is carrying a covered basket.*)

HJALMAR: Back already, Gina?
GINA: Yes. I'm in a hurry. (*Puts the basket down on a chair and takes off her coat and hat.*)
HJALMAR: Did you look in at Gregers's?
GINA: I did. It looks real nice in there. He fixed up the place real pretty, soon as he moved in.
HJALMAR: Oh?
GINA: Remember, he was to take care of everything himself? Well, he built a fire in the stove, but he hadn't opened the flue, so the whole room got filled with smoke. Phew! It smelled like —
HJALMAR: Oh dear —
GINA: Then do you know what he does? This really beats everything. He wanted to put out the fire, so he pours the water from the wash basin into the stove. The whole floor is sloppy with filth!
HJALMAR: I am sorry.
GINA: I've got the janitor's wife to clean up after him, pig as he is, but the room can't be lived in till this afternoon.
HJALMAR: Where is he now?
GINA: He said he was going out for a while.
HJALMAR: I went in there for a moment, too — right after you had left.
GINA: He told me. You've asked him for breakfast.
HJALMAR: Just a bit of a late morning meal. It's the first day and all. We can hardly do less. I am sure you have something.
GINA: I'll have to find something, at any rate.
HJALMAR: Be sure it's plenty, though. I think Relling and Molvik are coming, too. I ran into Relling on the stairs just now, and so of course I had to —

GINA: So we are to have those two as well.

HJALMAR: Good heavens, one or two more or less — can that make any difference?

EKDAL (*opens his door and looks in*): Listen, Hjalmar — (*Sees* GINA.) Well, never mind.

GINA: Do you want something, Grandpa?

EKDAL: No. It doesn't matter. H'm! (*Goes back inside his room.*)

GINA (*picking up her basket*): Make sure he doesn't go out.

HJALMAR: Yes, I will. — Say, Gina — how about some herring salad? I believe Relling and Molvik made a night of it again last night.

GINA: If only they don't get here too soon.

HJALMAR: I'm sure they won't. Just take your time.

GINA: Well, all right. Then you can work some in the meantime.

HJALMAR: I *am* working! I'm working as hard as I can!

GINA: All I mean is you'd have it out of the way for later. (*Goes into the kitchen.*)

(HJALMAR *picks up the photograph and the brush and works for a while — slowly and with evident distaste.*)

EKDAL (*peeks in, looks around, says in a low voice*): Pst! Are you busy?

HJALMAR: Yes. I am struggling with these everlasting pictures —

EKDAL: All right, all right. If you're busy, then you're busy. H'm! (*Goes back inside his room. The door remains open.*)

HJALMAR (*works in silence for a while, puts his brush down, walks over to* EKDAL's *door*): Are *you* busy, father?

EKDAL (*grumbling inside his room*): When *you* are busy, *I* am busy! H'm!

HJALMAR: Oh all right. (*Returns to his work.*)

EKDAL (*appears in his door again after a while*): H'm, Hjalmar, listen — I'm not so *terribly* busy, you know.

HJALMAR: I thought you were writing.

EKDAL: Dammit all! Can't that Gråberg wait a day or two? Didn't think it was a matter of life and death.

HJALMAR: Of course not. And you aren't a slave, after all.

EKDAL: And there is this other job in there —

HJALMAR: Just what I was thinking. Do you want to go in there now? Shall I open the door for you?

EKDAL: Good idea.

HJALMAR (*getting up*): Then we'd have that job out of the way.

EKDAL: Exactly. It has to be ready for tomorrow, anyway. It *is* tomorrow, isn't it?

HJALMAR: Sure it's tomorrow.

(*They slide the double doors open. The morning sun is shining through the skylight. Some pigeons are flying around; others are cooing on their perches. From farther inside the room the chickens are heard clucking once in a while.*)

HJALMAR: All right, father. Guess you can go ahead.

EKDAL (*entering the attic*): Aren't you coming?

HJALMAR: Yes, do you know — I almost think I will. (*Notices* GINA *in the kitchen door.*) I? No, I don't have the time. I have to work. But then there is this thing —

(*He pulls a cord. A curtain comes down from within the attic. Its lower part is made out of a strip of old sailcloth; its upper part is a piece of stretched-out fish net. The attic floor is now no longer visible.*)

HJALMAR (*returns to the table*): Now! Maybe I can have peace for a few minutes.

GINA: Is he fooling around in there again?

HJALMAR: Would you rather he went down to Madam Eriksen? (*Sitting down.*) Do you want anything? I thought you said —

GINA: I just wanted to ask you if you think we can set the table in here?

HJALMAR: Yes. There aren't any appointments this early, are there?

GINA: No — only those two sweethearts who want their picture taken.

HJALMAR: Damn! Couldn't they come some other time!

GINA: Goodness, Ekdal, they'll be here after dinner, when you're asleep.

HJALMAR: Oh, in that case it's all right. Yes, let's eat in here.

GINA: Fine. But there's no hurry with the table. You're welcome to use it some more.

HJALMAR: Can't you see I *am* using it?

GINA: Then you'll be all done for afterwards, you know. (*Goes into the kitchen.*)

(*Brief silence.*)

EKDAL (*in the door to the attic, inside the fish net*): Hjalmar!

HJALMAR: What?

EKDAL: Afraid we'll have to move the pail, after all.

HJALMAR: What else have I been saying all along?

EKDAL: H'm — h'm — h'm! (*Disappears inside again.*)

HJALMAR (*keeps on working for a moment, glances over towards the attic, half rises, as* HEDVIG *enters from the kitchen. He quickly sits down again*): What do you want?

HEDVIG: Just to be with you, father.

HJALMAR (*after a short while*): Seems to me like you're snooping around. Have you been told to watch me, perhaps?

HEDVIG: No, of course not.

HJALMAR: What is mother doing?

HEDVIG: Mother is in the middle of the herring salad. (*Comes over to the table.*) Isn't there any little thing I can help you with, father?

HJALMAR: Oh no. It is better I do it all alone — as long as my strength lasts. There is no need for you to worry about anything, Hedvig, as long as your father is allowed to keep his health.

HEDVIG: Oh father. I won't have you talk that horrid way. (*She walks around a bit, stops by the opening to the inner room and looks in.*)

HJALMAR: What is he doing in there?

HEDVIG: Looks like a new ladder up to the water pail.

HJALMAR: He'll never manage that by himself! And here I am condemned to sit — !

HEDVIG (*goes to him*): Give me the brush, father. I can do it.

HJALMAR: I won't hear of it. You'll just be ruining your eyes.

HEDVIG: No, I won't. Give me the brush.

HJALMAR (*getting up*): It would only be for a minute or two —

HEDVIG: What possible harm could that do? (*Takes the brush.*) There now. (*Sits down.*) And here is one I can use as model.

HJALMAR: But don't ruin your eyes! Do you hear me? I will not take the responsibility. It's all yours. I'm just telling you.

HEDVIG (*working*): Yes, of course.

HJALMAR: You are really very good at it, Hedvig. It will only be for a few minutes, you understand.

(*He slips into the attic by the edge of the curtain.* HEDVIG *keeps on working.* HJALMAR *and* EKDAL *can be heard talking behind the curtain.*)

HJALMAR (*appearing inside the net*): Hedvig, please give me the pliers on the shelf. And the chisel. (*Turns around.*) See here, father. Just let me show you what I have in mind first.

(HEDVIG *fetches the tools from the shelf and gives them to him.*)

HJALMAR: Thank you. It was a good thing I went in.

(*He leaves the doorway. Sounds of carpentering and conversation are heard from inside.* HEDVIG *remains watching them. After a while there is a knock on the entrance door. She does not notice.*)

GREGERS (*bareheaded and coatless, enters, stops near the door*): H'm!

HEDVIG (*turns around and walks towards him*): Good morning! Won't you please come in?

GREGERS: Thank you. (*Looks towards the attic.*) You seem to have workmen in the house.

HEDVIG: Oh no. It's just father and Grandpa. I'll tell them you're here.

GREGERS: Please don't. I'd rather wait a while. (*Sits down on the sofa.*)

HEDVIG: It's such a mess in here — (*Begins removing the photographs.*)

GREGERS: Never mind. Are they pictures you are retouching?

HEDVIG: Yes. It is something I help father with.

GREGERS: I hope you won't let me disturb you.

HEDVIG: I won't.

(*She moves the things more within her reach and resumes work.* GREGERS *watches her in silence.*)

GREGERS: Did the wild duck sleep well last night?

HEDVIG: Yes, thank you. I think so.

GREGERS (*turning towards the attic*): In daylight it looks quite different from last night when there was a moon.

HEDVIG: Yes, it varies so. In the morning it looks different than in the afternoon, and when it rains it looks different than when the sun is shining.

GREGERS: You have noticed that?

HEDVIG: Yes, of course.

GREGERS: Do you too spend much time with the wild duck?

HEDVIG: Yes, when I can.

GREGERS: I suppose you don't have much spare time, though. You are going to school, of course?

HEDVIG: Not any more. Father is afraid I'll ruin my eyes.

GREGERS: Then he reads with you himself?

HEDVIG: He has promised to, but he hasn't had the time yet.

GREGERS: But isn't there anyone else who can help you?

HEDVIG: Well, yes, there is Mr. Molvik, but he isn't always — you know — quite —

GREGERS: You mean he is drunk sometimes.

HEDVIG: I think so.

GREGERS: Well, in that case you have time for many things. And in there, I suppose, it's like a world all its own?

HEDVIG: Yes, quite. And there are so many strange things in there.

GREGERS: There are?

HEDVIG: Yes, there are big closets with books in them, and in many of the books there are pictures.

GREGERS: I see.

HEDVIG: And there is an old desk with drawers and drop-down leaves and a big clock with figures that come out. But the clock doesn't run any more.

GREGERS: So time has stopped in there where the wild duck lives?

HEDVIG: Yes. And there are old coloring sets and that sort of thing, and then all the books.

GREGERS: I expect you read the books.

HEDVIG: Yes, whenever I have a chance. But most of them are in English and I can't read that. But I look at the pictures. There is a great, big book that's called "Harrison's History of London." I think it is a hundred years old. There are ever so many pictures in it. In front it shows a picture of Death with an hourglass and a girl. I think that is horrible. But then there are all the pictures of churches and castles and streets and big ships that sail the seas.

GREGERS: Tell me — where do all those strange things come from?

HEDVIG: There was an old sea captain who used to live here. He brought them home. They called him The Flying Dutchman. And that's odd, I think, for he wasn't a Dutchman at all.

GREGERS: No?

HEDVIG: No. But finally he disappeared at sea, and all the things were left here.

GREGERS: Listen — when you sit in there looking at the pictures, don't you ever want to travel and see the real, big world for yourself?

HEDVIG: Oh no. I want to stay here at home always and help father and mother.

GREGERS: With the photographs?

HEDVIG: Not just with that. Best of all I'd like to learn how to engrave pictures like those in the English books.

GREGERS: H'm. And what does your father say to that?

HEDVIG: I don't think father likes the idea very much. He is funny about things like that. You know, he says I ought to learn basket-weaving and straw-plaiting. But I don't think that sounds like much of anything at all.

GREGERS: No, I don't think it does either.

HEDVIG: Though of course father is quite right in saying that if I had learned basket-weaving I could have made the new basket for the wild duck.

GREGERS: That's true. And that really ought to have been your job, you know.

HEDVIG: Yes. Because it is my wild duck.

GREGERS: So I hear.

HEDVIG: Oh yes. I own it. But father and Grandpa get to borrow it as often as they like.

GREGERS: So? And what do they do with it?

HEDVIG: Oh — they take care of it and build things for it and that sort of thing.

GREGERS: I see. For of course the wild duck is the noblest of all the animals in there.

HEDVIG: Yes, she is, for she is a real, wild bird. And then I feel sorrier for her than for any of the others, because she's all alone, poor thing.

GREGERS: No family, like the rabbits.

HEDVIG: No. And the chickens, they have so many they were little chicks together with. But she is all alone, with none of her own near by. And there is the strange thing about the wild duck. Nobody knows her and nobody knows where she is from.

GREGERS: And she has been down to the depths of the sea.

HEDVIG (*glances quickly at him, suppresses a smile, asks*): Why do you say "the depths of the sea"?

GREGERS: What should I say?

HEDVIG: You could say "the sea bottom" or "the bottom of the sea."

GREGERS: Can't I just as well say "the depths of the sea"?

HEDVIG: Yes, but I think it sounds so strange when other people say "the depths of the sea."

GREGERS: Why is that? Tell me.

HEDVIG: No, I won't, for it is so silly.

GREGERS: I don't think so. Please tell me why you smiled.

HEDVIG: It's because every time I think of what's in there — when it comes into my head all of a sudden, I mean — I always feel that the whole room and everything that's in it are the depths of the sea. But that's silly.

GREGERS: Don't say that.

HEDVIG: Yes, for it's just an old attic, you know.

GREGERS (*looking intently at her*): Are you sure?

HEDVIG (*surprised*): That it's an attic?

GREGERS: Yes. Are you sure it is?

(HEDVIG *stares at him in silence, her mouth open in astonishment.* GINA *enters from the kitchen with linen, silverware, etc., to set the table.*)

GREGERS (*getting up*): I am afraid I am too early for you.

GINA: Oh well. You have to be somewhere. Things are almost ready now, anyway. Clear the table, Hedvig.

(*During the next scene* HEDVIG *clears the table and* GINA *sets it.* GREGERS *seats himself in the armchair and starts leafing through an album of photographs.*)

GREGERS: I understand you know how to retouch, Mrs. Ekdal.

GINA (*looks at him out of the corner of her eye*): That's right.

GREGERS: That was fortunate.

GINA: How — fortunate?

GREGERS: I mean since Ekdal is a photographer.

HEDVIG: Mother knows how to take pictures, too.

GINA: Oh yes, I've had to learn *that* business, all right.

GREGERS: Perhaps it is you who are responsible for the daily routine?

GINA: Yes, when Ekdal himself doesn't have the time —

GREGERS: I suppose he busies himself a great deal with his old father?

GINA: Yes, and then it's not for a man like Ekdal to waste his time taking pictures of everybody and his grandmother.

GREGERS: I quite agree, but since he did choose this as his profession, shouldn't he — ?

GINA: You know just as well as I do, Mr. Werle, that Ekdal isn't just one of your common, ordinary photographers.

GREGERS: Of course not, but — nevertheless —

(*A shot is heard from the attic.*)

GREGERS (*jumps up*): What was that?

GINA: Ugh! There they go, firing away again!

GREGERS: They shoot, too?

HEDVIG: They go hunting.

GREGERS: What? (*Over by the door to the attic.*) Do you go hunting, Hjalmar?

HJALMAR (*inside the curtain*): Have you arrived? I didn't know — I've been so busy — (*To* HEDVIG.) And you — not letting us know — ! (*Comes into the studio.*)

GREGERS: Do you go shooting in the attic?

HJALMAR (*showing him a double-barreled pistol*): Oh, it's only this old thing.

GINA: You and Grandpa are going to have an accident with that pestol of yours one of these days.

HJALMAR (*irritated*): I believe I have told you that this kind of firearm is called a pistol.

GINA: I don't see that that makes it any better.

GREGERS: So you have taken up hunting, too, Hjalmar?

HJALMAR: Only a little rabbit hunting now and then. It's mostly for father's sake, you understand.

GINA: Menfolks are strange. They always need something to diverge themselves with.

HJALMAR (*grimly*): That's right. We always need something to divert ourselves with.

GINA: That's exactly what I'm saying.

HJALMAR: Oh well — ! H'm! (*To* GREGERS.) Well, you see, we're fortunate in that the attic is situated so that nobody can hear the shots.

(*Puts the pistol on the top shelf.*) Don't touch the pistol, Hedvig! Remember, one barrel is loaded!

GREGERS (*peering through the net*): You have a hunting rifle, too, I see.

HJALMAR: That's father's old gun. It doesn't work any more. There's something wrong with the lock. But it's rather fun to have it around all the same, for we take it apart and clean it once in a while and grease it and put it back together again. It's mostly father, of course, who amuses himself with things like that.

HEDVIG (*standing next to* GREGERS): Now you can get a good look at the wild duck.

GREGERS: I was just looking at it. One wing is drooping a bit, isn't it?

HJALMAR: Well that's not so strange. She was hit, you know.

GREGERS: And she drags her foot a little. Or doesn't she?

HJALMAR: Perhaps a little bit.

HEDVIG: Yes, for that is the foot the dog seized her by.

HJALMAR: But aside from that she has no other hurt or defect, and that's really quite remarkable when you consider that she has a charge of buckshot in her and has been between the teeth of a dog.

GREGERS (*with a glance at* HEDVIG): Yes, and been to the depths of the sea — for so long.

HEDVIG (*smiles*): Yes.

GINA (*busy at the table*): Oh yes, that precious wild duck. There sure is enough circumstance made over it.

HJALMAR: H'm. Will you be done setting the table soon?

GINA: In a minute. Hedvig, I need your help. (GINA *and* HEDVIG *go into the kitchen.*)

HJALMAR (*in a low voice*): You had better not watch father. He doesn't like it.

GREGERS (*leaves the attic door.*)

HJALMAR: And I ought to close this before the others arrive. (*Shoos the birds away with his hands.*) Shoo! Shoo — you! (*Raising the curtain and sliding the doors back.*) This arrangement is my own invention. It is really quite amusing to fool around with these things and to fix them when they get broken. And it's absolutely necessary to have something like it, for Gina won't stand for rabbits and chickens in the studio.

GREGERS: No, I suppose not. And perhaps the studio is your wife's department?

HJALMAR: I generally leave the daily run of the business to her. That gives me a chance to retire into the living room and give my thoughts to more important things.

GREGERS: What things, Hjalmar?

HJALMAR: I have been wondering why you haven't asked me that before. Or maybe you haven't heard about the invention?

GREGERS: Invention? No.

HJALMAR: Really? You haven't? Oh well — up there in the woods and wilderness —

GREGERS: So you have invented something!

HJALMAR: Not quite yet, but I am working on it. As you can well imagine, when I decided to devote myself to photography it was not my intent to do nothing but take portraits of all sorts of ordinary people.

GREGERS: I suppose not. Your wife just said the same thing.

HJALMAR: I made a pledge to myself that if I were to give my powers to this profession, I would raise it so high that it would become both an art and a science. That is how I decided to make some remarkable invention.

GREGERS: What is it? What does it do?

HJALMAR: Well, Gregers, you must not ask for details just yet. You see, it takes time. And don't think I am driven by vanity. I can truthfully say I am not working for my own sake. Far from it. It is my life's mission that is in my thoughts night and day.

GREGERS: What mission?

HJALMAR: The old man with the silver hair — can you forget him?

GREGERS: Yes, your poor father. But what exactly do you think you can do for him?

HJALMAR: I can resurrect his respect for himself by once again raising the name of Ekdal to fame and honor.

GREGERS: So that is your life's mission.

HJALMAR: Yes. I will rescue that shipwrecked man. For he was shipwrecked the moment the storm broke. During those terrible inquiries he was not himself. The pistol over yonder — the one we use to shoot rabbits with — it has played its part in the tragedy of the Ekdal family.

GREGERS: The pistol? Really?

HJALMAR: When sentence had been pronounced and he was to be confined — he had that pistol in his hand —

GREGERS: He tried to — !

HJALMAR: Yes, but didn't dare. He was a coward. So much of a wreck, so spiritually ruined was he already then. Can you understand it? He, an officer, the killer of nine bears, descended from two lieutenant colonels — I mean one after the other, of course — Can you understand it, Gregers?

GREGERS: I can indeed.

HJALMAR: Not I. — But the pistol came to figure in our family chronicle a second time. When he had begun to wear the garb of gray and sat there behind bolt and bar — oh, those were terrible days for me, believe me. I kept the shades down on both windows. When I looked out, I saw the sun shining as usual. I saw people in the street laughing and talking about nothing. I could not understand it. It seemed to me that all of existence ought to come to a standstill, as during an eclipse of the sun.

GREGERS: I felt that way when mother died.

HJALMAR: In such an hour Hjalmar Ekdal turned the pistol against himself —

GREGERS: You too were thinking of — ?

HJALMAR: Yes.

GREGERS: But you did not pull the trigger?

HJALMAR: No. In the decisive moment I won a victory over myself. I remained alive. Take my word for it: it requires courage to go on living in a situation like that.

GREGERS: That depends on how you look at it.

HJALMAR: No, it doesn't. At any rate, it all turned out to be for the best. For soon now I will finish my invention, and when I do, Doctor Relling thinks, as I do myself, that father will be allowed to wear his uniform again. I shall claim that as my only reward.

GREGERS: So it is this business with the uniform that mostly —

HJALMAR: Yes, to be able to wear it again is what he dreams of and longs for. You have no idea how it cuts me to the quick to see him. Whenever we have a little family celebration here, like Gina's and my wedding anniversary or whatever it may be, then the old man appears in his lieutenant's uniform from happier days. But no sooner is there a knock on the door than he scuttles back to his own little room as fast as his old legs will carry him. He doesn't dare to show himself to strangers, you know. A sight like that lacerates a son's heart, Gregers!

GREGERS: About when do you think the invention will be ready?

HJALMAR: Heavens, you must not ask for details like that. An invention, you see, is something you don't altogether control yourself. It is very largely a matter of inspiration — a sudden idea — and it is next to impossible to tell beforehand when that may come.

GREGERS: But it is progressing?

HJALMAR: Certainly, it is progressing. It occupies my thoughts every day. It fills me. Every afternoon, after dinner, I shut myself up in the living room to ponder in peace. I just can't be hurried; it won't do any good. That is what Relling says, too.

GREGERS: And you don't think that all this business in the attic interferes too much, distracts you from your work?

HJALMAR: No, no, no. Quite the contrary. You must not say a thing like that. After all, I cannot everlastingly be pursuing the same exhausting train of thought. I need something else, something to occupy me during the waiting period. The inspiration, the sudden flash of insight, don't you see? — when it comes, it comes.

GREGERS: My dear Hjalmar, I almost think there is something of the wild duck in you.

HJALMAR: The wild duck? How do you mean?

GREGERS: You have plunged down through the sea and got yourself entangled in the grasses on the bottom.

HJALMAR: Are you perhaps referring to the well-nigh fatal shot that lodged in father's wing and hit me, too?

GREGERS: Not to that so much. I won't say you are crippled. But you are in a poisonous marsh, Hjalmar. You have contracted an insidious disease and gone to the bottom to die in the dark.

HJALMAR: I? Die in the dark? Honestly, Gregers. You really shouldn't say such things.

GREGERS: Don't you worry. I'll get you up again. For I, too, have got a mission in life. I found it yesterday.

HJALMAR: That may well be, but I shall ask you kindly to leave me out of it. I assure you that — aside from my easily explainable melancholia, of course — I am as contented a man as anybody could wish to be.

GREGERS: The fact that you are — that is one of the symptoms of the poisoning.

HJALMAR: No, really, Gregers. Please don't talk to me any more about disease and poison. I am not used to that sort of talk. In my house we never discuss unpleasant topics.

GREGERS: That I can well believe.

HJALMAR: No, for it isn't good for me. And there is no marshy air here, as you call it. The roof may be low in the poor photographer's home — I know very well it is — and my lot is lowly. But I am an inventor, and a provider as well. That is what raises me above my humble circumstances. — Ah! Here's lunch!

(GINA *and* HEDVIG *enter with bottles of beer, a decanter of brandy, glasses, and other appurtenances. At the same moment,* RELLING *and* MOLVIK *come through the entrance door. Neither one wears hat or coat.* MOLVIK *is dressed in black.*)

GINA (*putting the things down on the table*): Well, you two arrive just in time.

RELLING: Molvik thought he could smell herring salad, and then there was no holding him. — Good morning again, Ekdal.

HJALMAR: Gregers, may I introduce you to Mr. Molvik — And Doctor — that's right, you two already know each other, don't you.

GREGERS: Slightly.

RELLING: Oh yes, young Mr. Werle. We used to do some skirmishing up at the Høydal works. I take it you have just moved in?

GREGERS: This morning.

RELLING: Well, Molvik and I live downstairs, so you don't have far to go for doctor and minister if you need them.

GREGERS: Thank you; maybe I shall. We were thirteen at the table yesterday.

HJALMAR: Come now! Please don't start any of that unpleasantness again!

RELLING: Calm down, Ekdal. You are immune.

HJALMAR: I hope so, for my family's sake. — Sit down. Let's eat, drink, and be merry.

GREGERS: Aren't we going to wait for your father?

HJALMAR: No, he'll eat later in his own room. Do sit down!

(*The men seat themselves and begin eating and drinking.* GINA *and* HEDVIG *wait on them.*)

RELLING: Molvik got pretty high last night, Mrs. Ekdal.

GINA: Again?

RELLING: Didn't you hear me bring him home?

GINA: Can't say I did.

RELLING: That's good, for Molvik was awful last night.

GINA: Is that true, Molvik?

MOLVIK: Let us consign last night's events to oblivion. They do not represent my better self.

RELLING (*to* GREGERS): It comes over him like an irresistible impulse. Then he has to go out and get drunk. You see, Molvik is demonic.

GREGERS: Demonic?

RELLING: That's right. Molvik is demonic.

GREGERS: H'm.

RELLING: And demonic natures aren't made to follow the straight and narrow path. They have to take off for the fields once in a while. — So you still stick it out up at that filthy old place?

GREGERS: So far.

RELLING: Did you ever collect on that claim you went around presenting?

GREGERS: Claim? (*Looks at him and understands.*) Oh I see.

HJALMAR: Have you been a bill collector, Gregers?

GREGERS: Oh nonsense.

RELLING: Oh yes, he has. He went around to all the cottages up there, trying to collect on something he called "the claim of the ideal."

GREGERS: I was young.

RELLING: You're right. You were very young. And the claim of the ideal — you never collected as long as I was up there.

GREGERS: Not since then, either.

RELLING: In that case, I suppose you have been wise enough to reduce the amount somewhat.

GREGERS: Never when I have to do with a real and genuine human being.

HJALMAR: I think that is reasonable enough. — Some butter, Gina.

RELLING: And a piece of bacon for Molvik.

MOLVIK: Ugh! Not bacon!

(*There is a knock from inside the door to the attic.*)

HJALMAR: Go and open, Hedvig. Father wants to get out.

(HEDVIG *opens the door a little.* OLD EKDAL *enters with the skin of a freshly flayed rabbit.* HEDVIG *closes the door after him.*)

EKDAL: Good morning, gentlemen! Good hunting today. Got me a big one.

HJALMAR: And you skinned it yourself, I see.

EKDAL: Salted it, too. It's nice, tender meat, rabbit is. It's sweet, y'know. Tastes like sugar. Good appetite, gentlemen! (*Goes into his room.*)

MOLVIK (*getting up*): Excuse me — I can't — Got to get downstairs —

RELLING: Drink soda water, you idiot!

MOLVIK: Uh — Uh — (*Hurries out, right rear.*)

RELLING (*to* HJALMAR): Let us drink to the old hunter.

HJALMAR (*touching* RELLING's *glass with his own*): For the sportsman on the brink of the grave — yes.

RELLING: For the gray-haired — (*Drinks.*) Tell me, is his hair gray or is it white?

HJALMAR: In between, I think. Though I don't think there are many hairs left on his head at all.

RELLING: Oh well. One can live happily with a wig, too. Ah, yes, Ekdal. You are really a very happy man. You have this beautiful ambition of yours to strive for —

HJALMAR: Believe me, I am striving.

RELLING: Then you have your excellent wife, shuffling about in slippered feet with that comfortable waddle of hers, making things nice and pleasant for you.

HJALMAR: Yes, Gina — (*Nods to her.*) — you are a good companion on life's journey.

GINA: Aw, you don't need to sit there and dissectate me!

RELLING: And your Hedvig, Ekdal.

HJALMAR (*moved*): Ah yes, the child! The child above all. Hedvig, come to me. (*Stroking her hair.*) What day is tomorrow?

HEDVIG (*playfully shaking him*): Oh, stop it, father!

HJALMAR: It's like a knife through my heart, when I consider how little we can do. Just a small celebration here in the attic.

HEDVIG: But that's just the way I like it!

RELLING: You wait till the invention is all done, Hedvig.

HJALMAR: Yes! Then you'll see, Hedvig. I have decided to secure your future. You shall be made comfortable for as long as you live. I will ask for something for you, something or other. That will be the impecunious inventor's sole reward.

HEDVIG (*whispers, her arms around his neck*): Oh you good, sweet father!

RELLING (*to* GREGERS): Well, now, don't you think it's nice for a change to sit down to a good table in a happy family circle?

HJALMAR: Yes, I really relish these hours at the table.

GREGERS: I, for one, don't like to breathe marsh air.

RELLING: Marsh air?

HJALMAR: Oh, don't start all that again!

GINA: I'll have you know there is no marsh air here, Mr. Werle. The place is aired every single day.

GREGERS (*leaving the table*): The stench I have in mind you don't get rid of by opening windows.

HJALMAR: Stench!

GINA: Yes, how do you like that, Ekdal!

RELLING: Begging your pardon — it wouldn't by any chance be you yourself who bring the stench with you from the Høydal mines?

GREGERS: It's just like you to call stench what I bring to this house.

RELLING (*walks over to* GREGERS): Listen here, Mr. Werle junior. I strongly suspect that you still carry the claim of the ideal around in your rear pocket.

GREGERS: I carry it in my heart.

RELLING: I don't care where the hell you carry it as long as you don't go bill collecting here while I am around.

GREGERS: And if I do so, nevertheless?

RELLING: Then you'll go head first down the stairs. Now you know!

HJALMAR: No, really, Relling — !

GREGERS: Go ahead! Throw me out!

GINA (*interposing*): No, we won't have any of that, Relling. But I will

say this to you, Mr. Werle, that it seems like you are not the right
person to come here and talk about stench after what you did to the
stove in your room this morning.

(*There is a knock on the door.*)

HEDVIG: Mother, someone's knocking.

HJALMAR: Oh yes, let's have customers on top of everything else —!

GINA: I'll handle it. (*Opens the door, gives a start, steps back*): Oh
dear!

(WERLE, *in a fur coat, steps inside.*)

WERLE: I beg your pardon, but I am told my son is here.

GINA (*swallowing hard*): Yes sir.

HJALMAR (*closer*): Sir, wouldn't you like to —?

WERLE: Thanks. I just want a word with my son.

GREGERS: Well. Here I am.

WERLE: I want to talk with you in your room.

GREGERS: In my room —? Oh, all right. (*Is about to leave.*)

GINA: Good Lord, no! That's not a fit place!

WERLE: All right; out here in the hall, then. I want to see you alone.

HJALMAR: You may do that right here, Mr. Werle. Relling, come into
the living room with me.

(HJALMAR *and* RELLING *go out, right front.* GINA *takes* HEDVIG
with her into the kitchen, left front.)

GREGERS (*after a brief silence*): Well. We are alone.

WERLE: You dropped some hints last night. And since you have moved
in with the Ekdals, I can only assume that you are planning something or other against me.

GREGERS: I plan to open Hjalmar Ekdal's eyes. He is to see his position
as it really is. That's all.

WERLE: Is that the life mission you mentioned yesterday?

GREGERS: Yes. You have left me no other.

WERLE: So you feel it is I who have twisted your mind, Gregers?

GREGERS: You have twisted my whole life. I am not thinking of all that
with mother. But it is you I can thank for the fact that I am being
haunted and driven by a guilty conscience.

WERLE: Ah, I see. So your conscience is ailing.

GREGERS: I should have opposed you the time you were laying traps for
Lieutenant Ekdal. I should have warned him, for I suspected how
things were going.

WERLE: Yes, in that case you certainly ought to have said something.

GREGERS: I didn't have the courage. I was a coward — frightened. I felt an unspeakable fear of you — both then and for a long, long time afterwards.

WERLE: That fear appears to have left you now.

GREGERS: Yes, fortunately. What has been done to Old Ekdal, both by me and by — others, for that there is no remedy. But Hjalmar I can rescue from the web of lies and deceit in which he is suffocating.

WERLE: Do you think that is a good thing to do?

GREGERS: I am sure it is.

WERLE: I take it you think Mr. Photographer Ekdal is the kind of man who will be grateful for your friendly services?

GREGERS: Yes! He is that kind of man.

WERLE: H'm. We'll see.

GREGERS: Besides, if I am to continue living, I have to find a way to heal my sick conscience.

WERLE: It will never get well. Your conscience has been sickly from the time you were a child. It's hereditary, Gregers. You have it from your mother. The only inheritance she left you.

GREGERS (*with a contemptuous half smile*): I see you still haven't forgotten your disappointment when you found out mother wasn't rich.

WERLE: Let's not change the subject. Am I to think, then, that you are firmly resolved to guide Hjalmar Ekdal into the path you consider the right one?

GREGERS: Yes. That is my firm intent.

WERLE: In that case I could have saved myself coming all the way up here. For then I suppose there is no point in my asking you to move back home again?

GREGERS: No.

WERLE: And you don't want to join the firm?

GREGERS: No.

WERLE: Very well. But since I am to marry again, your part of the estate will have to be paid you.

GREGERS (*quickly*): No, I don't want that.

WERLE: You don't want it?

GREGERS: I dare not, for my conscience's sake.

WERLE (*after a brief pause*): Are you going back up to Høydal?

GREGERS: No. I consider myself released from your service.

WERLE: But what do you want to do with yourself?

GREGERS: Accomplish my mission. Nothing else.

WERLE: But afterwards? What are you going to live on?

GREGERS: I have saved some of my salary.

WERLE: How long do you think that will last?

GREGERS: I think it will do for the time I have left.

WERLE: What is that supposed to mean?

GREGERS: I won't answer any more questions.
WERLE: Well, goodbye, Gregers.
GREGERS: Goodbye.

(WERLE *leaves.*)

HJALMAR (*looks in*): Did he leave?
GREGERS: Yes.

(HJALMAR *and* RELLING *enter from the living room,* GINA *and* HEDVIG *from the kitchen.*)

RELLING: Now that was a very successful breakfast.
GREGERS: Put on your coat, Hjalmar. I want you to take a long walk with me.
HJALMAR: Gladly. What did your father want? Did it have to do with me?
GREGERS: Just come. We'll talk. I'll go and get my coat. (*Goes out.*)
GINA: You shouldn't go with him, Ekdal.
RELLING: No, don't. Stay here.
HJALMAR (*taking his hat and coat*): What! When an old friend feels the need to open his heart for me in private — !
RELLING: But goddamit! Can't you see that the fellow is mad, cracked, insane!
GINA: Yes, listen to Relling. His mother used to have physicological fits, too.
HJALMAR: All the more reason why he needs a friend's alert eyes. (*To* GINA.) Be sure to have dinner ready at the usual time. Goodbye. (*Goes out.*)
RELLING: It's nothing less than a disaster that that man didn't go straight to hell down one of the shafts up at Høydal.
GINA: Heavens — ! Why do you say that?
RELLING (*mutters*): I have my reasons.
GINA: Do you really think young Werle is crazy?
RELLING: No, unfortunately. He is no madder than most people. He is sick, though.
GINA: What do you think is wrong with him?
RELLING: That I can tell you, Mrs. Ekdal. He suffers from an acute attack of moral integrity.
GINA: Moral integrity?
HEDVIG: Is that a disease?
RELLING: Yes, it is a national disease, but it occurs only sporadically. (*Nods to* GINA.) That was a good meal, thank you. (*Goes out.*)
GINA (*troubled, walks up and down*): Ugh! That Gregers Werle — he's always been a weird fish.

HEDVIG (*by the table, looks at her searchingly*): I think this is very strange.

ACT IV

(*The studio. Photographs have just been taken. A cloth-covered camera on a tripod, a couple of chairs, and a small table are standing about in the middle of the floor. Afternoon light. The sun is about to disappear. After a while darkness begins to fall.* •

GINA *stands in the open entrance door with a small box and a wet glass plate in her hand. She is talking to someone not in sight.*)

GINA: Absolutely. When I promise something, I keep it. I'll have the first dozen ready for you on Monday. — Goodbye.

(*Sounds of someone descending the stairs.* GINA *closes the door, puts the plate inside the box and the box into the camera.*)

HEDVIG (*enters from the kitchen*): Did they leave?
GINA (*putting things in order*): Yes, thank goodness. I finally got rid of them.
HEDVIG: Can you understand why father isn't back yet?
GINA: You're sure he is not down at Relling's?
HEDVIG: No, he is not there. I just went down the kitchen stairs to ask.
GINA: His food is getting cold and everything.
HEDVIG: Yes. And father who is always so particular about having dinner on time.
GINA: Oh well. You'll see he'll be back soon.
HEDVIG: I wish he'd come. Everything seems so strange.

(HJALMAR *enters from outside.*)

HEDVIG (*towards him*): Father! If you knew how we've been waiting for you!
GINA (*glancing at him*): You've been gone quite some time.
HJALMAR (*without looking at her*): Yes, I suppose I have.

(*He starts taking his coat off.* GINA *and* HEDVIG *both go to help him. He turns them away.*)

GINA: Maybe you and Werle had something to eat some place?
HJALMAR (*hanging up his coat*): No.
GINA (*towards the kitchen door*): I'll get your dinner.
HJALMAR: Never mind. I don't feel like eating now.

HEDVIG (*coming closer*): Are you sick, father?

HJALMAR: Sick? No, I'm not sick — exactly. We had a strenuous walk, Gregers and I.

GINA: You shouldn't do that, Ekdal. You aren't used to it.

HJALMAR: H'm. There are many things in life a man has to get used to. (*Paces up and down.*) Anybody here while I've been gone?

GINA: Only that engaged couple.

HJALMAR: No new appointments?

GINA: No, not today.

HEDVIG: There will be some tomorrow, father, I am sure.

HJALMAR: I hope you are right, for tomorrow I plan to go to work in earnest.

HEDVIG: Tomorrow! But don't you remember what day is tomorrow?

HJALMAR: That's right. Well, then, the day after tomorrow. From now on I'll do everything myself. I want to assume the entire work load.

GINA: Whatever for, Ekdal? That's only making yourself miserable. I'll manage the pictures. You just go on with the invention.

HEDVIG: And the wild duck, father. And the chickens and the rabbits and —

HJALMAR: Don't ever mention all that junk to me again! Starting tomorrow, I'll never more set foot in the attic.

HEDVIG: But father, you promised that tomorrow we're having a celebration —

HJALMAR: H'm. That's right. Day after tomorrow then. That damn wild duck! I'd like to wring its neck!

HEDVIG (*with a cry*): The wild duck!

GINA: Now I've heard everything!

HEDVIG (*shaking him*): But father — it's *my* wild duck!

HJALMAR: That's why I won't do it. I don't have the heart — for your sake, Hedvig. But deep down I feel I ought to do it. I shouldn't harbor under my roof a creature that has been in those hands.

GINA: For heaven's sake! Even if Grandpa *did* get it from that awful Pettersen.

HJALMAR (*walking up and down*): There are certain demands — what shall I call them? Let me say ideal demands — certain claims, that a man disregards only at the peril of his soul.

HEDVIG (*following after him*): But think — the wild duck! That poor wild duck!

HJALMAR (*halts*): Didn't I tell you I'll spare it — for your sake? Not a hair on its head will be — h'm. Well, as I said, I'll spare it. After all, there are bigger tasks awaiting me. But you ought to go out for a little walk, Hedvig. The twilight is just right for you.

HEDVIG: I don't care to go out now.

HJALMAR: Yes, do. Seems to me you are squinting. The fumes in here aren't good for you. The air is close under this roof.

HEDVIG: All right. I'll run down the kitchen stairs and walk around a bit. My hat and coat? Oh yes, in my room. Father, please — don't do anything bad to the wild duck while I'm gone!

HJALMAR: Not a feather shall be plucked from its head. (*Clutches her to him.*) You and I, Hedvig — we two! Be on your way now.

(HEDVIG *nods goodbye to her parents and goes out through the kitchen door.*)

HJALMAR (*pacing back and forth*): Gina.

GINA: Yes?

HJALMAR: Starting tomorrow — or let's say the day after tomorrow — I'd like to keep account of the housekeeping expenses myself.

GINA: So you want to keep the accounts too, now?

HJALMAR: Keep track of what we take in, at any rate.

GINA: Lord knows, that's easily done!

HJALMAR: One wouldn't think so. It seems to me you make the money go incredibly far. (*Stops and looks at her.*) How do you do it?

GINA: It's because Hedvig and I need so little.

HJALMAR: Is it true that father is overpaid for the copying work he does for Werle?

GINA: I couldn't say about that. I don't know the rates.

HJALMAR: Well, what *does* he get? In round figures. — I want to know.

GINA: It differs. I guess it comes to about what he costs us, plus a little extra in spending money.

HJALMAR: What he costs us! And you haven't told me that!

GINA: No, I couldn't, for you were so happy because he got everything from you.

HJALMAR: And it has really been Werle all the time!

GINA: Oh well. He can afford it.

HJALMAR: Light the lamp!

GINA (*lighting the lamp*): And as far as that is concerned, how do we know it is Werle himself? It may be Gråberg —

HJALMAR: Really, Gina. You know that isn't so. Why do you say a thing like that?

GINA: I don't know. I just thought —

HJALMAR: H'm!

GINA: It wasn't me who got Grandpa all that copying to do. It was Bertha, when she took service there.

HJALMAR: It sounds to me like your voice is trembling.

GINA (*putting the shade on the lamp*): Does it?

HJALMAR: And your hands are shaking. Aren't they?

GINA (*firmly*): You might as well tell me straight, Ekdal. What has he been saying about me?

HJALMAR: Is it true — *can* it be true — that there was some kind of affair between you and Werle while you were in his house?

GINA: That's not so. Not then. He was after me, though. And Mrs. Werle thought there was something going on, and she made a fuss and a big hullaballoo about it, and she beat me and pulled me around — and so I quit.

HJALMAR: But afterwards — !

GINA: Well, then I went to live with mother. And you see — mother — she wasn't all the woman you thought she was, Ekdal. She talked to me about this, that, and the other. For Werle was a widower by that time —

HJALMAR: And then — ?

GINA: You might as well know it, I guess. He didn't give up till he had his way.

HJALMAR (*striking his hands together*): And this is the mother of my child! How could you keep a thing like this from me?

GINA: Yes, I know it was wrong. I should have told you long ago, I suppose.

HJALMAR: You should have told me right away; that's what you should have. Then I would have known what sort of woman you were.

GINA: But would you have married me, irregardless?

HJALMAR: Of course, I wouldn't!

GINA: I didn't think so, and that's why I didn't dare to tell you. I had come to care for you, you know — a whole lot I cared for you. And I just couldn't see making myself as unhappy as all that —

HJALMAR (*walking about*): And this is my Hedvig's mother! And to know that everything I lay my eyes on here (*Kicks a chair.*) — my whole home — I owe to a favored predecessor! Oh, that seducer, that damn Werle!

GINA: Do you regret the fourteen-fifteen years we've had together?

HJALMAR (*fronting her*): Tell me if you haven't felt every day and every hour to be one long agony of repentance for that web of deceitful silence you have woven around me, like a spider? Answer me! Haven't you lived here in perpetual torture of guilt and remorse?

GINA: Bless you, Ekdal! I've been plenty busy with the house and the pictures —

HJALMAR: So you never cast a probing glance at your past?

GINA: No, to tell the truth, I had almost forgotten all those old stories.

HJALMAR: Oh, this dull, apathetic calm! There is something shocking about it. Not even repentant — !

GINA: Just tell me this, Ekdal. What do you think would have become of you if you hadn't got yourself a wife like me?

HJALMAR: Like you — !

GINA: Yes, for you know I have always been more practical and able to cope with things than you. Of course, I am a couple of years older —

HJALMAR: What would have become of me!

GINA: For you've got to admit you weren't living exactly right when you first met me.

HJALMAR: So you call that living wrong! Oh, what do you know about a man's feelings when he sorrows and despairs — especially a man of my fiery temperament.

GINA: No, I guess I don't know. And I don't mean to execrete you for it, either, for you turned into as decent a man as they come as soon as you got a house and a family of your own to take care of. And now we were getting on so nicely here, and Hedvig and I were just thinking that pretty soon we might spend some money on clothes for ourselves.

HJALMAR: Yes, in the swamp of deceit!

GINA: That that fellow ever poked his nose inside here!

HJALMAR: I, too, thought our home a pleasant one. That was a mistake. Where now do I gather the necessary inner resilience to bring my invention into the world of reality? Perhaps it will die with me. If it does, it will be your past, Gina, that has killed it.

GINA (*on the verge of tears*): Please, Ekdal — don't be saying such things! I that have all my days only tried to make things nice and pleasant for you!

HJALMAR: I ask — what happens now to the breadwinner's dream? As I reclined in there on the sofa, pondering the invention, it came to me that it was going to drain me of my last drop of vitality. I knew that the day the patent was issued and in my hands — that day would be my — my day of farewell. And then it was my dream that you were to live on as the late inventor's well-to-do widow.

GINA (*wiping her tears*): I won't have you talk that way, Ekdal. May the good Lord never let me live the day when I'm your widow!

HJALMAR: Oh what difference does it all make! It is all over now, anyway. Everything!

(GREGERS *cautiously opens the entrance door and peers in.*)

GREGERS: May I come in?

HJALMAR: Yes, do.

GREGERS (*goes up to them with a beaming, happy face, reaches out his hands to them*): Now, then — you dear people — ! (*Looks from one to the other, whispers to* HJALMAR:) It hasn't happened yet?

HJALMAR (*loud*): It has happened.

GREGERS: It has?

HJALMAR: I have lived through the bitterest moment of my life.

GREGERS: But also, I trust, its most exalted one.

HJALMAR: Anyway, it's done and over with.

GINA: May God forgive you, Mr. Werle.

GREGERS (*greatly bewildered*): But I don't understand —!

HJALMAR: What don't you understand?

GREGERS: As crucial a conversation as this — a conversation that is to be the foundation for a whole new way of life — a life, a partnership, in truth and frankness —

HJALMAR: I know. I know it very well.

GREGERS: I was so sure that when I came in here now I would be met with a splendor of revelation shining from both husband and wife. But all I see is this dull, heavy gloom —

GINA: So that's it. (*Removes the lamp shade.*)

GREGERS: You refuse to understand me, Mrs. Ekdal. Well, I suppose you need time. But you, Hjalmar? Surely, you must have felt a higher consecration in this great crisis.

HJALMAR: Of course I did. That is, in a way.

GREGERS: For surely nothing in the world can be compared to finding forgiveness in one's heart for her who has erred and lovingly lifting her up to one's own heights.

HJALMAR: Do you think a man so easily forgets the draught of wormwood I just drained?

GREGERS: An ordinary man, maybe not. But a man like you —!

HJALMAR: Oh, I know. But you must not rush me, Gregers. It takes time.

GREGERS: There is much of the wild duck in you, Hjalmar.

(RELLING *has entered.*)

RELLING: Ah! Here we go with the wild duck again!

HJALMAR: Mr. Werle's crippled prey — yes.

RELLING: Werle? Is it him you're talking about?

HJALMAR: About him — and about ourselves.

RELLING (*in a low voice, to* GREGERS): Damn you to hell!

HJALMAR: What are you saying?

RELLING: I am just expressing an ardent wish that this quack here would betake himself home. If he stays around he is likely to ruin both of you.

GREGERS: Those two cannot be ruined, Mr. Relling. Of Hjalmar I need say nothing. Him we know. But she, too, has surely in the depths of her being something reliable, something of integrity —

GINA (*almost crying*): Why didn't you leave me alone then?

RELLING (*to* GREGERS): Is it impertinent to ask exactly what you want in this house?

GREGERS: I want to lay the foundation for a true marriage.

RELLING: So you don't think the Ekdals' marriage is good enough as it is?

GREGERS: I daresay it is as good a marriage as most, unfortunately. But a true marriage it has yet to become.

HJALMAR: You have never had an eye for the claim of the ideal, Relling!

RELLING: Nonsense, boy! — Begging your pardon, Mr. Werle — how many — roughly — how many true marriages have you observed in your life?

GREGERS: Hardly a single one.

RELLING: Nor have I.

GREGERS: But I have seen a number of the other kind. And I have had occasion to witness what havoc a marriage like that can work in a pair of human beings.

HJALMAR: A man's whole moral foundation may crumble under his feet; that's the terrible thing.

RELLING: Well, I can't say I've ever been exactly married, so I can't judge about that. But I do know this, that the child belongs to marriage too. And you had better leave the child alone.

HJALMAR: Oh, Hedvig! My poor Hedvig!

RELLING: Yes — keep Hedvig out of it, you two! You are grown-ups. In God's name, do whatever fool things you like to your marriage. But I am warning you: be careful what you do to Hedvig. If you're not, there is no telling what may happen to her.

HJALMAR: Happen to her!

RELLING: Yes, she may bring a disaster upon herself — and perhaps on others, too.

GINA: But how can you tell about that, Relling?

HJALMAR: Are you saying there is some immediate danger to her eyes?

RELLING: This has nothing whatever to do with her eyes. Hedvig is in a difficult age. She may do all sorts of crazy things.

GINA: I know — she does already. She's taken to fooling around with the woodstove in the kitchen. Playing fire, she calls it. Sometimes I'm scared she'll burn the whole house down.

RELLING: There you are. I knew it.

GREGERS (*to* RELLING): But how do you explain a thing like that?

RELLING (*sullenly*): Her voice is changing, sir.

HJALMAR: As long as the child has *me* — ! As long as *my* head is above the ground!

(*There is a knock on the door.*)

GINA: Shhh, Ekdal. There are people outside.

(MRS. SØRBY *enters, wearing hat and coat.*)

MRS. SØRBY: Good evening!

GINA (*going to her*): Goodness! Is it you, Bertha!

MRS. SØRBY: So it is. Maybe it's inconvenient — ?

HJALMAR: Oh by no means! A messenger from *that* house — !

MRS. SØRBY (*to* GINA): Frankly, I had hoped you'd be without your menfolks this time of day. I've just dropped in to have a word with you about something and say goodbye.

GINA: You're going away?

MRS. SØRBY: Tomorrow morning — to Høydal. Mr. Werle left this afternoon. (*Casually, to* GREGERS.) He asked me to say hello.

GINA: Imagine — !

HJALMAR: So Mr. Werle has left? And you are going after him?

MRS. SØRBY: Yes. What do you say to that, Ekdal?

HJALMAR: Look out, is all I say.

GREGERS: I can explain. Father and Mrs. Sørby are getting married.

GINA: Oh Bertha! At long last!

RELLING (*his voice trembling a little*): Surely, this cannot be true?

MRS. SØRBY: Yes, my dear Relling, true it is.

RELLING: You want to get married again?

MRS. SØRBY: That's what it amounts to. Werle has got the license. We'll have a quiet little party up at the works.

GREGERS: I suppose I should tender my felicitations like a good stepson.

MRS. SØRBY: Thank you, if you really mean it. I hope this will be for the best for both Werle and myself.

RELLING: I am sure you have every reason to think it will. Mr. Werle never gets drunk — at least not to my knowledge. Nor do I believe he is in the habit of beating up his wife, like the late lamented horse doctor.

MRS. SØRBY: Let Sørby rest quietly in his grave. He had his good sides, too.

RELLING: Mr. Industrialist Werle has better ones, I am sure.

MRS. SØRBY: At least he has not thrown away what is best in himself. The man who does that must take the consequences.

RELLING: Tonight I'll go out with Molvik.

MRS. SØRBY: Don't do that, Relling. Don't — for my sake.

RELLING: There's nothing else to do. (*To* HJALMAR.) Want to come along?

GINA: No, thank you. Ekdal doesn't go in for excapades like that.

HJALMAR (*angrily, in a half whisper*): For heaven's sake! Keep your mouth shut!

RELLING: Goodbye — Mrs. Werle! (*Goes out.*)

GREGERS (*to* MRS. SØRBY): It appears that you and Doctor Relling know each other quite well?

MRS. SØRBY: Yes, we've known each other for a good many years. At one time it looked as if we might have made a match of it.

GREGERS: I'm sure it was lucky for you that you didn't.

MRS. SØRBY: You may well say that. But I've always been wary of acting on impulse. A woman can't just throw herself away, you know.

GREGERS: Aren't you afraid I'll let my father know about this old acquaintanceship?

MRS. SØRBY: Do you really believe I haven't told him myself?

GREGERS: Oh?

MRS. SØRBY: Your father knows every little thing people might say about me with any show of truth at all. I have told him everything. That was the first thing I did when I realized what his intentions were.

GREGERS: It seems to me you are more than usually frank.

MRS. SØRBY: I have always been frank. For us women that's the best policy.

HJALMAR: What do you say to that, Gina?

GINA: Oh, women differ. Some do it one way, others do it different.

MRS. SØRBY: Well, Gina, in my opinion I have followed the wiser course. And Werle hasn't kept back anything either. You see, that's what mainly brought us together. Now he can sit and talk to me as openly as a child. He has never been able to do that before. A healthy, vigorous man like him — all through his youth and all the best years of his life he had his ears drummed full with angry sermons. And very often sermons about sins he hadn't even committed — according to what I have been told.

GINA: That's the truth.

GREGERS: If you ladies want to pursue that topic any further, I had better absent myself.

MRS. SØRBY: You may just as well stay as far as that's concerned. I won't say another word. I just wanted you to know I haven't kept anything back or played him false in any way. Maybe people will say I am a very fortunate woman, and in a way of course that's true. But I don't think I am getting any more than I am giving. I'll certainly never desert him. And I can be of more service and use to him than anybody else, now that he'll soon be helpless.

HJALMAR: Will he be helpless?

GREGERS (*to* MRS. SØRBY): Don't say anything about that here.

MRS. SØRBY: It can't be kept secret any longer, much as he'd like to. He is going blind.

HJALMAR (*struck*): Blind? That's strange. He, too?

GINA: Lots of people go blind.

MRS. SØRBY: And I'm sure you can tell yourself what that must mean to a businessman. Well, I'll try to be his eyes, the best I know how. — But I can't stay any longer. I have so much to do right now. — Oh yes, What I wanted to tell you, Ekdal, is that if Werle can be of any service to you, all you need to do is to get in touch with Gråberg.

GREGERS: That is an offer I am sure Hjalmar Ekdal will decline.

MRS. SØRBY: Really? It seems to me he hasn't always been so —

GINA: Yes, Bertha. Ekdal doesn't need to accept anything more from Mr. Werle.

HJALMAR (*slowly, with weight*): Tell your husband-to-be from me, that in the very near future I intend to go to Mr. Gråberg —

GREGERS: What! You want to do that!

HJALMAR: — I say, go to Mr. Gråberg, and demand an account of the sum I owe his employer. I desire to pay this debt of honor — ha-ha-ha! — let us call it a debt of honor! Enough! I shall pay it all, with five per cent interest.

GINA: But Ekdal — goodness! We don't have that kind of money!

HJALMAR: Be so good as to inform your fiancé that I am working incessantly on my invention. Please tell him that what sustains my mind during this exhausting enterprise is my ambition to free myself from a painful burden of debt. This is why I am an inventor. The entire proceeds from my invention are to be devoted to liberating myself from the obligation to remunerate your husband-to-be for his expenses on behalf of my family.

MRS. SØRBY: Something has happened here.

HJALMAR: Indeed, something has.

MRS. SØRBY: Well, goodbye. I had something else I wanted to talk to you about, Gina, but that will have to wait till some other time. Goodbye.

(HJALMAR *and* GREGERS *return her greeting silently.* GINA *sees her to the door.*)

HJALMAR: Not beyond the threshold, Gina!

(MRS. SØRBY *leaves.* GINA *closes the door.*)

HJALMAR: There, now, Gregers. I have that burdensome debt off my chest.

GREGERS: You soon will, at any rate.

HJALMAR: I believe my attitude must be deemed the proper one.

GREGERS: You are the man I have always taken you to be.

HJALMAR: In certain cases it is impossible to disregard the claims of the ideal. As provider for my family, I am bound, of course, to find my course of action difficult and painful. Believe me, it is no joke for a man situated as I am, without means, to assume a debt of many years' standing — a debt, you might say, covered by the sands of oblivion. But never mind. The man in me demands his rights.

GREGERS (*placing his hand on his shoulder*): Dear Hjalmar — wasn't it a good thing that I came?

HJALMAR: Yes.

GREGERS: That your whole situation was made clear to you — wasn't that a good thing?

HJALMAR (*a bit impatiently*): Of course it was. But there is one thing that shocks my sense of justice.

GREGERS: What is that?

HJALMAR: It is this that — But I don't know that I ought to speak so freely about your father —

GREGERS: Don't let that worry you. Say what you want.

HJALMAR: All right. Well, you see, there is something shocking in the notion that now it's he and not I who realizes the true marriage.

GREGERS: How can you say a thing like that!

HJALMAR: Well, it is. For your father and Mrs. Sørby are about to solemnify a union built on full mutual confidence, on complete, unconditional frankness on both sides. They conceal nothing from each other, there are no deceitful silences, there has been declared, if I may put it so, mutual absolution between them.

GREGERS: Well, what of it?

HJALMAR: Well, then — it's all there! All the difficult conditions you yourself said are prerequisites for the building of a true marriage.

GREGERS: But that's in quite a different way, Hjalmar. Surely, you won't compare either yourself or Gina with those two — ? Oh I am sure you know what I mean.

HJALMAR: Yet I can't get away from the thought that in all this there is something that offends my sense of justice. It looks exactly as if there were no just order in the universe.

GINA: Ekdal, for God's sake, don't talk like that!

GREGERS: H'm. Let's not get involved in those issues.

HJALMAR: Though, on the other hand, I do in a way discern fate's ruling finger, too. He is going blind.

GINA: We don't know that yet.

HJALMAR: There is no doubt about it. At least, we ought not to doubt it, for in that very fact lies the proof of just retribution. He did once hoodwink a trusting fellow being.

GREGERS: I am afraid he has hoodwinked many.

HJALMAR: And here comes the inexorable, the inscrutable, claiming Werle's own eyes.

GINA: How you talk! I think it's scary.

HJALMAR: It is salutary at times to contemplate the night side of existence.

(HEDVIG, *dressed for the outside, enters. She is happy, breathless.*)

GINA: Back so soon?

HEDVIG: Yes. I didn't feel like walking any farther. It was a good thing, too, for I met somebody as I was coming in.

HJALMAR: Mrs. Sørby, I suppose.

HEDVIG: Yes.

HJALMAR (*pacing the floor*): I hope you have seen her for the last time.

(*Silence.* HEDVIG, *troubled, looks from one to the other in order to gauge their mood.*)

HEDVIG (*approaching* HJALMAR, *ingratiatingly*): Father?

HJALMAR: All right — what is it, Hedvig?

HEDVIG: Mrs. Sørby had something for me.

HJALMAR (*halts*): For you?

HEDVIG: Yes. Something for tomorrow.

GINA: Bertha always brings you a little something for your birthday.

HJALMAR: What is it?

HEDVIG: No, you're not to find out now. Mother is to give it to me in the morning, when she brings me breakfast in bed.

HJALMAR: What is all this mystification that I am to be kept in the dark about!

HEDVIG (*quickly*): I'll be glad to let you see it, father. It's a big letter. (*Takes the letter out of her coat pocket.*)

HJALMAR: A letter too?

HEDVIG: The letter is all there is. I suppose the other thing will come later. Just think — a letter! I never got a letter before. And it says "Miss" on the outside of it. (*Reads.*) "Miss Hedvig Ekdal." Just think — that's me!

HJALMAR: Let me see that letter.

HEDVIG: Here you are. (*Hands it to him.*)

HJALMAR: It's Werle's handwriting.

GINA: Are you sure, Ekdal?

HJALMAR: See for yourself.

GINA: How would I know?

HJALMAR: Hedvig? May I open the letter? Read it?

HEDVIG: If you like.

GINA: Not tonight, Ekdal. It's supposed to be for tomorrow.

HEDVIG (*in a low voice*): Please let him read it! It's bound to be something nice, and then father will be in a good mood, and everything will be pleasant again.

HJALMAR: You say I may open it?

HEDVIG: Yes, please, father. I'd like to know what it is about, too.

HJALMAR: Good. (*Opens the envelope, reads the letter inside. Appears confused.*) What *is* this — ?

GINA: What does it say?

HEDVIG: Please, father — tell us!

HJALMAR: Be quiet. (*Reads the letter again. He is pale, but his voice is controlled.*) It is a gift letter, Hedvig.

HEDVIG: Imagine! What is it I get?

HJALMAR: Read for yourself.

(HEDVIG *goes over to the lamp and reads.*)

HJALMAR (*in a low voice, clenches his fists*): The eyes, the eyes! And now that letter!

HEDVIG (*interrupting his reading*): Seems to me like it's Grandpa who gets it.

HJALMAR (*taking the letter away from her*): You, Gina — can you make any sense out of this?

GINA: I don't know a blessed thing about it. Why don't you just tell me?

HJALMAR: Werle writes to Hedvig that her old grandfather no longer needs to trouble himself with the copying work he has been doing, but that he may go to the office every month and draw one hundred crowns —

GREGERS: Aha!

HEDVIG: One hundred crowns, mother! I read that.

GINA: That will be nice for Grandpa.

HJALMAR: — one hundred crowns for as long as he needs it. That means, of course, till he closes his eyes.

GINA: So *he* is all taken care of, poor soul.

HJALMAR: Then it comes. You can't have read that far, Hedvig. After his death, that money will be yours.

HEDVIG: Mine? All of it?

HJALMAR: He writes that the same amount has been set aside for you for the rest of your life. Are you listening, Gina?

GINA: Yes, I hear.

HEDVIG: Just think — all the money I'll be getting! (*Shaking* HJAL-MAR's *arm*.) Father! Father! But aren't you glad?

HJALMAR (*going away from her*): Glad! (*Walking about*.) Oh what vistas, what perspectives, open up before me! It is Hedvig he is so generous to!

GINA: Well, she's the one with the birthday.

HEDVIG: And of course you will get it anyway, father! Don't you know I'll give it all to you and mother?

HJALMAR: To mother, yes! That's just it!

GREGERS: Hjalmar, this is a trap being prepared for you.

HJALMAR: You think this may be another trap?

GREGERS: When he was here this morning, he said, "Hjalmar Ekdal is not the man you think he is."

HJALMAR: Not the man — !

GREGERS: "You just wait and see," he said.

HJALMAR: You were to see me selling myself for money — !

HEDVIG: Mother, what *is* all this?

GINA: Go out and take your wraps off.

(HEDVIG, *about to cry, goes out into the kitchen*.)

GREGERS: Well, Hjalmar — now we shall see who is right — he or I.

HJALMAR (*slowly tearing the letter in two, putting the pieces down on the table*): Here is my answer.

GREGERS: Just as I thought.

HJALMAR (*to* GINA, *who is standing near the stove; in a low voice*): No more concealment now. If everything was over between you and him when you — came to care for me, as you call it, then why did he make it possible for us to get married?

GINA: I guess he thought he'd make free of the house.

HJALMAR: Just that? He wasn't worried about a certain possibility?

GINA: I don't know what you're talking about.

HJALMAR: I want to know — if your child has the right to live under my roof.

GINA (*drawing herself up, her eyes flashing*): You ask me that!

HJALMAR: Just tell me one thing. Is Hedvig mine or — ? — Well?

GINA (*looks at him with cold defiance*): I don't know.

HJALMAR (*with a slight tremble*): You don't know!

GINA: How can I? A woman like me!

HJALMAR (*quietly, turning away from her*): In that case I have nothing more to do in this house.

GREGERS: Think it over, Hjalmar!

HJALMAR (*putting his overcoat on*): For a man like me there is nothing to think over.

GREGERS: Yes, there is ever so much to think over. You three must stay together if you are to attain to the sacrificial spirit of sublime forgivingness.

HJALMAR: I don't want to attain it! Never! Never! My hat! (*Takes his hat.*) My house is in ruins about me. (*Bursts out crying.*) Gregers! I have no child!

HEDVIG (*who has opened the kitchen door*): Father! What are you saying!

GINA: Oh dear!

HJALMAR: Don't come near me, Hedvig! Go far away from me. I can't stand looking at you. Oh those eyes — ! Goodbye. (*Is about to go out.*)

HEDVIG (*clings to him, cries*): No! No! Don't leave me!

GINA: Look at the child, Ekdal! Look at the child!

HJALMAR: I will not! I cannot! I must get out — away from all this! (*He tears himself loose from* HEDVIG *and exits.*)

HEDVIG (*her eyes desperate*): He's leaving us, mother! He's leaving us! He'll never come back!

GINA: Just don't cry, Hedvig. Father will be back. You wait.

HEDVIG (*throws herself sobbing down on the sofa*): No! No! He'll never come back to us any more!

GREGERS: Do you believe I meant all for the best, Mrs. Ekdal?

GINA: Yes, I suppose you did, but God forgive you all the same.

HEDVIG (*on the sofa*): I want to die! What have I done to him, mother? You just have to get him back again!

GINA: Yes, yes, yes; only be quiet. I'll go out and look for him. (*Putting on her coat.*) Perhaps he's gone down to Relling's. But you're not to lie there, bawling like that. Promise?

HEDVIG (*sobbing convulsively*): All right, I'll stop, if only father comes home again.

GREGERS (*to* GINA, *who is leaving*): But would it not be better to let him fight his agony through by himself?

GINA: He can do that afterwards. First we've got to get the child quieted down. (*Goes out.*)

HEDVIG (*sitting up, drying her eyes*): Now you have to tell me what this is all about. Why doesn't father want me any more?

GREGERS: You must not ask that till you're big and grown-up.

HEDVIG (*sobbing*): But I just can't stay as miserable as this all the time till I'm grown up. — But I know what it is. Maybe I'm not really father's child.

GREGERS (*uneasily*): How could that be?

15101

HEDVIG: Mother might have found me. And now perhaps father has found out about it. I have read about things like that.

GREGERS: Well, if it really were so —

HEDVIG: I think he could love me just as much, regardless. More, almost. The wild duck is a gift, too, and I love her very, very much.

GREGERS (*glad to turn the conversation*): Oh yes, the wild duck. Let's talk about the wild duck, Hedvig.

HEDVIG: That poor wild duck. He can't stand the sight of her, either. Just think, he wants to wring her neck!

GREGERS: Oh, I don't think he'll do that.

HEDVIG: No, but he said it. And I think that was horrid of father, for I pray for the wild duck every night, that she may be kept safe from death and all that's evil.

GREGERS (*looks at her*): Do you usually say prayers at night?

HEDVIG: Yes, I do.

GREGERS: Who taught you that?

HEDVIG: Myself, for father was terribly sick once and had leeches on his neck, and then he said that death was his dread companion.

GREGERS: And — ?

HEDVIG: So I prayed for him when I went to bed. And I have done so ever since.

GREGERS: And now you pray for the wild duck, too?

HEDVIG: I thought it was best to mention her as well, for she was so sickly when we first got her.

GREGERS: Do you say morning prayers, too?

HEDVIG: Of course not.

GREGERS: Why is that so of course?

HEDVIG: Because it's light in the morning. There's not so much to be afraid of then.

GREGERS: And the wild duck you love so much — your father said he'd like to wring her neck?

HEDVIG: No, he said it would be better for him if he did, but he was going to spare her for my sake. And that was good of him.

GREGERS (*closer to her*): How would it be if you decided to sacrifice the wild duck for *his* sake?

HEDVIG (*getting up*): The wild duck!

GREGERS: What if you willingly gave up the dearest thing in the whole world for him?

HEDVIG: Do you think that would help?

GREGERS: Try it, Hedvig.

HEDVIG (*softly, with shining eyes*): Yes. I want to.

GREGERS: Do you think you have the right kind of strength for doing it?

HEDVIG: I shall ask Grandpa to shoot the wild duck for me.

GREGERS: Yes, do that. But not a word to your mother about this!

HEDVIG: Why not?

GREGERS: She doesn't understand us.

HEDVIG: The wild duck? I'll try it in the morning!

(GINA *enters from the hall.*)

HEDVIG (*towards her*): Did you find him, mother?

GINA: No, but I found out he's got Relling with him.

GREGERS: Are you sure?

GINA: Yes, the janitor's wife said so. Molvik's with them also.

GREGERS: Just now, when his soul so sorely needs to struggle in solitude — !

GINA (*taking off her coat*): Yes, men are funny. God knows where Relling is taking him! I ran over to Madam Eriksen's, but they aren't there.

HEDVIG (*struggling with her tears*): What if he never comes back!

GREGERS: He'll come back. I'll get word to him tomorrow, and then you'll see *how* he comes back. You count on that, Hedvig, and get a good night's sleep. Goodnight. (*Goes out.*)

HEDVIG (*throws herself sobbing on* GINA'S *neck*): Mother! Mother!

GINA (*patting her back, sighing*): Yes, Relling was right. This is what happens when crazy people come around pestering us with the claim of the ordeal.

ACT V

(*The studio. Cold, gray morning light. There is wet snow on the big panes of the skylight.*

GINA, *aproned, with broom and dust cloth in her hand, enters from the kitchen and goes towards the living room door.* HEDVIG *hurries in from the outside at the same moment.*)

GINA (*stops*): Well?

HEDVIG: Yes, mother, I almost think he's down at Relling's —

GINA: What did I tell you!

HEDVIG: — for the janitor's wife said she heard Relling bring two others home with him last night.

GINA: I knew it.

HEDVIG: But what good does it do, if he doesn't come up here to us?

GINA: I want to go down and have a talk with him, anyway.

(OLD EKDAL, *in dressing gown and slippers and with his lighted pipe, appears in the door to his room.*)

EKDAL: Eh — Hjalmar — ? Isn't Hjalmar here?

GINA: No, he is out, Grandpa.

EKDAL: So early? In this blizzard? Well, I can walk by myself in the morning, I can, if it comes to that.

(*He slides the attic door open.* HEDVIG *helps him. He enters. She closes the door behind him.*)

HEDVIG (*in a low voice*): Mother, what do you think will happen when poor Grandpa hears that father has left us?

GINA: Silly! Grandpa mustn't hear anything about it, of course. It was a good thing he wasn't home last night, during all that hullaballoo.

HEDVIG: Yes, but —

(GREGERS *enters.*)

GREGERS: Well? Have you traced him yet?

GINA: They say he's down at Relling's.

GREGERS: At Relling's! Has he really been out with those two?

GINA: It looks like it.

GREGERS: But he is so badly in need of solitude — to find himself in earnest —

GINA: Yes. I should think so, too.

(RELLING *enters.*)

HEDVIG (*goes towards him*): Is father with you?

GINA (*at the same time*): Is he down there?

RELLING: He certainly is.

HEDVIG: And you haven't told us!

RELLING: I know. I am a big, bad beast. But I had this other big, bad beast to take care of, too — I mean the demonic one. And after that, I just fell asleep — sound asleep —

GINA: What does Ekdal say today?

RELLING: Not a thing.

HEDVIG: Doesn't he say anything at all?

RELLING: Not a blessed word.

GREGERS: I think I understand that.

GINA: But what is he doing?

RELLING: He is on the sofa, snoring.

GINA: Oh. Yes, Ekdal does snore a lot.

HEDVIG: He's asleep? Can he sleep now?

RELLING: It certainly looks that way.

GREGERS: That's reasonable enough, after the spiritual turmoil he's just been through —

GINA: And he isn't used to be out revelling nights, either.

HEDVIG: It may be a good thing that he is sleeping, mother.

GINA: That's what I am thinking. Anyway, we'd better not wake him up too soon. Thank you, Relling. First of all I've got to clean things up a bit and make the place look nice. Come and help me, Hedvig. (*They go into the living room.*)

GREGERS (*turning to* RELLING): Can you account for the present spiritual unrest in Hjalmar Ekdal?

RELLING: To tell you the truth, I haven't noticed any spiritual unrest in him.

GREGERS: What? At such a turning point — When his whole life is acquiring a new basis? How can you think that a personality like Hjalmar Ekdal — ?

RELLING: Personality? He? If he ever had any tendency to sprout the kind of abnormal growth you call personality, I can assure you that all roots and tendrils were thoroughly extirpated in his boyhood.

GREGERS: That would indeed be strange, considering the loving up-bringing he enjoyed.

RELLING: By those two crackpot, hysterical spinster aunts of his, you mean?

GREGERS: Let me tell you that they were women who never forgot the claim of the ideal — though I suppose you'll just be making fun of me again.

RELLING: No, I'm not in the mood. I do know about them, though. He has often enough held forth about "his soul's two mothers." Personally, I don't think he has much to be grateful to them for. Ekdal's misfortune is that he has always been looked upon as a shining light in his own circle.

GREGERS: And you don't think he is that? I mean, when it comes to depth of soul?

RELLING: I have never noticed it. That his father thought so is one thing. The old lieutenant has been an idiot all his days.

GREGERS: He has all his days been a man with a childlike mind. That is what you don't understand.

RELLING: All right. But after dear, sweet Hjalmar had taken up study-ing — after a fashion — right away he was the light of the future among his friends, too. He was handsome enough, the rascal — red and white, just the way little shop-girls like the fellows. And he had this sentimental temperament and this warm-hearted voice, and he could give such pretty declamations of other people's poetry and other people's thoughts —

GREGERS (*indignantly*): Is this Hjalmar Ekdal you are describing?

RELLING: Yes, if you please. For this is what he looks like on the inside, the idol you are prostrating yourself for.

GREGERS: I didn't know I was as blind as all that.

RELLING: Well — not far from it. For you are sick, too, you see.

GREGERS: That is true.

RELLING: Yes it is. And yours is a complicated case. First, there is this pesky integrity fever you're suffering from, and then something worse — you are forever walking around in a delirium of adoration, always looking for something to admire outside of yourself.

GREGERS: Yes, there certainly wouldn't be much point in looking for it within myself.

RELLING: But you are always so hideously wrong about all those big, wonderful flies you see and hear buzzing around you. Once again you have entered a cottage with your claim of the ideal. People here just can't pay.

GREGERS: If this is the way you think of Hjalmar Ekdal, what sort of pleasure can you derive from your constant association with him?

RELLING: Oh well. I am supposed to be a kind of doctor, believe it or not, so the least I can do is to look after the poor patients I share quarters with.

GREGERS: Ah, I see. Hjalmar Ekdal is sick, too?

RELLING: Most people are, worse luck.

GREGERS: And what treatment do you apply in Hjalmar's case?

RELLING: My usual one. I see to it that his vital lie is kept up.

GREGERS: Vital — lie? I am not sure I heard what you said.

RELLING: That's right. I said the vital lie. You see, that's the stimulating principle.

GREGERS: May I ask with what vital lie you have infected Hjalmar?

RELLING: You may not. I never reveal professional secrets to quacks. You are capable of messing him up for me even more than you have. But the method is proven. I have used it with Molvik, too. I have made him demonic. That's the suppurative I have applied to *his* neck.

GREGERS: But *isn't* he demonic?

RELLING: What the hell does it mean — being demonic? It's just some nonsense I thought of to save his life. If I hadn't, the poor, pitiful swine would have succumbed to self-hatred and despair many a year ago. Not to mention the old lieutenant! Though he has found his own cure.

GREGERS: Lieutenant Ekdal? What about him?

RELLING: What do you think? There he is, the old slayer of bears, chasing rabbits in a dark attic. And yet, there isn't a happier hunter alive than that old man when he is playing with all that junk. The four or five dried-out Christmas trees he has saved are the whole big, wild Høydal forest to him. The rooster and the chickens are wild fowl in the tree tops, and the rabbits bouncing about on the floor are bears he's grappling with — the frisky old sportsman.

GREGERS: Ah, yes — that unfortunate old Lieutenant Ekdal. He has certainly had to compromise the ideals of his youth.

RELLING: While I think of it, Mr. Werle — don't use the foreign word "ideals." We have available a good native one: "lies."

GREGERS: You think the two things are related?

RELLING: About as closely as typhus and putrid fever.

GREGERS: Doctor Relling! I won't give up till I have rescued Hjalmar from your clutches!

RELLING: That might be his bad luck. Take his vital lie away from the average person, and you take his happiness, too. (*To* HEDVIG, *who enters from the living room.*) Well, now, little duck mother. I am going down to see if papa is still in bed pondering that wonderful invention of his. (*Goes out.*)

GREGERS (*approaching* HEDVIG): I can tell from looking at you that it has not yet been accomplished.

HEDVIG: What? Oh, that about the wild duck? No.

GREGERS: Your strength of purpose deserted you, I suppose, when the time for action had come.

HEDVIG: No, it wasn't that. But when I woke up this morning and remembered what we had talked about, it all seemed so strange.

GREGERS: Strange?

HEDVIG: Yes, I don't know — Last night, just at the time — I thought there was something very wonderful about it, but when I had slept and I thought about it again, it didn't seem like anything much.

GREGERS: I see. I could hardly expect you to grow up in this environment without injury to your soul.

HEDVIG: I don't care about that, if only father would come home again.

GREGERS: If only your eyes were opened to what gives life its worth — if only you possessed the true, joyful, brave, sacrificial spirit, then you'd see he'll return. But I still have faith in you, Hedvig. (*Goes out.*)

(HEDVIG *walks around aimlessly. She is about to enter the kitchen, when there is a knock on the inside of the door to the attic.* HEDVIG *opens the doors wide enough for* OLD EKDAL *to come out. She shuts them again.*)

EKDAL: H'm. Not much fun taking a walk by yourself, y'know.

HEDVIG: Wouldn't you like to go hunting, Grandpa?

EKDAL: It isn't hunting weather today. Too dark. Can hardly see a thing.

HEDVIG: Don't you ever want to shoot something beside rabbits?

EKDAL: Aren't the rabbits good enough, perhaps?

HEDVIG: Yes, but what about the wild duck?

EKDAL: Haw! So you're scared I'll shoot your wild duck? I'll never do that, Hedvig. Never.

HEDVIG: No, for I bet you don't know how. I've heard it's difficult to shoot wild ducks.

EKDAL: Don't know how! Should say I do!

HEDVIG: How would you do it, Grandpa? — I don't mean *my* wild duck, but another one.

EKDAL: Would try to get a shot in just below the breast; that's the best place. And try to shoot *against* the feathers, not *with*.

HEDVIG: Then they die?

EKDAL: Damn right they do — if you shoot right. — Well, better go in and dress up. H'm. Y'know. H'm — (*Goes into his own room.*)

(HEDVIG *waits a moment, glances towards the living room door, stands on tiptoe, takes the double-barreled pistol down from the shelf, looks at it.* GINA, *with broom and dust cloth, enters from the living room.* HEDVIG *quickly puts the pistol back, without* GINA's *noticing.*)

GINA: Don't fool with father's things, Hedvig.

HEDVIG (*leaving the shelf*): I just wanted to straighten up some.

GINA: Why don't you go into the kitchen and see if the coffee is keeping hot? I am taking a tray with me when I go down.

(HEDVIG *goes into the kitchen.* GINA *starts putting the studio in order. After a short while, the door to the outside is hesitantly opened and* HJALMAR *looks in. He is wearing a coat but no hat. He looks unkempt and unwashed. His eyes are dull and lusterless.*)

GINA (*stands staring at him, still with the broom in her hand*): Bless you, Ekdal — so you did come back, after all!

HJALMAR (*enters, answers in a dull voice*): I return — only to leave.

GINA: Yes, yes, I suppose. But good Lord! how you look!

HJALMAR: Look?

GINA: And your nice winter coat? I'd say that's done for.

HEDVIG (*in the kitchen door*): Mother, don't you want me to — (*sees* HJALMAR, *gives a shout of joy and runs towards him.*) Father! Father!

HJALMAR (*turning away, with a gesture*): Go away! Go away! (*To* GINA.) Get her away from me, I say!

GINA (*in a low voice*): Go into the living room, Hedvig.

(HEDVIG *leaves silently.*)

HJALMAR (*busy, pulling out the table drawer*): I need my books with me. Where are my books?

GINA: Which books?

HJALMAR: My scientific works, of course — the technical journals I need for my invention.

GINA (*looking on the shelf*): Do you mean these over here, with no covers on them?

HJALMAR: Yes, yes, of course.

GINA (*puts a pile of journals down on the table*): Don't you want me to get Hedvig to cut them open for you?

HJALMAR: No. Nobody needs to cut any pages for me.

(*Brief silence.*)

GINA: So you *are* going to leave us, Ekdal?

HJALMAR (*rummaging among the books*): That goes without saying, I should think.

GINA: All right.

HJALMAR (*violently*): For you can hardly expect me to want to stay where my heart is pierced every single hour of the day!

GINA: God forgive you for thinking so bad of me!

HJALMAR: Proof — !

GINA: Seems to me, you're the one who should bring proof.

HJALMAR: After a past like yours? There are certain claims — I might call them the claims of the ideal —

GINA: What about Grandpa? What is *he* going to do, poor man?

HJALMAR: I know my duty. The helpless one goes with me. I'll go out and make arrangements — H'm (*Hesitantly.*) Has anybody found my hat on the stairs?

GINA: No. Have you lost your hat?

HJALMAR: I most certainly had it on when I came home last night; there isn't the slightest doubt about that. But now I can't find it.

GINA: Good Lord! Where did you go with those two drunks?

HJALMAR: Oh, don't ask about inessentials. Do you think I'm in a mood for remembering details?

GINA: I only hope you haven't got a cold, Ekdal (*Goes into the kitchen.*)

HJALMAR (*speaking to himself, in a low voice, angrily, as he empties the drawer*): You're a scoundrel, Relling! — A villain is what you are! — Miserable traitor! — I'd gladly see you assassinated — !

(*He puts aside some old letters, discovers the torn gift letter from the day before, picks it up and looks at the two pieces, puts them down quickly as* GINA *enters.*)

GINA (*putting a tray with food down on the table*): Here's a drop of coffee, if you want it. And some salt meat sandwiches.

HJALMAR (*glancing at the tray*): Salt meat? Never under this roof! True it is, I haven't taken solid nourishment for almost twenty-four hours, but that can't be helped. — My notes! My incipient memoirs! Where is my diary — all my important papers! (*Opens the door to the living room, but steps back.*) If she isn't there, too!

GINA: Heavens, Ekdal. She's got to be somewhere.

HJALMAR: Leave! (*He makes room.* HEDVIG, *scared, enters the studio. With his hand on the door knob; to* GINA.) During the last moments I spend in my former home I wish to be spared the sight of intruders — (*Enters the living room.*)

HEDVIG (*starts, asks her mother in a low and trembling voice*): Does that mean me?

GINA: Stay in the kitchen, Hedvig, or no — go to your own room. (*To* HJALMAR, *as she enters the living room.*) Wait a minute, Ekdal. Don't make such a mess in the dresser. I know where everything is.

HEDVIG (*remains motionless for a moment, in helpless fright, presses her lips together not to cry, clenches her hands, whispers*): The wild duck!

(*She tiptoes over to the shelf and takes the pistol down, opens the doors to the inner attic, goes inside, closes behind her.* HJALMAR *and* GINA *are heard talking in the living room.*)

HJALMAR (*appears with some notebooks and a pile of old papers, which he puts down on the table*): The bag obviously won't be enough. There are thousands of things I need to take with me!

GINA (*entering with the bag*): Can't you leave most of it behind for the time being and just pick up a clean shirt and some underwear?

HJALMAR: Phew — ! These exhausting preparations — ! (*Takes off his overcoat and throws it on the sofa.*)

GINA: And there's the coffee getting cold too.

HJALMAR: H'm. (*Without thinking, he takes a sip, and then another one.*)

GINA (*dusting off the back of chairs*): How are you ever going to find a large enough attic for the rabbits?

HJALMAR: You mean I have to drag all those rabbits along, too?

GINA: Grandpa can't do without his rabbits — you know that as well as I do.

HJALMAR: He'll have to get used to that. I shall have to give up higher values in life than a bunch of rabbits.

GINA (*dusting off the shelf*): Shall I put the flute in for you?

HJALMAR: No. No flute for me. But give me my pistol.

GINA: You want that old pestol?

HJALMAR: Yes. My loaded pistol.

GINA (*looking for it*): It's gone. He must have taken it inside with him.

HJALMAR: Is he in the attic?

GINA: Sure, he's in the attic.

HJALMAR: H'm. The lonely grayhead — (*He eats a sandwich, empties his cup of coffee.*)

GINA: If only we hadn't rented that room, you could have moved in there.

HJALMAR: And stay under the same roof as — ! Never! Never again!

GINA: But couldn't you stay in the living room for a day or two? There you'd have everything to yourself.

HJALMAR: Not within these walls!

GINA: How about down at Relling's and Molvik's, then?

HJALMAR: Don't mention their names to me! I get sick just thinking about them. Oh no — it's out into the wind and the snowdrifts for me — to walk from house to house seeking shelter for father and myself.

GINA: But you have no hat, Ekdal! You've lost your hat, remember?

HJALMAR: Oh, those two abominations! Rich in nothing but every vice! A hat must be procured. (*Takes another sandwich.*) Arrangements must be made. After all, I don't intend to catch my death. (*Looks for something on the tray.*)

GINA: What are you looking for?

HJALMAR: Butter.

GINA: Just a moment. (*Goes out into the kitchen.*)

HJALMAR (*shouting after her*): Oh never mind. Dry bread is good enough for me.

GINA (*bringing a plate with butter*): Here. This is supposed to be freshly churned.

(*She pours him another cup of coffee. He sits down on the sofa, puts more butter on his bread, eats and drinks in silence.*)

HJALMAR (*after a pause*): Could I, without being disturbed by anyone — and I mean *anyone* — stay in the living room for a day or two?

GINA: You certainly can, if you want to.

HJALMAR: You see, I don't know how to get all of father's things moved out on such short notice.

GINA: And there is this, too, that first you'd have to tell him that you don't want to live together with the rest of us any more.

HJALMAR (*pushing his cup away*): Yes, yes — that, too. I shall have to go into all those intricate relationships once again, to explain — I must think, I must have air to breathe, I can't bear all the burdens in one single day.

GINA: Of course not. And in such awful weather too —

HJALMAR (*moving* WERLE'S *letter*): I notice this piece of paper still lying around.

GINA: Well, *I* haven't touched it.

HJALMAR: Not that it concerns *me* —

GINA: I'm sure *I* don't expect to make use of it —

HJALMAR: Nevertheless, I suppose we shouldn't let it get completely lost. In all the fuss of moving, something might easily —

GINA: I'll take care of it, Ekdal.

HJALMAR: For the gift letter belongs to father, first of all. It's his affair whether he wants to make use of it or not.

GINA (*with a sigh*): Yes, poor old Grandpa —

HJALMAR: Just to make sure — Is there any glue?

GINA (*walks over to the shelf*): Here's a bottle.

HJALMAR: And a brush?

GINA: Here. (*Brings him both.*)

HJALMAR (*picks up a pair of scissors*): Just a strip of paper on the back — (*Cuts and glues.*) Far be it from me to lay hands on somebody else's property — least of all the property of a poverty-stricken old man. — Well — not on — that other one's, either. — There, now! Leave it to dry for a while. And when it's dry, remove it. I don't want to see that document again — ever!

(GREGERS *enters.*)

GREGERS (*a little surprised*): What? So this is where you are, Hjalmar!

HJALMAR (*quickly gets up*): Sheer exhaustion drove me to sit down.

GREGERS: And I see you've had breakfast.

HJALMAR: The body, too, makes demands at times.

GREGERS: Well, what have you decided to do?

HJALMAR: For a man like me, there is only one way open. I am in the process of gathering up my most important possessions. Obviously, that takes time.

GINA (*a trifle impatient*): Do you want me to make the living room ready for you, or do you want me to pack the bag?

HJALMAR (*after an irritated glance at* GREGERS): Pack — and make the room ready.

GINA (*picking up the bag*): All right. I'll just put in the shirts and those other things. (*She goes into the living room, closing the door behind her.*)

GREGERS (*after a short silence*): I had no idea this would be the end of it. Is it really necessary for you to leave house and home?

HJALMAR (*paces restlessly up and down*): What do you want me to do? I am not made to be unhappy, Gregers. I require peace and security and comfort around me.

GREGERS: But you can have all that, Hjalmar. Just try. It seems to me there is a firm foundation to build upon now. Start all over again. And remember, you still have your invention to live for.

HJALMAR: Oh don't talk about that invention. It may take a long time yet.

GREGERS: So?

HJALMAR: Well, yes, for heaven's sake, what do you expect me to invent, anyway? The others have invented most of it already. It's getting more difficult every day.

GREGERS: But all the labor you have put into it — ?

HJALMAR: It was that dissipated Relling who got me started on it.

GREGERS: Relling?

HJALMAR: Yes, it was he who first called attention to my talent for making some fabulous invention or other in photography.

GREGERS: I see. It was Relling — !

HJALMAR: Ah — I have been so wonderfully happy about it. Not so much about the invention itself, but because Hedvig believed in it — believed with all the strength and power of a child's soul. — That is, I *thought* she did — fool as I was.

GREGERS: Can you really think that Hedvig would be false to you?

HJALMAR: I can believe anything now. It is Hedvig who is in the way. She it is who is shutting the sun out of my entire life.

GREGERS: Hedvig? You mean Hedvig? How in the world is she going to be an obstacle?

HJALMAR (*without answering*): I have loved that child more than I can ever say. You have no idea how happy I was whenever I came back to my humble dwelling and she rushed towards me with her sweet, squinting eyes. Ha, credulous fool that I was! She was so unspeakably dear to me — and so I lulled myself into the dream that I was equally dear to her.

GREGERS: You call that a dream?

HJALMAR: How can I tell? I can't get anything out of Gina. Besides, she completely lacks any sense of the ideal aspects of the issue. But to you I can open up, Gregers. It is this terrible doubt — perhaps Hedvig has never really loved me.

GREGERS: Maybe you'll receive proof — (*Listens.*) Shh! What's that? The wild duck?

HJALMAR: It's just quacking. Father's in the attic.

GREGERS: He is! (*Joy lights his face.*) I tell you again, Hjalmar — maybe you will find proof that your poor, misunderstood Hedvig has always loved you!

HJALMAR: Pah! What proof could she give? I dare not trust to mere asseverations.

GREGERS: Surely, Hedvig doesn't know what deceit is.

HJALMAR: Ah, Gregers — that is just what I cannot be certain of. Who knows what Gina and this Mrs. Sørby may have been whispering and scheming? And Hedvig's ears are big enough, believe you me. Maybe that gift letter didn't come as such a surprise to her. It seemed to me I noticed something like that.

GREGERS: Good heavens, Hjalmar! What kind of spirit is this that's taken possession of you!

HJALMAR: I have had my eyes opened. You just wait. It may turn out that the gift letter was just the beginning. Mrs. Sørby has always been very fond of Hedvig, and now, of course, it's in her power to do anything she likes for the child. They can take her away from me what day and hour they choose.

GREGERS: Hedvig will never leave you, Hjalmar. Never.

HJALMAR: Don't be too sure. If they beckon her with their arms full — ? And I who have loved her so infinitely much! I, whose greatest joy it was to take her tenderly by the hand and lead her, as one leads a frightened child through a dark and deserted room! Now I feel this painful certainty that the poor photographer in his attic has never really meant very much to her. She has only cleverly managed to keep on good terms with him while she bided her time.

GREGERS: You don't believe this, Hjalmar.

HJALMAR: That is just what is so terrible — I don't know what to believe — I'll never be able to find out! But do you really doubt that I am right? Ah, Gregers, you put too much trust in the claim of the ideal! If those others were to come now, with their ample offerings, and called to the child: Leave him; life awaits you here with us —

GREGERS (*quickly*): Yes, what then — ?

HJALMAR: If then I were to ask her: Hedvig, are you willing to give your life for me? (*Laughs scornfully.*) Oh yes — you'd find out soon enough what answer I'd get!

(*A pistol shot is heard from within the attic.*)

GREGERS (*with a shout of joy*): Hjalmar!

HJALMAR: Must he go shooting today — !

GINA (*enters*): Can't say I like this, Ekdal — Grandpa in there all by himself, banging away.

HJALMAR: I'll take a look —

GREGERS (*agitated, feelingly*): Wait! Do you know what that was?

HJALMAR: Yes, of course, I do.

GREGERS: No, you don't. But *I* know. It was the proof!

HJALMAR: What proof?

GREGERS: It was a child's sacrifice. She has got your father to shoot the wild duck.

HJALMAR: Shoot the wild duck!

GINA: Heavens — !

HJALMAR: Whatever for?

GREGERS: She wanted to sacrifice to you what she held dearest in the whole world. For then she thought you'd love her again.

HJALMAR (*softly, moved*): Oh that child!

GINA: What she thinks of!

GREGERS: All she wanted was your love, Hjalmar. Without it, life didn't seem possible to her.

GINA (*struggling with tears*): *Now*, do you see, Ekdal?

HJALMAR: Gina, where is she?

GINA (*sniffling*): Poor thing. She is sitting out in the kitchen, I guess.

HJALMAR (*walks to the kitchen door, flings it open, says*): Hedvig — come! Come to me! (*Looks around.*) No. She isn't here.

GINA: Then she must be in her own room.

HJALMAR (*offstage*): No, she isn't there, either. (*Re-entering the studio.*) She must have gone out.

GINA: Yes, for you know you didn't want to see hide nor hair of her in the house.

HJALMAR: If only she'd come back soon — so I can tell her — Now I feel that everything will be all right, Gregers. Now I think we can start life over again.

GREGERS (*quietly*): I knew it. Restitution would come through the child.

(*Old* EKDAL *appears in the door to his room. He is in full uniform and is buckling on his sabre.*)

HJALMAR (*surprised*): Father! You're in there!

GINA: Do you go shooting in your room, now, Grandpa?

EKDAL (*approaches indignantly*): So you're off hunting by yourself, are you Hjalmar?

HJALMAR (*tense, confused*): You mean it wasn't you who fired that shot in the attic just now?

EKDAL: I? Fired? H'm.

GREGERS (*shouts to* HJALMAR): She has shot the wild duck herself!

HJALMAR: What *is* this? (*He hurriedly slides the attic doors open, looks in, gives a loud cry.*) Hedvig!

GINA (*runs to the door*): Oh God! What is it?

HJALMAR (*going inside*): She is lying on the floor!

GREGERS: Lying — ! (*Follows* HJALMAR *inside.*)

GINA (*at the same time*): Hedvig! (*Enters the attic.*) No! No! No!

EKDAL: Ho-ho! So *she* has taken to hunting too, now!

(HJALMAR, GINA, *and* GREGERS *drag* HEDVIG *into the studio. Her trailing right hand clasps the pistol tightly.*)

HJALMAR (*beside himself*): The pistol went off! She's hit! Call for help! Help!

GINA (*running out into the hallway, shouts down*): Relling! Relling! Doctor Relling! Hurry up here, fast as you can!

(HJALMAR *and* GREGERS *put* HEDVIG *down on the sofa.*)

EKDAL (*quietly*): The woods avenge themselves.

HJALMAR (*on his knees beside* HEDVIG): She's coming to now. She is coming to. Oh yes, yes, yes —

GINA (*having returned*): Where's she hit? I can't see a thing.

(RELLING *enters hurriedly, followed by* MOLVIK. *The latter is without vest and tie, his tailcoat thrown open.*)

RELLING: What's the matter?

GINA: They say Hedvig has shot herself.

HJALMAR: Come and help us!

RELLING: Shot herself! (*He pulls the table back and begins to examine her.*)

HJALMAR (*still on his knees, looking anxiously at* RELLING): It can't be dangerous, can it, Relling? What, Relling? She hardly bleeds at all. It can't possibly be dangerous?

RELLING: How did this happen?

HJALMAR: Oh, I don't know —

GINA: She was going to shoot the wild duck.

RELLING: The wild duck?

HJALMAR: The pistol must have gone off.

RELLING: H'm. I see.

EKDAL: The woods avenge themselves. But I'm not afraid. (*Enters the attic and closes the doors behind him.*)

HJALMAR: Relling — why don't you say anything?

RELLING: The bullet has entered her chest.

HJALMAR: Yes, but she's coming to!

RELLING: Can't you see that Hedvig is dead?

GINA (*bursts into tears*): Oh, the child, the child — !

GREGERS (*hoarsely*): In the depths of the sea —

HJALMAR (*jumps to his feet*): She must live! I want her to live! For God's sake, Relling — just for a moment — just so I can tell her how unspeakably much I have loved her all the time!

RELLING: Her heart has been pierced. Internal hemorrhage. She died instantly.

HJALMAR: And I who chased her away from me like an animal! Frightened and lonely she crawled into the attic and died for love of me. (*Sobbing.*) Never to be able to make up for it! Never to tell her — ! (*Shakes his fists upwards.*) You! You above! If thou art at all — ! Why hast thou done this unto me?

GINA: Shhh, shhh. You mustn't make such a fuss. We had no right to keep her, I suppose.

MOLVIK: The child is not dead. It sleepeth.

RELLING: Rubbish!

HJALMAR (*quieting down, walks over to the sofa, looks at* HEDVIG, *his arms crossed*): There she lies, so stiff and still.

RELLING (*trying to release the pistol*): She holds on so tightly, I can't —

GINA: No, no, Relling. Don't break her fingers. Let the pestol be.

HJALMAR: Let her have it with her.

GINA: Yes, let her. But the child isn't going to lie out here for a show. She is going into her own little room, right now. Give me a hand, Ekdal.

(HJALMAR *and* GINA *carry* HEDVIG *between them.*)

HJALMAR (*carrying*): Gina, Gina — do you think you can bear this?

GINA: The one has to help the other. Seems to me like now we both have a share in her.

MOLVIK (*raising his arms, muttering*): Praise be the Lord, to dust thou returnest, to dust thou returnest —

RELLING (*whispers*): Shut up, man! You're drunk.

(HJALMAR *and* GINA *carry* HEDVIG *through the kitchen door.* RELLING *closes the door behind them.* MOLVIK *slinks quietly out into the hall.*)

RELLING (*goes up to* GREGERS): Nobody is going to tell me this was an accident.

GREGERS (*who has remained stunned, moving convulsively*): Who is to say how this terrible thing happened?

RELLING: There were powder burns on her dress. She must have placed the muzzle against her chest and pulled the trigger.

GREGERS: Hedvig has not died in vain. Did you notice how grief released what is great in him?

RELLING: There is a touch of greatness in most of us when we stand in sorrow by a corpse. How long do you think that will last with him?

GREGERS: As if it won't last and grow throughout the rest of his days!

RELLING: Within a year little Hedvig won't be anything to him but an occasion for spouting pretty sentiments.

GREGERS: And you dare say that about Hjalmar Ekdal!

RELLING: Let's talk about this again when the first grass has withered on her grave. You'll hear all about "the child so early taken from the father's heart." You'll see him wallow in sentimentality and self-admiration and self-pity. You just wait!

GREGERS: If you are right and I am wrong, life isn't worth living.

RELLING: Oh, life would be fairly tolerable if only we'd be spared these blasted bill collectors who come around pestering us paupers with the claim of the ideal.

GREGERS (*staring ahead*): In that case I am glad my destiny is what it is.

RELLING: Beg your pardon — what *is* your destiny?

GREGERS (*about to leave*): To be the thirteenth man at the table.

RELLING: The hell it is.

⌇⌇⌇ LIKE ALL of Ibsen's later plays, *The Wild Duck* appeared in book form (in 1884) before it was staged. Its earliest readers and audiences found it obscure and morbid, but its reputation has since risen. Today it is generally considered one of Ibsen's greatest plays in prose. Though for some critics this is not saying very much, the play's status is nevertheless remarkable, in view of its technical imperfections. The old romance between Mrs. Sørby and Dr. Relling is a plot excrescence, and Old Ekdal's vengeful woods introduce a note of irrelevant melodrama, but its gravest defect is Hjalmar Ekdal's character. Splendid though he is with beer and chamberlains, at times he lapses into mere caricature. This would not matter in some kinds of drama, but it matters here, for Ibsen writes in the naturalistic convention, which puts a premium on plausibility of character and incident. It is hard to accept Gregers Werle's continuing faith in the greatness of a man who almost without stop reveals his phoniness (sincere phoniness though it is). Gregers may be sick, but he is not supposed to be stupid.

For most critics, however, the play survives its imperfections. It may illuminate the sources of strength of naturalistic drama in general to try to answer why.

The Wild Duck stays close to Ibsen's usual pattern. A friend (sometimes a member) of a middle-class family returns after long absence and by his return triggers disastrous revelations. The action is nearly all exposition — the gradual discovery of the painful truth about the past concealed in the family's decorous and complacent present. We recognize the pattern from *Oedipus Rex*, and *The Wild Duck* does in fact share with Sophocles' play a tightness of structure, a concentration of meaningful events in small compass of time and space, made possible by the playwright's seizure of his story near its climax. The plot is a looking-back on the past responsible for the crisis in the present. It is drama of ripe condition, a "fifth act play" compared with the panoramic, expansive, chronologically developed Shakespearean drama.

But aside from its retrospective structure, *The Wild Duck* has little in common with classical tragedy. No kingdom trembles when Hjalmar Ekdal is in agony. He is too negligible to be the concern of gods, too meanly petty to be even wicked. Beside the language of traditional tragedy, dialogue here is small talk indeed and Hjalmar's eloquence merely absurd. The Ekdal studio is a small and shrunken world — banal, pathetic, ridiculous. But can it not be argued that the inapplicability of the yardstick of great tragedy to *The Wild Duck* is less a comment on the play than on modern man and his values?

If *The Wild Duck* is not in the tragic tradition, neither does it belong with those pat, once shocking, now commonplace, social messages that date such a large part of naturalistic drama of the last and this century, exposés of skeletons, today more dead than fearful, in Victorian closets. In the plays immediately preceding *The Wild Duck* Ibsen had dramatized the damage that contemporary institutions and attitudes were doing to the individual's self-realization, happiness, and integrity. But most people resented what they took to be Ibsen's attack on the entrenched sanctities of religion and marriage and majority rule and were scandalized by his reference (in *Ghosts*) to venereal disease. *The Wild Duck* records, with deceptive blandness, the meaning of the public reaction to its author's crusade for freedom and truth: most people not only don't want the truth about themselves; they are much better off with comfortable lies. Its mood is delicately balanced between two contrasting statements of the same single fact about man: Swift's virulent irony (in *A Tale of a Tub*) in defining "the sublime and refined point of felicity" as "the possession of being well deceived" and the compassionate excuse for the grieving women of Canterbury that T. S. Eliot puts into the mouth of Saint Thomas à Becket in *Murder in the Cathedral:* "Human kind cannot bear very much reality." Together with *An Enemy of the People, The Wild Duck* demonstrates Ibsen's near compulsive habit of seeing every issue from opposite sides. In the earlier play he had put much of himself into Dr. Stockman, the hearty, indomitable fighter for truth. Here he seems to parody his own reforming self in the character of the gloomy, neurotic Gregers Werle, whose officious mission of truth ends in a child's death.

But the play never surrenders the ambiguities of its precarious poise between tragedy and farce, pathos and cynicism, pity and laughter. It is skeptical and relativistic, not doctrinaire. For if it existed for the sake of telling us that everyman's happiness depends on illusion, then its spokesman appears oddly chosen. Dr. Relling, the common-sensical realist, is pretty much of a human wreck. To Mrs. Sørby, the play's most sensible character, he is a man who has "thrown away what is best in himself." He does not enter the play till it is more than half over — a late entrance for a protagonist. Though the action may be defined as the conflict between Relling and Gregers Werle for control over Hjalmar Ekdal, Relling never really occupies the center of the play; he remains a commentator rather than participant — chorus, not hero. The principle of "the vital lie," with which he is associated, is not a major plot issue, for only incidentally does Hedvig kill herself in order to restore her father's faith in his invention. In short, to see Relling as protagonist opposite Gregers's antagonist and to equate the play with his much-quoted piece of psychological wisdom, "Take his vital lie away from the average person, and you take his happiness, too," is to shatter the ambiguities inherent in his flawed personality and inferior plot position and, for that matter, in the shoddiness of his well intentioned formula for adjustment. The fact that he has the last word hardly settles any issues. At stake between him and Gregers is the Ekdal happiness. Truth conquers the protective lie, and the result, ironically, is disaster for the one innocent and wholly lovable character in the entire household. And as if to keep us from extracting any ulterior significance from these sordid events, Ibsen ends his play by having Relling's profanity explode the pretentious melodramatics of Gregers's belief — *his* vital lie — that he is the superfluous man, tragically chosen by destiny to bring bad luck to others. The play insists on its own meaninglessness.

Nor is its symbolism reducible to some simple formula for social or mental health. It teases. It doesn't teach. The wild duck, the play's major symbol, offers endless game for interpretive ingenuity.

What does it stand for? Escape from reality? Wounded innocence? The guilty past? Whom does it represent — and *for* whom? Gregers thinks Hjalmar is a wild duck, but aren't there ways in which the duck could be said to symbolize not only Molvik and Old Ekdal, but Hedvig and even Gregers himself, as well? May we ignore Relling's reference to Gina's "comfortable waddle?"

Perhaps all this is only to say that "meaning" in *The Wild Duck* is not to be sought in a concept but in such realities as Old Ekdal's reluctance to use the pronoun "I," in Hjalmar's uncut technical journals, in Gina's infinitely patient and competent housekeeping. Before the wild duck is anything else it is part of the Ekdal establishment — an object as real as the photographs and the flute and the herring salad. It presides in the attic world of fantasy and escape, a denizen of the depths of the sea, content among the shipwrecked skipper's assorted belongings. It is one of Ibsen's triumphs that the whole unlikely contrivance of the barnyard attic is both believable as solid fact and rich and beautiful in its suggestiveness. It convinces because it is comical and pitiful, haunting and bizarre, all at the same time. By defining the attitudes of the different members of the household to the attic one can both grasp the play's major unifying image and go a long way toward understanding the characters and their position vis à vis the issue of reality versus illusion. There is a poetry of naturalism, generated when human feeling impinges upon the commonplace. The Ekdal attic is an instance.

And it is not true that the stage language of naturalism banished poetry from the theater. There is in *The Wild Duck* careful organization of words for esthetic purposes. In addition to having a utilitarian value in suggesting milieu and in setting off Hjalmar's excursions into oratory, the drab dialogue also reveals subterranean levels of imagery that bear upon theme and character. The allusions to sight and blindness, darkness and light, that weave in and out of Hjalmar's and Gregers' speeches, reinforce the blindness motif in the plot and achieve effects of mordant irony: Gregers rejecting Relling's accurate estimate of Hjalmar's character with the words, "I didn't know I was as blind as all that"; Hjalmar refusing to "look at the child" after "he has had his eyes opened."

By visual imagination and verbal ironies *The Wild Duck* transcends the triviality of a snapshot of middle-class life and the simple-minded shrillness of a social tract. What it attains is neither tragedy's sublime affirmation of man's significance in a dark world, nor the proved lesson of the documentary thesis play, but a compassionate, unsentimental vision of small people suffering under the high price of truth.)

Bernard Shaw

ARMS AND THE MAN

A Pleasant Play

Characters

RAINA PETKOFF, *a young Bulgarian lady*
CATHERINE PETKOFF, *her mother*
LOUKA, *the Petkoffs' maid*
CAPTAIN BLUNTSCHLI, *a Swiss officer in the Serbian army*
A RUSSIAN OFFICER *in the Bulgarian army*
NICOLA, *the Petkoffs' butler*
PETKOFF, *Raina's father, a major in the Bulgarian army*
SERGIUS SARANOFF, *Raina's fiancé, a major in the Bulgarian army*

ACT I

(*Night: A lady's bedchamber in Bulgaria, in a small town near the Dragoman Pass, late in November in the year 1885. Through an open window with a little balcony a peak of the Balkans, wonderfully white and beautiful in the starlit snow, seems quite close at hand, though it is really miles away. The interior of the room is not like anything to be seen in the west of Europe. It is half rich Bulgarian, half cheap Viennese. Above the head of the bed, which stands against a little wall cutting off the left hand corner of the room, is a painted wooden shrine, blue and gold, with an ivory image of Christ, and a light hanging before it in a pierced metal ball suspended by three chains. The principal seat, placed towards the other side of the room and opposite the window, is a Turkish ottoman. The counterpane and hangings of the bed, the window curtains, the little carpet, and all the ornamental textile fabrics in the*

Reprinted by permission of the Public Trustee of the Estate of Bernard Shaw, and of The Society of Authors.

room are oriental and gorgeous; the paper on the walls is occidental and paltry. The washstand, against the wall on the side
nearest the ottoman and window, consists of an enamelled iron
basin with a pail beneath it in a painted metal frame, and a single
towel on the rail at the side. The dressing table, between the bed
and the window, is a common pine table, covered with a cloth of
many colours, with an expensive toilet mirror on it. The door is on
the side nearest the bed; and there is a chest of drawers between.
This chest of drawers is also covered by a variegated native cloth;
and on it there is a pile of paper backed novels, a box of chocolate
creams, and a miniature easel with a large photograph of an extremely handsome officer, whose lofty bearing and magnetic glance
can be felt even from the portrait. The room is lighted by a candle
on the chest of drawers, and another on the dressing table with a
box of matches beside it.

The window is hinged doorwise and stands wide open. Outside,
a pair of wooden shutters, opening outwards, also stand open. On
the balcony a young lady, intensely conscious of the romantic
beauty of the night, and of the fact that her own youth and
beauty are part of it, is gazing at the snowy Balkans. She is in her
nightgown, well covered by a long mantle of furs, worth, on a
moderate estimate, about three times the furniture of the room.

Her reverie is interrupted by her mother, CATHERINE PETKOFF,
a woman over forty, imperiously energetic, with magnificent black
hair and eyes, who might be a very splendid specimen of the wife
of a mountain farmer, but is determined to be a Viennese lady,
and to that end wears a fashionable tea gown on all occasions.)

CATHERINE (*entering hastily, full of good news*): Raina! (*She pronounces it Rah-eena, with the stress on the ee.*) Raina! (*She goes to
the bed, expecting to find* RAINA *there.*) Why, where — ?

(RAINA *looks into the room.*)

Heavens, child! are you out in the night air instead of in your bed?
Youll catch your death. Louka told me you were asleep.

RAINA (*dreamily*): I sent her away. I wanted to be alone. The stars are
so beautiful! What is the matter?

CATHERINE: Such news! There has been a battle.

RAINA (*her eyes dilating*): Ah! (*She comes eagerly to* CATHERINE.)

CATHERINE: A great battle at Slivnitza! A victory! And it was won by
Sergius.

RAINA (*with a cry of delight*): Ah! (*They embrace rapturously.*) Oh,
mother! (*Then, with sudden anxiety*) is father safe?

CATHERINE: Of course! he sends me the news. Sergius is the hero of the hour, the idol of the regiment.

RAINA: Tell me, tell me. How was it? (*Ecstatically*) Oh, mother! mother! mother! (*She pulls her mother down on the ottoman; and they kiss one another frantically.*)

CATHERINE (*with surging enthusiasm*): You cant guess how splendid it is. A cavalry charge! think of that! He defied our Russian commanders — acted without orders — led a charge on his own responsibility — headed it himself — was the first man to sweep through their guns. Cant you see it, Raina: our gallant splendid Bulgarians with their swords and eyes flashing, thundering down like an avalanche and scattering the wretched Serbs and their dandified Austrian officers like chaff. And you! you kept Sergius waiting a year before you would be betrothed to him. Oh, if you have a drop of Bulgarian blood in your veins, you will worship him when he comes back.

RAINA: What will he care for my poor little worship after the acclamations of a whole army of heroes? But no matter: I am so happy! so proud! (*She rises and walks about excitedly.*) It proves that all our ideas were real after all.

CATHERINE (*indignantly*): Our ideas real! What do you mean?

RAINA: Our ideas of what Sergius would do. Our patriotism. Our heroic ideals. I sometimes used to doubt whether they were anything but dreams. Oh, what faithless little creatures girls are! When I buckled on Sergius's sword he looked so noble: it was treason to think of disillusion or humiliation or failure. And yet — and yet — (*She sits down again suddenly.*) Promise me youll never tell him.

CATHERINE: Dont ask me for promises until I know what I'm promising.

RAINA: Well, it came into my head just as he was holding me in his arms and looking into my eyes, that perhaps we only had our heroic ideas because we are so fond of reading Byron and Pushkin, and because we were so delighted with the opera that season at Bucharest. Real life is so seldom like that! indeed never, as far as I knew it then. (*Remorsefully*) Only think, mother: I doubted him: I wondered whether all his heroic qualities and his soldiership might not prove mere imagination when he went into a real battle. I had an uneasy fear that he might cut a poor figure there beside all those clever officers from the Tsar's court.

CATHERINE: A poor figure! Shame on you! The Serbs have Austrian officers who are just as clever as the Russians; but we have beaten them in every battle for all that.

RAINA (*laughing and snuggling against her mother*): Yes: I was only a

prosaic little coward. Oh, to think that it was all true! that Sergius is
just as splendid and noble as he looks! that the world is really a
glorious world for women who can see its glory and men who can act
its romance! What happiness! what unspeakable fulfillment!

(*They are interrupted by the entry of* LOUKA, *a handsome proud
girl in a pretty Bulgarian peasant's dress with double apron, so de-
fiant that her servility to* RAINA *is almost insolent. She is afraid of*
CATHERINE, *but even with her goes as far as she dares.*)

LOUKA: If you please, madam, all the windows are to be closed and the
shutters made fast. They say there may be shooting in the streets.

(RAINA *and* CATHERINE *rise together, alarmed.*)

The Serbs are being chased right back through the pass; and they say
they may run into the town. Our cavalry will be after them; and our
people will be ready for them, you may be sure, now theyre running
away. (*She goes out on the balcony, and pulls the outside shutters
to; then steps back into the room.*)

CATHERINE (*businesslike, housekeeping instincts aroused*): I must see
that everything is made safe downstairs.

RAINA: I wish our people were not so cruel. What glory is there in killing wretched fugitives?

CATHERINE: Cruel! Do you suppose they would hesitate to kill you —
or worse?

RAINA (*to* LOUKA): Leave the shutters so that I can just close them if
I hear any noise.

CATHERINE (*authoritatively, turning on her way to the door*): Oh no,
dear: you must keep them fastened. You would be sure to drop off
to sleep and leave them open. Make them fast, Louka.

LOUKA: Yes, madam. (*She fastens them.*)

RAINA: Dont be anxious about me. The moment I hear a shot, I shall
blow out the candles and roll myself up in bed with my ears well
covered.

CATHERINE: Quite the wisest thing you can do, my love. Goodnight.

RAINA: Goodnight. (*Her emotion comes back for a moment.*) Wish
me joy. (*They kiss.*) This is the happiest night of my life — if only
there are no fugitives.

CATHERINE: Go to bed, dear; and dont think of them. (*She goes out.*)

LOUKA (*secretly to* RAINA): If you would like the shutters open, just
give them a push like this. (*She pushes them: they open: she pulls
them to again.*) One of them ought to be bolted at the bottom; but
the bolt's gone.

RAINA (*with dignity, reproving her*): Thanks, Louka; but we must do what we are told.

(LOUKA *makes a grimace.*)

Goodnight.

LOUKA (*carelessly*): Goodnight. (*She goes out, swaggering.*)

(RAINA, *left alone, takes off her fur cloak and throws it on the ottoman. Then she goes to the chest of drawers, and adores the portrait there with feelings that are beyond all expression. She does not kiss it or press it to her breast, or shew it any mark of bodily affection; but she takes it in her hands and elevates it, like a priestess.*)

RAINA (*looking up at the picture*): Oh, I shall never be unworthy of you any more, my soul's hero: never, never, never. (*She replaces it reverently. Then she selects a novel from the little pile of books. She turns over the leaves dreamily; finds her page; turns the book inside out at it; and, with a happy sigh, gets into bed and prepares to read herself to sleep. But before abandoning herself to fiction, she raises her eyes once more, thinking of the blessed reality, and murmurs.*) My hero! my hero!

(*A distant shot breaks the quiet of the night. She starts, listening; and two more shots, much nearer, follow, startling her so that she scrambles out of bed, and hastily blows out the candle on the chest of drawers. Then, putting her fingers in her ears, she runs to the dressing table, blows out the light there, and hurries back to bed in the dark, nothing being visible but the glimmer of the light in the pierced ball before the image, and the starlight seen through the slits at the top of the shutters. The firing breaks out again: there is a startling fusillade quite close at hand. Whilst it is still echoing, the shutters disappear, pulled open from without; and for an instant the rectangle of snowy starlight flashes out with the figure of a man silhouetted in black upon it. The shutters close immediately; and the room is dark again. But the silence is now broken by the sound of panting. Then there is a scratch; and the flame of a match is seen in the middle of the room.*)

RAINA (*crouching on the bed*): Who's there? (*The match is out instantly.*) Who's there? Who is that?

A MAN'S VOICE (*in the darkness, subduedly, but threateningly*): Sh — sh! Dont call out; or youll be shot. Be good; and no harm will happen to you.

(*She is heard leaving her bed, and making for the door.*)

Take care: it's no use trying to run away.

RAINA: But who —

THE VOICE (*warning*): Remember: if you raise your voice my revolver will go off. (*Commandingly*) Strike a light and let me see you. Do you hear?

(*Another moment of silence and darkness as she retreats to the chest of drawers. Then she lights a candle; and the mystery is at an end. He is a man of about 35, in a deplorable plight, bespattered with mud and blood and snow, his belt and the strap of his revolver case keeping together the torn ruins of the blue tunic of a Serbian artillery officer. All that the candlelight and his unwashed unkempt condition make it possible to discern is that he is of middling stature and undistinguished appearance, with strong neck and shoulders, roundish obstinate looking head covered with short crisp bronze curls, clear quick eyes and good brows and mouth, hopelessly prosaic nose like that of a strong minded baby, trim soldierlike carriage and energetic manner, and with all his wits about him in spite of his desperate predicament: even with a sense of the humor of it, without, however, the least intention of trifling with it or throwing away a chance. Reckoning up what he can guess about* RAINA: *her age, her social position, her character, and the extent to which she is frightened, he continues, more politely but still most determinedly.*)

Excuse my disturbing you; but you recognize my uniform? Serb! If I'm caught I shall be killed. (*Menacingly*) Do you understand that?

RAINA: Yes.

THE MAN: Well, I dont intend to get killed if I can help it. (*Still more formidably*) Do you understand that? (*He locks the door quickly but quietly.*)

RAINA (*disdainfully*): I suppose not. (*She draws herself up superbly, and looks him straight in the face, adding, with cutting emphasis*) Some soldiers, I know, are afraid to die.

THE MAN (*with grim goodhumor*): All of them, dear lady, all of them, believe me. It is our duty to live as long as we can. Now, if you raise an alarm —

RAINA (*cutting him short*): You will shoot me. How do you know that I am afraid to die?

THE MAN (*cunningly*): Ah; but suppose I dont shoot you, what will happen then? A lot of your cavalry will burst into this pretty room of yours and slaughter me here like a pig; for I'll fight like a demon:

they shant get me into the street to amuse themselves with: I know what they are. Are you prepared to receive that sort of company in your present undress?

(RAINA, *suddenly conscious of her nightgown, instinctively shrinks and gathers it more closely about her neck. He watches her and adds pitilessly*)

Hardly presentable, eh?

(*She turns to the ottoman. He raises his pistol instantly, and cries*)

Stop!

(*She stops.*)

Where are you going?

RAINA (*with dignified patience*): Only to get my cloak.

THE MAN (*passing swiftly to the ottoman and snatching the cloak*): A good idea! I'll keep the cloak; and youll take care that nobody comes in and sees you without it. This is a better weapon than the revolver: eh? (*He throws the pistol down on the ottoman.*)

RAINA (*revolted*): It is not the weapon of a gentleman!

THE MAN: It's good enough for a man with only you to stand between him and death. (*As they look at one another for a moment,* RAINA *hardly able to believe that even a Serbian officer can be so cynically and selfishly unchivalrous, they are startled by a sharp fusillade in the street. The chill of imminent death hushes the man's voice as he adds*) Do you hear? If you are going to bring those blackguards in on me you shall receive them as you are.

(*Clamor and disturbance. The pursuers in the street batter at the house door, shouting,* Open the door! Open the door! Wake up, will you! *A man servant's voice calls to them angrily from within,* This is Major Petkoff's house: you cant come in here; *but a renewal of the clamor, and a torrent of blows on the door, end with his letting a chain down with a clank, followed by a rush of heavy footsteps and a din of triumphant yells, dominated at last by the voice of* CATHERINE, *indignantly addressing an officer with* What does this mean, sir? Do you know where you are? *The noise subsides suddenly.*)

LOUKA (*outside, knocking at the bedroom door*): My lady! my lady! get up quick and open the door. If you dont they will break it down.

(*The fugitive throws up his head with the gesture of a man who sees that it is all over with him, and drops the manner he has been assuming to intimidate* RAINA.)

THE MAN (*sincerely and kindly*): No use, dear: I'm done for. (*Flinging the cloak to her*) Quick! wrap yourself up: they're coming.

RAINA: Oh, thank you. (*She wraps herself up with intense relief.*)

THE MAN (*between his teeth*): Dont mention it.

RAINA (*anxiously*): What will you do?

THE MAN (*grimly*): The first man in will find out. Keep out of the way; and dont look. It wont last long; but it will not be nice. (*He draws his sabre and faces the door, waiting.*)

RAINA (*impulsively*): I'll help you. I'll save you.

THE MAN: You cant.

RAINA: I can. I'll hide you. (*She drags him towards the window.*) Here! behind the curtains.

THE MAN (*yielding to her*): There's just half a chance, if you keep your head.

RAINA (*drawing the curtain before him*): S-sh! (*She makes for the ottoman.*)

THE MAN (*putting out his head*): Remember —

RAINA (*running back to him*): Yes?

THE MAN: — nine soldiers out of ten are born fools.

RAINA: Oh! (*She draws the curtain angrily before him.*)

THE MAN (*looking out at the other side*): If they find me, I promise you a fight: a devil of a fight.

(*She stamps at him. He disappears hastily. She takes off her cloak, and throws it across the foot of the bed. Then, with a sleepy, disturbed air, she opens the door.* LOUKA *enters excitedly.*)

LOUKA: One of those beasts of Serbs has been seen climbing up the waterpipe to your balcony. Our men want to search for him; and they are so wild and drunk and furious. (*She makes for the other side of the room to get as far from the door as possible.*) My lady says you are to dress at once and to — (*She sees the revolver lying on the ottoman, and stops, petrified.*)

RAINA (*as if annoyed at being disturbed*): They shall not search here. Why have they been let in?

CATHERINE (*coming in hastily*): Raina, darling, are you safe? Have you seen anyone or heard anything?

RAINA: I heard the shooting. Surely the soldiers will not dare come in here?

CATHERINE: I have found a Russian officer, thank Heaven: he knows

Sergius. (*Speaking through the door to someone outside*) Sir: will you come in now. My daughter will receive you.

(*A young Russian officer, in Bulgarian uniform, enters, sword in hand.*)

OFFICER (*with soft feline politeness and stiff military carriage*): Good evening, gracious lady. I am sorry to intrude; but there is a Serb hiding on the balcony. Will you and the gracious lady your mother please to withdraw whilst we search?

RAINA (*petulantly*): Nonsense, sir: you can see that there is no one on the balcony. (*She throws the shutters wide open and stands with her back to the curtain where the man is hidden, pointing to the moonlit balcony. A couple of shots are fired right under the window; and a bullet shatters the glass opposite* RAINA, *who winks and gasps, but stands her ground; whilst* CATHERINE *screams, and* THE OFFICER, *with a cry of* Take care! *rushes to the balcony.*)

THE OFFICER (*on the balcony, shouting savagely down to the street*): Cease firing there, you fools: do you hear? Cease firing, damn you! (*He glares down for a moment; then turns to* RAINA, *trying to resume his polite manner.*) Could anyone have got in without your knowledge? Were you asleep?

RAINA: No: I have not been to bed.

THE OFFICER (*impatiently, coming back into the room*): Your neighbors have their heads so full of runaway Serbs that they see them everywhere. (*Politely*) Gracious lady: a thousand pardons. Goodnight. (*Military bow, which* RAINA *returns coldly. Another to* CATHERINE, *who follows him out.*)

(RAINA *closes the shutters. She turns and sees* LOUKA, *who has been watching the scene curiously.*)

RAINA: Don't leave my mother, Louka, until the soldiers go away.

(LOUKA *glances at* RAINA, *at the ottoman, at the curtain; then purses her lips secretively, laughs insolently, and goes out.* RAINA, *highly offended by this demonstration, follows her to the door, and shuts it behind her with a slam, locking it violently. The man immediately steps out from behind the curtain, sheathing his sabre. Then, dismissing the danger from his mind in a business-like way, he comes affably to* RAINA.)

THE MAN: A narrow shave; but a miss is as good as a mile. Dear young lady: your servant to the death. I wish for your sake I had joined the Bulgarian army instead of the other one. I am not a native Serb.

RAINA (*haughtily*): No: you are one of the Austrians who set the Serbs on to rob us of our national liberty, and who officer their army for them. We hate them!

THE MAN: Austrian! not I. Dont hate me, dear young lady. I am a Swiss, fighting merely as a professional soldier. I joined the Serbs because they came first on the road from Switzerland. Be generous: youve beaten us hollow.

RAINA: Have I not been generous?

THE MAN: Noble! Heroic! But I'm not saved yet. This particular rush will soon pass through; but the pursuit will go on all night by fits and starts. I must take my chance to get off in a quiet interval. (*Pleasantly*) You dont mind my waiting just a minute or two, do you?

RAINA (*putting on her most genteel society manner*): Oh, not at all. Wont you sit down?

THE MAN: Thanks. (*He sits on the foot of the bed.*)

(RAINA *walks with studied elegance to the ottoman and sits down. Unfortunately she sits on the pistol, and jumps up with a shriek. The man, all nerves, shies like a frightened horse to the other side of the room.*)

THE MAN (*irritably*): Dont frighten me like that. What is it?

RAINA: Your revolver! It was staring that officer in the face all the time. What an escape!

THE MAN (*vexed at being unnecessarily terrified*): Oh, is that all?

RAINA (*staring at him rather superciliously as she conceives a poorer and poorer opinion of him, and feels proportionately more and more at her ease*): I am sorry I frightened you. (*She takes up the pistol and hands it to him.*) Pray take it to protect yourself against me.

THE MAN (*grinning wearily at the sarcasm as he takes the pistol*): No use, dear young lady; there's nothing in it. It's not loaded. (*He makes a grimace at it, and drops it despairingly into his revolver case.*)

RAINA: Load it by all means.

THE MAN: Ive no ammunition. What use are cartridges in battle? I always carry chocolate instead; and I finished the last cake of that hours ago.

RAINA (*outraged in her most cherished ideals of manhood*): Chocolate! Do you stuff your pockets with sweets — like a schoolboy — even in the field?

THE MAN (*grinning*): Yes: isnt it contemptible? (*Hungrily*) I wish I had some now.

RAINA: Allow me. (*She sails away scornfully to the chest of drawers,*) *and returns with the box of confectionery in her hand.*) I am sorry I have eaten them all except these. (*She offers him the box.*)

THE MAN (*ravenously*): Youre an angel! (*He gobbles the contents.*) Creams! Delicious! (*He looks anxiously to see whether there are any more. There are none: he can only scrape the box with his fingers and suck them. When that nourishment is exhausted he accepts the inevitable with pathetic goodhumor, and says, with grateful emotion*) Bless you, dear lady! You can always tell an old soldier by the inside of his holsters and cartridge boxes. The young ones carry pistols and cartridges: the old ones, grub. Thank you. (*He hands back the box. She snatches it contemptuously from him and throws it away. He shies again, as if she had meant to strike him.*) Ugh! Dont do things so suddenly, gracious lady. It's mean to revenge yourself because I frightened you just now.

RAINA (*loftily*): Frighten me! Do you know, sir, that though I am only a woman, I think I am at heart as brave as you.

THE MAN: I should think so. You havnt been under fire for three days as I have. I can stand two days without shewing it much; but no man can stand three days: I'm as nervous as a mouse. (*He sits down on the ottoman, and takes his head in his hands.*) Would you like to see me cry?

RAINA (*alarmed*): No.

THE MAN: If you would, all you have to do is to scold me just as if I were a little boy and you my nurse. If I were in camp now, theyd play all sorts of tricks on me.

RAINA (*a little moved*): I'm sorry. I wont scold you. (*Touched by the sympathy in her tone, he raises his head and looks gratefully at her: she immediately draws back and says stiffly*) You must excuse me: our soldiers are not like that. (*She moves away from the ottoman.*)

THE MAN: Oh yes they are. There are only two sorts of soldiers: old ones and young ones. Ive served fourteen years: half of your fellows never smelt powder before. Why, how is it that youve just beaten us? Sheer ignorance of the art of war, nothing else. (*Indignantly*) I never saw anything so unprofessional.

RAINA (*ironically*): Oh! was it unprofessional to beat you?

THE MAN: Well, come! is it professional to throw a regiment of cavalry on a battery of machine guns, with the dead certainty that if the guns go off not a horse or man will ever get within fifty yards of the fire? I couldn't believe my eyes when I saw it.

RAINA (*eagerly turning to him, as all her enthusiasm and her dreams of glory rush back on her*): Did you see the great cavalry charge? Oh, tell me about it. Describe it to me.

THE MAN: You never saw a cavalry charge, did you?

RAINA: How could I?

THE MAN: Ah, perhaps not. No: of course not! Well, it's a funny sight.
It's like slinging a handful of peas against a window pane: first one
comes; then two or three close behind him; and then all the rest in
a lump.

RAINA (*her eyes dilating as she raises her clasped hands ecstatically*):
Yes, first One! the bravest of the brave!

THE MAN (*prosaically*): Hm! you should see the poor devil pulling at
his horse.

RAINA: Why should he pull at his horse?

THE MAN (*impatient of so stupid a question*): It's running away with
him, of course: do you suppose the fellow wants to get there before
the others and be killed? Then they all come. You can tell the young
ones by their wildness and their slashing. The old ones come bunched
up under the number one guard: they know that theyre mere pro-
jectiles, and that it's no use trying to fight. The wounds are mostly
broken knees, from the horses cannoning together.

RAINA: Ugh! But I dont believe the first man is a coward. I know he is
a hero!

THE MAN (*goodhumoredly*): Thats what youd have said if youd seen
the first man in the charge today.

RAINA (*breathless, forgiving him everything*): Ah, I knew it! Tell me.
Tell me about him.

THE MAN: He did it like an operatic tenor. A regular handsome fellow,
with flashing eyes and lovely moustache, shouting his war-cry and
charging like Don Quixote at the windmills. We did laugh.

RAINA: You dared to laugh!

THE MAN: Yes; but when the sergeant ran up as white as a sheet, and
told us theyd sent us the wrong ammunition, and that we couldnt
fire a round for the next ten minutes, we laughed at the other side
of our mouths. I never felt so sick in my life; though Ive been in one
or two very tight places. And I hadnt even a revolver cartridge: only
chocolate. We'd no bayonets: nothing. Of course, they just cut us
to bits. And there was Don Quixote flourishing like a drum major,
thinking he'd done the cleverest thing ever known, whereas he ought
to be courtmartialled for it. Of all the fools ever let loose on a field
of battle, that man must be the very maddest. He and his regiment
simply committed suicide; only the pistol missed fire: thats all.

RAINA (*deeply wounded, but steadfastly loyal to her ideals*): Indeed!
Would you know him again if you saw him?

THE MAN: Shall I ever forget him!

(*She again goes to the chest of drawers. He watches her with a vague hope that she may have something more for him to eat. She takes the portrait from its stand and brings it to him.*)

RAINA: That is a photograph of the gentleman — the patriot and hero — to whom I am betrothed.

THE MAN (*recognizing it with a shock*): I'm really very sorry. (*Looking at her*) Was it fair to lead me on? (*He looks at the portrait again.*) Yes: thats Don Quixote: not a doubt of it. (*He stifles a laugh.*)

RAINA (*quickly*): Why do you laugh?

THE MAN (*apologetic, but still greatly tickled*): I didnt laugh, I assure you. At least I didnt mean to. But when I think of him charging the windmills and imagining he was doing the finest thing — (*He chokes with suppressed laughter.*)

RAINA (*sternly*): Give me back the portrait, sir.

THE MAN (*with sincere remorse*): Of course. Certainly. I'm really very sorry. (*He hands her the picture. She deliberately kisses it and looks him straight in the face before returning to the chest of drawers to replace it. He follows her, apologizing.*) Perhaps I'm quite wrong, you know: no doubt I am. Most likely he had got wind of the cartridge business somehow, and knew it was a safe job.

RAINA: That is to say, he was a pretender and a coward! You did not dare say that before.

THE MAN (*with a comic gesture of despair*): It's no use, dear lady: I cant make you see it from the professional point of view. (*As he turns away to get back to the ottoman, a couple of distant shots threaten renewed trouble.*)

RAINA (*sternly, as she sees him listening to the shots*): So much the better for you!

THE MAN (*turning*): How?

RAINA: You are my enemy; and you are at my mercy. What would I do if I were a professional soldier?

THE MAN: Ah, true, dear young lady: youre always right. I know how good youve been to me: to my last hour I shall remember those three chocolate creams. It was unsoldierly; but it was angelic.

RAINA (*coldly*): Thank you. And now I will do a soldierly thing. You cannot stay here after what you have just said about my future husband; but I will go out on the balcony and see whether it is safe for you to climb down into the street. (*She turns to the window.*)

THE MAN (*changing countenance*): Down that waterpipe! Stop! Wait! I cant! I darent! The very thought of it makes me giddy. I came up it fast enough with death behind me. But to face it now in cold blood — ! (*He sinks on the ottoman.*) It's no use: I give up: I'm beaten. Give the alarm. (*He drops his head on his hands in the deepest dejection.*)

RAINA (*disarmed by pity*): Come: dont be disheartened. (*She stoops over him almost maternally: he shakes his head.*) Oh, you are a very poor soldier: a chocolate cream soldier! Come, cheer up! it takes less courage to climb down than to face capture: remember that.

THE MAN (*dreamily, lulled by her voice*): No: capture only means death; and death is sleep: oh, sleep, sleep, sleep, undisturbed sleep! Climbing down the pipe means doing something — exerting myself — thinking! Death ten times over first.

RAINA (*softly and wonderingly, catching the rhythm of his weariness*): Are you as sleepy as that?

THE MAN: Ive not had two hours undisturbed sleep since I joined. I havnt closed my eyes for forty-eight hours.

RAINA (*at her wit's end*): But what am I to do with you?

THE MAN (*staggering up, roused by her desperation*): Of course. I must do something. (*He shakes himself; pulls himself together; and speaks with rallied vigor and courage.*) You see, sleep or no sleep, hunger or no hunger, tired or not tired, you can always do a thing when you know it must be done. Well, that pipe must be got down: (*he hits himself on the chest*) do you hear that, you chocolate cream soldier? (*He turns to the window.*)

RAINA (*anxiously*): But if you fall?

THE MAN: I shall sleep as if the stones were a feather bed. Goodbye. (*He makes boldly for the window; and his hand is on the shutter when there is a terrible burst of firing in the street beneath.*)

RAINA (*rushing to him*): Stop! (*She seizes him recklessly, and pulls him quite round.*) Theyll kill you.

THE MAN (*coolly, but attentively*): Never mind: this sort of thing is all in my day's work. I'm bound to take my chance. (*Decisively*) Now do what I tell you. Put out the candle; so that they shant see the light when I open the shutters. And keep away from the window, whatever you do. If they see me theyre sure to have a shot at me.

RAINA (*clinging to him*): Theyre sure to see you: it's bright moonlight. I'll save you. Oh, how can you be so indifferent! You want me to save you, dont you?

THE MAN: I really dont want to be troublesome.

(*She shakes him in her impatience.*)

I am not indifferent, dear young lady, I assure you. But how is it to be done?

RAINA: Come away from the window. (*She takes him firmly back to the middle of the room. The moment she releases him he turns mechanically towards the window again. She seizes him and turns him back, exclaiming*) Please!

(*He becomes motionless, like a hypnotized rabbit, his fatigue gaining fast on him. She releases him, and addresses him patronizingly.*)

Now listen. You must trust to our hospitality. You do not yet know in whose house you are. I am a Petkoff.

THE MAN: A pet what?

RAINA (*rather indignantly*): I mean that I belong to the family of the Petkoffs, the richest and best known in our country.

THE MAN: Oh, yes, of course. I beg your pardon. The Petkoffs, to be sure. How stupid of me!

RAINA: You know you never heard of them until this moment. How can you stoop to pretend!

THE MAN: Forgive me: I'm too tired to think; and the change of subject was too much for me. Dont scold me.

RAINA: I forgot. It might make you cry.

(*He nods, quite seriously. She pouts and then resumes her patronizing tone.*)

I must tell you that my father holds the highest command of any Bulgarian in our army. He is (*proudly*) a Major.

THE MAN (*pretending to be deeply impressed*): A Major! Bless me! Think of that!

RAINA: You shewed great ignorance in thinking that it was necessary to climb up to the balcony because ours is the only private house that has two rows of windows. There is a flight of stairs inside to get up and down by.

THE MAN: Stairs! How grand! You live in great luxury indeed, dear young lady.

RAINA: Do you know what a library is?

THE MAN: A library? A roomful of books?

RAINA: Yes. We have one, the only one in Bulgaria.

THE MAN: Actually a real library! I should like to see that.

RAINA (*affectedly*): I tell you these things to shew you that you are not in the house of ignorant country folk who would kill you the moment they saw your Serbian uniform, but among civilized people. We go to Bucharest every year for the opera season; and I have spent a whole month in Vienna.

THE MAN: I saw that, dear young lady. I saw at once that you knew the world.

RAINA: Have you ever seen the opera of Ernani?

THE MAN: Is that the one with the devil in it in red velvet, and a soldiers' chorus?

RAINA (*contemptuously*): No!

THE MAN (*stifling a heavy sigh of weariness*): Then I dont know it.

RAINA: I thought you might have remembered the great scene where Ernani, flying from his foes just as you are tonight, takes refuge in the castle of his bitterest enemy, an old Castilian noble. The noble refuses to give him up. His guest is sacred to him.

THE MAN (*quickly, waking up a little*): Have your people got that notion?

RAINA (*with dignity*): My mother and I can understand that notion, as you call it. And if instead of threatening me with your pistol as you did you had simply thrown yourself as a fugitive on our hospitality, you would have been as safe as in your father's house.

THE MAN: Quite sure?

RAINA (*turning her back on him in disgust*): Oh, it is useless to try to make you understand.

THE MAN: Dont be angry: you see how awkward it would be for me if there was any mistake. My father is a very hospitable man: he keeps six hotels; but I couldnt trust him as far as that. What about your father?

RAINA: He is away at Slivnitza fighting for his country. I answer for your safety. There is my hand in pledge of it. Will that reassure you? (*She offers him her hand.*)

THE MAN (*looking dubiously at his own hand*): Better not touch my hand, dear young lady. I must have a wash first.

RAINA (*touched*): That is very nice of you. I see that you are a gentleman.

THE MAN (*puzzled*): Eh?

RAINA: You must not think I am surprised. Bulgarians of really good standing — people in our position — wash their hands nearly every day. So you see I can appreciate your delicacy. You may take my hand. (*She offers it again.*)

THE MAN (*kissing it with his hands behind his back*): Thanks, gracious young lady: I feel safe at last. And now would you mind breaking the news to your mother? I had better not stay here secretly longer than is necessary.

RAINA: If you will be so good as to keep perfectly still whilst I am away.

THE MAN: Certainly. (*He sits down on the ottoman.*)

(RAINA *goes to the bed and wraps herself in the fur cloak. His eyes close. She goes to the door. Turning for a last look at him, she sees that he is dropping off to sleep.*)

RAINA (*at the door*): You are not going asleep, are you?

(*He murmurs inarticulately: she runs to him and shakes him.*)

Do you hear? Wake up: you are falling asleep.

THE MAN: Eh? Falling aslee — ? Oh no: not the least in the world: I was only thinking. It's all right: I'm wide awake.

RAINA (*severely*): Will you please stand up while I am away.

(*He rises reluctantly.*)

All the time, mind.

THE MAN (*standing unsteadily*): Certainly. Certainly: you may depend on me.

(RAINA *looks doubtfully at him. He smiles weakly. She goes reluctantly, turning again at the door, and almost catching him in the act of yawning. She goes out.*)

THE MAN (*drowsily*): Sleep, sleep, sleep, sleep, slee — (*The words trail off into a murmur. He wakes again with a shock on the point of falling.*) Where am I? Thats what I want to know: where am I? Must keep awake. Nothing keeps me awake except danger: remember that: (*intently*) danger, danger, danger, dan — (*trailing off again: another shock*) Wheres danger? Mus' find it. (*He starts off vaguely round the room in search of it.*) What am I looking for? Sleep — danger — dont know. (*He stumbles against the bed.*) Ah yes: now I know. All right now. I'm to go to bed, but not to sleep. Be sure not to sleep, because of danger. Not to lie down either, only sit down. (*He sits on the bed. A blissful expression comes into his face.*) Ah! (*With a happy sigh he sinks back at full length; lifts his boots into the bed with a final effort; and falls fast asleep instantly.*)

(CATHERINE *comes in, followed by* RAINA.)

RAINA (*looking at the ottoman*): He's gone! I left him here.

CATHERINE: Here! Then he must have climbed down from the —

RAINA (*seeing him*): Oh! (*She points.*)

CATHERINE (*scandalized*): Well! (*She strides to the bed,* RAINA *following until she is opposite her on the other side.*) He's fast asleep. The brute!

RAINA (*anxiously*): Sh!

CATHERINE (*shaking him*): Sir! (*Shaking him again, harder*) Sir!! (*Vehemently, shaking very hard*) Sir!!!

RAINA (*catching her arm*): Dont, mamma; the poor darling is worn out. Let him sleep.

CATHERINE (*letting him go, and turning amazed to* RAINA): The poor darling! Raina!!! (*She looks sternly at her daughter.*)

(*The man sleeps profoundly.*)

ACT II

(*The sixth of March, 1886. In the garden of* MAJOR PETKOFF'S *house. It is a fine spring morning: the garden looks fresh and pretty. Beyond the paling the tops of a couple of minarets can be seen, shewing that there is a valley there, with the little town in it. A few miles further the Balkan mountains rise and shut in the landscape. Looking towards them from within the garden, the side of the house is seen on the left, with a garden door reached by a little flight of steps. On the right the stable yard, with its gateway, encroaches on the garden. There are fruit bushes along the paling and house, covered with washing spread out to dry. A path runs by the house, and rises by two steps at the corner, where it turns out of sight. In the middle, a small table, with two bent wood chairs at it, is laid for breakfast with Turkish coffee pot, cups, rolls, etc.; but the cups have been used and the bread broken. There is a wooden garden seat against the wall on the right.*

LOUKA, smoking a cigaret, is standing between the table and the house, turning her back with angry disdain on a man servant who is lecturing her. He is a middle-aged man of cool temperament and low but clear and keen intelligence, with the complacency of the servant who values himself on his rank in servitude, and the imperturbability of the accurate calculator who has no illusions. He wears a white Bulgarian costume: jacket with embroidered border, sash, wide knickerbockers, and decorated gaiters. His head is shaved up to the crown, giving him a high Japanese forehead. His name is NICOLA.)

NICOLA: Be warned in time, Louka: mend your manners. I know the mistress. She is so grand that she never dreams that any servant could dare be disrespectful to her; but if she once suspects that you are defying her, out you go.

LOUKA: I do defy her. I will defy her. What do I care for her?

NICOLA: If you quarrel with the family, I never can marry you. It's the same as if you quarrelled with me!

LOUKA: You take her part against me, do you?

NICOLA (*sedately*): I shall always be dependent on the good will of the family. When I leave their service and start a shop in Sofia, their custom will be half my capital: their bad word would ruin me.

LOUKA: You have no spirit. I should like to catch them saying a word against me!

NICOLA (*pityingly*): I should have expected more sense from you, Louka. But youre young: youre young!

LOUKA: Yes; and you like me the better for it, dont you? But I know some family secrets they wouldnt care to have told, young as I am. Let them quarrel with me if they dare!

NICOLA (*with compassionate superiority*): Do you know what they would do if they heard you talk like that?

LOUKA: What could they do?

NICOLA: Discharge you for untruthfulness. Who would believe any stories you told after that? Who would give you another situation? Who in this house would dare be seen speaking to you ever again? How long would your father be left on his little farm?

(*She impatiently throws away the end of her cigaret, and stamps on it.*)

Child: you dont know the power such high people have over the like of you and me when we try to rise out of our poverty against them. (*He goes close to her and lowers his voice.*) Look at me, ten years in their service. Do you think I know no secrets? I know things about the mistress that she wouldnt have the master know for a thousand levas. I know things about him that she wouldnt let him hear the last of for six months if I blabbed them to her. I know things about Raina that would break off her match with Sergius if —

LOUKA (*turning on him quickly*): How do you know? I never told you!

NICOLA (*opening his eyes cunningly*): So thats your little secret, is it? I thought it might be something like that. Well, you take my advice and be respectful; and make the mistress feel that no matter what you know or dont know, she can depend on you to hold your tongue and serve the family faithfully. Thats what they like; and thats how youll make most out of them.

LOUKA (*with searching scorn*): You have the soul of a servant, Nicola.

NICOLA (*complacently*): Yes: thats the secret of success in service.

(*A loud knocking with a whip handle on a wooden door is heard from the stable yard.*)

MALE VOICE OUTSIDE: Hollo! Hollo there! Nicola!

LOUKA: Master! back from the war!

NICOLA (*quickly*): My word for it, Louka, the war's over. Off with you and get some fresh coffee. (*He runs out into the stable yard.*)

LOUKA (*as she collects the coffee pot and cups on the tray, and carries it into the house*): Youll never put the soul of a servant into me.

(MAJOR PETKOFF *comes from the stable yard, followed by* NICOLA. *He is a cheerful, excitable, insignificant, unpolished man of about fifty, naturally unambitious except as to his income and his importance in local society, but just now greatly pleased with the military rank which the war has thrust on him as a man of consequence in his town. The fever of plucky patriotism which the Serbian attack roused in all the Bulgarians has pulled him through the war; but he is obviously glad to be home again.*)

PETKOFF (*pointing to the table with his whip*): Breakfast out here, eh?

NICOLA: Yes, sir. The mistress and Miss Raina have just gone in.

PETKOFF (*sitting down and taking a roll*): Go in and say Ive come; and get me some fresh coffee.

NICOLA: It's coming, sir. (*He goes to the house door.* LOUKA, *with fresh coffee, a clean cup, and a brandy bottle on her tray, meets him.*) Have you told the mistress?

LOUKA: Yes: she's coming.

(NICOLA *goes into the house.* LOUKA *brings the coffee to the table.*)

PETKOFF: Well: the Serbs havnt run away with you, have they?

LOUKA: No, sir.

PETKOFF: Thats right. Have you brought me some cognac?

LOUKA (*putting the bottle on the table*): Here, sir.

PETKOFF: Thats right. (*He pours some into his coffee.*)

(CATHERINE, *who, having at this early hour made only a very perfunctory toilet, wears a Bulgarian apron over a once brilliant but now half worn-out dressing gown, and a colored handkerchief tied over her thick black hair, comes from the house with Turkish slippers on her bare feet, looking astonishingly handsome and stately under all the circumstances.* LOUKA *goes into the house.*)

CATHERINE: My dear Paul: what a surprise for us! (*She stoops over the back of his chair to kiss him.*) Have they brought you fresh coffee?

PETKOFF: Yes: Louka's been looking after me. The war's over. The treaty was signed three days ago at Bucharest; and the decree for our army to demobilize was issued yesterday.

CATHERINE (*springing erect, with flashing eyes*): Paul: have you let the Austrians force you to make peace?

PETKOFF (*submissively*): My dear: they didnt consult me. What could I do?

(*She sits down and turns away from him.*)

But of course we saw to it that the treaty was an honorable one. It declares peace —

CATHERINE (*outraged*): Peace!

PETKOFF (*appeasing her*): — but not friendly relations: remember that. They wanted to put that in; but I insisted on its being struck out. What more could I do?

CATHERINE: You could have annexed Serbia and made Prince Alexander Emperor of the Balkans. Thats what I would have done.

PETKOFF: I dont doubt it in the least, my dear. But I should have had to subdue the whole Austrian Empire first; and that would have kept me too long away from you. I missed you greatly.

CATHERINE (*relenting*): Ah! (*She stretches her hand affectionately across the table to squeeze his.*)

PETKOFF: And how have you been, my dear?

CATHERINE: Oh, my usual sore throats: thats all.

PETKOFF (*with conviction*): That comes from washing your neck every day. Ive often told you so.

CATHERINE: Nonsense, Paul!

PETKOFF (*over his coffee and cigaret*): I dont believe in going too far with these modern customs. All this washing cant be good for the health; it's not natural. There was an Englishman at Philippopolis who used to wet himself all over with cold water every morning when he got up. Disgusting! It all comes from the English: their climate makes them so dirty that they have to be perpetually washing themselves. Look at my father! he never had a bath in his life; and he lived to be ninety-eight, the healthiest man in Bulgaria. I dont mind a good wash once a week to keep up my position; but once a day is carrying the thing to a ridiculous extreme.

CATHERINE: You are a barbarian at heart still, Paul. I hope you behaved yourself before all those Russian officers.

PETKOFF: I did my best. I took care to let them know that we have a library.

CATHERINE: Ah; but you didnt tell them that we have an electric bell in it? I have had one put up.

PETKOFF: Whats an electric bell?

CATHERINE: You touch a button; something tinkles in the kitchen; and then Nicola comes up.

PETKOFF: Why not shout for him?

CATHERINE: Civilized people never shout for their servants. Ive learnt that while you were away.

PETKOFF: Well, I'll tell you something Ive learnt too. Civilized people dont hang out their washing to dry where visitors can see it: so youd better have all that (*indicating the clothes on the bushes*) put somewhere else.

CATHERINE: Oh, thats absurd, Paul: I don't believe really refined people notice such things.

SERGIUS (*knocking at the stable gates*): Gate, Nicola!

PETKOFF: Theres Sergius. (*Shouting*) Hollo, Nicola!

CATHERINE: Oh, dont shout, Paul: it really isnt nice.

PETKOFF: Bosh! (*He shouts louder than before.*) Nicola!

NICOLA (*appearing at the house door*): Yes, sir.

PETKOFF: Are you deaf? Dont you hear Major Saranoff knocking? Bring him round this way. (*He pronounces the name with the stress on the second syllable:* SARAHNOFF.)

NICOLA: Yes, Major. (*He goes into the stable yard.*)

PETKOFF: You must talk to him, my dear, until Raina takes him off our hands. He bores my life out about our not promoting him. Over my head, if you please.

CATHERINE: He certainly ought to be promoted when he marries Raina. Besides, the country should insist on having at least one native general.

PETKOFF: Yes; so that he could throw away whole brigades instead of regiments. It's no use, my dear: he hasnt the slightest chance of promotion until we're quite sure that the peace will be a lasting one.

NICOLA (*at the gate, announcing*): Major Sergius Saranoff! (*He goes into the house and returns presently with a third chair, which he places at the table. He then withdraws.*)

(MAJOR SERGIUS SARANOFF, *the original of the portrait in* RAINA's *room, is a tall romantically handsome man, with the physical hardihood, the high spirit, and the susceptible imagination of an untamed mountaineer chieftain. But his remarkable personal distinction is of a characteristically civilized type. The ridges of his eyebrows, curving with an interrogative twist round the projections at the outer corners; his jealously observant eye; his nose, thin, keen, and apprehensive in spite of the pugnacious high bridge and large nostril; his assertive chin would not be out of place in a Parisian salon, shewing that the clever imaginative barbarian has an acute critical faculty which has been thrown into intense activity by the arrival of western civilization in the Balkans. The result is precisely what the advent of nineteenth century thought first produced in England: to wit, Byronism. By his brooding on the perpetual failure, not only of others, but of himself, to live up to his ideals; by his consequent cynical scorn for humanity; by his jejune credulity as to the absolute validity of his concepts and the unworthiness of the world in disregarding them; by his wincings and mockeries under the sting of the petty disillusions which every hour spent among men brings to his sensitive observation, he has acquired the half tragic, half ironic air, the mysterious moodiness, the suggestion of a strange and terrible history that has left nothing but undying remorse, by which Childe Harold fascinated the grandmothers of his English contemporaries. It is clear that here or nowhere is* RAINA's *ideal hero.* CATHERINE *is hardly less enthusiastic about him than her daughter, and much less reserved in shewing her enthusiasm. As he enters from the stable gate, she rises effusively to greet him.* PETKOFF *is distinctly less disposed to make a fuss about him.*)

PETKOFF: Here already, Sergius! Glad to see you.

CATHERINE: My dear Sergius! (*She holds out both her hands.*)

SERGIUS (*kissing them with scrupulous gallantry*): My dear mother, if I may call you so.

PETKOFF (*drily*): Mother-in-law, Sergius: mother-in-law! Sit down; and have some coffee.

SERGIUS: Thank you: none for me. (*He gets away from the table with a certain distaste for* PETKOFF's *enjoyment of it, and posts himself with conscious dignity against the rail of the steps leading to the house.*)

CATHERINE: You look superb. The campaign has improved you, Sergius. Everybody here is mad about you. We were all wild with enthusiasm about that magnificent cavalry charge.

SERGIUS (*with grave irony*): Madam: it was the cradle and the grave of my military reputation.

CATHERINE: How so?

SERGIUS: I won the battle the wrong way when our worthy Russian generals were losing it the right way. In short, I upset their plans, and wounded their self-esteem. Two Cossack colonels had their regiments routed on the most correct principles of scientific warfare. Two major-generals got killed strictly according to military etiquette. The two colonels are now major-generals; and I am still a simple major.

CATHERINE: You shall not remain so, Sergius. The women are on your side; and they will see that justice is done you.

SERGIUS: It is too late. I have only waited for the peace to send in my resignation.

PETKOFF (*dropping his cup in his amazement*): Your resignation!

CATHERINE: Oh, you must withdraw it!

SERGIUS (*with resolute measured emphasis, folding his arms*): I never withdraw.

PETKOFF (*vexed*): Now who could have supposed you were going to do such a thing?

SERGIUS (*with fire*): Everyone that knew me. But enough of myself and my affairs. How is Raina; and where is Raina?

RAINA (*suddenly coming round the corner of the house and standing at the top of the steps in the path*): Raina is here.

(*She makes a charming picture as they turn to look at her. She wears an underdress of pale green silk, draped with an overdress of thin ecru canvas embroidered with gold. She is crowned with a dainty eastern cap of gold tinsel. SERGIUS goes impulsively to meet her. Posing regally, she presents her hand: he drops chivalrously on one knee and kisses it.*)

PETKOFF (*aside to* CATHERINE, *beaming with parental pride*): Pretty, isnt it? She always appears at the right moment.

CATHERINE (*impatiently*): Yes; she listens for it. It is an abominable habit.

(*SERGIUS leads* RAINA *forward with splendid gallantry. When they arrive at the table, she turns to him with a bend of the head: he bows; and thus they separate, he coming to his place and she going behind her father's chair.*)

RAINA (*stooping and kissing her father*): Dear father! Welcome home!

PETKOFF (*patting her cheek*): My little pet girl. (*He kisses her. She goes to the chair left by* NICOLA *for* SERGIUS, *and sits down.*)

CATHERINE: And so youre no longer a soldier, Sergius.

SERGIUS: I am no longer a soldier. Soldiering, my dear madam, is the coward's art of attacking mercilessly when you are strong, and keeping out of harm's way when you are weak. That is the whole secret of successful fighting. Get your enemy at a disadvantage; and never, on any account, fight him on equal terms.

PETKOFF: They wouldnt let us make a fair stand-up fight of it. How ever, I suppose soldiering has to be a trade like any other trade.

SERGIUS: Precisely. But I have no ambition to shine as a tradesman; so I have taken the advice of that bagman of a captain that settled the exchange of prisoners with us at Pirot, and given it up.

PETKOFF: What! that Swiss fellow? Sergius: I've often thought of that exchange since. He over-reached us about those horses.

SERGIUS: Of course he over-reached us. His father was a hotel and livery stable keeper; and he owed his first step to his knowledge of horse-dealing. (*With mock enthusiasm*) Ah, he was a soldier: every inch a soldier! If only I had bought the horses for my regiment instead of foolishly leading it into danger, I should have been a field-marshal now!

CATHERINE: A Swiss? What was he doing in the Serbian army?

PETKOFF: A volunteer, of course: keen on picking up his profession. (*Chuckling*) We shouldnt have been able to begin fighting if these foreigners hadnt shewn us how to do it: we knew nothing about it; and neither did the Serbs. Egad, there'd have been no war without them!

RAINA: Are there many Swiss officers in the Serbian Army?

PETKOFF: No. All Austrians, just as our officers were all Russians. This was the only Swiss I came across. I'll never trust a Swiss again. He humbugged us into giving him fifty ablebodied men for two hundred worn out chargers. They werent even eatable!

SERGIUS: We were two children in the hands of that consummate soldier, Major: simply two innocent little children.

RAINA: What was he like?

CATHERINE: Oh, Raina, what a silly question!

SERGIUS: He was like a commercial traveller in uniform. Bourgeois to his boots!

PETKOFF (*grinning*): Sergius: tell Catherine that queer story his friend told us about how he escaped after Slivnitza. You remember. About his being hid by two women.

SERGIUS (*with bitter irony*): Oh yes: quite a romance! He was serving in the very battery I so unprofessionally charged. Being a thorough soldier, he ran away like the rest of them, with our cavalry at his heels. To escape their sabres he climbed a waterpipe and made his way into the bedroom of a young Bulgarian lady. The young lady was enchanted by his persuasive commercial traveller's manners. She very modestly entertained him for an hour or so, and then called in her mother lest her conduct should appear unmaidenly. The old lady was equally fascinated; and the fugitive was sent on his way in the morning, disguised in an old coat belonging to the master of the house, who was away at the war.

RAINA (*rising with marked stateliness*): Your life in the camp has made you coarse, Sergius. I did not think you would have repeated such a story before me. (*She turns away coldly.*)

CATHERINE (*also rising*): She is right, Sergius. If such women exist, we should be spared the knowledge of them.

PETKOFF: Pooh! nonsense! what does it matter?

SERGIUS (*ashamed*): No, Petkoff: I was wrong. (*To* RAINA, *with earnest humility*) I beg your pardon. I have behaved abominably. Forgive me, Raina.

(*She bows reservedly.*)

And you too, madam.

(CATHERINE *bows graciously and sits down. He proceeds solemnly, again addressing* RAINA.)

The glimpses I have had of the seamy side of life during the last few months have made me cynical; but I should not have brought my cynicism here: least of all into your presence, Raina. I — (*Here, turning to the others, he is evidently going to begin a long speech when the Major interrupts him.*)

PETKOFF: Stuff and nonsense, Sergius! Thats quite enough fuss about nothing: a soldier's daughter should be able to stand up without flinching to a little strong conversation. (*He rises.*) Come: it's time for us to get to business. We have to make up our minds how those three regiments are to get back to Philippopolis: theres no forage for them on the Sofia route. (*He goes towards the house.*) Come along.

(SERGIUS *is about to follow him when* CATHERINE *rises and intervenes.*)

CATHERINE: Oh, Paul, cant you spare Sergius for a few moments? Raina has hardly seen him yet. Perhaps I can help you to settle about the regiments.

SERGIUS (*protesting*): My dear madam, impossible: you —

CATHERINE (*stopping him playfully*): You stay here, my dear Sergius: theres no hurry. I have a word or two to say to Paul.

(SERGIUS *instantly bows and steps back.*)

Now, dear (*taking* PETKOFF's *arm*): come and see the electric bell.

PETKOFF: Oh, very well, very well.

(*They go into the house together affectionately.* SERGIUS, *left alone with* RAINA, *looks anxiously at her, fearing that she is still offended. She smiles, and stretches out her arms to him.*)

SERGIUS (*hastening to her*): Am I forgiven?

RAINA (*placing her hands on his shoulders as she looks up at him with admiration and worship*): My hero! My king!

SERGIUS: My queen! (*He kisses her on the forehead.*)

RAINA: How I have envied you, Sergius! You have been out in the world, on the field of battle, able to prove yourself there worthy of any woman in the world; whilst I have had to sit at home inactive — dreaming — useless — doing nothing that could give me the right to call myself worthy of any man.

SERGIUS: Dearest: all my deeds have been yours. You inspired me. I have gone through the war like a knight in a tournament with his lady looking down at him!

RAINA: And you have never been absent from my thoughts for a moment. (*Very solemnly*) Sergius: I think we two have found the higher love. When I think of you, I feel that I could never do a base deed, or think an ignoble thought.

SERGIUS: My lady and my saint! (*He clasps her reverently.*)

RAINA (*returning his embrace*): My lord and my —

SERGIUS: Sh — sh! Let me be the worshipper, dear. You little know how unworthy even the best man is of a girl's pure passion!

RAINA: I trust you. I love you. You will never disappoint me, Sergius.

(LOUKA *is heard singing within the house. They quickly release each other.*)

I cant pretend to talk indifferently before her: my heart is too full.

(LOUKA *comes from the house with her tray. She goes to the table, and begins to clear it, with her back turned to them.*)

I will get my hat; and then we can go out until lunch time. Wouldnt you like that?

SERGIUS: Be quick. If you are away five minutes, it will seem five hours.

(RAINA *runs to the top of the steps, and turns there to exchange looks with him and wave him a kiss with both hands. He looks after her with emotion for a moment; then turns slowly away, his face radiant with the loftiest exaltation. The movement shifts his field of vision, into the corner of which there now comes the tail of* LOUKA's *double apron. His attention is arrested at once. He takes a stealthy look at her, and begins to twirl his moustache mischievously, with his left hand akimbo on his hip. Finally, striking the ground with his heels in something of a cavalry swagger, he strolls over to the other side of the table, opposite her, and says*)

Louka: do you know what the higher love is?

LOUKA (*astonished*): No, sir.

SERGIUS: Very fatiguing thing to keep up for any length of time, Louka. One feels the need of some relief after it.

LOUKA (*innocently*): Perhaps you would like some coffee, sir? (*She stretches her hand across the table for the coffee pot.*)

SERGIUS (*taking her hand*): Thank you, Louka.

LOUKA (*pretending to pull*): Oh, sir, you know I didnt mean that. I'm surprised at you!

SERGIUS (*coming clear of the table and drawing her with him*): I am surprised at myself, Louka. What would Sergius, the hero of Slivnitza, say if he saw me now? What would Sergius, the apostle of the higher love, say if he saw me now? What would the half dozen Sergiuses who keep popping in and out of this handsome figure of mine say if they caught us here? (*Letting go her hand and slipping his arm dexterously round her waist*) Do you consider my figure handsome, Louka?

LOUKA: Let me go, sir. I shall be disgraced. (*She struggles: he holds her inexorably.*) Oh, will you let go?

SERGIUS (*looking straight into her eyes*): No.

LOUKA: Then stand back where we cant be seen. Have you no common sense?

SERGIUS: Ah! thats reasonable. (*He takes her into the stable yard gateway, where they are hidden from the house.*)

LOUKA (*plaintively*): I may have been seen from the windows: Miss Raina is sure to be spying about after you.

SERGIUS (*stung: letting her go*): Take care, Louka. I may be worthless enough to betray the higher love; but do not you insult it.

LOUKA (*demurely*): Not for the world, sir, I'm sure. May I go on with my work, please, now?

SERGIUS (*again putting his arm round her*): You are a provoking little witch, Louka. If you were in love with me, would you spy out of windows on me?

LOUKA: Well, you see, sir, since you say you are half a dozen different gentlemen all at once, I should have a great deal to look after.

SERGIUS (*charmed*): Witty as well as pretty. (*He tries to kiss her.*)

LOUKA (*avoiding him*): No: I dont want your kisses. Gentlefolk are all alike: you making love to me behind Miss Raina's back; and she doing the same behind yours.

SERGIUS (*recoiling a step*): Louka!

LOUKA: It shews how little you really care.

SERGIUS (*dropping his familiarity, and speaking with freezing polite-*

ness): If our conversation is to continue, Louka, you will please remember that a gentleman does not discuss the conduct of the lady he is engaged to with her maid.

LOUKA: It's so hard to know what a gentleman considers right. I thought from your trying to kiss me that you had given up being so particular.

SERGIUS (*turning from her and striking his forehead as he comes back into the garden from the gateway*): Devil! devil!

LOUKA: Ha! ha! I expect one of the six of you is very like me, sir; though I am only Miss Raina's maid. (*She goes back to her work at the table, taking no further notice of him.*)

SERGIUS (*speaking to himself*): Which of the six is the real man? thats the question that torments me. One of them is a hero, another a buffoon, another a humbug, another perhaps a bit of a blackguard. (*He pauses, and looks furtively at* LOUKA *as he adds, with deep bitterness*) And one, at least, is a coward: jealous, like all cowards. (*He goes to the table.*) Louka.

LOUKA: Yes?

SERGIUS: Who is my rival?

LOUKA: You shall never get that out of me, for love or money.

SERGIUS: Why?

LOUKA: Never mind why. Besides, you would tell that I told you; and I should lose my place.

SERGIUS (*holding out his right hand in affirmation*): No! on the honor of a — (*He checks himself; and his hand drops, nerveless, as he concludes sardonically*) — of a man capable of behaving as I have been behaving for the last five minutes. Who is he?

LOUKA: I dont know. I never saw him. I only heard his voice through the door of her room.

SERGIUS: Damnation! How dare you?

LOUKA (*retreating*): Oh, I mean no harm: youve no right to take up my words like that. The mistress knows all about it. And I tell you that if that gentleman ever comes here again, Miss Raina will marry him, whether he likes it or not. I know the difference between the sort of manner you and she put on before one another and the real manner.

(SERGIUS *shivers as if she had stabbed him. Then, setting his face like iron, he strides grimly to her, and grips her above the elbows with both hands.*)

SERGIUS: Now listen you to me.

LOUKA (*wincing*): Not so tight: youre hurting me.

SERGIUS: That doesnt matter. You have stained my honor by making me a party to your eavesdropping. And you have betrayed your mistress.

LOUKA (*writhing*): Please —

SERGIUS: That shews that you are an abominable little clod of common clay, with the soul of a servant. (*He lets her go as if she were an unclean thing, and turns away, dusting his hands of her, to the bench by the wall, where he sits down with averted head, meditating gloomily.*)

LOUKA (*whimpering angrily with her hands up her sleeves, feeling her bruised arms*): You know how to hurt with your tongue as well as with your hands. But I dont care, now Ive found out that whatever clay I'm made of, youre made of the same. As for her, she's a liar; and her fine airs are a cheat; and I'm worth six of her. (*She shakes the pain off hardily; tosses her head; and sets to work to put the things on the tray.*)

(*He looks doubtfully at her. She finishes packing the tray, and laps the cloth over the edges, so as to carry all out together. As she stoops to lift it, he rises.*)

SERGIUS: Louka!

(*She stops and looks defiantly at him.*)

A gentleman has no right to hurt a woman under any circumstances. (*With profound humility, uncovering his head*) I beg your pardon.

LOUKA: That sort of apology may satisfy a lady. Of what use is it to a servant?

SERGIUS (*rudely crossed in his chivalry, throws it off with a bitter laugh, and says slightingly*): Oh! you wish to be paid for the hurt! (*He puts on his shako, and takes some money from his pocket.*)

LOUKA (*her eyes filling with tears in spite of herself*): No: I want my hurt made well.

SERGIUS (*sobered by her tone*): How?

(*She rolls up her left sleeve; clasps her arm with the thumb and fingers of her right hand; and looks down at the bruise. Then she raises her head and looks straight at him. Finally, with a superb gesture, she presents her arm to be kissed. Amazed, he looks at her; at the arm; at her again; hesitates; and then, with shuddering intensity, exclaims* Never! *and gets away as far as possible from her.*

Her arm drops. Without a word, and with unaffected dignity, she takes her tray, and is approaching the house when RAINA *re-*

turns, wearing a hat and jacket in the height of the Vienna fashion of the previous year, 1885. LOUKA *makes way proudly for her, and then goes into the house.*)

RAINA: I'm ready. Whats the matter? (*Gaily*) Have you been flirting with Louka?

SERGIUS (*hastily*): No, no. How can you think such a thing?

RAINA (*ashamed of herself*): Forgive me, dear: it was only a jest. I am so happy today.

(*He goes quickly to her, and kisses her hand remorsefully.* CATHERINE *comes out and calls to them from the top of the steps.*)

CATHERINE (*coming down to them*): I am sorry to disturb you, children; but Paul is distracted over those three regiments. He doesnt know how to send them to Philippopolis; and he objects to every suggestion of mine. You must go and help him, Sergius. He is in the library.

RAINA (*disappointed*): But we are just going out for a walk.

SERGIUS: I shall not be long. Wait for me just five minutes. (*He runs up the steps to the door.*)

RAINA (*following him to the foot of the steps and looking up at him with timid coquetry*): I shall go round and wait in full view of the library windows. Be sure you draw father's attention to me. If you are a moment longer than five minutes, I shall go in and fetch you, regiments or no regiments.

SERGIUS (*laughing*): Very well. (*He goes in.*)

(RAINA *watches him until he is out of her sight. Then, with a perceptible relaxation of manner, she begins to pace up and down the garden in a brown study.*)

CATHERINE: Imagine their meeting that Swiss and hearing the whole story! The very first thing your father asked for was the old coat we sent him off in. A nice mess you have got us into!

RAINA (*gazing thoughtfully at the gravel as she walks*): The little beast!

CATHERINE: Little beast! What little beast?

RAINA: To go and tell! Oh, if I had him here, I'd cram him with chocolate creams til he couldnt ever speak again!

CATHERINE: Dont talk such stuff. Tell me the truth, Raina. How long was he in your room before you came to me?

RAINA (*whisking round and recommencing her march in the opposite direction*): Oh, I forget.

CATHERINE: You cannot forget! Did he really climb up after the soldiers were gone: or was he there when that officer searched the room?

RAINA: No. Yes: I think he must have been there then.

CATHERINE: You think! Oh, Raina! Raina! Will anything ever make you straightforward? If Sergius finds out, it will be all over between you.

RAINA (*with cool impertinence*): Oh, I know Sergius is your pet. I sometimes wish you could marry him instead of me. You would just suit him. You would pet him, and spoil him, and mother him to perfection.

CATHERINE (*opening her eyes very widely indeed*): Well, upon my word!

RAINA (*capriciously: half to herself*): I always feel a longing to do or say something dreadful to him — to shock his propriety — to scandalize the five senses out of him. (*To* CATHERINE, *perversely*) I dont care whether he finds out about the chocolate cream soldier or not. I half hope he may. (*She again turns and strolls flippantly away up the path to the corner of the house.*)

CATHERINE: And what should I be able to say to your father, pray?

RAINA (*over her shoulder, from the top of the two steps*): Oh, poor father! As if he could help himself! (*She turns the corner and passes out of sight.*)

CATHERINE (*looking after her, her fingers itching*): Oh, if you were only ten years younger!

(LOUKA *comes from the house with a salver, which she carries hanging down by her side.*)

Well?

LOUKA: Theres a gentleman just called, madam. A Serbian officer.

CATHERINE (*flaming*): A Serb! And how dare he — (*checking herself bitterly*) Oh, I forgot. We are at peace now. I suppose we shall have them calling every day to pay their compliments. Well: if he is an officer why dont you tell your master? He is in the library with Major Saranoff. Why do you come to me?

LOUKA: But he asks for you, madam. And I dont think he knows who you are: he said the lady of the house. He gave me this little ticket for you. (*She takes a card out of her bosom; puts it on the salver; and offers it to* CATHERINE.)

CATHERINE (*reading*): "Captain Bluntschli"? Thats a German name.

LOUKA: Swiss, madam, I think.

CATHERINE (*with a bound that makes* LOUKA *jump back*): Swiss! What is he like?

LOUKA (*timidly*): He has a big carpet bag, madam.

CATHERINE: Oh Heavens! he's come to return the coat. Send him away: say we're not at home: ask him to leave his address and I'll write to him. Oh stop: that will never do. Wait! (*She throws herself into a chair to think it out.* LOUKA *waits.*) The master and Major Saranoff are busy in the library, arent they?

LOUKA: Yes, madam.

CATHERINE (*decisively*): Bring the gentleman out here at once. (*Peremptorily*) And be very polite to him. Dont delay. Here (*impatiently snatching the salver from her*): leave that here; and go straight back to him.

LOUKA: Yes, madam (*going*).

CATHERINE: Louka!

LOUKA (*stopping*): Yes, madam.

CATHERINE: Is the library door shut?

LOUKA: I think so, madam.

CATHERINE: If not, shut it as you pass through.

LOUKA: Yes, madam (*going*).

CATHERINE: Stop.

(LOUKA *stops.*)

He will have to go that way (*indicating the gate of the stable yard*). Tell Nicola to bring his bag here after him. Dont forget.

LOUKA (*surprised*): His bag?

CATHERINE: Yes: here: as soon as possible. (*Vehemently*) Be quick!

(LOUKA *runs into the house.* CATHERINE *snatches her apron off and throws it behind a bush. She then takes up the salver and uses it as a mirror, with the result that the handkerchief tied round her head follows the apron. A touch to her hair and a shake to her dressing gown make her presentable.*)

Oh, how? how? how can a man be such a fool! Such a moment to select!

(LOUKA *appears at the door of the house, announcing* CAPTAIN BLUNTSCHLI. *She stands aside at the top of the steps to let him pass before she goes in again. He is the man of the midnight adventure in* RAINA's *room, clean, well brushed, smartly uniformed, and out of trouble, but still unmistakably the same man. The moment* LOUKA's *back is turned,* CATHERINE *swoops on him with impetuous, urgent, coaxing appeal.*)

Captain Bluntschli: I am very glad to see you; but you must leave this house at once.

(*He raises his eyebrows.*)

My husband has just returned with my future son-in-law; and they know nothing. If they did, the consequences would be terrible. You are a foreigner: you do not feel our national animosities as we do. We still hate the Serbs: the effect of the peace on my husband has been to make him feel like a lion baulked of his prey. If he discovers our secret, he will never forgive me; and my daughter's life will hardly be safe. Will you, like the chivalrous gentleman and soldier you are, leave at once before he finds you here?

BLUNTSCHLI (*disappointed, but philosophical*): At once, gracious lady. I only came to thank you and return the coat you lent me. If you will allow me to take it out of my bag and leave it with your servant as I pass out, I need detain you no further. (*He turns to go into the house.*)

CATHERINE (*catching him by the sleeve*): Oh, you must not think of going back that way. (*Coaxing him across to the stable gates*) This is the shortest way out. Many thanks. So glad to have been of service to you. Goodbye.

BLUNTSCHLI: But my bag?

CATHERINE: It shall be sent on. You will leave me your address.

BLUNTSCHLI: True. Allow me. (*He takes out his cardcase, and stops to write his address, keeping* CATHERINE *in an agony of impatience. As he hands her the card,* PETKOFF, *hatless, rushes from the house in a fluster of hospitality, followed by* SERGIUS.)

PETKOFF (*as he hurries down the steps*): My dear Captain Bluntschli —

CATHERINE: Oh Heavens! (*She sinks on the seat against the wall.*)

PETKOFF (*too preoccupied to notice her as he shakes* BLUNTSCHLI'S *hand heartily*): Those stupid people of mine thought I was out here, instead of in the — haw! — library (*he cannot mention the library without betraying how proud he is of it*). I saw you through the window. I was wondering why you didnt come in. Saranoff is with me: you remember him, dont you?

SERGIUS (*saluting humorously, and then offering his hand with great charm of manner*): Welcome, our friend the enemy!

PETKOFF: No longer the enemy, happily. (*Rather anxiously*) I hope youve called as a friend, and not about horses or prisoners.

CATHERINE: Oh, quite as a friend, Paul. I was just asking Captain Bluntschli to stay to lunch; but he declares he must go at once.

SERGIUS (*sardonically*): Impossible, Bluntschli. We want you here badly. We have to send on three cavalry regiments to Philippopolis; and we dont in the least know how to do it.

BLUNTSCHLI (*suddenly attentive and businesslike*): Philippopolis? The forage is the trouble, I suppose.

PETKOFF (*eagerly*): Yes: thats it. (*To* SERGIUS) He sees the whole thing at once.

BLUNTSCHLI: I think I can shew you how to manage that.

SERGIUS: Invaluable man! Come along! (*Towering over* BLUNTSCHLI, *he puts his hand on his shoulder and takes him to the steps,* PETKOFF *following.*)

(RAINA *comes from the house as* BLUNTSCHLI *puts his foot on the first step.*)

RAINA: Oh! The chocolate cream soldier!

(BLUNTSCHLI *stands rigid.* SERGIUS, *amazed, looks at* RAINA, *then at* PETKOFF, *who looks back at him and then at his wife.*)

CATHERINE (*with commanding presence of mind*): My dear Raina, dont you see that we have a guest here? Captain Bluntschli: one of our new Serbian friends.

(RAINA *bows.* BLUNTSCHLI *bows.*)

RAINA: How silly of me! (*She comes down into the centre of the group, between* BLUNTSCHLI *and* PETKOFF.) I made a beautiful ornament this morning for the ice pudding; and that stupid Nicola has just put down a pile of plates on it and spoilt it. (*To* BLUNTSCHLI, *winningly*) I hope you didnt think that you were the chocolate cream soldier, Captain Bluntschli.

BLUNTSCHLI (*laughing*): I assure you I did. (*Stealing a whimsical glance at her*) Your explanation was a relief.

PETKOFF (*suspiciously, to* RAINA): And since when, pray, have you taken to cooking?

CATHERINE: Oh, whilst you were away. It is her latest fancy.

PETKOFF (*testily*): And has Nicola taken to drinking? He used to be careful enough. First he shews Captain Bluntschli out here when he knew quite well I was in the library; and then he goes downstairs and breaks Raina's chocolate soldier. He must —

(NICOLA *appears at the top of the steps with the bag. He descends; places it respectfully before* BLUNTSCHLI; *and waits for further orders. General amazement.* NICOLA, *unconscious of the effect he is producing, looks perfectly satisfied with himself. When* PETKOFF *recovers his power of speech, he breaks out at him with*)

Are you mad, Nicola?

NICOLA (*taken aback*): Sir?

PETKOFF: What have you brought that for?

NICOLA: My lady's orders, major. Louka told me that —

CATHERINE (*interrupting him*): My orders! Why should I order you to bring Captain Bluntschli's luggage out here? What are you thinking of, Nicola?

NICOLA (*after a moment's bewilderment, picking up the bag as he addresses* BLUNTSCHLI *with the very perfection of servile discretion*): I beg your pardon, captain, I am sure. (*To* CATHERINE) My fault, madam: I hope youll overlook it. (*He bows, and is going to the steps with the bag, when* PETKOFF *addresses him angrily.*)

PETKOFF: Youd better go and slam that bag, too, down on Miss Raina's ice pudding!

(*This is too much for* NICOLA. *The bag drops from his hand almost on his master's toes, eliciting a roar of*)

Begone, you butter-fingered donkey.

NICOLA (*snatching up the bag, and escaping into the house*): Yes, Major.

CATHERINE: Oh, never mind. Paul: dont be angry.

PETKOFF (*blustering*): Scoundrel! He's got out of hand while I was away. I'll teach him. Infernal blackguard! The sack next Saturday! I'll clear out the whole establishment — (*He is stifled by the caresses of his wife and daughter, who hang round his neck, petting him.*)

CATHERINE   Now, now, now, it

                        (*together*):

RAINA   Wow, wow, wow:

mustnt be angry. He meant
not on your first day at home.

no harm. Be good to please
I'll make another ice pudding.

me, dear. Sh-sh-sh-sh!
Tch-ch-ch!

PETKOFF (*yielding*): Oh well, never mind. Come, Bluntschli: lets have no more nonsense about going away. You know very well youre not going back to Switzerland yet. Until you do go back youll stay with us.

RAINA: Oh, do, Captain Bluntschli.

PETKOFF (*to* CATHERINE): Now, Catherine: it's of you he's afraid. Press him: and he'll stay.

CATHERINE: Of course I shall be only too delighted if (*appealingly*) Captain Bluntschli really wishes to stay. He knows my wishes.

BLUNTSCHLI (*in his driest military manner*): I am at madam's orders.

SERGIUS (*cordially*): That settles it!

PETKOFF (*heartily*): Of course!

RAINA: You see you must stay.

BLUNTSCHLI (*smiling*): Well, if I must, I must.

(*Gesture of despair from* CATHERINE.)

ACT III

(*In the library after lunch. It is not much of a library. Its literary equipment consists of a single fixed shelf stocked with old paper covered novels, broken backed, coffee stained, torn and thumbed; and a couple of little hanging shelves with a few gift books on them: the rest of the wall space being occupied by trophies of war and the chase. But it is a most comfortable sitting room. A row of three large windows shews a mountain panorama, just now seen in one of its friendliest aspects in the mellowing afternoon light. In the corner next the right hand window a square earthenware stove, a perfect tower of glistening pottery, rises nearly to the ceiling and guarantees plenty of warmth. The ottoman is like that in* RAINA's *room, and similarly placed; and the window seats are luxurious with decorated cushions. There is one object, however, hopelessly out of keeping with its surroundings. This is a small kitchen table, much the worse for wear, fitted as a writing table with an old canister full of pens, an eggcup filled with ink, and a deplorable scrap of heavily used pink blotting paper.*

At the side of this table, which stands to the left of anyone facing the window, BLUNTSCHLI *is hard at work with a couple of maps before him, writing orders. At the head of it sits* SERGIUS, *who is supposed to be also at work, but is actually gnawing the feather of a pen, and contemplating* BLUNTSCHLI's *quick, sure, businesslike progress with a mixture of envious irritation at his own incapacity and awestruck wonder at an ability which seems to him almost miraculous, though its prosaic character forbids him to esteem it.* THE MAJOR *is comfortably established on the ottoman, with a newspaper in his hand and the tube of his hookah within easy reach.* CATHERINE *sits at the stove, with her back to them, embroidering.* RAINA, *reclining on the divan, is gazing in a day-*

dream out at the Balkan landscape, with a neglected novel in her lap.

The door is on the same side as the stove, further from the window. The button of the electric bell is at the opposite side, behind BLUNTSCHLI.)

PETKOFF (*looking up from his paper to watch how they are getting on at the table*): Are you sure I cant help in any way, Bluntschli?

BLUNTSCHLI (*without interrupting his writing or looking up*): Quite sure, thank you. Saranoff and I will manage it.

SERGIUS (*grimly*): Yes: we'll manage it. He finds out what to do; draws up the orders; and I sign em. Division of labor! (BLUNTSCHLI *passes him a paper.*) Another one? Thank you. (*He plants the paper squarely before him; sets his chair carefully parallel to it; and signs with his cheek on his elbow and his protruded tongue following the movements of his pen.*) This hand is more accustomed to the sword than to the pen.

PETKOFF: It's very good of you, Bluntschli: it is indeed, to let yourself be put upon in this way. Now are you quite sure I can do nothing?

CATHERINE (*in a low warning tone*): You can stop interrupting, Paul.

PETKOFF (*starting and looking round at her*): Eh? Oh! Quite right, my love: Quite right. (*He takes his newspaper up again, but presently lets it drop.*) Ah, you havent been campaigning, Catherine: you dont know how pleasant it is for us to sit here, after a good lunch, with nothing to do but enjoy ourselves. Theres only one thing I want to make me thoroughly comfortable.

CATHERINE: What is that?

PETKOFF: My old coat. I'm not at home in this one: I feel as if I were on parade.

CATHERINE: My dear Paul, how absurd you are about that old coat! It must be hanging in the blue closet where you left it.

PETKOFF: My dear Catherine, I tell you Ive looked there. Am I to believe my own eyes or not?

(CATHERINE *rises and crosses the room to press the button of the electric bell.*)

What are you shewing off that bell for?

(*She looks at him majestically, and silently resumes her chair and her needlework.*)

My dear: if you think the obstinacy of your sex can make a coat out of two old dressing gowns of Raina's, your waterproof, and my mackintosh, youre mistaken. Thats exactly what the blue closet contains at present.

(NICOLA *presents himself.*)

CATHERINE: Nicola: go to the blue closet and bring your master's old coat here: the braided one he wears in the house.

NICOLA: Yes, madam. (*He goes out.*)

PETKOFF: Catherine.

CATHERINE: Yes, Paul.

PETKOFF: I bet you any piece of jewellery you like to order from Sofia against a week's housekeeping money that the coat isnt there.

CATHERINE: Done, Paul!

PETKOFF (*excited by the prospect of a gamble*): Come: heres an opportunity for some sport. Wholl bet on it? Bluntschli: I'll give you six to one.

BLUNTSCHLI (*imperturbably*): I would be robbing you, Major. Madam is sure to be right. (*Without looking up, he passes another batch of papers to* SERGIUS.)

SERGIUS (*also excited*): Bravo, Switzerland! Major: I bet my best charger against an Arab mare for Raina that Nicola finds the coat in the blue closet.

PETKOFF (*eagerly*): Your best char —

CATHERINE (*hastily interrupting him*): Don't be foolish, Paul. An Arabian mare will cost you 50,000 levas.

RAINA (*suddenly coming out of her picturesque revery*): Really, mother, if you are going to take the jewellery, I don't see why you should grudge me my Arab.

(NICOLA *comes back with the coat, and brings it to* PETKOFF, *who can hardly believe his eyes.*)

CATHERINE: Where was it, Nicola?

NICOLA: Hanging in the blue closet, madam.

PETKOFF: Well, I am d —

CATHERINE (*stopping him*): Paul!

PETKOFF: I could have sworn it wasnt there. Age is beginning to tell on me. I'm getting hallucinations. (*To* NICOLA) Here: help me to change. Excuse me, Bluntschli. (*He begins changing coats,* NICOLA *acting as valet.*) Remember: I didnt take that bet of yours, Sergius. Youd better give Raina that Arab steed yourself, since youve roused her expectations. Eh, Raina? (*He looks round at her; but she is again rapt in the landscape. With a little gush of parental affection and pride, he points her out to them, and says*) She's dreaming, as usual.

SERGIUS: Assuredly she shall not be the loser.

PETKOFF: So much the better for her. I shant come off so cheaply, I expect.

(*The change is now complete.* NICOLA *goes out with the discarded coat.*)

Ah, now I feel at home at last. (*He sits down and takes his newspaper with a grunt of relief.*)

BLUNTSCHLI (*to* SERGIUS, *handing a paper*): Thats the last order.

PETKOFF (*jumping up*): What! Finished?

BLUNTSCHLI: Finished.

PETKOFF (*with childlike envy*): Havnt you anything for me to sign?

BLUNTSCHLI: Not necessary. His signature will do.

PETKOFF (*inflating his chest and thumping it*): Ah well, I think weve done a thundering good day's work. Can I do anything more?

BLUNTSCHLI: You had better both see the fellows that are to take these. (SERGIUS *rises.*) Pack them off at once; and shew them that Ive marked on the orders the time they should hand them in by. Tell them that if they stop to drink or tell stories — if theyre five minutes late, theyll have the skin taken off their backs.

SERGIUS (*stiffening indignantly*): I'll say so. (*He strides to the door.*) And if one of them is man enough to spit in my face for insulting him, I'll buy his discharge and give him a pension. (*He goes out.*)

BLUNTSCHLI (*confidentially*): Just see that he talks to them properly, Major, will you?

PETKOFF (*officiously*): Quite right, Bluntschli, quite right. I'll see to it. (*He goes to the door importantly, but hesitates on the threshold.*) By the bye, Catherine, you may as well come too. Theyll be far more frightened of you than of me.

CATHERINE (*putting down her embroidery*): I daresay I had better. You would only splutter at them. (*She goes out,* PETKOFF *holding the door for her and following her.*)

BLUNTSCHLI: What an army! They make cannons out of cherry trees; and the officers send for their wives to keep discipline! (*He begins to fold and docket the papers.*)

(RAINA, *who has risen from the divan, marches slowly down the room with her hands clasped behind her, and looks mischievously at him.*)

RAINA: You look ever so much nicer than when we last met.

(*He looks up, surprised.*)

What have you done to yourself?

BLUNTSCHLI: Washed; brushed; good night's sleep and breakfast. Thats all.

RAINA: Did you get back safely that morning?

BLUNTSCHLI: Quite, thanks.

RAINA: Were they angry with you for running away from Sergius's charge?

BLUNTSCHLI (*grinning*): No: they were glad; because theyd all just run away themselves.

RAINA (*going to the table, and leaning over it towards him*): It must have made a lovely story for them: all that about me and my room.

BLUNTSCHLI: Capital story. But I only told it to one of them: a particular friend.

RAINA: On whose discretion you could absolutely rely?

BLUNTSCHLI: Absolutely.

RAINA: Hm! He told it all to my father and Sergius the day you exchanged the prisoners. (*She turns away and strolls carelessly across to the other side of the room.*)

BLUNTSCHLI (*deeply concerned, and half incredulous*): No! You dont mean that, do you?

RAINA (*turning, with sudden earnestness*): I do indeed. But they dont know that it was in this house you took refuge. If Sergius knew, he would challenge you and kill you in a duel.

BLUNTSCHLI: Bless me! then dont tell him.

RAINA: Please be serious, Captain Bluntschli. Can you not realize what it is to me to deceive him? I want to be quite perfect with Sergius: no meanness, no smallness, no deceit. My relation to him is the one really beautiful and noble part of my life. I hope you can understand that.

BLUNTSCHLI (*sceptically*): You mean that you wouldnt like him to find out that the story about the ice pudding was a — a — a — You know.

RAINA (*wincing*): Ah, dont talk of it in that flippant way. I lied: I know it. But I did it to save your life. He would have killed you. That was the second time I ever uttered a falsehood.

(BLUNTSCHLI *rises quickly and looks doubtfully and somewhat severely at her.*)

Do you remember the first time?

BLUNTSCHLI: I! No. Was I present?

RAINA: Yes; and I told the officer who was searching for you that you were not present.

BLUNTSCHLI: True. I should have remembered it.

RAINA (*greatly encouraged*): Ah, it is natural that you should forget it first. It cost you nothing: it cost me a lie! A lie!

(*She sits down on the ottoman, looking straight before her with her hands clasped round her knee.* BLUNTSCHLI, *quite touched, goes to the ottoman with a particularly reassuring and considerate air, and sits down beside her.*)

BLUNTSCHLI: My dear young lady, dont let this worry you. Remember: I'm a soldier. Now what are the two things that happen to a soldier so often that he comes to think nothing of them? One is hearing people tell lies (RAINA *recoils*) the other is getting his life saved in all sorts of ways by all sorts of people.

RAINA (*rising in indignant protest*): And so he becomes a creature incapable of faith and of gratitude.

BLUNTSCHLI (*making a wry face*): Do you like gratitude? I dont. If pity is akin to love, gratitude is akin to the other thing.

RAINA: Gratitude! (*Turning on him*) If you are incapable of gratitude you are incapable of any noble sentiment. Even animals are grateful. Oh, I see now exactly what you think of me! You were not surprised to hear me lie. To you it was something I probably did every day! every hour! That is how men think of women. (*She paces the room tragically.*)

BLUNTSCHLI (*dubiously*): Theres reason in everything. You said youd told only two lies in your whole life. Dear young lady: isnt that rather a short allowance? I'm quite a straightforward man myself; but it wouldn't last me a whole morning.

RAINA (*staring haughtily at him*): Do you know, sir, that you are insulting me?

BLUNTSCHLI: I cant help it. When you strike that noble attitude and speak in that thrilling voice, I admire you; but I find it impossible to believe a single word you say.

RAINA (*superbly*): Captain Bluntschli!

BLUNTSCHLI (*unmoved*): Yes?

RAINA (*standing over him, as if she could not believe her senses*): Do you mean what you said just now? Do you know what you said just now?

BLUNTSCHLI: I do.

RAINA (*gasping*): I! I!!! (*She points to herself incredulously, meaning* "I, Raina Petkoff tell lies!" *He meets her gaze unflinchingly. She suddenly sits down beside him, and adds, with a complete change of manner from the heroic to a babyish familiarity*) How did you find me out?

BLUNTSCHLI (*promptly*): Instinct, dear young lady. Instinct, and experience of the world.

RAINA (*wonderingly*): Do you know, you are the first man I ever met who did not take me seriously?

BLUNTSCHLI: You mean, dont you, that I am the first man that has ever taken you quite seriously?

RAINA: Yes: I suppose I do mean that. (*Cosily, quite at her ease with him*) How strange it is to be talked to in such a way! You know, Ive always gone on like that.

BLUNTSCHLI: You mean the — ?

RAINA: I mean the noble attitude and the thrilling voice.

(*They laugh together.*)

I did it when I was a tiny child to my nurse. She believed in it. I do it before my parents. They believe in it. I do it before Sergius. He believes in it.

BLUNTSCHLI: Yes: he's a little in that line himself, isnt he?

RAINA (*startled*): Oh! Do you think so?

BLUNTSCHLI: You know him better than I do.

RAINA: I wonder — I wonder is he? If I thought that — ! (*Discouraged*) Ah, well; what does it matter? I suppose, now youve found me out, you despise me.

BLUNTSCHLI (*warmly, rising*): No, my dear young lady, no, no, no a thousand times. It's part of your youth: part of your charm. I'm like all the rest of them: the nurse, your parents, Sergius: I'm your infatuated admirer.

RAINA (*pleased*): Really?

BLUNTSCHLI (*slapping his breast smartly with his hand, German fashion*): Hand aufs Herz! Really and truly.

RAINA (*very happy*): But what did you think of me for giving you my portrait?

BLUNTSCHLI (*astonished*): Your portrait! You never gave me your portrait.

RAINA (*quickly*): Do you mean to say you never got it?

BLUNTSCHLI: No. (*He sits down beside her, with renewed interest, and says, with some complacency*) When did you send it to me?

RAINA (*indignantly*): I did not send it to you. (*She turns her head away, and adds, reluctantly*) It was in the pocket of that coat.

BLUNTSCHLI (*pursing his lips and rounding his eyes*): Oh-o-oh! I never found it. It must be there still.

RAINA (*springing up*): There still! for my father to find the first time he puts his hand in his pocket! Oh, how could you be so stupid?

BLUNTSCHLI (*rising also*): It doesnt matter: I suppose it's only a photograph: how can he tell who it was intended for? Tell him he put it there himself.

RAINA (*bitterly*): Yes: that is so clever! isnt it? (*Distractedly*) Oh! what shall I do?

BLUNTSCHLI: Ah, I see. You wrote something on it. That was rash.

RAINA (*vexed almost to tears*): Oh, to have done such a thing for you, who care no more — except to laugh at me — oh! Are you sure nobody has touched it?

BLUNTSCHLI: Well, I cant be quite sure. You see, I couldnt carry it about with me all the time: one cant take much luggage on active service.

RAINA: What did you do with it?

BLUNTSCHLI: When I got through to Pirot I had to put it in safe keeping somehow. I thought of the railway cloak room; but thats the surest place to get looted in modern warfare. So I pawned it.

RAINA: Pawned it!!!

BLUNTSCHLI: I know it doesnt sound nice: but it was much the safest plan. I redeemed it the day before yesterday. Heaven only knows whether the pawnbroker cleared out the pockets or not.

RAINA (*furious: throwing the words right into his face*): You have a low shopkeeping mind. You think of things that would never come into a gentleman's head.

BLUNTSCHLI (*phlegmatically*): Thats the Swiss national character, dear lady. (*He returns to the table.*)

RAINA: Oh, I wish I had never met you. (*She flounces away, and sits at the window fuming.*)

(LOUKA *comes in with a heap of letters and telegrams on her salver, and crosses, with her bold free gait, to the table. Her left sleeve is looped up to the shoulder with a brooch, shewing her naked arm, with a broad gilt bracelet covering the bruise.*)

LOUKA (*to* BLUNTSCHLI): For you. (*She empties the salver with a fling on to the table.*) The messenger is waiting. (*She is determined not to be civil to an enemy, even if she must bring him his letters.*)

BLUNTSCHLI (*to* RAINA): Will you excuse me: the last postal delivery that reached me was three weeks ago. These are the subsequent accumulations. Four telegrams: a week old. (*He opens one.*) Oho! Bad news!

RAINA (*rising and advancing a little remorsefully*): Bad news?

BLUNTSCHLI: My father's dead. (*He looks at the telegram with his lips pursed, musing on the unexpected change in his arrangements.* LOUKA *crosses herself hastily.*)

RAINA: Oh, how very sad!

BLUNTSCHLI: Yes: I shall have to start for home in an hour. He has left a lot of big hotels behind him to be looked after. (*He takes up a fat letter in a long blue envelope.*) Here's a whacking letter from the family solicitor. (*He puts out the enclosures and glances over them.*) Great Heavens! Seventy! Two hundred! (*In a crescendo of dismay*) Four hundred! Four thousand!! Nine thousand six hundred!!! What on earth am I to do with them all?

RAINA (*timidly*): Nine thousand hotels?

BLUNTSCHLI: Hotels nonsense. If you only knew! Oh, it's too ridiculous! Excuse me: I must give my fellow orders about starting. (*He leaves the room hastily, with the documents in his hand.*)

LOUKA (*knowing instinctively that she can annoy* RAINA *by disparaging* BLUNTSCHLI): He has not much heart, that Swiss. He has not a word of grief for his poor father.

RAINA (*bitterly*): Grief! A man who has been doing nothing but killing people for years! What does he care? What does any soldier care? (*She goes to the door, restraining her tears with difficulty.*)

LOUKA: Major Saranoff has been fighting too; and he has plenty of heart left.

(RAINA, *at the door, draws herself up haughtily and goes out.*)

Aha! I thought you wouldnt get much feeling out of your soldier.

(*She is following* RAINA *when* NICOLA *enters with an armful of logs for the stove.*)

NICOLA (*grinning amorously at her*): Ive been trying all the afternoon to get a minute alone with you, my girl. (*His countenance changes as he notices her arm.*) Why, what fashion is that of wearing your sleeve, child?

LOUKA (*proudly*): My own fashion.

NICOLA: Indeed! If the mistress catches you, she'll talk to you. (*He puts the logs down, and seats himself comfortably on the ottoman.*)

LOUKA: Is that any reason why you should take it on yourself to talk to me?

NICOLA: Come! dont be contrary with me. Ive some good news for you.

(*She sits down beside him. He takes out some paper money.* LOUKA, *with an eager gleam in her eyes, tries to snatch it; but he shifts it quickly to his left hand, out of her reach.*)

See! a twenty leva bill! Sergius gave me that, out of pure swagger. A fool and his money are soon parted. Theres ten levas more. The Swiss gave me that for backing up the mistress' and Raina's lies

about him. He's no fool, he isnt. You should have heard old Catherine downstairs as polite as you please to me, telling me not to mind
the Major being a little impatient; for they knew what a good servant I was — after making a fool and a liar of me before them all!
The twenty will go to our savings; and you shall have the ten to
spend if youll only talk to me so as to remind me I'm a human being. I get tired of being a servant occasionally.

LOUKA: Yes: sell your manhood for 30 levas, and buy me for 10! (*Rising scornfully*) Keep your money. You were born to be a servant. I
was not. When you set up your shop you will only be everybody's
servant instead of somebody's servant. (*She goes moodily to the
table and seats herself regally in* SERGIUS's *chair*.)

NICOLA (*picking up his logs, and going to the stove*): Ah, wait til you
see. We shall have our evenings to ourselves; and I shall be master
in my own house, I promise you. (*He throws the logs down and
kneels at the stove*.)

LOUKA: You shall never be master in mine.

NICOLA (*turning, still on his knees, and squatting down rather forlornly
on his calves, daunted by her implacable disdain*): You have a great
ambition in you, Louka. Remember: if any luck comes to you, it
was I that made a woman of you.

LOUKA: You!

NICOLA (*scrambling up and going to her*): Yes, me. Who was it made
you give up wearing a couple of pounds of false black hair on your
head and reddening your lips and cheeks like any other Bulgarian
girl! I did. Who taught you to trim your nails, and keep your hands
clean, and be dainty about yourself, like a fine Russian lady! Me: do
you hear that? me!

(*She tosses her head defiantly; and he turns away, adding more
coolly*)

Ive often thought that if Raina were out of the way, and you just a
little less of a fool and Sergius just a little more of one, you might
come to be one of my grandest customers, instead of only being my
wife and costing me money.

LOUKA: I believe you would rather be my servant than my husband.
You would make more out of me. Oh, I know that soul of yours.

NICOLA (*going closer to her for greater emphasis*): Never you mind my
soul; but just listen to my advice. If you want to be a lady, your
present behaviour to me wont do at all, unless when we're alone.
It's too sharp and impudent; and impudence is a sort of familiarity:
it shews affection for me. And dont you try being high and mighty
with me, either. Youre like all country girls: you think it's genteel to

treat a servant the way I treat a stableboy. Thats only your ignorance; and dont you forget it. And dont be so ready to defy everybody. Act as if you expected to have your own way, not as if you expected to be ordered about. The way to get on as a lady is the same
as the way to get on as a servant: youve got to know your place:
thats the secret of it. And you may depend on me to know my place
if you get promoted. Think over it, my girl. I'll stand by you: one
servant should always stand by another.

LOUKA (*rising impatiently*): Oh, I must behave in my own way. You
take all the courage out of me with your coldblooded wisdom. Go
and put those logs in the fire: thats the sort of thing you understand.

(*Before* NICOLA *can retort,* SERGIUS *comes in. He checks himself a
moment on seeing* LOUKA; *then goes to the stove.*)

SERGIUS (*to* NICOLA): I am not in the way of your work, I hope.

NICOLA (*in a smooth, elderly manner*): Oh no, sir: thank you kindly.
I was only speaking to this foolish girl about her habit of running up
here to the library whenever she gets a chance, to look at the books.
Thats the worst of her education, sir: it gives her habits above her
station. (*To* LOUKA) Make that table tidy, Louka, for the Major.
(*He goes out sedately.*)

(LOUKA, *without looking at* SERGIUS, *pretends to arrange the papers on the table. He crosses slowly to her, and studies the arrangement of her sleeve reflectively.*)

SERGIUS: Let me see: is there a mark there? (*He turns up the bracelet
and sees the bruise made by his grasp. She stands motionless, not
looking at him: fascinated, but on her guard.*) Ffff! Does it hurt?

LOUKA: Yes.

SERGIUS: Shall I cure it?

LOUKA (*instantly withdrawing herself proudly, but still not looking at
him*): No. You cannot cure it now.

SERGIUS (*masterfully*): Quite sure? (*He makes a movement as if to
take her in his arms.*)

LOUKA: Dont trifle with me, please. An officer should not trifle with a
servant.

SERGIUS (*indicating the bruise with a merciless stroke of his fore-
finger*): That was no trifle, Louka.

LOUKA (*flinching; then looking at him for the first time*): Are you
sorry?

SERGIUS (*with measured emphasis, folding his arms*): I am never sorry.

LOUKA (*wistfully*): I wish I could believe a man could be as unlike a
woman as that. I wonder are you really a brave man?

SERGIUS (*unaffectedly, relaxing his attitude*): Yes: I am a brave man. My heart jumped like a woman's at the first shot; but in the charge I found that I was brave. Yes: that at least is real about me.

LOUKA: Did you find in the charge that the men whose fathers are poor like mine were any less brave than the men who are rich like you?

SERGIUS (*with bitter levity*): Not a bit. They all slashed and cursed and yelled like heroes. Psha! the courage to rage and kill is cheap. I have an English bull terrier who has as much of that sort of courage as the whole Bulgarian nation, and the whole Russian nation at its back. But he lets my groom thrash him, all the same. Thats your soldier all over! No, Louka: your poor men can cut throats; but they are afraid of their officers; they put up with insults and blows; they stand by and see one another punished like children: aye, and help to do it when they are ordered. And the officers!!! Well (*with a short harsh laugh*) I am an officer. Oh (*fervently*), give me the man who will defy to the death any power on earth or in heaven that sets itself up against his own will and conscience: he alone is the brave man.

LOUKA: How easy it is to talk! Men never seem to me to grow up: they all have schoolboy's ideas. You dont know what true courage is.

SERGIUS (*ironically*): Indeed! I am willing to be instructed. (*He sits on the ottoman, sprawling magnificently.*)

LOUKA: Look at me! How much am I allowed to have my own will? I have to get your room ready for you: to sweep and dust, to fetch and carry. How could that degrade me if it did not degrade you to have it done for you? But (*with subdued passion*) if I were Empress of Russia, above everyone in the world, then!! Ah then, though according to you I could shew no courage at all, you should see, you should see.

SERGIUS: What would you do, most noble Empress?

LOUKA: I would marry the man I loved, which no other queen in Europe has the courage to do. If I loved you, though you would be as far beneath me as I am beneath you, I would dare to be the equal of my inferior. Would you dare as much if you loved me? No: if you felt the beginnings of love for me you would not let it grow. You would not dare: you would marry a rich man's daughter because you would be afraid of what other people would say of you.

SERGIUS (*bounding up*): You lie: it is not so, by all the stars! If I loved you, and I were the Tsar himself, I would set you on the throne by my side. You know that I love another woman, a woman as high above you as heaven is above earth. And you are jealous of her.

LOUKA: I have no reason to be. She will never marry you now. The man I told you of has come back. She will marry the Swiss.

SERGIUS (*recoiling*): The Swiss!

LOUKA: A man worth ten of you. Then you can come to me; and I will refuse you. You are not good enough for me. (*She turns to the door.*)

SERGIUS (*springing after her and catching her fiercely in his arms*): I will kill the Swiss; and afterwards I will do as I please with you.

LOUKA (*in his arms, passive and steadfast*): The Swiss will kill you, perhaps. He has beaten you in love. He may beat you in war.

SERGIUS (*tormentedly*): Do you think I believe that she — she! whose worst thoughts are higher than your best ones, is capable of trifling with another man behind my back?

LOUKA: Do you think she would believe the Swiss if he told her now that I am in your arms?

SERGIUS (*releasing her in despair*): Damnation! Oh, damnation! Mockery! mockery everywhere! everything I think is mocked by everything I do! (*He strikes himself frantically on the breast.*) Coward! liar! fool! Shall I kill myself like a man, or live and pretend to laugh at myself?

(*She again turns to go.*)

Louka!

(*She stops near the door.*)

Remember: you belong to me.

LOUKA (*turning*): What does that mean? An insult?

SERGIUS (*commandingly*): It means that you love me, and that I have had you here in my arms, and will perhaps have you there again. Whether that is an insult I neither know nor care: take it as you please. But (*vehemently*) I will not be a coward and a trifler. If I choose to love you, I dare marry you, in spite of all Bulgaria. If these hands ever touch you again, they shall touch my affianced bride.

LOUKA: We shall see whether you dare keep your word. And take care. I will not wait long.

SERGIUS (*again folding his arms and standing motionless in the middle of the room*): Yes: we shall see. And you shall wait my pleasure.

(BLUNTSCHLI, *much preoccupied, with his papers still in his hand, enters, leaving the door open for* LOUKA *to go out. He goes across to the table, glancing at her as he passes.* SERGIUS, *without altering his resolute attitude, watches him steadily.* LOUKA *goes out, leaving the door open.*)

BLUNTSCHLI (*absently, sitting at the table as before, and putting down his papers*): Thats a remarkable-looking young woman.

SERGIUS (*gravely, without moving*): Captain Bluntschli.

BLUNTSCHLI: Eh?

SERGIUS: You have deceived me. You are my rival. I brook no rivals. At six o'clock I shall be in the drilling-ground on the Klissoura road, alone, on horseback, with my sabre. Do you understand?

BLUNTSCHLI (*staring, but sitting quite at his ease*): Oh, thank you: thats a cavalry man's proposal. I'm in the artillery; and I have the choice of weapons. If I go, I shall take a machine gun. And there shall be no mistake about the cartridges this time.

SERGIUS (*flushing, but with deadly coldness*): Take care, sir. It is not our custom in Bulgaria to allow invitations of that kind to be trifled with.

BLUNTSCHLI (*warmly*): Pooh! dont talk to me about Bulgaria. You dont know what fighting is. But have it your own way. Bring your sabre along. I'll meet you.

SERGIUS (*fiercely delighted to find his opponent a man of spirit*): Well said, Switzer. Shall I lend you my best horse?

BLUNTSCHLI: No: damn your horse! thank you all the same, my dear fellow.

(RAINA *comes in, and hears the next sentence.*)

I shall fight you on foot. Horseback's too dangerous; I dont want to kill you if I can help it.

RAINA (*hurrying forward anxiously*): I have heard what Captain Bluntschli said, Sergius. You are going to fight. Why?

(SERGIUS *turns away in silence, and goes to the stove, where he stands watching her as she continues, to* BLUNTSCHLI)

What about?

BLUNTSCHLI: I don't know: he hasn't told me. Better not interfere, dear young lady. No harm will be done: Ive often acted as sword instructor. He wont be able to touch me; and I'll not hurt him. It will save explanations. In the morning I shall be off home; and youll never see me or hear of me again. You and he will then make it up and live happily ever after.

RAINA (*turning away deeply hurt, almost with a sob in her voice*): I never said I wanted to see you again.

SERGIUS (*striding forward*): Ha! That is a confession.

RAINA (*haughtily*): What do you mean?

SERGIUS: You love that man!

RAINA (*scandalized*): Sergius!

SERGIUS: You allow him to make love to you behind my back, just as you treat me as your affianced husband behind his. Bluntschli: you knew our relations; and you deceived me. It is for that that I call you to account, not for having received favors I never enjoyed.

BLUNTSCHLI (*jumping up indignantly*): Stuff! Rubbish! I have received no favors. Why, the young lady doesnt even know whether I'm married or not.

RAINA (*forgetting herself*): Oh! (*Collapsing on the ottoman*) Are you?

SERGIUS: You see the young lady's concern, Captain Bluntschli. Denial is useless. You have enjoyed the privilege of being received in her own room, late at night —

BLUNTSCHLI (*interrupting him pepperily*): Yes, you blockhead! she received me with a pistol at her head. Your cavalry were at my heels. I'd have blown out her brains if she'd uttered a cry.

SERGIUS (*taken aback*): Bluntschli! Raina: is this true?

RAINA (*rising in wrathful majesty*): Oh, how dare you, how dare you?

BLUNTSCHLI: Apologize, man: apologize. (*He resumes his seat at the table.*)

SERGIUS (*with the old measured emphasis, folding his arms*): I never apologize!

RAINA (*passionately*): This is the doing of that friend of yours, Captain Bluntschli. It is he who is spreading this horrible story about me. (*She walks about excitedly.*)

BLUNTSCHLI: No: he's dead. Burnt alive.

RAINA (*stopping, shocked*): Burnt alive!

BLUNTSCHLI: Shot in the hip in a woodyard. Couldnt drag himself out. Your fellows' shells set the timber on fire and burnt him, with a half a dozen other poor devils in the same predicament.

RAINA: How horrible!

SERGIUS: And how ridiculous! Oh, war! war! the dream of patriots and heroes! A fraud, Bluntschli. A hollow sham, like love.

RAINA (*outraged*): Like love! You say that before me!

BLUNTSCHLI: Come, Saranoff: that matter is explained.

SERGIUS: A hollow sham, I say. Would you have come back here if nothing had passed between you except at the muzzle of your pistol? Raina is mistaken about your friend who was burnt. He was not my informant.

RAINA: Who then? (*Suddenly guessing the truth*) Ah, Louka! my maid! my servant! You were with her this morning all that time after — after — Oh, what sort of god is this I have been worshipping!

(*He meets her gaze with sardonic enjoyment of her disenchant-ment. Angered all the more, she goes closer to him, and says, in a lower, intenser tone*)

Do you know that I looked out of the window as I went upstairs, to have another sight of my hero; and I saw something I did not understand then. I know now that you were making love to her.

SERGIUS (*with grim humor*): You saw that?

RAINA: Only too well. (*She turns away, and throws herself on the divan under the centre window, quite overcome.*)

SERGIUS (*cynically*): Raina: our romance is shattered. Life's a farce.

BLUNTSCHLI (*to* RAINA, *whimsically*): You see: he's found himself out now.

SERGIUS (*going to him*): Bluntschli: I have allowed you to call me a blockhead. You may now call me a coward as well. I refuse to fight you. Do you know why?

BLUNTSCHLI: No; but it doesnt matter. I didnt ask the reason when you cried on; and I dont ask the reason now that you cry off. I'm a professional soldier! I fight when I have to, and am very glad to get out of it when I havent to. Youre only an amateur: you think fighting's an amusement.

SERGIUS (*sitting down at the table, nose to nose with him*): You shall hear the reason all the same, my professional. The reason is that it takes two men — real men — men of heart, blood and honor — to make a genuine combat. I could no more fight with you than I could make love to an ugly woman. Youve no magnetism: youre not a man: youre a machine.

BLUNTSCHLI (*apologetically*): Quite true, quite true. I always was that sort of chap. I'm very sorry.

SERGIUS: Psha!

BLUNTSCHLI: But now that youve found that life isnt a farce, but something quite sensible and serious, what further obstacle is there to your happiness?

RAINA (*rising*): You are very solicitous about my happiness and his. Do you forget his new love — Louka? It is not you that he must fight now, but his rival, Nicola.

SERGIUS: Rival!! (*Bouncing half across the room.*)

RAINA: Dont you know that theyre engaged?

SERGIUS: Nicola! Are fresh abysses opening? Nicola!

RAINA (*sarcastically*): A shocking sacrifice, isnt it? Such beauty! such intellect! such modesty! wasted on a middle-aged servant man. Really, Sergius, you cannot stand by and allow such a thing. It would be unworthy of your chivalry.

SERGIUS (*losing all self-control*): Viper! Viper! (*He rushes to and fro, raging.*)

BLUNTSCHLI: Look here, Saranoff: youre getting the worst of this.

RAINA (*getting angrier*): Do you realize what he has done, Captain Bluntschli? He has set this girl as a spy on us; and her reward is that he makes love to her.

SERGIUS: False! Monstrous!

RAINA: Monstrous! (*Confronting him*) Do you deny that she told you about Captain Bluntschli being in my room?

SERGIUS: No; but —

RAINA (*interrupting*): Do you deny that you were making love to her when she told you?

SERGIUS: No; but I tell you —

RAINA (*cutting him short contemptuously*): It is unnecessary to tell us anything more. That is quite enough for us. (*She turns away from him and sweeps majestically back to the window.*)

BLUNTSCHLI (*quietly, as* SERGIUS, *in an agony of mortification, sinks on the ottoman, clutching his averted head between his fists*): I told you you were getting the worst of it, Saranoff.

SERGIUS: Tiger cat!

RAINA (*running excitedly to* BLUNTSCHLI): You hear this man calling me names, Captain Bluntschli?

BLUNTSCHLI: What else can he do, dear lady? He must defend himself somehow. Come (*very persuasively*): dont quarrel. What good does it do?

(RAINA, *with a gasp, sits down on the ottoman, and after a vain effort to look vexedly at* BLUNTSCHLI, *falls a victim to her sense of humor, and actually leans back babyishly against the writhing shoulder of* SERGIUS.)

SERGIUS: Engaged to Nicola! Ha! ha! Ah well, Bluntschli, you are right to take this huge imposture of a world coolly.

RAINA (*quaintly to* BLUNTSCHLI, *with an intuitive guess at his state of mind*): I daresay you think us a couple of grown-up babies, dont you?

SERGIUS (*grinning savagely*): He does: he does. Swiss civilization nurse-tending Bulgarian barbarism, eh?

BLUNTSCHLI (*blushing*): Not at all, I assure you. I'm only very glad to get you two quieted. There! there! let's be pleasant and talk it over in a friendly way. Where is this other young lady?

RAINA: Listening at the door, probably.

SERGIUS (*shivering as if a bullet had struck him, and speaking with quiet but deep indignation*): I will prove that that, at least, is a calumny. (*He goes with dignity to the door and opens it. A yell of fury bursts from him as he looks out. He darts into the passage, and returns dragging in* LOUKA, *whom he flings violently against the table, exclaiming*) Judge her, Bluntschli. You, the cool impartial one: judge the eavesdropper.

(LOUKA *stands her ground, proud and silent.*)

BLUNTSCHLI (*shaking his head*): I mustnt judge her. I once listened myself outside a tent when there was a mutiny brewing. It's all a question of the degree of provocation. My life was at stake.

LOUKA: My love was at stake. I am not ashamed.

RAINA (*contemptuously*): Your love! Your curiosity, you mean.

LOUKA (*facing her and returning her contempt with interest*): My love, stronger than anything you can feel, even for your chocolate cream soldier.

SERGIUS (*with quick suspicion, to* LOUKA): What does that mean?

LOUKA (*fiercely*): It means —

SERGIUS (*interrupting her slightingly*): Oh, I remember: the ice pudding. A paltry taunt, girl!

(MAJOR PETKOFF *enters, in his shirtsleeves.*)

PETKOFF: Excuse my shirtsleeves, gentlemen. Raina: somebody has been wearing that coat of mine: I'll swear it. Somebody with a differently shaped back. It's all burst open at the sleeve. Your mother is mending it. I wish she'd make haste: I shall catch cold. (*He looks more attentively at them.*) Is anything the matter?

RAINA: No. (*She sits down at the stove, with a tranquil air.*)

SERGIUS: Oh no. (*He sits down at the end of the table, as at first.*)

BLUNTSCHLI (*who is already seated*): Nothing. Nothing.

PETKOFF (*sitting down on the ottoman in his old place*): Thats all right. (*He notices* LOUKA.) Anything the matter, Louka?

LOUKA: No, sir.

PETKOFF (*genially*): Thats all right. (*He sneezes.*) Go and ask your mistress for my coat, like a good girl, will you?

(NICOLA *enters with the coat.* LOUKA *makes a pretence of having business in the room by taking the little table with the hookah away to the wall near the windows.*)

RAINA (*rising quickly as she sees the coat on* NICOLA's *arm*): Here it is papa. Give it to me Nicola; and do you put some more wood on the fire. (*She takes the coat, and brings it to* THE MAJOR, *who stands up to put it on.* NICOLA *attends to the fire.*)

PETKOFF (*to* RAINA, *teasing her affectionately*): Aha! Going to be very good to poor old papa just for one day after his return from the wars, eh?

RAINA (*with solemn reproach*): Ah, how can you say that to me, father?

PETKOFF: Well, well, only a joke, little one. Come: give me a kiss.

(*She kisses him.*)

Now give me the coat.

RAINA: No: I am going to put it on for you. Turn your back.

(*He turns his back and feels behind him with his arms for the sleeves. She dexterously takes the photograph from the pocket and throws it on the table before* BLUNTSCHLI, *who covers it with a sheet of paper under the very nose of* SERGIUS, *who looks on amazed, with his suspicions roused in the highest degree. She then helps* PETKOFF *on with his coat.*)

There, dear! Now are you comfortable?

PETKOFF: Quite, little love. Thanks. (*He sits down; and* RAINA *returns to her seat near the stove.*) Oh, by the bye, Ive found something funny. Whats the meaning of this? (*He puts his hand into the picked pocket.*) Eh? Hallo! (*He tries the other pocket.*) Well, I could have sworn — ! (*Much puzzled, he tries the breast pocket.*) I wonder — (*trying the original pocket*) Where can it — ? (*He rises, exclaiming*) Your mother's taken it!

RAINA (*very red*): Taken what?

PETKOFF: Your photograph, with the inscription: "Raina, to her Chocolate Cream Soldier: a Souvenir." Now you know theres something more in this than meets the eye; and I'm going to find it out. (*Shouting*) Nicola!

NICOLA (*coming to him*): Sir!

PETKOFF: Did you spoil any pastry of Miss Raina's this morning?

NICOLA: You heard Miss Raina say that I did, sir.

PETKOFF: I know that, you idiot. Was it true?

NICOLA: I am sure Miss Raina is incapable of saying anything that is not true, sir.

PETKOFF: Are you? Then I'm not. (*Turning to the others*) Come: do you think I dont see it all? (*He goes to* SERGIUS, *and slaps him on the shoulder.*) Sergius: youre the chocolate cream soldier, arent you?

SERGIUS (*starting up*): I! A chocolate cream soldier! Certainly not.

PETKOFF: Not! (*He looks at them. They are all very serious and very conscious.*) Do you mean to tell me that Raina sends things like that to other men?

SERGIUS (*enigmatically*): The world is not such an innocent place as we used to think, Petkoff.

BLUNTSCHLI (*rising*): It's all right, Major. I'm the chocolate cream soldier.

(PETKOFF *and* SERGIUS *are equally astonished.*)

The gracious young lady saved my life by giving me chocolate creams when I was starving: shall I ever forget their flavour! My late friend Stolz told you the story at Pirot. I was the fugitive.

PETKOFF: You! (*He gasps.*) Sergius: do you remember how those two women went on this morning when we mentioned it?

(SERGIUS *smiles cynically.* PETKOFF *confronts* RAINA *severely.*)

Youre a nice young woman, arent you?

RAINA (*bitterly*): Major Saranoff has changed his mind. And when I wrote that on the photograph, I did not know that Captain Bluntschli was married.

BLUNTSCHLI (*startled into vehement protest*): I'm not married.

RAINA (*with deep reproach*): You said you were.

BLUNTSCHLI: I did not. I positively did not. I never was married in my life.

PETKOFF (*exasperated*): Raina: will you kindly inform me, if I am not asking too much, which of these gentlemen you are engaged to?

RAINA: To neither of them. This young lady (*introducing* LOUKA, *who faces them all proudly*) is the object of Major Saranoff's affections at present.

PETKOFF: Louka! Are you mad, Sergius? Why, this girl's engaged to Nicola.

NICOLA: I beg your pardon, sir. There is a mistake. Louka is not engaged to me.

PETKOFF: Not engaged to you, you scoundrel! Why, you had twenty-five levas from me on the day of your betrothal; and she had that gilt bracelet from Miss Raina.

NICOLA (*with cool unction*): We gave it out so, sir. But it was only to give Louka protection. She had a soul above her station; and I have been no more than her confidential servant. I intend, as you know, sir, to set up a shop later on in Sofia; and I look forward to her custom and recommendation should she marry into the nobility. (*He goes out with impressive discretion, leaving them all staring after him.*)

PETKOFF (*breaking the silence*): Well, I am — hm!

SERGIUS: This is either the finest heroism or the most crawling baseness. Which is it, Bluntschli?

BLUNTSCHLI: Never mind whether it's heroism or baseness. Nicola's the ablest man Ive met in Bulgaria. I'll make him manager of a hotel if he can speak French and German.

LOUKA (*suddenly breaking out at* SERGIUS): I have been insulted by everyone here. You set them the example. You owe me an apology.

(SERGIUS, *like a repeating clock of which the spring has been touched, immediately begins to fold his arms.*)

BLUNTSCHLI (*before he can speak*): It's no use. He never apologizes.

LOUKA: Not to you, his equal and his enemy. To me, his poor servant, he will not refuse to apologize.

SERGIUS (*approvingly*): You are right. (*He bends his knee in his grandest manner.*) Forgive me.

LOUKA: I forgive you. (*She timidly gives him her hand, which he kisses.*) That touch makes me your affianced wife.

SERGIUS (*springing up*): Ah! I forgot that.

LOUKA (*coldly*): You can withdraw if you like.

SERGIUS: Withdraw! Never! You belong to me. (*He puts his arm about her.*)

(CATHERINE *comes in and finds* LOUKA *in* SERGIUS' *arms, with all the rest gazing at them in bewildered astonishment.*)

CATHERINE: What does this mean?

(SERGIUS *releases* LOUKA.)

PETKOFF: Well, my dear, it appears that Sergius is going to marry Louka instead of Raina.

(*She is about to break out indignantly at him: he stops her by exclaiming testily*)

Dont blame me: Ive nothing to do with it. (*He retreats to the stove.*)

CATHERINE: Marry Louka! Sergius: you are bound by your word to us!

SERGIUS (*folding his arms*): Nothing binds me.

BLUNTSCHLI (*much pleased by this piece of common sense*): Saranoff: your hand. My congratulations. These heroics of yours have their practical side after all. (*To* LOUKA) Gracious young lady: the best wishes of a good Republican! (*He kisses her hand, to* RAINA'S *great disgust, and returns to his seat.*)

CATHERINE: Louka: you have been telling stories.

LOUKA: I have done Raina no harm.

CATHERINE (*haughtily*): Raina!

(RAINA, *equally indignant, almost snorts at the liberty.*)

LOUKA: I have a right to call her Raina: she calls me Louka. I told Major Saranoff she would never marry him if the Swiss gentleman came back.

BLUNTSCHLI (*rising, much surprised*): Hallo!

LOUKA (*turning to* RAINA): I thought you were fonder of him than of Sergius. You know best whether I was right.

BLUNTSCHLI: What nonsense! I assure you, my dear Major, my dear Madame, the gracious young lady simply saved my life, nothing else. She never cared two straws for me. Why, bless my heart and soul, look at the young lady and look at me. She, rich, young, beautiful, with her imagination full of fairy princes and noble natures and cavalry charges and goodness knows what! And I, a commonplace Swiss soldier who hardly knows what a decent life is after fifteen years of barracks and battles: a vagabond, a man who has spoiled all his chances in life through an incurably romantic disposition, a man —

SERGIUS (*starting as if a needle had pricked him and interrupting* BLUNTSCHLI *in incredulous amazement*): Excuse me, Bluntschli: what did you say had spoiled your chances in life?

BLUNTSCHLI (*promptly*): An incurably romantic disposition. I ran away from home twice when I was a boy. I went into the army instead of into my father's business. I climbed the balcony of this house when a man of sense would have dived into the nearest cellar. I came sneaking back here to have another look at the young lady when any other man of my age would have sent the coat back —

PETKOFF: My coat!

BLUNTSCHLI: — yes: thats the coat I mean — would have sent it back and gone quietly home. Do you suppose I am the sort of fellow a young girl falls in love with? Why, look at our ages! I'm thirty-four: I dont suppose the young lady is much over seventeen. (*This estimate produces a marked sensation, all the rest turning and staring at one another. He proceeds innocently.*) All that adventure which was life or death to me, was only a schoolgirl's game to her — chocolate creams and hide and seek. Heres the proof! (*He takes the photograph from the table.*) Now, I ask you, would a woman who took the affair seriously have sent me this and written on it "Raina, to her Chocolate Cream Soldier: a Souvenir"? (*He exhibits the photograph triumphantly, as if it settled the matter beyond all possibility of refutation.*)

PETKOFF: Thats what I was looking for. How the deuce did it get there? (*He comes from the stove to look at it, and sits down on the ottoman.*)

BLUNTSCHLI (*to* RAINA, *complacently*): I have put everything right, I hope, gracious young lady.

RAINA (*going to the table to face him*): I quite agree with your account of yourself. You are a romantic idiot.

(BLUNTSCHLI *is unspeakably taken back.*)

Next time, I hope you will know the difference between a schoolgirl of seventeen and a woman of twenty-three.

BLUNTSCHLI (*stupefied*): Twenty-three!

(RAINA *snaps the photograph contemptuously from his hand; tears it up; throws the pieces in his face; and sweeps back to her former place.*)

SERGIUS (*with grim enjoyment of his rival's discomfiture*): Bluntschli: my one last belief is gone. Your sagacity is a fraud, like everything else. You have less sense than even I!

BLUNTSCHLI (*overwhelmed*): Twenty-three! Twenty-three!! (*He considers.*) Hm! (*Swiftly making up his mind and coming to his host*) In that case, Major Petkoff, I beg to propose formally to become a suitor for your daughter's hand, in place of Major Saranoff retired.

RAINA: You dare!

BLUNTSCHLI: If you were twenty-three when you said those things to me this afternoon, I shall take them seriously.

CATHERINE (*loftily polite*): I doubt, sir, whether you quite realize either my daughter's position or that of Major Sergius Saranoff, whose place you propose to take. The Petkoffs and the Saranoffs are known as the richest and most important families in the country. Our position is almost historical: we can go back for twenty years.

PETKOFF: Oh, never mind that, Catherine. (*To* BLUNTSCHLI) We should be most happy, Bluntschli, if it were only a question of your position; but hang it, you know, Raina is accustomed to a very comfortable establishment. Sergius keeps twenty horses.

BLUNTSCHLI: But who wants twenty horses? We're not going to keep a circus.

CATHERINE (*severely*): My daughter, sir, is accustomed to a first-rate stable.

RAINA: Hush, mother: youre making me ridiculous.

BLUNTSCHLI: Oh well, if it comes to a question of an establishment, here goes! (*He darts impetuously to the table; seizes the papers in the blue envelope; and turns to* SERGIUS.) How many horses did you say?

SERGIUS: Twenty, noble Switzer.

BLUNTSCHLI: I have two hundred horses.

(*They are amazed.*)

How many carriages?

SERGIUS: Three.

BLUNTSCHLI: I have seventy. Twenty-four of them will hold twelve inside, besides two on the box, without counting the driver and conductor. How many tablecloths have you?

SERGIUS: How the deuce do I know?

BLUNTSCHLI: Have you four thousand?

SERGIUS: No.

BLUNTSCHLI: I have. I have nine thousand six hundred pairs of sheets and blankets, with two thousand four hundred eider-down quilts. I have ten thousand knives and forks, and the same quantity of dessert spoons. I have three hundred servants. I have six palatial establishments, besides two livery stables, a tea garden, and a private house. I have four medals for distinguished services; I have the rank of an officer and the standing of a gentleman; and I have three native languages. Shew me any man in Bulgaria that can offer as much!

PETKOFF (*with childish awe*): Are you Emperor of Switzerland?

BLUNTSCHLI: My rank is the highest known in Switzerland: I am a free citizen.

CATHERINE: Then, Captain Bluntschli, since you are my daughter's choice —

RAINA (*mutinously*): He's not.

CATHERINE (*ignoring her*): — I shall not stand in the way of her happiness.

(PETKOFF *is about to speak.*)

That is Major Petkoff's feeling also.

PETKOFF: Oh, I shall be only too glad. Two hundred horses! Whew!

SERGIUS: What says the lady?

RAINA (*pretending to sulk*): The lady says that he can keep his tablecloths and his omnibuses. I am not here to be sold to the highest bidder. (*She turns her back on him.*)

BLUNTSCHLI: I wont take that answer. I appealed to you as a fugitive, a beggar, and a starving man. You accepted me. You gave me your hand to kiss, your bed to sleep in, and your roof to shelter me.

RAINA: I did not give them to the Emperor of Switzerland.

BLUNTSCHLI: Thats just what I say. (*He catches her by the shoulders and turns her face-to-face with him.*) Now tell us whom you did give them to.

RAINA (*succumbing with a shy smile*): To my chocolate cream soldier.

BLUNTSCHLI (*with a boyish laugh of delight*): Thatll do. Thank you. (*He looks at his watch and suddenly becomes businesslike.*) Time's up, Major. Youve managed those regiments so well that youre sure to be asked to get rid of some of the infantry of the Timok division. Send them home by way of Lom Palanka. Saranoff: dont get married until I come back: I shall be here punctually at five in the evening on Tuesday fortnight. Gracious ladies (*his heels click*) good evening. (*He makes them a military bow, and goes.*)

SERGIUS: What a man! Is he a man!

When *Arms and the Man*, Shaw's fourth play, appeared on the London stage in 1894, its success was both qualified and ambiguous. Some took it to be just another funny farce, but the majority took offense at Shaw's ridicule of military heroism — not a proper subject for frivolity in imperial England. In 1898 the play appeared in a volume of seven plays by Shaw, entitled *Plays Pleasant and Unpleasant*, in which it belongs with the plays pleasant. The label suggests Shavian mischievousness.

Its setting is Bulgaria, to the Victorian Englishman a distant, exotic, and somewhat comical country, forever engaged in small and colorful wars with her equally semi-civilized neighbors. Shaw has considerable fun with the backwardness, sanitary and cultural, of the Petkoffs. The setting further makes the farce more acceptable, for anything might happen among these picturesque people, and it allows Shaw to satirize Western institutions and attitudes indirectly. Also, in Act I it introduces some key images. The view through Raina's bedroom window with the mountain peak "wonderfully white and beautiful in the starlit snow" and apparently "quite close at hand, though it is really miles away" parallels Raina's view of human ideals. The room's interior, "half rich Bulgarian, half cheap Viennese" with the "ornamental textile fabrics," "oriental and gorgeous," contrasting with the "occidental and paltry" wallpaper, anticipates a central conflict in the play and renders its opposing values ambiguous. Is the point that in the process of Westernization Bulgaria loses something of rich beauty? Or do the impending marriages at the end symbolize the union of East and West (though Louka is Bulgarian, her attitude to love resembles that of the Westerner Bluntschli more than it does Sergius's and Raina's) in a way that contrasts with the arbitrary and tasteless mixture of styles in the still-romantic Raina's room?

The room's appearance, at any rate, suggests the play's two poles of action. What is chronicled is the conversion, on the issues of war and love, of Raina and Sergius from romantic idealism to healthy realism. The Swiss Bluntschli, representing the sanity and practicality and egalitarianism of the West, serves as a kind of catalyst for the process. The conversion results in realignment of partners in love.

More is involved here than a clever game of musical chairs, kept going by such old-fashioned props of intrigue as Petkoff's coat and Raina's photograph. The regrouping of the four lovers is a dramatic metaphor of Sergius' and Raina's self-discovery. Before their conversion, they speak of love as a pure and noble feeling, far exalted above lust and infidelity, either in thought or deed. Raina "adores" Sergius' portrait in Act I, but "she does not kiss it or press it to her breast, or shew it any mark of bodily affection" (though it is a question if she would not have seemed more, not less, silly if she had done so). After Sergius' return, Raina waits for "the right moment" to appear, and the reunion of the lovers becomes, both in movement and in speech, a royal ceremony, splendid but completely unspontaneous. In obvious contrast is the earthy sensualism in the scene between Sergius and Louka that follows, but it is sensualism attended by cool, calm, hard-headed thinking. Sergius puts his arm around Louka.

LOUKA: Let me go, sir. I shall be disgraced. (*She struggles: he holds her inexorably.*) Oh, will you let me go?
SERGIUS (*looking straight into her eyes*): No.
LOUKA: Then stand back where we cant be seen. Have you no common sense?

Their encounter begins when Sergius observes that "the higher love" is a "very fatiguing thing to keep up," and a little later, Raina, in a similar mood, "undergoes a perceptible relaxation of manner" as soon as Sergius leaves her. Both change their attitude to love — and, therefore, to one another — as soon as they admit to themselves how artificial and exhausting their conventionally lofty attitudes have been and how deeply the two realists touch their true nature. That the alliances at the end represent a victory of egalitarian republicanism over aristocratic snobbery is part of the general pattern of change. They experience a similar change of attitude vis à vis war. Raina begins as a sententious idealist ("Some soldiers, I know, are afraid to die"), Sergius as the leader of a mad cavalry charge ("Suicide; only the pistol missed fire"). But from the fact that Sergius fails of promotion both learn that war is a business for unheroic professionals, and from Bluntschli they learn that it is, on the one hand, suffering (good friends get burned alive) and, on the other, a craft. A soldier's first duty is to survive, food is more important than arms, the best soldier is he who can get a cavalry regiment to Phillipopolis when there is no provender. The heroic connotations of the play's allusive title ply their ironies here.

But we should not oversimplify Shaw's theme. The play deflates impossibly idealistic attitudes toward love and war, but the realism it substitutes is not a "cheap" and "paltry" prosaic practical-mindedness. If Bluntschli is something as unromantic as hotel owner, his hotel is epically equipped. He is a realist, but he is distinguished from Nicola, the realist-in-excess. Bluntschli is, if only for a moment, "Emperor of Switzerland," whose "incurably romantic disposition" is directly responsible for almost every single plot development. One realizes with astonishment that the phrase is not coy, does not serve some paradox of Shaw's; testing it against what happens in the play proves it quite true. Nicola, on the other hand, has a servant's soul, whether he serves a single master or (as he intends some day) the general public. He is the cold-blooded shopkeeper, to whom Louka is more attractive as rich customer than as penniless wife. And what saves Sergius from the cynicism that besets him after his double disillusionment (war is a "fraud, . . . a hollow sham, like love") and restores him to his magnificently mannered old self is his engagement to Louka. The point is unmistakable — not that true love is unromantic, but that romantic love is unrealistic. The most significant dialogue in the entire play follows immediately upon Raina's peripety. When Bluntschli has exposed her sham attitudes, she says, "Do you know, you are the first man I ever met who did not take me seriously?" Bluntschli replies, "You mean, dont you, that I am the first man that has ever taken you quite seriously?" And Raina happily agrees that she does indeed mean that.)

Anton Chekhov

THREE SISTERS

Translated by Elisaveta Fen

Characters

PROZOROV, *Andrey Serghyeevich*
NATASHA (*Natalia Ivanovna*), *his fiancée, afterwards his wife*
OLGA (*Olga Serghyeevna, Olia*) ⎫
MASHA (*Maria Serghyeevna*) ⎬ *his sisters*
IRENA (*Irena Serghyeevna*) ⎭
KOOLYGHIN, *Fiodor Ilyich, master at the High School for boys,
      husband of Masha*
VERSHININ, *Alexandr Ignatyevich, Lieutenant-Colonel, Battery
      Commander*
TOOZENBACH, *Nikolai Lvovich, Baron, Lieutenant in the Army*
SOLIONY, *Vassily Vassilich, Captain*
CHEBUTYKIN, *Ivan Romanych, Army Doctor*
FEDOTIK, *Aleksey Petrovich, Second Lieutenant*
RODÉ, *Vladimir Karlovich, Second Lieutenant*
FERAPONT (*Ferapont Spiridonych*), *an old porter from the
      County Office*
ANFISA, *the Prozorovs' former nurse, an old woman of 80*

SCENE: *The action takes place in a county town.*

ACT I

(*A drawing-room in the Prozorovs' house; it is separated from a
large ballroom*[1] *at the back by a row of columns. It is midday;*

[1] A large room, sparsely furnished, used for receptions and dances in Russian houses.

Reprinted by permission of Penguin Books, Ltd.

*there is cheerful sunshine outside. In the ballroom the table is be-
ing laid for lunch.* OLGA, *wearing the regulation dark-blue dress of
a secondary school mistress, is correcting her pupils' work, standing or walking about as she does so.* MASHA, *in a black dress, is sitting reading a book, her hat on her lap.* IRENA, *in white, stands lost
in thought.*)

OLGA: It's exactly a year ago that Father died, isn't it? This very day,
the fifth of May — your Saint's day, Irena. I remember it was very
cold and it was snowing. I felt then as if I should never survive his
death; and you had fainted and were lying quite still, as if you were
dead. And now — a year's gone by, and we talk about it so easily.
You're wearing white, and your face is positively radiant. . . .

(*A clock strikes twelve.*)

The clock struck twelve then, too. (*A pause.*) I remember when
Father was being taken to the cemetery there was a military band,
and a salute with rifle fire. That was because he was a general, in
command of a brigade. And yet there weren't many people at the
funeral. Of course, it was raining hard, raining and snowing.

IRENA: Need we bring up all these memories?

(*Baron* TOOZENBACH, CHEBUTYKIN *and* SOLIONY *appear behind the
columns by the table in the ballroom.*)

OLGA: It's so warm to-day that we can keep the windows wide open,
and yet there aren't any leaves showing on the birch trees. Father
was made a brigadier eleven years ago, and then he left Moscow and
took us with him. I remember so well how everything in Moscow
was in blossom by now, everything was soaked in sunlight and
warmth. Eleven years have gone by, yet I remember everything
about it, as if we'd only left yesterday. Oh, Heavens! When I woke
up this morning and saw this flood of sunshine, all this spring sunshine, I felt so moved and so happy! I felt such a longing to get back
home to Moscow!

CHEBUTYKIN (*to* TOOZENBACH): The devil you have!

TOOZENBACH: It's nonsense, I agree.

MASHA (*absorbed in her book, whistles a tune under her breath*).

OLGA: Masha, do stop whistling! How can you? (*A pause.*) I suppose
I must get this continual headache because I have to go to school
every day and go on teaching right into the evening. I seem to have
the thoughts of someone quite old. Honestly, I've been feeling as if
my strength and youth were running out of me drop by drop, day
after day. Day after day, all these four years that I've been working

at the school. . . . I just have one longing and it seems to grow stronger and stronger. . . .

IRENA: If only we could go back to Moscow! Sell the house, finish with our life here, and go back to Moscow.

OLGA: Yes, Moscow! As soon as we possibly can.

(CHEBUTYKIN _and_ TOOZENBACH _laugh_.)

IRENA: I suppose Andrey will soon get a professorship. He isn't likely to go on living here. The only problem is our poor Masha.

OLGA: Masha can come and stay the whole summer with us every year in Moscow.

MASHA (_whistles a tune under her breath_).

IRENA: Everything will settle itself, with God's help. (_Looks through the window_.) What lovely weather it is to-day! Really, I don't know why there's such joy in my heart. I remembered this morning that it was my Saint's day, and suddenly I felt so happy, and I thought of the time when we were children, and Mother was still alive. And then such wonderful thoughts came to me, such wonderful stirring thoughts!

OLGA: You're so lovely to-day, you really do look most attractive. Masha looks pretty to-day, too. Andrey could be good-looking, but he's grown so stout. It doesn't suit him. As for me, I've just aged and grown a lot thinner. I suppose it's through getting so irritated with the girls at school. But to-day I'm at home, I'm free, and my headache's gone, and I feel much younger than I did yesterday. I'm only twenty-eight, after all. . . . I suppose everything that God wills must be right and good, but I can't help thinking sometimes that if I'd got married and stayed at home, it would have been a better thing for me. (_A pause_.) I would have been very fond of my husband.

TOOZENBACH (_to_ SOLIONY): Really, you talk such a lot of nonsense, I'm tired of listening to you. (_Comes into the drawing-room_.) I forgot to tell you: Vershinin, our new battery commander, is going to call on you to-day. (_Sits down by the piano_.)

OLGA: I'm very glad to hear it.

IRENA: Is he old?

TOOZENBACH: No, not particularly. Forty, forty-five at the most. (_Plays quietly_.) He seems a nice fellow. Certainly not a fool. His only weakness is that he talks too much.

IRENA: Is he interesting?

TOOZENBACH: He's all right, only he's got a wife, a mother-in-law and two little girls. What's more, she's his second wife. He calls on everybody and tells them that he's got a wife and two little girls.

He'll tell you about it, too, I'm sure of that. His wife seems to be a bit soft in the head. She wears a long plait like a girl, she is always philosophizing and talking in high-flown language, and then she often tries to commit suicide, apparently just to annoy her husband. I would have run away from a wife like that years ago, but he puts up with it, and just grumbles about it.

SOLIONY (*enters the drawing-room with* CHEBUTYKIN): Now I can only lift sixty pounds with one hand, but with two I can lift two hundred pounds, or even two hundred and forty. So I conclude from that that two men are not just twice as strong as one, but three times as strong, if not more.

CHEBUTYKIN (*reads the paper as he comes in*): Here's a recipe for falling hair . . . two ounces of naphthaline, half-a-bottle of methylated spirit . . . dissolve and apply once a day. . . . (*Writes it down in a notebook.*) Must make a note of it. (*To* SOLIONY.) Well, as I was trying to explain to you, you cork the bottle and pass a glass tube through the cork. Then you take a pinch of ordinary powdered alum, and . . .

IRENA: Ivan Romanych, dear Ivan Romanych!

CHEBUTYKIN: What is it, my child, what is it?

IRENA: Tell me, why is it I'm so happy to-day? Just as if I were sailing along in a boat with big white sails, and above me the wide, blue sky, and in the sky great white birds floating around?

CHEBUTYKIN (*kisses both her hands, tenderly*): My little white bird!

IRENA: You know, when I woke up this morning, and after I'd got up and washed, I suddenly felt as if everything in the world had become clear to me, and I knew the way I ought to live. I know it all now, my dear Ivan Romanych. Man must work by the sweat of his brow whatever his class, and that should make up the whole meaning and purpose of his life and happiness and contentment. Oh, how good it must be to be a workman, getting up with the sun and breaking stones by the roadside — or a shepherd — or a schoolmaster teaching the children — or an engine-driver on the railway. Good Heavens! it's better to be a mere ox or horse, and work, than the sort of young woman who wakes up at twelve, and drinks her coffee in bed, and then takes two hours dressing. . . . How dreadful! You know how you long for a cool drink in hot weather? Well, that's the way I long for work. And if I don't get up early from now on and really work, you can refuse to be friends with me any more, Ivan Romanych.

CHEBUTYKIN (*tenderly*): So I will, so I will. . . .

OLGA: Father taught us to get up at seven o'clock and so Irena always wakes up at seven — but then she stays in bed till at least nine, thinking about something or other. And with such a serious expression on her face, too! (*Laughs.*)

IRENA: You think it's strange when I look serious because you always think of me as a little girl. I'm twenty, you know!

TOOZENBACH: All this longing for work. . . . Heavens! how well I can understand it! I've never done a stroke of work in my life. I was born in Petersburg, an unfriendly, idle city — born into a family where work and worries were simply unknown. I remember a valet pulling off my boots for me when I came home from the cadet school. . . . I grumbled at the way he did it, and my mother looked on in admiration. She was quite surprised when other people looked at me in any other way. I was so carefully protected from work! But I doubt whether they succeeded in protecting me for good and all — yes, I doubt it very much! The time's come: there's a terrific thunder-cloud advancing upon us, a mighty storm is coming to freshen us up! Yes, it's coming all right, it's quite near already, and it's going to blow away all this idleness and indifference, and prejudice against work, this rot of boredom that our society is suffering from. I'm going to work, and in twenty-five or thirty years' time every man and woman will be working. Every one of us!

CHEBUTYKIN: I'm not going to work.

TOOZENBACH: You don't count.

SOLIONY: In twenty-five years' time you won't be alive, thank goodness. In a couple of years you'll die from a stroke — or I'll lose my temper with you and put a bullet in your head, my good fellow. (*Takes a scent bottle from his pocket and sprinkles the scent over his chest and hands.*)

CHEBUTYKIN (*laughs*): It's quite true that I never have done any work. Not a stroke since I left the university. I haven't even read a book, only newspapers. (*Takes another newspaper out of his pocket.*) For instance, here. . . . I know from the paper that there was a person called Dobroliubov, but what he wrote about I've not the faintest idea. . . . God alone knows. . . . (*Someone knocks on the floor from downstairs.*) There! They're calling me to come down: there's someone come to see me. I'll be back in a moment. . . . (*Goes out hurriedly, stroking his beard.*)

IRENA: He's up to one of his little games.

TOOZENBACH: Yes. He looked very solemn as he left. He's obviously going to give you a present.

IRENA: I do dislike that sort of thing. . . .

OLGA: Yes, isn't it dreadful? He's always doing something silly.

MASHA: "A green oak grows by a curving shore, And round that oak hangs a golden chain" . . . (*Gets up as she sings under her breath.*)

OLGA: You're sad to-day, Masha.

MASHA (*puts on her hat, singing*).

OLGA: Where are you going?

MASHA: Home.

IRENA: What a strange thing to do.

TOOZENBACH: What! Going away from your sister's party?

MASHA: What does it matter? I'll be back this evening. Good-bye, my darling. (*Kisses* IRENA.) And once again — I wish you all the happiness in the world. In the old days when Father was alive we used to have thirty or forty officers at our parties. What gay parties we had! And to-day — what have we got to-day? A man and a half, and the place is as quiet as a tomb. I'm going home. I'm depressed to-day, I'm sad, so don't listen to me. (*Laughs through her tears.*) We'll have a talk later, but good-bye for now, my dear. I'll go somewhere or other. . . .

IRENA (*displeased*): Really, you are a . . .

OLGA (*tearfully*): I understand you, Masha.

SOLIONY: If a man starts philosophizing, you call that philosophy, or possibly just sophistry, but if a woman or a couple of women start philosophizing you call that . . . what would you call it, now? Ask me another!

MASHA: What are you talking about? You are a disconcerting person!

SOLIONY: Nothing.

"He had no time to say 'Oh, oh!'
Before that bear had struck him low" . . .

(*A pause.*)

MASHA (*to* OLGA, *crossly*): Do stop snivelling!

(*Enter* ANFISA *and* FERAPONT, *the latter carrying a large cake.*)

ANFISA: Come along, my dear, this way. Come in, your boots are quite clean. (*To* IRENA.) A cake from Protopopov, at the Council Office.

IRENA: Thank you. Tell him I'm very grateful to him. (*Takes the cake.*)

FERAPONT: What's that?

IRENA (*louder*): Tell him I sent my thanks.

OLGA: Nanny, will you give him a piece of cake? Go along, Ferapont, they'll give you some cake.

FERAPONT: What's that?

ANFISA: Come along with me, Ferapont Spiridonych, my dear. Come along. (*Goes out with* FERAPONT.)

MASHA: I don't like that Protopopov fellow, Mihail Potapych, or Ivanych, or whatever it is. It's best not to invite him here.

IRENA: I haven't invited him.

MASHA: Thank goodness.

(Enter CHEBUTYKIN, *followed by a soldier carrying a silver samovar. Murmurs of astonishment and displeasure.)*

OLGA *(covering her face with her hands)*: A samovar! But this is dreadful! *(Goes through to the ballroom and stands by the table.)*

IRENA: My dear Ivan Romanych, what are you thinking about?

TOOZENBACH *(laughs)*: Didn't I tell you?

MASHA: Ivan Romanych, you really ought to be ashamed of yourself!

CHEBUTYKIN: My dear, sweet girls, I've no one in the world but you. You're dearer to me than anything in the world! I'm nearly sixty, I'm an old man, a lonely, utterly unimportant old man. The only thing that's worth anything in me is my love for you, and if it weren't for you, really I would have been dead long ago. *(To* IRENA.*)* My dear, my sweet little girl, haven't I known you since the very day you were born? Didn't I carry you about in my arms? . . . didn't I love your dear mother?

IRENA: But why do you get such expensive presents?

CHEBUTYKIN *(tearfully and crossly)*: Expensive presents! . . . Get along with you! *(To the orderly.)* Put the samovar over there. *(Mimics* IRENA.*)* Expensive presents!

(The orderly takes the samovar to the ballroom.)

ANFISA *(crosses the drawing-room)*: My dears, there's a strange colonel just arrived. He's taken off his coat and he's coming up now. Irenushka, do be nice and polite to him, won't you? *(In the doorway.)* And it's high time we had lunch, too. . . . Oh, dear! *(Goes out.)*

TOOZENBACH: It's Vershinin, I suppose.

(Enter VERSHININ.*)*

TOOZENBACH: Lieutenant-Colonel Vershinin!

VERSHININ *(to* MASHA *and* IRENA*)*: Allow me to introduce myself — Lieutenant-Colonel Vershinin. I'm so glad, so very glad to be here at last. How you've changed! Dear, dear, how you've changed!

IRENA: Please, do sit down. We're very pleased to see you, I'm sure.

VERSHININ *(gaily)*: I'm so glad to see you, so glad! But there were three of you, weren't there? — three sisters. I remember there were three little girls. I don't remember their faces, but I knew your father, Colonel Prozorov, and I remember he had three little girls.

Oh, yes, I saw them myself. I remember them quite well. How time flies! Dear, dear, how it flies!

TOOZENBACH: Alexandr Ignatyevich comes from Moscow.

IRENA: From Moscow? You come from Moscow?

VERSHININ: Yes, from Moscow. Your father was a battery commander there, and I was an officer in the same brigade. (*To* MASHA.) I seem to remember your face a little.

MASHA: I don't remember you at all.

IRENA: Olia, Olia! (*Calls toward the ballroom.*) Olia, do come!

(OLGA *enters from the ballroom.*)

IRENA: It seems that Lieutenant-Colonel Vershinin comes from Moscow.

VERSHININ: You must be Olga Serghyeevna, the eldest. And you are Maria. . . . And you are Irena, the youngest. . . .

OLGA: You come from Moscow?

VERSHININ: Yes. I studied in Moscow and entered the service there. I stayed there quite a long time, but then I was put in charge of a battery here — so I moved out here, you see. I don't really remember you, you know, I only remember that there were three sisters. I remember your father, though, I remember him very well. All I need to do is to close my eyes and I can see him standing there as if he were alive. I used to visit you in Moscow.

OLGA: I thought I remembered everybody, and yet . . .

VERSHININ: My Christian names are Alexandr Ignatyevich.

IRENA: Alexandr Ignatyevich, and you come from Moscow! Well, what a surprise!

OLGA: We're going to live there, you know.

IRENA: We hope to be there by the autumn. It's our home town, we were born there. . . . In Staraya Basmannaya Street.

(*Both laugh happily.*)

MASHA: Fancy meeting a fellow townsman so unexpectedly! (*Eagerly.*) I remember now. Do you remember, Olga, there was someone they used to call "the lovesick Major"? You were a Lieutenant then, weren't you, and you were in love with someone or other, and everyone used to tease you about it. They called you "Major" for some reason or other.

VERSHININ (*laughs*): That's it, that's it. . . . "The lovesick Major," that's what they called me.

MASHA: In those days you only had a moustache. . . . Oh, dear, how much older you look! (*Tearfully.*) How much older!

VERSHININ: Yes, I was still a young man in the days when they called me "the lovesick Major." I was in love then. It's different now.

OLGA: But you haven't got a single grey hair! You've aged, yes, but you're certainly not an old man.

VERSHININ: Nevertheless, I'm turned forty-two. Is it long since you left Moscow?

IRENA: Eleven years. Now what are you crying for, Masha, you funny girl? . . . (*Tearfully.*) You'll make me cry, too.

MASHA: I'm not crying. What was the street you lived in?

VERSHININ: In the Staraya Basmannaya.

OLGA: We did, too.

VERSHININ: At one time I lived in the Niemietzkaya Street. I used to walk from there to the Krasny Barracks, and I remember there was such a gloomy bridge I had to cross. I used to hear the noise of the water rushing under it. I remember how lonely and sad I felt there. (*A pause.*) But what a magnificently wide river you have here! It's a marvellous river!

OLGA: Yes, but this is a cold place. It's cold here, and there are too many mosquitoes.

VERSHININ: Really? I should have said you had a really good healthy climate here, a real Russian climate. Forest, river . . . birch-trees, too. The dear, unpretentious birch-trees — I love them more than any of the other trees. It's nice living here. But there's one rather strange thing, the station is fifteen miles from the town. And no one knows why.

SOLIONY: I know why it is. (*Everyone looks at him.*) Because if the station were nearer, it wouldn't be so far away, and as it is so far away, it can't be nearer. (*An awkward silence.*)

TOOZENBACH: You like your little joke, Vassily Vassilich.

OLGA: I'm sure I remember you now. I know I do.

VERSHININ: I knew your mother.

CHEBUTYKIN: She was a good woman, God bless her memory!

IRENA: Mamma was buried in Moscow.

OLGA: At the convent of Novo-Dievichye.

MASHA: You know, I'm even beginning to forget what she looked like. I suppose people will lose all memory of us in just the same way. We'll be forgotten.

VERSHININ: Yes, we shall all be forgotten. Such is our fate, and we can't do anything about it. And all the things that seem serious, important and full of meaning to us now will be forgotten one day — or anyway they won't seem important any more. (*A pause.*) It's strange to think that we're utterly unable to tell what will be re-

garded as great and important in the future and what will be
thought of as just paltry and ridiculous. Didn't the great discoveries
of Copernicus — or of Columbus, if you like — appear useless and
unimportant to begin with? — whereas some rubbish, written up by
an eccentric fool, was regarded as a revelation of great truth? It may
well be that in time to come the life we live to-day will seem strange
and uncomfortable and stupid and not too clean, either, and perhaps
even wicked. . . .

TOOZENBACH: Who can tell? It's just as possible that future generations will think that we lived our lives on a very high plane and remember us with respect. After all, we no longer have tortures and
public executions and invasions, though there's still a great deal of
suffering!

SOLIONY (*in a high-pitched voice as if calling to chickens*): Cluck,
cluck, cluck! There's nothing our good Baron loves as much as a
nice bit of philosophizing.

TOOZENBACH: Vassily Vassilich, will you kindly leave me alone?
(*Moves to another chair.*) It's becoming tiresome.

SOLIONY (*as before*): Cluck, cluck, cluck! . . .

TOOZENBACH (*to* VERSHININ): The suffering that we see around us —
and there's so much of it — itself proves that our society has at
least achieved a level of morality which is higher. . . .

VERSHININ: Yes, yes, of course.

CHEBUTYKIN: You said just now, Baron, that our age will be called
great; but people are small all the same. . . . (*Gets up.*) Look how
small I am.

(*A violin is played off stage.*)

MASHA: That's Andrey playing the violin; he's our brother, you know.

IRENA: We've got quite a clever brother. . . . We're expecting him
to be a professor. Papa was a military man, but Andrey chose an
academic career.

OLGA: We've been teasing him to-day. We think he's in love, just a
little.

IRENA: With a girl who lives down here. She'll be calling in to-day
most likely.

MASHA: The way she dresses herself is awful! It's not that her clothes
are just ugly and old-fashioned, they're simply pathetic. She'll put
on some weird-looking, bright yellow skirt with a crude sort of fringe
affair, and then a red blouse to go with it. And her cheeks look as
though they've been scrubbed, they're so shiny! Andrey's not in love
with her — I can't believe it; after all, he has got some taste. I
think he's just playing the fool, just to annoy us. I heard yesterday

that she's going to get married to Protopopov, the chairman of the local council. I thought it was an excellent idea. (*Calls through the side door.*) Andrey, come here, will you? Just for a moment, dear.

(*Enter* ANDREY.)

OLGA: This is my brother, Andrey Serghyeevich.

VERSHININ: Vershinin.

ANDREY: Prozorov. (*Wipes the perspiration from his face.*) I believe you've been appointed battery commander here?

OLGA: What do you think, dear? Alexandr Ignatyevich comes from Moscow.

ANDREY: Do you, really? Congratulations! You'll get no peace from my sisters now.

VERSHININ: I'm afraid your sisters must be getting tired of me already.

IRENA: Just look, Andrey gave me this little picture frame to-day. (*Shows him the frame.*) He made it himself.

VERSHININ (*looks at the frame, not knowing what to say*): Yes, it's . . . it's very nice indeed. . . .

IRENA: Do you see that little frame over the piano? He made that one, too.

(ANDREY *waves his hand impatiently and walks off.*)

OLGA: He's awfully clever, and he plays the violin, and he makes all sorts of things, too. In fact, he's very gifted all round. Andrey, please, don't go. He's got such a bad habit — always going off like this. Come here!

(MASHA *and* IRENA *take him by the arms and lead him back, laughing.*)

MASHA: Now just you come here!

ANDREY: Do leave me alone, please do!

MASHA: You are a silly! They used to call Alexandr Ignatyevich "the lovesick Major," and he didn't get annoyed.

VERSHININ: Not in the least.

MASHA: I feel like calling you a "lovesick fiddler."

IRENA: Or a "lovesick professor."

OLGA: He's fallen in love! Our Andriusha's in love!

IRENA (*clapping her hands*): Three cheers for Andriusha! Andriusha's in love!

CHEBUTYKIN (*comes up behind* ANDREY *and puts his arms round his waist*): "Nature created us for love alone." . . . (*Laughs loudly, still holding his paper in his hand.*)

ANDREY: That's enough of it, that's enough. . . . (*Wipes his face.*)

I couldn't get to sleep all night, and I'm not feeling too grand just now. I read till four o'clock, and then I went to bed, but nothing happened. I kept thinking about one thing and another . . . and it gets light so early; the sun just pours into my room. I'd like to translate a book from the English while I'm here during the summer.

VERSHININ: You read English, then?

ANDREY: Yes. My father — God bless his memory — used to simply wear us out with learning. It sounds silly, I know, but I must confess that since he died I've begun to grow stout, as if I'd been physically relieved of the strain. I've grown quite stout in a year. Yes, thanks to Father, my sisters and I know French and German and English, and Irena here knows Italian, too. But what an effort it all cost us!

MASHA: Knowing three languages in a town like this is an unnecessary luxury. In fact, not even a luxury, but just a sort of useless encumbrance . . . it's rather like having a sixth finger on your hand. We know a lot of stuff that's just useless.

VERSHININ: Really! (*Laughs.*) You know a lot of stuff that's useless! It seems to me that there's no place on earth, however dull and depressing it may be, where intelligence and education can be useless. Let us suppose that among the hundred thousand people in this town, all of them, no doubt, very backward and uncultured, there are just three people like yourselves. Obviously, you can't hope to triumph over all the mass of ignorance around you; as your life goes by, you'll have to keep giving in little by little until you get lost in the crowd, in the hundred thousand. Life will swallow you up, but you'll not quite disappear, you'll make some impression on it. After you've gone, perhaps six more people like you will turn up, then twelve, and so on, until in the end most people will have become like you. So in two or three hundred years life on this old earth of ours will have become marvellously beautiful. Man longs for a life like that, and if it isn't here yet, he must imagine it, wait for it, dream about it, prepare for it, he must know and see more than his father and his grandfather did. (*Laughs.*) And you're complaining because you know a lot of stuff that's useless.

MASHA (*takes off her hat*): I'll be staying to lunch.

IRENA (*with a sigh*): Really, someone should have written all that down.

(ANDREY *has left the room, unnoticed.*)

TOOZENBACH: You say that in time to come life will be marvellously beautiful. That's probably true. But in order to share in it now, at a distance so to speak, we must prepare for it and work for it.

VERSHININ (*gets up*): Yes. . . . What a lot of flowers you've got here! (*Looks round.*) And what a marvellous house! I do envy you! All my life I seem to have been pigging it in small flats, with two chairs and a sofa and a stove which always smokes. It's the flowers that I've missed in my life, flowers like these! . . . (*Rubs his hands.*) Oh, well, never mind!

TOOZENBACH: Yes, we must work. I suppose you're thinking I'm a sentimental German. But I assure you I'm not — I'm Russian. I don't speak a word of German. My father was brought up in the Greek Orthodox faith. (*A pause.*)

VERSHININ (*walks up and down the room*): You know, I often wonder what it would be like if you could start your life over again — deliberately, I mean, consciously. . . . Suppose you could put aside the life you'd lived already, as though it was just a sort of rough draft, and then start another one like a fair copy. If that happened, I think the thing you'd want most of all would be not to repeat yourself. You'd try at least to create a new environment for yourself, a flat like this one, for instance, with some flowers and plenty of light. . . . I have a wife, you know, and two little girls; and my wife's not very well, and all that. . . . Well, if I had to start my life all over again, I wouldn't marry. . . . No, no!

(*Enter* KOOLYGHIN, *in the uniform of a teacher.*)

KOOLYGHIN (*approaches* IRENA): Congratulations, dear sister — from the bottom of my heart, congratulations on your Saint's day. I wish you good health and everything a girl of your age ought to have! And allow me to present you with this little book. . . . (*Hands her a book.*) It's the history of our school covering the whole fifty years of its existence. I wrote it myself. Quite a trifle, of course — I wrote it in my spare time when I had nothing better to do — but I hope you'll read it nevertheless. Good morning to you all! (*To* VERSHININ.) Allow me to introduce myself. Koolyghin's the name; I'm a master at the secondary school here. And a town councillor. (*To* IRENA.) You'll find a list in the book of all the pupils who have completed their studies at our school during the last fifty years. *Feci quod potui, faciant meliora potentes.* (*Kisses* MASHA.)

IRENA: But you gave me this book last Easter!

KOOLYGHIN (*laughs*): Did I really? In that case, give it me back — or no, better give it to the Colonel. Please do take it, Colonel. Maybe you'll read it some time when you've nothing better to do.

VERSHININ: Thank you very much. (*Prepares to leave.*) I'm so very glad to have made your acquaintance. . . .

OLGA: You aren't going are you? . . . Really, you mustn't.

IRENA: But you'll stay and have lunch with us! Please do.

OLGA: Please do.

VERSHININ (*bows*): I see I've intruded on your Saint's day party. I didn't know. Forgive me for not offering you my congratulations. (*Goes into the ballroom with* OLGA.)

KOOLYGHIN: To-day is Sunday, my friends, a day of rest; let us rest and enjoy it, each according to his age and position in life! We shall have to roll up the carpets and put them away till the winter. . . . We must remember to put some naphthaline on them, or Persian powder. . . . The Romans enjoyed good health because they knew how to work *and* how to rest. They had *mens sana in corpore sano*. Their life had a definite shape, a form. . . . The director of the school says that the most important thing about life is form. . . . A thing that loses its form is finished — that's just as true of our ordinary, everyday lives. (*Takes* MASHA *by the waist and laughs*.) Masha loves me. My wife loves me. Yes, and the curtains will have to be put away with the carpets, too. . . . I'm cheerful to-day, I'm in quite excellent spirits. . . . Masha, we're invited to the director's at four o'clock to-day. A country walk has been arranged for the teachers and their families.

MASHA: I'm not going.

KOOLYGHIN (*distressed*): Masha, darling, why not?

MASHA: I'll tell you later. . . . (*Crossly*.) All right, I'll come, only leave me alone now. . . . (*Walks off*.)

KOOLYGHIN: And after the walk we shall all spend the evening at the director's house. In spite of weak health, that man is certainly sparing no pains to be sociable. A first-rate, thoroughly enlightened man! A most excellent person! After the conference yesterday he said to me: "I'm tired, Fiodor Ilyich. I'm tired!" (*Looks at the clock, then at his watch*.) Your clock is seven minutes fast. Yes, "I'm tired," he said.

(*The sound of the violin is heard off stage*.)

OLGA: Will you all come and sit down, please! Lunch is ready. There's a pie.

KOOLYGHIN: Ah, Olga, my dear girl! Last night I worked up to eleven o'clock, and I felt tired, but to-day I'm quite happy. (*Goes to the table in the ballroom*.) My dear Olga!

CHEBUTYKIN (*puts the newspaper in his pocket and combs his beard*): A pie? Excellent!

MASHA (*sternly to* CHEBUTYKIN): Remember, you mustn't take anything to drink to-day. Do you hear? It's bad for you.

CHEBUTYKIN: Never mind. I've got over that weakness long ago! I haven't done any heavy drinking for two years. (*Impatiently.*) Anyway, my dear, what does it matter?

MASHA: All the same, don't you dare to drink anything. Mind you don't now! (*Crossly, but taking care that her husband does not hear.*) So now I've got to spend another of these damnably boring evenings at the director's!

TOOZENBACH: I wouldn't go if I were you, and that's that.

CHEBUTYKIN: Don't you go, my dear.

MASHA: Don't go, indeed! Oh, what a damnable life! It's intolerable. . . . (*Goes into the ballroom.*)

CHEBUTYKIN (*follows her*): Well, well! . . .

SOLIONY (*as he passes* TOOZENBACH *on the way to the ballroom*): Cluck, cluck, cluck!

TOOZENBACH: Do stop it, Vassily Vassilich. I've really had enough of it. . . .

SOLIONY: Cluck, cluck, cluck! . . .

KOOLYGHIN (*gaily*): Your health, Colonel! I'm a schoolmaster . . . and I'm quite one of the family here, as it were. I'm Masha's husband. She's got a sweet nature, such a very sweet nature!

VERSHININ: I think I'll have a little of this dark vodka. (*Drinks.*) Your health! (*To* OLGA.) I do feel so happy with you people!

(*Only* IRENA *and* TOOZENBACH *remain in the drawing-room.*)

IRENA: Masha's a bit out of humour to-day. You know, she got married when she was eighteen, and then her husband seemed the cleverest man in the world to her. It's different now. He's the kindest of men, but not the cleverest.

OLGA (*impatiently*): Andrey, will you please come?

ANDREY (*off stage*): Just coming. (*Enters and goes to the table.*)

TOOZENBACH: What are you thinking about?

IRENA: Oh, nothing special. You know, I don't like this man Soliony, I'm quite afraid of him. Whenever he opens his mouth he says something silly.

TOOZENBACH: He's a strange fellow. I'm sorry for him, even though he irritates me. In fact, I feel more sorry for him than irritated. I think he's shy. When he's alone with me, he can be quite sensible and friendly, but in company he's offensive and bullying. Don't go over there just yet, let them get settled down at the table. Let me stay beside you for a bit. Tell me what you're thinking about. (*A pause.*) You're twenty . . . and I'm not thirty yet myself. What years and years we still have ahead of us, a whole long succession of years, all full of my love for you! . . .

IRENA: Don't talk to me about love, Nikolai Lvovich.

TOOZENBACH (*not listening*): Oh, I long so passionately for life, I long to work and strive so much, and all this longing is somehow mingled with my love for you, Irena. And just because you happen to be beautiful, life appears beautiful to me! What are you thinking about?

IRENA: You say that life is beautiful. Maybe it is — but what if it only seems to be beautiful? Our lives, I mean the lives of us three sisters, haven't been beautiful up to now. The truth is that life has been stifling us, like weeds in a garden. I'm afraid I'm crying. . . . So unnecessary. . . . (*Quickly dries her eyes and smiles.*) We must work, work! The reason we feel depressed and take such a gloomy view of life is that we've never known what it is to make a real effort. We're the children of parents who despised work. . . .

(*Enter* NATALIA IVANOVNA. *She is wearing a pink dress with a green belt.*)

NATASHA: They've gone in to lunch already. . . . I'm late. . . . (*Glances at herself in a mirror, adjusts her dress.*) My hair seems to be all right. . . . (*Catches sight of* IRENA.) My dear Irena Serghyeevna, congratulations! (*Gives her a vigorous and prolonged kiss.*) You've got such a lot of visitors. . . . I feel quite shy. . . . How do you do, Baron?

OLGA (*enters the drawing-room*): Oh, there you are, Natalia Ivanovna! How are you, my dear?

(*They kiss each other.*)

NATASHA: Congratulations! You've such a lot of people here, I feel dreadfully shy. . . .

OLGA: It's all right, they're all old friends. (*Alarmed, dropping her voice.*) You've got a green belt on! My dear, that's surely a mistake!

NATASHA: Why, is it a bad omen, or what?

OLGA: No, but it just doesn't go with your dress . . . it looks so strange. . . .

NATASHA (*tearfully*): Really? But it isn't really green, you know, it's a sort of dull colour. . . . (*Follows* OLGA *to the ballroom.*)

(*All are now seated at the table; the drawing-room is empty.*)

KOOLYGHIN: Irena, you know, I do wish you'd find yourself a good husband. In my view it's high time you got married.

CHEBUTYKIN: You ought to get yourself a nice little husband, too, Natalia Ivanovna.

KOOLYGHIN: Natalia Ivanovna already has a husband in view.

MASHA (*strikes her plate with her fork*): A glass of wine for me, please!

Three cheers for our jolly old life! We keep our end up, we do!

KOOLYGHIN: Masha, you won't get more than five out of ten for good conduct!

VERSHININ: I say, this liqueur's very nice. What is it made of?

SOLIONY: Black beetles!

IRENA: Ugh! ugh! How disgusting!

OLGA: We're having roast turkey for dinner to-night, and then apple tart. Thank goodness, I'll be here all day to-day . . . this evening, too. You must all come this evening.

VERSHININ: May I come in the evening, too?

IRENA: Yes, please do.

NATASHA: They don't stand on ceremony here.

CHEBUTYKIN: "Nature created us for love alone." . . . (*Laughs.*)

ANDREY (*crossly*): Will you stop it, please? Aren't you tired of it yet?

(FEDOTIK *and* RODÉ *come in with a large basket of flowers.*)

FEDOTIK: Just look here, they're having lunch already!

RODÉ (*in a loud voice*): Having their lunch? So they are, they're having lunch already.

FEDOTIK: Wait half a minute. (*Takes a snapshot.*) One! Just one minute more! . . . (*Takes another snapshot.*) Two! All over now.

(*They pick up the basket and go into the ballroom where they are greeted uproariously.*)

RODÉ (*loudly*): Congratulations, Irena Serghyeevna! I wish you all the best, everything you'd wish for yourself! Gorgeous weather to-day, absolutely marvellous. I've been out walking the whole morning with the boys. You do know that I teach gym at the high school, don't you? . . .

FEDOTIK: You may move now, Irena Serghyeevna, that is, if you want to. (*Takes a snapshot.*) You do look attractive to-day. (*Takes a top out of his pocket.*) By the way, look at this top. It's got a wonderful hum.

IRENA: What a sweet little thing!

MASHA: "A green oak grows by a curving shore, And round that oak hangs a golden chain." . . . A green chain around that oak. . . . (*Peevishly.*) Why do I keep on saying that? Those lines have been worrying me all day long!

KOOLYGHIN: Do you know, we're thirteen at table?

RODÉ (*loudly*): You don't really believe in these old superstitions, do you? (*Laughter.*)

KOOLYGHIN: When thirteen people sit down to table, it means that some of them are in love. Is it you, by any chance, Ivan Romanych?

CHEBUTYKIN: Oh, I'm just an old sinner. . . . But what I can't make out is why Natalia Ivanovna looks so embarrassed.

(*Loud laughter.* NATASHA *runs out into the drawing-room,* ANDREY *follows her.*)

ANDREY: Please, Natasha, don't take any notice of them! Stop . . . wait a moment. . . . Please!

NATASHA: I feel so ashamed. . . . I don't know what's the matter with me, and they're all laughing at me. It's awful of me to leave the table like that, but I couldn't help it. . . . I just couldn't. . . . (*Covers her face with her hands.*)

ANDREY: My dear girl, please, please don't get upset. Honestly, they don't mean any harm, they're just teasing. My dear, sweet girl, they're really good-natured folks, they all are, and they're fond of us both. Come over to the window, they can't see us there. . . . (*Looks round.*)

NATASHA: You see, I'm not used to being with a lot of people.

ANDREY: Oh, how young you are, Natasha, how wonderfully, beautifully young! My dear, sweet girl, don't get so upset! Do believe me, believe me. . . . I'm so happy, so full of love, of joy. . . . No, they can't see us here! They can't see us! How did I come to love you, when was it? . . . I don't understand anything. My precious, my sweet, my innocent girl, please — I want you to marry me! I love you, I love you as I've never loved anybody. . . . (*Kisses her.*)

(*Enter two officers and, seeing* NATASHA *and* ANDREY *kissing, stand and stare in amazement.*)

ACT II

(*The scene is the same as in Act I. It is eight o'clock in the evening. The faint sound of an accordion is heard coming from the street.*

The stage is unlit. Enter NATALIA IVANOVNA *in a dressing-gown, carrying a candle. She crosses the stage and stops by the door leading to* ANDREY'S *room.*)

NATASHA: What are you doing, Andriusha? Reading? It's all right, I only wanted to know. . . . (*Goes to another door, opens it, looks inside and shuts it again.*) No one's left a light anywhere. . . .

ANDREY (*enters with a book in his hand*): What is it, Natasha?

NATASHA: I was just going round to see if anyone had left a light anywhere. It's carnival week, and the servants are so excited about it

. . . anything might happen! You've got to watch them. Last night about twelve o'clock I happened to go into the dining-room, and — would you believe it? — there was a candle alight on the table. I've not found out who lit it. (*Puts the candle down.*) What time is it?

ANDREY (*glances at his watch*): Quarter past eight.

NATASHA: And Olga and Irena still out. They aren't back from work yet, poor things! Olga's still at some teachers' conference, and Irena's at the post office. (*Sighs.*) This morning I said to Irena: "Do take care of yourself, my dear." But she won't listen. Did you say it was a quarter past eight? I'm afraid Bobik is not at all well. Why does he get so cold? Yesterday he had a temperature, but to-day he feels quite cold when you touch him. . . . I'm so afraid!

ANDREY: It's all right, Natasha. The boy's well enough.

NATASHA: Still, I think he ought to have a special diet. I'm so anxious about him. By the way, they tell me that some carnival party's supposed to be coming here soon after nine. I'd rather they didn't come, Andriusha.

ANDREY: Well, I really don't know what I can do. They've been asked to come.

NATASHA: This morning the dear little fellow woke up and looked at me, and then suddenly he smiled. He recognized me, you see. "Good morning, Bobik," I said, "good morning, darling precious!" And then he laughed. Babies understand everything, you know, they understand us perfectly well. Anyway, Andriusha, I'll tell the servants not to let that carnival party in.

ANDREY (*irresolutely*): Well . . . it's really for my sisters to decide, isn't it? It's their house, after all.

NATASHA: Yes, it's their house as well. I'll tell them, too. . . . They're so kind. . . . (*Walks off.*) I've ordered sour milk for supper. The doctor says you ought to eat nothing but sour milk, or you'll never get any thinner. (*Stops.*) Bobik feels cold. I'm afraid his room is too cold for him. He ought to move into a warmer room, at least until the warm weather comes. Irena's room, for instance — that's just a perfect room for a baby: it's dry, and it gets the sun all day long. We must tell her: perhaps she'd share Olga's room for a bit. . . . In any case, she's never at home during the day, she only sleeps there. . . . (*A pause.*) Andriusha, why don't you say anything?

ANDREY: I was just day-dreaming. . . . There's nothing to say, anyway. . . .

NATASHA: Well. . . . What was it I was going to tell you? Oh, yes! Ferapont from the Council Office wants to see you about something.

ANDREY (*yawns*): Tell him to come up.

(NATASHA *goes out.* ANDREY, *bending over the candle which she has left behind, begins to read his book. Enter* FERAPONT *in an old shabby overcoat, his collar turned up, his ears muffled in a scarf.*)

ANDREY: Hullo, old chap! What did you want to see me about?

FERAPONT: The chairman's sent you the register and a letter or something. Here they are. (*Hands him the book and the letter.*)

ANDREY: Thanks. That's all right. Incidentally, why have you come so late? It's gone eight already.

FERAPONT: What's that?

ANDREY (*raising his voice*): I said, why have you come so late? It's gone eight already.

FERAPONT: That's right. It was still daylight when I came first, but they wouldn't let me see you. The master's engaged, they said. Well, if you're engaged, you're engaged. I'm not in a hurry. (*Thinking that* ANDREY *has said something.*) What's that?

ANDREY: Nothing. (*Turns over the pages of the register.*) Tomorrow's Friday, there's no meeting, but I'll go to the office just the same . . . do some work. I'm so bored at home! . . . (*A pause.*) Yes, my dear old fellow, how things do change, what a fraud life is! So strange! To-day I picked up this book, just out of boredom, because I hadn't anything to do. It's a copy of some lectures I attended at the University. . . . Good Heavens! Just think — I'm secretary of the local council now, and Protopopov's chairman, and the most I can ever hope for is to become a member of the council myself! I — a member of the local council! I, who dream every night that I'm a professor in Moscow University, a famous academician, the pride of all Russia!

FERAPONT: I'm sorry, I can't tell you. I don't hear very well.

ANDREY: If you could hear properly I don't think I'd be talking to you like this. I must talk to someone, but my wife doesn't seem to understand me, and as for my sisters . . . I'm afraid of them for some reason or other, I'm afraid of them laughing at me and pulling my leg. . . . I don't drink and I don't like going to pubs, but my word! how I'd enjoy an hour or so at Tyestov's, or the Great Moscow Restaurant! Yes, my dear fellow, I would indeed!

FERAPONT: The other day at the office a contractor was telling me about some business men who were eating pancakes in Moscow. One of them ate forty pancakes and died. It was either forty or fifty, I can't remember exactly.

ANDREY: You can sit in some huge restaurant in Moscow without knowing anyone, and no one knowing you; yet somehow you don't feel that you don't belong there. . . . Whereas here you know everybody, and everybody knows you, and yet you don't feel you belong here, you feel you don't belong at all. . . . You're lonely and you feel a stranger.

FERAPONT: What's that? (*A pause.*) It was the same man that told me — of course, he may have been lying — he said that there's an enormous rope stretched right across Moscow.

ANDREY: Whatever for?

FERAPONT: I'm sorry, I can't tell you. That's what he said.

ANDREY: What nonsense! (*Reads the book.*) Have you ever been to Moscow?

FERAPONT (*after a pause*): No. It wasn't God's wish. (*A pause.*) Shall I go now?

ANDREY: Yes, you may go. Good-bye. (FERAPONT *goes out.*) Good-bye. (*Reading.*) Come in the morning to take some letters. . . . You can go now. (*A pause.*) He's gone. (*A bell rings.*) Yes, that's how it is. . . . (*Stretches and slowly goes to his room.*)

(*Singing is heard off stage; a nurse is putting a baby to sleep. Enter* MASHA *and* VERSHININ. *While they talk together, a maid lights a lamp and candles in the ballroom.*)

MASHA: I don't know. (*A pause.*) I don't know. Habit's very important, of course. For instance, after Father died, for a long time we couldn't get accustomed to the idea that we hadn't any orderlies to wait on us. But, habit apart, I think it's quite right what I was saying. Perhaps it's different in other places, but in this town the military certainly do seem to be the nicest and most generous and best-mannered people.

VERSHININ: I'm thirsty. I could do with a nice glass of tea.

MASHA (*glances at her watch*): They'll bring it in presently. You see, they married me off when I was eighteen. I was afraid of my husband because he was a school-master, and I had only just left school myself. He seemed terribly learned then, very clever and important. Now it's quite different, unfortunately.

VERSHININ: Yes. . . . I see. . . .

MASHA: I don't say anything against my husband — I'm used to him now — but there are such a lot of vulgar and unpleasant and offensive people among the other civilians. Vulgarity upsets me, it makes me feel insulted, I actually suffer when I meet someone who lacks refinement and gentle manners, and courtesy. When I'm with the other teachers, my husband's friends, I just suffer.

VERSHININ: Yes, of course. But I should have thought that in a town like this the civilians and the army people were equally uninteresting. There's nothing to choose between them. If you talk to any educated person here, civilian or military, he'll generally tell you that he's just worn out. It's either his wife, or his house, or his estate, or his horse, or something. . . . We Russians are capable of such elevated thoughts — then why do we have such low ideals in practical life? Why is it, why?

MASHA: Why?

VERSHININ: Yes, why does his wife wear him out, why do his children wear him out? And what about *him* wearing out his wife and children?

MASHA: You're a bit low-spirited to-day, aren't you?

VERSHININ: Perhaps. I haven't had any dinner to-day. I've had nothing to eat since morning. One of my daughters is a bit off colour, and when the children are ill, I get so worried. I feel utterly conscience-stricken at having given them a mother like theirs. Oh, if only you could have seen her this morning! What a despicable woman! We started quarrelling at seven o'clock, and at nine I just walked out and slammed the door. (*A pause.*) I never talk about these things in the ordinary way. It's a strange thing, but you're the only person I feel I dare complain to. (*Kisses her hand.*) Don't be angry with me. I've nobody, nobody but you. . . . (*A pause.*)

MASHA: What a noise the wind's making in the stove! Just before Father died the wind howled in the chimney just like that.

VERSHININ: Are you superstitious?

MASHA: Yes.

VERSHININ: How strange. (*Kisses her hand.*) You really are a wonderful creature, a marvellous creature! Wonderful, marvellous! It's quite dark here, but I can see your eyes shining.

MASHA (*Moves to another chair*):There's more light over here.

VERSHININ: I love you, I love you, I love you. . . . I love your eyes, I love your movements. . . . I dream about them. A wonderful, marvellous being!

MASHA (*Laughing softly*): When you talk to me like that, somehow I can't help laughing, although I'm afraid at the same time. Don't say it again, please. (*Half-audibly.*) Well, no . . . go on. I don't mind. . . . (*Covers her face with her hands.*) I don't mind. . . . Someone's coming. . . . Let's talk about something else. . . .

(*Enter* IRENA *and* TOOZENBACH *through the ballroom.*)

TOOZENBACH: I have a triple-barrelled name — Baron Toozenbach-Krone-Alschauer — but actually I'm a Russian. I was baptized in the Greek-Orthodox faith, just like yourself. I haven't really got any German characteristics, except maybe the obstinate patient way I keep on pestering you. Look how I bring you home every evening.

IRENA: How tired I am!

TOOZENBACH: And I'll go on fetching you from the post office and bringing you home every evening for the next twenty years — unless you send me away. . . . (*Noticing* MASHA *and* VERSHININ, *with pleasure.*) Oh, it's you! How are you?

IRENA: Well, here I am, home at last! (*To* MASHA.) A woman came into the post office just before I left. She wanted to send a wire to her brother in Saratov to tell him her son had just died, but she couldn't remember the address. So we had to send the wire without an address, just to Saratov. She was crying and I was rude to her, for no reason at all. "I've no time to waste," I told her. So stupid of me. We're having the carnival crowd to-day, aren't we?

MASHA: Yes.

IRENA (*sits down*): How nice it is to rest! I am tired!

TOOZENBACH (*smiling*): When you come back from work, you look so young, so pathetic, somehow. . . . (*A pause.*)

IRENA: I'm tired. No, I don't like working at the post office, I don't like it at all.

MASHA: You've got thinner. . . . (*Whistles.*) You look younger, too, and your face looks quite boyish.

TOOZENBACH: It's the way she does her hair.

IRENA: I must look for another job. This one doesn't suit me. It hasn't got what I always longed for and dreamed about. It's the sort of work you do without inspiration, without even thinking.

(*Someone knocks at the floor from below.*)

That's the Doctor knocking. (*To* TOOZENBACH.) Will you answer him, dear? . . . I can't. . . . I'm so tired.

TOOZENBACH (*knocks on the floor.*)

IRENA: He'll be up in a moment. We must do something about all this. Andrey and the Doctor went to the club last night and lost at cards again. They say Andrey lost two hundred roubles.

MASHA (*with indifference*): Well, what are we to do about it?

IRENA: He lost a fortnight ago, and he lost in December, too. I wish to goodness he'd lose everything we've got, and soon, too, and then perhaps we'd move out of this place. Good Heavens, I dream of Moscow every night. Sometimes I feel as if I were going mad. (*Laughs.*) We're going to Moscow in June. How many months are there till June? . . . February, March, April, May . . . nearly half-a-year!

MASHA: We must take care that Natasha doesn't get to know about him losing at cards.

IRENA: I don't think she cares.

(*Enter* CHEBUTYKIN. *He has been resting on his bed since dinner and has only just got up. He combs his beard, then sits down at the table and takes out a newspaper.*)

MASHA: There he is. Has he paid his rent yet?
IRENA (*laughs*): No. Not a penny for the last eight months. I suppose he's forgotten.
MASHA (*laughs*): How solemn he looks sitting there!

(*They all laugh. A pause.*)

IRENA: Why don't you say something, Alexandr Ignatyevich?
VERSHININ: I don't know. I'm just longing for some tea. I'd give my life for a glass of tea! I've had nothing to eat since morning. . . .
CHEBUTYKIN: Irena Serghyeevna!
IRENA: What is it?
CHEBUTYKIN: Please come here. *Venez ici!* (IRENA *goes over to him and sits down at the table.*) I can't do without you.

(IRENA *lays out the cards for a game of patience.*)

VERSHININ: Well, if we can't have any tea, let's do a bit of philosophizing, anyway.
TOOZENBACH: Yes, let's. What about?
VERSHININ: What about? Well . . . let's try to imagine what life will be like after we're dead, say in two or three hundred years.
TOOZENBACH: All right, then. . . . After we're dead, people will fly about in balloons, the cut of their coats will be different, the sixth sense will be discovered, and possibly even developed and used, for all I know. . . . But I believe, life itself will remain the same; it will still be difficult and full of mystery and full of happiness. And in a thousand years' time people will still be sighing and complaining: "How hard this business of living is!" — and yet they'll still be scared of death and unwilling to die, just as they are now.
VERSHININ (*after a moment's thought*): Well, you know . . . how shall I put it? I think everything in the world is bound to change gradually — in fact, it's changing before our very eyes. In two or three hundred years, or maybe in a thousand years — it doesn't matter how long exactly — life will be different. It will be happy. Of course, we shan't be able to enjoy that future life, but all the same, what we're living for now is to create it, we work and . . . yes, we suffer in order to create it. That's the goal of our life, and you might say that's the only happiness we shall ever achieve.
MASHA (*laughs quietly.*)

TOOZENBACH: Why are you laughing?

MASHA: I don't know. I've been laughing all day to-day.

VERSHININ (*to* TOOZENBACH): I went to the same cadet school as you did but I never went on to the Military Academy. I read a great deal, of course, but I never know what books I ought to choose, and probably I read a lot of stuff that's not worth anything. But the longer I live the more I seem to long for knowledge. My hair's going grey and I'm getting on in years, and yet how little I know, how little! All the same, I think I do know one thing which is not only true but also most important. I'm sure of it. Oh, if only I could convince you that there's not going to be any happiness for our own generation, that there mustn't be and won't be. . . . We've just got to work and work. All the happiness is reserved for our descendants, our remote descendants. (*A pause.*) Anyway, if I'm not to be happy, then at least my children's children will be.

(FEDOTIK *and* RODÉ *enter the ballroom; they sit down and sing quietly, one of them playing on a guitar.*)

TOOZENBACH: So you won't even allow us to dream of happiness! But what if I *am* happy?

VERSHININ: You're not.

TOOZENBACH (*flinging up his hands and laughing*): We don't understand one another, that's obvious. How can I convince you?

MASHA (*laughs quietly.*)

TOOZENBACH (*holds up a finger to her*): Show a finger to her and she'll laugh! (*To* VERSHININ.) And life will be just the same as ever not merely in a couple of hundred years' time, but in a million years. Life doesn't change, it always goes on the same; it follows its own laws, which don't concern us, which we can't discover anyway. Think of the birds that migrate in the autumn, the cranes, for instance: they just fly on and on. It doesn't matter what sort of thoughts they've got in their heads, great thoughts or little thoughts, they just fly on and on, not knowing where or why. And they'll go on flying no matter how many philosophers they happen to have flying with them. Let them philosophize as much as they like, as long as they go on flying.

MASHA: Isn't there some meaning?

TOOZENBACH: Meaning? . . . Look out there, it's snowing. What's the meaning of that? (*A pause.*)

MASHA: I think a human being has got to have some faith, or at least he's got to seek faith. Otherwise his life will be empty, empty. . . . How can you live and not know why the cranes fly, why children are born, why the stars shine in the sky! . . . You must either know why you live, or else . . . nothing matters . . . everything's just wild grass. . . . (*A pause.*)

VERSHININ: All the same, I'm sorry my youth's over.

MASHA: "It's a bore to be alive in this world, friends," that's what Gogol says.

TOOZENBACH: And I feel like saying: it's hopeless arguing with you, friends! I give you up.

CHEBUTYKIN (*reads out of the paper*): Balsac's marriage took place at Berdichev.[1]

IRENA (*sings softly to herself.*)

CHEBUTYKIN: Must write this down in my notebook. (*Writes.*) Balsac's marriage took place at Berdichev. (*Reads on.*)

IRENA (*playing patience, pensively*): Balsac's marriage took place at Berdichev.

TOOZENBACH: Well, I've thrown in my hand. Did you know that I'd sent in my resignation, Maria Serghyeevna?

MASHA: Yes, I heard about it. I don't see anything good in it, either. I don't like civilians.

TOOZENBACH: Never mind. (*Gets up.*) What sort of a soldier do I make, anyway? I'm not even good-looking. Well, what does it matter? I'll work. I'd like to do such a hard day's work that when I came home in the evening I'd fall on my bed exhausted and go to sleep at once. (*Goes to the ballroom.*) I should think working men sleep well at nights!

FEDOTIK (*to* IRENA): I've got you some coloured crayons at Pyzhikov's, in Moscow Street. And this little penknife, too. . . .

IRENA: You still treat me as if I were a little girl. I wish you'd remember I'm grown up now. (*Takes the crayons and the penknife, joyfully.*) They're awfully nice!

FEDOTIK: Look, I bought a knife for myself, too. You see, it's got another blade here, and then another . . . this thing's for cleaning your ears, and these are nail-scissors, and this is for cleaning your nails. . . .

RODÉ (*in a loud voice*): Doctor, how old are you?

CHEBUTYKIN: I? Thirty-two.

(*Laughter.*)

FEDOTIK: I'll show you another kind of patience. (*Sets out the cards.*)

(*The samovar is brought in, and* ANFISA *attends to it. Shortly afterwards* NATASHA *comes in and begins to fuss around the table.*)

---

[1] A town in Western Russia well known for its almost exclusively Jewish population.

SOLIONY (*enters, bows to the company and sits down at the table.*)

VERSHININ: What a wind, though!

MASHA: Yes. I'm tired of winter! I've almost forgotten what summer is like.

IRENA (*playing patience*): I'm going to go out. We'll get to Moscow!

FEDOTIK: No, it's not going out. You see, the eight has to go on the two of spades. (*Laughs.*) That means you won't go to Moscow.

CHEBUTYKIN (*reads the paper*): Tzitzikar. Smallpox is raging. . . .

ANFISA (*goes up to* MASHA): Masha, the tea's ready, dear. (*To* VERSHININ.) Will you please come to the table, your Excellency? Forgive me, your name's slipped my memory. . . .

MASHA: Bring it here, Nanny. I'm not coming over there.

IRENA: Nanny!

ANFISA: Comi-ing!

NATASHA (*to* SOLIONY): You know, even tiny babies understand what we say perfectly well! "Good morning, Bobik," I said to him only today, "Good morning, my precious!" — and then he looked at me in such a special sort of way. You may say it's only a mother's imagination, but it isn't, I do assure you. No, no! He really is an extraordinary child!

SOLIONY: If that child were mine, I'd cook him up in a frying pan and eat him. (*Picks up his glass, goes into the drawing-room and sits down in a corner.*)

NATASHA (*covers her face with her hands*): What a rude, ill-mannered person!

MASHA: People who don't even notice whether it's summer or winter are lucky! I think I'd be indifferent to the weather if I were living in Moscow.

VERSHININ: I've just been reading the diary of some French cabinet minister — he wrote it in prison. He got sent to prison in connection with the Panama affair. He writes with such a passionate delight about the birds he can see through the prison window — the birds he never even noticed when he was a cabinet minister. Of course, now he's released he won't notice them any more. . . . And in the same way, you won't notice Moscow once you live there again. We're not happy and we can't be happy: we only want happiness.

TOOZENBACH (*picks up a box from the table*): I say, where are all the chocolates?

IRENA: Soliony's eaten them.

TOOZENBACH: All of them?

ANFISA (*serving* VERSHININ *with tea*): Here's a letter for you, Sir.

VERSHININ: For me? (*Takes the letter.*) From my daughter. (*Reads it.*) Yes, of course. . . . Forgive me, Maria Serghyeevna, I'll just leave quietly. I won't have any tea. (*Gets up, agitated.*) Always the same thing. . . .

MASHA: What is it? Secret?

VERSHININ (*in a low voice*): My wife's taken poison again. I must go. I'll get away without them seeing me. All this is so dreadfully unpleasant. (*Kisses* MASHA's *hand.*) My dear, good, sweet girl. . . . I'll go out this way, quietly. . . . (*Goes out.*)

ANFISA: Where's he off to? And I've just brought him some tea! What a queer fellow!

MASHA (*flaring up*): Leave me alone! Why do you keep worrying me? Why don't you leave me in peace? (*Goes to the table, cup in hand.*) I'm sick and tired of you, silly old woman!

ANFISA: Why. . . . I didn't mean to offend you, dear.

ANDREY'S VOICE (*off stage*): Anfisa!

ANFISA (*mimics him*): Anfisa! Sitting there in his den! . . . (*Goes out.*)

MASHA (*by the table in the ballroom, crossly*): Do let me sit down somewhere! (*Jumbles up the cards laid out on the table.*) You take up the whole table with your cards! Why don't you get on with your tea?

IRENA: How bad-tempered you are, Mashka!

MASHA: Well, if I'm bad-tempered, don't talk to me, then. Don't touch me!

CHEBUTYKIN (*laughs*): Don't touch her! . . . Take care you don't touch her!

MASHA: You may be sixty, but you're always gabbling some damn nonsense or other, just like a child. . . .

NATASHA (*sighs*): My dear Masha, need you use such expressions? You know, with your good looks you'd be thought so charming, even by the best people — yes, I honestly mean it — if only you wouldn't use these expressions of yours! Je vous prie, pardonnez moi, Marie, mais vous avez des manières un peu grossières.

TOOZENBACH (*with suppressed laughter*): Pass me . . . I say, will you please pass me. . . . Is that cognac over there, or what? . . .

NATASHA: Il parait que mon Bobik déjà ne dort pas. . . . I think he's awake. He's not been too well to-day. I must go and see him . . . excuse me. (*Goes out.*)

IRENA: I say, where has Alexandr Ignatyevich gone to?

MASHA: He's gone home. His wife's done something queer again.

TOOZENBACH (*goes over to* SOLIONY *with a decanter of cognac*): You always sit alone brooding over something or other — though what it's all about nobody knows. Well, let's make it up. Let's have cognac together. (*They drink.*) I suppose I'll have to play the piano all night to-night — a lot of rubbishy tunes, of course. . . . Never mind!

SOLIONY: Why did you say "let's make it up"? We haven't quarrelled.

TOOZENBACH: You always give me the feeling that there's something wrong between us. You're a strange character, no doubt about it.

SOLIONY (*recites*): "I am strange, but who's not so? Don't be angry, Aleko!"

TOOZENBACH: What's Aleko got to do with it? . . . (*A pause.*)

SOLIONY: When I'm alone with somebody I'm all right, I'm just like other people. But in company, I get depressed and shy, and . . . I talk all sorts of nonsense. All the same, I'm a good deal more honest and well-intentioned than plenty of others. I can prove I am.

TOOZENBACH: You often make me angry because you keep on pestering me when we're in company — but all the same, I do like you for some reason. . . . I'm going to get drunk to-night, whatever happens! Let's have another drink!

SOLIONY: Yes, let's. (*A pause.*) I've never had anything against you personally, Baron. But my temperament's rather like Lermontov's. (*In a low voice.*) I even look a little like Lermontov, I've been told. . . . (*Takes a scent bottle from his pocket and sprinkles some scent on his hands.*)

TOOZENBACH: I have sent in my resignation! Finished! I've been considering it for five years, and now I've made up my mind at last. I'm going to work.

SOLIONY (*recites*): "Don't be angry, Aleko. . . . Away, away with all your dreams!"

(*During the conversation* ANDREY *enters quietly with a book in his hand and sits down by the candle.*)

TOOZENBACH: I'm going to work!

CHEBUTYKIN (*comes into the drawing-room with* IRENA): And the food they treated me to was the genuine Caucasian stuff: onion soup, followed by chehartma — that's a meat dish, you know.

SOLIONY: Chereshma isn't meat at all; it's a plant, something like an onion.

CHEBUTYKIN: No-o, my dear friend. Chehartma isn't an onion, it's roast mutton.

SOLIONY: I tell you chereshma is a kind of onion.

CHEBUTYKIN: Well, why should I argue about it with you? You've never been to the Caucasus and you've never tasted chehartma.

SOLIONY: I haven't tasted it because I can't stand the smell of it. Chereshma stinks just like garlic.

ANDREY (*imploringly*): Do stop it, friends! Please stop it!

TOOZENBACH: When's the carnival crowd coming along?

IRENA: They promised to be here by nine — that means any moment now.

TOOZENBACH (*embraces* ANDREY *and sings*): "Ah, my beautiful porch, my lovely new porch, my . . ." [2]

ANDREY (*dances and sings*): "My new porch all made of maple-wood. . . ."

CHEBUTYKIN (*dances*): "With fancy carving over the door. . . ." (*Laughter.*)

TOOZENBACH (*kisses* ANDREY): Let's have a drink, the devil take it! Andriusha, let's drink to eternal friendship. I'll come with you when you go back to Moscow University.

SOLIONY: Which university? There are two universities in Moscow.

ANDREY: There's only one.

SOLIONY: I tell you there are two.

ANDREY: Never mind, make it three. The more the merrier.

SOLIONY: There are two universities in Moscow.

(*Murmurs of protest and cries of "Hush!"*)

There are two universities in Moscow, an old one and a new one. But if you don't want to listen to what I'm saying, if my conversation irritates you, I can keep silent. In fact I can go to another room. . . . (*Goes out through one of the doors.*)

TOOZENBACH: Bravo, bravo! (*Laughs.*) Let's get started, my friends, I'll play for you. What a funny creature that Soliony is! . . . (*Sits down at the piano and plays a waltz.*)

MASHA (*dances alone*): The Baron is drunk, the Baron is drunk, the Baron is drunk. . . .

(*Enter* NATASHA.)

NATASHA (*to* CHEBUTYKIN): Ivan Romanych! (*Speaks to him, then goes out quietly.* CHEBUTYKIN *touches* TOOZENBACH *on the shoulder and whispers to him.*)

IRENA: What is it?

CHEBUTYKIN: It's time we were going. Good-night.

IRENA: But really. . . . What about the carnival party?

ANDREY (*embarrassed*): The carnival party's not coming. You see, my dear, Natasha says that Bobik isn't very well, and so . . . Anyway, I don't know . . . and certainly don't care. . . .

IRENA (*shrugs her shoulders*): Bobik's not very well! . . .

MASHA: Never mind, we'll keep our end up! If they turn us out, out

---

[2] A traditional Russian dance-song.

we must go! (*To* IRENA.) It isn't Bobik who's not well, it's her. . . .
There! . . . (*Taps her forehead with her finger.*) Petty little
bourgeois housewife!

(ANDREY *goes to his room on the right.* CHEBUTYKIN *follows him.
The guests say good-bye in the ballroom.*)

FEDOTIK: What a pity! I'd been hoping to spend the evening here, but
of course, if the baby's ill. . . . I'll bring him some toys to-morrow.

RODÉ (*in a loud voice*): I had a good long sleep after lunch to-day on
purpose, I thought I'd be dancing all night. I mean to say, it's only
just nine o'clock.

MASHA: Let's go outside and talk it over. We can decide what to do
then.

(*Voices are heard saying* "Good-bye! God bless you!" *and* TOOZEN-
BACH *is heard laughing gaily. Everyone goes out.* ANFISA *and a
maid clear the table and put out the lights. The nurse sings to the
baby off stage. Enter* ANDREY, *wearing an overcoat and hat, followed by* CHEBUTYKIN. *They move quietly.*)

CHEBUTYKIN: I've never found time to get married, somehow . . .
partly because my life's just flashed past me like lightning, and
partly because I was always madly in love with your mother and she
was married. . . .

ANDREY: One shouldn't marry. One shouldn't marry because it's so
boring.

CHEBUTYKIN: That may be so, but what about loneliness? You can
philosophize as much as you like, dear boy, but loneliness is a dreadful thing. Although, really . . . well, it doesn't matter a damn, of
course! . . .

ANDREY: Let's get along quickly.

CHEBUTYKIN: What's the hurry? There's plenty of time.

ANDREY: I'm afraid my wife may try to stop me.

CHEBUTYKIN: Ah!

ANDREY: I won't play cards to-night, I'll just sit and watch. I'm not
feeling too well. . . . What ought I to do for this breathlessness,
Ivan Romanych?

CHEBUTYKIN: Why ask me, dear boy? I can't remember — I simply
don't know.

ANDREY: Let's go through the kitchen.

(*They go out. A bell rings. The ring is repeated, then voices and
laughter are heard.*)

IRENA (*coming in*): What's that?

ANFISA (*in a whisper*): The carnival party.

(*The bell rings again.*)

IRENA: Tell them there's no one at home, Nanny. Apologize to them.

(ANFISA *goes out.* IRENA *walks up and down the room, lost in thought. She seems agitated. Enter* SOLIONY.)

SOLIONY (*puzzled*): There's no one here. . . . Where is everybody?
IRENA: They've gone home.
SOLIONY: How strange! Then you're alone here?
IRENA: Yes, alone. (*A pause.*) Well . . . good-night.
SOLIONY: I know I behaved tactlessly just now, I lost control of myself. But you're different from the others, you stand out high above them — you're pure, you can see where the truth lies. . . . You're the only person in the world who can possibly understand me. I love you. . . . I love you with a deep, infinite . . .
IRENA: Do please go away. Good-night!
SOLIONY: I can't live without you. (*Follows her.*) Oh, it's such a delight just to look at you! (*With tears.*) Oh, my happiness! Your glorious, marvellous, entrancing eyes — eyes like no other woman's I've ever seen. . . .
IRENA (*coldly*): Please stop it, Vassily Vassilich!
SOLIONY: I've never spoken to you of my love before . . . it makes me feel as if I were living on a different planet. . . . (*Rubs his forehead.*) Never mind! I can't force you to love me, obviously. But I don't intend to have any rivals — successful rivals, I mean. . . . No, no! I swear to you by everything I hold sacred that if there's anyone else, I'll kill him. Oh, how wonderful you are!

(*Enter* NATASHA *carrying a candle.*)

NATASHA (*pokes her head into one room, then into another, but passes the door leading to her husband's room*): Andrey's reading in there. Better let him read. Forgive me, Vassily Vassilich, I didn't know you were here. I'm afraid I'm not properly dressed.
SOLIONY: I don't care. Good-bye. (*Goes out.*)
NATASHA: You must be tired, my poor dear girl. (*Kisses* IRENA.) You ought to go to bed earlier.
IRENA: Is Bobik asleep?
NATASHA: Yes, he's asleep. But he's not sleeping peacefully. By the way, my dear, I've been meaning to speak to you for some time but there's always been something . . . either you're not here, or I'm too busy. . . . You see, I think that Bobik's nursery is so cold and

damp. . . . And your room is just ideal for a baby. Darling, do you think you could move into Olga's room?

IRENA (*not understanding her*): Where to?

(*The sound of bells is heard outside, as a "troika" is driven up to the house.*)

NATASHA: You can share a room with Olia for the time being, and Bobik can have your room. He is such a darling! This morning I said to him: "Bobik, you're my very own! My very own!" And he just gazed at me with his dear little eyes. (*The door bell rings.*) That must be Olga. How late she is!

(*A maid comes up to* NATASHA *and whispers in her ear.*)

NATASHA: Protopopov! What a funny fellow! Protopopov's come to ask me to go for a drive with him. In a troika! (*Laughs.*) Aren't these men strange creatures! . . .

(*The door bell rings again.*)

Someone's ringing. Shall I go for a short drive? Just for a quarter of an hour? (*To the maid.*) Tell him I'll be down in a minute. (*The door bell rings.*) That's the bell again. I suppose it's Olga. (*Goes out.*)

(*The maid runs out;* IRENA *sits lost in thought. Enter* KOOLYGHIN *and* OLGA, *followed by* VERSHININ.)

KOOLYGHIN: Well! What's the meaning of this? You said you were going to have a party.

VERSHININ: It's a strange thing. I left here about half an hour ago, and they were expecting a carnival party then.

IRENA: They've all gone.

KOOLYGHIN: Masha's gone, too? Where has she gone to? And why is Protopopov waiting outside in a troika? Who's he waiting for?

IRENA: Please don't ask me questions. I'm tired.

KOOLYGHIN: You . . . spoilt child!

OLGA: The conference has only just ended. I'm quite worn out. The headmistress is ill and I'm deputizing for her. My head's aching, oh, my head, my head. . . . (*Sits down.*) Andrey lost two hundred roubles at cards last night. The whole town's talking about it. . . .

KOOLYGHIN: Yes, the conference exhausted me, too. (*Sits down.*)

VERSHININ: So now my wife's taken it into her head to try to frighten me. She tried to poison herself. However, everything's all right now, so I can relax, thank goodness. . . . So we've got to go away? Well, good-night to you, all the best. Fiodor Illych, would you care to come along with me somewhere or other? I can't stay at home to-night, I really can't. . . . Do come!

KOOLYGHIN: I'm tired. I don't think I'll come. (*Gets up.*) I'm tired. Has my wife gone home?

IRENA: I think so.

KOOLYGHIN (*kisses* IRENA's *hand*): Good-night. We can rest to-morrow and the day after to-morrow, two whole days! Well, I wish you all the best. (*Going out.*) How I long for some tea! I reckoned on spending the evening in congenial company, but — *o, fallacem hominum spem!* Always use the accusative case in exclamations.

VERSHININ: Well, it looks as if I'll have to go somewhere by myself. (*Goes out with* KOOLYGHIN, *whistling.*)

OLGA: My head aches, oh, my head. . . . Andrey lost at cards . . . the whole town's talking. . . . I'll go and lie down. (*Going out.*) To-morrow I'm free. Heavens, what a joy! To-morrow I'm free, and the day after to-morrow I'm free. . . . My head's aching, oh, my poor head. . . .

IRENA (*alone*): They've all gone. No one's left.

(*Someone is playing an accordion in the street. The nurse sings in the next room.*)

NATASHA (*crosses the ballroom, wearing a fur coat and cap. She is followed by the maid*): I'll be back in half an hour. I'm just going for a little drive. (*Goes out.*)

IRENA (*alone, with intense longing*): Moscow! Moscow! Moscow!

ACT III

(*A bedroom now shared by* OLGA *and* IRENA. *There are two beds, one on the right, the other on the left, each screened off from the center of the room. It is past two o'clock in the morning. Off stage the alarm is being sounded on account of a fire which has been raging for some time. The inmates of the house have not yet been to bed.* MASHA *is lying on a couch, dressed, as usual, in black.* OLGA *and* ANFISA *come in.*)

ANFISA: Now they're sitting down there, under the stairs. . . . I keep telling them to come upstairs, that they shouldn't sit down there, but they just cry. "We don't know where our Papa is," they say, "perhaps he's got burned in the fire." What an idea! And there are people in the yard, too . . . half dressed. . . .

OLGA (*takes a dress out of a wardrobe*): Take this grey frock, Nanny.

. . . And this one. . . . This blouse, too. . . . And this skirt. Oh, Heavens! what is happening! Apparently the whole of the Kirsanovsky Streets' been burnt down. . . . Take this . . . and this, too. . . . (*Throws the clothes into* ANFISA's *arms.*) The poor Vershinins had a fright. Their house only just escaped being burnt down. They'll have to spend the night here . . . we mustn't let them go home. Poor Fedotik's lost everything, he's got nothing left. . . .

ANFISA: I'd better call Ferapont, Oliushka, I can't carry all this.

OLGA (*rings*): No one takes any notice when I ring. (*Calls through the door.*) Is anyone there? Will someone come up, please!

(*A window, red with the glow of fire, can be seen through the open door. The sound of a passing fire engine is heard.*)

How dreadful it all is! And how tired of it I am! (*Enter* FERAPONT.) Take this downstairs please. . . . The Kolotilin girls are sitting under the stairs . . . give it to them. And this, too. . . .

FERAPONT: Very good, Madam. Moscow was burned down in 1812 just the same. Mercy on us! . . . Yes, the French were surprised all right.

OLGA: Go along now, take this down.

FERAPONT: Very good. (*Goes out.*)

OLGA: Give it all away, Nanny, dear. We won't keep anything, give it all away. . . . I'm so tired, I can hardly keep on my feet. We mustn't let the Vershinins go home. The little girls can sleep in the drawing-room, and Alexandr Ignatyevich can share the downstairs room with the Baron. Fedotik can go in with the Baron, too, or maybe he'd better sleep in the ballroom. The doctor's gone and got drunk — you'd think he'd done it on purpose; he's so hopelessly drunk that we can't let anyone go into his room. Vershinin's wife will have to go into the drawing-room, too.

ANFISA (*wearily*): Don't send me away, Oliushka, darling! Don't send me away!

OLGA: What nonsense you're talking, Nanny! No one's sending you away.

ANFISA (*leans her head against* OLGA's *breast*): My dearest girl! I do work, you know, I work as hard as I can. . . . I suppose now I'm getting weaker, I'll be told to go. But where can I go? Where? I'm eighty years old. I'm over eighty-one!

OLGA: You sit down for a while, Nanny. . . . You're tired, you poor dear. . . . (*Makes her sit down.*) Just rest a bit. You've turned quite pale.

(*Enter* NATASHA.)

NATASHA: They're saying we ought to start a subscription in aid of the victims of the fire. You know — form a society or something for the purpose. Well, why not? It's an excellent idea! In any case it's up to us to help the poor as best we can. Bobik and Sofochka are fast asleep as if nothing had happened. We've got such a crowd of people in the house; the place seems full of people whichever way you turn. There's 'flu about in the town. . . . I'm so afraid the children might catch it.

OLGA (*without listening to her*): You can't see the fire from this room; it's quiet in here.

NATASHA: Yes. . . . I suppose my hair is all over the place. (*Stands in front of the mirror.*) They say I've got stouter, but it's not true! I'm not a bit stouter. Masha's asleep . . . she's tired, poor girl. . . . (*To* ANFISA, *coldly.*) How dare you sit down in my presence? Get up! Get out of here! (ANFISA *goes out. A pause.*) I can't understand why you keep that old woman in the house.

OLGA (*taken aback*): Forgive me for saying it, but I can't understand how you . . .

NATASHA: She's quite useless here. She's just a peasant woman, her right place is in the country. You're spoiling her. I do like order in the home, I don't like having useless people about. (*Strokes* OLGA'S *cheek.*) You're tired, my poor dear! Our headmistress is tired! You know, when my Sofochka grows up and goes to school, I'll be frightened of you.

OLGA: I'm not going to be a headmistress.

NATASHA: You'll be asked to, Olechka. It's settled.

OLGA: I'll refuse. I couldn't do it. . . . I wouldn't be strong enough. (*Drinks water.*) You spoke so harshly to Nanny just now. . . . You must forgive me for saying so, but I just can't stand that sort of thing . . . it made me feel quite faint. . . .

NATASHA (*agitated*): Forgive me, Olia, forgive me. I didn't mean to upset you.

(MASHA *gets up, picks up a pillow and goes out in a huff.*)

OLGA: Please try to understand me, dear. . . . It may be that we've been brought up in a peculiar way, but anyway I just can't bear it. When people are treated like that, it gets me down, I feel quite ill. . . . I simply get unnerved. . . .

NATASHA: Forgive me, dear, forgive me! . . . (*Kisses her.*)

OLGA: Any cruel or tactless remark, even the slightest discourtesy, upsets me. . . .

NATASHA: It's quite true, I know I often say things which would be

better left unsaid — but you must agree with me, dear, that she'd
be better in the country somewhere.

OLGA: She's been with us for thirty years.

NATASHA: But she can't do any work now, can she? Either I don't understand you, or you don't want to understand me. She can't work,
she just sleeps or sits about.

OLGA: Well, let her sit about.

NATASHA (*in surprise*): What do you mean, let her sit about? Surely
she is a servant! (*Tearfully.*) No, I don't understand you, Olia! I
have a nurse for the children and a wet nurse and we share a maid
and a cook. Whatever do we want this old woman for? What for?

(*The alarm is sounded again.*)

OLGA: I've aged ten years to-night.

NATASHA: We must sort things out, Olia. You're working at your
school, and I'm working at home. You're teaching and I'm running
the house. And when I say anything about the servants, I know what
I'm talking about. . . . That old thief, that old witch must get out
of this house to-morrow! . . . (*Stamps her feet.*) How dare you
vex me so? How dare you? (*Recovering her self-control.*) Really, if
you don't move downstairs, we'll always be quarrelling. This is quite
dreadful!

(*Enter* KOOLYGHIN.)

KOOLYGHIN: Where's Masha? It's time we went home. They say the
fire's getting less fierce. (*Stretches.*) Only one block got burnt down,
but to begin with it looked as if the whole town was going to be set
on fire by that wind. (*Sits down.*) I'm so tired, Olechka, my dear.
You know, I've often thought that if I hadn't married Masha, I'd
have married you, Olechka. You're so kind. I'm worn out. (*Listens.*)

OLGA: What is it?

KOOLYGHIN: The doctor's got drunk just as if he'd done it on purpose.
Hopelessly drunk. . . . As if he'd done it on purpose. (*Gets up.*)
I think he's coming up here. . . . Can you hear him? Yes, he's
coming up. (*Laughs.*) What a fellow, really! . . . I'm going to hide
myself. (*Goes to the wardrobe and stands between it and the wall.*)
What a scoundrel!

OLGA: He's been off drinking for two years, and now suddenly he goes
and gets drunk. . . . (*Walks with* NATASHA *towards the back of
the room.*)

(CHEBUTYKIN *enters; walking firmly and soberly he crosses the
room, stops, looks round, then goes to the wash-stand and begins
to wash his hands.*)

CHEBUTYKIN (*glumly*): The devil take them all . . . all the lot of them! They think I can treat anything just because I'm a doctor, but I know positively nothing at all. I've forgotten everything I used to know. I remember nothing, positively nothing. . . . (OLGA and NATASHA *leave the room without his noticing.*) The devil take them! Last Wednesday I attended a woman at Zasyp. She died, and it's all my fault that she did die. Yes. . . . I used to know a thing or two twenty-five years ago, but now I don't remember anything. Not a thing! Perhaps I'm not a man at all, but I just imagine that I've got hands and feet and a head. Perhaps I don't exist at all, and I only imagine that I'm walking about and eating and sleeping. (*Weeps.*) Oh, if only I could simply stop existing! (*Stops crying, glumly.*) God knows. . . . The other day they were talking about Shakespeare and Voltaire at the club. . . . I haven't read either, never read a single line of either, but I tried to make out by my expression that I had. The others did the same. How petty it all is! How despicable! And then suddenly I thought of the woman I killed on Wednesday. It all came back to me, and I felt such a swine, so sick of myself that I went and got drunk. . . .

(*Enter* IRENA, VERSHININ *and* TOOZENBACH. TOOZENBACH *is wearing a fashionable new civilian suit.*)

IRENA: Let's sit down here for a while. No one will come in here.

VERSHININ: The whole town would have been burnt down but for the soldiers. They're a fine lot of fellows! (*Rubs his hands with pleasure.*) Excellent fellows! Yes, they're a fine lot!

KOOLYGHIN (*approaches them*): What's the time?

TOOZENBACH: It's gone three. It's beginning to get light.

IRENA: Everyone's sitting in the ballroom and nobody thinks of leaving. That man Soliony there, too. . . . (*To* CHEBUTYKIN.) You ought to go to bed, Doctor.

CHEBUTYKIN: I'm all right. . . . Thanks. . . . (*Combs his beard.*)

KOOLYGHIN (*laughs*): Half seas over, Ivan Romanych! (*Slaps him on the shoulder.*) You're a fine one! *In vino veritas,* as they used to say in Rome.

TOOZENBACH: Everyone keeps asking me to arrange a concert in aid of the victims of the fire.

IRENA: Well, who'd you get to perform in it?

TOOZENBACH: It could be done if we wanted to. Maria Serghyeevna plays the piano wonderfully well, in my opinion.

KOOLYGHIN: Yes, wonderfully well!

IRENA: She's forgotten how to. She hasn't played for three years. . . . or maybe it's four.

TOOZENBACH: Nobody understands music in this town, not a single person. But I do — I really do — and I assure you quite definitely that Maria Serghyeevna plays magnificently. She's almost a genius for it.

KOOLYGHIN: You're right, Baron. I'm very fond of Masha. She's such a nice girl.

TOOZENBACH: Fancy being able to play so exquisitely, and yet having nobody, nobody at all, to appreciate it!

KOOLYGHIN (*sighs*): Yes. . . . But would it be quite proper for her to play in a concert? (*A pause.*) I don't know anything about these matters, my friends. Perhaps it'll be perfectly all right. But you know, although our director is a good man, a very good man indeed, and most intelligent, I know that he does hold certain views. . . . Of course, this doesn't really concern him, but I'll have a word with him about it, all the same, if you like.

CHEBUTYKIN (*picks up a china clock and examines it.*)

VERSHININ: I've got my clothes in such a mess helping to put out the fire, I must look like nothing on earth. (*A pause.*) I believe they were saying yesterday that our brigade might be transferred to somewhere a long way away. Some said it was to be Poland, and some said it was Cheeta, in Siberia.

TOOZENBACH: I heard that, too. Well, the town will seem quite deserted.

IRENA: We'll go away, too!

CHEBUTYKIN (*drops clock and breaks it*): Smashed to smithereens!

(*A pause. Everyone looks upset and embarrassed.*)

KOOLYGHIN (*picks up the pieces*): Fancy breaking such a valuable thing! Ah, Ivan Romanych, Ivan Romanych! You'll get a bad mark for that!

IRENA: It was my mother's clock.

CHEBUTYKIN: Well, supposing it was. If it was your mother's, then it was your mother's. Perhaps I didn't smash it. Perhaps it only appears that I did. Perhaps it only appears to us that we exist, whereas in reality we don't exist at all. I don't know anything, no one knows anything. (*Stops at the door.*) Why are you staring at me? Natasha's having a nice little affair with Protopopov, and you don't see it. You sit here seeing nothing, and meanwhile Natasha's having a nice little affair with Protopopov. . . . (*Sings.*) Would you like a date? . . . (*Goes out.*)

VERSHININ: So. . . . (*Laughs.*) How odd it all is, really. (*A pause.*) When the fire started, I ran home as fast as I could. When I got near, I could see that our house was all right and out of danger, but the two little girls were standing there, in the doorway in their night clothes. Their mother wasn't there. People were rushing about, horses, dogs . . . and in the kiddies' faces I saw a frightened, anxious, appealing look, I don't know what! . . . My heart sank when I saw their faces. My God, I thought, what will these children have to go through in the course of their poor lives? And they may live a long time, too! I picked them up and ran back here with them, and all the time I was running, I was thinking the same thing: what will they have to go through? (*The alarm is sounded. A pause.*) When I got here, my wife was here already . . . angry, shouting!

(*Enter* MASHA *carrying a pillow; she sits down on the couch.*)

VERSHININ: And when my little girls were standing in the doorway with nothing on but their night clothes, and the street was red with the glow of the fire and full of terrifying noises, it struck me that the same sort of thing used to happen years ago, when armies used to make sudden raids on towns, and plunder them and set them on fire. . . . Anyway, is there any essential difference between things as they were and as they are now? And before very long, say, in another two or three hundred years, people may be looking at our present life just as we look at the past now, with horror and scorn. Our own times may seem uncouth to them, boring and frightfully uncomfortable and strange. . . . Oh, what a great life it'll be then, what a life! (*Laughs.*) Forgive me, I'm philosophizing my head off again . . . but may I go on, please? I'm bursting to philosophize just at the moment. I'm in the mood for it. (*A pause.*) You seem as if you've all gone to sleep. As I was saying: what a great life it will be in the future! Just try to imagine it. . . . At the present time there are only three people of your intellectual calibre in the whole of this town, but future generations will be more productive of people like you. They'll go on producing more and more of the same sort until at last the time will come when everything will be just as you'd wish it yourselves. People will live their lives in your way, and then even you may be outmoded, and a new lot will come along who will be even better than you are. . . . (*Laughs.*) I'm in quite a special mood to-day. I feel full of a tremendous urge to live. . . . (*Sings.*)

> "To Love all ages are in fee,
>   The passion's good for you and me." . . . (*Laughs.*)

MASHA (*sings*): Tara-tara-tara. . . .
VERSHININ: Tum-tum. . . .
MASHA: Tara-tara . . .

VERSHININ: Tum-tum, tum-tum. . . . (*Laughs.*)

(*Enter* FEDOTIK.)

FEDOTIK (*dancing about*): Burnt, burnt! Everything I've got burnt!

(*All laugh.*)

IRENA: It's hardly a joking matter. Has everything really been burnt?
FEDOTIK (*laughs*): Everything, completely. I've got nothing left. My guitar's burnt, my photographs are burnt, all my letters are burnt. Even the little note-book I was going to give you has been burnt.

(*Enter* SOLIONY.)

IRENA: No, please go away, Vassily Vassilich. You can't come in here.
SOLIONY: Can't I? Why can the Baron come in here if I can't?
VERSHININ: We really must go, all of us. What's the fire doing?
SOLIONY: It's dying down, they say. Well, I must say it's a peculiar thing that the Baron can come in here, and I can't. (*Takes a scent bottle from his pocket and sprinkles himself with scent.*)
VERSHININ: Tara-tara.
MASHA: Tum-tum, tum-tum.
VERSHININ (*laughs, to* SOLIONY): Let's go to the ballroom.
SOLIONY: Very well, we'll make a note of this. "I hardly need to make my moral yet more clear: That might be teasing geese, I fear!" [3] (*Looks at* TOOZENBACH.) Cluck, cluck, cluck! (*Goes out with* VERSHININ *and* FEDOTIK.)
IRENA: That Soliony has smoked the room out. . . . (*Puzzled.*) The Baron's asleep. Baron! Baron!
TOOZENBACH (*waking out of his doze*): I must be tired. The brick-works. . . . No, I'm not talking in my sleep. I really do intend to go to the brick-works and start working there quite soon. I've had a talk with the manager. (*To* IRENA, *tenderly.*) You are so pale, so beautiful, so fascinating. . . . Your pallor seems to light up the darkness around you, as if it were luminous, somehow. . . . You're sad, you're dissatisfied with the life you have to live. . . . Oh, come away with me, let's go away and work together!
MASHA: Nikolai Lvovich, I wish you'd go away.
TOOZENBACH (*laughs*): Oh, you're here, are you? I didn't see you. (*Kisses* IRENA's *hand.*) Good-bye, I'm going. You know as I look at you now, I keep thinking of the day — it was a long time ago, your Saint's day — when you talked to us about the joy of work. . . . You were so gay and high-spirited then. . . . And what a happy

[3] From Krylov's fable *Geese* (translated by Bernard Pares).

life I saw ahead of me! Where is it all now? (*Kisses her hand.*)
There are tears in your eyes. You should go to bed, it's beginning to
get light . . . it's almost morning. . . . Oh, if only I could give
my life for you!

MASHA: Nikolai Lvovich, please go away! Really now. . . .

TOOZENBACH: I'm going. (*Goes out.*)

MASHA (*lies down*): Are you asleep, Fiodor?

KOOLYGHIN: Eh?

MASHA: Why don't you go home?

KOOLYGHIN: My darling Masha, my sweet, my precious Masha. . . .

IRENA: She's tired. Let her rest a while, Fyedia.

KOOLYGHIN: I'll go in a moment. My wife, my dear, good wife! . . .
How I love you! . . . only you!

MASHA (*crossly*): *Amo, amas, amat, amamus, amatis, amant!*

KOOLYGHIN (*laughs*): Really, she's an amazing woman! — I've been
married to you for seven years, but I feel as if we were only married
yesterday. Yes, on my word of honour, I do! You really are amazing!
Oh, I'm so happy, happy, happy!

MASHA: And I'm so bored, bored, bored! (*Sits up.*) I can't get it out
of my head. . . . It's simply disgusting. It's like having a nail
driven into my head. No, I can't keep silent about it any more. It's
about Andrey. . . . He's actually mortgaged this house to a bank,
and his wife's got hold of all the money — and yet the house doesn't
belong to him, it belongs to all four of us! Surely, he must realize
that, if he's got any honesty.

KOOLYGHIN: Why bring all this up, Masha? Why bother about it now?
Andriusha owes money all round. . . . Leave him alone.

MASHA: Anyway, it's disgusting. (*Lies down.*)

KOOLYGHIN: Well, we aren't poor, Masha. I've got work, I teach at the
county school, I give private lessons in my spare time. . . . I'm
just a plain, honest man. . . . *Omnia mea mecum porto*, as they
say.

MASHA: I don't ask for anything, but I'm just disgusted by injustice.
(*A pause.*) Why don't you go home, Fiodor?

KOOLYGHIN (*kisses her*): You're tired. Just rest here for a while. . . .
I'll go home and wait for you. . . . Go to sleep. (*Goes to the
door.*) I'm happy, happy, happy! (*Goes out.*)

IRENA: The truth is that Andrey is getting to be shallow-minded. He's
aging and since he's been living with that woman he's lost all the
inspiration he used to have! Not long ago he was working for a
professorship, and yet yesterday he boasted of having at last been
elected a member of the County Council. Fancy him a member,
with Protopopov as chairman! They say the whole town's laughing

at him, he's the only one who doesn't know anything or see anything. And now, you see, everyone's at the fire, while he's just sitting in his room, not taking the slightest notice of it. Just playing his violin. (*Agitated.*) Oh, how dreadful it is, how dreadful, how dreadful! I can't bear it any longer, I can't, I really can't! . . .

(*Enter* OLGA. *She starts arranging things on her bedside table.*)

IRENA (*sobs loudly*): You must turn me out of here! Turn me out; I can't stand it any more!

OLGA (*alarmed*): What is it? What is it, darling?

IRENA (*sobbing*): Where. . . . Where has it all gone to? Where is it? Oh, God! I've forgotten. . . . I've forgotten everything . . . there's nothing but a muddle in my head. . . . I don't remember what the Italian for "window" is, or for "ceiling." . . . Every day I'm forgetting more and more, and life's slipping by, and it will never, never come back. . . . We shall never go to Moscow. . . . I can see that we shall never go. . . .

OLGA: Don't, my dear, don't. . . .

IRENA (*trying to control herself*): Oh, I'm so miserable! . . . I can't work, I won't work! I've had enough of it, enough! . . . First I worked on the telegraph, now I'm in the County Council office, and I hate and despise everything they give me to do there. . . . I'm twenty-three years old, I've been working all this time, and I feel as if my brain's dried up. I know I've got thinner and uglier and older, and I find no kind of satisfaction in anything, none at all. And the time's passing . . . and I feel as if I'm moving away from any hope of a genuine, fine life, I'm moving further and further away and sinking into a kind of abyss. I feel in despair, and I don't know why I'm still alive, why I haven't killed myself. . . .

OLGA: Don't cry, my dear child, don't cry. . . . It hurts me.

IRENA: I'm not crying any more. That's enough of it. Look, I'm not crying now. Enough of it, enough! . . .

OLGA: Darling, let me tell you something. . . . I just want to speak as your sister, as your friend. . . . That is, if you want my advice. . . . Why don't you marry the Baron?

IRENA (*weeps quietly.*)

OLGA: After all, you do respect him, you think a lot of him. . . . It's true, he's not good-looking, but he's such a decent, clean-minded sort of man. . . . After all, one doesn't marry for love, but to fulfil a duty. At least, I think so, and I'd marry even if I weren't in love. I'd marry anyone that proposed to me, as long as he was a decent man. I'd even marry an old man.

IRENA: I've been waiting all this time, imagining that we'd be moving to Moscow, and I'd meet the man I'm meant for there. I've dreamt about him and I've loved him in my dreams. . . . But it's all turned out to be nonsense . . . nonsense. . . .

OLGA (*embracing her*): My darling sweetheart, I understand everything perfectly. When the Baron resigned his commission and came to see us in his civilian clothes, I thought he looked so plain that I actually started to cry. . . . He asked me why I was crying. . . . How could I tell him? But, of course, if it were God's will that he should marry you, I'd feel perfectly happy about it. That's quite a different matter, quite different!

(NATASHA, *carrying a candle, comes out of the door on the right, crosses the stage and goes out through the door on the left without saying anything.*)

MASHA (*sits up*): She goes about looking as if she'd started the fire.

OLGA: You're silly, Masha. You're the stupidest person in our family. Forgive me for saying so.

(*A pause.*)

MASHA: My dear sisters, I've got something to confess to you. I must get some relief, I feel the need of it in my heart. I'll confess it to you two alone, and then never again, never to anybody! I'll tell you in a minute. (*In a low voice.*) It's a secret, but you'll have to know everything. I can't keep silent any more. (*A pause.*) I'm in love, in love. . . . I love that man. . . . You saw him here just now. . . . Well, what's the good? . . . I love Vershinin. . . .

OLGA (*goes behind her screen*): Don't say it. I don't want to hear it.

MASHA: Well, what's to be done? (*Holding her head.*) I thought he was queer at first, then I started to pity him . . . then I began to love him . . . love everything about him — his voice, his talk, his misfortunes, his two little girls. . . .

OLGA: Nevertheless, I don't want to hear it. You can say any nonsense you like, I'm not listening.

MASHA: Oh, you're stupid, Olia! If I love him, well — that's my fate! That's my destiny. . . . He loves me, too. It's all rather frightening, isn't it? Not a good thing, is it? (*Takes* IRENA *by the hand and draws her to her.*) Oh, my dear! . . . How are we going to live through the rest of our lives? What's going to become of us? When you read a novel, everything in it seems so old and obvious, but when you fall in love yourself, you suddenly discover that you don't really know anything, and you've got to make your own decisions. . . . My dear sisters, my dear sisters! . . . I've confessed it all to

you, and now I'll keep quiet. . . . I'll be like that madman in the
story by Gogol — silence . . . silence! . . .

(*Enter* ANDREY *followed by* FERAPONT.)

ANDREY (*crossly*): What do you want? I don't understand you.

FERAPONT (*stopping in the doorway, impatiently*): I've asked you
about ten times already, Andrey Serghyeevich.

ANDREY: In the first place, you're not to call me Andrey Serghyeevich
— call me "Your Honour."

FERAPONT: The firemen are asking Your Honour if they may drive
through your garden to get to the river. They've been going a long
way round all this time — it's a terrible business!

ANDREY: All right. Tell them it's all right. (FERAPONT *goes out.*) They
keep on plaguing me. Where's Olga? (OLGA *comes from behind the
screen.*) I wanted to see you. Will you give me the key to the cupboard? I've lost mine. You know the key I mean, the small one
you've got. . . .

(OLGA *silently hands him the key.* IRENA *goes behind the screen
on her side of the room.*)

ANDREY: What a terrific fire! It's going down though. That Ferapont
annoyed me, the devil take him! Silly thing he made me say. . . .
Telling him to call me "Your Honour"! . . . (*A pause.*) Why
don't you say anything, Olia? (*A pause.*) It's about time you
stopped this nonsense . . . sulking like this for no reason whatever. . . . You here, Masha? And Irena's here, too. That's excellent! We can talk it over then, frankly and once for all. What have
you got against me? What is it?

OLGA: Drop it now, Andriusha. Let's talk it over to-morrow. (*Agitated.*) What a dreadful night!

ANDREY (*in great embarrassment*): Don't get upset. I'm asking you
quite calmly, what have you got against me? Tell me frankly.

VERSHININ'S VOICE (*off stage*): Tum-tum-tum!

MASHA (*in a loud voice, getting up*): *Tara-tara-tara!* (*To* OLGA.) Good-
bye, Olia, God bless you! (*Goes behind the screen and kisses*
IRENA.) Sleep well. . . . Good-bye, Andrey. I should leave them
now, they're tired . . . talk it over to-morrow. . . . (*Goes out.*)

OLGA: Really, Andriusha, let's leave it till to-morrow. . . . (*Goes
behind the screen on her side of the room.*) It's time to go to bed.

ANDREY: I only want to say one thing, then I'll go. In a moment. . . .
First of all, you've got something against my wife, against Natasha.
I've always been conscious of it from the day we got married. Na-
tasha is a fine woman, she's honest and straightforward and high-

principled.' . . . That's my opinion. I love and respect my wife.
You understand that I respect her, and I expect others to respect
her, too. I repeat: she's an honest, high-principled woman, and all
your grievances against her — if you don't mind my saying so —
are just imagination, and nothing more. . . . (*A pause.*) Secondly,
you seem to be annoyed with me for not making myself a professor,
and not doing any academic work. But I'm working in the Council
Office, I'm a member of the County Council, and I feel my service
there is just as fine and valuable as any academic work I might do.
I'm a member of the County Council, and if you want to know, I'm
proud of it! (*A pause.*) Thirdly . . . there's something else I must
tell you. . . . I know I mortgaged the house without asking your
permission. . . . That was wrong, I admit it, and I ask you to forgive me. . . . I was driven to it by my debts. . . . I'm in debt for
about thirty-five thousand roubles. I don't play cards any more, I've
given it up long ago. . . . The only thing I can say to justify myself
is that you girls get an annuity, while I don't get anything . . . no
income, I mean. . . . (*A pause.*)

KOOLYGHIN (*calling through the door*): Is Masha there? She's not
there? (*Alarmed.*) Where can she be then? It's very strange. . . .
(*Goes away.*)

ANDREY: So you won't listen? Natasha is a good, honest woman, I tell
you. (*Walks up and down the stage, then stops.*) When I married
her, I thought we were going to be happy, I thought we should all
be happy. . . . But . . . oh, my God! . . . (*Weeps.*) My dear
sisters, my dear, good sisters, don't believe what I've been saying,
don't believe it. . . . (*Goes out.*)

KOOLYGHIN (*through the door, agitated*): Where's Masha? Isn't
Masha here? Extraordinary! (*Goes away.*)

(*The alarm is heard again. The stage is empty.*)

IRENA (*speaking from behind the screen*): Olia! Who's that knocking
on the floor?

OLGA: It's the doctor, Ivan Romanych. He's drunk.

IRENA: It's been one thing after another all night. (*A pause.*) Olia!
(*Peeps out from behind the screen.*) Have you heard? The troops
are being moved from the district . . . they're being sent somewhere a long way off.

OLGA: That's only a rumour.

IRENA: We'll be left quite alone then. . . . Olia!

OLGA: Well?

IRENA: Olia, darling, I do respect the Baron. . . . I think a lot of him,
he's a very good man. . . . I'll marry him, Olia, I'll agree to marry

him, if only we can go to Moscow! Let's go, please do let's go!
There's nowhere in all the world like Moscow. Let's go, Olia! Let's
go!

ACT IV

(*The old garden belonging to the Prozorovs' house. A river is seen
at the end of a long avenue of fir-trees, and on the far bank of the
river a forest. On the right of the stage there is a verandah with
a table on which champagne bottles and glasses have been left. It
is midday. From time to time people from the street pass through
the garden to get to the river. Five or six soldiers march through
quickly.*

CHEBUTYKIN, *radiating a mood of benevolence which does not
leave him throughout the act, is sitting in a chair in the garden.
He is wearing his army cap and is holding a walking stick, as if
ready to be called away at any moment.* KOOLYGHIN, *with a decoration round his neck and with his moustache shaved off,* TOOZEN-
BACH *and* IRENA *are standing on the verandah saying good-bye to*
FEDOTIK *and* RODÉ, *who are coming down the steps. Both officers
are in marching uniform.*)

TOOZENBACH (*embracing* FEDOTIK): You're a good fellow, Fedotik;
we've been good friends! (*Embraces* RODÉ.) Once more, then. . . .
Good-bye, my dear friends!

IRENA: Au revoir!

FEDOTIK: It's not "au revoir." It's good-bye. We shall never meet
again!

KOOLYGHIN: Who knows? (*Wipes his eyes, smiling.*) There! you've
made me cry.

IRENA: We'll meet some time.

FEDOTIK: Perhaps in ten or fifteen years' time. But then we'll hardly
know one another. . . . We shall just meet and say, "How are
you?" coldly. . . . (*Takes a snapshot.*) Wait a moment. . . .
Just one more, for the last time.

RODÉ (*embraces* TOOZENBACH): We're not likely to meet again. . . .
(*Kisses* IRENA's *hand.*) Thank you for everything . . . everything!

FEDOTIK (*annoyed*): Do just wait a second!

TOOZENBACH: We'll meet again if we're fated to meet. Do write to us.
Be sure to write.

RODÉ (*glancing round the garden*): Good-bye, trees! (*Shouts.*) Heigh-
ho! (*A pause.*) Good-bye, echo!

KOOLYGHIN: I wouldn't be surprised if you got married out there, in Poland. . . . You'll get a Polish wife, and she'll put her arms round you and say: Kohane![4] (*Laughs.*)

FEDOTIK (*glances at his watch*): There's less than an hour to go. Soliony is the only one from our battery who's going down the river on the barge. All the others are marching with the division. Three batteries are leaving to-day by road and three more to-morrow — then the town will be quite peaceful.

TOOZENBACH: Yes, and dreadfully dull, too.

RODÉ: By the way, where's Maria Serghyeevna?

KOOLYGHIN: She's somewhere in the garden.

FEDOTIK: We must say good-bye to her.

RODÉ: Good-bye. I really must go, or I'll burst into tears. (*Quickly embraces* TOOZENBACH *and* KOOLYGHIN, *kisses* IRENA's *hand.*) Life's been very pleasant here. . . .

FEDOTIK (*to* KOOLYGHIN): Here's something for a souvenir for you — a note-book with a pencil. . . . We'll go down to the river through here. (*They go off, glancing back.*)

RODÉ (*shouts*): Heigh-ho!

KOOLYGHIN (*shouts*): Good-bye!

(*At the back of the stage* FEDOTIK *and* RODÉ *meet* MASHA, *and say good-bye to her; she goes off with them.*)

IRENA: They've gone. . . . (*Sits down on the bottom step of the verandah.*)

CHEBUTYKIN: They forgot to say good-bye to me.

IRENA: Well, what about you?

CHEBUTYKIN: That's true, I forgot, too. Never mind, I'll be seeing them again quite soon. I'll be leaving to-morrow. Yes . . . only one more day. And then, in a year's time I'll be retiring. I'll come back here and finish the rest of my life near you. There's just one more year to go and then I get my pension. . . . (*Puts a newspaper in his pocket and takes out another.*) I'll come back here and lead a reformed life. I'll be a nice, quiet, well-behaved little man.

IRENA: Yes, it's really time you reformed, my dear friend. You ought to live a different sort of life, somehow.

CHEBUTYKIN: Yes. . . . I think so, too. (*Sings quietly.*) Tarara-boom-di-ay. . . . I'm sitting on a tomb-di-ay. . . .

KOOLYGHIN: Ivan Romanych is incorrigible! Incorrigible!

CHEBUTYKIN: Yes, you ought to have taken me in hand. You'd have reformed me!

---

4 A Polish word meaning "beloved."

IRENA: Fiodor's shaved his moustache off. I can't bear to look at him.

KOOLYGHIN: Why not?

CHEBUTYKIN: If I could just tell you what your face looks like now — but I daren't.

KOOLYGHIN: Well! Such are the conventions of life! *Modus vivendi,* you know. The director shaved his moustache off, so I shaved mine off when they gave me an inspectorship. No one likes it, but personally I'm quite indifferent. I'm content. Whether I've got a moustache or not, it's all the same to me. (*Sits down.*)

ANDREY (*passes across the back of the stage pushing a pram with a child asleep in it.*)

IRENA: Ivan Romanych, my dear friend, I'm awfully worried about something. You were out in the town garden last night — tell me what happened there?

CHEBUTYKIN: What happened? Nothing. Just a trifling thing. (*Reads his paper.*) It doesn't matter anyway.

KOOLYGHIN: They say that Soliony and the Baron met in the town garden outside the theatre last night and . . .

TOOZENBACH: Don't please! What's the good? . . . (*Waves his hand at him deprecatingly and goes into the house.*)

KOOLYGHIN: It was outside the theatre. . . . Soliony started badgering the Baron, and he lost patience and said something that offended him.

CHEBUTYKIN: I don't know anything about it. It's all nonsense.

KOOLYGHIN: A school-master once wrote "nonsense" in Russian over a pupil's essay, and the pupil puzzled over it, thinking it was a Latin word. (*Laughs.*) Frightfully funny, you know! They say that Soliony's in love with Irena and that he got to hate the Baron more and more. . . . Well, that's understandable. Irena's a very nice girl. She's a bit like Masha, she tends to get wrapped up in her own thoughts. (*To* IRENA.) But your disposition is more easy-going than Masha's. And yet Masha has a very nice disposition, too. I love her, I love my Masha.

(*From the back of the stage comes a shout: "Heigh-ho!"*)

IRENA (*starts*): Anything seems to startle me to-day. (*A pause.*) I've got everything ready, too. I'm sending my luggage off after lunch. The Baron and I are going to get married to-morrow, and directly afterwards we're moving to the brick-works, and the day after to-morrow I'm starting work at the school. So our new life will begin, God willing! When I was sitting for my teacher's diploma, I suddenly started crying for sheer joy, with a sort of feeling of blessedness. . . . (*A pause.*) The carrier will be coming for my luggage in a minute. . . .

KOOLYGHIN: That's all very well, but somehow I can't feel that it's meant to be serious. All ideas and theories, but nothing really serious. Anyway, I wish you luck from the bottom of my heart.

CHEBUTYKIN (*moved*): My dearest girl, my precious child! You've gone on so far ahead of me, I'll never catch you up now. I've got left behind like a bird which has grown too old and can't keep up with the rest of the flock. Fly away, my dears, fly away, and God be with you! (*A pause.*) It's a pity you've shaved your moustache off, Fiodor Illyich.

KOOLYGHIN: Don't keep on about it, please! (*Sighs.*) Well, the soldiers will be leaving to-day, and everything will go back to what it was before. Anyway, whatever they say, Masha is a good, loyal wife. Yes, I love her dearly and I'm thankful for what God has given me. Fate treats people so differently. For instance, there's an excise clerk here called Kozyrev. He was at school with me and he was expelled in his fifth year because he just couldn't grasp the *ut consecutivum.* He's dreadfully hard up now, and in bad health, too, and whenever I meet him, I just say to him: "Hullo, *ut consecutivum!*" "Yes," he replies, "that's just the trouble — *consecutivum*" . . . and he starts coughing. Whereas I — I've been lucky all my life. I'm happy, I've actually been awarded the order of Saint Stanislav, second class — and now I'm teaching the children the same old *ut consecutivum.* Of course, I'm clever, cleverer than plenty of other people, but happiness does not consist of merely being clever. . . .

(*In the house someone plays "The Maiden's Prayer."*)

IRENA: To-morrow night I shan't have to listen to "The Maiden's Prayer." I shan't have to meet Protopopov. . . . (*A pause.*) By the way, he's in the sitting-room. He's come again.

KOOLYGHIN: Hasn't our headmistress arrived yet?

IRENA: No, we've sent for her. If you only knew how difficult it is for me to live here by myself, without Olia! She lives at the school now; she's the headmistress and she's busy the whole day. And I'm here alone, bored, with nothing to do, and I hate the very room I live in. So I've just made up my mind — if I'm really not going to be able to live in Moscow, that's that. It's my fate, that's all. Nothing can be done about it. It's God's will, everything that happens, and that's the truth. Nikolai Lvovich proposed to me. . . . Well, I thought it over, and I made up my mind. He's such a nice man, it's really extraordinary how nice he is. . . . And then suddenly I felt as though my soul had grown wings, I felt more cheerful and so re-

lieved somehow that I wanted to work again. Just to start work!
. . . Only something happened yesterday, and now I feel as though
something mysterious is hanging over me. . . .

CHEBUTYKIN: Nonsense!

NATASHA (*speaking through the window*): Our headmistress!

KOOLYGHIN: Our headmistress has arrived! Let's go indoors.

(*Goes indoors with* IRENA.)

CHEBUTYKIN (*reads his paper and sings quietly to himself*): Tarara-
boom-di-ay. . . . I'm sitting on a tomb-di-ay. . . .

(MASHA *walks up to him;* ANDREY *passes across the back of the
stage pushing the pram.*)

MASHA: You look very comfortable sitting here. . . .

CHEBUTYKIN: Well, why not? Anything happening?

MASHA (*sits down*): No, nothing. (*A pause.*) Tell me something.
Were you in love with my mother?

CHEBUTYKIN: Yes, very much in love.

MASHA: Did she love you?

CHEBUTYKIN (*after a pause*): I can't remember now.

MASHA: Is my man here? Our cook Marfa always used to call her
policeman "my man." Is he here?

CHEBUTYKIN: Not yet.

MASHA: When you have to take your happiness in snatches, in little
bits, as I do, and then lose it, as I've lost it, you gradually get
hardened and bad-tempered. (*Points at her breast.*) Something's
boiling over inside me, here. (*Looking at* ANDREY, *who again crosses
the stage with the pram.*) There's Andrey, our dear brother. . . .
All our hopes are gone. It's the same as when thousands of people
haul a huge bell up into a tower. Untold labour and money is spent
on it, and then suddenly it falls and gets smashed. Suddenly, without rhyme or reason. It was the same with Andrey. . . .

ANDREY: When are they going to settle down in the house? They're
making such a row.

CHEBUTYKIN: They will soon. (*Looks at his watch.*) This is an old-
fashioned watch: it strikes. . . . (*Winds his watch which then
strikes.*) The first, second and fifth batteries will be leaving punctually at one o'clock. (*A pause.*) And I shall leave to-morrow.

ANDREY: For good?

CHEBUTYKIN: I don't know. I may return in about a year. Although,
God knows . . . it's all the same. . . .

(*The sounds of a harp and a violin are heard.*)

ANDREY: The town will seem quite empty. Life will be snuffed out like a candle. (*A pause.*) Something happened yesterday outside the theatre; everybody's talking about it. I'm the only one that doesn't seem to know about it.

CHEBUTYKIN: It was nothing. A lot of nonsense. Soliony started badgering the Baron, or something. The Baron lost his temper and insulted him, and in the end Soliony had to challenge him to a duel. (*Looks at his watch.*) I think it's time to go. . . . At half-past twelve, in the forest over there, on the other side of the river. . . . Bang-bang! (*Laughs.*) Soliony imagines he's like Lermontov. He actually writes poems. But, joking apart, this is his third duel.

MASHA: Whose third duel?

CHEBUTYKIN: Soliony's.

MASHA: What about the Baron?

CHEBUTYKIN: Well, what about him? (*A pause.*)

MASHA: My thoughts are all in a muddle. . . . But what I mean to say is that they shouldn't be allowed to fight. He might wound the Baron or even kill him.

CHEBUTYKIN: The Baron's a good enough fellow, but what does it really matter if there's one Baron more or less in the world? Well, let it be! It's all the same. (*The shouts of "Ah-oo!" and "Heigh-ho!" are heard from beyond the garden.*) That's Skvortsov, the second, shouting from the boat. He can wait.

ANDREY: I think it's simply immoral to fight a duel, or even to be present at one as a doctor.

CHEBUTYKIN: That's only how it seems. . . . We don't exist, nothing exists, it only seems to us that we do. . . . And what difference does it make?

MASHA: Talk, talk, nothing but talk all day long! . . . (*Starts to go.*) Having to live in this awful climate with the snow threatening to fall at any moment, and then on the top of it having to listen to all this sort of talk. . . . (*Stops.*) I won't go into the house, I can't bear going in there. . . . Will you let me know when Vershinin comes? . . . (*Walks off along the avenue.*) Look, the birds are beginning to fly away already! (*Looks up.*) Swans or geese. . . . Dear birds, happy birds. . . . (*Goes off.*)

ANDREY: Our house will seem quite deserted. The officers will go, you'll go, my sister will get married, and I'll be left alone in the house.

CHEBUTYKIN: What about your wife?

(*Enter* FERAPONT *with some papers.*)

ANDREY: My wife is my wife. She's a good, decent sort of woman . . . she's really very kind, too, but there's something about her which pulls her down to the level of an animal . . . a sort of mean, blind, thick-skinned animal — anyway, not a human being. I'm telling you this as a friend, the only person I can talk openly to. I love Natasha, it's true. But at times she appears to me so utterly vulgar, that I feel quite bewildered by it, and then I can't understand why, for what reasons I love her — or, anyway, did love her.

CHEBUTYKIN (*gets up*): Well, dear boy, I'm going away to-morrow and it may be we shall never see each other again. So I'll give you a bit of advice. Put on your hat, take a walking stick, and go away. . . . Go away, and don't ever look back. And the further you go, the better.

(SOLIONY *passes across the back of the stage accompanied by two officers. Seeing* CHEBUTYKIN, *he turns towards him, while the officers walk on.*)

SOLIONY: It's time, Doctor. Half past twelve already. (*Shakes hands with* ANDREY.)

CHEBUTYKIN: In a moment. Oh, I'm tired of you all. (*To* ANDREY.) Andriusha, if anyone asks for me, tell them I'll be back presently. (*Sighs.*) Oh-ho-ho!

SOLIONY: "He had no time to say 'Oh, oh!'
Before that bear had struck him low." . . .

(*Walks off with him.*) What are you groaning about, old man?

CHEBUTYKIN: Oh, well!

SOLIONY: How do you feel?

CHEBUTYKIN (*crossly*): Like a last year's bird's-nest.

SOLIONY: You needn't be so agitated about it, old boy. I shan't indulge in anything much, I'll just scorch his wings a little, like a woodcock's. (*Takes out a scent bottle and sprinkles scent over his hands.*) I've used up a whole bottle to-day, but my hands still smell. They smell like a corpse. (*A pause.*) Yes. . . . Do you remember that poem of Lermontov's?

"And he, rebellious, seeks a storm,
As if in storms there were tranquillity." . . .

CHEBUTYKIN: Yes.

"He had no time to say 'Oh, oh!'
Before that bear had struck him low."

(*Goes out with* SOLIONY. *Shouts of* "Heigh-ho!" *and* "Ah-oo!" *are heard. Enter* ANDREY *and* FERAPONT.)

FERAPONT: Will you sign these papers, please?

ANDREY (*with irritation*): Leave me alone! Leave me alone, for Heaven's sake. (*Goes off with the pram.*)

FERAPONT: Well, what am I supposed to do with the papers then? They are meant to be signed, aren't they? (*Goes to back of stage.*)

(*Enter* IRENA *and* TOOZENBACH, *the latter wearing a straw hat.* KOOLYGHIN *crosses the stage, calling:* "Ah-oo! Masha! Ah-oo!")

TOOZENBACH: I think he's the only person in the whole town who's glad that the army is leaving.

IRENA: That's quite understandable, really. (*A pause.*) The town will look quite empty.

TOOZENBACH: My dear, I'll be back in a moment.

IRENA: Where are you going?

TOOZENBACH: I must slip back to the town, and then . . . I want to see some of my colleagues off.

IRENA: It's not true. . . . Nikolai, why are you so absent-minded to-day? (*A pause.*) What happened outside the theatre last night?

TOOZENBACH (*with a movement of impatience*): I'll be back in an hour. . . . I'll be back with you again. (*Kisses her hands.*) My treasure! . . . (*Gazes into her eyes.*) It's five years since I first began to love you, and still I can't get used to it, and you seem more beautiful every day. What wonderful, lovely hair! What marvellous eyes! I'll take you away to-morrow. We'll work, we'll be rich, my dreams will come to life again. And you'll be happy! But — there's only one "but," only one — you don't love me!

IRENA: I can't help that! I'll be your wife, I'll be loyal and obedient to you, but I can't love you. . . . What's to be done? (*Weeps.*) I've never loved anyone in my life. Oh, I've had such dreams about being in love! I've been dreaming about it for ever so long, day and night . . . but somehow my soul seems like an expensive piano which someone has locked up and the key's got lost. (*A pause.*) Your eyes are so restless.

TOOZENBACH: I was awake all night. Not that there's anything to be afraid of in my life, nothing threatening. . . . Only the thought of that lost key torments me and keeps me awake. Say something to me. . . . (*A pause.*) Say something!

IRENA: What? What am I to say? What?

TOOZENBACH: Anything.

IRENA: Don't, my dear, don't. . . . (*A pause.*)

TOOZENBACH: Such trifles, such silly little things sometimes become so important suddenly, for no apparent reason! You laugh at them, just as you always have done, you still regard them as trifles, and yet you suddenly find they're in control, and you haven't the power to stop them. But don't let us talk about all that! Really, I feel quite elated. I feel as if I was seeing those fir-trees and maples and birches for the first time in my life. They all seem to be looking at me with a sort of inquisitive look and waiting for something. What beautiful trees — and how beautiful, when you think of it, life ought to be with trees like these! (*Shouts of "Ah-oo! Heigh-ho!" are heard.*) I must go, it's time. . . . Look at that dead tree, it's all dried-up, but it's still swaying in the wind along with the others. And in the same way, it seems to me that, if I die, I shall still have a share in life somehow or other. Goodbye, my dear. . . . (*Kisses her hands.*) Your papers, the ones you gave me, are on my desk, under the calendar.

IRENA: I'm coming with you.

TOOZENBACH (*alarmed*): No, no! (*Goes off quickly, then stops in the avenue.*) Irena!

IRENA: What?

TOOZENBACH (*not knowing what to say*): I didn't have any coffee this morning. Will you tell them to get some ready for me? (*Goes off quickly.*)

(IRENA *stands, lost in thought, then goes to the back of the stage and sits down on a swing. Enter* ANDREY *with the pram;* FERAPONT *appears.*)

FERAPONT: Andrey Serghyeech, the papers aren't mine, you know, they're the office papers. I didn't make them up.

ANDREY: Oh, where has all my past life gone to? — the time when I was young and gay and clever, when I used to have fine dreams and great thoughts, and the present and the future were bright with hope? Why do we become so dull and commonplace and uninteresting almost before we've begun to live? Why do we get lazy, indifferent, useless, unhappy? . . . This town's been in existence for two hundred years; a hundred thousand people live in it, but there's not one who's any different from all the others! There's never been a scholar or an artist or a saint in this place, never a single man sufficiently outstanding to make you feel passionately that you wanted to emulate him. People here do nothing but eat, drink and sleep. . . . Then they die and some more take their places, and they eat, drink and sleep, too, — and just to introduce a bit of variety into their lives, so as to avoid getting completely stupid with boredom, they indulge in their disgusting gossip and vodka and gambling and law-suits. The wives deceive their husbands, and the husbands lie to their wives, and pretend they don't see anything and don't hear anything. . . . And all this overwhelming vulgarity and pettiness crushes the children and puts out any spark they might have in them, so that they, too, become miserable, half-dead creatures, just like one another and just like their parents! . . . (*To* FERAPONT, *crossly.*) What do you want?

FERAPONT: What? Here are the papers to sign.

ANDREY: What a nuisance you are!

FERAPONT (*hands him the papers*): The porter at the finance department told me just now . . . he said last winter they had two hundred degrees of frost in Petersburg.

ANDREY: I hate the life I live at present, but oh! the sense of elation when I think of the future! Then I feel so light-hearted, such a sense of release! I seem to see light ahead, light and freedom. I see myself free, and my children, too, — free from idleness, free from *kvass*, free from eternal meals of goose and cabbage, free from after-dinner naps, free from all this degrading parasitism! . . .

FERAPONT: They say two thousand people were frozen to death. They say everyone was scared stiff. It was either in Petersburg or in Moscow, I can't remember exactly.

ANDREY (*with sudden emotion, tenderly*): My dear sisters, my dear good sisters! (*Tearfully.*) Masha, my dear sister! . . .

NATASHA (*through the window*): Who's that talking so loudly there? Is that you, Andriusha? You'll wake Sofochka. *Il ne faut pas faire du bruit, la Sophie est dormie déjà. Vous êtes un ours.* (*Getting angry.*) If you want to talk, give the pram to someone else. Ferapont, take the pram from the master.

FERAPONT: Yes, Madam. (*Takes the pram.*)

ANDREY (*shamefacedly*): I was talking quietly.

NATASHA (*in the window, caressing her small son*): Bobik! Naughty Bobik! Aren't you a naughty boy!

ANDREY (*glancing through the papers*): All right, I'll go through them and sign them if they need it. You can take them back to the office later. (*Goes into the house, reading the papers.*)

(FERAPONT *wheels the pram into the garden.*)

NATASHA (*in the window*): What's Mummy's name, Bobik? You darling! And who's that lady? Auntie Olia. Say: "Hullo, Auntie Olia."

(*Two street musicians, a man and a girl, enter and begin to play on a violin and a harp;* VERSHININ, OLGA *and* ANFISA *come out of the house and listen in silence for a few moments; then* IRENA *approaches them.*)

OLGA: Our garden's like a public road; everybody goes through it. Nanny, give something to the musicians.

ANFISA (*giving them money*): Go along now, God bless you, good people! (*The musicians bow and go away.*) Poor, homeless folk! Whoever would go dragging round the streets playing tunes if he had enough to eat? (*To* IRENA.) How are you, Irenushka? (*Kisses her.*) Ah, my child, what a life I'm having! Such comfort! In a large flat at the school with Oliushka — and no rent to pay, either! The Lord's been kind to me in my old age. I've never had such a comfortable time in my life, old sinner that I am! A big flat, and no rent to pay, and a whole room to myself, with my own bed. All free. Sometimes when I wake up in the night I begin to think, and then — Oh, Lord! Oh, Holy Mother of God! — there's no one happier in the world than me!

VERSHININ (*glances at his watch*): We shall be starting in a moment, Olga Serghyeevna. It's time I went. (*A pause.*) I wish you all the happiness in the world . . . everything. . . . Where's Maria Serghyeevna?

IRENA: She's somewhere in the garden. I'll go and look for her.

VERSHININ: That's kind of you. I really must hurry.

ANFISA: I'll come and help to look for her. (*Calls out.*) Mashenka, ah-oo! (*Goes with* IRENA *towards the far end of the garden.*) Ah-oo! Ah-oo!

VERSHININ: Everything comes to an end. Well, here we are — and now it's going to be "good-bye." (*Looks at his watch.*) The city gave us a sort of farewell lunch. There was champagne, and the mayor made a speech, and I ate and listened, but in spirit I was with you here. . . . (*Glances round the garden.*) I've grown so . . . so accustomed to you.

OLGA: Shall we meet again some day, I wonder?

VERSHININ: Most likely not! (*A pause.*) My wife and the two little girls will be staying on here for a month or two. Please, if anything happens, if they need anything. . . .

OLGA: Yes, yes, of course. You needn't worry about that. (*A pause.*) To-morrow there won't be a single officer or soldier in the town. . . . All that will be just a memory, and, of course, a new life will begin for us here. . . . (*A pause.*) Nothing ever happens as we'd like it to. I didn't want to be a headmistress, and yet now I am one. It means we shan't be going to live in Moscow. . . .

VERSHININ: Well. . . . Thank you for everything. Forgive me if ever I've done anything. . . . I've talked a lot too much, far too much. . . . Forgive me for that, don't think too unkindly of me.

OLGA (*wipes her eyes*): Now . . . why is Masha so long coming?

VERSHININ: What else can I tell you now it's time to say "good-bye"? What shall I philosophize about now? . . . (*Laughs.*) Yes, life is difficult. It seems quite hopeless for a lot of us, just a kind of impasse. . . . And yet you must admit that it is gradually getting easier and brighter, and it's clear that the time isn't far off when the light will spread everywhere. (*Looks at his watch.*) Time, it's time for me to go. . . . In the old days the human race was always making war, its entire existence was taken up with campaigns, advances, retreats, victories. . . . But now all that's out of date, and in its place there's a huge vacuum, clamouring to be filled. Humanity is passionately seeking something to fill it with and, of course, it will find something some day. Oh! If only it would happen soon! (*A pause.*) If only we could educate the industrious people and make the educated people industrious. . . . (*Looks at his watch.*) I really must go. . . .

OLGA: Here she comes!

(*Enter* MASHA.)

VERSHININ: I've come to say good-bye. . . .

(OLGA *walks off and stands a little to one side so as not to interfere with their leave-taking.*)

MASHA (*looking into his face*): Good-bye! . . . (*A long kiss.*)

OLGA: That'll do, that'll do.

MASHA (*sobs loudly.*)

VERSHININ: Write to me. . . . Don't forget me! Let me go . . . it's time. Olga Serghyeevna, please take her away . . . I must go . . . I'm late already. . . . (*Deeply moved, kisses* OLGA's *hands, then embraces* MASHA *once again and goes out quickly.*)

OLGA: That'll do, Masha! Don't, my dear, don't. . . .

(*Enter* KOOLYGHIN.)

KOOLYGHIN (*embarrassed*): Never mind, let her cry, let her. . . . My dear Masha, my dear, sweet Masha. . . . You're my wife, and I'm happy in spite of everything. . . . I'm not complaining, I've no reproach to make — not a single one. . . . Olga here is my witness. . . . We'll start our life over again in the same old way, and you won't hear a word from me . . . not a hint. . . .

MASHA (*suppressing her sobs*): "A green oak grows by a curving shore, And round that oak hangs a golden chain." . . . "A golden chain round that oak." . . . Oh, I'm going mad. . . . By a curving shore . . . a green oak. . . .

OLGA: Calm yourself, Masha, calm yourself. . . . Give her some water.

MASHA: I'm not crying any more. . . .

KOOLYGHIN: She's not crying any more . . . she's a good girl.

(*The hollow sound of a gun-shot is heard in the distance.*)

MASHA: "A green oak grows by a curving shore, And round that oak hangs a golden chain." . . . A green cat . . . a green oak . . . I've got it all mixed up. . . . (*Drinks water.*) My life's messed up. . . . I don't want anything now. . . . I'll calm down in a moment. . . . it doesn't matter. . . . What *is* "the curving shore"? Why does it keep coming into my head all the time? My thoughts are all mixed up.

(*Enter* IRENA.)

OLGA: Calm down, Masha. That's right . . . good girl! . . . Let's go indoors.

MASHA (*irritably*): I'm not going in there! (*Sobs, but immediately checks herself.*) I don't go into that house now, and I'm not going to. . . .

IRENA: Let's sit down together for a moment, and not talk about anything. I'm going away to-morrow, you know. . . .

(*A pause.*)

KOOLYGHIN: Yesterday I took away a false beard and a moustache from a boy in the third form. I've got them here. (*Puts them on.*) Do I look like our German teacher? . . . (*Laughs.*) I do, don't I? The boys are funny.

MASHA: It's true, you do look like that German of yours.

OLGA (*laughs*): Yes, he does.

(MASHA *cries.*)

IRENA: That's enough, Masha!

KOOLYGHIN: Very much like him, I think!

(*Enter* NATASHA.)

NATASHA (*to the maid*): What? Oh, yes. Mr. Protopopov is going to keep an eye on Sofochka, and Andrey Serghyeevich is going to take Bobik out in the pram. What a lot of work these children make! . . . (*To* IRENA.) Irena, you're really leaving to-morrow? What a pity! Do stay just another week, won't you? (*Catching sight of* KOOLYGHIN, *shrieks; he laughs and takes off the false beard and moustache.*) Get away with you! How you scared me! (*To* IRENA.) I've grown so accustomed to you being here. . . . You mustn't think it's going to be easy for me to be without you. I'll get Andrey and his old violin to move into your room: he can saw away at it as much as he likes there. And then we'll move Sofochka into his room. She's such a wonderful child, really! Such a lovely little girl! This morning she looked at me with such a sweet expression, and then she said: "Ma-mma!"

KOOLYGHIN: It's quite true, she is a beautiful child.

NATASHA: So to-morrow I'll be alone here. (*Sighs.*) I'll have this fir-tree avenue cut down first, then that maple tree over there. It looks so awful in the evenings. . . . (*To* IRENA.) My dear, that belt you're wearing doesn't suit you at all. Not at all in good taste. You want something brighter to go with that dress. . . . I'll tell them to put flowers all round here, lots of flowers, so that we get plenty of scent from them. . . . (*Sternly.*) Why is there a fork lying on this seat? (*Going into the house, to the maid.*) Why is that fork left on the seat there? (*Shouts.*) Don't answer me back!

KOOLYGHIN: There she goes again.

(*A band plays a military march off stage; all listen.*)

OLGA: They're going.

(*Enter* CHEBUTYKIN.)

MASHA: The soldiers are going. Well. . . . Happy journey to them! (*To her husband.*) We must go home. . . . Where's my hat and cape? . . .

KOOLYGHIN: I took them indoors. I'll bring them at once.

OLGA: Yes, we can go home now. It's time.

CHEBUTYKIN: Olga Serghyeevna!

OLGA: What is it? (*A pause.*) What?

CHEBUTYKIN: Nothing. . . . I don't know quite how to tell you. . . . (*Whispers into her ear.*)

OLGA (*frightened*): It can't be true!

CHEBUTYKIN: Yes . . . a bad business. . . . I'm so tired . . . quite worn out. . . . I don't want to say another word. . . . (*With annoyance.*) Anyway, nothing matters! . . .

MASHA: What's happened?

OLGA (*puts her arms round* IRENA): What a dreadful day! . . . I don't know how to tell you, dear. . . .

IRENA: What is it? Tell me quickly, what is it? For Heaven's sake! . . . (*Cries.*)

CHEBUTYKIN: The Baron's just been killed in a duel.

IRENA (*cries quietly*): I knew it, I knew it. . . .

CHEBUTYKIN (*goes to the back of the stage and sits down*): I'm tired. . . . (*Takes a newspaper out of his pocket.*) Let them cry for a bit. . . . (*Sings quietly to himself.*) Tarara-boom-di-ay, I'm sitting on a tomb-di-ay. . . . What difference does it make? . . .

(*The three sisters stand huddled together.*)

MASHA: Oh, listen to that band! They're leaving us . . . one of them's gone for good . . . for ever! We're left alone . . . to start our lives all over again. We must go on living . . . we must go on living. . . .

IRENA (*puts her head on* OLGA'S *breast*): Some day people will know why such things happen, and what the purpose of all this suffering is. . . . Then there won't be any more riddles. . . . Meanwhile we must go on living . . . and working. Yes, we must just go on working! To-morrow I'll go away alone and teach in a school somewhere; I'll give my life to people who need it. . . . It's autumn now, winter will soon be here, and the snow will cover everything . . . but I'll go on working and working! . . .

OLGA (*puts her arms round both her sisters*): How cheerfully and jauntily that band's playing — really I feel as if I wanted to live! Merciful God! The years will pass, and we shall all be gone for good and quite forgotten. . . . Our faces and our voices will be forgotten and people won't even know that there were once three of us here. . . . But our sufferings may mean happiness for the people who come after us. . . . There'll be a time when peace and happiness reign in the world, and then we shall be remembered kindly and blessed. No, my dear sisters, life isn't finished for us yet! We're going to live! The band is playing so cheerfully and joyfully — maybe, if we wait a little longer, we shall find out why we live, why we suffer. . . . Oh, if we only knew, if only we knew!

(*The music grows fainter and fainter.* KOOLYGHIN, *smiling happily, brings out the hat and the cape.* ANDREY *enters; he is pushing the pram with* BOBIK *sitting in it.*)

CHEBUTYKIN (*sings quietly to himself*): Tarara-boom-di-ay. . . . I'm sitting on a tomb-di-ay. . . . (*Reads the paper.*) What does it matter? Nothing matters!

OLGA: If only we knew, if only we knew! . . .

WHEN *Three Sisters* was first performed by the Stanislavsky ensemble at the Moscow Art Theater in 1901, even Chekhov's own friends were less than enthusiastic. One can, perhaps, understand why, for the greatness of the play may not reveal itself readily; it is achieved against such heavy odds. The play seems to lack plot, and its main characters are lethargic melancholiacs, sometimes pathetic, sometimes laughable, invariably frustrated, musing upon themselves and a vague future in rhapsodic tirades no one listens to, making ineffectual little gestures toward happiness, wasting their small lives in boredom and apathy. How can there be greatness here? One might conceive of Chekhov telling himself that life, after all, does not run in plots, but readers who have learned to admire the plot structures of *Oedipus Rex*, *Macbeth*, and *Tartuffe* will retort that absolute realism is an impossibility in art, that life is formless and art nothing if not form, and that realism as a literary ideal therefore should not be measured against standards of stenographic or photographic reproductions of petty life in the raw.

This is all true, but it does not finish Chekhov. He knew — the plays prove it — that a dramatist is an artist who gives form to his vision of life in scenic action. If Chekhov seems difficult or dull, it is not because his plays lack action, but because their kind of action differs from that of most other traditionally great plays. He writes not about what happens to people but about what does not happen to them (which, of course, for literary purposes is a kind of happening). In Ibsen there is a core of melodrama that makes for suspense and coherent action, in Shaw the tonic of clashing ideologies, in Strindberg the nightmarish fascination of evil ghosts. In Chekhov there are only gray little lives captured with perfect sharpness of vision. The dismal drabness, the wearying, frustrating monotony — that is life. "All I wanted to do," Chekhov wrote to a friend, "was to say to people, 'Have a look at yourselves and see how bad and dreary your lives are!' The important thing is that people should realize that, for when they do, they will certainly create a better life for themselves." Chekhov is forever staging Thoreau's "lives of quiet desperation." That nothing great happens to people who are not great is precisely the point. Chekhov was rightly irritated when he heard his plays called gloomy and tragic.

Still, one does not quite explain Chekhov's art by talking of the action of non-happening. Perhaps this is why so much has been written about mood and atmosphere in his plays: a blend of pity for good people caught in the rut of existence, of irony and gentle laughter at their absorption in their frustrations and their inability to free themselves and act on their idealism, of knowledge of the isolation of the human heart. Because there is no plot that continuously demands to be furthered, scenes and speeches can be allowed to play themselves out in the varying tempos and little irrelevancies by which life proceeds in the ordinary living room. Compared to Chekhov's, Ibsen's domestic scenes may seem crude and contrived. But the emphasis on the delicate atmosphere that surrounds these fragile lives has obscured Chekhov's command of action. Things, after all, do happen in his plays. In *Three Sisters* visitors call, gifts are given, lunches eaten, pictures taken, papers signed, jokes told, babies wheeled, love made, fires seen. And these little events, though not causally nor logically connected, constitute more than a random phase in an infinite progress of triviality. They make an action which points backward (life in Moscow) and forward (what will life be like for the sisters from now on?) and yet has definite beginning and end. In general terms, it is an action of good life atrophying and mean life succeeding; in specific terms, the gradual disappointment of the sisters' hope for a better life. Season and circumstance of the first and the last act not only set the limits for the action; they also define the nature of its movement.

From the mass of events that fills the interval, five main strands of action emerge. Each of the first four involves a Prozorov, and each ends in passive frustration. There is the love of Masha and Vershinin — romantic, mature, and adulterous. In double contrast, there is Toozenbach's legitimate but unreciprocated love for Irena. There is Olga's rise to the headmistress-ship she doesn't want, the making of an old maid. And there is Andrey's moral dissolution, marked by the lessening of his ambition and his surrender to his wife. The wife's, Natasha's, is the fifth, the non-Prozorov action. She is the play's antagonist, whose rise to power we see at four different stages. The coarseness of her being and the nature of her development are evident in the growing frequency of her remarks in French, the language of the gentility she makes pretense to, and by the impression she somehow gives of aging faster than her sisters-in-law. The action spans five years — long enough for Natasha to change from flustered girl to formidable matron.

Around these opposite dramatic movements Chekhov weaves the texture of his play. He juxtaposes scenes that subtly modify one another by varying in tempo and mood. Near the opening of the play Olga's passionate outburst of longing for Moscow is interrupted by Chebutykin's and Toozenbach's voices from the adjoining room: "The devil you have! — It's nonsense, I agree." We have no idea what they are talking about, but in context the seven words assume tremendous dramatic voltage. Near the end of the second act the idiotic argument between Soliony and Chebutykin is followed by a little interlude of pleasant though equally silly dancing and singing. Then comes another nonsense argument — about the number of universities in Moscow. Then there are again movement and physical activity as the entertainment is cut short by Natasha's demand that everyone leave so little Bobik can have quiet. The stage, crowded a moment ago, is empty. Then Andrey and Soliony dispiritedly discuss marriage; then Soliony tries to make love to Irena. The sequence of discordant little scenes continues till Natasha (devoted mother a few minutes ago) goes out for a sleigh ride with her admirer and Irena is left alone and the words "Moscow! Moscow! Moscow!" fall from her lips in an agony of longing. A succession of such scenes does not constitute a plot in any ordinary sense, but in the shifts from farce to pathos, from triviality to importance, from activity and dramatic progress to bickering stasis, and from ensemble scene to soliloquy, the sequence builds a scenic image that both commands instant belief as reality and embodies Chekhov's theme about the attrition of soul in the meaninglessness of everyday. "Meaning?" says Toozenbach once when Masha suggests that existence has some purpose. "Look out there, it's snowing. What's the meaning of that?"

Just beyond the pettiness on stage is the outside world, represented by the pressures of unseen characters. To list them and decide how they affect the characters we *do* see is to become aware of an added dimension in the play, a kind of natural force, built-in facts of a life that systematically defeats human happiness.

Symbolism is still another strand in the rich texture. The frequent pauses, the anecdotes nobody listens to, the philosophical discussions that end nowhere, the fragments of song and poetry that nobody understands, the way remarks have of being misunderstood or of just missing being relevant to the talk of the moment — these are eminently performable dialogue symbols of human isolation. Chebutykin's and Soliony's speeches are particularly striking instances of the way the dialogue emphasizes failure in human communication. Generally, the verbal symbolism eludes precise interpretation and is for that reason all the more effective. Specifying which characters can be considered birds of passage and in what sense is not only unnecessary but ruinous. The power of the image goes beyond any symbolic function and resists reduction to mere meaning. It carries its own weight as tonal element.

The scenic symbols are more definite in significance. The military uniforms, Chebutykin's unrelated clippings of newspaper trivia, the cards in the game of patience, Natasha's sinister appearance with a lighted candle during the fire, Soliony's ominously futile bottle of perfume — all are images of central abstracts in the play. At the same time, they are the stuff of reality: acts, facts, objects — things that *are* before they signify and that signify at all only because they so unmistakably are.

The chief symbol in the play is Moscow — the object of the sisters' dream of escape. But Moscow is a curiously indeterminate quality. Nobody seems really to know it. One of our chief informants is old, befuddled Ferapont. Is it true that a rope is stretched across the city? If so, what for? How many universities are there? Do Moscow merchants kill themselves on pancakes? It is the city where love waits for Irena and where Andrey will become a professor, but to Vershinin it is a city of gloomy bridges, without birch trees. How real is the city of the sisters' longing? To ask the question is to doubt the validity of their frustration, to suggest that they build their sorrow on an illusion and are escaping from a reality they could improve upon had they but the will and the strength to face it. The question is never answered, but in its ambivalence lies much of Chekhov's poetic realism.

Three Sisters proves nothing — except, perhaps, that life can be dreary, and we need no playwright to tell us that. Almost its last words are Chebutykin's, the chorus-like voice of total negation, whose life has become so meaningless that he denies existence itself. The only answer to his nihilistic mutter that "nothing matters" is Olga's "If only we knew, if only we knew!" Knew what? Whether Chebutykin is right, that nothing matters? Or, the meaning of suffering? The wish is cryptic, but the stage image in which it is uttered suggests that all three sisters share it.

There are people — sensible people among them — who find *Three Sisters* a big bore: "four acts about not going to Moscow." But the reader who is tempted to dismiss the play because he feels that people in reality are not so ineffectual and so passively unhappy as Chekhov's ("Why, in the name of heaven, don't they just *go!*") might keep in mind that the criterion for literary excellence is not a statistical average. Chekhov's dramatic world came into being at least partly because of his exasperation with the lack of purpose and dignity in the lives of a certain class of Russian society at a certain time (a reason which has endeared him to Soviet critics). The fact that his exasperation was justified is irrelevant here, as are the causes for the middle-class lassitude. What *is* relevant is that in recording his sympathetic-ironic attitude to its victims Chekhov created human beings whose little tragicomedies of attrition somehow resemble our own.

August Strindberg
THE GHOST SONATA
Translated by Elizabeth Sprigge

Characters

THE OLD MAN, *Hummel, a Company Director*

THE STUDENT, *Arkenholtz*

THE MILKMAID, *an apparition*

THE CARETAKER'S WIFE

THE CARETAKER

THE LADY IN BLACK, *the daughter of the Caretaker's Wife and the Dead Man. Also referred to as the Dark Lady*

THE COLONEL

THE MUMMY, *the Colonel's wife*

THE GIRL, *the Colonel's daughter, actually the daughter of the Old Man*

THE ARISTOCRAT, *Baron Skanskorg. Engaged to the Lady in Black*

JOHANSSON, *the Old Man's servant*

BENGTSSON, *the Colonel's servant*

THE FIANCÉE, *a white-haired old woman, once betrothed to the Old Man*

THE COOK

A MAIDSERVANT

BEGGARS

SCENE I

Outside the house. The corner of the façade of a modern house, showing the ground floor above, and the street in front. The

Reprinted by permission of Willis Kingsley Wing. Copyright © 1951, by Prentice-Hall, Inc. All rights whatsoever in this play are strictly reserved and any applications for performances, etc. should be made to Willis Kingsley Wing, 24 E. 38th Street, New York 16, N.Y.

ground floor terminates on the right in the Round Room, above which, on the first floor, is a balcony with a flagstaff. The windows of the Round Room face the street in front of the house, and at the corner look on to the suggestion of a side-street running toward the back. At the beginning of the scene the blinds of the Round Room are down. When, later, they are raised, the white marble statue of a young woman can be seen, surrounded with palms and brightly lighted by rays of sunshine.

To the left of the Round Room is the Hyacinth Room; its window filled with pots of hyacinths, blue, white and pink. Further left, at the back, is an imposing double front door with laurels in tubs on either side of it. The doors are wide open, showing a staircase of white marble with a banister of mahogany and brass. To the left of the front door is another ground-floor window, with a window-mirror.[1] On the balcony rail in the corner above the Round Room are a blue silk quilt and two white pillows. The windows to the left of this are hung with white sheets.[2]

In the foreground, in front of the house, is a green bench; to the right a street drinking-fountain, to the left an advertisement column.

It is a bright Sunday morning, and as the curtain rises the bells of several churches, some near, some far away, are ringing.

On the staircase the LADY IN BLACK *stands motionless.*

The CARETAKER'S WIFE *sweeps the doorstep, then polishes the brass on the door and waters the laurels.*

In a wheel-chair by the advertisement column sits the OLD MAN, *reading a newspaper. His hair and beard are white and he wears spectacles.*

The MILKMAID *comes round the corner on the right, carrying milk bottles in a wire basket. She is wearing a summer dress with brown shoes, black stockings and a white cap. She takes off her cap and hangs it on the fountain, wipes the perspiration from her forehead, washes her hands and arranges her hair, using the water as a mirror.*

A steamship bell is heard, and now and then the silence is broken by the deep notes of an organ in a nearby church.

After a few moments, when all is silent and the MILKMAID *has finished her toilet, the* STUDENT *enters from the left. He has had a sleepless night and is unshaven. He goes straight up to the fountain. There is a pause before he speaks.*

---

[1] Set at an angle inside the window, so as to show what is going on in the street.
[2] Sign of mourning.

STUDENT: May I have the cup?

(*The* MILKMAID *clutches the cup to her.*)

Haven't you finished yet?

(*The* MILKMAID *looks at him with horror.*)

OLD MAN (*to himself*): Who's he talking to? I don't see anybody. Is he crazy? (*He goes on watching them in great astonishment.*)

STUDENT (*to the* MILKMAID): What are you staring at? Do I look so terrible? Well, I've had no sleep, and of course you think I've been making a night of it . . .

(*The* MILKMAID *stays just as she is.*)

You think I've been drinking, eh? Do I smell of liquor?

(*The* MILKMAID *does not change.*)

I haven't shaved, I know. Give me a drink of water, girl. I've earned it. (*Pause.*) Oh well, I suppose I'll have to tell you. I spent the whole night dressing wounds and looking after the injured. You see, I was there when that house collapsed last night. Now you know.

(*The* MILKMAID *rinses the cup and gives him a drink.*)

Thanks.

(*The* MILKMAID *stands motionless. Slowly.*)

Will you do me a great favor? (*Pause.*) The thing is, my eyes, as you can see, are inflamed, but my hands have been touching wounds and corpses, so it would be dangerous to put them near my eyes. Will you take my handkerchief — it's quite clean — and dip it in the fresh water and bathe my eyes? Will you do this? Will you play the good Samaritan?

(*The* MILKMAID *hesitates, but does as he bids.*)

Thank you, my dear. (*He takes out his purse. She makes a gesture of refusal.*) Forgive my stupidity, but I'm only half-awake. . . .

(*The* MILKMAID *disappears.*)

OLD MAN (*to the* STUDENT): Excuse me speaking to you, but I heard you say you were at the scene of the accident last night. I was just reading about it in the paper.

STUDENT: Is it in the paper already?

OLD MAN: The whole thing, including your portrait. But they regret that they have been unable to find out the name of the splendid young student. . . .

STUDENT: Really? (*Glances at the paper.*) Yes, that's me. Well I never!

OLD MAN: Who was it you were talking to just now?

STUDENT: Didn't you see? (*Pause.*)

OLD MAN: Would it be impertinent to inquire — what in fact your name is?

STUDENT: What would be the point? I don't care for publicity. If you get any praise, there's always disapproval too. The art of running people down has been developed to such a pitch. . . . Besides, I don't want any reward.

OLD MAN: You're well off, perhaps.

STUDENT: No, indeed. On the contrary, I'm very poor.

OLD MAN: Do you know, it seems to me I've heard your voice before. When I was young I had a friend who pronounced certain words just as you do. I've never met anyone else with quite that pronunciation. Only him — and you. Are you by any chance related to Mr. Arkenholtz, the merchant?

STUDENT: He was my father.

OLD MAN: Strange are the paths of fate. I saw you when you were an infant, under very painful circumstances.

STUDENT: Yes, I understand I came into the world in the middle of a bankruptcy.

OLD MAN: Just that.

STUDENT: Perhaps I might ask your name.

OLD MAN: I am Mr. Hummel.

STUDENT: Are you the? . . . I remember that . . .

OLD MAN: Have you often heard my name mentioned in your family?

STUDENT: Yes.

OLD MAN: And mentioned perhaps with a certain aversion?

(*The* STUDENT *is silent.*)

Yes, I can imagine it. You were told, I suppose, that I was the man who ruined your father? All who ruin themselves through foolish speculations consider they were ruined by those they couldn't fool. (*Pause.*) Now these are the facts. Your father robbed me of seventeen thousand crowns — the whole of my savings at that time.

STUDENT: It's queer that the same story can be told in two such different ways.

OLD MAN: You surely don't believe I'm telling you what isn't true?

STUDENT: What am I to believe? My father didn't lie.

OLD MAN: That is so true. A father never lies. But I too am a father, and so it follows . . .

STUDENT: What are you driving at?

OLD MAN: I saved your father from disaster, and he repaid me with all the frightful hatred that is born of an obligation to be grateful. He taught his family to speak ill of me.

STUDENT: Perhaps you made him ungrateful by poisoning your help with unnecessary humiliation.

OLD MAN: All help is humiliating, sir.

STUDENT: What do you want from me?

OLD MAN: I'm not asking for the money, but if you will render me a few small services, I shall consider myself well paid. You see that I am a cripple. Some say it is my own fault; others lay the blame on my parents. I prefer to blame life itself, with its pitfalls. For if you escape one snare, you fall headlong into another. In any case, I am unable to climb stairs or ring doorbells, and that is why I am asking you to help me.

STUDENT: What can I do?

OLD MAN: To begin with, push my chair so that I can read those play-bills. I want to see what is on tonight.

STUDENT (*pushing the chair*): Haven't you got an attendant?

OLD MAN: Yes, but he has gone on an errand. He'll be back soon. Are you a medical student?

STUDENT: No, I am studying languages, but I don't know at all what I'm going to do.

OLD MAN: Aha! Are you good at mathematics?

STUDENT: Yes, fairly.

OLD MAN: Good. Perhaps you would like a job.

STUDENT: Yes, why not?

OLD MAN: Splendid. (*He studies the playbills.*) They are doing *The Valkyrie* for the matinée. That means the Colonel will be there with his daughter, and as he always sits at the end of the sixth row, I'll put you next to him. Go to that telephone kiosk please and order a ticket for seat eighty-two in the sixth row.

STUDENT: Am I to go to the Opera in the middle of the day?

OLD MAN: Yes. Do as I tell you and things will go well with you. I want to see you happy, rich and honored. Your début last night as the brave rescuer will make you famous by tomorrow and then your name will be worth something.

STUDENT (*going to the telephone kiosk*): What an odd adventure!

OLD MAN: Are you a gambler?

STUDENT: Yes, unfortunately.

OLD MAN: We'll make it fortunately. Go on now, telephone.

(*The* STUDENT *goes. The* OLD MAN *reads his paper. The* LADY IN BLACK *comes out on to the pavement and talks to the* CARE- TAKER'S WIFE. *The* OLD MAN *listens, but the audience hears noth- ing. The* STUDENT *returns.*)

Did you fix it up?

STUDENT: It's done.

OLD MAN: You see that house?

STUDENT: Yes, I've been looking at it a lot. I passed it yesterday when the sun was shining on the windowpanes, and I imagined all the beauty and elegance there must be inside. I said to my companion: "Think of living up there in the top flat, with a beautiful young wife, two pretty little children and an income of twenty thousand crowns a year."

OLD MAN: So that's what you said. That's what you said. Well, well! I too am very fond of this house.

STUDENT: Do you speculate in houses?

OLD MAN: Mm — yes. But not in the way you mean.

STUDENT: Do you know the people who live here?

OLD MAN: Every one of them. At my age one knows everybody, and their parents and grandparents too, and one's always related to them in some way or other. I am just eighty, but no one knows me — not really. I take an interest in human destiny.

(*The blinds of the Round Room are drawn up. The* COLONEL *is seen, wearing mufti. He looks at the thermometer outside one of the windows, then turns back into the room and stands in front of the marble statue.*)

Look, that's the Colonel, whom you will sit next to this afternoon.

STUDENT: Is he — the Colonel? I don't understand any of this, but it's like a fairy story.

OLD MAN: My whole life's like a book of fairy stories, sir. And although the stories are different, they are held together by one thread, and the main theme constantly recurs.

STUDENT: Who is that marble statue of?

OLD MAN: That, naturally, is his wife.

STUDENT: Was she such a wonderful person?

OLD MAN: Er . . . yes.

STUDENT: Tell me.

OLD MAN: We can't judge people, young man. If I were to tell you that she left him, that he beat her, that she returned to him and mar- ried him a second time, and that now she is sitting inside there like a mummy, worshipping her own statue — then you would think me crazy.

STUDENT: I don't understand.

OLD MAN: I didn't think you would. Well, then we have the window with the hyacinths. His daughter lives there. She has gone out for a ride, but she will be home soon.

STUDENT: And who is the dark lady talking to the caretaker?

OLD MAN: Well, that's a bit complicated, but it is connected with the dead man, up there where you see the white sheets.

STUDENT: Why, who was he?

OLD MAN: A human being like you or me, but the most conspicuous thing about him was his vanity. If you were a Sunday child, you would see him presently come out of that door to look at the Consulate flag flying at half-mast. He was, you understand, a Consul, and he reveled in coronets and lions and plumed hats and colored ribbons.

STUDENT: Sunday child, you say? I'm told I was born on a Sunday.

OLD MAN: No, were you really? I might have known it. I saw it from the color of your eyes. Then you can see what others can't. Have you noticed that?

STUDENT: I don't know what others do see, but at times. . . . Oh, but one doesn't talk of such things!

OLD MAN: I was almost sure of it. But you can talk to me, because I understand such things.

STUDENT: Yesterday, for instance . . . I was drawn to that obscure little street where later on the house collapsed. I went there and stopped in front of that building which I had never seen before. Then I noticed a crack in the wall. . . . I heard the floor boards snapping. . . . I dashed over and picked up a child that was passing under the wall. . . . The next moment the house collapsed. I was saved, but in my arms, which I thought held the child, was nothing at all.

OLD MAN: Yes, yes, just as I thought. Tell me something. Why were you gesticulating that way just now by the fountain? And why were you talking to yourself?

STUDENT: Didn't you see the milkmaid I was talking to?

OLD MAN (*in horror*): Milkmaid?

STUDENT: Surely. The girl who handed me the cup.

OLD MAN: Really? So that's what was going on. Ah well, I haven't second sight, but there are things I can do.

(THE FIANCÉE *is now seen to sit down by the window which has the window-mirror.*)

Look at that old woman in the window. Do you see her? Well, she was my fiancée once, sixty years ago. I was twenty. Don't be alarmed. She doesn't recognize me. We see one another every day, and it makes no impression on me, although once we vowed to love one another eternally. Eternally!

STUDENT: How foolish you were in those days! We never talk to our girls like that.

OLD MAN: Forgive us, young man. We didn't know any better. But can you see that that old woman was once young and beautiful?

STUDENT: It doesn't show. And yet there's some charm in her looks. I can't see her eyes.

(*The* CARETAKER'S WIFE *comes out with a basket of chopped fir branches.*[3])

OLD MAN: Ah, the caretaker's wife! That dark lady is her daughter by the dead man. That's why her husband was given the job of caretaker. But the dark lady has a suitor, who is an aristocrat with great expectations. He is in the process of getting a divorce — from his present wife, you understand. She's presenting him with a stone mansion in order to be rid of him. This aristocratic suitor is the son-in-law of the dead man, and you can see his bedclothes being aired on the balcony upstairs. It is complicated, I must say.

STUDENT: It's fearfully complicated.

OLD MAN: Yes, that it is, internally and externally, although it looks quite simple.

STUDENT: But then who was the dead man?

OLD MAN: You asked me that just now, and I answered. If you were to look round the corner, where the tradesmen's entrance is, you would see a lot of poor people whom he used to help — when it suited him.

STUDENT: He was a kind man then.

OLD MAN: Yes — sometimes.

STUDENT: Not always?

OLD MAN: No-o. That's the way of people. Now, sir, will you push my chair a little, so that it gets into the sun. I'm horribly cold. When you're never able to move about, the blood congeals. I'm going to die soon, I know that, but I have a few things to do first. Take my hand and feel how cold I am.

STUDENT (*taking it*): Yes, inconceivably. (*He shrinks back, trying in vain to free his hand.*)

OLD MAN: Don't leave me. I am tired now and lonely, but I haven't always been like this, you know. I have an enormously long life be-

---

[3] It was customary in Sweden to strew the ground with these for a funeral.

hind me, enormously long. I have made people unhappy and people have made me unhappy — the one cancels out the other — but before I die I want to see you happy. Our fates are entwined through your father — and other things.

STUDENT: Let go of my hand. You are taking all my strength. You are freezing me. What do you want with me?

OLD MAN (*letting go*): Be patient and you shall see and understand. Here comes the young lady.

(*They watch the* GIRL *approaching, though the audience cannot yet see her.*)

STUDENT: The Colonel's daughter?

OLD MAN: His daughter — yes. Look at her. Have you ever seen such a masterpiece?

STUDENT: She is like the marble statue in there.

OLD MAN: That's her mother, you know.

STUDENT: You are right. Never have I seen such a woman of woman born. Happy the man who may lead her to the altar and his home.

OLD MAN: You can see it. Not everyone recognizes her beauty. So, then, it is written.

(*The* GIRL *enters, wearing an English riding habit. Without noticing anyone she walks slowly to the door, where she stops to say a few words to the* CARETAKER'S WIFE. *Then she goes into the house. The* STUDENT *covers his eyes with his hand.*)

OLD MAN: Are you weeping?

STUDENT: In the face of what's hopeless there can be nothing but despair.

OLD MAN: I can open doors and hearts, if only I find an arm to do my will. Serve me and you shall have power.

STUDENT: Is it a bargain? Am I to sell my soul?

OLD MAN: Sell nothing. Listen. All my life I have *taken*. Now I have a craving to give — give. But no one will accept. I am rich, very rich, but I have no heirs, except for a good-for-nothing who torments the life out of me. Become my son. Inherit me while I am still alive. Enjoy life so that I can watch, at least from a distance.

STUDENT: What am I to do?

OLD MAN: First go to *The Valkyrie.*

STUDENT: That's settled. What else?

OLD MAN: This evening you must be in there — in the Round Room.

STUDENT: How am I to get there?

OLD MAN: By way of *The Valkyrie.*

STUDENT: Why have you chosen me as your medium? Did you know me before?

OLD MAN: Yes, of course. I have had my eye on you for a long time. But now look up there at the balcony. The maid is hoisting the flag to half-mast for the Consul. And now she is turning the bedclothes. Do you see that blue quilt? It was made for two to sleep under, but now it covers only one.

(*The* GIRL, *having changed her dress, appears in the window and waters the hyacinths.*)

There is my little girl. Look at her, look! She is talking to the flowers. Is she not like that blue hyacinth herself? She gives them drink — nothing but pure water, and they transform the water into color and fragrance. Now here comes the Colonel with the newspaper. He is showing her the bit about the house that collapsed. Now he's pointing to your portrait. She's not indifferent. She's reading of your brave deed. . . .

I believe it's clouding over. If it turns to rain I shall be in a pretty fix, unless Johansson comes back soon.

(*It grows cloudy and dark. The* FIANCÉE *at the window-mirror closes her window.*)

Now my fiancée is closing the window. Seventy-nine years old. The window-mirror is the only mirror she uses, because in it she sees not herself, but the world outside — in two directions. But the world can see her; she hasn't thought of that. Anyhow she's a handsome old woman.

(*Now the* DEAD MAN, *wrapped in a winding sheet, comes out of the door.*)

STUDENT: Good God, what do I see?

OLD MAN: What do you see?

STUDENT: Don't *you* see? There, in the doorway, the dead man?

OLD MAN: I see nothing, but I expected this. Tell me.

STUDENT: He is coming out into the street. (*Pause.*) Now he is turning his head and looking up at the flag.

OLD MAN: What did I tell you? You may be sure he'll count the wreaths and read the visiting cards. Woe to him who's missing.

STUDENT: Now he's turning the corner.

OLD MAN: He's gone to count the poor at the back door. The poor are in the nature of a decoration, you see. "Followed by the blessings of many." Well, he's not going to have my blessing. Between ourselves he was a great scoundrel.

STUDENT: But charitable.

OLD MAN: A charitable scoundrel, always thinking of his grand funeral. When he knew his end was near, he cheated the State out of fifty thousand crowns. Now his daughter has relations with another woman's husband and is wondering about the Will. Yes, the scoundrel can hear every word we're saying, and he's welcome to it. Ah, here comes Johansson!

(JOHANSSON *enters.*)

Report!

(JOHANSSON *speaks, but the audience does not hear.*)

Not at home, eh? You are an ass. And the telegram? Nothing? Go on. . . . At six this evening? That's good. Special edition, you say? With his name in full. Arkenholtz, a student, born . . . parents . . . That's splendid. . . . I think it's beginning to rain. . . . What did he say about it? So — so. He wouldn't? Well, he must. Here comes the aristocrat. Push me round the corner, Johansson, so I can hear what the poor are saying. And, Arkenholtz, you wait for me here. Understand? (*To* JOHANSSON.) Hurry up now, hurry up.

(JOHANSSON *wheels the chair round the corner. The* STUDENT *remains watching the* GIRL, *who is now loosening the earth round the hyacinths. The* ARISTOCRAT, *wearing mourning, comes in and speaks to the* DARK LADY, *who has been walking to and fro on the pavement.*)

ARISTOCRAT: But what can we do about it? We shall have to wait.

LADY: I can't wait.

ARISTOCRAT: You can't? Well then, go into the country.

LADY: I don't want to do that.

ARISTOCRAT: Come over here or they will hear what we are saying.

(*They move toward the advertisement column and continue their conversation inaudibly.* JOHANSSON *returns.*)

JOHANSSON (*to the* STUDENT): My master asks you not to forget that other thing, sir.

STUDENT (*hesitating*): Look here . . . first of all tell me . . . who is your master?

JOHANSSON: Well, he's so many things, and he has been everything.

STUDENT: Is he a wise man?

JOHANSSON: Depends what that is. He says all his life he's been looking for a Sunday child, but that may not be true.

STUDENT: What does he want? He's grasping, isn't he?

JOHANSSON: It's power he wants. The whole day long he rides round in his chariot like the god Thor himself. He looks at houses, pulls them down, opens up new streets, builds squares. . . . But he breaks into houses too, sneaks through windows, plays havoc with human destinies, kills his enemies — and never forgives. Can you imagine it, sir? This miserable cripple was once a Don Juan — although he always lost his women.

STUDENT: How do you account for that?

JOHANSSON: You see he's so cunning he makes the women leave him when he's tired of them. But what he's most like now is a horse-thief in the human market. He steals human beings in all sorts of different ways. He literally stole me out of the hands of the law. Well, as a matter of fact I'd made a slip — hm, yes — and only he knew about it. Instead of getting me put in gaol, he turned me into a slave. I slave — for my food alone, and that's none of the best.

STUDENT: Then what is it he means to do in this house?

JOHANSSON: I'm not going to talk about that. It's too complicated.

STUDENT: I think I'd better get away from it all.

(*The* GIRL *drops a bracelet out the window.*)

JOHANSSON: Look! The young lady has dropped her bracelet out of the window.

(*The* STUDENT *goes slowly over, picks up the bracelet and returns it to the* GIRL, *who thanks him stiffly. The* STUDENT *goes back to* JOHANSSON.)

So you mean to get away. That's not so easy as you think, once he's got you in his net. And he's afraid of nothing between heaven and earth — yes, of one thing he is — of one person rather. . . .

STUDENT: Don't tell me. I think perhaps I know.

JOHANSSON: How can you know?

STUDENT: I'm guessing. Is it a little milkmaid he's afraid of?

JOHANSSON: He turns his head the other way whenever he meets a milk cart. Besides, he talks in his sleep. It seems he was once in Hamburg. . . .

STUDENT: Can one trust this man?

JOHANSSON: You can trust him — to do anything.

STUDENT: What's he doing now round the corner?

JOHANSSON: Listening to the poor. Sowing a little word, loosening one stone at a time, till the house falls down — metaphorically speaking. You see I'm an educated man. I was once a book-seller. . . . Do you still mean to go away?

STUDENT: I don't like to be ungrateful. He saved my father once, and now he only asks a small service in return.

JOHANSSON: What is that?

STUDENT: I am to go to *The Valkyrie*.

JOHANSSON: That's beyond me. But he's always up to new tricks. Look at him now, talking to that policeman. He is always thick with the police. He uses them, gets them involved in his interests, holds them with false promises and expectations, while all the time he's pumping them. You'll see that before the day is over he'll be received in the Round Room.

STUDENT: What does he want there? What connection has he with the Colonel?

JOHANSSON: I think I can guess, but I'm not sure. You'll see for yourself once you're in there.

STUDENT: I shall never be in there.

JOHANSSON: That depends on yourself. Go to *The Valkyrie*.

STUDENT: Is that the way?

JOHANSSON: Yes, if he said so. Look. Look at him in his war chariot, drawn in triumph by the beggars, who get nothing for their pains but the hint of a treat at his funeral.

(*The* OLD MAN *appears standing up in his wheel-chair, drawn by one of the beggars and followed by the rest.*)

OLD MAN: Hail the noble youth who, at the risk of his own life, saved so many others in yesterday's accident. Three cheers for Arkenholtz!

(*The* BEGGARS *bare their heads but do not cheer. The* GIRL *at the window waves her handkerchief. The* COLONEL *gazes from the window of the Round Room. The* OLD WOMAN *rises at her window. The* MAID *on the balcony hoists the flag to the top.*)

Clap your hands, citizens. True, it is Sunday, but the ass in the pit and the ear in the corn field will absolve us. And although I am not a Sunday child, I have the gift of prophecy and also that of healing. Once I brought a drowned person back to life. That was in Hamburg on a Sunday morning just like this. . . .

(*The* MILKMAID *enters, seen only by the* STUDENT *and the* OLD MAN. *She raises her arms like one who is drowning and gazes fixedly at the* OLD MAN. *He sits down, then crumples up, stricken with horror.*)

Johansson! Take me away! Quick! . . . Arkenholtz, don't forget *The Valkyrie*.

STUDENT: What is all this?

JOHANSSON: We shall see. We shall see.

SCENE II

*Inside the Round Room. At the back is a white porcelain stove.
On either side of it are a mirror, a pendulum clock and candela-
bra. On the right of the stove is the entrance to the hall beyond
which is a glimpse of a room furnished in green and mahogany.
On the left of the stove is the door to a cupboard, papered like
the wall. The statue, shaded by palms, has a curtain which can be
drawn to conceal it.*

*A door on the left leads into the Hyacinth Room, where the
GIRL sits reading.*

*The back of the COLONEL can be seen, as he sits in the Green
Room, writing.*

*BENGTSSON, the Colonel's servant, comes in from the hall. He
is wearing livery, and is followed by JOHANSSON, dressed as a
waiter.*

BENGTSSON: Now you'll have to serve the tea, Johansson, while I take
the coats. Have you ever done it before?

JOHANSSON: It's true I push a war chariot in the daytime, as you know,
but in the evenings I go as a waiter to receptions and so forth. It's
always been my dream to get into this house. They're queer people
here, aren't they?

BENGTSSON: Ye-es. A bit out of the ordinary anyhow.

JOHANSSON: Is it to be a musical party or what?

BENGTSSON: The usual ghost supper, as we call it. They drink tea and
don't say a word — or else the Colonel does all the talking. And
they crunch their biscuits, all at the same time. It sounds like rats
in an attic.

JOHANSSON: Why do you call it the ghost supper?

BENGTSSON: They look like ghosts. And they've kept this up for twenty
years, always the same people saying the same things or saying nothing at all for fear of being found out.

JOHANSSON: Isn't there a mistress of the house?

BENGTSSON: Oh yes, but she's crazy. She sits in a cupboard because her
eyes can't bear the light. (*He points to the papered door.*) She sits
in there.

JOHANSSON: In there?

BENGTSSON: Well, I told you they were a bit out of the ordinary.

JOHANSSON: But then — what does she look like?

BENGTSSON: Like a mummy. Do you want to have a look at her? (*He opens the door.*) There she is.

(*The figure of the* COLONEL'S WIFE *is seen, white and shrivelled into a* MUMMY.)

JOHANSSON: Oh my God!

MUMMY (*babbling*): Why do you open the door? Haven't I told you to keep it closed?

BENGTSSON (*in a wheedling tone*): Ta, ta, ta, ta. Be a good girl now, then you'll get something nice. Pretty Polly.

MUMMY (*parrot-like*): Pretty Polly. Are you there, Jacob? Currrrr!

BENGTSSON: She thinks she's a parrot, and maybe she's right. (*To the* MUMMY.) Whistle for us, Polly.

(*The* MUMMY *whistles.*)

JOHANSSON: Well, I've seen a few things in my day, but this beats everything.

BENGTSSON: You see, when a house gets old, it grows moldy, and when people stay a long time together and torment each other they go mad. The mistress of the house — shut up, Polly! — that mummy there, has been living here for forty years — same husband, same furniture, same relatives, same friends. (*He closes the papered door.*) And the goings-on in this house — well, they're beyond me. Look at that statue — that's her when she was young.

JOHANSSON: Good Lord! Is that the mummy?

BENGTSSON: Yes. It's enough to make you weep. And somehow, carried away by her own imagination or something, she's got to be a bit like a parrot — the way she talks and the way she can't stand cripples or sick people. She can't stand the sight of her own daughter, because she's sick.

JOHANSSON: Is the young lady sick?

BENGTSSON: Didn't you know that?

JOHANSSON: No. And the Colonel, who is he?

BENGTSSON: You'll see.

JOHANSSON (*looking at the statue*): It's horrible to think that . . . How old is she now?

BENGTSSON: Nobody knows. But it's said that when she was thirty-five she looked nineteen, and that's what she made the Colonel believe she was — here in this very house. Do you know what that black Japanese screen by the couch is for? They call it the death-screen, and when someone's going to die, they put it round — same as in a hospital.

JOHANSSON: What a horrible house! And the student was longing to get in, as if it were paradise.

BENGTSSON: What student? Oh, I know. The one who's coming here this evening. The Colonel and the young lady happened to meet him at the Opera, and both of them took a fancy to him. Hm. Now it's my turn to ask questions. Who is your master — the man in the wheelchair?

JOHANSSON: Well, he . . . er . . . Is he coming here too?

BENGTSSON: He hasn't been invited.

JOHANSSON: He'll come uninvited — if need be.

(*The* OLD MAN *appears in the hall on crutches, wearing a frock-coat and top-hat. He steals forward and listens.*)

BENGTSSON: He's a regular old devil, isn't he?

JOHANSSON: Up to the ears.

BENGTSSON: He looks like old Nick himself.

JOHANSSON: And he must be a wizard too, for he goes through locked doors.

(*The* OLD MAN *comes forward and takes hold of* JOHANSSON *by the ear.*)

OLD MAN: Rascal — take care! (*To* BENGTSSON.) Tell the Colonel I am here.

BENGTSSON: But we are expecting guests.

OLD MAN: I know. But my visit is as good as expected, if not exactly looked forward to.

BENGTSSON: I see. What name shall I say? Mr. Hummel?

OLD MAN: Exactly. Yes.

(BENGTSSON *crosses the hall to the Green Room, the door of which he closes behind him.*)

(*To* JOHANSSON.) Get out!

(JOHANSSON *hesitates.*)

Get out!

(JOHANSSON *disappears into the hall. The* OLD MAN *inspects the room and stops in front of the statue in much astonishment.*)

Amelia! It is she — she!

MUMMY (*from the cupboard*): Prrr-etty Polly.

(*The* OLD MAN *starts.*)

OLD MAN: What was that? Is there a parrot in the room? I don't see it.

MUMMY: Are you there, Jacob?

OLD MAN: The house is haunted.

MUMMY: Jacob!

OLD MAN: I'm scared. So these are the kind of secrets they guard in this house. (*With his back turned to the cupboard he stands looking at a portrait.*) There he is — he!

(*The* MUMMY *comes out behind the* OLD MAN *and gives a pull at his wig.*)

MUMMY: Currrrr! Is it . . . ? Currrrr!

OLD MAN (*jumping out of his skin*): God in heaven! Who is it?

MUMMY (*in a natural voice*): Is it Jacob?

OLD MAN: Yes, my name is Jacob.

MUMMY (*with emotion*): And my name is Amelia.

OLD MAN: No, no, no . . . Oh my God!

MUMMY: That's how I look. Yes. (*Pointing to the statue.*) And that's how I *did* look. Life opens one's eyes, does it not? I live mostly in the cupboard to avoid seeing and being seen. . . . But, Jacob, what do you want here?

OLD MAN: My child. Our child.

MUMMY: There she is.

OLD MAN: Where?

MUMMY: There — in the Hyacinth Room.

OLD MAN (*looking at the* GIRL): Yes, that is she. (*Pause.*) And what about her father — the Colonel, I mean — your husband?

MUMMY: Once, when I was angry with him, I told him everything.

OLD MAN: Well. . . . ?

MUMMY: He didn't believe me. He just said: "That's what all wives say when they want to murder their husbands." It was a terrible crime none the less. It has falsified his whole life — his family tree too. Sometimes I take a look in the Peerage, and then I say to myself: Here she is, going about with a false birth certificate like some servant girl, and for such things people are sent to the reformatory.

OLD MAN: Many do it. I seem to remember your own date of birth was given incorrectly.

MUMMY: My mother made me do that. I was not to blame. And in our crime, *you* played the biggest part.

OLD MAN: No. Your husband caused that crime, when he took my fiancée from me. I was born one who cannot forgive until he has punished. That was to me an imperative duty — and is so still.

MUMMY: What are you expecting to find in this house? What do you want? How did you get in? Is it to do with my daughter? If you touch her, you shall die.

OLD MAN: I mean well by her.

MUMMY: Then you must spare her father.

OLD MAN: No.

MUMMY: Then you shall die. In this room, behind that screen.

OLD MAN: That may be. But I can't let go once I've got my teeth into a thing.

MUMMY: You want to marry her to that student. Why? He is nothing and has nothing.

OLD MAN: He will be rich, through me.

MUMMY: Have you been invited here tonight?

OLD MAN: No, but I propose to get myself an invitation to this ghost supper.

MUMMY: Do you know who is coming?

OLD MAN: Not exactly.

MUMMY: The Baron. The man who lives up above — whose father-in-law was buried this afternoon.

OLD MAN: The man who is getting a divorce in order to marry the daughter of the Caretaker's wife . . . The man who used to be — your lover.

MUMMY: Another guest will be your former fiancée, who was seduced by my husband.

OLD MAN: A select gathering.

MUMMY: Oh God, if only we might die, might die!

OLD MAN: Then why have you stayed together?

MUMMY: Crime and secrets and guilt bind us together. We have broken our bonds and gone our own ways, times without number, but we are always drawn together again.

OLD MAN: I think the Colonel is coming.

MUMMY: Then I will go in to Adèle. (*Pause.*) Jacob, mind what you do. Spare him. (*Pause. She goes into the Hyacinth Room and disappears.*)

(*The* COLONEL *enters, cold and reserved, with a letter in his hand.*)

COLONEL: Be seated, please.

(*Slowly the* OLD MAN *sits down. Pause. The* COLONEL *stares at him.*)

You wrote this letter, sir?

OLD MAN: I did.

COLONEL: Your name is Hummel?

OLD MAN: It is. (*Pause.*)

COLONEL: As I understand, you have bought in all my unpaid promissory notes. I can only conclude that I am in your hands. What do you want?

OLD MAN: I want payment, in one way or another.

COLONEL: In what way?

OLD MAN: A very simple one. Let us not mention the money. Just bear with me in your house as a guest.

COLONEL: If so little will satisfy you . . .

OLD MAN: Thank you.

COLONEL: What else?

OLD MAN: Dismiss Bengtsson.

COLONEL: Why should I do that? My devoted servant, who has been with me a lifetime, who has the national medal for long and faithful service — why should I do that?

OLD MAN: That's how you see him — full of excellent qualities. He is not the man he appears to be.

COLONEL: Who is?

OLD MAN (*taken aback*): True. But Bengtsson must go.

COLONEL: Are you going to run my house?

OLD MAN: Yes. Since everything here belongs to me — furniture, curtains, dinner service, linen . . . and more too.

COLONEL: How do you mean — more?

OLD MAN: Everything. I own everything here. It is mine.

COLONEL: Very well, it is yours. But my family escutcheon and my good name remain my own.

OLD MAN: No, not even those. (*Pause.*) You are not a nobleman.

COLONEL: How dare you!

OLD MAN (*producing a document*): If you read this extract from *The Armorial Gazette*, you will see that the family whose name you are using has been extinct for a hundred years.

COLONEL: I have heard rumors to this effect, but I inherited the name from my father. (*Reads.*) It is true. You are right. I am not a nobleman. Then I must take off my signet ring. It is true, it belongs to you. (*Gives it to him.*) There you are.

OLD MAN (*pocketing the ring*): Now we will continue. You are not a Colonel either.

COLONEL: I am not . . . ?

OLD MAN: No. You once held the temporary rank of Colonel in the American Volunteer Force, but after the war in Cuba and the reorganization of the Army, all such titles were abolished.

COLONEL: Is this true?

OLD MAN (*indicating his pocket*): Do you want to read it?

COLONEL: No, that's not necessary. Who are you, and what right have you to sit there stripping me in this fashion?

OLD MAN: You will see. But as far as stripping you goes . . . do you know who you are?

COLONEL: How dare you?

OLD MAN: Take off that wig and have a look at yourself in the mirror. But take your teeth out at the same time and shave off your moustache. Let Bengtsson unlace your metal stays and perhaps a certain X.Y.Z., a lackey, will recognize himself. The fellow who was a cupboard lover in a certain kitchen . . .

(*The* COLONEL *reaches for the bell on the table, but* HUMMEL *checks him.*)

Don't touch that bell, and don't call Bengtsson. If you do, I'll have him arrested. (*Pause.*) And now the guests are beginning to arrive. Keep your composure and we will continue to play our old parts for a while.

COLONEL: Who are you? I recognize your voice and eyes.

OLD MAN: Don't try to find out. Keep silent and obey.

(*The* STUDENT *enters and bows to the* COLONEL.)

STUDENT: How do you do, sir.

COLONEL: Welcome to my house, young man. Your splendid behavior at that great disaster has brought your name to everybody's lips, and I count it an honor to receive you in my home.

STUDENT: My humble descent, sir . . . Your illustrious name and noble birth. . . .

COLONEL: May I introduce Mr. Arkenholtz — Mr. Hummel. If you will join the ladies in here, Mr. Arkenholtz — I must conclude my conversation with Mr. Hummel.

(*He shows the* STUDENT *into the Hyacinth Room, where he remains visible, talking shyly to the* GIRL.)

A splendid young man, musical, sings, writes poetry. If he only had blue blood in him, if he were of the same station, I don't think I should object . . .

OLD MAN: To what?

COLONEL: To my daughter . . .

OLD MAN: *Your* daughter! But apropos of that, why does she spend all her time in there?

COLONEL: She insists on being in the Hyacinth Room except when she is out-of-doors. It's a peculiarity of hers. Ah, here comes Miss Beatrice von Holsteinkrona — a charming woman, a pillar of the Church, with just enough money of her own to suit her birth and position.

OLD MAN (*to himself*): My fiancée.

(*The* FIANCÉE *enters, looking a little crazy.*)

COLONEL: Miss Holsteinkrona — Mr. Hummel.

(The FIANCÉE *curtseys and takes a seat. The* ARISTOCRAT *enters and seats himself. He wears mourning and looks mysterious.*)

Baron Skanskorg . . .

OLD MAN (*aside, without rising*): That's the jewel-thief, I think. (*To the* COLONEL.) If you bring in the Mummy, the party will be complete.

COLONEL (*at the door of the Hyacinth Room*): Polly!

MUMMY (*entering*): Currrrr . . . !

COLONEL: Are the young people to come in too?

OLD MAN: No, not the young people. They shall be spared.

(*They all sit silent in a circle.*)

COLONEL: Shall we have the tea brought in?

OLD MAN: What's the use? No one wants tea. Why should we pretend about it?

COLONEL: Then shall we talk?

OLD MAN: Talk of the weather, which we know? Inquire about each other's health, which we know just as well? I prefer silence — then one can hear thoughts and see the past. Silence cannot hide anything — but words can. I read the other day that differences of language originated among savages for the purpose of keeping one tribe's secrets hidden from another. Every language therefore is a code, and he who finds the key can understand every language in the world. But this does not prevent secrets from being exposed without a key, specially when there is a question of paternity to be proved. Proof in a Court of Law is another matter. Two false witnesses suffice to prove anything about which they are agreed, but one does not take witnesses along on the kind of explorations I have in mind. Nature herself has instilled in human beings a sense of modesty which tries to hide what should be hidden, but we slip into situations unintentionally, and by chance sometimes the deepest secret is divulged — the mask torn from the impostor, the villain exposed. . . .

(*Pause. All look at each other in silence.*)

What a silence there is now!

(*Long silence.*)

Here, for instance, in this honorable house, in this elegant home, where beauty, wealth and culture are united. . . .

(*Long silence.*)

All of us now sitting here know who we are — do we not? There's no need for me to tell you. And you know me, although you pretend ignorance. (*He indicates the Hyacinth Room.*) In there is my daughter. *Mine* — you know that too. She had lost the desire to live, without knowing why. The fact is she was withering away in this air charged with crime and deceit and falseness of every kind. That is why I looked for a friend for her in whose company she might enjoy the light and warmth of noble deeds.

(*Long silence.*)

That was my mission in this house: to pull up the weeds, to expose the crimes, to settle all accounts, so that those young people might start afresh in this home, which is my gift to them.

(*Long silence.*)

Now I am going to grant safe-conduct, to each of you in his and her proper time and turn. Whoever stays I shall have arrested.

(*Long silence.*)

Do you hear the clock ticking like a death-watch beetle in the wall? Do you hear what it says? "It's time, it's time, it's time." When it strikes, in a few moments, your time will be up. Then you can go, but not before. It's raising its arm against you before it strikes. Listen! It is warning you. "The clock can strike." And I can strike too. (*He strikes the table with one of his crutches.*) Do you hear?

(*Silence. The* MUMMY *goes up to the clock and stops it, then speaks in a normal and serious voice.*)

MUMMY: But I can stop time in its course. I can wipe out the past and undo what is done. But not with bribes, not with threats — only through suffering and repentance. (*She goes up to the* OLD MAN.) We are miserable human beings, that we know. We have erred and we have sinned, we like all the rest. We are not what we seem, because at bottom we are better than ourselves, since we detest our sins. But when you, Jacob Hummel, with your false name, choose to sit in judgment over us, you prove yourself worse than us miserable sinners. For you are not the one you appear to be. You are a thief of human souls. You stole me once with false promises. You murdered the Consul who was buried today; you strangled him with debts.

You have stolen the student, binding him by the pretence of a claim on his father, who never owed you a farthing.

(*Having tried to rise and speak, the* OLD MAN *sinks back in his chair and crumples up more and more as she goes on.*)

But there is one dark spot in your life which I am not quite sure about, although I have my suspicions. I think Bengtsson knows. (*She rings the bell on the table.*)

OLD MAN: No, not Bengtsson, not him.

MUMMY: So he does know. (*She rings again.*)

(*The* MILKMAID *appears in the hallway door, unseen by all but the* OLD MAN, *who shrinks back in horror. The* MILKMAID *vanishes as* BENGTSSON *enters.*)

Do you know this man, Bengtsson?

BENGTSSON: Yes, I know him and he knows me. Life, as you are aware, has its ups and downs. I have been in his service; another time he was in mine. For two whole years he was a sponger in my kitchen. As he had to be away by three, the dinner was got ready at two, and the family had to eat the warmed-up leavings of that brute. He drank the soup stock, which the cook then filled up with water. He sat out there like a vampire, sucking the marrow out of the house, so that we became like skeletons. And he nearly got us put in prison when we called the cook a thief. Later I met this man in Hamburg under another name. He was a usurer then, a blood-sucker. But while he was there he was charged with having lured a young girl out on to the ice so as to drown her, because she had seen him commit a crime he was afraid would be discovered. . . .

(*The* MUMMY *passes her hand over the* OLD MAN's *face.*)

MUMMY: This is you. Now give up the notes and the Will.

(JOHANSSON *appears in the hallway door and watches the scene with great interest, knowing he is now to be freed from slavery. The* OLD MAN *produces a bundle of papers and throws it on the table. The* MUMMY *goes over and strokes his back.*)

Parrot. Are you there, Jacob?

OLD MAN (*like a parrot*): Jacob is here. Pretty Polly. Currrrr!

MUMMY: May the clock strike?

OLD MAN (*with a clucking sound*): The clock may strike. (*Imitating a cuckoo clock.*) Cuckoo, cuckoo, cuckoo. . . .

(*The* MUMMY *opens the cupboard door.*)

MUMMY: Now the clock has struck. Rise, and enter the cupboard where I have spent twenty years repenting our crime. A rope is hanging there, which you can take as the one with which you strangled the Consul, and with which you meant to strangle your benefactor. . . . Go!

(*The* OLD MAN *goes in to the cupboard. The* MUMMY *closes the door.*)

Bengtsson! Put up the screen — the death-screen.

(BENGTSSON *places the screen in front of the door.*)

It is finished. God have mercy on his soul.
ALL: Amen. (*Long silence.*)

(*The* GIRL *and the* STUDENT *appear in the Hyacinth Room. She has a harp, on which he plays a prelude, and then accompanies the* STUDENT'S *recitation.*)

STUDENT: *I saw the sun. To me it seemed*
that I beheld the Hidden.
Men must reap what they have sown;
blest is he whose deeds are good.
Deeds which you have wrought in fury,
cannot in evil find redress.
Comfort him you have distressed
with loving-kindness — this will heal.
No fear has he who does no ill.
Sweet is innocence.

SCENE III

Inside the Hyacinth Room. The general effect of the room is exotic and oriental. There are hyacinths everywhere, of every color, some in pots, some with the bulbs in glass vases and the roots going down into the water.

On top of the tiled stove is a large seated Buddha, in whose lap rests a bulb from which rises the stem of a shallot (Allium ascalonicum), bearing its globular cluster of white, starlike flowers.

On the right is an open door, leading into the Round Room, where the COLONEL *and the* MUMMY *are seated, inactive and silent. A part of the death-screen is also visible.*

On the left is a door to the pantry and kitchen.

The STUDENT *and the* GIRL (Adèle) *are beside the table; he standing, she seated with her harp.*

GIRL: Now sing to my flowers.

STUDENT: Is this the flower of your soul?

GIRL: The one and only. Do you too love the hyacinth?

STUDENT: I love it above all other flowers — its virginal shape rising straight and slender out of the bulb, resting on the water and sending its pure white roots down into the colorless fluid. I love its colors: the snow-white, pure as innocence, the yellow honey-sweet, the youthful pink, the ripe red, but best of all the blue — the dewy blue, deep-eyed and full of faith. I love them all, more than gold or pearls. I have loved them ever since I was a child, have worshipped them because they have all the fine qualities I lack. . . . And yet . . .

GIRL: Go on.

STUDENT: My love is not returned, for these beautiful blossoms hate me.

GIRL: How do you mean?

STUDENT: Their fragrance, strong and pure as the early winds of spring which have passed over melting snows, confuses my senses, deafens me, blinds me, thrusts me out of the room, bombards me with poisoned arrows that wound my heart and set my head on fire. Do you know the legend of that flower?

GIRL: Tell it to me.

STUDENT: First its meaning. The bulb is the earth, resting on the water or buried in the soil. Then the stalk rises, straight as the axis of the world, and at the top are the six-pointed star-flowers.

GIRL: Above the earth — the stars. Oh, that is wonderful! Where did you learn this? How did you find it out?

STUDENT: Let me think . . . In your eyes. And so, you see, it is an image of the Cosmos. This is why Buddha sits holding the earth-bulb, his eyes brooding as he watches it grow, outward and upward, transforming itself into a heaven. This poor earth will become a heaven. It is for this that Buddha waits.

GIRL: I see it now. Is not the snowflake six-pointed too like the hyacinth flower?

STUDENT: You are right. The snowflakes must be falling stars.

GIRL: And the snowdrop is a snow-star, grown out of snow.

STUDENT: But the largest and most beautiful of all the stars in the firmament, the golden-red Sirius, is the narcissus with its gold and red chalice and its six white rays.

GIRL: Have you seen the shallot in bloom?

STUDENT: Indeed I have. It bears its blossoms within a ball, a globe like the celestial one, strewn with white stars.

GIRL: Oh how glorious! Whose thought was that?

STUDENT: Yours.

GIRL: Yours.

STUDENT: Ours. We have given birth to it together. We are wedded.

GIRL: Not yet.

STUDENT: What's still to do?

GIRL: Waiting, ordeals, patience.

STUDENT: Very well. Put me to the test. (*Pause.*) Tell me. Why do your parents sit in there so silently, not saying a single word?

GIRL: Because they have nothing to say to each other, and because neither believes what the other says. This is how my father puts it: What's the point of talking, when neither of us can fool the other?

STUDENT: What a horrible thing to hear!

GIRL: Here comes the Cook. Look at her, how big and fat she is.

(*They watch the* COOK, *although the audience cannot yet see her.*)

STUDENT: What does she want?

GIRL: To ask me about the dinner. I have to do the housekeeping as my mother's ill.

STUDENT: What have we to do with the kitchen?

GIRL: We must eat. Look at the Cook. I can't bear the sight of her.

STUDENT: Who is that ogress?

GIRL: She belongs to the Hummel family of vampires. She is eating us.

STUDENT: Why don't you dismiss her?

GIRL: She won't go. We have no control over her. We've got her for our sins. Can't you see that we are pining and wasting away?

STUDENT: Don't you get enough to eat?

GIRL: Yes, we get many dishes, but all the strength has gone. She boils the nourishment out of the meat and gives us the fibre and water, while she drinks the stock herself. And when there's a roast, she first boils out the marrow, eats the gravy and drinks the juices herself. Everything she touches loses its savor. It's as if she sucked with her eyes. We get the grounds when she has drunk the coffee. She drinks the wine and fills the bottles up with water.

STUDENT: Send her packing.

GIRL: We can't.

STUDENT: Why not?

GIRL: We don't know. She won't go. No one has any control over her. She has taken all our strength from us.

STUDENT: May I get rid of her?

GIRL: No. It must be as it is. Here she is. She will ask me what is to be for dinner. I shall tell her. She will make objections and get her own way.

STUDENT: Let her do the ordering herself then.

GIRL: She won't do that.

STUDENT: What an extraordinary house! It is bewitched.

GIRL: Yes. But now she is turning back, because she has seen you.

THE COOK (*in the doorway*): No, that wasn't the reason. (*She grins, showing all her teeth.*)

STUDENT: Get out!

COOK: When it suits me. (*Pause.*) It does suit me now. (*She disappears.*)

GIRL: Don't lose your temper. Practice patience. She is one of the ordeals we have to go through in this house. You see, we have a housemaid too, whom we have to clean up after.

STUDENT: I am done for. *Cor in æthere.* Music!

GIRL: Wait.

STUDENT: Music!

GIRL: Patience. This room is called the room of ordeals. It looks beautiful, but it is full of defects.

STUDENT: Really? Well, such things must be seen to. It is very beautiful, but a little cold. Why don't you have a fire?

GIRL: Because it smokes.

STUDENT: Can't you have the chimney swept?

GIRL: It doesn't help. You see that writing-desk there?

STUDENT: An unusually fine piece.

GIRL: But it wobbles. Every day I put a piece of cork under that leg, and every day the housemaid takes it away when she sweeps and I have to cut a new piece. The penholder is covered with ink every morning and so is the inkstand. I have to clean them up every morning after that woman, as sure as the sun rises. (*Pause.*) What's the worst job you can think of?

STUDENT: To count the washing. Ugh!

GIRL: That I have to do. Ugh!

STUDENT: What else?

GIRL: To be waked in the middle of the night and have to get up and see to the window, which the housemaid has left banging.

STUDENT: What else?

GIRL: To get up on a ladder and tie the cord on the damper[4] which the housemaid has torn off.

[4] Damper to the big stove.

STUDENT: What else?

GIRL: To sweep after her, to dust after her, to light the fire in the stove when all she's done is throw in some wood. To see to the damper, to wipe the glasses, to lay the table over again, to open the bottles, to see that the rooms are aired, to remake my bed, to rinse the water-bottle when it's green with sediment, to buy matches and soap which are always lacking, to wipe the chimneys and trim the wicks to keep the lamps from smoking — and so that they don't go out when we have company, I have to fill them myself. . . .

STUDENT: Music!

GIRL: Wait. The labor comes first. The labor of keeping the dirt of life at a distance.

STUDENT: But you are wealthy and have two servants.

GIRL: It doesn't help. Even if we had three. Living is hard work, and sometimes I grow tired. (*Pause.*) Think then if there were a nursery as well.

STUDENT: The greatest of joys.

GIRL: And the costliest. Is life worth so much hardship?

STUDENT: That must depend on the reward you expect for your labors. I would not shrink from anything to win your hand.

GIRL: Don't say that. You can never have me.

STUDENT: Why not?

GIRL: You mustn't ask. (*Pause.*)

STUDENT: You dropped your bracelet out of the window. . . .

GIRL: Because my hand has grown so thin. (*Pause.*)

(*The* COOK *appears with a Japanese bottle in her hand.*)

There she is — the one who devours me and all of us.

STUDENT: What has she in her hand?

GIRL: It is the bottle of coloring matter that has letters like scorpions on it. It is the soy which turns water into soup and takes the place of gravy. She makes cabbage soup with it — and mock-turtle soup too.

STUDENT (*to* COOK): Get out!

COOK: You drain us of sap, and we drain you. We take the blood and leave you the water, but colored . . . colored. I am going now, but all the same I shall stay, as long as I please. (*She goes out.*)

STUDENT: Why did Bengtsson get a medal?

GIRL: For his great merits.

STUDENT: Has he no defects?

GIRL: Yes, great ones. But you don't get a medal for them.

(*They smile.*)

STUDENT: You have many secrets in this house.

GIRL: As in all others. Permit us to keep ours.

STUDENT: Don't you approve of candor?

GIRL: Yes — within reason.

STUDENT: Sometimes I'm seized with a raging desire to say all I think. But I know the world would go to pieces if one were completely candid. (*Pause.*) I went to a funeral the other day . . . in church. It was very solemn and beautiful.

GIRL: Was it Mr. Hummel's?

STUDENT: My false benefactor's — yes. At the head of the coffin stood an old friend of the deceased. He carried the mace. I was deeply impressed by the dignified manner and moving words of the clergyman. I cried. We all cried. Afterwards we went to a tavern, and there I learned that the man with the mace had been in love with the dead man's son. . . .

(*The* GIRL *stares at him, trying to understand.*)

And that the dead man had borrowed money from his son's admirer. (*Pause.*) Next day the clergyman was arrested for embezzling the church funds. A pretty story.

GIRL: Oh . . . ! (*Pause.*)

STUDENT: Do you know how I am thinking about you now?

GIRL: Don't tell me, or I shall die.

STUDENT: I must, or I shall die.

GIRL: It is in asylums that people say everything they think.

STUDENT: Exactly. My father finished up in an asylum.

GIRL: Was he ill?

STUDENT: No, he was well, but he was mad. You see, he broke out once — in these circumstances. Like all of us, he was surrounded with a circle of acquaintances; he called them friends for short. They were a lot of rotters, of course, as most people are, but he had to have some society — he couldn't get on all alone. Well, as you know, in everyday life no one tells people what he thinks of them, and he didn't either. He knew perfectly well what frauds they were — he'd sounded the depths of their deceit — but as he was a wise and well-bred man, he was always courteous to them. Then one day he gave a big party. It was in the evening and he was tired by the day's work and by the strain of holding his tongue and at the same time talking rubbish with his guests. . . .

(*The* GIRL *is frightened.*)

Well, at the dinner table he rapped for silence, raised his glass, and began to speak. Then something loosed the trigger. He made an enormous speech in which he stripped the whole company naked, one after the other, and told them of all their treachery. Then, tired out, he sat down on the table and told them all to go to hell.

GIRL: Oh!

STUDENT: I was there, and I shall never forget what happened then. Father and Mother came to blows, the guests rushed for the door . . . and my father was taken to a madhouse, where he died. (*Pause.*) Water that is still too long stagnates, and so it is in this house too. There is something stagnating here. And yet I thought it was paradise itself that first time I saw you coming in here. There I stood that Sunday morning, gazing in. I saw a Colonel who was no Colonel. I had a benefactor who was a thief and had to hang himself. I saw a mummy who was not a mummy and an old maid — what of the maidenhood, by the way? Where is beauty to be found? In nature, and in my own mind, when it is in its Sunday clothes. Where are honor and faith? In fairy-tales and children's fancies. Where is anything that fulfills its promise? In my imagination. Now your flowers have poisoned me and I have given the poison back to you. I asked you to become my wife in a home full of poetry and song and music. Then the Cook came. . . . *Sursum Corda!* Try once more to strike fire and glory out of the golden harp. Try, I beg you, I implore you on my knees. (*Pause.*) Then I will do it myself. (*He picks up the harp, but the strings give no sound.*) It is dumb and deaf. To think that the most beautiful flowers are so poisonous, are the most poisonous. The curse lies over the whole of creation, over life itself. Why will you not be my bride? Because the very life-spring within you is sick . . . now I can feel that vampire in the kitchen beginning to suck me. I believe she is a Lamia, one of those that suck the blood of children. It is always in the kitchen quarters that the seed-leaves of the children are nipped, if it has not already happened in the bedroom. There are poisons that destroy the sight and poisons that open the eyes. I seem to have been born with the latter kind, for I cannot see what is ugly as beautiful, nor call evil good. I cannot. Jesus Christ descended into hell. That was His pilgrimage on earth — to this madhouse, this prison, this charnel-house, this earth. And the madmen killed Him when He wanted to set them free; but the robber they let go. The robber always gets the sympathy. Woe! Woe to us all. Saviour of the world, save us! We perish.

(*And now the* GIRL *has drooped, and it is seen that she is dying. She rings.* BENGTSSON *enters.*)

GIRL: Bring the screen. Quick. I am dying.

(BENGTSSON *comes back with the screen, opens it and arranges it in front of the* GIRL.)

STUDENT: The Liberator is coming. Welcome, pale and gentle one. Sleep, you lovely, innocent, doomed creature, suffering for no fault of your own. Sleep without dreaming, and when you wake again . . . may you be greeted by a sun that does not burn, in a home without dust, by friends without stain, by a love without flaw. You wise and gentle Buddha, sitting there waiting for a Heaven to sprout from the earth, grant us patience in our ordeal and purity of will, so that this hope may not be confounded.

(*The strings of the harp hum softly and a white light fills the room.*)

> I saw the sun. To me it seemed
> that I beheld the Hidden.
> Men must reap what they have sown;
> blest is he whose deeds are good.
> Deeds which you have wrought in fury,
> cannot in evil find redress.
> Comfort him you have distressed
> with loving-kindness — this will heal.
> No fear has he who does no ill.
> Sweet is innocence.

(*A faint moaning is heard behind the screen.*)

You poor little child, child of this world of illusion, guilt, suffering, and death, this world of endless change, disappointment, and pain. May the Lord of Heaven be merciful to you upon your journey.

(*The room disappears. Böcklin's picture* The Island of the Dead *is seen in the distance, and from the island comes music, soft, sweet, and melancholy.*)

WHEN Strindberg wrote *The Ghost Sonata* (in 1907) his Intimate Theater in Stockholm had just opened and he was worried about its success, his domestic arrangements were made trying by problems with servants (one reason, perhaps, for the prominent and rather obtusely ridiculed "kitchen imagery" in the play), and he suffered from a severe attack of psoriasis (a painful skin disease) of the hands. *The Ghost Sonata*, he wrote to his German translator, had been written "with bleeding hands."

The difficulties one experiences with *The Ghost Sonata* could be due to something we might call the inertia of literary taste. Perhaps the play baffles because it seems so unlike the kind of plays with which we are familiar, plays like *The Wild Duck, Three Sisters,* and *A View From the Bridge,* in which people much like ourselves suffer and triumph, are good and evil, sick and sane, noble and ignoble, act or fail to act, in a world much like our own. If we get past our initial sense of being lost among incoherent and inexplicable events, we may begin to recognize familiar themes. Strindberg, too, looks behind the façade of middle-class life and uncovers its moral iniquities. Like Ibsen's, his characters are guilt-haunted captives of their past. And his picture of life stagnating and rotting in a petty and sordid everyday — where people torture one another with silences, and where "the labor of keeping the dirt of life at a distance" saps the good and the young — is close to Chekhov's.

Still, the differences between *The Ghost Sonata* and naturalistic plays are obvious. Strindberg's play is not an authentic image of what actual life appears to be. It deals with the irrational, the mystical, in human life; it is scarcely a coincidence that it is roughly contemporary with the birth of psychoanalysis. Strindberg's stage is more than a setting for the action. It is plastic and fluid, responsive to the playwright's shifting phantasmagoria, an integral part of the play. To move from *Three Sisters* to *The Ghost Sonata* is to leave the familiar living room, drab, perhaps, and stifling, but safely *real,* and to enter a nightmare where ordinary realities appear in new and changing shapes and grotesque combinations, all the more disturbing for being recognizable as their ordinary selves behind the distortions. Clocks and screens and a bottle of soya sauce loom larger than life in Strindberg's ghostly dream. And yet, they are not symbols. They are nothing but themselves, only, somehow, more frighteningly so than in real life; they are solidly there, as things, but imbued with more than thing-like power. And *as* things they will not allow us to think the nightmare unreal. Here horror is a commonplace, normality a dread beyond comprehension and remedy. It is of the essence of Strindberg's art that his ultimate "ghost" is a lazy and impudent cook. The ordinary is both ordinary and supernatural, both tiresome and terrifying.

The reader who still feels that the play "doesn't make sense" may take the dream metaphor a step further. If in Ibsen, Shaw, Chekhov, and Miller our position as audience is that of unobserved observer, fly on the living room wall, in *The Ghost Sonata* it may be thought of as that of troubled dreamer. And dreams are not required to make sense. That they do not is often what makes them most compelling.

The Ghost Sonata has come to be regarded as a pioneer specimen of a kind of drama that has been given the name *expressionistic*. The term is not Strindberg's, it is unlikely that he ever heard it applied to his plays, but it is as meaningful as such labels ever are. Expressionists do not try to copy nature, don't care to make a cow look like a cow. They express themselves, turn reality inside out, fragmentize it, bring its meaning (to them) to the surface, record the feel of experience in bone and nerve. They claim for their subjectivity as much reality as does the scientist for his objectivity. Suppose you don't like liver or colonial furniture (the expressionist may say). What is for you the truer statement about these things: that liver has a certain color, texture, chemical composition, nutritional value, price per pound? Or that it makes you sick? That American colonial is characterized by certain lines and shapes and finishes, a certain use of maple wood? Or that it is ugly? Isn't the second statement in each case as true as the first? Isn't it as important, since it takes account of your feelings? Isn't it at any rate worth expressing?

The distortions of objective reality in this art — sometimes to the point of the unrecognizability of pure abstractionism — serve to universalize it. The emphasis is on the feeling rather than on the real-life object that happens to occasion the feeling. "Abstractionism," says a modern practitioner, "can touch many springs in the human spirit, whereas reality can touch only one." The same premise underlies expressionism — though it is surrealistic rather than non-realistic, like abstractionism. In expressing himself the artist expresses every man's subjectivity, articulates the inarticulate, helps us for the moment exercise our human potential. "We don't live in reality," says Strindberg, "but in what we take reality to be." Perhaps the theory of expressionism is best summed up in the answer a painter acquaintance of Strindberg's gave to a technology-minded friend's suggestion that in an age of photography paint and brush were old-fashioned and inaccurate tools for recording truth: "As long as the camera can't enter heaven and hell," said Edvard Munch, "people will keep on painting and other people keep on looking at what they paint." In *The Ghost Sonata* Strindberg enters hell.

Hell (in this connection) is a state of mind, a climate of the soul, something experienced rather than understood. The musical term "sonata" in the title suggests a work that calls for a sensory and emotional response to its evocation of evil — not for explanation.

The play's theme is the universality of evil, the suffering of the innocent, the ambiguity of human motives. The Old Man seems to be a satanic figure — the Mummy calls him "a thief of human souls" — but we cannot really be sure that he is not also the would-be redeemer of his natural daughter and the benefactor of the young man whose father he once wronged (or did he?). The anguish of sin and shame that constitutes the human condition in this most mercilessly dark of all Strindberg's plays is expressed in personal relationships seen as a vast and complicated network of mutual guilt and recrimination.* This is the master image of the play, and it explains why some of the structurally most important characters are little more than names. Their function is to be strands in the web of universal sin. Their anonymity furthers that function.

The play's world is a world of deceptions. Act I begins in hope and promise as a penniless young hero is befriended by a wealthy old man on a bright Sunday morning. But the sun disappears, the kindly benefactor appears as a stricken Thor, the blustering heathen god of wrath and war, and the blessing of being a Sunday child amounts only to seeing ghosts from the Old Man's evil past. The second "movement" of the sonata marks the seeming fulfillment of the Student's hopes. He enters the elegant apartment house and meets his beloved. But the remainder of the act disillusions hope in a sequence of disclosure and counter-disclosure. The Old Man's exposure of his victims and the purgation of his sinful past are frustrated at their moment of apparent fruition in a dramatization of something close to Christ's "Judge not, that ye be not judged." Acting outside of time, the insane Mummy suddenly turns sane savior, and the wise benefactor hangs himself — the unmasker unmasked.

---

* It may be as well to clarify those relationships here. To do so is not to "get" the play; it is not even a necessary step toward adequate response. But the relationships are so involved and so implausible (as realism) that they are likely to be obstacles to enjoyment if left unclarified.

There are two sets of relationships, both adulterous and both involving an illegitimate daughter. (1) The Janitor's Wife is the mother of the Dark Lady by the Dead Man (the Consul). The Dark Lady is engaged to be married to Baron Skanskorg (the Aristocrat) and is apparently pregnant with his child. The Baron is getting a divorce from another daughter (presumably legitimate) of the Dead Man. (2) The Mummy is the wife of the Colonel and the mother of the Girl by the Old Man (Hummel). The Old Man seduced the Mummy in revenge for the Colonel's seduction of the Old Man's Fiancée. The two sets of relationships are linked by still another illicit affair: that between the Mummy and the Baron. (The Old Man's relationship with the Student and the Student's father, with Johansson and Bengtsson, and with the Milkmaid, while part of the general mesh of past and hidden crimes, do not concern these love entanglements.)

But the company stands revealed: a seduced virgin; a jewel thief turned baron about to enter a mésalliance; a host who is fake father, fake officer, fake nobleman, whose very appearance is faked by means of wig, false teeth, and iron corset; an adulterous wife; a master who once was servant and a servant who once was master.

In the third movement, the house of promised happiness has shrunk to a room of desperate but passive suffering, the Hyacinth room of ordeals, beautiful but fatal, where the mysterious poetry of love decays to complaints about servants and housekeeping, where flowers sicken and the Girl dies. Here rules the same vampire evil that had seemed to die with the Old Man, and the suffering of the beautiful and the innocent is presided over by a statue of Buddha, incarnating that infinite patience with which weary mankind must await the miraculous liberation from the curse of life.

Anticipation, disillusionment, suffering — these are the phases of life. Existence, poisoned at the roots, is paralysis in the contemplation of one's own damnation or slow dystrophy in the endless execution of small and distasteful domestic tasks. The kitchen is in charge of a giant, undismissible slattern, whose actions contradict her calling: she grows fat on the food she should serve others. There is no restoration of the ruined house, no atonement for the Old Man, the Mummy, or the Colonel. Salvation is hardly more than a pious hope and a prayer set to soft music before a sentimental picture. The action does not include the Christian redemption the ending hints at. The burden of life is too heavy to bear; blessed are those who, like the Girl, find release in death. "Oh God, if only we might die, might die!" cries the Mummy. But the sleep of death is denied these tormented souls. They are ghosts, miserably, hopelessly, immortal.

Philosophically, the pervasive gloom of *The Ghost Sonata* may not survive scrutiny. The play is not, as far as reader or spectator can discover, based on any rational, coherent system of thought. It asserts, or, rather, it shows — it does not prove. On the other hand, that Strindberg has not philosophized his vision renders it immune to rational criticism. It does not presume to conform to its tenets and can refuse to be judged on its terms. That may be its strength. Its sense-defying manipulation of fragments of reality weaves a spell for those who once have shared, if only in a dream, the awareness of evil at the very core of human existence. It haunts our imagination long after our daylight minds have granted or refused to grant assent to its ghastly judgment.)❧

Luigi Pirandello

SIX CHARACTERS IN SEARCH OF AN AUTHOR

A Comedy in the Making

English Version by Edward Storer

Characters of the Comedy in the Making

THE FATHER	THE BOY
THE MOTHER	THE CHILD
THE STEP-DAUGHTER	(*The last two do not speak*)
THE SON	MADAME PACE

Actors of the Company

THE MANAGER	OTHER ACTORS AND ACTRESSES
LEADING LADY	PROPERTY MAN
LEADING MAN	PROMPTER
SECOND LADY	MACHINIST
LEAD	MANAGER'S SECRETARY
L'INGÉNUE	DOOR-KEEPER
JUVENILE LEAD	SCENE-SHIFTERS

SCENE: *Daytime. The stage of a theater.*

N. B. *The Comedy is without acts or scenes. The performance is interrupted once, without the curtain being lowered, when the*

From the book *Naked Masks: Five Plays* by Luigi Pirandello, edited by Eric Bentley. Copyright, 1922, by E. P. Dutton & Co., Inc. Renewal, 1950, in the names of Stefano, Fausto & Lietta Pirandello. Dutton Paperback Series. Reprinted by permission of the publishers.

253

*manager and the chief characters withdraw to arrange a scenario.
A second interruption of the action takes place when, by mistake,
the stage hands let the curtain down.*

ACT I

(*The spectators will find the curtain raised and the stage as it
usually is during the day time. It will be half dark, and empty,
so that from the beginning the public may have the impression
of an impromptu performance.*

Prompter's box and a small table and chair for the MANAGER.

*Two other small tables and several chairs scattered about as
during rehearsals.*

The ACTORS *and* ACTRESSES *of the company enter from the
back of the stage: first one, then another, then two together; nine
or ten in all. They are about to rehearse a Pirandello play:* Mixing
It Up.* *Some of the company move off towards their dressing
rooms. The* PROMPTER, *who has the "book" under his arm, is
waiting for the* MANAGER *in order to begin the rehearsal.*

The ACTORS *and* ACTRESSES, *some standing, some sitting, chat
and smoke. One perhaps reads a paper; another cons his part.*

Finally, the MANAGER *enters and goes to the table prepared for
him. His* SECRETARY *brings him his mail, through which he
glances. The* PROMPTER *takes his seat, turns on a light, and opens
the "book."*)

THE MANAGER (*throwing a letter down on the table*): I can't see. (*To*
PROPERTY MAN.) Let's have a little light, please!

PROPERTY MAN: Yes sir, yes, at once. (*A light comes down on to the
stage.*)

THE MANAGER (*clapping his hands*): Come along! Come along! Second
act of "Mixing It Up." (*Sits down.*)

(*The* ACTORS *and* ACTRESSES *go from the front of the stage to the
wings, all except the three who are to begin the rehearsal.*)

THE PROMPTER (*reading the "book"*): "Leo Gala's house. A curious
room serving as dining-room and study."

THE MANAGER (*to* PROPERTY MAN): Fix up the old red room.

PROPERTY MAN (*noting it down*): Red set. All right!

THE PROMPTER (*continuing to read from the "book"*): "Table already

* i.e. *Il giuoco delle parti.*

laid and writing desk with books and papers. Book-shelves. Exit rear to Leo's bedroom. Exit left to kitchen. Principal exit to right."

THE MANAGER (*energetically*): Well, you understand: The principal exit over there; here, the kitchen. (*Turning to actor who is to play the part of* SOCRATES.) You make your entrances and exits here. (*To* PROPERTY MAN.) The baize doors at the rear, and curtains.

PROPERTY MAN (*noting it down*): Right!

PROMPTER (*reading as before*): "When the curtain rises, Leo Gala, dressed in cook's cap and apron is busy beating an egg in a cup. Philip, also dressed as a cook, is beating another egg. Guido Venanzi is seated and listening."

LEADING MAN (*to* MANAGER): Excuse me, but must I absolutely wear a cook's cap?

THE MANAGER (*annoyed*): I imagine so. It says so there anyway. (*Pointing to the "book."*)

LEADING MAN: But it's ridiculous!

THE MANAGER (*jumping up in a rage*): Ridiculous? Ridiculous? Is it my fault if France won't send us any more good comedies, and we are reduced to putting on Pirandello's works, where nobody understands anything, and where the author plays the fool with us all? (*The* ACTORS *grin. The* MANAGER *goes to* LEADING MAN *and shouts.*) Yes sir, you put on the cook's cap and beat eggs. Do you suppose that with all this egg-beating business you are on an ordinary stage? Get that out of your head. You represent the shell of the eggs you are beating! (*Laughter and comments among the* ACTORS.) Silence! and listen to my explanations, please! (*To* LEADING MAN.) "The empty form of reason without the fullness of instinct, which is blind." — You stand for reason, your wife is instinct. It's a mixing up of the parts, according to which you who act your own part become the puppet of yourself. Do you understand?

LEADING MAN: I'm hanged if I do.

THE MANAGER: Neither do I. But let's get on with it. It's sure to be a glorious failure anyway. (*Confidentially.*) But I say, please face three-quarters. Otherwise, what with the abstruseness of the dialogue, and the public that won't be able to hear you, the whole thing will go to hell. Come on! come on!

PROMPTER: Pardon sir, may I get into my box? There's a bit of a draught.

THE MANAGER: Yes, yes, of course!

(*At this point, the* DOOR-KEEPER *has entered from the stage door and advances towards the* MANAGER's *table, taking off his braided cap. During this manoeuvre, the* SIX CHARACTERS *enter, and stop by the door at back of stage, so that when the* DOOR-KEEPER *is about to announce their coming to the* MANAGER, *they are already on the stage. A tenuous light surrounds them, almost as if irradiated by them — the faint breath of their fantastic reality.*

This light will disappear when they come forward towards the actors. They preserve, however, something of the dream lightness in which they seem almost suspended; but this does not detract from the essential reality of their forms and expressions.

He who is known as THE FATHER *is a man of about 50: hair, reddish in color, thin at the temples; he is not bald, however; thick moustaches, falling over his still fresh mouth, which often opens in an empty and uncertain smile. He is fattish, pale; with an especially wide forehead. He has blue, oval-shaped eyes, very clear and piercing. Wears light trousers and a dark jacket. He is alternatively mellifluous and violent in his manner.*

THE MOTHER *seems crushed and terrified as if by an intolerable weight of shame and abasement. She is dressed in modest black and wears a thick widow's veil of crêpe. When she lifts this, she reveals a wax-like face. She always keeps her eyes downcast.*

THE STEP-DAUGHTER *is dashing, almost impudent, beautiful. She wears mourning too, but with great elegance. She shows contempt for the timid half-frightened manner of the wretched* BOY *(14 years old, and also dressed in black); on the other hand, she displays a lively tenderness for her little sister,* THE CHILD *(about four), who is dressed in white, with a black silk sash at the waist.*

THE SON *(22) tall, severe in his attitude of contempt for* THE FATHER, *supercilious and indifferent to* THE MOTHER. *He looks as if he had come on the stage against his will.)*

DOOR-KEEPER *(cap in hand)*: Excuse me, sir . . .

THE MANAGER *(rudely)*: Eh? What is it?

DOOR-KEEPER *(timidly)*: These people are asking for you, sir.

THE MANAGER *(furious)*: I am rehearsing, and you know perfectly well no one's allowed to come in during rehearsals! *(Turning to the* CHARACTERS.*)* Who are you, please? What do you want?

THE FATHER *(coming forward a little, followed by the others who seem embarrassed)*: As a matter of fact . . . we have come here in search of an author . . .

THE MANAGER *(half angry, half amazed)*: An author? What author?

THE FATHER: Any author, sir.

THE MANAGER: But there's no author here. We are not rehearsing a new piece.

THE STEP-DAUGHTER (*vivaciously*): So much the better, so much the better! We can be your new piece.

AN ACTOR (*coming forward from the others*): Oh, do you hear that?

THE FATHER (*to* STEP-DAUGHTER): Yes, but if the author isn't here . . . (*To* MANAGER.) unless you would be willing . . .

THE MANAGER: You are trying to be funny.

THE FATHER: No, for Heaven's sake, what are you saying? We bring you a drama, sir.

THE STEP-DAUGHTER: We may be your fortune.

THE MANAGER: Will you oblige me by going away? We haven't time to waste with mad people.

THE FATHER (*mellifluously*): Oh sir, you know well that life is full of infinite absurdities, which, strangely enough, do not even need to appear plausible, since they are true.

THE MANAGER: What the devil is he talking about?

THE FATHER: I say that to reverse the ordinary process may well be considered a madness: that is, to create credible situations, in order that they may appear true. But permit me to observe that if this be madness, it is the sole *raison d'être* of your profession, gentlemen. (*The* ACTORS *look hurt and perplexed.*)

THE MANAGER (*getting up and looking at him*): So our profession seems to you one worthy of madmen then?

THE FATHER: Well, to make seem true that which isn't true . . . without any need . . . for a joke as it were . . . Isn't that your mission, gentlemen: to give life to fantastic characters on the stage?

THE MANAGER (*interpreting the rising anger of the* COMPANY): But I would beg you to believe, my dear sir, that the profession of the comedian is a noble one. If today, as things go, the playwrights give us stupid comedies to play and puppets to represent instead of men, remember we are proud to have given life to immortal works here on these very boards! (*The* ACTORS, *satisfied, applaud their* MANAGER.)

THE FATHER (*interrupting furiously*): Exactly, perfectly, to living beings more alive than those who breathe and wear clothes: beings less real perhaps, but truer! I agree with you entirely. (*The* ACTORS *look at one another in amazement.*)

THE MANAGER: But what do you mean? Before, you said . . .

THE FATHER: No, excuse me, I meant it for you, sir, who were crying out that you had no time to lose with madmen, while no one better than yourself knows that nature uses the instrument of human fantasy in order to pursue her high creative purpose.

THE MANAGER: Very well, — but where does all this take us?

THE FATHER: Nowhere! It is merely to show you that one is born to life in many forms, in many shapes, as tree, or as stone, as water, as butterfly, or as woman. So one may also be born a character in a play.

THE MANAGER (*with feigned comic dismay*): So you and these other friends of yours have been born characters?

THE FATHER: Exactly, and alive as you see! (MANAGER *and* ACTORS *burst out laughing.*)

THE FATHER (*hurt*): I am sorry you laugh, because we carry in us a drama, as you can guess from this woman here veiled in black.

THE MANAGER (*losing patience at last and almost indignant*): Oh, chuck it! Get away please! Clear out of here! (*To* PROPERTY MAN.) ·For Heaven's sake, turn them out!

THE FATHER (*resisting*): No, no, look here, we . . .

THE MANAGER (*roaring*): We come here to work, you know.

LEADING ACTOR: One cannot let oneself be made such a fool of.

THE FATHER (*determined, coming forward*): I marvel at your incredulity, gentlemen. Are you not accustomed to see the characters created by an author spring to life in yourselves and face each other? Just because there is no "book" (*pointing to the* PROMPTER'S box) which contains us, you refuse to believe . . .

THE STEP-DAUGHTER (*advances towards* MANAGER, *smiling and coquettish*): Believe me, we are really six most interesting characters, sir; side-tracked however.

THE FATHER: Yes, that is the word! (*To* MANAGER *all at once.*) In the sense, that is, that the author who created us alive no longer wished, or was no longer able, materially to put us into a work of art. And this was a real crime, sir; because he who has had the luck to be born a character can laugh even at death. He cannot die. The man, the writer, the instrument of the creation will die, but his creation does not die. And to live for ever, it does not need to have extraordinary gifts or to be able to work wonders. Who was Sancho Panza? Who was Don Abbondio? Yet they live eternally because — live germs as they were — they had the fortune to find a fecundating matrix, a fantasy which could raise and nourish them: make them live for ever!

THE MANAGER: That is quite all right. But what do you want here, all of you?

THE FATHER: We want to live.

THE MANAGER (*ironically*): For Eternity?

THE FATHER: No, sir, only for a moment . . . in you.

AN ACTOR: Just listen to him!

LEADING LADY: They want to live, in us . . . !

JUVENILE LEAD (*pointing to the* STEP-DAUGHTER): I've no objection, as far as that one is concerned!

THE FATHER: Look here! look here! The comedy has to be made. (*To the* MANAGER.) But if you and your actors are willing, we can soon concert it among ourselves.

THE MANAGER (*annoyed*): But what do you want to concert? We don't go in for concerts here. Here we play dramas and comedies!

THE FATHER: Exactly! That is just why we have come to you.

THE MANAGER: And where is the "book"?

THE FATHER: It is in us! (*The* ACTORS *laugh.*) The drama is in us, and we are the drama. We are impatient to play it. Our inner passion drives us on to this.

THE STEP-DAUGHTER (*disdainful, alluring, treacherous, full of impudence*): My passion, sir! Ah, if you only knew! My passion for him! (*Points to the* FATHER *and makes a pretence of embracing him. Then she breaks out into a loud laugh.*)

THE FATHER (*angrily*): Behave yourself! And please don't laugh in that fashion.

THE STEP-DAUGHTER: With your permission, gentlemen, I, who am a two months' orphan, will show you how I can dance and sing. (*Sings and then dances* Prenez garde à Tchou-Tchin-Tchou.)

> Les chinois sont un peuple malin,
> De Shangaï à Pékin,
> Ils ont mis des écriteaux partout:
> Prenez garde à Tchou-Tchin-Tchou.

ACTORS *and* ACTRESSES: Bravo! Well done! Tip-top!

THE MANAGER: Silence! This isn't a café concert, you know! (*Turning to the* FATHER *in consternation.*) Is she mad?

THE FATHER: Mad? No, she's worse than mad.

THE STEP-DAUGHTER (*to* MANAGER): Worse? Worse? Listen! Stage this drama for us at once! Then you will see that at a certain moment I . . . when this little darling here. . . . (*Takes the* CHILD *by the hand and leads her to the* MANAGER.) Isn't she a dear? (*Takes her up and kisses her.*) Darling! Darling! (*Puts her down again and adds feelingly.*) Well, when God suddenly takes this dear little child away from that poor mother there; and this imbecile here (*seizing hold of the* BOY *roughly and pushing him forward*) does the stupidest things, like the fool he is, you will see me run away. Yes, gentlemen, I shall be off. But the moment hasn't arrived yet. After what has taken place between him and me (*indicates the*

FATHER *with a horrible wink*) I can't remain any longer in this society, to have to witness the anguish of this mother here for that fool. . . . (*Indicates the* SON.) Look at him! Look at him! See how indifferent, how frigid he is, because he is the legitimate son. He despises me, despises him (*pointing to the* BOY), despises this baby here; because . . . we are bastards. (*Goes to the* MOTHER *and embraces her.*) And he doesn't want to recognize her as his mother — she who is the common mother of us all. He looks down upon her as if she were only the mother of us three bastards. Wretch! (*She says all this very rapidly, excitedly. At the word "bastards" she raises her voice, and almost spits out the final "Wretch!"*)

THE MOTHER (*to the* MANAGER, *in anguish*): In the name of these two little children, I beg you. . . . (*She grows faint and is about to fall.*) Oh God!

THE FATHER (*coming forward to support her as do some of the* ACTORS): Quick, a chair, a chair for this poor widow!

THE ACTORS: Is it true? Has she really fainted?

THE MANAGER: Quick, a chair! Here!

(*One of the* ACTORS *brings a chair, the* OTHERS *proffer assistance. The* MOTHER *tries to prevent the* FATHER *from lifting the veil which covers her face.*)

THE FATHER: Look at her! Look at her!

THE MOTHER: No, no; stop it please!

THE FATHER (*raising her veil*): Let them see you!

THE MOTHER (*rising and covering her face with her hands, in desperation*): I beg you, sir, to prevent this man from carrying out his plan which is loathsome to me.

THE MANAGER (*dumbfounded*): I don't understand at all. What is the situation? Is this lady your wife? (*To the* FATHER.)

THE FATHER: Yes, gentlemen: my wife!

THE MANAGER: But how can she be a widow if you are alive? (*The* ACTORS *find relief for their astonishment in a loud laugh.*)

THE FATHER: Don't laugh! Don't laugh like that, for Heaven's sake. Her drama lies just here in this: she has had a lover, a man who ought to be here.

THE MOTHER (*with a cry*): No! No!

THE STEP-DAUGHTER: Fortunately for her, he is dead. Two months ago as I said. We are in mourning, as you see.

THE FATHER: He isn't here you see, not because he is dead. He isn't here — look at her a moment and you will understand — because her drama isn't a drama of the love of two men for whom she was incapable of feeling anything except possibly a little gratitude —

gratitude not for me but for the other. She isn't a woman, she is a mother, and her drama — powerful sir, I assure you — lies, as a matter of fact, all in these four children she has had by two men.

THE MOTHER: I had them? Have you got the courage to say that I wanted them? (*To the* COMPANY.) It was his doing. It was he who gave me that other man, who forced me to go away with him.

THE STEP-DAUGHTER: It isn't true.

THE MOTHER (*startled*): Not true, isn't it?

THE STEP-DAUGHTER: No, it isn't true, it just isn't true.

THE MOTHER: And what can you know about it?

THE STEP-DAUGHTER: It isn't true. Don't believe it. (*To* MANAGER.) Do you know why she says so? For that fellow there. (*Indicates the* SON.) She tortures herself, destroys herself on account of the neglect of that son there; and she wants him to believe that if she abandoned him when he was only two years old, it was because he (*indicates the* FATHER) made her do so.

THE MOTHER (*vigorously*): He forced me to it, and I call God to witness it. (*To the* MANAGER.) Ask him (*indicates* HUSBAND) if it isn't true. Let him speak. You (*to* DAUGHTER) are not in a position to know anything about it.

THE STEP-DAUGHTER: I know you lived in peace and happiness with my father while he lived. Can you deny it?

THE MOTHER: No, I don't deny it. . . .

THE STEP-DAUGHTER: He was always full of affection and kindness for you. (*To the* BOY, *angrily*.) It's true, isn't it? Tell them! Why don't you speak, you little fool?

THE MOTHER: Leave the poor boy alone. Why do you want to make me appear ungrateful, daughter? I don't want to offend your father. I have answered him that I didn't abandon my house and my son through any fault of mine, nor from any wilful passion.

THE FATHER: It is true. It was my doing.

LEADING MAN (*to the* COMPANY): What a spectacle!

LEADING LADY: We are the audience this time.

JUVENILE LEAD: For once, in a way.

THE MANAGER (*beginning to get really interested*): Let's hear them out. Listen!

THE SON: Oh yes, you're going to hear a fine bit now. He will talk to you of the Demon of Experiment.

THE FATHER: You are a cynical imbecile. I've told you so already a hundred times. (*To the* MANAGER.) He tries to make fun of me on account of this expression which I have found to excuse myself with.

THE SON (*with disgust*): Yes, phrases! phrases!

THE FATHER: Phrases! Isn't everyone consoled when faced with a trouble or fact he doesn't understand, by a word, some simple word, which tells us nothing and yet calms us?

THE STEP-DAUGHTER: Even in the case of remorse. In fact, especially then.

THE FATHER: Remorse? No, that isn't true. I've done more than use words to quieten the remorse in me.

THE STEP-DAUGHTER: Yes, there was a bit of money too. Yes, yes, a bit of money. There were the hundred lire he was about to offer me in payment, gentlemen. . . . (*Sensation of horror among the* ACTORS.)

THE SON (*to the* STEP-DAUGHTER): This is vile.

THE STEP-DAUGHTER: Vile? There they were in a pale blue envelope on a little mahogany table in the back of Madame Pace's shop. You know Madame Pace — one of those ladies who attract poor girls of good family into their ateliers, under the pretext of their selling *robes et manteaux*.

THE SON: And he thinks he has bought the right to tyrannize over us all with those hundred lire he was going to pay; but which, fortunately — note this, gentlemen — he had no chance of paying.

THE STEP-DAUGHTER: It was a near thing, though, you know! (*Laughs ironically.*)

THE MOTHER (*protesting*): Shame, my daughter, shame!

THE STEP-DAUGHTER: Shame indeed! This is my revenge! I am dying to live that scene . . . The room . . . I see it . . . Here is the window with the mantles exposed, there the divan, the looking-glass, a screen, there in front of the window the little mahogany table with the blue envelope containing one hundred lire. I see it. I see it. I could take hold of it. . . . But you, gentlemen, you ought to turn your backs now: I am almost nude, you know. But I don't blush: I leave that to him. (*Indicating* FATHER.)

THE MANAGER: I don't understand this at all.

THE FATHER: Naturally enough. I would ask you, sir, to exercise your authority a little here, and let me speak before you believe all she is trying to blame me with. Let me explain.

THE STEP-DAUGHTER: Ah yes, explain it in your own way.

THE FATHER: But don't you see that in the whole trouble lies here? In words, words. Each one of us has within him a whole world of things, each man of us his own special world. And how can we ever come to an understanding if I put in the words I utter the sense and value of things as I see them; while you who listen to me must inevitably translate them according to the conception of things each one of you has within himself. We think we understand each other, but we never really do. Look here! This woman (*indicating the* MOTHER) takes all my pity for her as a specially ferocious form of cruelty.

THE MOTHER: But you drove me away.

THE FATHER: Do you hear her? I drove her away! She believes I really sent her away.

THE MOTHER: You know how to talk, and I don't; but, believe me, sir (*to* MANAGER), after he had married me . . . who knows why? . . . I was a poor insignificant woman. . . .

THE FATHER: But, good Heavens! it was just for your humility that I married you. I loved this simplicity in you. (*He stops when he sees she makes signs to contradict him, opens his arms wide in sign of desperation, seeing how hopeless it is to make himself understood.*) You see she denies it. Her mental deafness, believe me, is phenomenal, the limit: (*touches his forehead*) deaf, deaf, mentally deaf! She has plenty of feeling. Oh yes, a good heart for the children; but the brain — deaf, to the point of desperation ——!

THE STEP-DAUGHTER: Yes, but ask him how his intelligence has helped us.

THE FATHER: If we could see all the evil that may spring from good, what should we do? (*At this point the* LEADING LADY, *who is biting her lips with rage at seeing the* LEADING MAN *flirting with the* STEP-DAUGHTER, *comes forward and speaks to the* MANAGER.)

LEADING LADY: Excuse me, but are we going to rehearse today?

MANAGER: Of course, of course; but let's hear them out.

JUVENILE LEAD: This is something quite new.

L'INGÉNUE: Most interesting!

LEADING LADY: Yes, for the people who like that kind of thing. (*Casts a glance at* LEADING MAN.)

THE MANAGER (*to* FATHER): You must please explain yourself quite clearly. (*Sits down.*)

THE FATHER: Very well then: listen! I had in my service a poor man, a clerk, a secretary of mine, full of devotion, who became friends with her. (*Indicating the* MOTHER.) They understood one another, were kindred souls in fact, without, however, the least suspicion of any evil existing. They were incapable even of thinking of it.

THE STEP-DAUGHTER: So he thought of it — for them!

THE FATHER: That's not true. I meant to do good to them — and to myself, I confess, at the same time. Things had come to the point that I could not say a word to either of them without their making a mute appeal, one to the other, with their eyes. I could see them silently asking each other how I was to be kept in countenance,

how I was to be kept quiet. And this, believe me, was just about
enough of itself to keep me in a constant rage, to exasperate me
beyond measure.

THE MANAGER: And why didn't you send him away then — this secretary of yours?

THE FATHER: Precisely what I did, sir. And then I had to watch this
poor woman drifting forlornly about the house like an animal
without a master, like an animal one has taken in out of pity.

THE MOTHER: Ah yes . . . !

THE FATHER (*suddenly turning to the* MOTHER): It's true about the
son anyway, isn't it?

THE MOTHER: He took my son away from me first of all.

THE FATHER: But not from cruelty. I did it so that he should grow
up healthy and strong by living in the country.

THE STEP-DAUGHTER (*pointing to him ironically*): As one can see.

THE FATHER (*quickly*): Is it my fault if he has grown up like this?
I sent him to a wet nurse in the country, a peasant, as *she* did not
seem to me strong enough, though she is of humble origin. That
was, anyway, the reason I married her. Unpleasant all this may
be, but how can it be helped? My mistake possibly, but there we
are! All my life I have had these confounded aspirations towards
a certain moral sanity. (*At this point the* STEP-DAUGHTER *bursts
into a noisy laugh.*) Oh, stop it! Stop it! I can't stand it.

THE MANAGER: Yes, please stop it, for Heaven's sake.

THE STEP-DAUGHTER: But imagine moral sanity from him, if you
please — the client of certain ateliers like that of Madame Pace!

THE FATHER: Fool! That is the proof that I am a man! This seeming
contradiction, gentlemen, is the strongest proof that I stand here
a live man before you. Why, it is just for this very incongruity in
my nature that I have had to suffer what I have. I could not live
by the side of that woman (*indicating the* MOTHER) any longer;
but not so much for the boredom she inspired me with as for the
pity I felt for her.

THE MOTHER: And so he turned me out —.

THE FATHER: — well provided for! Yes, I sent her to that man,
gentlemen . . . to let her go free of me.

THE MOTHER: And to free himself.

THE FATHER: Yes, I admit it. It was also a liberation for me. But
great evil has come of it. I meant well when I did it; and I did it
more for her sake than mine. I swear it. (*Crosses his arms on his
chest; then turns suddenly to the* MOTHER.) Did I ever lose sight
of you until that other man carried you off to another town, like
the angry fool he was? And on account of my pure interest in you

. . . my pure interest, I repeat, that had no base motive in it . . . I watched with the tenderest concern the new family that grew up around her. She can bear witness to this. (*Points to the* STEP-DAUGHTER.)

THE STEP-DAUGHTER: Oh yes, that's true enough. When I was a kiddie, so so high, you know, with plaits over my shoulders and knickers longer than my skirts, I used to see him waiting outside the school for me to come out. He came to see how I was growing up.

THE FATHER: This is infamous, shameful!

THE STEP-DAUGHTER: No. Why?

THE FATHER: Infamous! infamous! (*Then excitedly to* MANAGER *explaining.*) After she (*indicating* MOTHER) went away, my house seemed suddenly empty. She was my incubus, but she filled my house. I was like a dazed fly alone in the empty rooms. This boy here (*indicating the* SON) was educated away from home, and when he came back, he seemed to me to be no more mine. With no mother to stand between him and me, he grew up entirely for himself, on his own, apart, with no tie of intellect or affection binding him to me. And then — strange but true — I was driven, by curiosity at first and then by some tender sentiment, towards her family, which had come into being through my will. The thought of her began gradually to fill up the emptiness I felt all around me. I wanted to know if she were happy in living out the simple daily duties of life. I wanted to think of her as fortunate and happy because far away from the complicated torments of my spirit. And so, to have proof of this, I used to watch that child coming out of school.

THE STEP-DAUGHTER: Yes, yes. True. He used to follow me in the street and smiled at me, waved his hand, like this. I would look at him with interest, wondering who he might be. I told my mother, who guessed at once. (*The* MOTHER *agrees with a nod.*) Then she didn't want to send me to school for some days; and when I finally went back, there he was again — looking so ridiculous — with a paper parcel in his hands. He came close to me, caressed me, and drew out a fine straw hat from the parcel, with a bouquet of flowers — all for me!

THE MANAGER: A bit discursive this, you know!

THE SON (*contemptuously*): Literature! Literature!

THE FATHER: Literature indeed! This is life, this is passion!

THE MANAGER: It may be, but it won't act.

THE FATHER: I agree. This is only the part leading up. I don't suggest this should be staged. She (*pointing to the* STEP-DAUGHTER), as you see, is no longer the flapper with plaits down her back —.

THE STEP-DAUGHTER: — and the knickers showing below the skirt!

THE FATHER: The drama is coming now, sir; something new, complex, most interesting.

THE STEP-DAUGHTER: As soon as my father died . . .

THE FATHER: — there was absolute misery for them. They came back here, unknown to me. Through her stupidity! (*Pointing to the* MOTHER.) It is true she can barely write her own name; but she could anyhow have got her daughter to write to me that they were in need . . .

THE MOTHER: And how was I to divine all this sentiment in him?

THE FATHER: That is exactly your mistake, never to have guessed any of my sentiments.

THE MOTHER: After so many years apart, and all that had happened . . .

THE FATHER: Was it my fault if that fellow carried you away? It happened quite suddenly; for after he had obtained some job or other, I could find no trace of them; and so, not unnaturally, my interest in them dwindled. But the drama culminated unforeseen and violent on their return, when I was impelled by my miserable flesh that still lives. . . . Ah! what misery, what wretchedness is that of the man who is alone and disdains debasing *liaisons!* Not old enough to do without women, and not young enough to go and look for one without shame. Misery? It's worse than misery; it's a horror; for no woman can any longer give him love; and when a man feels this. . . . One ought to do without, you say? Yes, yes, I know. Each of us when he appears before his fellows is clothed in a certain dignity. But every man knows what unconfessable things pass within the secrecy of his own heart. One gives way to the temptation, only to rise from it again, afterwards, with a great eagerness to re-establish one's dignity, as if it were a tombstone to place on the grave of one's shame, and a monument to hide and sign the memory of our weaknesses. Everybody's in the same case. Some folks haven't the courage to say certain things, that's all!

THE STEP-DAUGHTER: All appear to have the courage to do them though.

THE FATHER: Yes, but in secret. Therefore, you want more courage to say these things. Let a man but speak these things out, and folks at once label him a cynic. But it isn't true. He is like all the others, better indeed, because he isn't afraid to reveal with the light of the intelligence the red shame of human bestiality on which most men close their eyes so as not to see it.

Woman — for example, look at her case! She turns tantalizing inviting glances on you. You seize her. No sooner does she feel

herself in your grasp than she closes her eyes. It is the sign of her
mission, the sign by which she says to man: "Blind yourself, for
I am blind."

THE STEP-DAUGHTER: Sometimes she can close them no more: when
she no longer feels the need of hiding her shame to herself, but
dry-eyed and dispassionately, sees only that of the man who has
blinded himself without love. Oh, all these intellectual complica-
tions make me sick, disgust me — all this philosophy that uncovers
the beast in man, and then seeks to save him, excuse him . . . I
can't stand it, sir. When a man seeks to "simplify" life bestially,
throwing aside every relic of humanity, every chaste aspiration,
every pure feeling, all sense of ideality, duty, modesty, shame . . .
then nothing is more revolting and nauseous than a certain kind
of remorse — crocodiles' tears, that's what it is.

THE MANAGER: Let's come to the point. This is only discussion.

THE FATHER: Very good, sir! But a fact is like a sack which won't
stand up when it's empty. In order that it may stand up, one has
to put into it the reason and sentiment which have caused it to
exist. I couldn't possibly know that after the death of that man,
they had decided to return here, that they were in misery, and that
she (*pointing to the* MOTHER) had gone to work as a modiste, and
at a shop of the type of that of Madame Pace.

THE STEP-DAUGHTER: A real high-class modiste, you must know, gentlemen. In appearance, she works for the leaders of the best society;
but she arranges matters so that these elegant ladies serve her
purpose . . . without prejudice to other ladies who are . . . well
. . . only so so.

THE MOTHER: You will believe me, gentlemen, that it never entered
my mind that the old hag offered me work because she had her
eye on my daughter.

THE STEP-DAUGHTER: Poor mamma! Do you know, sir, what that
woman did when I brought her back the work my mother had
finished? She would point out to me that I had torn one of my
frocks, and she would give it back to my mother to mend. It was
I who paid for it, always I; while this poor creature here believed
she was sacrificing herself for me and these two children here,
sitting up at night sewing Madame Pace's robes.

THE MANAGER: And one day you met there . . .

THE STEP-DAUGHTER: Him, him. Yes sir, an old client. There's a scene
for you to play! Superb!

THE FATHER: She, the Mother arrived just then . . .

THE STEP-DAUGHTER (*treacherously*): Almost in time!

THE FATHER (*crying out*): No, in time! in time! Fortunately I recognized her . . . in time. And I took them back home with me to my house. You can imagine now her position and mine; she, as you see her; and I who cannot look her in the face.

THE STEP-DAUGHTER: Absurd! How can I possibly be expected — after that — to be a modest young miss, a fit person to go with his confounded aspirations for "a solid moral sanity"?

THE FATHER: For the drama lies all in this — in the conscience that I have, that each one of us has. We believe this conscience to be a single thing, but it is many-sided. There is one for this person, and another for that. Diverse consciences. So we have this illusion of being one person for all, of having a personality that is unique in all our acts. But it isn't true. We perceive this when, tragically perhaps, in something we do, we are as it were, suspended, caught up in the air on a kind of hook. Then we perceive that all of us was not in that act, and that it would be an atrocious injustice to judge us by that action alone, as if all our existence were summed up in that one deed. Now do you understand the perfidy of this girl? She surprised me in a place, where she ought not to have known me, just as I could not exist for her; and she now seeks to attach to me a reality such as I could never suppose I should have to assume for her in a shameful and fleeting moment of my life. I feel this above all else. And the drama, you will see, acquires a tremendous value from this point. Then there is the position of the others . . . his. . . . (*Indicating the* SON.)

THE SON (*shrugging his shoulders scornfully*): Leave me alone! I don't come into this.

THE FATHER: What? You don't come into this?

THE SON: I've got nothing to do with it, and don't want to have; because you know well enough I wasn't made to be mixed up in all this with the rest of you.

THE STEP-DAUGHTER: We are only vulgar folk! He is the fine gentleman. You may have noticed, Mr. Manager, that I fix him now and again with a look of scorn while he lowers his eyes — for he knows the evil he has done me.

THE SON (*scarcely looking at her*): I?

THE STEP-DAUGHTER: You! you! I owe my life on the streets to you. Did you or did you not deny us, with your behavior, I won't say the intimacy of home, but even that mere hospitality which makes guests feel at their ease? We were intruders who had come to disturb the kingdom of your legitimacy. I should like to have you witness, Mr. Manager, certain scenes between him and me. He says I have tyrannized over everyone. But it was just his behavior which made me insist on the reason for which I had come into the house, — this reason he calls "vile" — into his house, with my mother who is his mother too. And I came as mistress of the house.

THE SON: It's easy for them to put me always in the wrong. But imagine, gentlemen, the position of a son, whose fate it is to see arrive one day at his home a young woman of impudent bearing, a young woman who inquires for his father, with whom who knows what business she has. This young man has then to witness her return bolder than ever, accompanied by that child there. He is obliged to watch her treat his father in an equivocal and confidential manner. She asks money of him in a way that lets one suppose he must give it to her, *must*, do you understand, because he has every obligation to do so.

THE FATHER: But I have, as a matter of fact, this obligation. I owe it to your mother.

THE SON: How should I know? When had I ever seen or heard of her? One day there arrive with her (*indicating* STEP-DAUGHTER) that lad and this baby here. I am told: "This is *your* mother too, you know." I divine from her manner (*indicating* STEP-DAUGHTER *again*) why it is they have come home. I had rather not say what I feel and think about it. I shouldn't even care to confess to myself. No action can therefore be hoped for from me in this affair. Believe me, Mr. Manager, I am an "unrealized" character, dramatically speaking; and I find myself not at all at ease in their company. Leave me out of it, I beg you.

THE FATHER: What? It is just because you are so that . . .

THE SON: How do you know what I am like? When did you ever bother your head about me?

THE FATHER: I admit it. I admit it. But isn't that a situation in itself? This aloofness of yours which is so cruel to me and to your mother, who returns home and sees you almost for the first time grown up, who doesn't recognize you but knows you are her son. . . . (*Pointing out the* MOTHER *to the* MANAGER.) See, she's crying!

THE STEP-DAUGHTER (*angrily, stamping her foot*): Like a fool!

THE FATHER (*indicating* STEP-DAUGHTER): She can't stand him you know. (*Then referring again to the* SON.) He says he doesn't come into the affair, whereas he is really the hinge of the whole action. Look at that lad who is always clinging to his mother, frightened and humiliated. It is on account of this fellow here. Possibly his situation is the most painful of all. He feels himself a stranger more than the others. The poor little chap feels mortified, humiliated at being brought into a home out of charity as it were. (*In con-*

fidence.) He is the image of his father. Hardly talks at all. Humble and quiet.

THE MANAGER: Oh, we'll cut him out. You've no notion what a nuisance boys are on the stage. . . .

THE FATHER: He disappears soon, you know. And the baby too. She is the first to vanish from the scene. The drama consists finally in this: when that mother re-enters my house, her family born outside of it, and shall we say superimposed on the original, ends with the death of the little girl, the tragedy of the boy and the flight of the elder daughter. It cannot go on, because it is foreign to its surroundings. So after much torment, we three remain: I, the mother, that son. Then, owing to the disappearance of that extraneous family, we too find ourselves strange to one another. We find we are living in an atmosphere of mortal desolation which is the revenge, as he (*indicating* SON) scornfully said of the Demon of Experiment, that unfortunately hides in me. Thus, sir, you see when faith is lacking, it becomes impossible to create certain states of happiness, for we lack the necessary humility. Vaingloriously, we try to substitute ourselves for this faith, creating thus for the rest of the world a reality which we believe after their fashion, while, actually, it doesn't exist. For each one of us has his own reality to be respected before God, even when it is harmful to one's very self.

THE MANAGER: There is something in what you say. I assure you all this interests me very much. I begin to think there's the stuff for a drama in all this, and not a bad drama either.

THE STEP-DAUGHTER (*coming forward*): When you've got a character like me.

THE FATHER (*shutting her up, all excited to learn the decision of the* MANAGER): You be quiet!

THE MANAGER (*reflecting, heedless of interruption*): It's new . . . hem . . . yes. . . .

THE FATHER: Absolutely new!

THE MANAGER: You've got a nerve though, I must say, to come here and fling it at me like this . . .

THE FATHER: You will understand, sir, born as we are for the stage . . .

THE MANAGER: Are you amateur actors then?

THE FATHER: No. I say born for the stage, because . . .

THE MANAGER: Oh, nonsense. You're an old hand, you know.

THE FATHER: No sir, no. We act that rôle for which we have been cast, that rôle which we are given in life. And in my own case, passion itself, as usually happens, becomes a trifle theatrical when it is exalted.

THE MANAGER: Well, well, that will do. But you see, without an author. . . . I could give you the address of an author if you like . . .

THE FATHER: No, no. Look here! You must be the author.

THE MANAGER: I? What are you talking about?

THE FATHER: Yes, you, you! Why not?

THE MANAGER: Because I have never been an author: that's why.

THE FATHER: Then why not turn author now? Everybody does it. You don't want any special qualities. Your task is made much easier by the fact that we are all here alive before you. . . .

THE MANAGER: It won't do.

THE FATHER: What? When you see us live our drama. . . .

THE MANAGER: Yes, that's all right. But you want someone to write it.

THE FATHER: No, no. Someone to take it down, possibly, while we play it, scene by scene! It will be enough to sketch it out at first, and then try it over.

THE MANAGER: Well . . . I am almost tempted. It's a bit of an idea. One might have a shot at it.

THE FATHER: Of course. You'll see what scenes will come out of it. I can give you one, at once . . .

THE MANAGER: By Jove, it tempts me. I'd like to have a go at it. Let's try it out. Come with me to my office. (*Turning to the* ACTORS.) You are at liberty for a bit, but don't step out of the theatre for long. In a quarter of an hour, twenty minutes, all back here again! (*To the* FATHER.) We'll see what can be done. Who knows if we don't get something really extraordinary out of it?

THE FATHER: There's no doubt about it. They (*indicating the* CHAR-ACTERS) had better come with us too, hadn't they?

THE MANAGER: Yes, yes. Come on! come on! (*Moves away and then turning to the* ACTORS.) Be punctual, please! (MANAGER *and the* SIX CHARACTERS *cross the stage and go off. The other* ACTORS *remain, looking at one another in astonishment.*)

LEADING MAN: Is he serious? What the devil does he want to do?

JUVENILE LEAD: This is rank madness.

THIRD ACTOR: Does he expect to knock up a drama in five minutes?

JUVENILE LEAD: Like the improvisers!

LEADING LADY: If he thinks I'm going to take part in a joke like this. . . .

JUVENILE LEAD: I'm out of it anyway.

FOURTH ACTOR: I should like to know who they are. (*Alludes to* CHARACTERS.)

THIRD ACTOR: What do you suppose? Madmen or rascals!

JUVENILE LEAD: And he takes them seriously!

L'INGÉNUE: Vanity! He fancies himself as an author now.

LEADING MAN: It's absolutely unheard of. If the stage has come to this . . . well I'm . . .

FIFTH ACTOR: It's rather a joke.

THIRD ACTOR: Well, we'll see what's going to happen next.

(*Thus talking, the* ACTORS *leave the stage; some going out by the little door at the back; others retiring to their dressing-rooms.*
The curtain remains up.
The action of the play is suspended for twenty minutes.)

ACT II

The stage call-bells ring to warn the company that the play is about to begin again.

The STEP-DAUGHTER *comes out of the* MANAGER'S *office along with the* CHILD *and the* BOY. *As she comes out of the office, she cries:* —

Nonsense! nonsense! Do it yourselves! I'm not going to mix myself up in this mess. (*Turning to the* CHILD *and coming quickly with her on to the stage.*) Come on, Rosetta, let's run!

(*The* BOY *follows them slowly, remaining a little behind and seeming perplexed.*)

THE STEP-DAUGHTER (*stops, bends over the* CHILD *and takes the latter's face between her hands*): My little darling! You're frightened, aren't you? You don't know where we are, do you? (*Pretending to reply to a question of the* CHILD.) What is the stage? It's a place, baby, you know, where people play at being serious, a place where they act comedies. We've got to act a comedy now, dead serious, you know; and you're in it also, little one. (*Embraces her, pressing the little head to her breast, and rocking the* CHILD *for a moment.*) Oh darling, darling, what a horrid comedy you've got to play! What a wretched part they've found for you! A garden . . . a fountain . . . look . . . just suppose, kiddie, it's here. Where, you say? Why, right here in the middle. It's all pretense you know. That's the trouble, my pet: it's all make-believe here. It's better to imagine it though, because if they fix it up for you, it'll only be painted cardboard, painted cardboard for the rockery, the water, the plants. . . . Ah, but I think a baby like this one would sooner have a make-believe fountain than a real one, so she could play with it. What a joke it'll be for the others! But for you, alas! not quite such a joke: you who are real, baby dear, and really play by a real fountain that is big and green and beautiful, with ever so many bamboos around it that are reflected in the water, and a whole lot of little ducks swimming about. . . . No, Rosetta, no, your mother doesn't bother about you on account of that wretch of a son there. I'm in the devil of a temper, and as for that lad. . . . (*Seizes* BOY *by the arm to force him to take one of his hands out of his pockets.*) What have you got there? What are you hiding? (*Pulls his hand out of his pocket, looks into it and catches the glint of a revolver.*) Ah! where did you get this? (*The* BOY, *very pale in the face, looks at her, but does not answer.*) Idiot! If I'd been in your place, instead of killing myself, I'd have shot one of those two, or both of them: father and son.

(*The* FATHER *enters from the office, all excited from his work. The* MANAGER *follows him.*)

THE FATHER: Come on, come on dear! Come here for a minute! We've arranged everything. It's all fixed up.

THE MANAGER (*also excited*): If you please, young lady, there are one or two points to settle still. Will you come along?

THE STEP-DAUGHTER (*following him towards the office*): Ouff! what's the good, if you've arranged everything.

(*The* FATHER, MANAGER *and* STEP-DAUGHTER *go back into the office again* [*off*] *for a moment. At the same time, the* SON *followed by the* MOTHER, *comes out.*)

THE SON (*looking at the three entering office*): Oh this is fine, fine! And to think I can't even get away!

(*The* MOTHER *attempts to look at him, but lowers her eyes immediately when he turns away from her. She then sits down. The* BOY *and the* CHILD *approach her. She casts a glance again at the* SON, *and speaks with humble tones, trying to draw him into conversation.*)

THE MOTHER: And isn't my punishment the worst of all? (*Then seeing from the* SON's *manner that he will not bother himself about her.*) My God! Why are you so cruel? Isn't it enough for one person to support all this torment? Must you then insist on others seeing it also?

THE SON (*half to himself, meaning the* MOTHER *to hear, however*): And they want to put it on the stage! If there was at least a reason for it! He thinks he has got at the meaning of it all. Just as if each one of us in every circumstance of life couldn't find his own explanation of it! (*Pauses.*) He complains he was discovered in a place where he ought not to have been seen, in a moment of his life which ought to have remained hidden and kept out of the reach of that convention which he has to maintain for other people. And what about my case? Haven't I had to reveal what no son ought ever to reveal: how father and mother live and are man and wife for themselves quite apart from that idea of father and mother which we give them? When this idea is revealed, our life is then linked at one point only to that man and that woman; and as such it should shame them, shouldn't it?

(*The* MOTHER *hides her face in her hands. From the dressing-rooms and the little door at the back of the stage the* ACTORS *and* STAGE MANAGER *return, followed by the* PROPERTY MAN, *and the* PROMPTER. *At the same moment, the* MANAGER *comes out of his office, accompanied by the* FATHER *and the* STEP-DAUGHTER.)

THE MANAGER: Come on, come on, ladies and gentlemen! Heh! you there, machinist!

MACHINIST: Yes sir?

THE MANAGER: Fix up the white parlor with the floral decorations. Two wings and a drop with a door will do. Hurry up!

(*The* MACHINIST *runs off at once to prepare the scene, and arranges it while the* MANAGER *talks with the* STAGE MANAGER, *the* PROPERTY MAN, *and the* PROMPTER *on matters of detail.*)

THE MANAGER (*to* PROPERTY MAN): Just have a look, and see if there isn't a sofa or divan in the wardrobe . . .

PROPERTY MAN: There's the green one.

THE STEP-DAUGHTER: No no! Green won't do. It was yellow, ornamented with flowers — very large! and most comfortable!

PROPERTY MAN: There isn't one like that.

THE MANAGER: It doesn't matter. Use the one we've got.

THE STEP-DAUGHTER: Doesn't matter? It's most important!

THE MANAGER: We're only trying it now. Please don't interfere. (*To* PROPERTY MAN.) See if we've got a shop window — long and narrowish.

THE STEP-DAUGHTER: And the little table! The little mahogany table for the pale blue envelope!

PROPERTY MAN (*to* MANAGER): There's that little gilt one.

THE MANAGER: That'll do fine.

THE FATHER: A mirror.

THE STEP-DAUGHTER: And the screen! We must have a screen. Otherwise how can I manage?

PROPERTY MAN: That's all right, Miss. We've got any amount of them.

THE MANAGER (*to the* STEP-DAUGHTER): We want some clothes pegs too, don't we?

THE STEP-DAUGHTER: Yes, several, several!

THE MANAGER: See how many we've got and bring them all.

PROPERTY MAN: All right!

(*The* PROPERTY MAN *hurries off to obey his orders. While he is putting the things in their places, the* MANAGER *talks to the* PROMPTER *and then with the* CHARACTERS *and the* ACTORS.)

THE MANAGER (*to* PROMPTER): Take your seat. Look here: this is the outline of the scenes, act by act. (*Hands him some sheets of paper.*) And now I'm going to ask you to do something out of the ordinary.

PROMPTER: Take it down in shorthand?

THE MANAGER (*pleasantly surprised*): Exactly! Can you do shorthand?

PROMPTER: Yes, a little.

THE MANAGER: Good! (*Turning to a* STAGE HAND.) Go and get some paper from my office, plenty, as much as you can find.

(*The* STAGE HAND *goes off, and soon returns with a handful of paper which he gives to the* PROMPTER.)

THE MANAGER (*to* PROMPTER): You follow the scenes as we play them, and try and get the points down, at any rate the most important ones. (*Then addressing the* ACTORS.) Clear the stage, ladies and gentlemen! Come over here (*pointing to the left*) and listen attentively.

LEADING LADY: But, excuse me, we. . . .

THE MANAGER (*guessing her thought*): Don't worry! You won't have to improvise.

LEADING MAN: What have we to do then?

THE MANAGER: Nothing. For the moment you just watch and listen. Everybody will get his part written out afterwards. At present we're going to try the thing as best we can. They're going to act now.

THE FATHER (*as if fallen from the clouds into the confusion of the stage*): We? What do you mean, if you please, by a rehearsal?

THE MANAGER: A rehearsal for them. (*Points to the* ACTORS.)

THE FATHER: But since we are the characters . . .

THE MANAGER: All right: "characters" then, if you insist on calling yourselves such. But here, my dear sir, the characters don't act. Here the actors do the acting. The characters are there, in the "book" (*pointing towards* PROMPTER'S *box*) — when there is a "book"!

THE FATHER: I won't contradict you; but excuse me, the actors aren't the characters. They want to be, they pretend to be, don't they? Now if these gentlemen here are fortunate enough to have us alive before them . . .

THE MANAGER: Oh this is grand! You want to come before the public yourselves then?

THE FATHER: As we are. . . .

THE MANAGER: I can assure you it would be a magnificent spectacle!

LEADING MAN: What's the use of us here anyway then?

THE MANAGER: You're not going to pretend that you can act? It makes me laugh! (*The* ACTORS *laugh.*) There, you see, they are laughing at the notion. But, by the way, I must cast the parts. That won't be difficult. They cast themselves. (*To the* SECOND LADY LEAD.) You play the Mother. (*To the* FATHER.) We must find her a name.

THE FATHER: Amalia, sir.

THE MANAGER: But that is the real name of your wife. We don't want to call her by her real name.

THE FATHER: Why ever not, if it is her name? . . . Still, perhaps, if that lady must. . . . (*Makes a slight motion of the hand to indicate the* SECOND LADY LEAD.) I see this woman here (*means the* MOTHER) as Amalia. But do as you like. (*Gets more and more confused.*) I don't know what to say to you. Already, I begin to hear my own words ring false, as if they had another sound. . . .

THE MANAGER: Don't you worry about it. It'll be our job to find the right tones. And as for her name, if you want her Amalia, Amalia it shall be; and if you don't like it, we'll find another! For the moment though, we'll call the characters in this way: (*To* JUVENILE LEAD.) You are the Son. (*To the* LEADING LADY.) You naturally are the Step-Daughter. . . .

THE STEP-DAUGHTER (*excitedly*): What? what? I, that woman there? (*Bursts out laughing.*)

THE MANAGER (*angry*): What is there to laugh at?

LEADING LADY (*indignant*): Nobody has ever dared to laugh at me. I insist on being treated with respect; otherwise I go away.

THE STEP-DAUGHTER: No, no, excuse me . . . I am not laughing at you. . . .

THE MANAGER (*to* STEP-DAUGHTER): You ought to feel honored to be played by. . .

LEADING LADY (*at once, contemptuously*): "That woman there" . . .

THE STEP-DAUGHTER: But I wasn't speaking of you, you know. I was speaking of myself — whom I can't see at all in you! That is all. I don't know . . . but . . . you . . . aren't in the least like me. . . .

THE FATHER: True. Here's the point. Look here, sir, our temperaments, our souls. . . .

THE MANAGER: Temperament, soul, be hanged! Do you suppose the spirit of the piece is in you? Nothing of the kind!

THE FATHER: What, haven't we our own temperaments, our own souls?

THE MANAGER: Not at all. Your soul or whatever you like to call it takes shape here. The actors give body and form to it, voice and gesture. And my actors — I may tell you — have given expression to much more lofty material than this little drama of yours, which may or may not hold up on the stage. But if it does, the merit of it, believe me, will be due to my actors.

THE FATHER: I don't dare contradict you, sir; but, believe me, it is a terrible suffering for us who are as we are, with these bodies of ours, these features to see. . . .

THE MANAGER (*cutting him short and out of patience*): Good heavens! The make-up will remedy all that, man, the make-up. . . .

THE FATHER: Maybe. But the voice, tne gestures . . .

THE MANAGER: Now, look here! On the stage, you as yourself, cannot exist. The actor here acts you, and that's an end to it!

THE FATHER: I understand. And now I think I see why our author who conceived us as we are, all alive, didn't want to put us on the stage after all. I haven't the least desire to offend your actors. Far from it! But when I think that I am to be acted by . . . I don't know by whom. . . .

LEADING MAN (*on his dignity*): By me, if you've no objection!

THE FATHER (*humbly, mellifluously*): Honored, I assure you, sir. (*Bows.*) Still, I must say that try as this gentleman may, with all his good will and wonderful art, to absorb me into himself. . . .

LEADING MAN: Oh chuck it! "Wonderful art!" Withdraw that, please!

THE FATHER: The performance he will give, even doing his best with make-up to look like me. . . .

LEADING MAN: It will certainly be a bit difficult! (*The* ACTORS *laugh.*)

THE FATHER: Exactly! It will be difficult to act me as I really am. The effect will be rather — apart from the make-up — according as to how he supposes I am, as he senses me — if he does sense me — and not as I inside of myself feel myself to be. It seems to me then that account should be taken of this by everyone whose duty it may become to criticize us. . . .

THE MANAGER: Heavens! The man's starting to think about the critics now! Let them say what they like. It's up to us to put on the play if we can. (*Looking around.*) Come on! come on! Is the stage set? (*To the* ACTORS *and* CHARACTERS.) Stand back — stand back! Let me see, and don't let's lose any more time! (*To the* STEP-DAUGHTER.) Is it all right as it is now?

THE STEP-DAUGHTER: Well, to tell the truth, I don't recognize the scene.

THE MANAGER: My dear lady, you can't possibly suppose that we can construct that shop of Madame Pace piece by piece here? (*To the* FATHER.) You said a white room with flowered wall paper, didn't you?

THE FATHER: Yes.

THE MANAGER: Well then. We've got the furniture right more or less. Bring that little table a bit further forward. (*The* STAGE HANDS *obey the order. To* PROPERTY MAN.) You go and find an envelope, if possible, a pale blue one; and give it to that gentleman. (*Indicates* FATHER.)

PROPERTY MAN: An ordinary envelope?

MANAGER *and* FATHER: Yes, yes, an ordinary envelope.

PROPERTY MAN: At once, sir (*Exit.*)

THE MANAGER: Ready, everyone! First scene — the Young Lady. (*The* LEADING LADY *comes forward.*) No, no, you must wait. I meant her. (*Indicating the* STEP-DAUGHTER.) You just watch —

THE STEP-DAUGHTER (*adding at once*): How I shall play it, how I shall live it! . . .

LEADING LADY (*offended*): I shall live it also, you may be sure, as soon as I begin!

THE MANAGER (*with his hands to his head*): Ladies and gentlemen, if you please! No more useless discussions! Scene I: the young lady with Madame Pace: Oh! (*Looks around as if lost.*) And this Madame Pace, where is she?

THE FATHER: She isn't with us, sir.

THE MANAGER: Then what the devil's to be done?

THE FATHER: But she is alive too.

THE MANAGER: Yes, but where is she?

THE FATHER: One minute. Let me speak! (*Turning to the* ACTRESSES.) If these ladies would be so good as to give me their hats for a moment. . . .

THE ACTRESSES (*half surprised, half laughing, in chorus*): What? Why? Our hats? What does he say?

THE MANAGER: What are you going to do with the ladies' hats? (*The* ACTORS *laugh.*)

THE FATHER: Oh nothing. I just want to put them on these pegs for a moment. And one of the ladies will be so kind as to take off her mantle. . . .

THE ACTORS: Oh, what d'you think of that? Only the mantle? He must be mad.

SOME ACTRESSES: But why? Mantles as well?

THE FATHER: To hang them up here for a moment. Please be so kind, will you?

THE ACTRESSES (*taking off their hats, one or two also their cloaks, and going to hang them on the racks*): After all, why not? There you are! This is really funny. We've got to put them on show.

THE FATHER: Exactly; just like that, on show.

THE MANAGER: May we know why?

THE FATHER: I'll tell you. Who knows if, by arranging the stage for her, she does not come here herself, attracted by the very articles of her trade? (*Inviting the* ACTORS *to look towards the exit at back of stage.*) Look! Look!

(*The door at the back of stage opens and* MADAME PACE *enters and takes a few steps forward. She is a fat, oldish woman with puffy oxygenated hair. She is rouged and powdered, dressed with a comical elegance in black silk. Round her waist is a long silver chain from which hangs a pair of scissors. The* STEP-DAUGHTER *runs over to her at once amid the stupor of the* ACTORS.)

THE STEP-DAUGHTER (*turning towards her*): There she is! There she is!

THE FATHER (*radiant*): It's she! I said so, didn't I? There she is!

THE MANAGER (*conquering his surprise, and then becoming indignant*): What sort of a trick is this?

LEADING MAN (*almost at the same time*): What's going to happen next?

JUVENILE LEAD: Where does *she* come from?

L'INGÉNUE: They've been holding her in reserve, I guess.

LEADING LADY: A vulgar trick!

THE FATHER (*dominating the protests*): Excuse me, all of you! Why are you so anxious to destroy in the name of a vulgar, common-place sense of truth, this reality which comes to birth attracted and formed by the magic of the stage itself, which has indeed more right to live here than you, since it is much truer than you — if you don't mind my saying so? Which is the actress among you who is to play Madame Pace? Well, here is Madame Pace herself. And you will allow, I fancy, that the actress who acts her will be less true than this woman here, who is herself in person. You see my daughter recognized her and went over to her at once. Now you're going to witness the scene!

(*But the scene between the* STEP-DAUGHTER *and* MADAME PACE *has already begun despite the protest of the actors and the reply of the* FATHER. *It has begun quietly, naturally, in a manner impossible for the stage. So when the* ACTORS, *called to attention by the* FATHER, *turn round and see* MADAME PACE, *who has placed one hand under the* STEP-DAUGHTER'S *chin to raise her head, they observe her at first with great attention, but hearing her speak in an unintelligible manner their interest begins to wane.*)

THE MANAGER: Well? well?

LEADING MAN: What does she say?

LEADING LADY: One can't hear a word.

JUVENILE LEAD: Louder! Louder please!

THE STEP-DAUGHTER (*leaving* MADAME PACE, *who smiles a Sphinx-like smile, and advancing towards the* ACTORS): Louder? Louder? What are you talking about? These aren't matters which can be shouted at the top of one's voice. If I have spoken them out loud, is was to shame him and have my revenge. (*Indicates* FATHER.) But for Madame it's quite a different matter.

THE MANAGER: Indeed? indeed? But here, you know, people have got to make themselves heard, my dear. Even we who are on the stage can't hear you. What will it be when the public's in the theatre? And anyway, you can very well speak up now among yourselves, since we shan't be present to listen to you as we are now. You've got to pretend to be alone in a room at the back of a shop where no one can hear you.

(*The* STEP-DAUGHTER *coquettishly and with a touch of malice makes a sign of disagreement two or three times with her finger.*)

THE MANAGER: What do you mean by no?

THE STEP-DAUGHTER (*sotto voce, mysteriously*): There's someone who will hear us if she (*indicating* MADAME PACE) speaks out loud.

THE MANAGER (*in consternation*): What? Have you got someone else to spring on us now? (*The* ACTORS *burst out laughing.*)

THE FATHER: No, no sir. She is alluding to me. I've got to be here — there behind that door, in waiting; and Madame Pace knows it. In fact, if you will allow me, I'll go there at once, so I can be quite ready. (*Moves away.*)

THE MANAGER (*stopping him*): No! Wait! wait! We must observe the conventions of the theatre. Before you are ready. . . .

THE STEP-DAUGHTER (*interrupting him*): No, get on with it at once!

I'm just dying, I tell you, to act this scene. If he's ready, I'm more than ready.

THE MANAGER (*shouting*): But, my dear young lady, first of all, we must have the scene between you and this lady. . . . (*Indicates* MADAME PACE.) Do you understand? . . .

THE STEP-DAUGHTER: Good Heavens! She's been telling me what you know already: that mamma's work is badly done again, that the material's ruined; and that if I want her to continue to help us in our misery I must be patient. . . .

MADAME PACE (*coming forward with an air of great importance*): Yes indeed, sir, I no wanta take advantage of her, I no wanta be hard. . . .

(*Note.* MADAME PACE *is supposed to talk in a jargon half Italian, half English.*)

THE MANAGER (*alarmed*): What? What? She talks like that? (*The* ACTORS *burst out laughing again.*)

THE STEP-DAUGHTER (*also laughing*): Yes yes, that's the way she talks, half English, half Italian! Most comical it is!

MADAME PACE: Itta seem not verra polite gentlemen laugha atta me eeff I trya best speaka English.

THE MANAGER: *Diamine!* Of course! Of course! Let her talk like that! Just what we want. Talk just like that, Madame, if you please! The effect will be certain. Exactly what was wanted to put a little comic relief into the crudity of the situation. Of course she talks like that! Magnificent!

THE STEP-DAUGHTER: Magnificent? Certainly! When certain suggestions are made to one in language of that kind, the effect is certain, since it seems almost a joke. One feels inclined to laugh when one hears her talk about an "old signore" "who wanta talka nicely with you." Nice old signore, eh, Madame?

MADAME PACE: Not so old my dear, not so old! And even if you no lika him, he won't make any scandal!

THE MOTHER (*jumping up amid the amazement and consternation of the* ACTORS *who had not been noticing her. They move to restrain her*): You old devil! You murderess!

THE STEP-DAUGHTER (*running over to calm her* MOTHER): Calm yourself, Mother, calm yourself! Please don't. . . .

THE FATHER (*going to her also at the same time*): Calm yourself! Don't get excited! Sit down now!

THE MOTHER: Well then, take that woman away out of my sight!

THE STEP-DAUGHTER (*to* MANAGER): It is impossible for my mother to remain here.

THE FATHER (*to* MANAGER): They can't be here together. And for this reason, you see: that woman there was not with us when we came. . . . If they are on together, the whole thing is given away inevitably, as you see.

THE MANAGER: It doesn't matter. This is only a first rough sketch — just to get an idea of the various points of the scene, even confusedly. . . . (*Turning to the* MOTHER *and leading her to her chair.*) Come along, my dear lady, sit down now, and let's get on with the scene. . . .

(*Meanwhile, the* STEP-DAUGHTER, *coming forward again, turns to* MADAME PACE.)

THE STEP-DAUGHTER: Come on, Madame, come on!

MADAME PACE (*offended*): No, no, *grazie*. I not do anything witha your mother present.

THE STEP-DAUGHTER: Nonsense! Introduce this "old signore" who wants to talk nicely to me. (*Addressing the* COMPANY *imperiously.*) We've got to do this scene one way or another, haven't we? Come on! (*To* MADAME PACE.) You can go!

MADAME PACE: Ah yes! I go'way! I go'way! Certainly! (*Exits furious.*)

THE STEP-DAUGHTER (*to the* FATHER): Now you make your entry. No, you needn't go over here. Come here. Let's suppose you've already come in. Like that, yes! I'm here with bowed head, modest like. Come on! Out with your voice! Say "Good morning, Miss" in that peculiar tone, that special tone. . . .

THE MANAGER: Excuse me, but are you the Manager, or am I? (*To the* FATHER, *who looks undecided and perplexed.*) Get on with it, man! Go down there to the back of the stage. You needn't go off. Then come right forward here.

(*The* FATHER *does as he is told, looking troubled and perplexed at first. But as soon as he begins to move, the reality of the action affects him, and he begins to smile and to be more natural. The* ACTORS *watch intently.*)

THE MANAGER (*sotto voce, quickly to the* PROMPTER *in his box*): Ready! ready? Get ready to write now.

THE FATHER (*coming forward and speaking in a different tone*): Good afternoon, Miss!

THE STEP-DAUGHTER (*head bowed down slightly, with restrained disgust*): Good afternoon!

THE FATHER (*looks under her hat which partly covers her face. Perceiving she is very young, he makes an exclamation, partly of surprise, partly of fear lest he compromise himself in a risky ad-*

venture): Ah . . . but . . . ah . . . I say . . . this is not the first time that you have come here, is it?

THE STEP-DAUGHTER (*modestly*): No sir.

THE FATHER: You've been here before, eh? (*Then seeing her nod .agreement.*) More than once? (*Waits for her to answer, looks under her hat, smiles, and then says.*) Well then, there's no need to be so shy, is there? May I take off your hat?

THE STEP-DAUGHTER (*anticipating him and with veiled disgust*): No sir . . . I'll do it myself. (*Takes it off quickly.*)

(*The* MOTHER, *who watches the progress of the scene with the* SON *and the other two children who cling to her, is on thorns; and follows with varying expressions of sorrow, indignation, anxiety, and horror the words and actions of the other two. From time to time she hides her face in her hands and sobs.*)

THE MOTHER: Oh, my God, my God!

THE FATHER (*playing his part with a touch of gallantry*): Give it to me! I'll put it down. (*Takes hat from her hands.*) But a dear little head like yours ought to have a smarter hat. Come and help me choose one from the stock, won't you?

L'INGÉNUE (*interrupting*): I say . . . those are our hats you know.

THE MANAGER (*furious*): Silence! silence! Don't try and be funny, if you please. . . . We're playing the scene now I'd have you notice. (*To the* STEP-DAUGHTER.) Begin again, please!

THE STEP-DAUGHTER (*continuing*): No thank you, sir.

THE FATHER: Oh, come now. Don't talk like that. You must take it. I shall be upset if you don't. There are some lovely little hats here; and then — Madame will be pleased. She expects it, anyway, you know.

THE STEP-DAUGHTER: No, no! I couldn't wear it!

THE FATHER: Oh, you're thinking about what they'd say at home if they saw you come in with a new hat? My dear girl, there's always a way round these little matters, you know.

THE STEP-DAUGHTER (*all keyed up*): No, it's not that. I couldn't wear it because I am . . . as you see . . . you might have noticed . . . (*Showing her black dress.*)

THE FATHER: . . . in mourning! Of course: I beg your pardon: I'm frightfully sorry. . . .

THE STEP-DAUGHTER (*forcing herself to conquer her indignation and nausea*): Stop! Stop! It's I who must thank you. There's no need for you to feel mortified or specially sorry. Don't think any more of what I've said. (*Tries to smile.*) I must forget that I am dressed so. . . .

THE MANAGER (*interrupting and turning to the* PROMPTER): Stop a
minute! Stop! Don't write that down. Cut out that last bit. (*Then
to the* FATHER *and* STEP-DAUGHTER.) Fine! it's going fine! (*To the*
FATHER *only.*) And now you can go on as we arranged. (*To the*
ACTORS.) Pretty good that scene, where he offers her the hat, eh?

THE STEP-DAUGHTER: The best's coming now. Why can't we go on?

THE MANAGER: Have a little patience! (*To the* ACTORS.) Of course,
it must be treated rather lightly.

LEADING MAN: Still, with a bit of go in it!

LEADING LADY: Of course! It's easy enough! (*To* LEADING MAN.)
Shall you and I try it now?

LEADING MAN: Why, yes! I'll prepare my entrance. (*Exit in order to
make his entrance.*)

THE MANAGER (*to* LEADING LADY): See here! The scene between you
and Madame Pace is finished. I'll have it written out properly after.
You remain here . . . oh, where are you going?

LEADING LADY: One minute. I want to put my hat on again. (*Goes
over to hat-rack and puts her hat on her head.*)

THE MANAGER: Good! You stay here with your head bowed down a
bit.

THE STEP-DAUGHTER: But she isn't dressed in black.

LEADING LADY: But I shall be, and much more effectively than you.

THE MANAGER (*to* STEP-DAUGHTER): Be quiet please, and watch!
You'll be able to learn something. (*Clapping his hands.*) Come on!
come on! Entrance, please!

(*The door at rear of stage opens, and the* LEADING MAN *enters
with the lively manner of an old gallant. The rendering of the
scene by the* ACTORS *from the very first words is seen to be quite a
different thing, though it has not in any way the air of a parody.
Naturally, the* STEP-DAUGHTER *and the* FATHER, *not being able to
recognize themselves in the* LEADING LADY *and the* LEADING MAN,
*who deliver their words in different tones and with a different
psychology, express, sometimes with smiles, sometimes with gestures, the impression they receive.*)

LEADING MAN: Good afternoon, Miss. . . .

THE FATHER (*at once unable to contain himself*): No!

(*The* STEP-DAUGHTER *noticing the way the* LEADING MAN *enters,
bursts out laughing.*)

THE MANAGER (*furious*): Silence! And you please just stop that laughing. If we go on like this, we shall never finish.

THE STEP-DAUGHTER: Forgive me, sir, but it's natural enough. This lady (*indicating* LEADING LADY) stands there still; but if she is supposed to be me, I can assure you that if I heard anyone say "Good afternoon" in that manner and in that tone, I should burst out laughing as I did.

THE FATHER: Yes, yes, the manner, the tone. . . .

THE MANAGER: Nonsense! Rubbish! Stand aside and let me see the action.

LEADING MAN: If I've got to represent an old fellow who's coming into a house of an equivocal character. . . .

THE MANAGER: Don't listen to them, for Heaven's sake! Do it again! It goes fine. (*Waiting for the* ACTORS *to begin again.*) Well?

LEADING MAN: Good afternoon, Miss.

LEADING LADY: Good afternoon.

LEADING MAN (*imitating the gesture of the* FATHER *when he looked under the hat, and then expressing quite clearly first satisfaction and then fear*): Ah, but . . . I say . . . this is not the first time that you have come here, is it?

THE MANAGER: Good, but not quite so heavily. Like this. (*Acts himself.*) "This isn't the first time that you have come here" . . . (*To* LEADING LADY.) And you say: "No, sir."

LEADING LADY: No, sir.

LEADING MAN: You've been here before, more than once.

THE MANAGER: No, no, stop! Let her nod "yes" first. "You've been here before, eh?" (*The* LEADING LADY *lifts up her head slightly and closes her eyes as though in disgust. Then she inclines her head twice.*)

THE STEP-DAUGHTER (*unable to contain herself*): Oh my God! (*Puts a hand to her mouth to prevent herself from laughing.*)

THE MANAGER (*turning round*): What's the matter?

THE STEP-DAUGHTER: Nothing, nothing!

THE MANAGER (*to* LEADING MAN): Go on!

LEADING MAN: You've been here before, eh? Well then, there's no need to be so shy, is there? May I take off your hat?

(*The* LEADING MAN *says this last speech in such a tone and with such gestures that the* STEP-DAUGHTER, *though she has her hand to her mouth, cannot keep from laughing.*)

LEADING LADY (*indignant*): I'm not going to stop here to be made a fool of by that woman there.

LEADING MAN: Neither am I! I'm through with it!

THE MANAGER (*shouting to* STEP-DAUGHTER): Silence! for once and all, I tell you!

THE STEP-DAUGHTER: Forgive me! forgive me!

THE MANAGER: You haven't any manners: that's what it is! You go too far.

THE FATHER (*endeavoring to intervene*): Yes, it's true, but excuse her. . . .

THE MANAGER: Excuse what? It's absolutely disgusting.

THE FATHER: Yes, sir, but believe me, it has such a strange effect when. . . .

THE MANAGER: Strange? Why strange? Where is it strange?

THE FATHER: No, sir; I admire your actors — this gentleman here, this lady; but they are certainly not us!

THE MANAGER: I should hope not. Evidently they cannot be you, if they are actors.

THE FATHER: Just so: actors! Both of them act our parts exceedingly well. But, believe me, it produces quite a different effect on us. They want to be us, but they aren't, all the same.

THE MANAGER: What is it then anyway?

THE FATHER: Something that is . . . that is theirs — and no longer ours . . .

THE MANAGER: But naturally, inevitably. I've told you so already.

THE FATHER: Yes, I understand . . . I understand . . .

THE MANAGER: Well then, let's have no more of it! (*Turning to the* ACTORS.) We'll have the rehearsals by ourselves, afterwards, in the ordinary way. I never could stand rehearsing with the author present. He's never satisfied! (*Turning to* FATHER *and* STEP-DAUGHTER.) Come on! Let's get on with it again; and try and see if you can't keep from laughing.

THE STEP-DAUGHTER: Oh, I shan't laugh any more. There's a nice little bit coming for me now: you'll see.

THE MANAGER: Well then: when she says "Don't think any more of what I've said, I must forget, etc.," you (*addressing the* FATHER) come in sharp with "I understand, I understand"; and then you ask her . . .

THE STEP-DAUGHTER (*interrupting*): What?

THE MANAGER: Why she is in mourning.

THE STEP-DAUGHTER: Not at all! See here: when I told him that it was useless for me to be thinking about my wearing mourning, do you know how he answered me? "Ah well," he said, "then let's take off this little frock."

THE MANAGER: Great! Just what we want, to make a riot in the theatre!

THE STEP-DAUGHTER: But it's the truth!

THE MANAGER: What does that matter? Acting is our business here. Truth up to a certain point, but no further.

THE STEP-DAUGHTER: What do you want to do then?

THE MANAGER: You'll see, you'll see! Leave it to me.

THE STEP-DAUGHTER: No sir! What you want to do is to piece together a little romantic sentimental scene out of my disgust, out of all the reasons, each more cruel and viler than the other, why I am what I am. He is to ask me why I'm in mourning; and I'm to answer with tears in my eyes, that it is just two months since papa died. No sir, no! He's got to say to me; as he did say: "Well, let's take off this little dress at once." And I, with my two months' mourning in my heart, went there behind that screen, and with these fingers tingling with shame . . .

THE MANAGER (*running his hands through his hair*): For Heaven's sake! What are you saying?

THE STEP-DAUGHTER (*crying out excitedly*): The truth! The truth!

THE MANAGER: It may be. I don't deny it, and I can understand all your horror; but you must surely see that you can't have this kind of thing on the stage. It won't go.

THE STEP-DAUGHTER: Not possible, eh? Very well! I'm much obliged to you — but I'm off!

THE MANAGER: Now be reasonable! Don't lose your temper!

THE STEP-DAUGHTER: I won't stop here! I won't! I can see you've fixed it all up with him in your office. All this talk about what is possible for the stage . . . I understand! He wants to get at his complicated "cerebral drama," to have his famous remorses and torments acted; but I want to act my part, *my part!*

THE MANAGER (*annoyed, shaking his shoulders*): Ah! Just *your* part! But, if you will pardon me, there are other parts than yours: His (*indicating the* FATHER) and hers (*indicating the* MOTHER)! On the stage you can't have a character becoming too prominent and overshadowing all the others. The thing is to pack them all into a neat little framework and then act what is actable. I am aware of the fact that everyone has his own interior life which he wants very much to put forward. But the difficulty lies in this fact: to set out just so much as is necessary for the stage, taking the other characters into consideration, and at the same time hint at the unrevealed interior life of each. I am willing to admit, my dear young lady, that from your point of view it would be a fine idea if each character could tell the public all his troubles in a nice monologue or a regular one hour lecture. (*Good humoredly.*) You must restrain yourself, my dear, and in your own interest, too; because this fury of yours, this exaggerated disgust you show, may make a bad impression, you know. After you have confessed to me that there were others before him at Madame Pace's and more than once . . .

THE STEP-DAUGHTER (*bowing her head, impressed*): It's true. But remember those others mean him for me all the same.

THE MANAGER (*not understanding*): What? The others? What do you mean?

THE STEP-DAUGHTER: For one who has gone wrong, sir, he who was responsible for the first fault is responsible for all that follow. He is responsible for my faults, was, even before I was born. Look at him, and see if it isn't true!

THE MANAGER: Well, well! And does the weight of so much responsibility seem nothing to you? Give him a chance to act it, to get it over!

THE STEP-DAUGHTER: How? How can he act all his "noble remorses," all his "moral torments," if you want to spare him the horror of being discovered one day — after he had asked her what he did ask her — in the arms of her, that already fallen woman, that child, sir, that child he used to watch come out of school? (*she is moved.*)

(*The* MOTHER *at this point is overcome with emotion, and breaks out into a fit of crying. All are touched. A long pause.*)

THE STEP-DAUGHTER (*as soon as the* MOTHER *becomes a little quieter, adds resolutely and gravely*): At present, we are unknown to the public. Tomorrow, you will act us as you wish, treating us in your own manner. But do you really want to see drama, do you want to see it flash out as it really did?

THE MANAGER: Of course! That's just what I do want, so I can use as much of it as is possible.

THE STEP-DAUGHTER: Well then, ask that Mother there to leave us.

THE MOTHER (*changing her low plaint into a sharp cry*): No! No! Don't permit it, sir, don't permit it!

THE MANAGER: But it's only to try it.

THE MOTHER: I can't bear it. I can't.

THE MANAGER: But since it has happened already . . . I don't understand!

THE MOTHER: It's taking place now. It happens all the time. My torment isn't a pretended one. I live and feel every minute of my torture. Those two children there — have you heard them speak? They can't speak any more. They cling to me to keep up my torment actual and vivid for me. But for themselves, they do not exist, they aren't any more. And she (*indicating the* STEP-DAUGHTER) has run away, she has left me, and is lost. If I now see her here before me, it is only to renew for me the tortures I have suffered for her too.

THE FATHER: The eternal moment! She (*indicating the* STEP-DAUGH-TER) is here to catch me, fix me, and hold me eternally in the stocks for that one fleeting and shameful moment of my life. She can't give it up! And you sir, cannot either fairly spare me it.

THE MANAGER: I never said I didn't want to act it. It will form, as a matter of fact, the nucleus of the whole first act right up to her surprise. (*Indicates the* MOTHER.)

THE FATHER: Just so! This is my punishment: the passion in all of us that must culminate in her final cry.

THE STEP-DAUGHTER: I can hear it still in my ears. It's driven me mad, that cry! — You can put me on as you like; it doesn't matter. Fully dressed, if you like — provided I have at least the arm bare; because, standing like this (*she goes close to the* FATHER *and leans her head on his breast*) with my head so, and my arms round his neck, I saw a vein pulsing in my arm here; and then, as if that live vein had awakened disgust in me, I closed my eyes like this, and let my head sink on his breast. (*Turning to the* MOTHER.) Cry out mother! Cry out! (*Buries head in* FATHER'S *breast, and with her shoulders raised as if to prevent her hearing the cry, adds in tones of intense emotion.*) Cry out as you did then!

THE MOTHER (*coming forward to separate them*): No! My daughter, my daughter! (*And after having pulled her away from him.*) You brute! you brute! She is my daughter! Don't you see she's my daughter?

THE MANAGER (*walking backwards towards footlights*): Fine! fine! Damned good! And then, of course — curtain!

THE FATHER (*going towards him excitedly*): Yes, of course, because that's the way it really happened.

THE MANAGER (*convinced and pleased*): Oh, yes, no doubt about it. Curtain here, curtain!

(*At the reiterated cry of the* MANAGER, *the* MACHINIST *lets the curtain down, leaving the* MANAGER *and the* FATHER *in front of it before the footlights.*)

THE MANAGER: The darned idiot! I said "curtain" to show the act should end there, and he goes and lets it down in earnest. (*To the* FATHER, *while he pulls the curtain back to go on to the stage again.*) Yes, yes, it's all right. Effect certain! That's the right ending. I'll guarantee the first act at any rate.

ACT III

When the curtain goes up again, it is seen that the stage hands have shifted the bit of scenery used in the last part, and have rigged up instead at the back of the stage a drop, with some trees, and one or two wings. A portion of a fountain basin is visible. The MOTHER *is sitting on the right with the two children by her side. The* SON *is on the same side, but away from the others. He seems bored, angry, and full of shame. The* FATHER *and the* STEP-DAUGHTER *are also seated towards the right front. On the other side (left) are the* ACTORS, *much in the positions they occupied before the curtain was lowered. Only the* MANAGER *is standing up in the middle of the stage, with his hand closed over his mouth in the act of meditating.*

THE MANAGER (*shaking his shoulders after a brief pause*): Ah yes: the second act! Leave it to me, leave it all to me as we arranged, and you'll see! It'll go fine!

THE STEP-DAUGHTER: Our entry into his house (*indicates* FATHER) in spite of him . . . (*indicates the* SON).

THE MANAGER (*out of patience*): Leave it to me, I tell you!

THE STEP-DAUGHTER: Do let it be clear, at any rate, that it is in spite of my wishes.

THE MOTHER (*from her corner, shaking her head*): For all the good that's come of it. . . .

THE STEP-DAUGHTER (*turning towards her quickly*): It doesn't matter. The more harm done us, the more remorse for him.

THE MANAGER (*impatiently*): I understand! Good Heavens! I understand! I'm taking it into account.

THE MOTHER (*supplicatingly*): I beg you, sir, to let it appear quite plain that for conscience' sake I did try in every way. . . .

THE STEP-DAUGHTER (*interrupting indignantly and continuing for the* MOTHER): . . . to pacify me, to dissuade me from spiting him. (*To* MANAGER.) Do as she wants: satisfy her, because it is true! I enjoy it immensely. Anyhow, as you can see, the meeker she is, the more she tries to get at his heart, the more distant and aloof does he become.

THE MANAGER: Are we going to begin this second act or not?

THE STEP-DAUGHTER: I'm not going to talk any more now. But I must tell you this: you can't have the whole action take place in the garden, as you suggest. It isn't possible!

THE MANAGER: Why not?

THE STEP-DAUGHTER: Because he (*indicates the* SON *again*) is always shut up alone in his room. And then there's all the part of that poor dazed-looking boy there which takes place indoors.

THE MANAGER: Maybe! On the other hand, you will understand — we can't change scenes three or four times in one act.

THE LEADING MAN: They used to once.

THE MANAGER: Yes, when the public was up to the level of that child there.

THE LEADING LADY: It makes the illusion easier.

THE FATHER (*irritated*): The illusion! For Heaven's sake, don't say illusion. Please don't use that word, which is particularly painful for us.

THE MANAGER (*astounded*): And why, if you please?

THE FATHER: It's painful, cruel, really cruel; and you ought to understand that.

THE MANAGER: But why? What ought we to say then? The illusion, I tell you, sir, which we've got to create for the audience. . . .

THE LEADING MAN: With our acting.

THE MANAGER: The illusion of a reality.

THE FATHER: I understand; but you, perhaps, do not understand us. Forgive me! You see . . . here for you and your actors, the thing is only — and rightly so . . . a kind of game. . . .

THE LEADING LADY (*interrupting indignantly*): A game! We're not children here, if you please! We are serious actors.

THE FATHER: I don't deny it. What I mean is the game, or play, of your art, which has to give, as the gentleman says, a perfect illusion of reality.

THE MANAGER: Precisely — !

THE FATHER: Now, if you consider the fact that we (*indicates himself and the other five* CHARACTERS), as we are, have no other reality outside of this illusion. . . .

THE MANAGER (*astonished, looking at his* ACTORS, *who are also amazed*): And what does that mean?

THE FATHER (*after watching them for a moment with a wan smile*): As I say, sir, that which is a game of art for you is our sole reality. (*Brief pause. He goes a step or two nearer the* MANAGER *and adds.*) But not only for us, you know, by the way. Just you think it over well. (*Looks him in the eyes.*) Can you tell me who you are?

THE MANAGER (*perplexed, half smiling*): What? Who am I? I am myself.

THE FATHER: And if I were to tell you that that isn't true, because you and I . . . ?

THE MANAGER: I should say you were mad — ! (*The* ACTORS *laugh.*)

THE FATHER: You're quite right to laugh: because we are all making believe here. (*To* MANAGER.) And you can therefore object that it's only for a joke that that gentleman there (*indicates the* LEADING MAN), who naturally is himself, has to be me, who am on the contrary myself — this thing you see here. You see I've caught you in a trap! (*The* ACTORS *laugh.*)

THE MANAGER (*annoyed*): But we've had all this over once before. Do you want to begin again?

THE FATHER: No, no! That wasn't my meaning! In fact, I should like to request you to abandon this game of art (*looking at the* LEADING LADY *as if anticipating her*) which you are accustomed to play here with your actors, and to ask you seriously once again: who are you?

THE MANAGER (*astonished and irritated, turning to his* ACTORS): If this fellow here hasn't got a nerve! A man who calls himself a character comes and asks me who I am!

THE FATHER (*with dignity, but not offended*): A character, sir, may always ask a man who he is. Because a character has really a life of his own, marked with his especial characteristics; for which reason he is always "somebody." But a man — I'm not speaking of you now — may very well be "nobody."

THE MANAGER: Yes, but you are asking these questions of me, the boss, the manager! Do you understand?

THE FATHER: But only in order to know if you, as you really are now, see yourself as you once were with all the illusions that were yours then, with all the things both inside and outside of you as they seemed to you — as they were then indeed for you. Well, sir, if you think of all those illusions that mean nothing to you now, of all those things which don't even *seem* to you to exist any more, while once they *were* for you, don't you feel that — I won't say these boards — but the very earth under your feet is sinking away from you when you reflect that in the same way this *you* as you feel it today — all this present reality of yours — is fated to seem a mere illusion to you tomorrow?

THE MANAGER (*without having understood much, but astonished by the specious argument*): Well, well! And where does all this take us anyway?

THE FATHER: Oh, nowhere! It's only to show you that if we (*indicating the* CHARACTERS) have no other reality beyond the illusion, you too must not count overmuch on your reality as you feel it today, since, like that of yesterday, it may prove an illusion for you tomorrow.

THE MANAGER (*determining to make fun of him*): Ah, excellent!

Then you'll be saying next that you, with this comedy of yours that you brought here to act, are truer and more real than I am.

THE FATHER (*with the greatest seriousness*): But of course; without doubt!

THE MANAGER: Ah, really?

THE FATHER: Why, I thought you'd understand that from the beginning.

THE MANAGER: More real than I?

THE FATHER: If your reality can change from one day to another. . . .

THE MANAGER: But everyone knows it can change. It is always changing, the same as anyone else's.

THE FATHER (*with a cry*): No, sir, not ours! Look here! That is the very difference! Our reality doesn't change: it can't change! It can't be other than what it is, because it is already fixed for ever. It's terrible. Ours is an immutable reality which should make you shudder when you approach us if you are really conscious of the fact that your reality is a mere transitory and fleeting illusion, taking this form today and that tomorrow, according to the conditions, according to your will, your sentiments, which in turn are controlled by an intellect that shows them to you today in one manner and tomorrow. . . . who knows how? . . . Illusions of reality represented in this fatuous comedy of life that never ends, nor can ever end! Because if tomorrow it were to end . . . then why, all would be finished.

THE MANAGER: Oh for God's sake, will you *at least* finish with this philosophizing and let us try and shape this comedy which you yourself have brought me here? You argue and philosophize a bit too much, my dear sir. You know you seem to me almost, almost. . . . (*Stops and looks him over from head to foot.*) Ah, by the way, I think you introduced yourself to me as a — what shall . . . we say — a "character," created by an author who did not afterward care to make a drama of his own creations.

THE FATHER: It is the simple truth, sir.

THE MANAGER: Nonsense! Cut that out, please! None of us believes it, because it isn't a thing, as you must recognize yourself, which one can believe seriously. If you want to know, it seems to me you are trying to imitate the manner of a certain author whom I heartily detest — I warn you — although I have unfortunately bound myself to put on one of his works. As a matter of fact, I was just starting to rehearse it, when you arrived. (*Turning to the* ACTORS.) And this is what we've gained — out of the frying-pan into the fire!

THE FATHER: I don't know to what author you may be alluding, but believe me I feel what I think; and I seem to be philosophizing only for those who do not think what they feel, because they blind themselves with their own sentiment. I know that for many people this self-blinding seems much more "human"; but the contrary is really true. For man never reasons so much and becomes so introspective as when he suffers; since he is anxious to get at the cause of his sufferings, to learn who has produced them, and whether it is just or unjust that he should have to bear them. On the other hand, when he is happy, he takes his happiness as it comes and doesn't analyze it, just as if happiness were his right. The animals suffer without reasoning about their sufferings. But take the case of a man who suffers and begins to reason about it. Oh no! it can't be allowed! Let him suffer like an animal, and then — ah yet, he is "human"!

THE MANAGER: Look here! Look here! You're off again, philosophizing worse than ever.

THE FATHER: Because I suffer, sir! I'm not philosophizing: I'm crying aloud the reason of my sufferings.

THE MANAGER (*makes brusque movement as he is taken with a new idea*): I should like to know if anyone has ever heard of a character who gets right out of his part and perorates and speechifies as you do. Have you ever heard of a case? I haven't.

THE FATHER: You have never met such a case, sir, because authors, as a rule, hide the labor of their creations. When the characters are really alive before their author, the latter does nothing but follow them in their action, in other words, in the situations which they suggest to him; and he has to will them the way they will themselves — for there's trouble if he doesn't. When a character is born, he acquires at once such an independence, even of his own author, that he can be imagined by everybody even in many other situations where the author never dreamed of placing him; and so he acquires for himself a meaning which the author never thought of giving him.

THE MANAGER: Yes, yes, I know this.

THE FATHER: What is there then to marvel at in us? Imagine such a misfortune for characters as I have described to you: to be born of an author's fantasy, and be denied life by him; and then answer me if these characters left alive, and yet without life, weren't right in doing what they did do and are doing now, after they have attempted everything in their power to persuade him to give them their stage life. We've all tried him in turn, I, she (*indicating the* STEP-DAUGHTER) and she (*indicating the* MOTHER).

THE STEP-DAUGHTER: It's true. I too have sought to tempt him, many,

many times, when he has been sitting at his writing table, feeling a bit melancholy, at the twilight hour. He would sit in his arm-chair too lazy to switch on the light, and all the shadows that crept into his room were full of our presence coming to tempt him. (*As if she saw herself still there by the writing table, and was annoyed by the presence of the* ACTORS.) Oh, if you would only go away, go away and leave us alone — mother here with that son of hers — I with that Child — that Boy there always alone — and then I with him (*just hints at the* FATHER) — and then I alone, alone . . . in those shadows! (*Makes a sudden movement as if in the vision she has of herself illuminating those shadows she wanted to seize hold of herself.*) Ah! my life! my life! Oh, what scenes we proposed to him — and I tempted him more than any of the others!

THE FATHER: Maybe. But perhaps it was your fault that he refused to give us life: because you were too insistent, too troublesome.

THE STEP-DAUGHTER: Nonsense! Didn't he make me so himself? (*Goes close to the* MANAGER *to tell him as if in confidence.*) In my opinion he abandoned us in a fit of depression, of disgust for the ordinary theatre as the public knows it and likes it.

THE SON: Exactly what it was, sir; exactly that!

THE FATHER: Not at all! Don't believe it for a minute. Listen to me! You'll be doing quite right to modify, as you suggest, the excesses both of this girl here, who wants to do too much, and of this young man, who won't do anything at all.

THE SON: No, nothing!

THE MANAGER: You too get over the mark occasionally, my dear sir, if I may say so.

THE FATHER: I? When? Where?

THE MANAGER: Always! Continuously! Then there's this insistence of yours in trying to make us believe you are a character. And then too, you must really argue and philosophize less, you know, much less.

THE FATHER: Well, if you want to take away from me the possibility of representing the torment of my spirit which never gives me peace, you will be suppressing me: that's all. Every true man, sir, who is a little above the level of the beasts and plants does not live for the sake of living, without knowing how to live; but he lives so as to give a meaning and a value of his own to life. For me this is *everything*. I cannot give up this, just to represent a mere fact as she (*indicating the* STEP-DAUGHTER) wants. It's all very well for her, since her "vendetta" lies in the "fact." I'm not going to do it. It destroys my *raison d'être*.

THE MANAGER: Your *raison d'être!* Oh, we're going ahead fine! First she starts off, and then you jump in. At this rate, we'll never finish.

THE FATHER: Now, don't be offended! Have it your own way — provided, however, that within the limits of the parts you assign us each one's sacrifice isn't too great.

THE MANAGER: You've got to understand that you can't go on arguing at your own pleasure. Drama is action, sir, action and not confounded philosophy.

THE FATHER: All right. I'll do just as much arguing and philosophizing as everybody does when he is considering his own torments.

THE MANAGER: If the drama permits! But for Heaven's sake, man, let's get along and come to the scene.

THE STEP-DAUGHTER: It seems to me we've got too much action with our coming into his house. (*Indicating* FATHER.) You said, before, you couldn't change the scene every five minutes.

THE MANAGER: Of course not. What we've got to do is to combine and group up all the facts in one simultaneous, close-knit, action. We can't have it as you want, with your little brother wandering like a ghost from room to room, hiding behind doors and meditating a project which — what did you say it did to him?

THE STEP-DAUGHTER: Consumes him, sir, wastes him away!

THE MANAGER: Well, it may be. And then at the same time, you want the little girl there to be playing in the garden . . . one in the house, and the other in the garden: isn't that it?

THE STEP-DAUGHTER: Yes, in the sun, in the sun! That is my only pleasure: to see her happy and careless in the garden after the misery and squalor of the horrible room where we all four slept together. And I had to sleep with her — I, do you understand? — with my vile contaminated body next to hers; with her folding me fast in her loving little arms. In the garden, whenever she spied me, she would run to take me by the hand. She didn't care for the big flowers, only the little ones; and she loved to show me them and pet me.

THE MANAGER: Well then, we'll have it in the garden. Everything shall happen in the garden; and we'll group the other scenes there. (*Calls a* STAGE HAND.) Here, a backcloth with trees and something to do as a fountain basin. (*Turning round to look at the back of the stage.*) Ah, you've fixed it up. Good! (*To* STEP-DAUGHTER.) This is just to give an idea, of course. The Boy, instead of hiding behind the doors, will wander about here in the garden, hiding behind the trees. But it's going to be rather difficult to find a child to do that scene with you where she shows you the flowers. (*Turning to the* BOY.) Come forward a little, will you please? Let's try it now! Come along! come along! (*Then seeing him come shyly forward, full of fear and looking lost.*) It's a nice business, this lad here. What's the matter with him? We'll have to give him a word or two to say. (*Goes close to him, puts a hand on his shoulders, and leads him behind one of the trees.*) Come on! come on! Let me see you a little! Hide here . . . yes, like that. Try and show your head just a little as if you were looking for someone. . . . (*Goes back to observe the effect, when the* BOY *at once goes through the action.*) Excellent! fine! (*Turning to* STEP-DAUGHTER.) Suppose the little girl there were to surprise him as he looks round, and run over to him, so we could give him a word or two to say?

THE STEP-DAUGHTER: It's useless to hope he will speak, as long as that fellow there is here. . . . (*Indicates the* SON.) You must send him away first.

THE SON (*jumping up*): Delighted! Delighted! I don't ask for anything better. (*Begins to move away.*)

THE MANAGER (*at once stopping him*): No! No! Where are you going? Wait a bit!

(*The* MOTHER *gets up alarmed and terrified at the thought that he is really about to go away. Instinctively she lifts her arms to prevent him, without, however, leaving her seat.*)

THE SON (*to* MANAGER *who stops him*): I've got nothing to do with this affair. Let me go please! Let me go!

THE MANAGER: What do you mean by saying you've got nothing to do with this?

THE STEP-DAUGHTER (*calmly, with irony*): Don't bother to stop him: he won't go away.

THE FATHER: He has to act the terrible scene in the garden with his mother.

THE SON (*suddenly resolute and with dignity*): I shall act nothing at all. I've said so from the very beginning. (*To the* MANAGER.) Let me go!

THE STEP-DAUGHTER (*going over to the* MANAGER): Allow me? (*Puts down the* MANAGER's *arm which is restraining the* SON.) Well, go away then, if you want to! (*The* SON *looks at her with contempt and hatred. She laughs and says.*) You see, he can't, he can't go away! He is obliged to stay here, indissolubly bound to the chain. If I, who fly off when that happens which has to happen, because I can't bear him — if I am still here and support that face and expression of his, you can well imagine that he is unable to move. He has to remain here, has to stop with that nice father of his, and that mother whose only son he is. (*Turning to the* MOTHER.) Come

on, mother, come along! (*Turning to* MANAGER *to indicate her.*)
You see, she was getting up to keep him back. (*To the* MOTHER,
beckoning her with her hand.) Come on! come on! (*Then to*
MANAGER.) You can imagine how little she wants to show these
actors of yours what she really feels; but so eager is she to get near
him that. . . . There, you see? She is willing to act her part. (*And
in fact, the* MOTHER *approaches him; and as soon as the* STEP-
DAUGHTER *has finished speaking, opens her arms to signify that she
consents.*)

THE SON (*suddenly*): No! no! If I can't go away, then I'll stop here;
but I repeat: I act nothing!

THE FATHER (*to* MANAGER *excitedly*): You can force him, sir.

THE SON: Nobody can force me.

THE FATHER: I can.

THE STEP-DAUGHTER: Wait a minute, wait . . . First of all, the baby
has to go to the fountain. . . . (*Runs to take the* CHILD *and leads
her to the fountain.*)

THE MANAGER: Yes, yes of course; that's it. Both at the same time.

(*The* SECOND LADY LEAD *and the* JUVENILE LEAD *at this point
separate themselves from the group of* ACTORS. *One watches the*
MOTHER *attentively; the other moves about studying the movements and manner of the* SON *whom he will have to act.*)

THE SON (*to* MANAGER): What do you mean by both at the same
time? It isn't right. There was no scene between me and her.
(*Indicates the* MOTHER.) Ask her how it was!

THE MOTHER: Yes, it's true. I had come into his room. . . .

THE SON: Into my room, do you understand? Nothing to do with the
garden.

THE MANAGER: It doesn't matter. Haven't I told you we've got to
group the action?

THE SON (*observing the* JUVENILE LEAD *studying him*): What do
you want?

THE JUVENILE LEAD: Nothing! I was just looking at you.

THE SON (*turning towards the* SECOND LADY LEAD): Ah! she's at it
too: to re-act her part! (*Indicating the* MOTHER.)

THE MANAGER: Exactly! And it seems to me that you ought to be
grateful to them for their interest.

THE SON: Yes, but haven't you yet perceived that it isn't possible
to live in front of a mirror which not only freezes us with the
image of ourselves, but throws our likeness back at us with a
horrible grimace?

THE FATHER: That is true, absolutely true. You must see that.

THE MANAGER (*to* SECOND LADY LEAD *and* JUVENILE LEAD): He's right! Move away from them!

THE SON: Do as you like. I'm out of this!

THE MANAGER: Be quiet, you, will you? And let me hear your mother! (*To* MOTHER.) You were saying you had entered. . . .

THE MOTHER: Yes, into his room, because I couldn't stand it any longer. I went to empty my heart to him of all the anguish that tortures me. . . . But as soon as he saw me come in. . . .

THE SON: Nothing happened! There was no scene. I went away, that's all! I don't care for scenes!

THE MOTHER: It's true, true. That's how it was.

THE MANAGER: Well now, we've got to do this bit between you and him. It's indispensable.

THE MOTHER: I'm ready . . . when you are ready. If you could only find a chance for me to tell him what I feel here in my heart.

THE FATHER (*going to* SON *in a great rage*): You'll do this for your mother, for your mother, do you understand?

THE SON (*quite determined*): I do nothing!

THE FATHER (*taking hold of him and shaking him*): For God's sake, do as I tell you! Don't you hear your mother asking you for a favor? Haven't you even got the guts to be a son?

THE SON (*taking hold of the* FATHER): No! No! And for God's sake stop it, or else. . . . (*General agitation. The* MOTHER, *frightened, tries to separate them.*)

THE MOTHER (*pleading*): Please! please!

THE FATHER (*not leaving hold of the* SON): You've got to obey, do you hear?

THE SON (*almost crying from rage*): What does it mean, this madness you've got? (*They separate.*) Have you no decency, that you insist on showing everyone our shame? I won't do it! I won't! And I stand for the will of our author in this. He didn't want to put us on the stage, after all!

THE MANAGER: Man alive! You came here . . .

THE SON (*indicating* FATHER): He did! I didn't!

THE MANAGER: Aren't you here now?

THE SON: It was his wish, and he dragged us along with him. He's told you not only the things that did happen, but also things that have never happened at all.

THE MANAGER: Well, tell me then what did happen. You went out of your room without saying a word?

THE SON: Without a word, so as to avoid a scene!

THE MANAGER: And then what did you do?

THE SON: Nothing . . . walking in the garden. . . . (*Hesitates for a moment with expression of gloom.*)

THE MANAGER (*coming closer to him, interested by his extraordinary reserve*): Well, well . . . walking in the garden. . . .

THE SON (*exasperated*): Why on earth do you insist? It's horrible!

(*The* MOTHER *trembles, sobs, and looks towards the fountain.*)

THE MANAGER (*slowly observing the glance and turning towards the* SON *with increasing apprehension*): The baby?

THE SON: There in the fountain. . . .

THE FATHER (*pointing with tender pity to the* MOTHER): She was following him at the moment. . . .

THE MANAGER (*to the* SON *anxiously*): And then you. . . .

THE SON: I ran over to her; I was jumping in to drag her out when I saw something that froze my blood . . . the boy standing stock still, with eyes like a madman's, watching his little drowned sister, in the fountain! (*The* STEP-DAUGHTER *bends over the fountain to hide the* CHILD. *She sobs.*) Then. . . . (*A revolver shot rings out behind the trees where the* BOY *is hidden.*)

THE MOTHER (*with a cry of terror runs over in that direction together with several of the* ACTORS *amid general confusion*): My son! My son! (*Then amid the cries and exclamations one hears her voice.*) Help! Help!

THE MANAGER (*pushing the* ACTORS *aside while they lift up the* BOY *and carry him off*): Is he really wounded?

SOME ACTORS: He's dead! dead!

OTHER ACTORS: No, no, it's only make believe, it's only pretense!

THE FATHER (*with a terrible cry*): Pretense? Reality, sir, reality!

THE MANAGER: Pretense? Reality? To hell with it all! Never in my life has such a thing happened to me. I've lost a whole day over these people, a whole day!

Six Characters in Search of an Author (1921) remains in the memory as the image of the real-life theater of illusionism invaded by the "fantastic reality" of imaginative truth. Pirandello, perhaps as thinking a playwright as there ever was, yet subordinates philosophy to action — the action of the six characters usurping the stage. That he does is the secret of the play's success as play of ideas. We contemplate facing mirrors. The eye is lost, the mind reels, in the infinitely reciprocal vistas of play and reality, actors and characters, illusion and truth. And the play's brilliance as drama is the containment of all its riddles and paradoxes within the one image of the invaded theater.

Not surprisingly, *Six Characters* has been provocative and controversial ever since its first appearance. Though it established Pirandello's fame, there were some, then as now, whom it irritated as a scoreless cerebral game. Others, friendly or hostile, saw in it only a new way of presenting the old middle-class domestic tragedy of past guilt and present anguish — Ibsen with a gimmick. Such views appear inadequate to explain the fact that *Six Characters* has been one of the most seminal plays of our time. In America it has influenced such theatricalist pieces as O'Neill's *Great God Brown* and *Marco Millions*, Thornton Wilder's *Our Town*, and Tennessee Williams' *Glass Menagerie*. It has anticipated much of the mood and manner of today's "absurd" drama. It has been partly responsible for the current scorn of straightforward realism in the theater as unimaginative and old-fashioned photographism. But its family connections run backward, too, for even the avant-garde has a way of slipping into place in the continuum of our dramatic tradition. The play-within-the-play device is traditional. The play's form has been partly suggested by that of the sixteenth- and seventeenth-century Italian *commedia dell' arte*, a playful, earthy drama of dialogue improvisation over stock characters, situations, and plots. Like expressionistic drama *Six Characters* shatters the surface of experience without abandoning the fragments in pursuit of symbol and myth. Its immediate historical context was the "grotesque" theater movement in Italy during and immediately after World War I, whose leader was Luigi Chiarelli and the aim and method of which was to mock and shock conventional sensibilities and institutions while proclaiming universal meaninglessness. But most significant of all is the play's relationship to the serious naturalistic drama of the previous generation.

That drama — Ibsenism and Chekhovianism rather than Ibsen's and Chekhov's own plays — stimulated Pirandello into revolutionizing dramatic form, but he did not simply react against it. He applied to it a new viewpoint. In a sense, what *Six Characters in Search of an Author* does is to put on trial the reality the nineteenth century had taken for granted: the reality of positivist science, matter in motion governed by discoverable, stable laws. It does not bring in a verdict of guilt; Pirandello's thought and art are both too subtle for that. It gives a vote of no confidence. In an important preface to the play, which he wrote in 1925, Pirandello contrasts playwrights to whom it is "enough to present a man or a woman and what is special and characteristic about them simply for the pleasure of presenting them" with those "others, who, beyond such pleasure, feel a more profound spiritual need on whose account they admit only figures, affairs, landscapes which have been soaked, so to speak, in a particular sense of life and acquire from it a universal value." Among these latter, "philosophical," writers he includes himself. His plays suggest that we should interpret this to mean that the concatenation of scene, event, and character that constitutes theme or mood within the realistic convention of scenic and psychological plausibility yielded no "particular sense of life" for him. Just as Strindberg's expressionistic chamber plays today seem more contemporary with our own sense of life than his historical and his naturalistic plays, so is the peculiar quality of Pirandello's modernity precisely his disaffection with the realistic theater of the first generation of modern masters. The particular sense of life that animates *Six Characters* derives from Pirandello's use of the theater itself to challenge the reality his predecessors had made it their artistic end to record as honestly as possible. His making playwriting conscious of itself as medium has been his most important original contribution to modern drama. Ever since, we have been getting plays of double vision: not just (to paraphrase Francis Fergusson) the stage seen as real-life parlor, but the real-life parlor seen as stage — a shifting and multiple stage at that. It is not Pirandello's fault that much of this drama has been mere toying with cleverness. Rather, the number of imitations suggests that the theatricalist convention invites and sometimes allows expression of a reality particularly meaningful to an age haunted by disaster, space, and relativity.

When the Manager, at the end of the play, complains that he has "lost a whole day," his sentiment strikes us as ironic, because our view is more inclusive than his. It is Pirandello's theatricalism that provides that more inclusive view. The Manager is interested in the play the six characters bring him only as long as he senses a hit. At the end he abandons them to the strange limbo in which their author left them. But *we* see that the aborted play-within is not the whole play. The burden of the whole is the tension and interplay between the framing and the framed action — not the family agony, but the family agony *seeking expression in the theater*. Hence, "A Comedy in the Making." The plot that unites the six characters, the web of jealousy, shame, scorn, guilt, rage, and inarticulate, childish sorrow, the demonstration that good intentions may have evil consequences, all this is neither comic nor in the making. The tragedy is rather that the script is finished and can never more be changed. But the Manager's effort to reduce raw suffering to a play *is* comic, because it offers the incongruous spectacle of the irascible, confident, bustlingly effective man of the theater being defeated by a play more real, in the Platonic sense, than reality itself. Since the core of the larger play is here, the point will bear illustration.

The curtain that falls at the end of Act II falls simultaneously in two distinct plays and, falling, brings them together without reconciling them. The crude matter-of-factness of the physical stage and its personnel dispels the purer reality of the family torment. Theatrical expedience, "effective drama," interrupts the characters' "eternal moment" of agony, the terrible scene in Madame Pace's shop that is a debased version of the recognition scene in older tragedy (recognition of identity bringing about recognition of unwitting guilt in an incestuous situation). The ironies proliferate as one ponders the scene. Beings who have no life except as characters in a play are betrayed by heavy-handed theatrical technique. The Manager does not believe in the reality only his craft can bestow. He loses his temper with an underling who is only trying to translate the projected play into theatrical actuality (itself a concept of ironic paradox). The psychological and moral realities of the inner play suddenly accommodate box office demands for a thrilling act climax, with the result that everything comes to a screeching halt. Where does reality end and art begin? The characters rehearse their reality, while the real-life troupe distort it into an actable play and finally close the curtain on both. We witness simultaneously a play about a rehearsal and one about a husband who ceded his wife to her lover with dreadful consequences for husband, wife, lover, and both sets of children. Clearly, there is a sense in which the rehearsal of *Mixing It Up* (there is such a play, Pirandello wrote it in 1918) has not been interrupted at all! The end impression is fireworks rather than incandescence.

But the bewildering doubt, the teasing skepticism, is the play's metaphysical point. The image of the invaded theater is a dramatization of relativism. And the built-in paradox of philosophical relativism is that any assertion of its validity necessarily forgoes all claim to being considered absolutely valid. For to hold that the statement "Everything is relative" is true is also to hold that no truth is absolute, including the assertion of relativity itself. This, of course, is a sophism, and people who don't like to be made dizzy by sophisms don't like Pirandello. What they fail to see is the disturbing truth of the drama of relativity: that it is man's doom to live with and in the metaphysical uncertainty. The passion (as distinct from the intellectualism) of a Pirandello play is man's cry of protest against his condition: perched on the sharp edge of paradox.

What is more, the metaphysical sophism has an esthetic counterpart. To consider it we must begin with a point of ethics. As ethics, the play implies a radical doctrine of human irresponsibility. For if identity is discontinuous, as the Father insists, no one is accountable for his past. The Father refuses to be judged by the degrading moment in the dress shop, because the visitor to Madame Pace's establishment was not his "true" self. In fact, he has no true self; there is no such thing. Art (ethics becoming esthetics), says the Father, is permanence, life ceaseless change, and it is his misfortune that as "character," a figure of literary art, he has been arrested in a single, disgraceful moment. The sordid assignation, the child in the fountain — these are forever. And like the figures on Keats' Grecian urn, only grimly so, these too do "tease us out of thought/As doth eternity." But if, as "character," the Father can rightly claim to be "less real perhaps, but truer" than the Manager and everyone else in the empirical, non-art reality of change, it follows — and this is the sophism — that the truth of art necessarily falsifies life, for when flux freezes as "eternal moment" it is no longer flux. The very essence of experience forever eludes art.

And so *Six Characters in Search of an Author* may be said to embody also the artist's unresolvable dilemma. The primary dramatic conflict between company and characters, invaded and invader, is a fable of artistic creation, with the Manager as a kind of semi-comical middle man, resentful, interested, again resentful, a mocking but painful self-portrait of the author haunted by shapes he can neither give life to nor exorcise.

"All that lives," says Pirandello in the Preface, "by the fact of living, has a form, and by the same token must die — except the work of art which lives forever in so far as it *is* form." Again paradox. His play, according to his own account, grew out of his futile search for a form for the six characters of his imagination. He made living art out of his inability to do so.

W. B. Yeats
PURGATORY

Characters

A BOY
AN OLD MAN

SCENE: *A ruined house and a bare tree in the background.*

BOY: Half-door, hall door,
    Hither and thither day and night,
    Hill or hollow, shouldering this pack,
    Hearing you talk.
OLD MAN: Study that house.
    I think about its jokes and stories;
    I try to remember what the butler
    Said to a drunken gamekeeper
    In mid-October, but I cannot.
    If I cannot, none living can.
    Where are the jokes and stories of a house,
    Its threshold gone to patch a pig-sty?
BOY: So you have come this path before?
OLD MAN: The moonlight falls upon the path,
    The shadow of a cloud upon the house,
    And that's symbolical; study that tree,
    What is it like?

From *Collected Plays of W. B. Yeats.* Copyright © 1952, by The Macmillian Company, and used with their permission. Canadian rights granted by Mrs. W. B. Yeats and The Macmillan Company of Canada, Ltd., through the offices of A. P. Watt & Son.

BOY: A silly old man.

OLD MAN: It's like — no matter what it's like.
I saw it a year ago stripped bare as now,
So I chose a better trade.
I saw it fifty years ago
Before the thunderbolt had riven it,
Green leaves, ripe leaves, leaves thick as butter,
Fat, greasy life. Stand there and look,
Because there is somebody in that house.

(*The* BOY *puts down pack and stands in the doorway.*)

BOY: There's nobody here.

OLD MAN: There's somebody there.

BOY: The floor is gone, the window's gone,
And where there should be roof there's sky,
And here's a bit of an egg-shell thrown
Out of a jackdaw's nest.

OLD MAN: But there are some
That do not care what's gone, what's left:
The souls of Purgatory that come back
To habitations and familiar spots.

BOY: Your wits are out again.

OLD MAN: Re-live
Their transgressions, and that not once
But many times; they know at last
The consequence of those trangressions
Whether upon others or upon themselves;
Upon others, others may bring help,
For when the consequence is at an end
The dream must end; if upon themselves,
There is no help but in themselves
And in the mercy of God.

BOY: I have had enough!
Talk to the jackdaws, if talk you must.

OLD MAN: Stop! Sit there upon that stone.
That is the house where I was born.

BOY: The big old house that was burnt down?

OLD MAN: My mother that was your grand-dam owned it,
This scenery and this countryside,
Kennel and stable, horse and hound —
She had a horse at the Curragh, and there met
My father, a groom in the training stable,
Looked at him and married him.

Her mother never spoke to her again,
And she did right.
BOY: What's right and wrong?
  My grand-dad got the girl and the money.
OLD MAN: Looked at him and married him,
  And he squandered everything she had.
  She never knew the worst, because
  She died in giving birth to me,
  But now she knows it all, being dead.
  Great people lived and died in this house;
  Magistrates, colonels, members of Parliament,
  Captains and Governors, and long ago
  Men that had fought at Aughrim and the Boyne.
  Some that had gone on Government work
  To London or to India came home to die,
  Or came from London every spring
  To look at the may-blossom in the park.
  They had loved the trees that he cut down
  To pay what he had lost at cards
  Or spent on horses, drink and women;
  Had loved the house, had loved all
  The intricate passages of the house,
  But he killed the house; to kill a house
  Where great men grew up, married, died,
  I here declare a capital offence.
BOY: My God, but you had luck! Grand clothes,
  And maybe a grand horse to ride.
OLD MAN: That he might keep me upon his level
  He never sent me to school, but some
  Half-loved me for my half of her:
  A gamekeeper's wife taught me to read,
  A Catholic curate taught me Latin.
  There were old books and books made fine
  By eighteenth-century French binding, books
  Modern and ancient, books by the ton.
BOY: What education have you given me?
OLD MAN: I gave the education that befits
  A bastard that a pedlar got
  Upon a tinker's daughter in a ditch.
  When I had come to sixteen years old
  My father burned down the house when drunk.
BOY: But that is my age, sixteen years old,
  At the Puck Fair.

OLD MAN: And everything was burnt;
   Books, library, all were burnt.
BOY: Is what I have heard upon the road the truth,
   That you killed him in the burning house?
OLD MAN: There's nobody here but our two selves?
BOY: Nobody, Father.
OLD MAN: I stuck him with a knife,
   That knife that cuts my dinner now,
   And after that I left him in the fire.
   They dragged him out, somebody saw
   The knife-wound but could not be certain
   Because the body was all black and charred.
   Then some that were his drunken friends
   Swore they would put me upon trial,
   Spoke of quarrels, a threat I had made.
   The gamekeeper gave me some old clothes,
   I ran away, worked here and there
   Till I became a pedlar on the roads,
   No good trade, but good enough
   Because I am my father's son,
   Because of what I did or may do.
   Listen to the hoof-beats! Listen, listen!
BOY: I cannot hear a sound.
OLD MAN: Beat! Beat!
   This night is the anniversary
   Of my mother's wedding night,
   Or of the night wherein I was begotten.
   My father is riding from the public-house,
   A whiskey-bottle under his arm.

(A *window is lit showing a young girl.*)

   Look at the window; she stands there
   Listening, the servants are all in bed,
   She is alone, he has stayed late
   Bragging and drinking in the public-house.
BOY: There's nothing but an empty gap in the wall.
   You have made it up. No, you are mad!
   You are getting madder every day.
OLD MAN: It's louder now because he rides
   Upon a gravelled avenue
   All grass to-day. The hoof-beat stops,
   He has gone to the other side of the house,

Gone to the stable, put the horse up.
She has gone down to open the door.
This night she is no better than her man
And does not mind that he is half drunk,
She is mad about him. They mount the stairs.
She brings him into her own chamber.
And that is the marriage-chamber now.
The window is dimly lit again.

Do not let him touch you! It is not true
That drunken men cannot beget,
And if he touch he must beget
And you must bear his murderer.
Deaf! Both deaf! If I should throw
A stick or a stone they would not hear;
And that's a proof my wits are out.
But there's a problem: she must live
Through everything in exact detail,
Driven to it by remorse, and yet
Can she renew the sexual act
And find no pleasure in it, and if not,
If pleasure and remorse must both be there,
Which is the greater?
                            I lack schooling.
Go fetch Tertullian; he and I
Will ravel all that problem out
Whilst those two lie upon the mattress
Begetting me.
                      Come back! Come back!
And so you thought to slip away,
My bag of money between your fingers,
And that I could not talk and see!
You have been rummaging in the pack.

(*The light in the window has faded out.*)

BOY: You never gave me my right share.
OLD MAN: And had I given it, young as you are,
     You would have spent it upon drink.
BOY: What if I did? I had a right
     To get it and spend it as I chose.
OLD MAN: Give me that bag and no more words.
BOY: I will not.
OLD MAN: I will break your fingers.

(*They struggle for the bag. In the struggle it drops, scattering the money. The* OLD MAN *staggers but does not fall. They stand looking at each other. The window is lit up. A man is seen pouring whiskey into a glass.*)

BOY: What if I killed you? You killed my grand-dad,
　　Because you were young and he was old.
　　Now I am young and you are old.
OLD MAN (*staring at window*): Better-looking, those sixteen years ——
BOY: What are you muttering?
OLD MAN:　　　　　　　　　　　Younger — and yet
　　She should have known he was not her kind.
BOY: What are you saying? Out with it!

(OLD MAN *points to window.*)

　　My God! The window is lit up
　　And somebody stands there, although
　　The floorboards are all burnt away.
OLD MAN: The window is lit up because my father
　　Has come to find a glass for his whiskey.
　　He leans there like some tired beast.
BOY: A dead, living, murdered man!
OLD MAN: "Then the bride-sleep fell upon Adam":
　　Where did I read those words?
　　　　　　　　　　　　　　And yet
　　There's nothing leaning in the window
　　But the impression upon my mother's mind;
　　Being dead she is alone in her remorse.
BOY: A body that was a bundle of old bones
　　Before I was born. Horrible! Horrible!

(*He covers his eyes.*)

OLD MAN: That beast there would know nothing, being nothing,
　　If I should kill a man under the window
　　He would not even turn his head.

(*He stabs the* BOY.)

　　My father and my son on the same jack-knife!
　　That finishes — there — there — there —

(*He stabs again and again. The window grows dark.*)

　　"Hush-a-bye baby, thy father's a knight,
　　Thy mother a lady, lovely and bright."

No, that is something that I read in a book,
And if I sing it must be to my mother,
And I lack rhyme.

(*The stage has grown dark except where the tree stands in white light.*)

    Study that tree.
It stands there like a purified soul,
All cold, sweet, glistening light.
Dear mother, the window is dark again,
But you are in the light because
I finished all that consequence.
I killed that lad because had he grown up
He would have struck a woman's fancy,
Begot, and passed pollution on.

I am a wretched foul old man
And therefore harmless. When I have stuck
This old jack-knife into a sod
And pulled it out all bright again,
And picked up all the money that he dropped,
I'll to a distant place, and there
Tell my old jokes among new men.

(*He cleans the knife and begins to pick up money.*)

Hoof-beats! Dear God,
How quickly it returns — beat — beat — !

Her mind cannot hold up that dream.
Twice a murderer and all for nothing,
And she must animate that dead night
Not once but many times!

    O God,
Release my mother's soul from its dream!
Mankind can do no more. Appease
The misery of the living and the remorse of the dead.

PURGATORY was written in 1938 and produced at the Abbey Theater in Dublin in the same year, a few months before Yeats's death.

An old pedlar and his bastard son arrive at the ruins of a country house that once belonged to the old man's mother. As, in a ghostly return of the past, the drunken sexual revelry in which the old man was begotten repeats itself behind the lighted windows, the pedlar stabs his son to death with the same knife he killed his father with years before. But discontinuing the befouled family line has not "finished all that consequence": the drunken groom once more rides home, the debased union is about to recur, and the pedlar realizes that only God's mercy can release his mother from the purgatory of endlessly repeating her sin.

There are affinities here both with *Oedipus Rex* (which Yeats translated) — the family tragedy, the parricide motif, the return of the past — and with the form and mood of a play like *The Ghost Sonata*. It dramatizes a conflict between values, the aristocratic idealism of the middle generation (the pedlar) against the materialism of grandfather and grandson. The idealism issues in a futile murder and in awareness of endless suffering. Its religious implications do not, in spite of the play's title, seem particularly Catholic in postulating purgatory as a reliving of past transgression. But — again like *The Ghost Sonata* — *Purgatory* cannot really be explained. To read it as thesis, religious or otherwise, is to violate its integrity as image, single, simple, brief, a tableau of two men, a bare tree, and a ruined house.

The tree, looking like "a silly old man," suggests the sterility of the pedlar's life. He has been reduced to trade, an occupation antithetical to that of his ancestors:

> Great people lived and died in this house;
> Magistrates, colonels, members of Parliament,
> Captains and Governors, and long ago
> Men that had fought at Aughrim and the Boyne.
> Some that had gone on government work
> To London or to India came home to die,
> Or came from London every spring
> To look at the may-blossom in the park.

The groom, his father, had ruined all that, wasted his wife's wealth, and, in a fire suggestive of the lust that drove him and his wife together, destroyed the house itself. For this he died:

> to kill a house
> Where great men grew up, married, died,
> I here declare a capital offence.

After the pedlar has killed his son, he thinks he will have cancelled the past when he has

stuck
This old jack-knife into a sod
And pulled it out all bright again.

But the soil does not purge. It is rather as if the cleansing of the knife is a third stabbing, compounded, perhaps, by the stabber's picking up the money that represents the values by which his two earlier victims lived. At any rate, it is just at this moment that the fired house, the symbol of ruined tradition, proves stronger than the expiatory act.

Yeats was opposed to the contemporary drama of naturalism, the Ibsen school of play-writing. With its emphasis on character and on real-life problems and its commitment to a dialogue that reproduced as faithfully as possible the inarticulateness of ordinary people, it seemed to him like a stale, ugly, soul-starving, unimaginative "mimicry of the restless surface of reality." He wanted a spiritual drama, a pure form that would be an end in itself because it would tap the roots of man's primeval consciousness, a dance-like ritual, deliberately distancing itself from the beholder, a symbolic, characterless, nonpopular drama for small and select audiences. In the aristocratic plays of the traditional Japanese Noh theater, highly stylized and formalized in gesture and chant, using masks rather than mimicry and make-up, Yeats found inspiration for his own nonrealistic, esoteric plays of the later part of his career. Of these plays, *Purgatory*, the next to the last, is perhaps the most immediately meaningful to an audience uninitiate in Yeats's symbolism and mysticism. No arcane, extraneous knowledge is required to respond to its supernatural sights and sounds, to the almost colloquial terseness of its free and flexible four-beat lines, in which the irregular sequence of iambs and trochees suggests the pedlar's tenseness, to the poignant drama represented by the old lullaby he sings after he has killed his son, and to its reverberating relevance to the whole play:

"Hush-a-bye baby, thy father's a knight,
Thy mother a lady, lovely and bright."

Bertolt Brecht

THE GOOD WOMAN
OF SETZUAN

An English Version by Eric Bentley

Characters

WONG, *a water seller*
THREE GODS
SHEN TE, *a prostitute, later a shopkeeper*
MRS. SHIN, *former owner of Shen Te's shop*
A FAMILY OF EIGHT (*husband, wife, brother, sister-in-law, grand-father, nephew, niece, boy*)
AN UNEMPLOYED MAN
A CARPENTER
MRS. MI TZU, *Shen Te's landlady*
YANG SUN, *an unemployed pilot, later a factory manager*
AN OLD WHORE
A POLICEMAN
AN OLD MAN
AN OLD WOMAN, *his wife*
MR. SHU FU, *a barber*
MRS. YANG, *mother of Yang Sun*
GENTLEMEN, VOICES, CHILDREN (3), etcetera.

Copyright © 1947, 1948, 1961, by Eric Bentley. Originally published in the volume *Parables for the Theater* by the University of Minnesota Press, Minneapolis. Included in *Seven Plays by Bertolt Brecht*, edited and with an introduction by Eric Bentley, published by Grove Press, Inc., 1961. Reprinted by permission.

PROLOGUE

(*At the gates of the half-westernized city of Setzuan.* Evening.* WONG *the Water Seller introduces himself to the audience.*)

WONG: I sell water here in the city of Setzuan. It isn't easy. When water is scarce, I have long distances to go in search of it, and when it is plentiful, I have no income. But in our part of the world there is nothing unusual about poverty. Many people think only the gods can save the situation. And I hear from a cattle merchant — who travels a lot — that some of the highest gods are on their way here at this very moment. Informed sources have it that heaven is quite disturbed at all the complaining. I've been coming out here to the city gates for three days now to bid these gods welcome. I want to be the first to greet them. What about those fellows over there? No, no, they *work*. And that one there has ink on his fingers, he's no god, he must be a clerk from the cement factory. *Those* two are another story. They look as though they'd like to beat you. But gods don't need to beat you, do they? (*Enter* THREE GODS.) What about those three? Old-fashioned clothes — dust on their feet — they *must* be gods! (*He throws himself at their feet.*) Do with me what you will, illustrious ones!

FIRST GOD (*with an ear trumpet*): Ah! (*He is pleased.*) So we were expected?

WONG (*giving them water*): Oh, yes. And I *knew* you'd come.

FIRST GOD: We need somewhere to stay the night. You know of a place?

WONG: The whole town is at your service, illustrious ones! What sort of a place would you like?

(*The* GODS *eye each other.*)

FIRST GOD: Just try the first house you come to, my son.

WONG: That would be Mr. Fo's place.

FIRST GOD: Mr. Fo.

WONG: One moment! (*He knocks at the first house.*)

VOICE FROM MR. FO'S: No!

(WONG *returns a little nervously.*)

* So Brecht's first MS. Brecht must later have learned that Setzuan (usually spelled Szechwan) is not a city but a province and he adjusted the printed German text. I have kept the earlier reading as such mythology seems to me more Brechtian than Brecht's own second thoughts. — E.B.

WONG: It's too bad. Mr. Fo isn't in. And his servants don't dare do a thing without his consent. He'll have a fit when he finds out who they turned away, won't he?

FIRST GOD (*smiling*): He will, won't he?

WONG: One moment! The next house is Mr. Cheng's. Won't he be thrilled?

FIRST GOD: Mr. Cheng.

(WONG *knocks.*)

VOICE FROM MR. CHENG'S: Keep your gods. We have our own troubles!

WONG (*back with the* GODS): Mr. Cheng is very sorry, but he has a houseful of relations. I think some of them are a bad lot, and naturally, he wouldn't like you to see them.

THIRD GOD: Are we so terrible?

WONG: Well, only with bad people, of course. Everyone knows the province of Kwan is always having floods.

SECOND GOD: Really? How's *that?*

WONG: Why, because they're so irreligious.

SECOND GOD: Rubbish. It's because they neglected the dam.

FIRST GOD (*to* SECOND): Sh! (*To* WONG.) You're still in hopes, aren't you, my son?

WONG: Certainly. All Setzuan is competing for the honor! What happened up to now is pure coincidence. I'll be back. (*He walks away, but then stands undecided.*)

SECOND GOD: What did I tell you?

THIRD GOD: It *could* be pure coincidence.

SECOND GOD: The same coincidence in Shun, Kwan, and Setzuan? People just aren't religious any more, let's face the fact. Our mission has failed!

FIRST GOD: Oh come, we might run into a good person any minute.

THIRD GOD: How did the resolution read? (*Unrolling a scroll and reading from it.*) "The world can stay as it is if enough people are found living lives worthy of human beings." Good people, that is. Well, what about this Water Seller himself? *He's* good, or I'm very much mistaken.

SECOND GOD: You're very much mistaken. When he gave us a drink, I had the impression there was something odd about the cup. Well, look! (*He shows the cup to the* FIRST GOD.)

FIRST GOD: A false bottom!

SECOND GOD: The man is a swindler.

FIRST GOD: Very well, count *him* out. That's one man among millions. And as a matter of fact, we only need one on *our* side. These atheists are saying, "The world must be changed because no one can *be* good

and *stay* good." No one, eh? I say: let us find one — just one — and
we have those fellows where we want them!

THIRD GOD (*to* WONG): Water Seller, is it so hard to find a place to
stay?

WONG: Nothing could be easier. It's just me. I don't go about it right.

THIRD GOD: Really? (*He returns to the others. A* GENTLEMAN *passes
by.*)

WONG: Oh dear, they're catching on. (*He accosts the* GENTLEMAN.)
Excuse the intrusion, dear sir, but three gods have just turned up.
Three of the very highest. They need a place for the night. Seize this
rare opportunity — to have real gods as your guests!

GENTLEMAN (*laughing*): A new way of finding free rooms for a gang
of crooks.

(*Exit* GENTLEMAN.)

WONG (*shouting at him*): Godless rascal! Have you no religion, gentlemen of Setzuan? (*Pause.*) Patience, illustrious ones! (*Pause.*)
There's only one person left. Shen Te, the prostitute. She *can't* say
no. (*Calls up to a window.*) Shen Te!

(SHEN TE *opens the shutters and looks out.*)

WONG: *They're* here, and nobody wants them. Will you take them?

SHEN TE: Oh, no, Wong, I'm expecting a gentleman.

WONG: Can't you forget about him for tonight?

SHEN TE: The rent has to be paid by tomorrow or I'll be out on the
street.

WONG: This is no time for calculation, Shen Te.

SHEN TE: Stomachs rumble even on the Emperor's birthday, Wong.

WONG: Setzuan is one big dung hill!

SHEN TE: Oh, very well! I'll hide till my gentleman has come and gone.
Then I'll take them. (*She disappears.*)

WONG: They mustn't see her gentleman or they'll know what she is.

FIRST GOD (*who hasn't heard any of this*): I think it's hopeless.

(*They approach* WONG.)

WONG (*jumping, as he finds them behind him*): A room has been
found, illustrious ones! (*He wipes sweat off his brow.*)

SECOND GOD: Oh, good.

THIRD GOD: Let's see it.

WONG (*nervously*): Just a minute. It has to be tidied up a bit.

THIRD GOD: Then we'll sit down here and wait.

WONG (*still more nervous*): No, no! (*Holding himself back.*) Too
much traffic, you know.

THIRD GOD (*with a smile*): Of course, if you *want* us to move.

(*They retire a little. They sit on a doorstep.* WONG *sits on the ground.*)

WONG (*after a deep breath*): You'll be staying with a single girl — the finest human being in Setzuan!

THIRD GOD: That's nice.

WONG (*to the audience*): They gave me such a look when I picked up my cup just now.

THIRD GOD: You're worn out, Wong.

WONG: A little, maybe.

FIRST GOD: Do people here have a hard time of it?

WONG: The good ones do.

FIRST GOD: What about yourself?

WONG: You mean I'm not good. That's true. And I don't have an easy time either!

(*During this dialogue, a* GENTLEMAN *has turned up in front of* SHEN TE'S *house, and has whistled several times. Each time* WONG *has given a start.*)

THIRD GOD (*to* WONG, *softly*): Psst! I think he's gone now.

WONG (*confused and surprised*): Ye-e-es.

(*The* GENTLEMAN *has left now, and* SHEN TE *has come down to the street.*)

SHEN TE (*softly*): Wong!

(*Getting no answer, she goes off down the street.* WONG *arrives just too late, forgetting his carrying pole.*)

WONG (*softly*): Shen Te! Shen Te! (*To himself.*) So she's gone off to earn the rent. Oh dear, I can't go to the gods *again* with no room to offer them. Having failed in the service of the gods, I shall run to my den in the sewer pipe down by the river and hide from their sight!

(*He rushes off.* SHEN TE *returns, looking for him, but finding the gods. She stops in confusion.*)

SHEN TE: You are the illustrious ones? My name is Shen Te. It would please me very much if my simple room could be of use to you.

THIRD GOD: Where is the Water Seller, Miss . . . Shen Te?

SHEN TE: I missed him, somehow.

FIRST GOD: Oh, he probably thought you weren't coming, and was afraid of telling us.

THIRD GOD (*picking up the carrying pole*): We'll leave this with you. He'll be needing it.

(*Led by* SHEN TE, *they go into the house. It grows dark, then light. Dawn. Again escorted by* SHEN TE, *who leads them through the half-light with a little lamp, the* GODS *take their leave.*)

FIRST GOD: Thank you, thank you, dear Shen Te, for your elegant hospitality! We shall not forget! And give our thanks to the Water Seller — he showed us a good human being.

SHEN TE: Oh, I'm not good. Let me tell you something: when Wong asked me to put you up, I hesitated.

FIRST GOD: It's all right to hesitate if you then go ahead! And in giving us that room you did much more than you knew. You proved that good people still exist, a point that has been disputed of late — even in heaven. Farewell!

SECOND GOD: Farewell!

THIRD GOD: Farewell!

SHEN TE: Stop, illustrious ones! I'm not sure you're right. I'd like to be good, it's true, but there's the rent to pay. And that's not all: I sell myself for a living. Even so I can't make ends meet, there's too much competition. I'd like to honor my father and mother and speak nothing but the truth and not covet my neighbor's house. I should love to stay with one man. But how? How is it done? Even breaking only a *few* of your commandments, I can hardly manage.

FIRST GOD (*clearing his throat*): These thoughts are but, um, the misgivings of an unusually good woman!

THIRD GOD: Goodbye, Shen Te! Give our regards to the Water Seller!

SECOND GOD: And above all: be good! Farewell!

FIRST GOD: Farewell!

THIRD GOD: Farewell!

(*They start to wave goodbye.*)

SHEN TE: But everything is so expensive, I don't feel sure I can do it!

SECOND GOD: That's not in our sphere. We never meddle with economics.

THIRD GOD: One moment.

(*They stop.*)

Isn't it true she might do better if she had more money?

SECOND GOD: Come, come! How could we ever account for it Up Above?

FIRST GOD: Oh, there are ways.

(*They put their heads together and confer in dumb show.*)

(*To* SHEN TE, *with embarrassment.*) As you say you can't pay your rent, well, um, we're not paupers, so of course we *insist* on paying for our room. (*Awkwardly thrusting money into her hands.*) There! (*Quickly.*) But don't tell anyone! The incident is open to misinterpretation.

SECOND GOD: It certainly is!

FIRST GOD (*defensively*): But there's no law against it! It was never decreed that a god mustn't pay hotel bills!

(*The* GODS *leave.*)

SCENE 1

(*A small tobacco shop. The shop is not as yet completely furnished and hasn't started doing business.*)

SHEN TE (*to the audience*): It's three days now since the gods left. When they said they wanted to pay for the room, I looked down at my hand, and there was more than a thousand silver dollars! I bought a tobacco shop with the money, and moved in yesterday. I don't own the building, of course, but I can pay the rent, and I hope to do a lot of good here. Beginning with Mrs. Shin, who's just coming across the square with her pot. She had the shop before me, and yesterday she dropped in to ask for rice for her children.

(*Enter* MRS. SHIN. *Both women bow.*)

How do you do, Mrs. Shin.

MRS. SHIN: How do you do, Miss Shen Te. You like your new home?

SHEN TE: Indeed, yes. Did your children have a good night?

MRS. SHIN: In that hovel? The youngest is coughing already.

SHEN TE: Oh, dear!

MRS. SHIN: You're going to learn a thing or two in these slums.

SHEN TE: Slums? That's not what you said when you sold me the shop!

MRS. SHIN: Now don't start nagging! Robbing me and my innocent children of their home and then calling it a slum! That's the limit! (*She weeps.*)

SHEN TE (*tactfully*): I'll get your rice.

MRS. SHIN: And a little cash while you're at it.

SHEN TE: I'm afraid I haven't sold anything yet.

MRS. SHIN (*screeching*): I've got to have it. Strip the clothes from my back and then cut my throat, will you? I know what I'll do: I'll leave my children on your doorstep! (*She snatches the pot out of* SHEN TE's *hands.*)

SHEN TE: Please don't be angry. You'll spill the rice.

(*Enter an elderly* HUSBAND *and* WIFE *with their shabbily-dressed* NEPHEW.)

WIFE: Shen Te, dear! You've come into money, they tell me. And we haven't a roof over our heads! A tobacco shop. We had one too. But it's gone. Could we spend the night here, do you think?

NEPHEW (*appraising the shop*): Not bad!

WIFE: He's our nephew. We're inseparable!

MRS. SHIN: And who are these . . . ladies and gentlemen?

SHEN TE: They put me up when I first came in from the country. (*To the audience.*) Of course, when my small purse was empty, they put me out on the street, and they may be afraid I'll do the same to them. (*To the newcomers, kindly.*) Come in, and welcome, though I've only one little room for you — it's behind the shop.

HUSBAND: That'll do. Don't worry.

WIFE (*bringing* SHEN TE *some tea*): We'll stay over here, so we won't be in your way. Did you make it a tobacco shop in memory of your first real home? We can certainly give you a hint or two! That's one reason we came.

MRS. SHIN (*to* SHEN TE): Very nice! As long as you have a few customers too!

HUSBAND: Sh! A customer!

(*Enter an* UNEMPLOYED MAN, *in rags.*)

UNEMPLOYED MAN: Excuse me. I'm unemployed.

(MRS. SHIN *laughs.*)

SHEN TE: Can I help you?

UNEMPLOYED MAN: Have you any damaged cigarettes? I thought there might be some damage when you're unpacking.

WIFE: What nerve, begging for tobacco! (*Rhetorically.*) Why don't they ask for bread?

UNEMPLOYED MAN: Bread is expensive. One cigarette butt and I'll be a new man.

SHEN TE (*giving him cigarettes*): That's very important — to be a new man. You'll be my first customer and bring me luck.

(*The* UNEMPLOYED MAN *quickly lights a cigarette, inhales, and goes off, coughing.*)

WIFE: Was that right, Shen Te, dear?

MRS. SHIN: If this is the opening of a shop, you can hold the closing at the end of the week.

HUSBAND: I bet he had money on him.

SHEN TE: Oh, no, he said he hadn't!

NEPHEW: How d'you know he wasn't lying?

SHEN TE (*angrily*): How do you know he was?

WIFE (*wagging her head*): You're too good, Shen Te, dear. If you're going to keep this shop, you'll have to learn to say No.

HUSBAND: Tell them the place isn't yours to dispose of. Belongs to . . . some relative who insists on all accounts being strictly in order . . .

MRS. SHIN: That's right! What do you think you are — a philanthropist?

SHEN TE (*laughing*): Very well, suppose I ask you for my rice back, Mrs. Shin?

WIFE (*combatively, at* MRS. SHIN): So that's *her* rice?

(*Enter the* CARPENTER, *a small man.*)

MRS. SHIN (*who, at the sight of him, starts to hurry away*): See you tomorrow, Miss Shen Te! (*Exit* MRS. SHIN.)

CARPENTER: Mrs. Shin, it's you I want!

WIFE (*to* SHEN TE): Has she some claim on you?

SHEN TE: She's hungry. That's a claim.

CARPENTER: Are you the new tenant? And filling up the shelves already? Well, they're not yours, till they're paid for, ma'am. I'm the carpenter, so I should know.

SHEN TE: I took the shop "furnishings included."

CARPENTER: You're in league with that Mrs. Shin, of course. All right: I demand my hundred silver dollars.

SHEN TE: I'm afraid I haven't got a hundred silver dollars.

CARPENTER: Then you'll find it. Or I'll have you arrested.

WIFE (*whispering to* SHEN TE): That relative: make it a cousin.

SHEN TE: Can't it wait till next month?

CARPENTER: No!

SHEN TE: Be a little patient, Mr. Carpenter, I can't settle all claims at once.

CARPENTER: Who's patient with me? (*He grabs a shelf from the wall.*) Pay up — or I take the shelves back!

WIFE: Shen Te! Dear! Why don't you let your . . . cousin settle this affair? (*To* CARPENTER.) Put your claim in writing. Shen Te's cousin will see you get paid.

CARPENTER (*derisively*): Cousin, eh?

HUSBAND: Cousin, yes.

CARPENTER: I know these cousins!

NEPHEW: Don't be silly. He's a personal friend of mine.

HUSBAND: What a man! Sharp as a razor!

CARPENTER: All right. I'll put my claim in writing. (*Puts shelf on floor, sits on it, writes out bill.*)

WIFE (*to* SHEN TE): He'd tear the dress off your back to get his shelves. Never recognize a claim! That's my motto.

SHEN TE: He's done a job, and wants something in return. It's shameful that I can't give it to him. What will the gods say?

HUSBAND: You did your bit when you took *us* in.

(*Enter the* BROTHER, *limping, and the* SISTER-IN-LAW, *pregnant.*)

BROTHER (*to* HUSBAND *and* WIFE): So this is where you're hiding out! There's family feeling for you! Leaving us on the corner!

WIFE (*embarrassed, to* SHEN TE): It's my brother and his wife. (*To them.*) Now stop grumbling, and sit quietly in that corner. (*To* SHEN TE.) It can't be helped. She's in her fifth month.

SHEN TE: Oh yes. Welcome!

WIFE (*to the couple*): Say thank you.

(*They mutter something.*)

The cups are there. (*To* SHEN TE.) Lucky you bought this shop when you did!

SHEN TE (*laughing and bringing tea*): Lucky indeed!

(*Enter* MRS. MI TZU, *the landlady.*)

MRS. MI TZU: Miss Shen Te? I am Mrs. Mi Tzu, your landlady. I hope our relationship will be a happy one? I like to think I give my tenants modern, personalized service. Here is your lease. (*To the others, as* SHEN TE *reads the lease.*) There's nothing like the opening of a little shop, is there? A moment of true beauty! (*She is looking around.*) Not very much on the shelves, of course. But everything in the gods' good time! Where are your references, Miss Shen Te?

SHEN TE: Do I *have* to have references?

MRS. MI TZU: After all, I haven't a notion who you are!

HUSBAND: Oh, *we'd* be glad to vouch for Miss Shen Te! We'd go through fire for her!

MRS. MI TZU: And who may *you* be?

HUSBAND (*stammering*): Ma Fu, tobacco dealer.

MRS. MI TZU: Where is your shop, Mr. . . . Ma Fu?

HUSBAND: Well, um, I haven't a shop — I've just sold it.

MRS. MI TZU: I see. (*To* SHEN TE.) Is there no one else that knows you?

WIFE (*whispering to* SHEN TE): Your cousin! Your cousin!

MRS. MI TZU: This is a respectable house, Miss Shen Te. I never sign a lease without certain assurances.

SHEN TE (*slowly, her eyes downcast*): I have . . . a cousin.

MRS. MI TZU: On the square? Let's go over and see him. What does he do?

SHEN TE (*as before*): He lives . . . in another city.

WIFE (*prompting*): Didn't you say he was in Shung?

SHEN TE: That's right. Shung.

HUSBAND (*prompting*): I had his name on the tip of my tongue. Mr. . . .

SHEN TE (*with an effort*): Mr. . . . Shui . . . Ta.

HUSBAND: That's it! Tall, skinny fellow!

SHEN TE: Shui Ta!

NEPHEW (*to* CARPENTER): You were in touch with him, weren't you? About the shelves?

CARPENTER (*surlily*): Give him this bill. (*He hands it over.*) I'll be back in the morning. (*Exit* CARPENTER.)

NEPHEW (*calling after him, but with his eyes on* MRS. MI TZU): Don't worry! Mr. Shui Ta pays on the nail!

MRS. MI TZU (*looking closely at* SHEN TE): I'll be happy to make his acquaintance, Miss Shen Te. (*Exit* MRS. MI TZU.)

(*Pause.*)

WIFE: By tomorrow morning she'll know more about you than you do yourself.

SISTER-IN-LAW (*to* NEPHEW): This thing isn't built to last.

(*Enter* GRANDFATHER.)

WIFE: It's Grandfather! (*To* SHEN TE.) Such a good old soul!

(*The* BOY *enters.*)

BOY (*over his shoulder*): Here they are!

WIFE: And the boy, how he's grown! But he always could eat enough for ten.

(*Enter the* NIECE.)

WIFE (*to* SHEN TE): Our little niece from the country. There are more of us now than in your time. The less we had, the more there were of us; the more there were of us, the less we had. Give me the key.

We must protect ourselves from unwanted guests. (*She takes the key and locks the door.*) Just make yourself at home. I'll light the little lamp.

NEPHEW (*a big joke*): I hope her cousin doesn't drop in tonight! The strict Mr. Shui Ta!

(SISTER-IN-LAW *laughs.*)

BROTHER (*reaching for a cigarette*): One cigarette more or less . . .

HUSBAND: One cigarette more or less.

(*They pile into the cigarettes. The* BROTHER *hands a jug of wine round.*)

NEPHEW: Mr. Shui Ta'll pay for it!

GRANDFATHER (*gravely, to* SHEN TE): How do you do?

(SHEN TE, *a little taken aback by the belatedness of the greeting, bows. She has the* CARPENTER's *bill in one hand, the landlady's lease in the other.*)

WIFE: How about a bit of a song? To keep Shen Te's spirits up?

NEPHEW: Good idea. Grandfather: you start!

Song of the Smoke

GRANDFATHER:

I used to think (before old age beset me)
    That brains could fill the pantry of the poor.
But where did all my cerebration get me?
    I'm just as hungry as I was before.
            So what's the use?
              See the smoke float free
              Into ever colder coldness!
              It's the same with me.

HUSBAND:

The straight and narrow path leads to disaster
    And so the crooked path I tried to tread.
That got me to disaster even faster.
    (They say we shall be happy when we're dead.)
              So what's the use, etc.

NIECE:

You older people, full of expectation,
    At any moment now you'll walk the plank!
The future's for the younger generation!
    Yes, even if that future is a blank.
              So what's the use, etc.

NEPHEW (*to the* BROTHER): Where'd you get that wine?

SISTER-IN-LAW (*answering for the* BROTHER): He pawned the sack of tobacco.

HUSBAND (*stepping in*): What? That tobacco was all we had to fall back on! You pig!

BROTHER: *You'd* call a man a pig because your wife was frigid! Did you refuse to drink it?

(*They fight. The shelves fall over.*)

SHEN TE (*imploringly*): Oh, don't! Don't break everything! Take it, take it all, but don't destroy a gift from the gods!

WIFE (*disparagingly*): This shop isn't big enough. I should never have mentioned it to Uncle and the others. When *they* arrive, it's going to be disgustingly overcrowded.

SISTER-IN-LAW: And did you hear our gracious hostess? She cools off quick!

(*Voices outside. Knocking at the door.*)

UNCLE'S VOICE: Open the door!

WIFE: Uncle? Is that you, Uncle?

UNCLE'S VOICE: Certainly, it's me. Auntie says to tell you she'll have the children here in ten minutes.

WIFE (*to* SHEN TE): I'll have to let him in.

SHEN TE (*who scarcely hears her*):
   The little lifeboat is swiftly sent down
   Too many men too greedily
   Hold on to it as they drown.

Scene 1A

(WONG's *den in a sewer pipe.*)

WONG (*crouching there*): All quiet! It's four days now since I left the city. The gods passed this way on the second day. I heard their steps on the bridge over there. They must be a long way off by this time, so I'm safe.

(*Breathing a sigh of relief, he curls up and goes to sleep. In his dream the pipe becomes transparent, and the* GODS *appear.*)

(*Raising an arm, as if in self-defense.*) I know, I know, illustrious ones! I found no one to give you a room — not in all Setzuan! There, it's out. Please continue on your way!

FIRST GOD (*mildly*): But you did find someone. Someone who took us in for the night, watched over us in our sleep, and in the early morning lighted us down to the street with a lamp.

WONG: It was . . . Shen Te, that took you in?

THIRD GOD: Who else?

WONG: And I ran away! "She isn't coming," I thought, "she just can't afford it."

GODS (*singing*):
O you feeble, well-intentioned, and yet feeble chap!
Where there's need the fellow thinks there is no goodness!
When there's danger he thinks courage starts to ebb away!
Some people only see the seamy side!
What hasty judgment! What premature desperation!

WONG: I'm *very* ashamed, illustrious ones.

FIRST GOD: Do us a favor, Water Seller. Go back to Setzuan. Find Shen Te, and give us a report on her. We hear that she's come into a little money. Show interest in her goodness — for no one can be good for long if goodness is not in demand. Meanwhile we shall continue the search, and find other good people. After which, the idle chatter about the impossibility of goodness will stop!

(*The* GODS *vanish.*)

SCENE 2

(*A knocking.*)

WIFE: Shen Te! Someone at the door. Where is she anyway?

NEPHEW: She must be getting the breakfast. Mr. Shui Ta will pay for it.

(*The* WIFE *laughs and shuffles to the door. Enter* MR. SHUI TA *and the* CARPENTER.)

WIFE: Who is it?

SHUI TA: I am Miss Shen Te's cousin.

WIFE: What?

SHUI TA: My name is Shui Ta.

WIFE: Her cousin?

NEPHEW: Her cousin?

NIECE: But that was a joke. She hasn't got a cousin.

HUSBAND: So early in the morning?

BROTHER: What's all the noise?

SISTER-IN-LAW: This fellow says he's her cousin.

BROTHER: Tell him to prove it.

NEPHEW: Right. If you're Shen Te's cousin, prove it by getting the breakfast.

SHUI TA (*whose regime begins as he puts out the lamp to save oil. Loudly, to all present, asleep or awake*): Would you all please get dressed! Customers will be coming! I wish to open my shop!

HUSBAND: *Your* shop? Doesn't it belong to our good friend Shen Te?

(SHUI TA *shakes his head.*)

SISTER-IN-LAW: So we've been cheated. Where *is* the little liar?

SHUI TA: Miss Shen Te has been delayed. She wishes me to tell you there will be nothing she can do — now I am here.

WIFE (*bowled over*): I thought she was *good!*

NEPHEW: Do you have to believe *him*?

HUSBAND: *I* don't.

NEPHEW: Then do something.

HUSBAND: Certainly! I'll send out a search party at once. You, you, you, and you, go out and look for Shen Te.

(*As the* GRANDFATHER *rises and makes for the door.*)

Not you, Grandfather, you and I will hold the fort.

SHUI TA: You won't find Miss Shen Te. She has suspended her hospitable activity for an unlimited period. There are too many of you. She asked me to say: this is a tobacco shop, not a gold mine.

HUSBAND: Shen Te never said a thing like that. Boy, food! There's a bakery on the corner. Stuff your shirt full when they're not looking!

SISTER-IN-LAW: Don't overlook the raspberry tarts.

HUSBAND: And don't let the policeman see you.

(*The* BOY *leaves.*)

SHUI TA: Don't you depend on this shop now? Then why give it a bad name, by stealing from the bakery?

NEPHEW: Don't listen to him. Let's find Shen Te. She'll give him a piece of her mind.

SISTER-IN-LAW: Don't forget to leave us some breakfast.

(BROTHER, SISTER-IN-LAW, *and* NEPHEW *leave.*)

SHUI TA (*to the* CARPENTER): You see, Mr. Carpenter, nothing has changed since the poet, eleven hundred years ago, penned these lines:

A governor was asked what was needed
To save the freezing people in the city.

He replied:
"A blanket ten thousand feet long
To cover the city and all its suburbs."

(*He starts to tidy up the shop.*)

CARPENTER: Your cousin owes me money. I've got witnesses. For the shelves.

SHUI TA: Yes, I have your bill. (*He takes it out of his pocket.*) Isn't a hundred silver dollars rather a lot?

CARPENTER: No deductions! I have a wife and children.

SHUI TA: How many children?

CARPENTER: Three.

SHUI TA: I'll make you an offer. Twenty silver dollars.

(*The* HUSBAND *laughs.*)

CARPENTER: You're crazy. Those shelves are real walnut.

SHUI TA: Very well. Take them away.

CARPENTER: What?

SHUI TA: They cost too much. Please take them away.

WIFE: Not bad! (*And she, too, is laughing.*)

CARPENTER (*a little bewildered*): Call Shen Te, someone! (*To* SHUI TA.) She's *good!*

SHUI TA: Certainly. She's ruined.

CARPENTER (*provoked into taking some of the shelves*): All right, you can keep your tobacco on the floor.

SHUI TA (*to the* HUSBAND): Help him with the shelves.

HUSBAND (*grins and carries one shelf over to the door where the* CAR-PENTER *now is*): Goodbye, shelves!

CARPENTER (*to the* HUSBAND): You dog! You want my family to starve?

SHUI TA: I repeat my offer. I have no desire to keep my tobacco on the floor. Twenty silver dollars.

CARPENTER (*with desperate aggressiveness*): One hundred!

(SHUI TA *shows indifference, looks through the window. The* HUS-BAND *picks up several shelves.*)

(*To* HUSBAND.) You needn't smash them against the doorpost, you idiot! (*To* SHUI TA.) These shelves were made to measure. They're no use anywhere else!

SHUI TA: Precisely.

(*The* WIFE *squeals with pleasure.*)

CARPENTER (*giving up, sullenly*): Take the shelves. Pay what you want to pay.

SHUI TA (*smoothly*): Twenty silver dollars.

(*He places two large coins on the table. The* CARPENTER *picks them up.*)

HUSBAND (*brings the shelves back in*): And quite enough too!

CARPENTER (*slinking off*): Quite enough to get drunk on.

HUSBAND (*happily*): Well, we got rid of *him!*

WIFE (*weeping with fun, gives a rendition of the dialogue just spoken*): "Real walnut," says he. "Very well, take them away," says his lordship. "I have children," says he. "Twenty silver dollars," says his lordship. "They're no use anywhere else," says he. "Precisely," said his lordship! (*She dissolves into shrieks of merriment.*)

SHUI TA: And now: go!

HUSBAND: What's that?

SHUI TA: You're thieves, parasites. I'm giving you this chance. Go!

HUSBAND (*summoning all his ancestral dignity*): That sort deserves no answer. Besides, one should never shout on an empty stomach.

WIFE: Where's that boy?

SHUI TA: Exactly. The boy. I want no stolen goods in this shop. (*Very loudly.*) I strongly advise you to leave! (*But they remain seated, noses in the air. Quietly.*) As you wish.

(SHUI TA *goes to the door. A* POLICEMAN *appears.* SHUI TA *bows.*)

I am addressing the officer in charge of this precinct?

POLICEMAN: That's right, Mr., um . . . what was the name, sir?

SHUI TA: Mr. Shui Ta.

POLICEMAN: Yes, of course, sir.

(*They exchange a smile.*)

SHUI TA: Nice weather we're having.

POLICEMAN: A little on the warm side, sir.

SHUI TA: Oh, a little on the warm side.

HUSBAND (*whispering to the* WIFE): If he keeps it up till the boy's back, we're done for. (*Tries to signal* SHUI TA.)

SHUI TA (*ignoring the signal*): Weather, of course, is one thing indoors, another out on the dusty street!

POLICEMAN: Oh, quite another, sir!

WIFE (*to the* HUSBAND): It's all right as long as he's standing in the doorway — the boy will see him.

SHUI TA: Step inside for a moment! It's quite cool indoors. My cousin and I have just opened the place. And we attach the greatest importance to being on good terms with the, um, authorities.

POLICEMAN (*entering*): Thank you, Mr. Shui Ta. It *is* cool!

HUSBAND (*whispering to the* WIFE): And now the boy won't see him.

SHUI TA (*showing* HUSBAND *and* WIFE *to the* POLICEMAN): Visitors, I think my cousin knows them. They were just leaving.

HUSBAND (*defeated*): Ye-e-es, we were . . . just leaving.

SHUI TA: I'll tell my cousin you couldn't wait.

(*Noise from the street. Shouts of "Stop, thief!"*)

POLICEMAN: What's that?

(*The* BOY *is in the doorway with cakes and buns and rolls spilling out of his shirt. The* WIFE *signals desperately to him to leave. He gets the idea.*)

No, you don't! (*He grabs the* BOY *by the collar.*) Where's all this from?

BOY (*vaguely pointing*): Down the street.

POLICEMAN (*grimly*): So that's it. (*Prepares to arrest the* BOY.)

WIFE (*stepping in*): And *we* knew nothing about it. (*To the* BOY.) Nasty little thief!

POLICEMAN (*dryly*): Can you clarify the situation, Mr. Shui Ta?

(SHUI TA *is silent.*)

POLICEMAN (*who understands silence*): Aha. You're all coming with me — to the station.

SHUI TA: I can hardly say how sorry I am that *my* establishment . . .

WIFE: Oh, he saw the boy leave not ten minutes ago!

SHUI TA: And to conceal the theft asked a policeman in?

POLICEMAN: Don't listen to her, Mr. Shui Ta, I'll be happy to relieve you of their presence one and all! (*To all three.*) Out! (*He drives them before him.*)

GRANDFATHER (*leaving last. Gravely*): Good morning!

POLICEMAN: Good morning!

(SHUI TA, *left alone, continues to tidy up.* MRS. MI TZU *breezes in.*)

MRS. MI TZU: *You're* her cousin, are you? Then have the goodness to explain what all this means — police dragging people from a respectable house! By what right does your Miss Shen Te turn my property into a house of assignation? — Well, as you see, I know all!

SHUI TA: Yes. My cousin has the worst possible reputation: that of being poor.

MRS. MI TZU: No sentimental rubbish, Mr. Shui Ta. Your cousin was a common . . .

SHUI TA: Pauper. Let's use the uglier word.

MRS. MI TZU: I'm speaking of her conduct, not her earnings. But there must have *been* earnings, or how did she buy all this? Several elderly gentlemen took care of it, I suppose. I repeat: this is a respectable house! I have tenants who prefer not to live under the same roof with such a person.

SHUI TA (*quietly*): How much do you want?

MRS. MI TZU (*he is ahead of her now*): I beg your pardon.

SHUI TA: To reassure yourself. To reassure your tenants. How much will it cost?

MRS. MI TZU: You're a cool customer.

SHUI TA (*picking up the lease*): The rent is high. (*He reads on.*) I assume it's payable by the month?

MRS. MI TZU: Not in her case.

SHUI TA (*looking up*): What?

MRS. MI TZU: Six months rent payable in advance. Two hundred silver dollars.

SHUI TA: Six . . . ! Sheer usury! And where am I to find it?

MRS. MI TZU: You should have thought of that before.

SHUI TA: Have you no heart, Mrs. Mi Tzu? It's true Shen Te acted foolishly, being kind to all those people, but she'll improve with time. I'll see to it she does. She'll work her fingers to the bone to pay her rent, and all the time be as quiet as a mouse, as humble as a fly.

MRS. MI TZU: Her social background . . .

SHUI TA: Out of the depths! She came out of the depths! And before she'll go back there, she'll work, sacrifice, shrink from nothing. . . . Such a tenant is worth her weight in gold, Mrs. Mi Tzu.

MRS. MI TZU: It's silver we were talking about, Mr. Shui Ta. Two hundred silver dollars or . . .

(*Enter the* POLICEMAN.)

POLICEMAN: Am I intruding, Mr. Shui Ta?

MRS. MI TZU: This tobacco shop is well-known to the police, I see.

POLICEMAN: Mr. Shui Ta has done us a service, Mrs. Mi Tzu. I am here to present our official felicitations!

MRS. MI TZU: That means less than nothing to me, sir. Mr. Shui Ta, all I can say is: I hope your cousin will find my terms acceptable. Good day, gentlemen. (*Exit.*)

SHUI TA: Good day, ma'am.

(*Pause.*)

POLICEMAN: Mrs. Mi Tzu a bit of a stumbling block, sir?

SHUI TA: She wants six months' rent in advance.

POLICEMAN: And you haven't got it, eh?

(SHUI TA *is silent.*)

But surely you can get it, sir? A man like you?

SHUI TA: What about a woman like Shen Te?

POLICEMAN: You're not staying, sir?

SHUI TA: No, and I won't be back. Do you smoke?

POLICEMAN (*taking two cigars, and placing them both in his pocket*):
Thank you, sir — I see your point. Miss Shen Te — let's mince no
words — Miss Shen Te lived by selling herself. "What else could
she have done?" you ask. "How else was she to pay the rent?" True.
But the fact remains, Mr. Shui Ta, it is not respectable. Why not?
A very deep question. But, in the first place, love — love isn't bought
and sold like cigars, Mr. Shui Ta. In the second place, it isn't respectable to go waltzing off with someone that's paying his way, so
to speak — it must be for love! Thirdly and lastly, as the proverb has
it: not for a handful of rice but for love! (*Pause. He is thinking
hard.*) "Well," you may say, "and what good is all this wisdom if
the milk's already spilt?" Miss Shen Te is what she is. Is *where*
she is. We have to face the fact that if she doesn't get hold of six
months' rent pronto, she'll be back on the streets. The question
then as I see it — everything in this world is a matter of opinion —
the question as I see it is: *how* is she to get hold of this rent? How?
Mr. Shui Ta: I don't know. (*Pause.*) I take that back, sir. It's just
come to me. A husband. We must find her a husband!

(*Enter a little* OLD WOMAN.)

OLD WOMAN: A good cheap cigar for my husband, we'll have been
married forty years tomorrow and we're having a little celebration.

SHUI TA: Forty years? And you still want to celebrate?

OLD WOMAN: As much as we can afford to. We have the carpet shop
across the square. We'll be good neighbors, I hope?

SHUI TA: I hope so too.

POLICEMAN (*who keeps making discoveries*): Mr. Shui Ta, you know
what we need? We need capital. And how do we acquire capital?
We get married.

SHUI TA (*to* OLD WOMAN): I'm afraid I've been pestering this gentleman with my personal worries.

POLICEMAN (*lyrically*): We can't pay six months' rent, so what do we
do? We marry money.

SHUI TA: That might not be easy.

POLICEMAN: Oh, I don't know. She's a good match. Has a nice, growing business. (*To the* OLD WOMAN.) What do you think?

OLD WOMAN (*undecided*): Well —

POLICEMAN: Should she put an ad in the paper?

OLD WOMAN (*not eager to commit herself*): Well, if *she* agrees —

POLICEMAN: I'll write it for her. *You* lend us a hand, and *we* write an ad for you! (*He chuckles away to himself, takes out his notebook, wets the stump of a pencil between his lips, and writes away.*)

SHUI TA (*slowly*): Not a bad idea.

POLICEMAN: "What . . . *respectable* . . . man . . . with small capital . . . widower . . . not excluded . . . desires . . . marriage . . . into flourishing . . . tobacco shop?" And now let's add: "am . . . pretty . . ." No! . . . "Prepossessing appearance."

SHUI TA: If you don't think that's an exaggeration?

OLD WOMAN: Oh, not a bit. I've seen her.

(*The* POLICEMAN *tears the page out of his notebook, and hands it over to* SHUI TA.)

SHUI TA (*with horror in his voice*): How much luck we need to keep our heads above water! How many ideas! How many friends! (*To the* POLICEMAN.) Thank you, sir. I think I see my way clear.

SCENE 3

(*Evening in the municipal park. Noise of a plane overhead.* YANG SUN, *a young man in rags, is following the plane with his eyes: one can tell that the machine is describing a curve above the park.* YANG SUN *then takes a rope out of his pocket, looking anxiously about him as he does so. He moves toward a large willow. Enter* TWO PROSTITUTES, *one old, the other the* NIECE *whom we have already met.*)

NIECE: Hello. Coming with me?

YANG SUN (*taken aback*): If you'd like to buy me a dinner.

OLD WHORE: Buy you a dinner! (*To the* NIECE.) Oh, we know him — it's the unemployed pilot. Waste no time on him!

NIECE: But he's the only man left in the park. And it's going to rain.

OLD WHORE: Oh, how do you know?

(*And they pass by.* YANG SUN *again looks about him, again takes his rope, and this time throws it round a branch of the willow tree. Again he is interrupted. It is the* TWO PROSTITUTES *returning — and in such a hurry they don't notice him.*)

NIECE: It's going to pour!

(*Enter* SHEN TE.)

OLD WHORE: There's that *gorgon* Shen Te! That *drove* your family out into the cold!

NIECE: It wasn't her. It was that cousin of hers. She offered to *pay* for the cakes. I've nothing against her.

OLD WHORE: I have, though. (*So that* SHEN TE *can hear.*) Now where could the little lady be off to? She may be rich now but that won't stop her snatching our young men, will it?

SHEN TE: I'm going to the tearoom by the pond.

NIECE: Is it true what they say? You're marrying a widower — with three children?

SHEN TE: Yes. I'm just going to see him.

YANG SUN (*his patience at breaking point*): Move on there! This is a park, not a whorehouse!

OLD WHORE: Shut your mouth!

(*But the* TWO PROSTITUTES *leave.*)

YANG SUN: Even in the farthest corner of the park, even when it's raining, you can't get rid of them! (*He spits.*)

SHEN TE (*overhearing this*): And what right have you to scold them? (*But at this point she sees the rope.*) Oh!

YANG SUN: Well, what are you staring at?

SHEN TE: That rope. What is it for?

YANG SUN: Think! Think! I haven't a penny. Even if I had, I wouldn't spend it on you. I'd buy a drink of water.

(*The rain starts.*)

SHEN TE (*still looking at the rope*): What is the rope for? You mustn't!

YANG SUN: What's it to you? Clear out!

SHEN TE (*irrelevantly*): It's raining.

YANG SUN: Well, don't try to come under this tree.

SHEN TE: Oh, no. (*She stays in the rain.*)

YANG SUN: Now go away. (*Pause.*) For one thing, I don't like your looks, you're bow-legged.

SHEN TE (*indignantly*): That's not true!

YANG SUN: Well, don't show 'em to me. Look, it's raining. You better come under this tree.

(*Slowly, she takes shelter under the tree.*)

SHEN TE: Why did you want to do it?

YANG SUN: You really want to know? (*Pause.*) To get rid of you! (*Pause.*) You know what a flyer is?

SHEN TE: Oh yes, I've met a lot of pilots. At the tearoom.

YANG SUN: You call *them* flyers? Think they know what a machine *is?* Just 'cause they have leather helmets? They gave the airfield director a bribe, that's the way *those* fellows got in the air! Try one of them out sometime. "Go up to two thousand feet," tell him, "then let it fall, then pick it up again with a flick of the wrist at the last moment." Know what he'll say to that? "It's not in my contract." Then again, there's the landing problem. It's like landing on your own backside. It's no different, planes are human. Those fools don't understand. (*Pause.*) And I'm the biggest fool for reading the book on flying in the Peking school and skipping the page where it says: "we've got enough flyers and we don't need you." I'm a mail pilot and no mail. You understand that?

SHEN TE (*shyly*): Yes. I do.

YANG SUN: No, you don't. You'd never understand that.

SHEN TE: When we were little we had a crane with a broken wing. He made friends with us and was very good-natured about our jokes. He would strut along behind us and call out to stop us going too fast for him. But every spring and autumn when the cranes flew over the villages in great swarms, he got quite restless. (*Pause.*) I understood that. (*She bursts out crying.*)

YANG SUN: Don't!

SHEN TE (*quieting down*): No.

YANG SUN: It's bad for the complexion.

SHEN TE (*sniffing*): I've stopped.

(*She dries her tears on her big sleeve. Leaning against the tree, but not looking at her, he reaches for her face.*)

YANG SUN: You can't even wipe your own face. (*He is wiping it for her with his handkerchief. Pause.*)

SHEN TE (*still sobbing*): I don't know *anything!*

YANG SUN: You interrupted me! What for?

SHEN TE: It's such a rainy day. You only wanted to do . . . *that* because it's such a rainy day.

(*To the audience.*)

In our country
The evenings should never be somber
High bridges over rivers
The grey hour between night and morning
And the long, long winter:
Such things are dangerous
For, with all the misery,

A very little is enough
And men throw away an unbearable life.

(*Pause.*)

YANG SUN: Talk about yourself for a change.

SHEN TE: What about me? I have a shop.

YANG SUN (*incredulous*): You have a shop, do you? Never thought of walking the streets?

SHEN TE: I *did* walk the streets. Now I have a shop.

YANG SUN (*ironically*): A gift of the gods, I suppose!

SHEN TE: How did you know?

YANG SUN (*even more ironical*): One fine evening the gods turned up saying: here's some money!

SHEN TE (*quickly*): One fine morning.

YANG SUN (*fed up*): This isn't much of an entertainment.

(*Pause.*)

SHEN TE: I can play the zither a little. (*Pause.*) And I can mimic men. (*Pause.*) I got the shop, so the first thing I did was to give my zither away. I can be as stupid as a fish now, I said to myself, and it won't matter.

I'm rich now, I said
I walk alone, I sleep alone
For a whole year, I said
I'll have nothing to do with a man.

YANG SUN: And now you're marrying one! The one at the tearoom by the pond?

(SHEN TE *is silent.*)

YANG SUN: What do you know about love?

SHEN TE: Everything.

YANG SUN: Nothing. (*Pause.*) Or d'you just mean you enjoyed it?

SHEN TE: No.

YANG SUN (*again without turning to look at her, he strokes her cheek with his hand*): You like that?

SHEN TE: Yes.

YANG SUN (*breaking off*): You're easily satisfied, I must say. (*Pause.*) What a town!

SHEN TE: You have no friends?

YANG SUN (*defensively*): Yes, I have! (*Change of tone.*) But they don't want to hear I'm still unemployed. "What?" they ask. "Is there still water in the sea?" You have friends?

SHEN TE (*hesitating*): Just a . . . cousin.

YANG SUN: Watch him carefully.

SHEN TE: He only came once. Then he went away. He won't be back.

(YANG SUN *is looking away*.)

But to be without hope, they say, is to be without goodness!

(*Pause*.)

YANG SUN: Go on talking. A voice is a voice.

SHEN TE: Once, when I was a little girl, I fell, with a load of brushwood. An old man picked me up. He gave me a penny too. Isn't it funny how people who don't have very much like to give some of it away? They must like to show what they can do, and how could they show it better than by being kind? Being wicked is just like being clumsy. When we sing a song, or build a machine, or plant some rice, we're being kind. You're kind.

YANG SUN: You make it sound easy.

SHEN TE: Oh, no. (*Little pause*.) Oh! A drop of rain!

YANG SUN: Where'd you feel it?

SHEN TE: Between the eyes.

YANG SUN: Near the right eye? Or the left?

SHEN TE: Near the left eye.

YANG SUN: Oh, good. (*He is getting sleepy*.) So you're through with men, eh?

SHEN TE (*with a smile*): But I'm not bow-legged.

YANG SUN: Perhaps not.

SHEN TE: Definitely not.

(*Pause*.)

YANG SUN (*leaning wearily against the willow*): I haven't had a drop to drink all day, I haven't eaten anything for two days. I couldn't love you if I tried.

(*Pause*.)

SHEN TE: I like it in the rain.

(Enter WONG the Water Seller, singing.)

The Song of the Water Seller in the Rain

"Buy my water," I am yelling
And my fury restraining

For no water I'm selling
'Cause it's raining, 'cause it's raining!
  I keep yelling: "Buy my water!"
  But no one's buying
  Athirst and dying
  And drinking and paying!
  Buy water!
  Buy water, you dogs!

Nice to dream of lovely weather!
Think of all the consternation
Were there no precipitation
Half a dozen years together!
Can't you hear them shrieking: "Water!"
Pretending they adore me!
They all would go down on their knees before me!
Down on your knees!
Go down on your knees, you dogs!

What are lawns and hedges thinking?
What are fields and forests saying?
"At the cloud's breast we are drinking!
And we've no idea who's paying!"
  I keep yelling: "Buy my water!"
  But no one's buying
  Athirst and dying
  And drinking and paying!
  Buy water!
  Buy water, you dogs!

(*The rain has stopped now.* SHEN TE *sees* WONG *and runs toward him.*)

SHEN TE: Wong! You're back! Your carrying pole's at the shop.

WONG: Oh, thank you, Shen Te. And how is life treating *you*?

SHEN TE: I've just met a brave and clever man. And I want to buy him a cup of your water.

WONG (*bitterly*): Throw back your head and open your mouth and you'll have all the water you need —

SHEN TE (*tenderly*):
  I want *your* water, Wong
  The water that has tired you so
  The water that you carried all this way
  The water that is hard to sell because it's been raining

I need it for the young man over there — he's a flyer!
>A flyer is a bold man:
>Braving the storms
>In company with the clouds
>He crosses the heavens
>And brings to friends in far-away lands
>The friendly mail!

(*She pays* WONG, *and runs over to* YANG SUN *with the cup. But* YANG SUN *is fast asleep.*)

(*Calling to* WONG, *with a laugh.*) He's fallen asleep! Despair and rain and I have worn him out!

Scene 3A

(WONG's *den. The sewer pipe is transparent, and the* GODS *again appear to* WONG *in a dream.*)

WONG (*radiant*): I've seen her, illustrious ones! And she hasn't changed!

FIRST GOD: That's good to hear.

WONG: She loves someone.

FIRST GOD: Let's hope the experience gives her the strength to stay good!

WONG: It does. She's doing good deeds all the time.

FIRST GOD: Ah? What sort? What sort of good deeds, Wong?

WONG: Well, she has a kind word for everybody.

FIRST GOD (*eagerly*): And then?

WONG: Hardly anyone leaves her shop without tobacco in his pocket — even if he can't pay for it.

FIRST GOD: Not bad at all. Next?

WONG: She's putting up a family of eight.

FIRST GOD (*gleefully, to the* SECOND GOD): Eight! (*To* WONG.) And that's not all, of course!

WONG: She bought a cup of water from me even though it was raining.

FIRST GOD: Yes, yes, yes, all these smaller good deeds!

WONG: Even they run into money. A little tobacco shop doesn't make so much.

FIRST GOD (*sententiously*): A prudent gardener works miracles on the smallest plot.

WONG: She hands out rice every morning. That eats up half her earnings.

FIRST GOD (*a little disappointed*): Well, as a beginning . . .

WONG: They call her the Angel of the Slums — whatever the Carpenter may say!

FIRST GOD: What's this? A carpenter speaks ill of her?

WONG: Oh, he only says her shelves weren't paid for in full.

SECOND GOD (*who has a bad cold and can't pronounce his n's and m's*): What's this? Not paying a carpenter? Why was that?

WONG: I suppose she didn't have the money.

SECOND GOD (*severely*): One pays what one owes, that's in our book of rules! First the letter of the law, then the spirit!

WONG: But it wasn't Shen Te, illustrious ones, it was her cousin. She called *him* in to help.

SECOND GOD: Then her cousin must never darken her threshold again!

WONG: Very well, illustrious ones! But in fairness to Shen Te, let me say that her cousin is a businessman.

FIRST GOD: Perhaps we should inquire what is customary? I find business quite unintelligible. But everybody's doing it. Business! Did the Seven Good Kings do business? Did Kung the Just sell fish?

SECOND GOD: In any case, such a thing must not occur again!

(*The* GODS *start to leave.*)

THIRD GOD: Forgive us for taking this tone with you, Wong, we haven't been getting enough sleep. The rich recommend us to the poor, and the poor tell us they haven't enough room.

SECOND GOD: Feeble, feeble, the best of them!

FIRST GOD: No great deeds! No heroic daring!

THIRD GOD: On such a *small* scale!

SECOND GOD: Sincere, yes, but what is actually *achieved?*

(*One can no longer hear them.*)

WONG (*calling after them*): I've thought of something, illustrious ones: Perhaps you shouldn't ask — too — much — all — at — once!

SCENE 4

(*The square in front of* SHEN TE'S *tobacco shop. Beside* SHEN TE'S *place, two other shops are seen: the carpet shop and a barber's. Morning. Outside* SHEN TE'S *the* GRANDFATHER, *the* SISTER-IN-LAW, *the* UNEMPLOYED MAN, *and* MRS. SHIN *stand waiting.*)

SISTER-IN-LAW: She's been out all night again.

MRS. SHIN: No sooner did we get rid of that crazy cousin of hers than

Shen Te herself starts carrying on! Maybe she does give us an ounce of rice now and then, but can you depend on her? Can you depend on her?

(*Loud voices from the Barber's.*)

VOICE OF SHU FU: What are you doing in my shop? Get out — at once!
VOICE OF WONG: But sir. They all let me sell . . .

(WONG *comes staggering out of the barber's shop pursued by* MR. SHU FU, *the barber, a fat man carrying a heavy curling iron.*)

SHU FU: Get out, I said! Pestering my customers with your slimy old water! Get out! Take your cup!

(*He holds out the cup.* WONG *reaches out for it.* MR. SHU FU *strikes his hand with the curling iron, which is hot.* WONG *howls.*)

You had it coming, my man!

(*Puffing, he returns to his shop. The* UNEMPLOYED MAN *picks up the cup and gives it to* WONG.)

UNEMPLOYED MAN: You can report that to the police.
WONG: My hand! It's smashed up!
UNEMPLOYED MAN: Any bones broken?
WONG: I can't move my fingers.
UNEMPLOYED MAN: Sit down. I'll put some water on it.

(WONG *sits.*)

MRS. SHIN: The water won't cost you anything.
SISTER-IN-LAW: You might have got a bandage from Miss Shen Te till she took to staying out all night. It's a scandal.
MRS. SHIN (*despondently*): If you ask me, she's forgotten we ever existed!

(*Enter* SHEN TE *down the street, with a dish of rice.*)

SHEN TE (*to the audience*): How wonderful to see Setzuan in the early morning! I always used to stay in bed with my dirty blanket over my head afraid to wake up. This morning I saw the newspapers being delivered by little boys, the streets being washed by strong men, and fresh vegetables coming in from the country on ox carts. It's a long walk from where Yang Sun lives, but I feel lighter at every step. They say you walk on air when you're in love, but it's even better walking on the rough earth, on the hard cement. In the early morning, the old city looks like a great rubbish heap. Nice, though — with all its little lights. And the sky, so pink, so transparent, before the dust comes and muddies it! What a lot you miss if you never see your city rising from its slumbers like an honest old crafts-man pumping his lungs full of air and reaching for his tools, as the poet says! (*Cheerfully, to her waiting guests.*) Good morning, every-one, here's your rice! (*Distributing the rice, she comes upon* WONG.) Good morning, Wong, I'm quite lightheaded today. On my way over, I looked at myself in all the shop windows. I'd love to be beautiful.

(*She slips into the carpet shop.* MR. SHU FU *has just emerged from his shop.*)

SHU FU (*to the audience*): It surprises me how beautiful Miss Shen Te is looking today! I never gave her a passing thought before. But now I've been gazing upon her comely form for exactly three minutes! I begin to suspect I am in love with her. She is overpoweringly attrac-tive! (*Crossly, to* WONG.) Be off with you, rascal!

(*He returns to his shop.* SHEN TE *comes back out of the carpet shop with the* OLD MAN *its proprietor and his wife — whom we have already met — the* OLD WOMAN. SHEN TE *is wearing a shawl. The* OLD MAN *is holding up a looking glass for her.*)

OLD WOMAN: Isn't it lovely? We'll give you a reduction because there's a little hole in it.

SHEN TE (*looking at another shawl on the* OLD WOMAN's *arm*): The other one's nice too.

OLD WOMAN (*smiling*): Too bad there's no hole in that!

SHEN TE: That's right. My shop doesn't make very much.

OLD WOMAN: And your good deeds eat it all up! Be more careful, my dear . . .

SHEN TE (*trying on the shawl with the hole*): Just now, I'm light-headed! Does the color suit me?

OLD WOMAN: You'd better ask a man.

SHEN TE (*to the* OLD MAN): Does the color suit me?

OLD MAN: You'd better ask your young friend.

SHEN TE: I'd like to have your opinion.

OLD MAN: It suits you, very well. But wear it this way: the dull side out.

(SHEN TE *pays up.*)

OLD WOMAN: If you decide you don't like it, you can exchange it. (*She pulls* SHEN TE *to one side.*) Has he got money?

SHEN TE (*with a laugh*): Yang Sun? Oh, no.

OLD WOMAN: Then how're you going to pay your rent?

SHEN TE: I'd forgotten about that.

OLD WOMAN: And next Monday is the first of the month! Miss Shen Te, I've got something to say to you. After we (*indicating her husband*) got to know you, we had our doubts about that marriage ad. We thought it would be better if you'd let *us* help you. Out of our savings. We reckon we could lend you two hundred silver dollars. We don't need anything in writing — you could pledge us your tobacco stock.

SHEN TE: You're prepared to lend money to a person like me?

OLD WOMAN: It's folks like you that need it. We'd think twice about lending anything to your cousin.

OLD MAN (*coming up*): All settled, my dear?

SHEN TE: I wish the gods could have heard what your wife was just saying, Mr. Ma. They're looking for good people who're happy — and helping me makes you happy because you know it was love that got me into difficulties!

(*The old couple smile knowingly at each other.*)

OLD MAN: And here's the money, Miss Shen Te.

(*He hands her an envelope. SHEN TE takes it. She bows. They bow back. They return to their shop.*)

SHEN TE (*holding up her envelope*): Look, Wong, here's six months' rent! Don't you believe in miracles now? And how do you like my new shawl?

WONG: For the young fellow I saw you with in the park?

(SHEN TE *nods.*)

MRS. SHIN: Never mind all that. It's time you took a look at his hand!

SHEN TE: Have you hurt your hand?

MRS. SHIN: That barber smashed it with his hot curling iron. Right in front of our eyes.

SHEN TE (*shocked at herself*): And I never noticed! We must get you to a doctor this minute or who knows what will happen?

UNEMPLOYED MAN: It's not a doctor he should see, it's a judge. He can ask for compensation. The barber's filthy rich.

WONG: You think I have a chance?

MRS. SHIN (*with relish*): If it's really good and smashed. But is it?

WONG: I think so. It's very swollen. Could I get a pension?

MRS. SHIN: You'd need a witness.

WONG: Well, you all saw it. You could all testify.

(*He looks round. The* UNEMPLOYED MAN, *the* GRANDFATHER, *and the* SISTER-IN-LAW *are all sitting against the wall of the shop eating rice. Their concentration on eating is complete.*)

SHEN TE (*to* MRS. SHIN): You saw it yourself.

MRS. SHIN: I want nothin' to do with the police. It's against my principles.

SHEN TE (*to* SISTER-IN-LAW): What about you?

SISTER-IN-LAW: Me? I wasn't looking.

SHEN TE (*to the* GRANDFATHER, *coaxingly*): Grandfather, *you'll* testify, won't you?

SISTER-IN-LAW: And a lot of good that will do. He's simple-minded.

SHEN TE (*to the* UNEMPLOYED MAN): You seem to be the only witness left.

UNEMPLOYED MAN: My testimony would only hurt him. I've been picked up twice for begging.

SHEN TE: Your brother is assaulted, and you shut your eyes?
  He is hit, cries out in pain, and you are silent?
  The beast prowls, chooses and seizes his victim, and you say:
  "Because we showed no displeasure, he has spared us."
If no one present will be a witness, I will. I'll say *I* saw it.

MRS. SHIN (*solemnly*): The name for that is perjury.

WONG: I don't know if I can accept that. Though maybe I'll have to. (*Looking at his hand.*) Is it swollen enough, do you think? The swelling's not going down?

UNEMPLOYED MAN: No, no, the swelling's holding up well.

WONG: Yes. It's *more* swollen if anything. Maybe my wrist is broken after all. I'd better see a judge at once.

(*Holding his hand very carefully, and fixing his eyes on it, he runs off.* MRS. SHIN *goes quickly into the barber's shop.*)

UNEMPLOYED MAN (*seeing her*): She is getting on the right side of Mr. Shu Fu.

SISTER-IN-LAW: You and I can't change the world, Shen Te.

SHEN TE: Go away! Go away all of you!

(*The* UNEMPLOYED MAN, *the* SISTER-IN-LAW, *and the* GRANDFATHER *stalk off, eating and sulking.*)

(*To the audience.*)

They've stopped answering
They stay put
They do as they're told
They don't care

Nothing can make them look up
But the smell of food.

(*Enter* MRS. YANG, YANG SUN'S *mother, out of breath.*)

MRS. YANG: Miss. Shen Te. My son has told me everything. I am Mrs. Yang, Sun's mother. Just think. He's got an offer. Of a job as a pilot. A letter has just come. From the director of the airfield in Peking!

SHEN TE: So he can fly again? Isn't that wonderful!

MRS. YANG (*less breathlessly all the time*): They won't give him the job for nothing. They want five hundred silver dollars.

SHEN TE: We can't let money stand in his way, Mrs. Yang!

MRS. YANG: If only you could help him out!

SHEN TE: I have the shop. I can try! (*She embraces* MRS. YANG.) I happen to have two hundred with me now. Take it. (*She gives her the old couple's money.*) It was a loan but they said I could repay it with my tobacco stock.

MRS. YANG: And they were calling Sun the Dead Pilot of Setzuan! A friend in need!

SHEN TE: We must find another three hundred.

MRS. YANG: How?

SHEN TE: Let me think. (*Slowly.*) I know someone who can help. I didn't want to call on his services again, he's hard and cunning. But a flyer must fly. And I'll make this the last time.

(*Distant sound of a plane.*)

MRS. YANG: If the man you mentioned can do it. . . . Oh, look, there's the morning mail plane, heading for Peking!

SHEN TE: The pilot can see us, let's wave!

(*They wave. The noise of the engine is louder.*)

MRS. YANG: You know that pilot up there?

SHEN TE: Wave, Mrs. Yang! I know the pilot who *will* be up there. He gave up hope. But he'll do it now. One man to raise himself above the misery, above us all.

(*To the audience.*)

Yang Sun, my lover:
Braving the storms
In company with the clouds
Crossing the heavens
And bringing to friends in far-away lands
The friendly mail!

Scene 4A

(*In front of the inner curtain. Enter* SHEN TE, *carrying* SHUI TA'S *mask. She sings.*)

The Song of Defenselessness

In our country
A useful man needs luck
Only if he finds strong backers can he prove himself useful
The good can't defend themselves and
Even the gods are defenseless.

Oh, why don't the gods have their own ammunition
And launch against badness their own expedition
Enthroning the good and preventing sedition
And bringing the world to a peaceful condition?

Oh, why don't the gods do the buying and selling
Injustice forbidding, starvation dispelling
Give bread to each city and joy to each dwelling?
Oh, why don't the gods do the buying and selling?

(*She puts on* SHUI TA'S *mask and sings in his voice.*)

You can only help one of your luckless brothers
By trampling down a dozen others

Why is it the gods do not feel indignation
And come down in fury to end exploitation
Defeat all defeat and forbid desperation
Refusing to tolerate such toleration?

Why is it?

SCENE 5

(SHEN TE'S *tobacco shop. Behind the counter,* MR. SHUI TA, *reading the paper.* MRS. SHIN *is cleaning up. She talks and he takes no notice.*)

MRS. SHIN: And when certain rumors get about, what *happens* to a little place like this? It goes to pot. I know. So, if you want my advice, Mr. Shui Ta, find out just what exactly has been going on between Miss Shen Te and that Yang Sun from Yellow Street. And remember: a certain interest in Miss Shen Te has been expressed by the barber next door, a man with twelve houses and only one wife, who, for that matter, is likely to drop off at any time. A certain interest has been expressed. (*She relishes the phrase.*) He was even inquiring about her means and, if *that* doesn't prove a man is getting serious, what would? (*Still getting no response, she leaves with her bucket.*)

YANG SUN'S VOICE: Is that Miss Shen Te's tobacco shop?

MRS. SHIN'S VOICE: Yes, it is, but it's Mr. Shui Ta who's here today.

(SHUI TA *runs to the looking glass with the short, light steps of* SHEN TE, *and is just about to start primping, when he realizes his mistake, and turns away, with a short laugh. Enter* YANG SUN. MRS. SHIN *enters behind him and slips into the back room to eavesdrop.*)

YANG SUN: I am Yang Sun.

(SHUI TA *bows.*)

Is Miss Shen Te in?

SHUI TA: No.

YANG SUN: I guess you know our relationship? (*He is inspecting the stock.*) Quite a place! And I thought she was just talking big. I'll be flying again, all right. (*He takes a cigar, solicits and receives a light from* SHUI TA.) You think we can squeeze the other three hundred out of the tobacco stock?

SHUI TA: May I ask if it is your intention to sell at once?

YANG SUN: It was decent of her to come out with the two hundred but they aren't much use with the other three hundred still missing.

SHUI TA: Shen Te was overhasty promising so much. She might have to sell the shop itself to raise it. Haste, they say, is the wind that blows the house down.

YANG SUN: Oh, she isn't a girl to keep a man waiting. For one thing or the other, if you take my meaning.

SHUI TA: I take your meaning.

YANG SUN (*leering*): Uh, huh.

SHUI TA: Would you explain what the five hundred silver dollars are for?

YANG SUN: Trying to sound me out? Very well. The director of the Peking airfield is a friend of mine from flying school. I give him five hundred: he gets me the job.

SHUI TA: The price is high.

YANG SUN: Not as these things go. He'll have to fire one of the present pilots — for negligence. Only the man he has in mind isn't negligent. Not easy, you understand. You needn't mention that part of it to Shen Te.

SHUI TA (*looking intently at* YANG SUN): Mr. Yang Sun, you are asking my cousin to give up her possessions, leave her friends, and place her entire fate in your hands. I presume you intend to marry her?

YANG SUN: I'd be prepared to.

(*Slight pause.*)

SHUI TA: Those two hundred silver dollars would pay the rent here for six months. If you were Shen Te wouldn't you be tempted to continue in business?

YANG SUN: What? Can you imagine Yang Sun the Flyer behind a counter? (*In an oily voice.*) "A strong cigar or a mild one, worthy sir?" Not in this century!

SHUI TA: My cousin wishes to follow the promptings of her heart, and, from her own point of view, she may even have what is called the right to love. Accordingly, she has commissioned me to help you to this post. There is nothing here that I am not empowered to turn immediately into cash. Mrs. Mi Tzu, the landlady, will advise me about the sale.

(*Enter* MRS. MI TZU.)

MRS. MI TZU: Good morning, Mr. Shui Ta, you wish to see me about the rent? As you know it falls due the day after tomorrow.

SHUI TA: Circumstances have changed, Mrs. Mi Tzu: my cousin is getting married. Her future husband here, Mr. Yang Sun, will be taking her to Peking. I am interested in selling the tobacco stock.

MRS. MI TZU: How much are you asking, Mr. Shui Ta?

YANG SUN: Three hundred sil —

SHUI TA: Five hundred silver dollars.

MRS. MI TZU: How much did she pay for it, Mr. Shui Ta?

SHUI TA: A thousand. And very little has been sold.

MRS. MI TZU: She was robbed. But I'll make you a special offer if you'll promise to be out by the day after tomorrow. Three hundred silver dollars.

YANG SUN (*shrugging*): Take it, man, take it.

SHUI TA: It is not enough.

YANG SUN: Why not? Why not? Certainly, it's enough.

SHUI TA: Five hundred silver dollars.

YANG SUN: But why? We only need three!

SHUI TA (*to* MRS. MI TZU): Excuse me. (*Takes* YANG SUN *on one side.*)

The tobacco stock is pledged to the old couple who gave my cousin the two hundred.

YANG SUN: Is it in writing?

SHUI TA: No.

YANG SUN (*to* MRS. MI TZU): Three hundred will do.

MRS. MI TZU: Of course, I need an assurance that Miss Shen Te is not in debt.

YANG SUN: Mr. Shui Ta?

SHUI TA: She is not in debt.

YANG SUN: When can you let us have the money?

MRS. MI TZU: The day after tomorrow. And remember: I'm doing this because I have a soft spot in my heart for young lovers! (*Exit.*)

YANG SUN (*calling after her*): Boxes, jars and sacks — three hundred for the lot and the pain's over! (*To* SHUI TA.) Where else can we raise money by the day after tomorrow?

SHUI TA: Nowhere. Haven't you enough for the trip and the first few weeks?

YANG SUN: Oh, certainly.

SHUI TA: How much, exactly?

YANG SUN: Oh, I'll dig it up, if I have to steal it.

SHUI TA: I see.

YANG SUN: Well, don't fall off the roof. I'll get to Peking somehow.

SHUI TA: Two people can't travel for nothing.

YANG SUN (*not giving* SHUI TA *a chance to answer*): I'm leaving *her* behind. No millstones round *my* neck!

SHUI TA: Oh.

YANG SUN: Don't look at me like that!

SHUI TA: How precisely is my cousin to live?

YANG SUN: Oh, you'll think of something.

SHUI TA: A small request, Mr. Yang Sun. Leave the two hundred silver dollars here until you can show me two tickets for Peking.

YANG SUN: You learn to mind your own business, Mr. Shui Ta.

SHUI TA: I'm afraid Miss Shen Te may not wish to sell the shop when she discovers that . . .

YANG SUN: You don't know women. She'll want to. Even then.

SHUI TA (*a slight outburst*): She is a human being, sir! And not devoid of common sense!

YANG SUN: Shen Te is a woman: she *is* devoid of common sense. I only have to lay my hand on her shoulder, and church bells ring.

SHUI TA (*with difficulty*): Mr. Yang Sun!

YANG SUN: Mr. Shui Whatever-it-is!

SHUI TA: My cousin is devoted to you . . . because . . .

YANG SUN: Because I have my hands on her breasts. Give me a cigar.

(*He takes one for himself, stuffs a few more in his pocket, then changes his mind and takes the whole box.*) Tell her I'll marry her, then bring me the three hundred. Or let her bring it. One or the other. (*Exit.*)

MRS. SHIN (*sticking her head out of the back room*): Well, he has your cousin under his thumb, and doesn't care if all Yellow Street knows it!

SHUI TA (*crying out*): I've lost my shop! And he doesn't love me! (*He runs berserk through the room, repeating these lines incoherently. Then stops suddenly, and addresses* MRS. SHIN.) Mrs. Shin, you grew up in the gutter, like me. Are we lacking in hardness? I doubt it. If you steal a penny from me, I'll take you by the throat till you spit it out! You'd do the same to me. The times are bad, this city is hell, but we're like ants, we keep coming, up and up the walls, however smooth! Till bad luck comes. Being in love, for instance. *One* weakness is enough, and love is the deadliest.

MRS. SHIN (*emerging from the back room*): You should have a little talk with Mr. Shu Fu the Barber. He's a real gentleman and just the thing for your cousin. (*She runs off.*)

SHUI TA:

A caress becomes a stranglehold
A sigh of love turns to a cry of fear
Why are there vultures circling in the air?
A girl is going to meet her lover.

(SHUI TA *sits down and* MR. SHU FU *enters with* MRS. SHIN.)

Mr. Shu Fu?

SHU FU: Mr. Shui Ta.

(*They both bow.*)

SHUI TA: I am told that you have expressed a certain interest in my cousin Shen Te. Let me set aside all propriety and confess: she is at this moment in grave danger.

SHU FU: Oh, dear!

SHUI TA: She has lost her shop, Mr. Shu Fu.

SHU FU: The charm of Miss Shen Te, Mr. Shui Ta, derives from the goodness, not of her shop, but of her heart. Men call her the Angel of the Slums.

SHUI TA: Yet her goodness has cost her two hundred silver dollars in a single day: we must put a stop to it.

SHU FU: Permit me to differ, Mr. Shui Ta. Let us rather, open wide the gates to such goodness! Every morning, with pleasure tinged by affection, I watch her charitable ministrations. For they are hungry, and she giveth them to eat! Four of them, to be precise. Why only four? I ask. Why not four hundred? I hear she has been seeking shelter for the homeless. What about my humble cabins behind the cattle run? They are at her disposal. And so forth. And so on. Mr. Shui Ta, do you think Miss Shen Te could be persuaded to listen to certain ideas of mine? Ideas like these?

SHUI TA: Mr. Shu Fu, she would be honored.

(*Enter* WONG *and the* POLICEMAN. MR. SHU FU *turns abruptly away and studies the shelves.*)

WONG: Is Miss Shen Te here?

SHUI TA: No.

WONG: I am Wong the Water Seller. You are Mr. Shui Ta?

SHUI TA: I am.

WONG: I am a friend of Shen Te's.

SHUI TA: An intimate friend, I hear.

WONG (*to the* POLICEMAN): You see? (*To* SHUI TA.) It's because of my hand.

POLICEMAN: He hurt his hand, sir, that's a fact.

SHUI TA (*quickly*): You need a sling, I see. (*He takes a shawl from the back room, and throws it to* WONG.)

WONG: But that's her new shawl!

SHUI TA: She has no more use for it.

WONG: But she bought it to please someone!

SHUI TA: It happens to be no longer necessary.

WONG (*making the sling*): She is my only witness.

POLICEMAN: Mr. Shui Ta, your cousin is supposed to have seen the Barber hit the Water Seller with a curling iron.

SHUI TA: I'm afraid my cousin was not present at the time.

WONG: But she was, sir! Just ask her! Isn't she in?

SHUI TA (*gravely*): Mr. Wong, my cousin has her own troubles. You wouldn't wish her to add to them by committing perjury?

WONG: But it was she that told me to go to the judge!

SHUI TA: Was the judge supposed to heal your hand?

(MR. SHU FU *turns quickly around.* SHUI TA *bows to* SHU FU, *and vice versa.*)

WONG (*taking the sling off, and putting it back*): I see how it is.

POLICEMAN: Well, I'll be on my way. (*To* WONG.) And you be careful. If Mr. Shu Fu wasn't a man who tempers justice with mercy, as the saying is, you'd be in jail for libel. Be off with you!

(*Exit* WONG, *followed by* POLICEMAN.)

SHUI TA: Profound apologies, Mr. Shu Fu.

SHU FU: Not at all, Mr. Shui Ta. (*Pointing to the shawl.*) The episode is over?

SHUI TA: It may take her time to recover. There are some fresh wounds.

SHU FU: We shall be discreet. Delicate. A short vacation could be arranged . . .

SHUI TA: First, of course, you and she would have to talk things over.

SHU FU: At a small supper in a small, but high-class, restaurant.

SHUI TA: I'll go and find her. (*Exit into back room.*)

MRS. SHIN (*sticking her head in again*): Time for congratulations, Mr. Shu Fu?

SHU FU: Ah, Mrs. Shin! Please inform Miss Shen Te's guests they may take shelter in the cabins behind the cattle run!

(MRS. SHIN *nods, grinning.*)

(*To the audience.*) Well? What do you think of me, ladies and gentlemen? What could a man do more? Could he be less selfish? More farsighted? A small supper in a small but . . . Does that bring rather vulgar and clumsy thoughts into your mind? Ts, ts, ts. Nothing of the sort will occur. She won't even be touched. Not even accidentally while passing the salt. An exchange of ideas only. Over the flowers on the table — white chrysanthemums, by the way (*He writes down a note of this.*) — yes, over the white chrysanthemums, two young souls will . . . shall I say "find each other"? We shall NOT exploit the misfortune of others. Understanding? Yes. An offer of assistance? Certainly. But quietly. Almost inaudibly. Perhaps with a single glance. A glance that could also — mean more.

MRS. SHIN (*coming forward*): Everything under control, Mr. Shu Fu?

SHU FU: Oh, Mrs. Shin, what do you know about this worthless rascal Yang Sun?

MRS. SHIN: Why, he's the most worthless rascal . . .

SHU FU: Is he really? You're sure? (*As she opens her mouth.*) From now on, he doesn't exist! Can't be found anywhere!

(*Enter* YANG SUN.)

YANG SUN: What's been going on here?

MRS. SHIN: Shall I call Mr. Shui Ta, Mr. Shu Fu? He wouldn't want strangers in here!

SHU FU: Mr. Shui Ta is in conference with Miss Shen Te. Not to be disturbed!

YANG SUN: Shen Te here? I didn't see her come in. What kind of conference?

SHU FU (*not letting him enter the back room*): Patience, dear sir! And if by chance I have an inkling who you are, pray take note that Miss Shen Te and I are about to announce our engagement.

YANG SUN: What?

MRS. SHIN: You didn't expect that, did you?

(YANG SUN *is trying to push past the barber into the back room when* SHEN TE *comes out.*)

SHU FU: My dear Shen Te, ten thousand apologies! Perhaps you . . .

YANG SUN: What is it, Shen Te? Have you gone crazy?

SHEN TE (*breathless*): My cousin and Mr. Shu Fu have come to an understanding. They wish me to hear Mr. Shu Fu's plans for helping the poor.

YANG SUN: Your cousin wants to part us.

SHEN TE: Yes.

YANG SUN: And you've agreed to it?

SHEN TE: Yes.

YANG SUN: They told you I was bad.

(SHEN TE *is silent.*)

And suppose I am. Does that make me need you less? I'm low, Shen Te, I have no money, I don't do the right thing but at least I put up a fight! (*He is near her now, and speaks in an undertone.*) Have you no eyes? Look at him. Have you forgotten already?

SHEN TE: No.

YANG SUN: How it was raining?

SHEN TE: No.

YANG SUN: How you cut me down from the willow tree? Bought me water? Promised me money to fly with?

SHEN TE (*shakily*): Yang Sun, what do you want?

YANG SUN: I want you to come with me.

SHEN TE (*in a small voice*): Forgive me, Mr. Shu Fu, I want to go with Mr. Yang Sun.

YANG SUN: We're lovers you know. Give me the key to the shop.

(SHEN TE *takes the key from around her neck.* YANG SUN *puts it on the counter. To* MRS. SHIN.)

Leave it under the mat when you're through. Let's go, Shen Te.

SHU FU: But this is rape! Mr. Shui Ta!!

YANG SUN (*to* SHEN TE): Tell him not to shout.

SHEN TE: Please don't shout for my cousin, Mr. Shu Fu. He doesn't agree with me, I know, but he's wrong. (*To the audience.*)

I want to go with the man I love
I don't want to count the cost

I don't want to consider if it's wise
I don't want to know if he loves me
I want to go with the man I love.

YANG SUN: That's the spirit.

(*And the couple leave.*)

Scene 5A

(*In front of the inner curtain.* SHEN TE *in her wedding clothes, on the way to her wedding.*)

SHEN TE: Something terrible has happened. As I left the shop with Yang Sun, I found the old carpet dealer's wife waiting in the street, trembling all over. She told me her husband had taken to his bed — sick with all the worry and excitement over the two hundred silver dollars they lent me. She said it would be best if I gave it back now. Of course, I had to say I would. She said she couldn't quite trust my cousin Shui Ta or even my fiancé Yang Sun. There were tears in her eyes. With my emotions in an uproar, I threw myself into Yang Sun's arms, I couldn't resist him. The things he'd said to Shui Ta had taught Shen Te nothing. Sinking into his arms, I said to myself:

To let no one perish, not even oneself
To fill everyone with happiness, even oneself
Is so good

How could I have forgotten those two old people? Yang Sun swept me away like a small hurricane. But he's not a bad man, and he loves me. He'd rather work in the cement factory than owe his flying to a crime. Though, of course, flying *is* a great passion with Sun. Now, on the way to my wedding, I waver between fear and joy.

SCENE 6

(*The "private dining room" on the upper floor of a cheap restaurant in a poor section of town. With* SHEN TE: *the* GRANDFATHER, *the* SISTER-IN-LAW, *the* NIECE, MRS. SHIN, *the* UNEMPLOYED MAN. *In a corner, alone, a* PRIEST. *A* WAITER *pouring wine. Downstage,* YANG SUN *talking to his mother. He wears a dinner jacket.*)

YANG SUN: Bad news, Mamma. She came right out and told me she can't sell the shop for me. Some idiot is bringing a claim because he lent her the two hundred she gave you.

MRS. YANG: What did *you* say? Of course, you can't marry her now.

YANG SUN: It's no use saying anything to *her*. I've sent for her cousin, Mr. Shui Ta. He said there was nothing in writing.

MRS. YANG: Good idea. I'll go out and look for him. Keep an eye on things.

(*Exit* MRS. YANG. SHEN TE *has been pouring wine.*)

SHEN TE (*to the audience, pitcher in hand*): I wasn't mistaken in him. He's bearing up well. Though it must have been an awful blow — giving up flying. I do love him so. (*Calling across the room to him.*) Sun, you haven't drunk a toast with the bride!

YANG SUN: What do we drink to?

SHEN TE: Why, to the future!

YANG SUN: When the bridegroom's dinner jacket won't be a hired one!

SHEN TE: But when the bride's dress will still get rained on sometimes!

YANG SUN: To everything we ever wished for!

SHEN TE: May all our dreams come true!

(*They drink.*)

YANG SUN (*with loud conviviality*): And now, friends, before the wedding gets under way, I have to ask the bride a few questions. I've no idea what kind of a wife she'll make, and it worries me. (*Wheeling on* SHEN TE.) For example. Can you make five cups of tea with three tea leaves?

SHEN TE: No.

YANG SUN: So I won't be getting very much tea. Can you sleep on a straw mattress the size of that book? (*He points to the large volume the* PRIEST *is reading.*)

SHEN TE: The two of us?

YANG SUN: The one of you.

SHEN TE: In that case, no.

YANG SUN: What a wife! I'm shocked!

(*While the audience is laughing, his mother returns. With a shrug of her shoulders, she tells* YANG SUN *the expected guest hasn't arrived. The* PRIEST *shuts the book with a bang, and makes for the door.*)

MRS. YANG: Where are *you* off to? It's only a matter of minutes.

PRIEST (*watch in hand*): Time goes on, Mrs. Yang, and I've another wedding to attend to. Also a funeral.

MRS. YANG (*irately*): D'you think we planned it this way? I was hoping to manage with one pitcher of wine, and we've run through two already. (*Points to empty pitcher. Loudly.*) My dear Shen Te, I don't know where your cousin can be keeping himself!

SHEN TE: My cousin?

MRS. YANG: Certainly. I'm old fashioned enough to think such a close relative should attend the wedding.

SHEN TE: Oh, Sun, is it the three hundred silver dollars?

YANG SUN (*not looking her in the eye*): Are you deaf? Mother says she's old fashioned. And I say I'm considerate. We'll wait another fifteen minutes.

HUSBAND: Another fifteen minutes.

MRS. YANG (*addressing the company*): Now you all know, don't you, that my son is getting a job as a mail pilot?

SISTER-IN-LAW: In Peking, too, isn't it?

MRS. YANG: In Peking, too! The two of us are moving to Peking!

SHEN TE: Sun, tell your mother Peking is out of the question now.

YANG SUN: Your cousin'll tell her. If he agrees. I don't agree.

SHEN TE (*amazed, and dismayed*): Sun!

YANG SUN: I hate this godforsaken Setzuan. What people! Know what they look like when I half close my eyes? Horses! Whinnying, fretting, stamping, screwing their necks up! (*Loudly.*) And what is it the thunder says? They are su-per-flu-ous! (*He hammers out the syllables.*) They've run their last race! They can go trample themselves to death! (*Pause.*) I've got to get out of here.

SHEN TE: But I've promised the money to the old couple.

YANG SUN: And since you always do the wrong thing, it's lucky your cousin's coming. Have another drink.

SHEN TE (*quietly*): My cousin can't be coming.

YANG SUN: How d'you mean?

SHEN TE: My cousin can't be where I am.

YANG SUN: Quite a conundrum!

SHEN TE (*desperately*): Sun, I'm the one that loves you. Not my cousin. He was thinking of the job in Peking when he promised you the old couple's money —

YANG SUN: Right. And that's why he's bringing the three hundred silver dollars. Here — to my wedding.

SHEN TE: He is not bringing the three hundred silver dollars.

YANG SUN: Huh? What makes you think that?

SHEN TE (*looking into his eyes*): He says you only bought one ticket to Peking.

(*Short pause.*)

YANG SUN: That was yesterday. (*He pulls two tickets part way out of his inside pocket, making her look under his coat.*) Two tickets. I don't want Mother to know. She'll get left behind. I sold her furniture to buy these tickets, so you see . . .

SHEN TE: But what's to become of the old couple?

YANG SUN: What's to become of me? Have another drink. Or do you believe in moderation? If I drink, I fly again. And if you drink, you may learn to understand me.

SHEN TE: You want to fly. But I can't help you.

YANG SUN: "Here's a plane, my darling — but it's only got one wing!"

(*The* WAITER *enters.*)

WAITER: Mrs. Yang! Mrs. Yang!

MRS. YANG: Yes?

WAITER: Another pitcher of wine, ma'am?

MRS. YANG: We have enough, thanks. Drinking makes me sweat.

WAITER: Would you mind paying, ma'am?

MRS. YANG (*to everyone*): Just be patient a few moments longer, everyone, Mr. Shui Ta is on his way over! (*To the* WAITER.) Don't be a spoilsport.

WAITER: I can't let you leave till you've paid your bill, ma'am.

MRS. YANG: But they know me here!

WAITER: That's just it.

PRIEST (*ponderously getting up*): I humbly take my leave. (*And he does.*)

MRS. YANG (*to the others, desperately*): Stay where you are, everybody! The priest says he'll be back in two minutes!

YANG SUN: It's no good, Mamma. Ladies and gentlemen, Mr. Shui Ta still hasn't arrived and the priest has gone home. We won't detain you any longer.

(*They are leaving now.*)

GRANDFATHER (*in the doorway, having forgotten to put his glass down*): To the bride! (*He drinks, puts down the glass, and follows the others.*)

(*Pause.*)

SHEN TE: Shall I go too?

YANG SUN: You? Aren't you the bride? Isn't this your wedding? (*He drags her across the room, tearing her wedding dress.*) If we can wait, you can wait. Mother calls me her falcon. She wants to see me in the clouds. But I think it may be St. Nevercome's Day before she'll go to the door and see my plane thunder by. (*Pause. He pretends the guests are still present.*) Why such a lull in the conversation, ladies and gentlemen? Don't you like it here? The ceremony is only slightly postponed — because an important guest is expected at any moment. Also because the bride doesn't know what love is. While we're waiting, the bridegroom will sing a little song. (*He does so.*)

The Song of St. Nevercome's Day

On a certain day, as is generally known,
    One and all will be shouting: Hooray, hooray!
For the beggar maid's son has a solid-gold throne
    And the day is St. Nevercome's Day
On St. Nevercome's, Nevercome's, Nevercome's Day
    He'll sit on his solid-gone throne

Oh, hooray, hooray! That day goodness will pay!
    That day badness will cost you your head!
And merit and money will smile and be funny
    While exchanging salt and bread
On St. Nevercome's, Nevercome's, Nevercome's Day
    While exchanging salt and bread

And the grass, oh, the grass will look down at the sky
    And the pebbles will roll up the stream
And all men will be good without batting an eye
    They will make of our earth a dream
On St. Nevercome's, Nevercome's, Nevercome's Day
    They will make of our earth a dream

And as for me, that's the day I shall be
    A flyer and one of the best
Unemployed man, you will have work to do
    Washerwoman, you'll get your rest
On St. Nevercome's, Nevercome's, Nevercome's Day
    Washerwoman, you'll get your rest.

MRS. YANG: It looks like he's not coming.

(*The three of them sit looking at the door.*)

Scene 6A

(WONG's *den. The sewer pipe is again transparent and again the* GODS *appear to* WONG *in a dream.*)

WONG: I'm so glad you've come, illustrious ones. It's Shen Te. She's in great trouble from following the rule about loving thy neighbor. Perhaps she's *too* good for this world!

FIRST GOD: Nonsense! You are eaten up by lice and doubts!

WONG: Forgive me, illustrious one, I only meant you might deign to intervene.

FIRST GOD: Out of the question! My colleague here intervened in some squabble or other only yesterday. (*He points to the* THIRD GOD *who has a black eye.*) The results are before us!

WONG: She had to call on her cousin again. But not even he could help. I'm afraid the shop is done for.

THIRD GOD (*a little concerned*): Perhaps we should help after all?

FIRST GOD: The gods help those that help themselves.

WONG: What if we *can't* help ourselves, illustrious ones?

(*Slight pause.*)

SECOND GOD: Try, anyway! Suffering ennobles!

FIRST GOD: Our faith in Shen Te is unshaken!

THIRD GOD: We certainly haven't found any *other* good people. You can see where we spend our nights from the straw on our clothes.

WONG: You might help her find her way by —

FIRST GOD: The good man finds his own way here below!

SECOND GOD: The good woman too.

FIRST GOD: The heavier the burden, the greater her strength!

THIRD GOD: We're only onlookers, you know.

FIRST GOD: And everything will be all right in the end, O ye of little faith!

(*They are gradually disappearing through these last lines.*)

SCENE 7

(*The yard behind* SHEN TE'S *shop. A few articles of furniture on a cart.* SHEN TE *and* MRS. SHIN *are taking the washing off the line.*)

MRS. SHIN: If you ask me, you should fight tooth and nail to keep the shop.

SHEN TE: How can I? I have to sell the tobacco to pay back the two hundred silver dollars today.

MRS. SHIN: No husband, no tobacco, no house and home! What are you going to live on?

SHEN TE: I can work. I can sort tobacco.

MRS. SHIN: Hey, look, Mr. Shui Ta's trousers! He must have left here stark naked!

SHEN TE: Oh, he may have another pair, Mrs. Shin.

MRS. SHIN: But if he's gone for good as you say, why has he left his pants behind?

SHEN TE: Maybe he's thrown them away.

MRS. SHIN: Can I take them?

SHEN TE: Oh, no.

(*Enter* MR. SHU FU, *running.*)

SHU FU: Not a word! Total silence! I know all. You have sacrificed your own love and happiness so as not to hurt a dear old couple who had put their trust in you! Not in vain does this district — for all its malevolent tongues! — call you the Angel of the Slums! That young man couldn't rise to your level, so you left him. And now, when I see you closing up the little shop, that veritable haven of rest for the multitude, well, I cannot, I cannot let it pass. Morning after morning I have stood watching in the doorway not unmoved — while you graciously handed out rice to the wretched. Is that never to happen again? Is the good woman of Setzuan to disappear? If only you would allow *me* to assist you! Now don't say anything! No assurances, no exclamations of gratitude! (*He has taken out his check book.*) Here! A blank check. (*He places it on the cart.*) Just my signature. Fill it out as you wish. Any sum in the world. I herewith retire from the scene, quietly, unobtrusively, making no claims, on tiptoe, full of veneration, absolutely selflessly . . . (*He has gone.*)

MRS. SHIN: Well! You're saved. There's always some idiot of a man . . . Now hurry! Put down a thousand silver dollars and let me fly to the bank before he comes to his senses.

SHEN TE: I can pay you for the washing without any check.

MRS. SHIN: What? You're not going to cash it just because you might have to marry him? Are you crazy? Men like him *want* to be led by the nose! Are you still thinking of that flyer? All Yellow Street knows how he treated you!

SHEN TE:

When I heard his cunning laugh, I was afraid

But when I saw the holes in his shoes, I loved him dearly.

MRS. SHIN: Defending that good for nothing after all that's happened!

SHEN TE (*staggering as she holds some of the washing*): Oh!

MRS. SHIN (*taking the washing from her, dryly*): So you feel dizzy when you stretch and bend? There couldn't be a little visitor on the way? If that's it, you can forget Mr. Shu Fu's blank check: it wasn't meant for a christening present!

(*She goes to the back with a basket.* SHEN TE'S *eyes follow* MRS. SHIN *for a moment. Then she looks down at her own body, feels her stomach, and a great joy comes into her eyes.*)

SHEN TE: O joy! A new human being is on the way. The world awaits him. In the cities the people say: he's got to be reckoned with, this new human being! (*She imagines a little boy to be present, and introduces him to the audience.*)

This is my son, the well-known flyer!
Say: Welcome
To the conqueror of unknown mountains and unreachable regions
Who brings us our mail across the impassable deserts!

(*She leads him up and down by the hand.*) Take a look at the world, my son. That's a tree. Tree, yes. Say: "Hello, tree!" And bow. Like this. (*She bows.*) Now you know each other. And, look, here comes the Water Seller. He's a friend, give him your hand. A cup of fresh water for my little son, please. Yes, it *is* a warm day. (*Handing the cup.*) Oh dear, a policeman, we'll have to make a circle round *him*. Perhaps we can pick a few cherries over there in the rich Mr. Pung's garden. But we mustn't be seen. You want cherries? Just like children with fathers. No, no, you can't go straight at them like that. Don't pull. We must learn to be reasonable. Well, have it your own way. (*She has let him make for the cherries.*) Can you reach? Where to put them? Your mouth is the best place. (*She tries one herself.*) Mmm, they're good. But the policeman, we must run! (*They run.*) Yes, back to the street. Calm now, so no one will notice us. (*Walking the street with her child, she sings.*)

Once a plum — 'twas in Japan —
Made a conquest of a man
But the man's turn soon did come
For he gobbled up the plum

(*Enter* WONG, *with a* CHILD *by the hand. He coughs.*)

SHEN TE: Wong!

WONG: It's about the Carpenter, Shen Te. He's lost his shop, and he's been drinking. His children are on the streets. This is one. Can you help?

SHEN TE (*to the child*): Come here, little man. (*Takes him down to the footlights. To the audience.*)

You there! A man is asking you for shelter!
A man of tomorrow says: what about today?
His friend the conqueror, whom you know,
Is his advocate!

(*To* WONG.) He can live in Mr. Shu Fu's cabins. I may have to go there myself. I'm going to have a baby. That's a secret — don't tell

Yang Sun — we'd only be in his way. Can you find the Carpenter for me?

WONG: I knew you'd think of something. (*To the* CHILD.) Goodbye, son, I'm going for your father.

SHEN TE: What about your hand, Wong? I wanted to help, but my cousin . . .

WONG: Oh, I can get along with one hand, don't worry. (*He shows how he can handle his pole with his left hand alone.*)

SHEN TE: But your right hand! Look, take this cart, sell everything that's on it, and go to the doctor with the money . . .

WONG: She's still good. But first I'll bring the Carpenter. I'll pick up the cart when I get back. (*Exit* WONG.)

SHEN TE (*to the* CHILD): Sit down over here, son, till your father comes.

(*The* CHILD *sits crosslegged on the ground. Enter the* HUSBAND *and* WIFE, *each dragging a large, full sack.*)

WIFE (*furtively*): You're alone, Shen Te, dear?

(SHEN TE *nods. The* WIFE *beckons to the* NEPHEW *offstage. He comes on with another sack.*)

Your cousin's away?

(SHEN TE *nods.*)

He's not coming back?

SHEN TE: No. I'm giving up the shop.

WIFE: That's why we're here. We want to know if we can leave these things in your new home. Will you do us this favor?

SHEN TE: Why, yes, I'd be glad to.

HUSBAND (*cryptically*): And if anyone asks about them, say they're yours.

SHEN TE: Would anyone ask?

WIFE (*with a glance back at her* HUSBAND): Oh, someone might. The police, for instance. They don't seem to like us. Where can we put it?

SHEN TE: Well, I'd rather not get in any more trouble . . .

WIFE: Listen to her! The good woman of Setzuan!

(SHEN TE *is silent.*)

HUSBAND: There's enough tobacco in those sacks to give us a new start in life. We could have our own tobacco factory!

SHEN TE (*slowly*): You'll have to put them in the back room.

(*The sacks are taken offstage, where the* CHILD *is left alone. Shyly glancing about him, he goes to the garbage can, starts playing with the contents, and eating some of the scraps. The others return.*)

WIFE: We're counting on you, Shen Te!

SHEN TE: Yes. (*She sees the* CHILD *and is shocked.*)

HUSBAND: We'll see you in Mr. Shu Fu's cabins.

NEPHEW: The day after tomorrow.

SHEN TE: Yes. Now, go. Go! I'm not feeling well.

(*Exeunt all three, virtually pushed off.*)

He is eating the refuse in the garbage can!
Only look at his little grey mouth!

(*Pause. Music.*)

As this is the world *my* son will enter
I will study to defend him.
To be good to you, my son,
I shall be a tigress to all others
If I have to.
And I shall have to.

(*She starts to go.*) One more time, then. I hope really the last.

(*Exit* SHEN TE, *taking* SHUI TA'S *trousers.* MRS. SHIN *enters and watches her with marked interest. Enter the* SISTER-IN-LAW *and the* GRANDFATHER.)

SISTER-IN-LAW: So it's true, the shop has closed down. And the furniture's in the back yard. It's the end of the road!

MRS. SHIN (*pompously*): The fruit of high living, selfishness, and sensuality! Down the primrose path to Mr. Shu Fu's cabins — with you!

SISTER-IN-LAW: Cabins? Rat holes! He gave them to us because his soap supplies only went mouldy there!

(*Enter the* UNEMPLOYED MAN.)

UNEMPLOYED MAN: Shen Te is moving?

SISTER-IN-LAW: Yes. She was sneaking away.

MRS. SHIN: She's ashamed of herself, and no wonder!

UNEMPLOYED MAN: Tell her to call Mr. Shui Ta or she's done for this time!

SISTER-IN-LAW: Tell her to call Mr. Shui Ta or *we're* done for this time!

(*Enter* WONG *and* CARPENTER, *the latter with a* CHILD *on each hand.*)

CARPENTER: So we'll have a roof over our heads for a change!

MRS. SHIN: Roof? Whose roof?

CARPENTER: Mr. Shu Fu's cabins. And we have little Feng to thank for it. (FENG, *we find, is the name of the child already there; his* FATHER *now takes him. To the other two.*) Bow to your little brother, you two! (*The* CARPENTER *and the two new arrivals bow to* FENG.)

(*Enter* SHUI TA.)

UNEMPLOYED MAN: Sst! Mr. Shui Ta!

(*Pause.*)

SHUI TA: And what is this crowd here for, may I ask?

WONG: How do you do, Mr. Shui Ta? This is the Carpenter. Miss Shen Te promised him space in Mr. Shu Fu's cabins.

SHUI TA: That will not be possible.

CARPENTER: We can't go there after all?

SHUI TA: All the space is needed for other purposes.

SISTER-IN-LAW: You mean we have to get out? But we've got nowhere to go.

SHUI TA: Miss Shen Te finds it possible to provide employment. If the proposition interests you, you may stay in the cabins.

SISTER-IN-LAW (*with distaste*): You mean *work*? Work for Miss Shen Te?

SHUI TA: Making tobacco, yes. There are three bales here already. Would you like to get them?

SISTER-IN-LAW (*trying to bluster*): We have our own tobacco! We were in the tobacco business before you were born!

SHUI TA (*to the* CARPENTER *and the* UNEMPLOYED MAN): You *don't* have your own tobacco. What about you?

(*The* CARPENTER *and the* UNEMPLOYED MAN *get the point, and go for the sacks. Enter* MRS. MI TZU.)

MRS. MI TZU: Mr. Shui Ta? I've brought you your three hundred silver dollars.

SHUI TA: I'll sign your lease instead. I've decided not to sell.

MRS. MI TZU: What? You don't need the money for that flyer?

SHUI TA: No.

MRS. MI TZU: And you can pay six months' rent?

SHUI TA (*takes the barber's blank check from the cart and fills it out*): Here is a check for ten thousand silver dollars. On Mr. Shu Fu's account. Look! (*He shows her the signature on the check.*) Your six months' rent will be in your hands by seven this evening. And now, if you'll excuse me.

MRS. MI TZU: So it's Mr. Shu Fu now. The flyer has been given his walking papers. These modern girls! In my day they'd have said she was flighty. That poor, deserted Mr. Yang Sun!

(*Exit* MRS. MI TZU. *The* CARPENTER *and the* UNEMPLOYED MAN *drag the three sacks back on the stage.*)

CARPENTER (*to* SHUI TA): I don't know why I'm doing this for you.

SHUI TA: Perhaps your children want to eat, Mr. Carpenter.

SISTER-IN-LAW (*catching sight of the sacks*): Was my brother-in-law here?

MRS. SHIN: Yes, he was.

SISTER-IN-LAW: I thought as much. I know those sacks! That's our tobacco!

SHUI TA: Really? I thought it came from my back room? Shall we consult the police on the point?

SISTER-IN-LAW (*defeated*): No.

SHUI TA: Perhaps you will show me the way to Mr. Shu Fu's cabins?

(SHUI TA *goes off, followed by the* CARPENTER *and his two older children, the* SISTER-IN-LAW, *the* GRANDFATHER, *and the* UNEMPLOYED MAN. *Each of the last three drags a sack. Enter* OLD MAN *and* OLD WOMAN.)

MRS. SHIN: A pair of pants — missing from the clothes line one minute — and next minute on the honorable backside of Mr. Shui Ta!

OLD WOMAN: We thought Miss Shen Te was here.

MRS. SHIN (*preoccupied*): Well, she's not.

OLD MAN: There was something she was going to give us.

WONG: She was going to help me too. (*Looking at his hand.*) It'll be too late soon. But she'll be back. This cousin has never stayed long.

MRS. SHIN (*approaching a conclusion*): No, he hasn't, has he?

Scene 7A

(*The sewer pipe:* WONG *asleep. In his dream, he tells the* GODS *his fears. The* GODS *seem tired from all their travels. They stop for a moment and look over their shoulders at the Water Seller.*)

WONG: Illustrious ones, I've been having a bad dream. Our beloved Shen Te was in great distress in the rushes down by the rivers — the spot where the bodies of suicides are washed up. She kept staggering and holding her head down as if she was carrying something and it was dragging her down into the mud. When I called out to her, she said she had to take your Book of Rules to the other side, and not get it wet, or the ink would all come off. You had talked to her about the virtues, you know, the time she gave you shelter in Setzuan.

THIRD GOD: Well, but what do you suggest, my dear Wong?

WONG: Maybe a little relaxation of the rules, Benevolent One, in view of the bad times.

THIRD GOD: As for instance?

WONG: Well, um, good-will, for instance, might do instead of love?

THIRD GOD: I'm afraid that would create new problems.

WONG: Or, instead of justice, good sportsmanship?

THIRD GOD: That would only mean more work.

WONG: Instead of honor, outward propriety?

THIRD GOD: Still more work! No, no! The rules will have to stand, my dear Wong!

(*Wearily shaking their heads, all three journey on.*)

SCENE 8

(SHUI TA's *tobacco factory in* SHU FU's *cabins. Huddled together behind bars, several families, mostly women and children. Among these people the* SISTER-IN-LAW, *the* GRANDFATHER, *the* CARPENTER, *and his three children. Enter* MRS. YANG *followed by* YANG SUN.)

MRS. YANG (*to the audience*): There's something I just *have* to tell you: strength and wisdom are wonderful things. The strong and wise Mr. Shui Ta has transformed my son from a dissipated good-for-nothing into a model citizen. As you may have heard, Mr. Shui Ta opened a small tobacco factory near the cattle runs. It flourished. Three months ago — I shall never forget it — I asked for an appointment, and Mr. Shui Ta agreed to see us — me and my son. I can see him now as he came through the door to meet us . . .

(*Enter* SHUI TA, *from a door.*)

SHUI TA: What can I do for you, Mrs. Yang?

MRS. YANG: This morning the police came to the house. We find you've brought an action for breach of promise of marriage. In the name of Shen Te. You also claim that Sun came by two hundred silver dollars by improper means.

SHUI TA: That is correct.

MRS. YANG: Mr. Shui Ta, the money's all gone. When the Peking job didn't materialize, he ran through it all in three days. I know he's a good-for-nothing. He sold my furniture. He was moving to Peking without me. Miss Shen Te thought highly of him at one time.

SHUI TA: What do *you* say, Mr. Yang Sun?

YANG SUN: The money's gone.

SHUI TA (*to* MRS. YANG): Mrs. Yang, in consideration of my cousin's incomprehensible weakness for your son, I am prepared to give him another chance. He can have a job — here. The two hundred silver dollars will be taken out of his wages.

YANG SUN: So it's the factory or jail?

SHUI TA: Take your choice.

YANG SUN: May I speak with Shen Te?

SHUI TA: You may not.

(*Pause.*)

YANG SUN (*sullenly*): Show me where to go.

MRS. YANG: Mr. Shui Ta, you are kindness itself: the gods will reward you! (*To* YANG SUN.) And honest work will make a man of you, my boy.

(YANG SUN *follows* SHUI TA *into the factory.* MRS. YANG *comes down again to the footlights.*)

Actually, honest work didn't agree with him — at first. And he got no opportunity to distinguish himself till — in the third week — when the wages were being paid. . . .

(SHUI TA *has a bag of money. Standing next to his foreman — the former* UNEMPLOYED MAN — *he counts out the wages. It is* YANG SUN's *turn.*)

UNEMPLOYED MAN (*reading*): Carpenter, six silver dollars. Yang Sun, six silver dollars.

YANG SUN (*quietly*): Excuse me, sir. I don't think it can be more than five. May I see? (*He takes the foreman's list.*) It says six working days. But that's a mistake, sir. I took a day off for court business. And I won't take what I haven't earned, however miserable the pay is!

UNEMPLOYED MAN: Yang Sun. Five silver dollars. (*To* SHUI TA.) A rare case, Mr. Shui Ta!

SHUI TA: How is it the book says six when it should say five?

UNEMPLOYED MAN: I must've made a mistake, Mr. Shui Ta. (*With a look at* YANG SUN.) It won't happen again.

SHUI TA (*taking* YANG SUN *aside*): You don't hold back, do you? You give your all to the firm. You're even honest. Do the foreman's mistakes always favor the workers?

YANG SUN: He does have . . . friends.

SHUI TA: Thank you. May I offer you any little recompense?

YANG SUN: Give me a trial period of one week, and I'll prove my intelligence is worth more to you than my strength.

MRS. YANG (*still down at the footlights*): Fighting words, fighting words! That evening, I said to Sun: "If you're a flyer, then fly, my falcon! Rise in the world!" And he got to be foreman. Yes, in Mr. Shui Ta's tobacco factory, he worked real miracles.

(*We see* YANG SUN *with his legs apart standing behind the workers who are handing along a basket of raw tobacco above their heads.*)

YANG SUN: Faster! Faster! You, there, d'you think you can just stand around now you're not foreman any more? It'll be your job to lead us in song. Sing!

(UNEMPLOYED MAN *starts singing. The others join in the refrain.*)

Song of the Eighth Elephant

Chang had seven elephants — all much the same —
    But then there was Little Brother
The seven, they were wild, Little Brother, he was tame
    And to guard them Chang chose Little Brother
        Run faster!
        Mr. Chang has a forest park
        Which must be cleared before tonight
        And already it's growing dark!

When the seven elephants cleared that forest park
    Mr. Chang rode high on Little Brother
While the seven toiled and moiled till dark
    On his big behind sat Little Brother
        Dig faster!
        Mr. Chang has a forest park
        Which must be cleared before tonight
        And already it's growing dark!

And the seven elephants worked many an hour
    Till none of them could work another
Old Chang, he looked sour, on the seven, he did glower
    But gave a pound of rice to Little Brother
        What was that?
        Mr. Chang has a forest park
        Which must be cleared before tonight
        And already it's growing dark!

And the seven elephants hadn't any tusks
  The one that had the tusks was Little Brother!
Seven are no match for one, if the one has a gun!
  How old Chang did laugh at Little Brother!
    Keep on digging!
    Mr. Chang has a forest park·
    Which must be cleared before tonight
    And already it's growing dark!

(*Smoking a cigar,* SHUI TA *strolls by.* YANG SUN, *laughing, has joined in the refrain of the third stanza and speeded up the tempo of the last stanza by clapping his hands.*)

MRS. YANG: And that's why I say: strength and wisdom are wonderful things. It took the strong and wise Mr. Shui Ta to bring out the best in Yang Sun. A real superior man is like a bell. If you ring it, it rings, and if you don't, it don't, as the saying is.

SCENE 9

(SHEN TE'S *shop, now an office with club chairs and fine carpets. It is raining.* SHUI TA, *now fat, is just dismissing the* OLD MAN *and* OLD WOMAN. MRS. SHIN, *in obviously new clothes, looks on, smirking.*)

SHUI TA: No! I can NOT tell you when we expect her back.

OLD WOMAN: The two hundred silver dollars came today. In an envelope. There was no letter, but it must be from Shen Te. We want to write and thank her. May we have her address?

SHUI TA: I'm afraid I haven't got it.

OLD MAN (*pulling* OLD WOMAN's *sleeve*): Let's be going.

OLD WOMAN: She's got to come back some time! (*They move off, uncertainly, worried.* SHUI TA *bows.*)

MRS. SHIN: They lost the carpet shop because they couldn't pay their taxes. The money arrived too late.

SHUI TA: They could have come to me.

MRS. SHIN: People don't like coming to you.

SHUI TA (*sits suddenly, one hand to his head*): I'm dizzy.

MRS. SHIN: After all, you *are* in your seventh month. But old Mrs. Shin will be there in your hour of trial! (*She cackles feebly.*)

SHUI TA (*in a stifled voice*): Can I count on that?

MRS. SHIN: We all have our price, and mine won't be too high for the great Mr. Shui Ta! (*She opens* SHUI TA's *collar.*)

SHUI TA: It's for the child's sake. All of this.

MRS. SHIN: "All for the child," of course.

SHUI TA: I'm so fat. People must notice.

MRS. SHIN: Oh no, they think it's 'cause you're rich.

SHUI TA (*more feelingly*): What will happen to the child?

MRS. SHIN: You ask that nine times a day. Why, it'll have the best that money can buy!

SHUI TA: He must never see Shui Ta.

MRS. SHIN: Oh, no. Always Shen Te.

SHUI TA: What about the neighbors? There are rumors, aren't there?

MRS. SHIN: As long as Mr. Shu Fu doesn't find out, there's nothing to worry about. Drink this.

(*Enter* YANG SUN *in a smart business suit, and carrying a businessman's brief case.* SHUI TA *is more or less in* MRS. SHIN's *arms.*)

YANG SUN (*surprised*): I seem to be in the way.

SHUI TA (*ignoring this, rises with an effort*): Till tomorrow, Mrs. Shin.

(MRS. SHIN *leaves with a smile, putting her new gloves on.*)

YANG SUN: Gloves now! She couldn't be fleecing you? And since when did *you* have a private life? (*Taking a paper from the brief case.*) You haven't been at your best lately, and things are getting out of hand. The police want to close us down. They say that at the most they can only permit twice the lawful number of workers.

SHUI TA (*evasively*): The cabins are quite good enough.

YANG SUN: For the workers maybe, not for the tobacco. They're too damp. We must take over some of Mrs. Mi Tzu's buildings.

SHUI TA: Her price is double what I can pay.

YANG SUN: Not unconditionally. If she has me to stroke her knees she'll come down.

SHUI TA: I'll never agree to that.

YANG SUN: What's wrong? Is it the rain? You get so irritable whenever it rains.

SHUI TA: Never! I will never . . .

YANG SUN: Mrs. Mi Tzu'll be here in five minutes. *You* fix it. And Shu Fu will be with her. . . . What's all that noise?

(*During the above dialogue,* WONG *is heard off stage calling:* "The good Shen Te, where is she? Which of you has seen Shen Te, good people? Where is Shen Te?" *A knock. Enter* WONG.)

WONG: Mr. Shui Ta, I've come to ask when Miss Shen Te will be back, it's six months now . . . There are rumors. People say something's happened to her.

SHUI TA: I'm busy. Come back next week.

WONG (*excited*): In the morning there was always rice on her doorstep — for the needy. It's been there again lately!

SHUI TA: And what do people conclude from this?

WONG: That Shen Te is still in Setzuan! She's been . . . (*He breaks off.*)

SHUI TA: She's been what? Mr. Wong, if you're Shen Te's friend, talk a little less about her, that's my advice to you.

WONG: I don't want your advice! Before she disappeared, Miss Shen Te told me something very important — she's pregnant!

YANG SUN: What? What was that?

SHUI TA (*quickly*): The man is lying.

WONG: A good woman isn't so easily forgotten, Mr. Shui Ta.

(*He leaves.* SHUI TA *goes quickly into the back room.*)

YANG SUN (*to the audience*): Shen Te pregnant? So that's why. Her cousin sent her away, so I wouldn't get wind of it. I have a son, a Yang appears on the scene, and what happens? Mother and child vanish into thin air! That scoundrel, that unspeakable . . . (*The sound of sobbing is heard from the back room.*) What was that? Someone sobbing? Who was it? Mr. Shui Ta the Tobacco King doesn't weep his heart out. And where does the rice come from that's on the doorstep in the morning?

(SHUI TA *returns. He goes to the door and looks out into the rain.*)

Where is she?

SHUI TA: Sh! It's nine o'clock. But the rain's so heavy, you can't hear a thing.

YANG SUN: What do you want to hear?

SHUI TA: The mail plane.

YANG SUN: What?

SHUI TA: I've been told *you* wanted to fly at one time. Is that all forgotten?

YANG SUN: Flying mail is night work. I prefer the daytime. And the firm is very dear to me — after all it belongs to my ex-fiancée, even if she's not around. And she's not, is she?

SHUI TA: What do you mean by that?

YANG SUN: Oh, well, let's say I haven't altogether — lost interest.

SHUI TA: My cousin might like to know that.

YANG SUN: I might not be indifferent — if I found she was being kept under lock and key.

SHUI TA: By whom?

YANG SUN: By you.

SHUI TA: What could you do about it?

YANG SUN: I could submit for discussion — my position in the firm.

SHUI TA: You are now my Manager. In return for a more appropriate position, you might agree to drop the enquiry into your ex-fiancée's whereabouts?

YANG SUN: I might.

SHUI TA: What position *would* be more appropriate?

YANG SUN: The one at the top.

SHUI TA: My own? (*Silence.*) And if I preferred to throw you out on your neck?

YANG SUN: I'd come back on my feet. With suitable escort.

SHUI TA: The police?

YANG SUN: The police.

SHUI TA: And when the police found no one?

YANG SUN: I might ask them not to overlook the back room. (*Ending the pretense.*) In short, Mr. Shui Ta, my interest in this young woman has not been officially terminated. I should like to see more of her. (*Into* SHUI TA's *face.*) Besides, she's pregnant and needs a friend. (*He moves to the door.*) I shall talk about it with the Water Seller. (*Exit.*)

(SHUI TA *is rigid for a moment, then he quickly goes into the back room. He returns with* SHEN TE's *belongings: underwear, etc. He takes a long look at the shawl of the previous scene. He then wraps the things in a bundle which, upon hearing a noise, he hides under the table. Enter* MRS. MI TZU *and* MR. SHU FU. *They put away their umbrellas and galoshes.*)

MRS. MI TZU: I thought your manager was here, Mr. Shui Ta. He combines charm with business in a way that can only be to the advantage of all of us.

SHU FU: You sent for us, Mr. Shui Ta?

SHUI TA: The factory is in trouble.

SHU FU: It always is.

SHUI TA: The police are threatening to close us down unless I can show that the extension of our facilities is imminent.

SHU FU: Mr. Shui Ta, I'm sick and tired of your constantly expanding projects. I place cabins at your cousin's disposal; you make a factory of them. I hand your cousin a check; you present it. Your cousin disappears and you find the cabins too small and talk of yet more . . .

SHUI TA: Mr. Shu Fu, I'm authorized to inform you that Miss Shen Te's return is now imminent.

SHU FU: Imminent? It's becoming his favorite word.

MRS. MI TZU: Yes, what does it mean?

SHUI TA: Mrs. Mi Tzu, I can pay you exactly half what you asked for your buildings. Are you ready to inform the police that I am taking them over?

MRS. MI TZU: Certainly, if I can take over your manager.

SHU FU: What?

MRS. MI TZU: He's so efficient.

SHUI TA: I'm afraid I need Mr. Yang Sun.

MRS. MI TZU: So do I.

SHUI TA: He will call on you tomorrow.

SHU FU: So much the better. With Shen Te likely to turn up at any moment, the presence of that young man is hardly in good taste.

SHUI TA: So we have reached a settlement. In what was once the good Shen Te's little shop we are laying the foundations for the great Mr. Shui Ta's twelve magnificent super tobacco markets. You will bear in mind that though they call me the Tobacco King of Setzuan, it is my cousin's interests that have been served . . .

VOICES (*off*): The police, the police! Going to the tobacco shop! Something must have happened! (*etcetera.*)

(*Enter* YANG SUN, WONG, *and the* POLICEMAN.)

POLICEMAN: Quiet there, quiet, quiet! (*They quiet down.*) I'm sorry, Mr. Shui Ta, but there's a report that you've been depriving Miss Shen Te of her freedom. Not that I believe all I hear, but the whole city's in an uproar.

SHUI TA: That's a lie.

POLICEMAN: Mr. Yang Sun has testified that he heard someone sobbing in the back room.

SHU FU: Mrs. Mi Tzu and myself will testify that no one here has been sobbing.

MRS. MI TZU: We have been quietly smoking our cigars.

POLICEMAN: Mr. Shui Ta, I'm afraid I shall have to take a look at that room. (*He does so. The room is empty.*) No one there, of course, sir.

YANG SUN: But I heard sobbing. What's that? (*He finds the clothes.*)

WONG: Those are Shen Te's things. (*To crowd.*) Shen Te's clothes are here!

VOICES (*Off. In sequence*): Shen Te's clothes! They've been found under the table! Body of murdered girl still missing! Tobacco King suspected!

POLICEMAN: Mr. Shui Ta, unless you can tell us where the girl is, I'll have to ask you to come along.

SHUI TA: I do not know.

POLICEMAN: I can't say how sorry I am, Mr. Shui Ta. (*He shows him the door.*)

SHUI TA: Everything will be cleared up in no time. There are still judges in Setzuan.

YANG SUN: I heard sobbing!

Scene 9A

(WONG's *den. For the last time, the* GODS *appear to the Water Seller in his dream. They have changed and show signs of a long journey, extreme fatigue, and plenty of mishaps. The* FIRST *no longer has a hat; the* THIRD *has lost a leg; all* THREE *are barefoot.*)

WONG: Illustrious ones, at last you're here. Shen Te's been gone for months and today her cousin's been arrested. They think he murdered her to get the shop. But I had a dream and in this dream Shen Te said her cousin was keeping her prisoner. You must find her for us, illustrious ones!

FIRST GOD: We've found very few good people anywhere, and even they didn't keep it up. Shen Te is still the only one that stayed good.

SECOND GOD: If she *has* stayed good.

WONG: Certainly she has. But she's vanished.

FIRST GOD: That's the last straw. All is lost!

SECOND GOD: A little moderation, dear colleague!

FIRST GOD (*plaintively*): What's the good of moderation now? If she can't be found, we'll have to resign! The world is a terrible place! Nothing but misery, vulgarity, and waste! Even the countryside isn't what it used to be. The trees are getting their heads chopped off by telephone wires, and there's such a noise from all the gunfire, and I can't stand those heavy clouds of smoke, and —

THIRD GOD: The place is absolutely unlivable! Good intentions bring people to the brink of the abyss, and good deeds push them over the edge. I'm afraid our book of rules is destined for the scrap heap —

SECOND GOD: It's people! They're a worthless lot!

THIRD GOD: The world is too cold!

SECOND GOD: It's people! They are too weak!

FIRST GOD: Dignity, dear colleagues, dignity! Never despair! As for this world, didn't we agree that we only have to find one human being who can stand the place? Well, we found her. True, we lost her again. We must find her again, that's all! And at once!

(*They disappear.*)

SCENE 10

(*Courtroom. Groups:* SHU FU *and* MRS. MI TZU; YANG SUN *and* MRS. YANG; WONG, *the* CARPENTER, *the* GRANDFATHER, *the* NIECE, *the* OLD MAN, *the* OLD WOMAN; MRS. SHIN, *the* POLICEMAN; *the* UNEMPLOYED MAN, *the* SISTER-IN-LAW.)

OLD MAN: So much power isn't good for one man.

UNEMPLOYED MAN: And he's going to open twelve super tobacco markets!

WIFE: One of the judges is a friend of Mr. Shu Fu's.

SISTER-IN-LAW: Another one accepted a present from Mr. Shui Ta only last night. A great fat goose.

OLD WOMAN (*to* WONG): And Shen Te is nowhere to be found.

WONG: Only the gods will ever know the truth.

POLICEMAN: Order in the court! My lords the judges!

(*Enter the* THREE GODS *in judges' robes. We overhear their conversation as they pass along the footlights to their bench.*)

THIRD GOD: We'll never get away with it, our certificates were so badly forged.

SECOND GOD: My predecessor's "sudden indigestion" will certainly cause comment.

FIRST GOD: But he *had* just eaten a whole goose.

UNEMPLOYED MAN: Look at that! *New* judges!

WONG: New judges. And what good ones!

(*The* THIRD GOD *hears this, and turns to smile at* WONG. *The* GODS *sit. The* FIRST GOD *beats on the bench with his gavel. The* POLICEMAN *brings in* SHUI TA *who walks with lordly steps. He is whistled at.*)

POLICEMAN (*to* SHUI TA): Be prepared for a surprise. The judges have been changed.

(SHUI TA *turns quickly round, looks at them, and staggers.*)

NIECE: What's the matter now?

WIFE: The great Tobacco King nearly fainted.

HUSBAND: Yes, as soon as he saw the new judges.

WONG: Does *he* know who they are?

(SHUI TA *picks himself up, and the proceedings open.*)

FIRST GOD: Defendant Shui Ta, you are accused of doing away with your cousin Shen Te in order to take possession of her business. Do you plead guilty or not guilty?

SHUI TA: Not guilty, my lord.

FIRST GOD (*thumbing through the documents of the case*): The first witness is the Policeman. I shall ask him to tell us something of the respective reputations of Miss Shen Te and Mr. Shui Ta.

POLICEMAN: Miss Shen Te was a young lady who aimed to please, my lord. She liked to live and let live, as the saying goes. Mr. Shui Ta, on the other hand, is a man of principle. Though the generosity of Miss Shen Te forced him at times to abandon half measures, unlike the girl, he was always on the side of the law, my lord. One time, he even unmasked a gang of thieves to whom his too trustful cousin had given shelter. The evidence, in short, my lord, proves that Mr. Shui Ta was *incapable* of the crime of which he stands accused!

FIRST GOD: I see. And are there others who could testify along, shall we say, the same lines?

(SHU FU *rises.*)

POLICEMAN (*whispering to* GODS): Mr. Shu Fu — a very important person.

FIRST GOD (*inviting him to speak*): Mr. Shu Fu!

SHU FU: Mr. Shui Ta is a businessman, my lord. Need I say more?

FIRST GOD: Yes.

SHU FU: Very well, I will. He is Vice President of the Council of Commerce and is about to be elected a Justice of the Peace. (*He returns to his seat.*)

WONG: Elected! *He* gave him the job!

(*With a gesture the* FIRST GOD *asks who* MRS. MI TZU *is.*)

POLICEMAN: Another very important person. Mrs. Mi Tzu.

FIRST GOD (*inviting her to speak*): Mrs. Mi Tzu!

MRS. MI TZU: My lord, as Chairman of the Committee on Social Work, I wish to call attention to just a couple of eloquent facts: Mr. Shui Ta not only has erected a model factory with model housing in our city, he is a regular contributor to our home for the disabled. (*She returns to her seat.*)

POLICEMAN (*whispering*): And she's a great friend of the judge that ate the goose!

FIRST GOD (*to the* POLICEMAN): Oh, thank you. What next? (*To the Court, genially.*) Oh, yes. We should find out if any of the evidence is less favorable to the Defendant.

(WONG, *the* CARPENTER, *the* OLD MAN, *the* OLD WOMAN, *the* UN-EMPLOYED MAN, *the* SISTER-IN-LAW, *and the* NIECE *come forward.*)

POLICEMAN (*whispering*): Just the riff raff, my lord.

FIRST GOD (*addressing the "riff raff"*): Well, um, riff raff — do you know anything of the Defendant, Mr. Shui Ta?

WONG: Too much, my lord.

UNEMPLOYED MAN: What don't we know, my lord?

CARPENTER: He ruined us.

SISTER-IN-LAW: He's a cheat.

NIECE: Liar.

WIFE: Thief.

BOY: Blackmailer.

BROTHER: Murderer.

FIRST GOD: Thank you. We should now let the Defendant state his point of view.

SHUI TA: I only came on the scene when Shen Te was in danger of losing what I had understood was a gift from the gods. Because I did the filthy jobs which someone had to do, they hate me. My activities were held down to the minimum, my lord.

SISTER-IN-LAW: He had us arrested!

SHUI TA: Certainly. You stole from the bakery!

SISTER-IN-LAW: Such concern for the bakery! You didn't want the shop for yourself, I suppose!

SHUI TA: I didn't want the shop overrun with parasites.

SISTER-IN-LAW: We had nowhere else to go.

SHUI TA: There were too many of you.

WONG: What about this old couple: Were *they* parasites?

OLD MAN: We lost our shop because of you!

SISTER-IN-LAW: And we gave your cousin money!

SHUI TA: My cousin's fiancé was a flyer. The money had to go to *him*.

WONG: Did you care whether he flew or not? Did you care whether she married him or not? You wanted her to marry someone else! (*He points at* SHU FU.)

SHUI TA: The flyer unexpectedly turned out to be a scoundrel.

YANG SUN (*jumping up*): Which was the reason you made him your Manager?

SHUI TA: Later on he improved.

WONG: And when he improved, you sold him to her? (*He points out* MRS. MI TZU.)

SHUI TA: She wouldn't let me have her premises unless she had him to stroke her knees!

MRS. MI TZU: What? The man's a pathological liar. (*To him.*) Don't mention my property to me as long as you live! Murderer! (*She rustles off, in high dudgeon.*)

YANG SUN (*pushing in*): My lord, I wish to speak for the Defendant.

SISTER-IN-LAW: Naturally. He's your employer.

UNEMPLOYED MAN: And the worst slave driver in the country.

MRS. YANG: That's a lie! My lord, Mr. Shui Ta is a great man. He . . .

YANG SUN: He's this and he's that, but he is not a murderer, my lord. Just fifteen minutes before his arrest I heard Shen Te's voice in his own back room.

FIRST GOD: Oh? Tell us more!

YANG SUN: I heard sobbing, my lord!

FIRST GOD: But lots of women sob, we've been finding.

YANG SUN: Could I fail to recognize her voice?

SHU FU: No, you made her sob so often yourself, young man!

YANG SUN: Yes. But I also made her happy. Till he (*pointing at* SHUI TA) decided to sell her to you!

SHUI TA: Because you didn't love her.

WONG: Oh, no: it was for the money, my lord!

SHUI TA: And what was the money for, my lord? For the poor! And for Shen Te so she could go on being good!

WONG: For the poor? That he sent to his sweatshops? And why didn't you let Shen Te be good when you signed the big check?

SHUI TA: For the child's sake, my lord.

CARPENTER: What about *my* children? What did he do about them?

(SHUI TA *is silent.*)

WONG: The shop was to be a fountain of goodness. That was the gods' idea. You came and spoiled it!

SHUI TA: If I hadn't, it would have run dry!

MRS. SHIN: There's a lot in that, my lord.

WONG: What have you done with the good Shen Te, bad man? She *was* good, my lords, she was, I swear it! (*He raises his hand in an oath.*)

THIRD GOD: What's happened to your hand, Water Seller?

WONG (*pointing to* SHUI TA): It's all his fault, my lord, *she* was going to send me to a doctor — (*To* SHUI TA.) You were her worst enemy!

SHUI TA: I was her only friend!

WONG: Where is she then? Tell us where your good friend is!

(*The excitement of this exchange has run through the whole crowd.*)

ALL: Yes, where is she? Where is Shen Te? (*etcetera.*)

SHUI TA: Shen Te had to go.

WONG: Where? Where to?

SHUI TA: I cannot tell you! I cannot tell you!

ALL: Why? Why did she have to go away? (*etcetera.*)

WONG (*into the din with the first words, but talking on beyond the others*): Why not, why not? Why did she have to go away?

SHUI TA (*shouting*): Because you'd all have torn her to shreds, that's why! My lords, I have a request. Clear the court! When only the judges remain, I will make a confession.

ALL (*except* WONG, *who is silent, struck by the new turn of events*): So he's guilty? He's confessing! (*etcetera.*)

FIRST GOD (*using the gavel*): Clear the court!

POLICEMAN: Clear the court!

WONG: Mr. Shui Ta has met his match this time.

MRS. SHIN (*with a gesture toward the judges*): You're in for a little surprise.

(*The court is cleared. Silence.*)

SHUI TA: Illustrious ones!

(*The* GODS *look at each other, not quite believing their ears.*)

SHUI TA: Yes, I recognize you!

SECOND GOD (*taking matters in hand, sternly*): What have you done with our good woman of Setzuan?

SHUI TA: I have a terrible confession to make: I am she! (*He takes off his mask, and tears away his clothes.* SHEN TE *stands there.*)

SECOND GOD: Shen Te!

SHEN TE: Shen Te, yes. Shui Ta *and* Shen Te. Both.

Your injunction
To be good and yet to live
Was a thunderbolt:
It has torn me in two
I can't tell how it was
But to be good to others
And myself at the same time
I could not do it
Your world is not an easy one, illustrious ones!
When we extend our hand to a beggar, he tears it off for us
When we help the lost, we are lost ourselves.
And so
Since not to eat is to die

Who can long refuse to be bad?
As I lay prostrate beneath the weight of good intentions
Ruin stared me in the face
It was when I was unjust that I ate good meat
And hobnobbed with the mighty
Why?
Why are bad deeds rewarded?
Good ones punished?
I enjoyed giving
I truly wished to be the Angel of the Slums
But washed by a foster-mother in the water of the gutter
I developed a sharp eye
The time came when pity was a thorn in my side
And, later, when kind words turned to ashes in my mouth
And anger took over
I became a wolf
Find me guilty, then, illustrious ones,
But know:
All that I have done I did
To help my neighbor
To love my lover
And to keep my little one from want
For your great, godly deeds, I was too poor, too small.

(*Pause.*)

FIRST GOD (*shocked*): Don't go on making yourself miserable, Shen Te! We're overjoyed to have found you!

SHEN TE: I'm telling you I'm the bad man who committed all those crimes!

FIRST GOD (*using — or failing to use — his ear trumpet*): The good woman who did all those good deeds?

SHEN TE: Yes, but the bad man too!

FIRST GOD (*as if something had dawned*): Unfortunate coincidences! Heartless neighbors!

THIRD GOD (*shouting in his ear*): But how is she to continue?

FIRST GOD: Continue? Well, she's a strong, healthy girl . . .

SECOND GOD: You didn't hear what she said!

FIRST GOD: I heard every word! She is confused, that's all! (*He begins to bluster.*) And what about this book of rules — we can't renounce our rules, can we? (*More quietly.*) Should the world be changed? How? By whom? The world should *not* be changed! (*At a sign from him, the lights turn pink, and music plays.*)

And now the hour of parting is at hand.
Dost thou behold, Shen Te, yon fleecy cloud?
It is our chariot. At a sign from me
'Twill come and take us back from whence we came
Above the azure vault and silver stars . . .

SHEN TE: No! Don't go, illustrious ones!
FIRST GOD:
Our cloud has landed now in yonder field
From whence it will transport us back to heaven.
Farewell, Shen Te, let not thy courage fail thee . . .

(*Exeunt* GODS.)

SHEN TE: What about the old couple? They've lost their shop! What about the Water Seller and his hand? And I've got to defend myself against the barber, because I don't love him! And against Sun, because I do love him! How? How?

(SHEN TE's *eyes follow the* GODS *as they are imagined to step into a cloud which rises and moves forward over the orchestra and up beyond the balcony.*)

FIRST GOD (*from on high*): We have faith in you, Shen Te!
SHEN TE: There'll be a child. And he'll have to be fed. I can't stay here. Where shall I go?
FIRST GOD: Continue to be good, good woman of Setzuan!
SHEN TE: I need my bad cousin!
FIRST GOD: But not very often!
SHEN TE: Once a week at least!
FIRST GOD: Once a month will be quite enough!
SHEN TE (*shrieking*): No, no! Help!

(*But the cloud continues to recede as the* GODS *sing.*)

Valedictory Hymn

What rapture, oh, it is to know
    A good thing when you see it
And having seen a good thing, oh,
    What rapture 'tis to flee it

Be good, sweet maid of Setzuan
    Let Shui Ta be clever
Departing, we forget the man
    Remember your endeavor

Because through all the length of days
    Her goodness faileth never

Sing hallelujah! May Shen Te's
Good name live on forever!

SHEN TE: Help!

BRECHT WROTE *The Good Woman of Setzuan* between 1938
and 1941. Directly, the play does not reflect the momentous political
and military events contemporary with its genesis, but its underlying
cynicism and flippant, almost gay, despair may perhaps be said to be
typical of at least one side of the modern temper. For all its quaint
and charming Chinese ways, its humor of incident and character, its
verbal high spirits, it is an acid rather than a pleasant play. Its issues
are ultimately metaphysical and deadly serious. If we do not sense
this, it may be because we are misled by the play's form.

Brecht's dramatic art differs from all the three main styles of
modern drama. It does not belong with the tight and tidy catas-
trophe-centered drama of the Greeks, reintroduced in modern times
by Ibsen; nor with the plotless and apparently diffuse plays of mood
and atmosphere that characterize the school of Chekhov; nor with
the fluid theatricality and surrealistic fantasies of Strindbergian expressionism. It has more in common with Shakespearean drama, developing its plot on a broad and crowded canvas and by a time
scheme unconfined by the rigors of the retrospective technique and
unities. Since telling a story is the chief artistic end of this drama it
has been called (by Brecht himself) the "epic" theater — epic in
the sense not of nobly heroic and magnificent but simply of "narrative." It breaks with Ibsenite naturalism also in its frank disavowal
of illusionism. The spectator, says Brecht, should not watch a play in
a trance of gripping make-believe; the play has a social function to
perform, and to that end it must engage the spectator's mind as well
as his senses and his emotions. The superbly simple expository device of Wang's opening speech, the characters' direct address to the
audience, the spontaneous songs, the flashbacks and the "A" scenes,
the quick sequence of scenes, all these remind us we are watching
a spectacle that tells a story for our thoughtful enjoyment and moral
benefit, and not life being lived. Life-likeness and plausibility are
not esthetic issues. The argument that it is psychologically uncon-
vincing that a character as good as Shen Te at will can assume and
maintain the attitudes and practices of hard and unscrupulous Shui
Ta refuses to take the play on Brecht's terms. In order to preserve
the sovereignty of our reason Brecht wants us *not* to "identify"
with the characters. Though the two playwrights certainly have

little enough in common in most other respects, Brecht and Yeats share a belief in the value of establishing esthetic distance between play and spectator.

All this is not to deny *The Good Woman of Setzuan* a quality of realism obviously lacking in Strindberg's nightmare and in Yeats's emblematic tableau. Brecht's Setzuan may be visited by traveling gods, but it is also a town of heat and stench, pilferers and prostitutes, unpaid bills and unfed children. And what happens in it, despite its unusualness, has the austere coherence of causality in the real world.

Perhaps the best term for such a play is Brecht's own. He called it "a parable play," that is, a kind of fable, a story that insists less on being true in any literal sense than on having significance and hence truth beyond its surface facts. It is neither symbolical nor allegorical, for we are not expected to transliterate people and events back into another level or dimension of meaning, in which concretes return to the abstracts that bred them. It may be possible to do so (perhaps rain stands for love, flying for free and noble service of one's fellow men, Yang Sun for ruthless careerism, Shu Fu and Mrs. Mi Tzu for capitalism, etc.), but the play's meaning does not depend on such symbol-finding. Rather, the story is representative, archetypal. Its meaning is the sum and meaning of its events, but the events constitute a pattern shared by other events. A law of life emerges. The plot bears testimony to a general rule.

The rule is simply that the world is so arranged that the good can't win. Goodness and success are mutually exclusive.

> Goodness will pay,
> And merit and money will smile and be funny
> While exchanging salt and bread

— only on St. Nevercome's Day. Only a gift of the gods can make goodness affluent, and no sooner has it become so than it is taken advantage of by parasites and capitalists. For goodness not only to continue to be good but even to survive, it has to sprout a second, antithetical personality; Shen Te must disappear in Shui Ta. (One wonders if the change of sex implies a comment on the ethics of men and women.) There is a profound and sad sense in which the charge against Shui Ta is true: he has indeed "imprisoned" or "done away with" Shen Te. And when Shen Te tells Yang Sun that "My cousin can't be where I am," she is stating the bitter truth about human existence. The waterseller Wong has a chorus-like function in the play, and his opening soliloquy anticipates this truth in the paradox that points up man's hopeless entrapment: "When water is

scarce, I have long distances to go in search of it, and when it is
plentiful, I have no income." The world is so rigged that man suffers
and fails unless he submerges his natural goodness and becomes a
businessman like Shui Ta, paying starvation wages to his employees
and housing them in damp river-bank hovels. You can't win on other
terms.

This, perhaps, is no more than a cynical lesson of life. The play's
metaphysical acerbity, its challenge of the cosmic order, enters
when we consider the role of the three gods. They are kindly per-
sonages, but they are stuffily fatuous and ineffectual. The First God's
ear trumpet is relevant in this connection. The nature of their very
divinity becomes suspect in their opening dialogue with Wong:

WONG: . . . Everyone knows the province of Kwan is always having
    floods.
SECOND GOD: Really? How's *that?*
WONG: Why, because they're so irreligious.
SECOND GOD: Rubbish. It's because they neglected the dam.

But it is this same Second God who admonishes Shen Te to "Be
good" and who, when she pleads, "But everything is so expensive. I
don't feel sure I can do it!" loftily answers, "That's not in our
sphere. We never meddle with economics." It is quite in character
when the gods are delighted to learn at the end that defendant
and alleged victim are identical, brush aside Shen Te's confession of
the inhumanities she committed as Shui Ta, and vanish on a pink
cloud, deaf to Shen Te's final desperate "Help!" The divine order,
Brecht seems to suggest, is at fault precisely because it does *not*
meddle in economics. We recall his Marxism.

The premise for the whole plot is that "the rules" will have to
be changed if the gods fail to find a person who is and remains
good. It is even suggested in one speech (by the First God, in the
Prologue) that the gods' own existence depends on such a person.
At any rate, they are clearly delighted with Shen Te. They are so
delighted, in fact, that the cruelest paradox of all turns out to be
that it is Shen Te's own goodness that keep things as they are, bad
rules and all. It is as if the parable means not only that goodness
is continually being defeated, but that it defeats itself. Shen Te
versus the world order — the issue is not without its ironic ambiguities. Is goodness goodness only in a fallen world? Would it be
meaningless if the rules were changed, making things easier for
man? Who, in the end, has the best of the argument: the benign
but foolish gods, the atheists whom they set out to confute, or em-
battled Shen Te? Where the grandeur lies is obvious.)

Tennessee Williams

THE GLASS MENAGERIE

Nobody, not even the rain, has such small hands.

E. E. CUMMINGS

Characters

> AMANDA WINGFIELD, *the mother*
> LAURA WINGFIELD, *her daughter*
> TOM WINGFIELD, *her son*
> JIM O'CONNOR, *the gentleman caller*

SCENE: *An alley in St. Louis*

PART I. *Preparation for a Gentleman Caller.*
PART II. *The Gentleman Calls.*

TIME: *Now and the Past.*

SCENE ONE

(*The Wingfield apartment is in the rear of the building, one of those vast hive-like conglomerations of cellular living-units that flower as warty growths in overcrowded urban centers of lower middle-class population and are symptomatic of the impulse of this largest and fundamentally enslaved section of American society to avoid fluidity and differentiation and to exist and function as one interfused mass of automatism.*

Copyright 1945 by Tennessee Williams and Edwina D. Williams. All rights strictly reserved. Reprinted from *Six Modern American Plays* by permission of Random House, Inc.

The apartment faces an alley and is entered by a fire-escape, a structure whose name is a touch of accidental poetic truth, for all of these huge buildings are always burning with the slow and implacable fires of human desperation. The fire-escape is included in the set — that is, the landing of it and steps descending from it.

The scene is memory and is therefore nonrealistic. Memory takes a lot of poetic license. It omits some details; others are exaggerated, according to the emotional value of the articles it touches, for memory is seated predominantly in the heart. The interior is therefore rather dim and poetic.

At the rise of the curtain, the audience is faced with the dark, grim rear wall of the Wingfield tenement. This building, which runs parallel to the footlights, is flanked on both sides by dark, narrow alleys which run into murky canyons of tangled clotheslines, garbage cans and the sinister latticework of neighboring fire-escapes. It is up and down these side alleys that exterior entrances and exits are made, during the play. At the end of TOM'S *opening commentary, the dark tenement wall slowly reveals (by means of a transparency) the interior of the ground floor Wingfield apartment.*

Downstage is the living room, which also serves as a sleeping room for LAURA, *the sofa unfolding to make her bed. Upstage, center, and divided by a wide arch or second proscenium with transparent faded portieres (or second curtain), is the dining room. In an old-fashioned what-not in the living room are seen scores of transparent glass animals. A blown-up photograph of the father hangs on the wall of the living room, facing the audience, to the left of the archway. It is the face of a very handsome young man in a doughboy's First World War cap. He is gallantly smiling, ineluctably smiling, as if to say, "I will be smiling forever."*

The audience hears and sees the opening scene in the dining room through both the transparent fourth wall of the building and the transparent gauze portieres of the dining-room arch. It is during this revealing scene that the fourth wall slowly ascends, out of sight. This transparent exterior wall is not brought down again until the very end of the play, during TOM'S *final speech.*

The narrator is an undisguised convention of the play. He takes whatever license with dramatic convention as is convenient to his purposes.

TOM *enters dressed as a merchant sailor from alley, stage left, and strolls across the front of the stage to the fire-escape. There he stops and lights a cigarette. He addresses the audience.)*

TOM: Yes, I have tricks in my pocket, I have things up my sleeve. But I am the opposite of a stage magician. He gives you illusion that has the appearance of truth. I give you truth in the pleasant disguise of illusion. To begin with, I turn back time. I reverse it to that quaint period, the thirties, when the huge middle class of America was matriculating in a school for the blind. Their eyes had failed them, or they had failed their eyes, and so they were having their fingers pressed forcibly down on the fiery Braille alphabet of a dissolving economy. In Spain there was revolution. Here there was only shouting and confusion. In Spain there was Guernica. Here there were disturbances of labor, sometimes pretty violent, in otherwise peaceful cities such as Chicago, Cleveland, Saint Louis. . . . This is the social background of the play.

(MUSIC.)

The play is memory. Being a memory play, it is dimly lighted, it is sentimental, it is not realistic. In memory everything seems to happen to music. That explains the fiddle in the wings. I am the narrator of the play, and also a character in it. The other characters are my mother, Amanda, my sister, Laura, and a gentleman caller who appears in the final scenes. He is the most realistic character in the play, being an emissary from a world of reality that we were somehow set apart from. But since I have a poet's weakness for symbols, I am using this character also as a symbol; he is the long delayed but always expected something that we live for. There is a fifth character in the play who doesn't appear except in this larger-than-life photograph over the mantel. This is our father who left us a long time ago. He was a telephone man who fell in love with long distances; he gave up his job with the telephone company and skipped the light fantastic out of town . . . The last we heard of him was a picture post-card from Mazatlan, on the Pacific coast of Mexico, containing a message of two words — "Hello — Goodbye!" and no address. I think the rest of the play will explain itself. . . .

(AMANDA'S *voice becomes audible through the portieres.*)

(LEGEND ON SCREEN: "OÙ SONT LES NEIGES.")

(*He divides the portieres and enters the upstage area.*)

(AMANDA *and* LAURA *are seated at a drop-leaf table. Eating is indicated by gestures without food or utensils.* AMANDA *faces the audience.* TOM *and* LAURA *are seated in profile.*)

(*The interior has lit up softly and through the scrim we see* AMANDA *and* LAURA *seated at the table in the upstage area.*)

AMANDA (*calling*): Tom?

TOM: Yes, Mother.

AMANDA: We can't say grace until you come to the table!

TOM: Coming, Mother. (*He bows slightly and withdraws, reappearing a few moments later in his place at the table.*)

AMANDA (*to her son*): Honey, don't push with your fingers. If you have to push with something, the thing to push with is a crust of bread. And chew — chew! Animals have sections in their stomachs which enable them to digest food without mastication, but human beings are supposed to chew their food before they swallow it down. Eat food leisurely, son, and really enjoy it. A well-cooked meal has lots of delicate flavors that have to be held in the mouth for appreciation. So chew your food and give your salivary glands a chance to function!

(TOM *deliberately lays his imaginary fork down and pushes his chair back from the table.*)

TOM: I haven't enjoyed one bite of this dinner because of your constant directions on how to eat it. It's you that makes me rush through meals with your hawk-like attention to every bite I take. Sickening — spoils my appetite — all this discussion of animals' secretion — salivary glands — mastication!

AMANDA (*lightly*): Temperament like a Metropolitan star! (*He rises and crosses downstage.*) You're not excused from the table.

TOM: I'm getting a cigarette.

AMANDA: You smoke too much.

(LAURA *rises.*)

LAURA: I'll bring in the blanc mange.

(*He remains standing with his cigarette by the portieres during the following.*)

AMANDA (*rising*): No, sister, no, sister — you be the lady this time and I'll be the darky.

LAURA: I'm already up.

AMANDA: Resume your seat, little sister — I want you to stay fresh and pretty — for gentlemen callers!

LAURA: I'm not expecting any gentlemen callers.

AMANDA (*crossing out to kitchenette. Airily*): Sometimes they come

when they are least expected! Why, I remember one Sunday afternoon in Blue Mountain — (*Enters kitchenette.*)

TOM: I know what's coming!

LAURA: Yes. But let her tell it.

TOM: Again?

LAURA: She loves to tell it.

(AMANDA *returns with bowl of dessert.*)

AMANDA: One Sunday afternoon in Blue Mountain — your mother
received — *seventeen!* — gentlemen callers! Why, sometimes there
weren't chairs enough to accommodate them all. We had to send
the nigger over to bring in folding chairs from the parish house.

TOM (*remaining at portieres*): How did you entertain those gentlemen
callers?

AMANDA: I understood the art of conversation!

TOM: I bet you could talk.

AMANDA: Girls in those days *knew* how to talk, I can tell you.

TOM: Yes?

(IMAGE: AMANDA AS A GIRL ON A PORCH, GREETING CALLERS.)

AMANDA: They knew how to entertain their gentlemen callers. It wasn't
enough for a girl to be possessed of a pretty face and a graceful
figure — although I wasn't slighted in either respect. She also
needed to have a nimble wit and a tongue to meet all occasions.

TOM: What did you talk about?

AMANDA: Things of importance going on in the world! Never anything
coarse or common or vulgar. (*She addresses* TOM *as though he
were seated in the vacant chair at the table though he remains by
portieres. He plays this scene as though he held the book.*) My
callers were gentlemen — all! Among my callers were some of the
most prominent young planters of the Mississippi Delta — planters
and sons of planters!

(TOM *motions for music and a spot of light on* AMANDA.)

(*Her eyes lift, her face glows, her voice becomes rich and elegiac.*)

(SCREEN LEGEND: "OÙ SONT LES NEIGES.")

There was young Champ Laughlin who later became vice-president
of the Delta Planters Bank. Hadley Stevenson who was drowned in
Moon Lake and left his widow one hundred and fifty thousand in
Government bonds. There were the Cutrere brothers, Wesley and
Bates. Bates was one of my bright particular beaux! He got in a

quarrel with that wild Wainright boy. They shot it out on the floor of Moon Lake Casino. Bates was shot through the stomach. Died in the ambulance on his way to Memphis. His widow was also well-provided for, came into eight or ten thousand acres, that's all. She married him on the rebound — never loved her — carried my picture on him the night he died! And there was that boy that every girl in the Delta had set her cap for! That beautiful, brilliant young Fitzhugh boy from Greene County!

TOM: What did he leave his widow?

AMANDA: He never married! Gracious, you talk as though all of my old admirers had turned up their toes to the daisies!

TOM: Isn't this the first you've mentioned that still survives?

AMANDA: That Fitzhugh boy went North and made a fortune — came to be known as the Wolf of Wall Street! He had the Midas touch, whatever he touched turned to gold! And I could have been Mrs. Duncan J. Fitzhugh, mind you! But — I picked your *father!*

LAURA (*rising*): Mother, let me clear the table.

AMANDA: No, dear, you go in front and study your typewriter chart. Or practice your shorthand a little. Stay fresh and pretty! — It's almost time for our gentlemen callers to start arriving. (*She flounces girlishly toward the kitchenette.*) How many do you suppose we're going to entertain this afternoon?

(TOM *throws down the paper and jumps up with a groan.*)

LAURA (*alone in the dining room*): I don't believe we're going to receive any, Mother.

AMANDA (*reappearing, airily*): What? No one — not one? You must be joking! (LAURA *nervously echoes her laugh. She slips in a fugitive manner through the half-open portieres and draws them gently behind her. A shaft of very clear light is thrown on her face against the faded tapestry of the curtains.* MUSIC: "THE GLASS MENAGERIE" UNDER FAINTLY. *Lightly.*) Not one gentlement caller? It can't be true! There must be a flood, there must have been a tornado!

LAURA: It isn't a flood, it's not a tornado, Mother. I'm just not popular like you were in Blue Mountain. . . . (TOM *utters another groan.* LAURA *glances at him with a faint, apologetic smile. Her voice catching a little.*) Mother's afraid I'm going to be an old maid.

THE SCENE DIMS OUT WITH "GLASS MENAGERIE" MUSIC.

SCENE TWO

(*"Laura, Haven't You Ever Liked Some Boy?"*

   On the dark stage the screen is lighted with the image of blue roses.

   Gradually LAURA's *figure becomes apparent and the screen goes out.*

   The music subsides.

   LAURA *is seated in the delicate ivory chair at the small claw-foot table.*

   She wears a dress of soft violet material for a kimono — her hair tied back from her forehead with a ribbon.

   She is washing and polishing her collection of glass.

   AMANDA *appears on the fire-escape steps. At the sound of her ascent,* LAURA *catches her breath, thrusts the bowl of ornaments away and seats herself stiffly before the diagram of the typewriter keyboard as though it held her spellbound. Something has happened to* AMANDA. *It is written in her face as she climbs to the landing: a look that is grim and hopeless and a little absurd.*

   She has on one of those cheap or imitation velvety-looking cloth coats with imitation fur collar. Her hat is five or six years old, one of those dreadful cloche hats that were worn in the late twenties and she is clasping an enormous black patent-leather pocketbook with nickel clasp and initials. This is her full-dress outfit, the one she usually wears to the D.A.R.

   Before entering she looks through the door.

   She purses her lips, opens her eyes wide, rolls them upward and shakes her head.

   Then she slowly lets herself in the door. Seeing her mother's expression LAURA *touches her lips with a nervous gesture.*)

LAURA: Hello, Mother, I was — (*She makes a nervous gesture toward the chart on the wall.* AMANDA *leans against the shut door and stares at* LAURA *with a martyred look.*)

AMANDA: Deception? Deception? (*She slowly removes her hat and gloves, continuing the swift suffering stare. She lets the hat and gloves fall on the floor — a bit of acting.*)

LAURA (*shakily*): How was the D.A.R. meeting? (AMANDA *slowly opens her purse and removes a dainty white handkerchief which she shakes out delicately and delicately touches to her lips and nostrils.*) Didn't you go to the D.A.R. meeting, Mother?

AMANDA (*faintly, almost inaudibly*): — No. — No. (*Then more forc-*

ibly. I did not have the strength — to go to the D.A.R. In fact, I did not have the courage! I wanted to find a hole in the ground and hide myself in it forever! (*She crosses slowly to the wall and removes the diagram of the typewriter keyboard. She holds it in front of her for a second, staring at it sweetly and sorrowfully — then bites her lips and tears it in two pieces.*)

LAURA (*faintly*): Why did you do that, Mother? (AMANDA *repeats the same procedure with the chart of the Gregg Alphabet.*) Why are you —

AMANDA: Why? Why? How old are you, Laura?

LAURA: Mother, you know my age.

AMANDA: I thought that you were an adult; it seems that I was mistaken. (*She crosses slowly to the sofa and sinks down and stares at* LAURA.)

LAURA: Please don't stare at me, Mother.

(AMANDA *closes her eyes and lowers her head. Count ten.*)

AMANDA: What are we going to do, what is going to become of us, what is the future?

(*Count ten.*)

LAURA: Has something happened, Mother? (AMANDA *draws a long breath and takes out the handkerchief again. Dabbing process.*) Mother, has — something happened?

AMANDA: I'll be all right in a minute. I'm just bewildered — (*Count five.*) — by life. . . .

LAURA: Mother, I wish that you would tell me what's happened!

AMANDA: As you know, I was supposed to be inducted into my office at the D.A.R. this afternoon. (IMAGE: A SWARM OF TYPEWRITERS.) But I stopped off at Rubicam's Business College to speak to your teachers about your having a cold and ask them what progress they thought you were making down there.

LAURA: Oh. . . .

AMANDA: I went to the typing instructor and introduced myself as your mother. She didn't know who you were. Wingfield, she said. We don't have any such student enrolled at the school! I assured her she did, that you had been going to classes since early in January. "I wonder," she said, "if you could be talking about that terribly shy little girl who dropped out of school after only a few days' attendance?" "No," I said, "Laura, my daughter, has been going to school every day for the past six weeks!" "Excuse me," she said. She took the attendance book out and there was your name, unmistakably printed, and all the dates you were absent until they decided that you had dropped out of school. I still said, "No, there must have been some mistake! There must have been some mix-up in the records!" And she said, "No — I remember her perfectly now. Her hands shook so that she couldn't hit the right keys! The first time we gave a speed-test, she broke down completely — was sick at the stomach and almost had to be carried into the wash-room! After that morning she never showed up any more. We phoned the house but never got any answer — while I was working at Famous and Barr, I suppose, demonstrating those — Oh!" I felt so weak I could barely keep on my feet! I had to sit down while they got me a glass of water! Fifty dollars' tuition, all of our plans — my hopes and ambitions for you — just gone up the spout, just gone up the spout like that. (LAURA *draws a long breath and gets awkwardly to her feet. She crosses to the victrola and winds it up.*) What are you doing?

LAURA: Oh! (*She releases the handle and returns to her seat.*)

AMANDA: Laura, where have you been going when you've gone out pretending that you were going to business college?

LAURA: I've just been going out walking.

AMANDA: That's not true.

LAURA: It is. I just went walking.

AMANDA: Walking? Walking? In winter? Deliberately courting pneumonia in that light coat? Where did you walk to, Laura?

LAURA: All sorts of places — mostly in the park.

AMANDA: Even after you'd started catching that cold?

LAURA: It was the lesser of two evils, Mother. (IMAGE: WINTER SCENE IN PARK.) I couldn't go back up. I — threw up — on the floor!

AMANDA: From half past seven till after five every day you mean to tell me you walked around in the park, because you wanted to make me think that you were still going to Rubicam's Business College?

LAURA: It wasn't as bad as it sounds. I went inside places to get warmed up.

AMANDA: Inside where?

LAURA: I went in the art museum and the bird-houses at the Zoo. I visited the penguins every day! Sometimes I did without lunch and went to the movies. Lately I've been spending most of my afternoons in the Jewel-box, that big glass house where they raise the tropical flowers.

AMANDA: You did all this to deceive me, just for the deception? (LAURA *looks down.*) Why?

LAURA: Mother, when you're disappointed, you get that awful suffering look on your face, like the picture of Jesus' mother in the museum!

AMANDA: Hush!

LAURA: I couldn't face it.

(*Pause. A whisper of strings.*)

(LEGEND: "THE CRUST OF HUMILITY.")

AMANDA (*hopelessly fingering the huge pocketbook*): So what are we going to do the rest of our lives? Stay home and watch the parades go by? Amuse ourselves with the glass menagerie, darling? Eternally play those worn-out phonograph records your father left as a painful reminder of him? We won't have a business career — we've given that up because it gave us nervous indigestion! (*Laughs wearily.*) What is there left but dependency all our lives? I know so well what becomes of unmarried women who aren't prepared to occupy a position. I've seen such pitiful cases in the South — barely tolerated spinsters living upon the grudging patronage of sister's husband or brother's wife! — stuck away in some little mouse-trap of a room — encouraged by one in-law to visit another — little birdlike women without any nest — eating the crust of humility all their life! Is that the future that we've mapped out for ourselves? I swear it's the only alternative I can think of! It isn't a very pleasant alternative, is it? Of course — some girls *do marry*. (LAURA *twists her hands nervously.*) Haven't you ever liked some boy?

LAURA: Yes. I liked one once. (*Rises.*) I came across his picture a while ago.

AMANDA (*with some interest*): He gave you his picture?

LAURA: No, it's in the year-book.

AMANDA (*disappointed*): Oh — a high-school boy.

(SCREEN IMAGE: JIM AS HIGH-SCHOOL HERO BEARING A SILVER CUP.)

LAURA: Yes. His name was Jim. (LAURA *lifts the heavy annual from the claw-foot table.*) Here he is in *The Pirates of Penzance*.

AMANDA (*absently*): The what?

LAURA: The operetta the senior class put on. He had a wonderful voice and we sat across the aisle from each other Mondays, Wednesdays and Fridays in the Aud. Here he is with the silver cup for debating! See his grin?

AMANDA (*absently*): He must have had a jolly disposition.

LAURA: He used to call me — Blue Roses.

(IMAGE: BLUE ROSES.)

AMANDA: Why did he call you such a name as that?

LAURA: When I had that attack of pleurosis — he asked me what was the matter when I came back. I said pleurosis — he thought that I said Blue Roses! So that's what he always called me after that. Whenever he saw me, he'd holler, "Hello, Blue Roses!" I didn't care for the girl that he went out with. Emily Meisenbach. Emily was the best-dressed girl at Soldan. She never struck me, though, as being sincere . . . It says in the Personal Section — they're engaged. That's — six years ago! They must be married by now.

AMANDA: Girls that aren't cut out for business careers usually wind up married to some nice man. (*Gets up with a spark of revival.*) Sister, that's what you'll do!

(LAURA *utters a startled, doubtful laugh. She reaches quickly for a piece of glass.*)

LAURA: But, Mother —

AMANDA: Yes? (*Crossing to photograph.*)

LAURA (*in a tone of frightened apology*): I'm — crippled!

(IMAGE: SCREEN.)

AMANDA: Nonsense! Laura, I've told you never, never to use that word. Why, you're not crippled, you just have a little defect — hardly noticeable, even! When people have some slight disadvantage like that, they cultivate other things to make up for it — develop charm — and vivacity — and — *charm!* That's all you have to do! (*She turns again to the photograph.*) One thing your father had *plenty of* — was *charm!*

(TOM *motions to the fiddle in the wings.*)

THE SCENE FADES OUT WITH MUSIC

SCENE THREE

LEGEND ON SCREEN: "AFTER THE FIASCO —"

(TOM *speaks from the fire-escape landing.*)

TOM: After the fiasco at Rubicam's Business College, the idea of getting a gentleman caller for Laura began to play a more important part in

Mother's calculations. It became an obsession. Like some archetype of the universal unconscious, the image of the gentleman caller haunted our small apartment. . . . (IMAGE: YOUNG MAN AT DOOR WITH FLOWERS.) An evening at home rarely passed without some allusion to this image, this spectre, this hope. . . . Even when he wasn't mentioned, his presence hung in Mother's preoccupied look and in my sister's frightened, apologetic manner — hung like a sentence passed upon the Wingfields! Mother was a woman of action as well as words. She began to take logical steps in the planned direction. Late that winter and in the early spring — realizing that extra money would be needed to properly feather the nest and plume the bird — she conducted a vigorous campaign on the telephone, roping in subscribers to one of those magazines for matrons called *The Home-maker's Companion*, the type of journal that features the serialized sublimations of ladies of letters who think in terms of delicate cup-like breasts, slim, tapering waists, rich, creamy thighs, eyes like wood-smoke in autumn, fingers that soothe and caress like strains of music, bodies as powerful as Etruscan sculpture.

(SCREEN IMAGE: GLAMOR MAGAZINE COVER.)

(AMANDA *enters with phone on long extension cord. She is spotted in the dim stage.*)

AMANDA: Ida Scott? This is Amanda Wingfield! We *missed* you at the D.A.R. last Monday! I said to myself: She's probably suffering with that sinus condition! How is that sinus condition? Horrors! Heaven have mercy! — You're a Christian martyr, yes, that's what you are, a Christian martyr! Well, I just now happened to notice that your subscription to the *Companion's* about to expire! Yes, it expires with the next issue, honey! — just when that wonderful new serial by Bessie Mae Hopper is getting off to such an exciting start. Oh, honey, it's something that you can't miss! You remember how *Gone With the Wind* took everybody by storm? You simply couldn't go out if you hadn't read it. All everybody *talked* was Scarlett O'Hara. Well, this is a book that critics already compare to *Gone With the Wind*. It's the *Gone With the Wind* of the post-World War generation! — What? — Burning? — Oh, honey, don't let them burn, go take a look in the oven and I'll hold the wire! Heavens — I think she's hung up!

DIM OUT

(LEGEND ON SCREEN: "YOU THINK I'M IN LOVE WITH CONTINENTAL SHOEMAKERS?")

(*Before the stage is lighted, the violent voices of* TOM *and* AMANDA *are heard.*)

(*They are quarreling behind the portieres. In front of them stands* LAURA *with clenched hands and panicky expression.*)

(*A clear pool of light on her figure throughout this scene.*)

TOM: What in Christ's name am I —

AMANDA (*shrilly*): Don't you use that —

TOM: Supposed to do!

AMANDA: Expression! Not in my —

TOM: Ohhh!

AMANDA: Presence! Have you gone out of your senses?

TOM: I have, that's true, *driven* out!

AMANDA: What is the matter with you, you — big — big — IDIOT!

TOM: Look — I've got *no thing*, no single thing —

AMANDA: Lower your voice!

TOM: In my life here that I can call my OWN! Everything is —

AMANDA: Stop that shouting!

TOM: Yesterday you confiscated my books! You had the nerve to —

AMANDA: I took that horrible novel back to the library — yes! That hideous book by that insane Mr. Lawrence. (TOM *laughs wildly.*) I cannot control the output of diseased minds or people who cater to them — (TOM *laughs still more wildly.*) BUT I WON'T ALLOW SUCH FILTH BROUGHT INTO MY HOUSE! No, no, no, no, no!

TOM: House, house! Who pays rent on it, who makes a slave of himself to —

AMANDA (*fairly screeching*): Don't you DARE to —

TOM: No, no, I mustn't say things! *I've* got to just —

AMANDA: Let me tell you —

TOM: I don't want to hear any more! (*He tears the portieres open. The upstage area is lit with a turgid smoky red glow.*)

(AMANDA'S *hair is in metal curlers and she wears a very old bathrobe, much too large for her slight figure, a relic of the faithless Mr. Wingfield.*)

(*An upright typewriter and a wild disarray of manuscripts is on the drop-leaf table. The quarrel was probably precipitated by* AMANDA'S *interruption of his creative labor. A chair lying overthrown on the floor.*)

(*Their gesticulating shadows are cast on the ceiling by the fiery glow.*)

AMANDA: You *will* hear more, you —

TOM: No, I won't hear more, I'm going out!

AMANDA: You come right back in —

TOM: Out, out out! Because I'm —

AMANDA: Come back here, Tom Wingfield! I'm not through talking to you!

TOM: Oh, go —

LAURA (*desperately*): — Tom!

AMANDA: You're going to listen, and no more insolence from you! I'm at the end of my patience! (*He comes back toward her.*)

TOM: What do you think I'm at? Aren't I supposed to have any patience to reach the end of, Mother? I know, I know. It seems unimportant to you, what I'm *doing* — what I *want* to do — having a little *difference* between them! You don't think that —

AMANDA: I think you've been doing things that you're ashamed of. That's why you act like this. I don't believe that you go every night to the movies. Nobody goes to the movies night after night. Nobody in their right minds goes to the movies as often as you pretend to. People don't go to the movies at nearly midnight, and movies don't let out at two A.M. Come in stumbling. Muttering to yourself like a maniac! You get three hours sleep and then go to work. Oh, I can picture the way you're doing down there. Moping, doping, because you're in no condition.

TOM (*wildly*): No, I'm in no condition!

AMANDA: What right have you got to jeopardize your job? Jeopardize the security of us all? How do you think we'd manage if you were —

TOM: Listen! You think I'm crazy *about* the *warehouse?* (*He bends fiercely toward her slight figure.*) You think I'm in love with the Continental Shoemakers? You think I want to spend fifty-five *years* down there in that — *celotex interior!* with — *fluorescent* — *tubes!* Look! I'd rather somebody picked up a crowbar and battered out my brains — than go back mornings! I *go!* Every time you come in yelling that God damn *"Rise and Shine!"* *"Rise and Shine!"* I say to myself, "How *lucky dead* people are!" But I get up. I *go!* For sixty-five dollars a month I give up all that I dream of doing and being *ever!* And you say self — *self's* all I ever think of. Why, listen, if self is what I thought of, Mother, I'd be where he is — GONE! (*Pointing to father's picture.*) As far as the system of transportation reaches! (*He starts past her. She grabs his arm.*) Don't grab at me, Mother!

AMANDA: Where are you going?

TOM: I'm going to the *movies!*

AMANDA: I don't believe that lie!

TOM (*crouching toward her, overtowering her tiny figure. She backs away, gasping*): I'm going to opium dens! Yes, opium dens, dens of vice and criminals' hang-outs, Mother. I've joined the Hogan gang, I'm a hired assassin, I carry a tommy-gun in a violin case! I run a string of cat-houses in the Valley! They call me Killer, Killer Wingfield, I'm leading a double-life, a simple, honest warehouse worker by day, by night, a dynamic *czar* of the *underworld, Mother.* I go to gambling casinos, I spin away fortunes on the roulette table! I wear a patch over one eye and a false mustache, sometimes I put on green whiskers. On those occasions they call me — *El Diablo!* Oh, I could tell you things to make you sleepless! My enemies plan to dynamite this place. They're going to blow us all sky-high some night! I'll be glad, very happy, and so will you! You'll go up, up on a broomstick, over Blue Mountain with seventeen gentlemen callers! You ugly — babbling old — *witch.* . . . (*He goes through a series of violent, clumsy movements, seizing his overcoat, lunging to the door, pulling it fiercely open. The women watch him, aghast. His arm catches in the sleeve of the coat as he struggles to pull it on. For a moment he is pinioned by the bulky garment. With an outraged groan he tears the coat off again, splitting the shoulder of it, and hurls it across the room. It strikes against the shelf of* LAURA'S *glass collection, there is a tinkle of shattering glass.* LAURA *cries out as if wounded.*

(MUSIC LEGEND: "THE GLASS MENAGERIE.")

LAURA (*shrilly*): My glass! — menagerie. . . . (*She covers her face and turns away.*)

(*But* AMANDA *is still stunned and stupefied by the "ugly witch" so that she barely notices this occurrence. Now she recovers her speech.*)

AMANDA (*in an awful voice*): I won't speak to you — until you apologize! (*She crosses through portieres and draws them together behind her.* TOM *is left with* LAURA. LAURA *clings weakly to the mantel with her face averted.* TOM *stares at her stupidly for a moment. Then he crosses to shelf. Drops awkwardly to his knees to collect the fallen glass, glancing at* LAURA *as if he would speak but couldn't.*)

"*The Glass Menagerie*" *steals in as*

THE SCENE DIMS OUT

SCENE FOUR

(The interior is dark. Faint light in the alley.

A deep-voiced bell in a church is tolling the hour of five as the scene commences.

TOM *appears at the top of the alley. After each solemn boom of the bell in the tower, he shakes a little noise-maker or rattle as if to express the tiny spasm of man in contrast to the sustained power and dignity of the Almighty. This and the unsteadiness of his advance make it evident that he has been drinking.*

As he climbs the few steps to the fire-escape landing light steals up inside. LAURA *appears in night-dress, observing* TOM'S *empty bed in the front room.*

TOM *fishes in his pockets for the door-key, removing a motley assortment of articles in the search, including a perfect shower of movie-ticket stubs and an empty bottle. At last he finds the key, but just as he is about to insert it, it slips from his fingers. He strikes a match and crouches below the door.)*

TOM (*bitterly*): One crack — and it falls through!

(LAURA *opens the door.*)

LAURA: Tom! Tom, what are you doing?

TOM: Looking for a door-key.

LAURA: Where have you been all this time?

TOM: I have been to the movies.

LAURA: All this time at the movies?

TOM: There was a very long program. There was a Garbo picture and a Mickey Mouse and a travelogue and a newsreel and a preview of coming attractions. And there was an organ solo and a collection for the milk-fund — simultaneously — which ended up in a terrible fight between a fat lady and an usher!

LAURA (*innocently*): Did you have to stay through everything?

TOM: Of course! And, oh, I forgot! There was a big stage show! The headliner on this stage show was Malvolio the Magician. He performed wonderful tricks, many of them, such as pouring water back and forth between pitchers. First it turned to wine and then it turned to beer and then it turned to whiskey. I know it was whiskey it finally turned into because he needed somebody to come up out of the audience to help him, and I came up — both shows! It was Kentucky Straight Bourbon. A very generous fellow, he gave souvenirs. (*He pulls from his back pocket a shimmering rain-*

bow-colored scarf.) He gave me this. This is his magic scarf. You can have it, Laura. You wave it over a canary cage and you get a bowl of gold-fish. You wave it over the gold-fish bowl and they fly away canaries. . . . But the wonderfullest trick of all was the coffin trick. We nailed him into a coffin and he got out of the coffin without removing one nail. (*He has come inside.*) There is a trick that would come in handy for me — get me out of this 2 by 4 situation!(*Flops onto bed and starts removing shoes.*)

LAURA: Tom — Shhh!

TOM: What you shushing me for?

LAURA: You'll wake up Mother.

TOM: Goody, goody! Pay 'er back for all those "Rise an' Shines." (*Lies down, groaning.*) You know it don't take much intelligence to get yourself into a nailed-up coffin, Laura. But who in hell ever got himself out of one without removing one nail?

(*As if in answer, the father's grinning photograph lights up.*)

SCENE DIMS OUT

(*Immediately following: The church bell is heard striking six. At the sixth stroke the alarm clock goes off in* AMANDA's *room, and after a few moments we hear her calling: "Rise and Shine! Rise and Shine! Laura, go tell your brother to rise and shine!"*)

TOM (*Sitting up slowly*): I'll rise — but I won't shine.

(*The light increases.*)

AMANDA: Laura, tell your brother his coffee is ready.

(LAURA *slips into front room.*)

LAURA: Tom! it's nearly seven. Don't make Mother nervous. (*He stares at her stupidly. Beseechingly.*) Tom, speak to Mother this morning. Make up with her, apologize, speak to her!

TOM: She won't to me. It's her that started not speaking.

LAURA: If you just say you're sorry she'll start speaking.

TOM: Her not speaking — is that such a tragedy?

LAURA: Please — please!

AMANDA (*calling from kitchenette*): Laura, are you going to do what I asked you to do, or do I have to get dressed and go out myself?

LAURA: Going, going — soon as I get on my coat! (*She pulls on a shapeless felt hat with nervous, jerky movement, pleadingly glancing at* TOM. *Rushes awkwardly for coat. The coat is one of* AMANDA's, *inaccurately made-over, the sleeves too short for* LAURA.) Butter and what else?

AMANDA (*entering upstage*): Just butter. Tell them to charge it.

LAURA: Mother, they make such faces when I do that.

AMANDA: Stick and stones may break our bones, but the expression on Mr. Garfinkel's face won't harm us! Tell your brother his coffee is getting cold.

LAURA (*at door*): Do what I asked you, will you, will you, Tom?

(*He looks sullenly away.*)

AMANDA: Laura, go now or just don't go at all!

LAURA (*rushing out*): Going — going! (*A second later she cries out. TOM springs up and crosses to the door. AMANDA rushes anxiously in. TOM opens the door.*)

TOM: Laura?

LAURA: I'm all right. I slipped, but I'm all right.

AMANDA (*peering anxiously after her*): If anyone breaks a leg on those fire-escape steps, the landlord ought to be sued for every cent he possesses! (*She shuts door. Remembers she isn't speaking and returns to other room.*)

(*As TOM enters listlessly for his coffee, she turns her back to him and stands rigidly facing the window on the gloomy gray vault of the areaway. Its light on her face with its aged but childish features is cruelly sharp, satirical as a Daumier print.*)

(MUSIC UNDER: "AVE MARIA.")

(TOM *glances sheepishly but sullenly at her averted figure and slumps at the table. The coffee is scalding hot; he sips it and gasps and spits it back in the cup. At his gasp, AMANDA catches her breath and half turns. Then catches herself and turns back to window.*)

(TOM *blows on his coffee, glancing sidewise at his mother. She clears her throat. TOM clears his. He starts to rise. Sinks back down again, scratches his head, clears his throat again. AMANDA coughs. TOM raises his cup in both hands to blow on it, his eyes staring over the rim of it at his mother for several moments. Then he slowly sets the cup down and awkwardly and hesitantly rises from the chair.*)

TOM (*hoarsely*): Mother. I — I apologize. Mother. (AMANDA *draws a quick, shuddering breath. Her face works grotesquely. She breaks into childlike tears.*) I'm sorry for what I said, for everything that I said, I didn't mean it.

AMANDA (*sobbingly*): My devotion has made me a witch and so I make myself hateful to my children!

TOM: No, you *don't.*

AMANDA: I worry so much, don't sleep, it makes me nervous!

TOM (*gently*): I understand that.

AMANDA: I've had to put up a solitary battle all these years. But you're my right-hand bower! Don't fall down, don't fail!

TOM (*gently*): I try, Mother.

AMANDA (*with great enthusiasm*): Try and you will SUCCEED! (*The notion makes her breathless.*) Why, you — you're just *full* of natural endowments! Both of my children — they're *unusual* children! Don't you think I know it? I'm so — *proud!* Happy and — feel I've — so much to be thankful for but — Promise me one thing, son!

TOM: What, Mother?

AMANDA: Promise, son, you'll — never be a drunkard!

TOM (*turns to her grinning*): I will never be a drunkard, Mother.

AMANDA: That's what frightened me so, that you'd be drinking! Eat a bowl of Purina!

TOM: Just coffee, Mother.

AMANDA: Shredded wheat biscuit?

TOM: No. No, Mother, just coffee.

AMANDA: You can't put in a day's work on an empty stomach. You've got ten minutes — don't gulp! Drinking too-hot liquids makes cancer of the stomach. . . . Put cream in.

TOM: No, thank you.

AMANDA: To cool it.

TOM: No! No, thank you, I want it black.

AMANDA: I know, but it's not good for you. We have to do all that we can to build ourselves up. In these trying times we live in, all that we have to cling to is — each other. . . . That's why it's so important to — Tom, I — I sent out your sister so I could discuss something with you. If you hadn't spoken I would have spoken to you. (*Sits down.*)

TOM (*gently*): What is it, Mother, that you want to discuss?

AMANDA: *Laura!*

(TOM *puts his cup down slowly.*)

(LEGEND ON SCREEN: "LAURA.")

(MUSIC: "THE GLASS MENAGERIE.")

TOM: — Oh. — Laura . . .

AMANDA (*touching his sleeve*): You know how Laura is. So quiet but — still water runs deep! She notices things and I think she

— broods about them. (TOM *looks up*). A few days ago I came in and she was crying.

TOM: What about?

AMANDA: You.

TOM: Me?

AMANDA: She has an idea that you're not happy here.

TOM: What gave her that idea?

AMANDA: What gives her any idea? However, you do act strangely. I — I'm not criticizing, understand *that!* I know your ambitions do not lie in the warehouse, that like everybody in the whole wide world — you've had to — make sacrifices, but — Tom — Tom — life's not easy, it calls for — Spartan endurance! There's so many things in my heart that I cannot describe to you! I've never told you but I — *loved* your father. . . .

TOM (*gently*): I know that, Mother.

AMANDA: And you — when I see you taking after his ways! Staying out late — and — well, you *had* been drinking the night you were in that — terrifying condition! Laura says that you hate the apartment and that you go out nights to get away from it! Is that true, Tom?

TOM: No. You say there's so much in your heart that you can't describe to me. That's true of me, too. There' so much in my heart that I can't describe to *you!* So let's respect each other's —

AMANDA: But, why — *why*, Tom — are you always so *restless?* Where do you go to, nights?

TOM: I — go to the movies.

AMANDA: Why do you go to the movies so much, Tom?

TOM: I go to the movies because — I like adventure. Adventure is something I don't have much of at work, so I go to the movies.

AMANDA: But, Tom, you go to the movies *entirely* too *much!*

TOM: I like a lot of adventure.

(AMANDA *looks baffled, then hurt. As the familiar inquisition resumes he becomes hard and impatient again.* AMANDA *slips back into her querulous attitude toward him.*)

(IMAGE ON SCREEN: SAILING VESSEL WITH JOLLY ROGER.)

AMANDA: Most young men find adventure in their careers.

TOM: Then most young men are not employed in a warehouse.

AMANDA: The world is full of young men employed in warehouses and offices and factories.

TOM: Do all of them find adventure in their careers?

AMANDA: They do or they do without it! Not everybody has a craze for adventure.

TOM: Man is by instinct a lover, a hunter, a fighter, and none of those instincts are given much play at the warehouse!

AMANDA: Man is by instinct! Don't quote instinct to me! Instinct is something that people have got away from! It belongs to animals! Christian adults don't want it!

TOM: What do Christian adults want, then, Mother?

AMANDA: Superior things! Things of the mind and the spirit! Only animals have to satisfy instincts! Surely your aims are somewhat higher than theirs! Than monkeys — pigs —

TOM: I reckon they're not.

AMANDA: You're joking. However, that isn't what I wanted to discuss.

TOM (*rising*): I haven't much time.

AMANDA (*pushing his shoulders*): Sit down.

TOM: You want me to punch in red at the warehouse, Mother?

AMANDA: You have five minutes. I want to talk about Laura.

(LEGEND: "PLANS AND PROVISIONS.")

TOM: All right! What about Laura?

AMANDA: We have to be making plans and provisions for her. She's older than you, two years, and nothing has happened. She just drifts along doing nothing. It frightens me terribly how she just drifts along.

TOM: I guess she's the type that people call home girls.

AMANDA: There's no such type, and if there is, it's a pity! That is unless the home is hers, with a husband!

TOM: What?

AMANDA: Oh, I can see the handwriting on the wall as plain as I see the nose in front of my face! It's terrifying! More and more you remind me of your father! He was out all hours without explanation — Then *left! Good-bye!* And me with a bag to hold. I saw that letter you got from the Merchant Marine. I know what you're dreaming of. I'm not standing here blindfolded. Very well, then. Then *do* it! But not till there's somebody to take your place.

TOM: What do you mean?

AMANDA: I mean that as soon as Laura has got somebody to take care of her, married, a home of her own, independent — why, then you'll be free to go wherever you please, on land, on sea, whichever way the wind blows you! But until that time you've got to look out for your sister. I don't say me because I'm old and don't matter! I say for your sister because she's young and dependent. I put her in business college — a dismal failure! Frightened her so it made her sick to her stomach. I took her over to the Young People's League at the church. Another fiasco. She spoke to nobody, nobody spoke to her. Now all she does is fool with those pieces of glass and play those worn-out records. What kind of a life is that for a girl to lead?

TOM: What can I do about it?

AMANDA: Overcome selfishness! Self, self, self is all that you ever think of! (TOM *springs up and crosses to get his coat. It is ugly and bulky. He pulls on a cap with earmuffs.*) Where is your muffler? Put your wool muffler on! (*He snatches it angrily from the closet and tosses it around his neck and pulls both ends tight.*) Tom! I haven't said what I had in mind to ask you.

TOM: I'm too late to —

AMANDA (*catching his arm — very importunately. Then shyly*): Down at the warehouse, aren't there some — nice young men?

TOM: No!

AMANDA: There *must* be — *some* . . .

TOM: Mother —

(*Gesture.*)

AMANDA: Find out one that's clean-living — doesn't drink and — ask him out for sister!

TOM: What?

AMANDA: For *sister!* To *meet!* Get *acquainted!*

TOM (*stamping to door*): Oh, my go-osh!

AMANDA: Will you? (*He opens door. Imploringly.*) Will you? (*He starts down.*) Will you? Will you, dear?

TOM (*calling back*): YES!

(AMANDA *closes the door hesitantly and with a troubled but faintly hopeful expression.*)

(SCREEN IMAGE: GLAMOR MAGAZINE COVER.)

(*Spot* AMANDA *at phone.*)

AMANDA: Ella Cartwright? This is Amanda Wingfield! How are you, honey? How is that kidney condition? (*Count five.*) Horrors! (*Count five.*) You're a Christian martyr, yes, honey, that's what you are, a Christian martyr! Well, I just happened to notice in my little red book that your subscription to the *Companion* has just run out! I knew that you wouldn't want to miss out on the wonderful serial starting in this new issue. It's by Bessie Mae Hopper, the first thing she's written since *Honeymoon for Three*.

Wasn't that a strange and interesting story? Well, this one is even lovelier, I believe. It has a sophisticated society background. It's all about the horsey set on Long Island!

FADE OUT

SCENE FIVE

LEGEND ON SCREEN: "ANNUNCIATION." *Fade with music.*

(*It is early dusk of a spring evening. Supper has just been finished in the Wingfield apartment.* AMANDA *and* LAURA *in light colored dresses are removing dishes from the table, in the upstage area, which is shadowy, their movements formalized almost as a dance or ritual, their moving forms as pale and silent as moths.*

TOM, *in white shirt and trousers, rises from the table and crosses toward the fire-escape.*)

AMANDA (*as he passes her*): Son, will you do me a favor?
TOM: What?
AMANDA: Comb your hair! You look so pretty when your hair is combed! (TOM *slouches on sofa with evening paper. Enormous caption "Franco Triumphs".*) There is only one respect in which I would like you to emulate your father.
TOM: What respect is that?
AMANDA: The care he always took of his appearance. He never allowed himself to look untidy. (*He throws down the paper and crosses to fire-escape.*) Where are you going?
TOM: I'm going out to smoke.
AMANDA: You smoke too much. A pack a day at fifteen cents a pack. How much would that amount to in a month? Thirty times fifteen is how much, Tom? Figure it out and you will be astounded at what you could save. Enough to give you a night-school course in accounting at Washington U! Just think what a wonderful thing that would be for you, son!

(TOM *is unmoved by the thought.*)

TOM: I'd rather smoke. (*He steps out on landing, letting the screen door slam.*)
AMANDA (*sharply*): I know! That's the tragedy of it. . . . (*Alone, she turns to look at her husband's picture.*)

(DANCE MUSIC: "ALL THE WORLD IS WAITING FOR THE SUNRISE!")

TOM (*to the audience*): Across the alley from us was the Paradise Dance Hall. On evenings in spring the windows and doors were open and the music came outdoors. Sometimes the lights were turned out except for a large glass sphere that hung from the ceiling. It would turn slowly about and filter the dusk with delicate rainbow colors. Then the orchestra played a waltz or a tango, something that had a slow and sensuous rhythm. Couples would come outside, to the relative privacy of the alley. You could see them kissing behind ash-pits and telephone poles. This was the compensation for lives that passed like mine, without any change or adventure. Adventure and change were imminent in this year. They were waiting around the corner for all these kids. Suspended in the mist over Berchtesgaden, caught in the folds of Chamberlain's umbrella — In Spain there was Guernica! But here there was only hot swing music and liquor, dance halls, bars, and movies, and sex that hung in the gloom like a chandelier and flooded the world with brief, deceptive rainbows. . . . All the world was waiting for bombardments!

(AMANDA *turns from the picture and comes outside.*)

AMANDA (*Sighing*). A fire-escape landing's a poor excuse for a porch. (*She spreads a newspaper on a step and sits down, gracefully and demurely as if she were settling into a swing on a Mississippi veranda.*) What are you looking at?

TOM: The moon.

AMANDA: Is there a moon this evening?

TOM: It's rising over Garfinkel's Delicatessen.

AMANDA: So it is! A little silver slipper of a moon. Have you made a wish on it yet?

TOM: Um-hum.

AMANDA: What did you wish for?

TOM: That's a secret.

AMANDA: A secret, huh? Well, I won't tell mine either. I will be just as mysterious as you.

TOM: I bet I can guess what yours is.

AMANDA: Is my head so transparent?

TOM: You're not a sphinx.

AMANDA: No, I don't have secrets. I'll tell you what I wished for on the moon. Success and happiness for my precious children! I wish for that whenever there's a moon, and when there isn't a moon, I wish for it, too.

TOM: I thought perhaps you wished for a gentleman caller.

AMANDA: Why do you say that?

TOM: Don't you remember asking me to fetch one?

AMANDA: I remember suggesting that it would be nice for your sister if you brought home some nice young man from the warehouse. I think I've made that suggestion more than once.

TOM: Yes, you have made it repeatedly.

AMANDA: Well?

TOM: We are going to have one.

AMANDA: *What?*

TOM: A gentleman caller!

(THE ANNUNCIATION IS CELEBRATED WITH MUSIC.)

(AMANDA *rises.*)

(IMAGE ON SCREEN: CALLER WITH BOUQUET.)

AMANDA: You mean you have asked some nice young man to come over?

TOM: Yep. I've asked him to dinner.

AMANDA: You really did?

TOM: I did!

AMANDA: You did, and did he — *accept?*

TOM: He did!

AMANDA: Well, well — well, well! That's — lovely!

TOM: I thought that you would be pleased.

AMANDA: It's definite, then?

TOM: Very definite.

AMANDA: Soon?

TOM: Very soon.

AMANDA: For heaven's sake, stop putting on and tell me some things, will you?

TOM: What things do you want me to tell you?

AMANDA: *Naturally* I would like to know when he's *coming!*

TOM: He's coming tomorrow.

AMANDA: *Tomorrow?*

TOM: Yep. Tomorrow.

AMANDA: But, Tom!

TOM: Yes, Mother?

AMANDA: Tomorrow gives me no time!

TOM: Time for what?

AMANDA: Preparations! Why didn't you phone me at once, as soon as you asked him, the minute that he accepted? Then, don't you see, I could have been getting ready!

TOM: You don't have to make any fuss.

AMANDA: Oh, Tom, Tom, Tom, of course I have to make a fuss! I

want things nice, not sloppy! Not thrown together. I'll certainly have
to do some fast thinking, won't I?

TOM: I don't see why you have to think at all.

AMANDA: You just don't know. We can't have a gentleman caller in
a pig-sty! All my wedding silver has to be polished, the monogrammed
table linen ought to be laundered! The windows have to be washed
and fresh curtains put up. And how about clothes? We have to *wear*
something, don't we?

TOM: Mother, this boy is no one to make a fuss over!

AMANDA: Do you realize he's the first young man we've introduced to
your sister? It's terrible, dreadful, disgraceful that poor little sister
has never received a single gentleman caller! Tom, come inside! [*She
opens the screen door.*]

TOM: What for?

AMANDA: I want to ask you some things.

TOM: If you're going to make such a fuss, I'll call it off, I'll tell him
not to come.

AMANDA: You certainly won't do anything of the kind. Nothing offends
people worse than broken engagements. It simply means I'll have
to work like a Turk! We won't be brilliant, but we'll pass inspection.
Come on inside. (TOM *follows, groaning.*) Sit down.

TOM: Any particular place you would like me to sit?

AMANDA: Thank heavens I've got that new sofa! I'm also making
payments on a floor lamp I'll have sent out! And put the chintz
covers on, they'll brighten things up! Of course I'd hoped to have
these walls re-papered. . . . What is the young man's name?

TOM: His name is O'Connor.

AMANDA: That, of course, means fish —tomorrow is Friday! I'll have
that salmon loaf — with Durkee's dressing! What does he do? He
works at the warehouse?

TOM: Of course! How else would I —

AMANDA: Tom, he — doesn't drink?

TOM: Why do you ask me that?

AMANDA: Your father *did!*

TOM: Don't get started on that!

AMANDA: He *does* drink, then?

TOM: Not that I know of!

AMANDA: Make sure, be certain! The last thing I want for my daughter's a boy who drinks!

TOM: Aren't you being a little premature? Mr. O'Connor has not yet
appeared on the scene!

AMANDA: But will tomorrow. To meet your sister, and what do I

know about his character? Nothing! Old maids are better off than
  wives of drunkards!

TOM: Oh, my God!

AMANDA: Be still!

TOM (*leaning forward to whisper*): Lots of fellows meet girls whom
  they don't marry!

AMANDA: Oh, talk sensibly, Tom — and don't be sarcastic! (*She has
  gotten a hairbrush.*)

TOM: What are you doing?

AMANDA: I'm brushing that cow-lick down! What is this young man's
  position at the warehouse?

TOM (*submitting grimly to the brush and the interrogation*): This
  young man's position is that of a shipping clerk, Mother.

AMANDA: Sounds to me like a fairly responsible job, the sort of a
  job *you* would be in if you just had more *get-up*. What is his
  salary? Have you got any idea?

TOM: I would judge it to be approximately eighty-five dollars a
  month.

AMANDA: Well — not princely, but —

TOM: Twenty more than I make.

AMANDA: Yes, how well I know! But for a family man, eighty-five
  dollars a month is not much more than you can just get by on. . . .

TOM: Yes, but Mr. O'Connor is not a family man.

AMANDA: He might be, mightn't he? Some time in the future?

TOM: I see. Plans and provisions.

AMANDA: You are the only young man that I know of who ignores
  the fact that the future becomes the present, the present the past,
  and the past turns into everlasting regret if you don't plan for it!

TOM: I will think that over and see what I can make of it.

AMANDA: Don't be supercilious with your mother! Tell me some more
  about this — what do you call him?

TOM: James D. O'Connor. The D. is for Delaney.

AMANDA: Irish on *both* sides! *Gracious!* And doesn't drink?

TOM: Shall I call him up and ask him right this minute?

AMANDA: The only way to find out about those things is to make discreet inquiries at the proper moment. When I was a girl in Blue
  Mountain and it was suspected that a young man drank, the girl
  whose attentions he had been receiving, if any girl *was*, would
  sometimes speak to the minister of his church, or rather her father
  would if her father was living, and sort of feel him out on the young
  man's character. That is the way such things are discreetly handled
  to keep a young woman from making a tragic mistake!

TOM: Then how did you happen to make a tragic mistake?

AMANDA: That innocent look of your father's had everyone fooled! He *smiled* — the world was *enchanted!* No girl can do worse than put herself at the mercy of a handsome appearance! I hope that Mr. O'Connor is not too good-looking.

TOM: No, he's not too good-looking. He's covered with freckles and hasn't too much of a nose.

AMANDA: He's not right-down homely, though?

TOM: Not right-down homely. Just medium homely, I'd say.

AMANDA: Character's what to look for in a man.

TOM: That's what I've always said, Mother.

AMANDA: You've never said anything of the kind and I suspect you would never give it a thought.

TOM: Don't be suspicious of me.

AMANDA: At least I hope he's the type that's up and coming.

TOM: I think he really goes in for self-improvement.

AMANDA: What reason have you to think so?

TOM: He goes to night school.

AMANDA (*beaming*): Splendid! What does he do, I mean study?

TOM: Radio engineering and public speaking!

AMANDA: Then he has visions of being advanced in the world! Any young man who studies public speaking is aiming to have an executive job some day! And radio engineering? A thing for the future! Both of these facts are very illuminating. Those are the sort of things that a mother should know concerning any young man who comes to call on her daughter. Seriously or — not.

TOM: One little warning. He doesn't know about Laura. I didn't let on that we had dark ulterior motives. I just said, why don't you come have dinner with us? He said okay and that was the whole conversation.

AMANDA: I bet it was! You're eloquent as an oyster. However, he'll know about Laura when he gets here. When he sees how lovely and sweet and pretty she is, he'll thank his lucky stars he was asked to dinner.

TOM: Mother, you mustn't expect too much of Laura.

AMANDA: What do you mean?

TOM: Laura seems all those things to you and me because she's ours and we love her. We don't even notice she's crippled any more.

AMANDA: Don't say crippled! You know that I never allow that word to be used!

TOM: But face facts, Mother. She is and — that's not all —

AMANDA: What do you mean "not all"?

TOM: Laura is very different from other girls.

AMANDA: I think the difference is all to her advantage.

TOM: Not quite all — in the eyes of others — strangers — she's terribly shy and lives in a world of her own and those things make her seem a little peculiar to people outside the house.

AMANDA: Don't say peculiar.

TOM: Face the facts. She is.

(THE DANCE-HALL MUSIC CHANGES TO A TANGO THAT HAS A MINOR AND SOMEWHAT OMINOUS TONE.)

AMANDA: In what way is she peculiar — may I ask?

TOM (*gently*): She lives in a world of her own — a world of — little glass ornaments, Mother. . . . (*Gets up.* AMANDA *remains holding brush, looking at him, troubled.*) She plays old phonograph records and — that's about all — (*He glances at himself in the mirror and crosses to door.*)

AMANDA (*sharply*): Where are you going?

TOM: I'm going to the movies. (*Out screen door.*)

AMANDA: Not to the movies, every night to the movies! (*Follows quickly to screen door.*) I don't believe you always go to the movies! (*He is gone.* AMANDA *looks worriedly after him for a moment. Then vitality and optimism return and she turns from the door. Crossing to portieres.*) Laura! Laura! (LAURA *answers from kitchenette.*)

LAURA: Yes, Mother.

AMANDA: Let those dishes go and come in front! (LAURA *appears with dish towel. Gaily.*) Laura, come here and make a wish on the moon!

LAURA (*entering*): Moon — moon?

AMANDA: A little silver slipper of a moon. Look over your left shoulder, Laura, and make a wish! (LAURA *looks faintly puzzled as if called out of sleep.* AMANDA *seizes her shoulders and turns her at an angle by the door.*) No! Now, darling, *wish!*

LAURA: What shall I wish for, Mother?

AMANDA (*her voice trembling and her eyes suddenly filling with tears*): Happiness! Good Fortune!

(*The violin rises and the stage dims out.*)

SCENE SIX

(IMAGE: HIGH SCHOOL HERO.)

TOM: And so the following evening I brought Jim home to dinner. I had known Jim slightly in high school. In high school Jim was a hero. He had tremendous Irish good nature and vitality with the scrubbed and polished look of white chinaware. He seemed to move in a continual spotlight. He was a star in basketball, captain of the debating club, president of the senior class and the glee club and he sang the male lead in the annual light operas. He was always running or bounding, never just walking. He seemed always at the point of defeating the law of gravity. He was shooting with such velocity through his adolescence that you would logically expect him to arrive at nothing short of the White House by the time he was thirty. But Jim apparently ran into more interference after his graduation from Soldan. His speed had definitely slowed. Six years after he left high school he was holding a job that wasn't much better than mine.

(IMAGE: CLERK.)

He was the only one at the warehouse with whom I was on friendly terms. I was valuable to him as someone who could remember his former glory, who had seen him win basketball games and the silver cup in debating. He knew of my secret practice of retiring to a cabinet of the washroom to work on poems when business was slack in the warehouse. He called me Shakespeare. And while the other boys in the warehouse regarded me with suspicious hostility, Jim took a humorous attitude toward me. Gradually his attitude affected the others, their hostility wore off and they also began to smile at me as people smile at an oddly fashioned dog who trots across their path at some distance.

I knew that Jim and Laura had known each other at Soldan, and I had heard Laura speak admiringly of his voice. I didn't know if Jim remembered her or not. In high school Laura had been as unobtrusive as Jim had been astonishing. If he did remember Laura, it was not as my sister, for when I asked him to dinner, he grinned and said, "You know, Shakespeare, I never thought of you as having folks!"

He was about to discover that I did. . . .

(LIGHT UP STAGE.)

(LEGEND ON SCREEN: "THE ACCENT OF A COMING FOOT.")

(*Friday evening. It is about five o'clock of a late spring evening which comes "scattering poems in the sky."*)

(*A delicate lemony light is in the Wingfield apartment.*)

(*AMANDA has worked like a Turk in preparation for the gentleman caller. The results are astonishing. The new floor lamp with its rose-silk shade is in place, a colored paper lantern conceals the broken light fixture in the ceiling, new billowing white curtains are at the windows, chintz covers are on chairs and sofa, a pair of new sofa pillows make their initial appearance.*)

(*Open boxes and tissue paper are scattered on the floor.*)

(LAURA *stands in the middle with lifted arms while* AMANDA *crouches before her, adjusting the hem of the new dress, devout and ritualistic. The dress is colored and designed by memory. The arrangement of* LAURA's *hair is changed; it is softer and more becoming. A fragile, unearthly prettiness has come out in* LAURA: *she is like a piece of translucent glass touched by light, given a momentary radiance, not actual, not lasting.*)

AMANDA (*impatiently*): Why are you trembling?

LAURA: Mother, you've made me so nervous!

AMANDA: How have I made you nervous?

LAURA: By all this fuss! You make it seem so important!

AMANDA: I don't understand you, Laura. You couldn't be satisfied with just sitting home, and yet whenever I try to arrange something for you, you seem to resist it. (*She gets up.*) Now take a look at yourself. No, wait! Wait just a moment — I have an idea!

LAURA: What is it now?

(AMANDA *produces two powder puffs which she wraps in handkerchiefs and stuffs in* LAURA's *bosom.*)

LAURA: Mother, what are you doing?

AMANDA: They call them "Gay Deceivers"!

LAURA: I won't wear them!

AMANDA: You will!

LAURA: Why should I?

AMANDA: Because, to be painfully honest, your chest is flat.

LAURA: You make it seem like we were setting a trap.

AMANDA: All pretty girls are a trap, a pretty trap, and men expect them to be. (LEGEND: "A PRETTY TRAP.") Now look at yourself, young lady. This is the prettiest you will ever be! I've got to fix myself now! You're going to be surprised by your mother's appearance! (*She crosses through portieres, humming gaily.*)

(LAURA *moves slowly to the long mirror and stares solemnly at herself.*)

(*A wind blows the white curtains inward in a slow, graceful motion and with a faint, sorrowful sighing.*)

AMANDA (*off stage*): It isn't dark enough yet. (*She turns slowly before the mirror with a troubled look.*)

(LEGEND ON SCREENS "THIS IS MY SISTER: CELEBRATE HER WITH STRINGS!" MUSIC.)

AMANDA (*laughing, off*): I'm going to show you something. I'm going to make a spectacular appearance!

LAURA: What is it, Mother?

AMANDA: Possess your soul in patience — you will see! Something I've resurrected from that old trunk! Styles haven't changed so terribly much after all. . . . (*She parts the portieres.*) Now just look at your mother! (*She wears a girlish frock of yellowed voile with a blue silk sash. She carries a bunch of jonquils — the legend of her youth is nearly revived. Feverishly*) This is the dress in which I led the cotillion. Won the cakewalk twice at Sunset Hill, wore one spring to the Governor's ball in Jackson! See how I sashayed around the ballroom, Laura? (*She raises her skirt and does a mincing step around the room.*) I wore it on Sundays for my gentlemen callers! I had it on the day I met your father — I had malaria fever all that spring. The change of climate from East Tennessee to the Delta — weakened resistance — I had a little temperature all the time — not enough to be serious — just enough to make me restless and giddy! Invitations poured in — parties all over the Delta! — "Stay in bed," said Mother, "you have fever!" — but I just wouldn't. — I took quinine but kept on going, going! — Evenings, dances! — Afternoons, long, long rides! Picnics — lovely! — So lovely, that country in May. — All lacy with dogwood, literally flooded with jonquils! — That was the spring I had the craze for jonquils. Jonquils became an absolute obsession. Mother said, "Honey, there's no more room for jonquils." And still I kept on bringing in more jonquils. Whenever, wherever I saw them, I'd say, "Stop! Stop! I see jonquils!" I made the young men help me gather the jonquils! It was a joke, Amanda and her jonquils! Finally there were no more vases to hold them, every available space was filled with jonquils. No vases to hold them? All right, I'll hold them myself! And then I — (*She stops in front of the picture. MUSIC.*) met your father! Malaria fever and jonquils and then — this — boy. . . . (*She switches on the rose-colored lamp.*) I hope they get here before it starts to rain. (*She crosses upstage and places the jonquils in bowl on table.*) I gave your brother a little extra change so he and Mr. O'Connor could take the service car home.

LAURA (*with altered look*): What did you say his name was?

AMANDA: O'Connor.

LAURA: What is his first name?

AMANDA: I don't remember. Oh, yes, I do. It was — Jim!

(LAURA *sways slightly and catches hold of a chair.*)

(LEGEND ON SCREEN: "NOT JIM!")

LAURA (*faintly*): Not — Jim!

AMANDA: Yes, that was it, it was Jim! I've never known a Jim that wasn't nice!

(MUSIC: OMINOUS.)

LAURA: Are you sure his name is Jim O'Connor?

AMANDA: Yes. Why?

LAURA: Is he the one that Tom used to know in high school?

AMANDA: He didn't say so. I think he just got to know him at the warehouse.

LAURA: There was a Jim O'Connor we both knew in high school — (*Then, with effort.*) If that is the one that Tom is bringing to dinner — you'll have to excuse me, I won't come to the table.

AMANDA: What sort of nonsense is this?

LAURA: You asked me once if I'd ever liked a boy. Don't you remember I showed you this boy's picture?

AMANDA: You mean the boy you showed me in the year book?

LAURA: Yes, that boy.

AMANDA: Laura, Laura, were you in love with that boy?

LAURA: I don't know, Mother. All I know is I couldn't sit at the table if it was him!

AMANDA: It won't be him! It isn't the least bit likely. But whether it is or not, you will come to the table. You will not be excused.

LAURA: I'll have to be, Mother.

AMANDA: I don't intend to humor your silliness, Laura. I've had too much from you and your brother, both! So just sit down and compose yourself till they come. Tom has forgotten his key so you'll have to let them in, when they arrive.

LAURA (*panicky*): Oh, Mother — *you* answer the door!

AMANDA (*lightly*): I'll be in the kitchen — busy!

LAURA: Oh, Mother, please answer the door, don't make me do it!

AMANDA (*crossing into kitchenette*): I've got to fix the dressing for the salmon. Fuss, fuss — silliness! — over a gentleman caller!

(*Door swings shut.* LAURA *is left alone.*)

(LEGEND: "TERROR!")

(*She utters a low moan and turns off the lamp — sits stiffly on the edge of the sofa, knotting her fingers together.*)

(LEGEND ON SCREEN: "THE OPENING OF A DOOR!")

(TOM *and* JIM *appear on the fire-escape steps and climb to landing. Hearing their approach,* LAURA *rises with a panicky gesture. She retreats to the portieres.*)

(*The doorbell.* LAURA *catches her breath and touches her throat. Low drums.*)

AMANDA (*calling*): Laura, sweetheart! The door!

(LAURA *stares at it without moving.*)

JIM: I think we just beat the rain.

TOM: Uh-huh. (*He rings again, nervously.* JIM *whistles and fishes for a cigarette.*)

AMANDA (*very, very gaily*): Laura, that is your brother and Mr. O'Connor! Will you let them in, darling?

(LAURA *crosses toward kitchenette door.*)

LAURA (*breathlessly*): Mother — you go to the door!

(AMANDA *steps out of kitchenette and stares furiously at* LAURA. *She points imperiously at the door.*)

LAURA: Please, please!

AMANDA (*in a fierce whisper*): What is the matter with you, you silly thing?

LAURA (*desperately*): Please, you answer it, *please!*

AMANDA: I told you I wasn't going to humor you, Laura. Why have you chosen this moment to lose your mind?

LAURA: Please, please, please, you go!

AMANDA: You'll have to go to the door because I can't!

LAURA (*despairingly*): I can't either!

AMANDA: *Why?*

LAURA: I'm *sick!*

AMANDA: I'm sick, too — of your nonsense! Why can't you and your brother be normal people? Fantastic whims and behavior! (TOM *gives a long ring.*) Preposterous goings on! Can you give me one reason — (*Calls out lyrically.*) COMING! JUST ONE SECOND! — why should you be afraid to open a door? Now you answer it, Laura!

LAURA: Oh, oh, oh . . . (*She returns through the portieres. Darts to the victrola and winds it frantically and turns it on.*)

AMANDA: Laura Wingfield, you march right to that door!

LAURA: Yes — yes, Mother!

(*A faraway, scratchy rendition of "Dardanella" softens the air and gives her strength to move through it. She slips to the door and draws it cautiously open.*)

(TOM *enters with the caller,* JIM O'CONNOR.)

TOM: Laura, this is Jim. Jim, this is my sister, Laura.

JIM (*stepping inside*): I didn't know that Shakespeare had a sister!

LAURA (*retreating stiff and trembling from the door*): How — how do you do?

JIM (*heartily extending his hand*): Okay!

(LAURA *touches it hesitantly with hers.*)

JIM: Your hand's *cold*, Laura!

LAURA: Yes, well — I've been playing the victrola. . . .

JIM: Must have been playing classical music on it! You ought to play a little hot swing music to warm you up!

LAURA: Excuse me — I haven't finished playing the victrola. . . .

(*She turns awkwardly and hurries into the front room. She pauses a second by the victrola. Then catches her breath and darts through the portieres like a frightened deer.*)

JIM (*grinning*): What was the matter?

TOM: Oh — with Laura? Laura is — terribly shy.

JIM: Shy, huh? It's unusual to meet a shy girl nowadays. I don't believe you ever mentioned you had a sister.

TOM: Well, now you know. I have one. Here is the *Post Dispatch*. You want a piece of it?

JIM: Uh-huh.

TOM: What piece? The comics?

JIM: Sports! (*Glances at it.*) Ole Dizzy Dean is on his bad behavior.

TOM (*disinterest*): Yeah? (*Lights cigarette and crosses back to fire-escape door.*)

JIM: Where are *you* going?

TOM: I'm going out on the terrace.

JIM (*goes after him*): You know, Shakespeare — I'm going to sell you a bill of goods!

TOM: What goods?

JIM: A course I'm taking.

TOM: Huh?

JIM: In public speaking! You and me, we're not the warehouse type.

TOM: Thanks — that's good news. But what has public speaking got to do with it?

JIM: It fits you for — executive positions!

TOM: Awww.

JIM: I tell you it's done a helluva lot for me.

(IMAGE: EXECUTIVE AT DESK.)

TOM: In what respect?

JIM: In every! Ask yourself what is the difference between you an' me and men in the office down front? Brains? — No! — Ability? — No! Then what? Just one little thing —

TOM: What is that one little thing?

JIM: Primarily it amounts to — social poise! Being able to square up to people and hold your own on any social level!

AMANDA (off stage): Tom?

TOM: Yes, Mother?

AMANDA: Is that you and Mr. O'Connor?

TOM: Yes, Mother.

AMANDA: Well, you just make yourselves comfortable in there.

TOM: Yes, Mother.

AMANDA: Ask Mr. O'Connor if he would like to wash his hands.

JIM: Aw, no — no — thank you — I took care of that at the warehouse. Tom —

TOM: Yes?

JIM: Mr. Mendoza was speaking to me about you.

TOM: Favorably?

JIM: What do you think?

TOM: Well —

JIM: You're going to be out of a job if you don't wake up.

TOM: I am waking up —

JIM: You show no signs.

TOM: The signs are interior.

(IMAGE ON SCREEN: THE SAILING VESSEL WITH JOLLY ROGER AGAIN.)

TOM: I'm planning to change. (He leans over the rail speaking with quiet exhilaration. The incandescent marquees and signs of the first-run movie houses light his face from across the alley. He looks like a voyager.) I'm right at the point of committing myself to a future that doesn't include the warehouse and Mr. Mendoza or even a night-school course in public speaking.

JIM: What are you gassing about?

TOM: I'm tired of the movies.

JIM: Movies!

TOM: Yes, movies! Look at them — (*A wave toward the marvels of Grand Avenue.*) All of those glamorous people — having adventures — hogging it all, gobbling the whole thing up! You know what happens? People go to the *movies* instead of *moving!* Hollywood characters are supposed to have all the adventures for everybody in America, while everybody in America sits in a dark room and watches them have them! Yes, until there's a war. That's when adventure becomes available to the masses! *Everyone's* dish, not only Gable's! Then the people in the dark room come out of the dark room to have some adventures themselves — Goody, goody! — It's our turn now, to go to the South Sea Island — to make a safari — to be exotic, far-off! — But I'm not patient. I don't want to wait till then. I'm tried of the *movies* and I am *about* to *move!*

JIM (*incredulously*): Move?

TOM: Yes.

JIM: When?

TOM: Soon!

JIM: Where? Where?

(THEME THREE MUSIC SEEMS TO ANSWER THE QUESTION, WHILE TOM THINKS IT OVER. HE SEARCHES AMONG HIS POCKETS.)

TOM: I'm starting to boil inside. I know I seem dreamy, but inside — well, I'm boiling! Whenever I pick up a shoe, I shudder a little thinking how short life is and what I am doing! — Whatever that means. I know it doesn't mean shoes — except as something to wear on a traveler's feet! (*Finds paper.*) Look —

JIM: What?

TOM: I'm a member.

JIM (*reading*): The Union of Merchant Seamen.

TOM: I paid my dues this month, instead of the light bill.

JIM: You will regret it when they turn the lights off.

TOM: I won't be here.

JIM: How about your mother?

TOM: I'm like my father. The bastard son of a bastard! See how he grins? And he's been absent going on sixteen years!

JIM: You're just talking, you drip. How does your mother feel about it?

TOM: Shhh! — Here comes Mother! Mother is not acquainted with my plans!

AMANDA (*enters portieres*): Where are you all?

TOM: On the terrace, Mother.

(*They start inside. She advances to them.* TOM *is distinctly shocked at her appearance. Even* JIM *blinks a little. He is making his first contact with girlish Southern vivacity and in spite of the night-school course in public speaking is somewhat thrown off the beam by the unexpected outlay of social charm.*)

(*Certain responses are attempted by* JIM *but are swept aside by* AMANDA'S *gay laughter and chatter.* TOM *is embarrassed but after the first shock* JIM *reacts very warmly. Grins and chuckles, is altogether won over.*)

(IMAGE: AMANDA AS A GIRL.)

AMANDA (*coyly smiling, shaking her girlish ringlets*): Well, well, well, so this is Mr. O'Connor. Introductions entirely unnecessary. I've heard so much about you from my boy. I finally said to him, Tom — good gracious! — why don't you bring this paragon to supper? I'd like to meet this nice young man at the warehouse! — Instead of just hearing him sing your praises so much! I don't know why my son is so stand-offish — that's not Southern behavior! Let's sit down and — I think we could stand a little more air in here! Tom, leave the door open. I felt a nice fresh breeze a moment ago. Where has it gone to? Mmm, so warm already! And not quite summer, even. We're going to burn up when summer really gets started. However, we're having — we're having a very light supper. I think light things are better fo' this time of year. The same as light clothes are. Light clothes an' light food are what warm weather calls fo'. You know our blood gets so thick during th' winter — it takes a while fo' us to *adjust* ou'selves! — when the season changes . . . It's come so quick this year. I wasn't prepared. All of a sudden — heavens! Already summer! — I ran to the trunk an' pulled out this light dress — Terribly old! Historical almost! But feels so good — so good an' co-ol, y'know. . . .

TOM: Mother —

AMANDA: Yes, honey?

TOM: How about — supper?

AMANDA: Honey, you go ask Sister if supper is ready! You know that Sister is in full charge of supper! Tell her you hungry boys are waiting for it. (*To* JIM.) Have you met Laura?

JIM: She —

AMANDA: Let you in? Oh, good, you've met already! It's rare for a girl as sweet an' pretty as Laura to be domestic! But Laura is, thank heavens, not only pretty but also very domestic. I'm not at all. I never was a bit. I never could make a thing but angel-food cake. Well, in the South we had so many servants. Gone, gone, gone. All vestige of gracious living! Gone completely! I wasn't prepared for what the future brought me. All of my gentlemen callers were sons of planters and so of course I assumed that I would be married to one and raise my family on a large piece of land with plenty of servants. But man proposes — and woman accepts the proposal! — To vary that old, old saying a little bit — I married no planter! I married a man who worked for the telephone company! — That gallantly smiling gentleman over there! (*Points to the picture.*) A telephone man who — fell in love with long-distance! — Now he travels and I don't even know where! — But what am I going on for about my — tribulations? Tell me yours — I hope you don't have any! Tom?

TOM (*returning*): Yes, Mother?

AMANDA: Is supper nearly ready?

TOM: It looks to me like supper is on the table.

AMANDA: Let me look — (*She rises prettily and looks through portieres.*) Oh, lovely! — But where is Sister?

TOM: Laura is not feeling well and she says that she thinks she'd better not come to the table.

AMANDA: What? — Nonsense! — Laura? Oh, Laura!

LAURA (*Off stage, faintly*): Yes, Mother.

AMANDA: You really must come to the table. We won't be seated until you come to the table! Come in, Mr. O'Connor. You sit over there, and I'll — Laura? Laura Wingfield! You're keeping us waiting, honey! We can't say grace until you come to the table!

(*The back door is pushed weakly open and* LAURA *comes in. She is obviously quite faint, her lips trembling, her eyes wide and staring. She moves unsteadily toward the table.*)

(LEGEND: "TERROR!")

(*Outside a summer storm is coming abruptly. The white curtains billow inward at the windows and there is a sorrowful murmur and deep blue dusk.*)

(LAURA *suddenly stumbles — she catches at a chair with a faint moan.*)

TOM: Laura!

AMANDA: Laura! (*There is a clap of thunder.*) (LEGEND: "AH!") (*Despairingly*). Why, Laura, you *are* sick, darling! Tom, help your sister into the living room, dear! Sit in the living room, Laura —

rest on the sofa. Well! (*To the gentleman caller.*) Standing over the hot stove made her ill! — I told her that it was just too warm this evening, but — (TOM *comes back in.* LAURA *is on the sofa.*) Is Laura all right now?

TOM: Yes.

AMANDA: What *is* that? Rain? A nice cool rain has come up! (*She gives the gentleman caller a frightened look.*) I think we may — have grace — now . . . (TOM *looks at her stupidly.*) Tom, honey — you say grace!

TOM: Oh . . . "For these and all thy mercies —" (*They bow their heads,* AMANDA *stealing a nervous glance at* JIM. *In the living room* LAURA, *stretched on the sofa, clenches her hand to her lips, to hold back a shuddering sob.*) God's Holy Name be praised —

THE SCENE DIMS OUT

SCENE SEVEN

(A Souvenir.)

(*Half an hour later. Dinner is just being finished in the upstage area which is concealed by the drawn portieres.*

As the curtain rises LAURA *is still huddled upon the sofa, her feet drawn under her, her head resting on a pale blue pillow, her eyes wide and mysteriously watchful. The new floor lamp with its shade of rose-colored silk gives a soft, becoming light to her face, bringing out the fragile, unearthly prettiness which usually escapes attention. There is a steady murmur of rain, but it is slackening and stops soon after the scene begins; the air outside becomes pale and luminous as the moon breaks out.*

A moment after the curtain rises, the lights in both rooms flicker and go out.)

JIM: Hey, there, Mr. Light Bulb!

(AMANDA *laughs nervously.*)

(LEGEND: "SUSPENSION OF A PUBLIC SERVICE.")

AMANDA: Where was Moses when the lights went out? Ha-ha. Do you know the answer to that one, Mr. O'Connor?

JIM: No, Ma'am, what's the answer?

AMANDA: In the dark! (JIM *laughs appreciably.*) Everybody sit still. I'll light the candles. Isn't it lucky we have them on the table? Where's a match? Which of you gentlemen can provide a match?

JIM: Here.

AMANDA: Thank you, sir.

JIM: Not at all, Ma'am!

AMANDA: I guess the fuse has burnt out. Mr. O'Connor, can you tell a burnt-out fuse? I know I can't and Tom is a total loss when it comes to mechanics. (SOUND: GETTING UP: VOICES RECEDE A LITTLE TO KITCHENETTE.) Oh, be careful you don't bump into something. We don't want our gentleman caller to break his neck. Now wouldn't that be a fine howdy-do?

JIM: Ha-ha! Where is the fuse-box?

AMANDA: Right here next to the stove. Can you see anything?

JIM: Just a minute.

AMANDA: Isn't electricity a mysterious thing? Wasn't it Benjamin Franklin who tied a key to a kite? We live in such a mysterious universe, don't we? Some people say that science clears up all the mysteries for us. In my opinion it only creates more! Have you found it yet?

JIM: No, Ma'am. All these fuses look okay to me.

AMANDA: Tom!

TOM: Yes, Mother?

AMANDA: That light bill I gave you several days ago. The one I told you we got the notices about?

TOM: Oh. — Yeah.

(LEGEND: "HA!")

AMANDA: You didn't neglect to pay it by any chance?

TOM: Why, I —

AMANDA: Didn't! I might have known it!

JIM: Shakespeare probably wrote a poem on that light bill, Mrs. Wingfield.

AMANDA: I might have known better than to trust him with it! There's such a high price for negligence in this world!

JIM: Maybe the poem will win a ten-dollar prize.

AMANDA: We'll just have to spend the remainder of the evening in the nineteenth century, before Mr. Edison made the Mazda lamp!

JIM: Candlelight is my favorite kind of light.

AMANDA: That shows you're romantic! But that's no excuse for Tom. Well, we got through dinner. Very considerate of them to let us get through dinner before they plunged us into everlasting darkness, wasn't it, Mr. O'Connor?

JIM: Ha-ha!

AMANDA: Tom, as a penalty for your carelessness you can help me with the dishes.

JIM: Let me give you a hand.

AMANDA: Indeed you will not!

JIM: I ought to be good for something.

AMANDA: Good for something? (*Her tone is rhapsodic.*) You? Why, Mr. O'Connor, nobody, *nobody's* given me this much entertainment in years — as you have!

JIM: Aw, now, Mrs. Wingfield!

AMANDA: I'm not exaggerating, not one bit! But Sister is all by her lonesome. You go keep her company in the parlor! I'll give you this lovely old candelabrum that used to be on the altar at the church of the Heavenly Rest. It was melted a little out of shape when the church burnt down. Lightning struck it one spring. Gypsy Jones was holding a revival at the time and he intimated that the church was destroyed because the Episcopalians gave card parties.

JIM: Ha-ha.

AMANDA: And how about coaxing Sister to drink a little wine? I think it would be good for her! Can you carry both at once?

JIM: Sure. I'm Superman!

AMANDA: Now, Thomas, get into this apron!

(*The door of kitchenette swings closed on* AMANDA's *gay laughter; the flickering light approaches the portieres.*)

(LAURA *sits up nervously as he enters. Her speech at first is low and breathless from the almost intolerable strain of being alone with a stranger.*)

(THE LEGEND. "I DON'T SUPPOSE YOU REMEMBER ME AT ALL!")

(*In her first speeches in this scene, before* JIM's *warmth overcomes her paralyzing shyness,* LAURA's *voice is thin and breathless as though she has just run up a steep flight of stairs.*)

(JIM's *attitude is gently humorous. In playing this scene it should be stressed that while the incident is apparently unimportant, it is to* LAURA *the climax of her secret life.*)

JIM: Hello, there, Laura.

LAURA (*faintly*): Hello. (*She clears her throat.*)

JIM: How are you feeling now? Better?

LAURA: Yes. Yes, thank you.

JIM: This is for you. A little dandelion wine. (*He extends it toward her with extravagant gallantry.*)

LAURA: Thank you.

JIM: Drink it — but don't get drunk! (*He laughs heartily.* LAURA *takes the glass uncertainly; laughs shyly.*) Where shall I set the candles?

LAURA: Oh — oh, anywhere . . .

JIM: How about here on the floor? Any objections?

LAURA: No.

JIM: I'll spread a newspaper under to catch the drippings. I like to sit on the floor. Mind if I do?

LAURA: Oh, no.

JIM: Give me a pillow?

LAURA: What?

JIM: A pillow!

LAURA: Oh . . . (*Hands him one quickly.*)

JIM: How about you? Don't you like to sit on the floor?

LAURA: Oh — yes.

JIM: Why don't you, then?

LAURA: I — will.

JIM: Take a pillow! (LAURA *does. Sits on the other side of the candelabrum.* JIM *crosses his legs and smiles engagingly at her.*) I can't hardly see you sitting way over there.

LAURA: I can — see you.

JIM: I know, but that's not fair, I'm in the limelight. (LAURA *moves her pillow closer.*) Good! Now I can see you! Comfortable?

LAURA: Yes.

JIM: So am I. Comfortable as a cow. Will you have some gum?

LAURA: No, thank you.

JIM: I think that I will indulge, with your permission. (*Musingly unwraps it and holds it up.*) Think of the fortune made by the guy that invented the first piece of chewing gum. Amazing, huh? The Wrigley Building is one of the sights of Chicago. — I saw it summer before last when I went up to the Century of Progress. Did you take in the Century of Progress?

LAURA: No, I didn't.

JIM: Well, it was quite a wonderful exposition. What impressed me most was the Hall of Science. Gives you an idea of what the future will be in America, even more wonderful than the present time is! (*Pause. Smiling at her.*) Your brother tells me you're shy. Is that right, Laura?

LAURA: I — don't know.

JIM: I judge you to be an old-fashioned type of girl. Well, I think that's a pretty good type to be. Hope you don't think I'm being too personal — do you?

LAURA (*hastily, out of embarrassment*): I believe I *will* take a piece of gum, if you — don't mind. (*Clearing her throat.*) Mr. O'Connor, have you — kept up with your singing?

JIM: Singing? Me?

LAURA: Yes. I remember what a beautiful voice you had.

JIM: When did you hear me sing?

(VOICE OFF STAGE IN THE PAUSE.)

VOICE (*off stage*):

> O blow, ye winds, heigh-ho,
> A-roving I will go!
>   I'm off to my love
>   With a boxing glove —
> Ten thousand miles away!

JIM: You say you've heard me sing?

LAURA: Oh, yes! Yes, very often . . . I — don't suppose you remember me — at all?

JIM (*smiling doubtfully*): You know I have an idea I've seen you before. I had that idea soon as you opened the door. It seemed almost like I was about to remember your name. But the name that I started to call you — wasn't a name! And so I stopped myself before I said it.

LAURA: Wasn't it — Blue Roses?

JIM: (*springs up. Grinning*): Blue Roses! My gosh, yes — Blue Roses! That's what I had on my tongue when you opened the door! Isn't it funny what tricks your memory plays? I didn't connect you with the high school somehow or other. But that's where it was; it was high school. I didn't even know you were Shakespeare's sister! Gosh, I'm sorry.

LAURA: I didn't expect you to. You — barely knew me!

JIM: But we did have a speaking acquaintance, huh?

LAURA: Yes, we — spoke to each other.

JIM: When did you recognize me?

LAURA: Oh, right away!

JIM: Soon as I came in the door?

LAURA: When I heard your name I thought it was probably you. I knew that Tom used to know you a little in high school. So when you came in the door — Well, then I was — sure.

JIM: Why didn't you *say* something, then?

LAURA (*breathlessly*): I didn't know what to say, I was — too surprised!

JIM: For goodness' sakes! You know, this sure is funny!

LAURA: Yes! Yes, isn't it, though . . .

JIM: Didn't we have a class in something together?

LAURA: Yes, we did.

JIM: What class was that?

LAURA: It was — singing — Chorus!

JIM: Aw!

LAURA: I sat across the aisle from you in the Aud.

JIM: Aw.

LAURA: Mondays, Wednesdays and Fridays.

JIM: Now I remember — you always came in late.

LAURA: Yes, it was so hard for me, getting upstairs. I had that brace on my leg — it clumped so loud!

JIM: I never heard any clumping.

LAURA (*wincing at the recollection*): To me it sounded like — thunder!

JIM: Well, well, well, I never even noticed.

LAURA: And everybody was seated before I came in. I had to walk in front of all those people. My seat was in the back row. I had to go clumping all the way up the aisle with everyone watching!

JIM: You shouldn't have been self-conscious.

LAURA: I know, but I was. It was always such a relief when the singing started.

JIM: Aw, yes, I've placed you now! I used to call you Blue Roses. How was it that I got started calling you that?

LAURA: I was out of school a little while with pleurosis. When I came back you asked me what was the matter. I said I had pleurosis — you thought I said Blue Roses. That's what you always called me after that!

JIM: I hope you didn't mind.

LAURA: Oh, no — I liked it. You see, I wasn't acquainted with many — people. . . .

JIM: As I remember you sort of stuck by yourself.

LAURA: I — I — never had much luck at — making friends.

JIM: I don't see why you wouldn't.

LAURA: Well, I — started out badly.

JIM: You mean being —

LAURA: Yes, it sort of — stood between me —

JIM: You shouldn't have let it!

LAURA: I know, but it did, and —

JIM: You were shy with people!

LAURA: I tried not to be but never could —

JIM: Overcome it?

LAURA: No, I — I never could!

JIM: I guess being shy is something you have to work out of kind of gradually.

LAURA: (*sorrowfully*): Yes — I guess it —

JIM: Takes time!

LAURA: Yes —

JIM: People are not so dreadful when you know them. That's what you have to remember! And everybody has problems, not just you, but practically everybody has got some problems. You think of yourself as having the only problems, as being the only one who is disappointed. But just look around you and you will see lots of people as disappointed as you are. For instance, I hoped when I was going to high school that I would be further along at this time, six years later, than I am now — You remember that wonderful write-up I had in *The Torch?*

LAURA: Yes! (*She rises and crosses to table.*)

JIM: It said I was bound to succeed in anything I went into! (LAURA *returns with the annual.*) Holy Jeez! *The Torch!* (*He accepts it reverently. They smile across it with mutual wonder.* LAURA *crouches beside him and they begin to turn through it.* LAURA's *shyness is dissolving in his warmth.*)

LAURA: Here you are in *Pirates of Penzance!*

JIM (*wistfully*): I sang the baritone lead in that operetta.

LAURA (*rapidly*): So — *beautifully!*

JIM (*protesting*): Aw —

LAURA: Yes, yes — beautifully — beautifully!

JIM: You heard me?

LAURA: All three times!

JIM: No!

LAURA: Yes!

JIM: All three performances?

LAURA (*Looking down*): Yes.

JIM: Why?

LAURA: I — wanted to ask you to — autograph my program.

JIM: Why didn't you ask me to?

LAURA: You were always surrounded by your own friends so much that I never had a chance to.

JIM: You should have just —

LAURA: Well, I — thought you might think I was —

JIM: Thought I might think you was — what?

LAURA: Oh —

JIM (*with reflective relish*): I was beleaguered by females in those days.

LAURA: You were terribly popular!

JIM: Yeah —

LAURA: You had such a — friendly way —

JIM: I was spoiled in high school.

LAURA: Everybody — liked you!

JIM: Including you?

LAURA: I — yes, I — I did, too — (*She gently closes the book in her lap.*)

JIM: Well, well, well! — Give me that program, Laura. (*She hands it to him. He signs it with a flourish.*) There you are — better late than never!

LAURA: Oh, I — what a — surprise!

JIM: My signature isn't worth very much right now. But some day — maybe — it will increase in value! Being disappointed is one thing and being discouraged is something else. I am disappointed but I am not discouraged. I'm twenty-three years old. How old are you?

LAURA: I'll be twenty-four in June.

JIM: That's not old age!

LAURA: No, but —

JIM: You finished high school?

LAURA (*with difficulty*): I didn't go back.

JIM: You mean you dropped out?

LAURA: I made bad grades in my final examinations. (*She rises and replaces the book and the program. Her voice strained.*) How is — Emily Meisenbach getting along?

JIM: Oh, that kraut-head!

LAURA: Why do you call her that?

JIM: That's what she was.

LAURA: You're not still — going with her?

JIM: I never see her.

LAURA: It said in the Personal Section that you were — engaged!

JIM: I know, but I wasn't impressed by that — propaganda!

LAURA: It wasn't — the truth?

JIM: Only in Emily's optimistic opinion!

LAURA: Oh —

(LEGEND: "WHAT HAVE YOU DONE SINCE HIGH SCHOOL?")

(JIM *lights a cigarette and leans indolently back on his elbows smiling at* LAURA *with a warmth and charm which lights her inwardly with altar candles. She remains by the table and turns in her hands a piece of glass to cover her tumult.*)

JIM (*after several reflective puffs on a cigarette*): What have you done since high school? (*She seems not to hear him.*) Huh? (LAURA *looks up.*) I said what have you done since high school, Laura?

LAURA: Nothing much.

JIM: You must have been doing something these six long years.

LAURA: Yes.

JIM: Well, then, such as what?

LAURA: I took a business course at business college —

JIM: How did that work out?

LAURA: Well, not very — well — I had to drop out, it gave me — indigestion —

(JIM *laughs gently.*)

JIM: What are you doing now?

LAURA: I don't do anything — much. Oh, please don't think I sit around doing nothing! My glass collection takes up a good deal of my time. Glass is something you have to take good care of.

JIM: What did you say — about glass?

LAURA: Collection I said — I have one — (*She clears her throat and turns away again, acutely shy.*)

JIM: (*abruptly*): You know what I judge to be the trouble with you? Inferiority complex! Know what that is? That's what they call it when someone low-rates himself! I understand it because I had it, too. Although my case was not so aggravated as yours seems to be. I had it until I took up public speaking, developed my voice, and learned that I had an aptitude for science. Before that time I never thought of myself as being outstanding in any way whatsoever! Now I've never made a regular study of it, but I have a friend who says I can analyze people better than doctors that make a profession of it. I don't claim that to be necessarily true, but I can sure guess a person's psychology, Laura! (*Takes out his gum.*) Excuse me, Laura. I always take it out when the flavor is gone. I'll use this scrap of paper to wrap it in. I know how it is to get it stuck on a shoe. Yep — that's what I judge to be your principal trouble. A lack of confidence in yourself as a person. You don't have the proper amount of faith in yourself. I'm basing that fact on a number of your remarks and also on certain observations I've made. For instance that clumping you thought was so awful in high school. You say that you even dreaded to walk into class. You see what you did? You dropped out of school, you gave up an education because of a clump, which as far as I know was practically non-existent! A little physical defect is what you have. Hardly noticeable even! Magnified thousands of times by imagination! You know what my strong advice to you is? Think of yourself as *superior* in some way!

LAURA: In what way would I think?

JIM: Why, man alive, Laura! Just look about you a little. What do you see? A world full of common people! All of 'em born and all of 'em going to die! Which of them has one-tenth of your good points! Or mine! Or anyone else's, as far as that goes — Gosh! Everybody excels in some one thing. Some in many! (*Unconsciously glances at himself in the mirror.*) All you've got to do is discover in *what!* Take me, for instance. (*He adjusts his tie at the mirror.*) My interest happens to lie in electro-dynamics. I'm taking a course in radio engineering at night school, Laura, on top of a fairly responsible job at the warehouse. I'm taking that course and studying public speaking.

LAURA: Ohhhh.

JIM: Because I believe in the future of television! (*Turning back to her.*) I wish to be ready to go up right along with it. Therefore I'm planning to get in on the ground floor. In fact, I've already made the right connections and all that remains is for the industry itself to get under way! Full steam — (*His eyes are starry.*) *Knowledge* — Zzzzzp! *Money* — Zzzzzzp! — *Power!* That's the cycle democracy is built on! (*His attitude is convincingly dynamic.* LAURA *stares at him, even her shyness eclipsed in her absolute wonder. He suddenly grins.*) I guess you think I think a lot of myself!

LAURA: No — o-o-o, I —

JIM: Now how about you? Isn't there something you take more interest in than anything else?

LAURA: Well, I do — as I said — have my — glass collection —

(*A peal of girlish laughter from the kitchen.*)

JIM: I'm not right sure I know what you're talking about. What kind of glass is it?

LAURA: Little articles of it, they're ornaments mostly! Most of them are little animals made out of glass, the tiniest little animals in the world. Mother calls them a glass menagerie! Here's an example of one, if you'd like to see it! This one is one of the oldest. It's nearly thirteen. (*He stretches out his hand.*) (MUSIC: "THE GLASS MENAGERIE.") Oh, be careful — if you breathe, it breaks!

JIM: I'd better not take it. I'm pretty clumsy with things.

LAURA: Go on, I trust you with him! (*Places it in his palm.*) There now — you're holding him gently! Hold him over the light, he loves the light! You see how the light shines through him?

JIM: It sure does shine!

LAURA: I shouldn't be partial, but he is my favorite one.

JIM: What kind of a thing is this one supposed to be?

LAURA: Haven't you noticed the single horn on his forehead?

JIM: A unicorn, huh?

LAURA: Mmm-hmmm!

JIM: Unicorns, aren't they extinct in the modern world?

LAURA: I know!

JIM: Poor little fellow, he must feel sort of lonesome.

LAURA (*smiling*): Well, if he does he doesn't complain about it. He stays on a shelf with some horses that don't have horns and all of them seem to get along nicely together.

JIM: How do you know?

LAURA (*lightly*): I haven't heard any arguments among them!

JIM (*grinning*): No arguments, huh? Well, that's a pretty good sign! Where shall I set him?

LAURA: Put him on the table. They all like a change of scenery once in a while!

JIM (*stretching*): Well, well, well, well — Look how big my shadow is when I stretch!

LAURA: Oh, oh, yes — it stretches across the ceiling!

JIM (*crossing to door*): I think it's stopped raining. (*Opens fire-escape door.*) Where does the music come from?

LAURA: From the Paradise Dance Hall across the alley.

JIM: How about cutting the rug a little, Miss Wingfield?

LAURA: Oh, I —

JIM: Or is your program filled up? Let me have a look at it. (*Grasps imaginary card.*) Why, every dance is taken! I'll just have to scratch some out. (WALTZ MUSIC: "LA GOLONDRINA") Ahhh, a waltz! (*He executes some sweeping turns by himself then holds his arms toward* LAURA.)

LAURA (*breathlessly*): I — can't dance!

JIM: There you go, that inferiority stuff!

LAURA: I've never danced in my life!

JIM: Come on, try!

LAURA: Oh, but I'd step on you!

JIM: I'm not made out of glass.

LAURA: How — how — how do we start?

JIM: Just leave it to me. You hold your arms out a little.

LAURA: Like this?

JIM: A little bit higher. Right. Now don't tighten up, that's the main thing about it — relax.

LAURA (*laughing breathlessly*): It's hard not to.

JIM: Okay.

LAURA: I'm afraid you can't budge me.

JIM: What do you bet I can't? (*He swings her into motion.*)

LAURA: Goodness, yes, you can!

JIM: Let yourself go, now, Laura, just let yourself go.

LAURA: I'm —

JIM: Come on!

LAURA: Trying!

JIM: Not so stiff — Easy does it!

LAURA: I know but I'm —

JIM: Loosen th' backbone! There now, that's a lot better.

LAURA: Am I?

JIM: Lots, lots better! (*He moves her about the room in a clumsy waltz.*)

LAURA: Oh, my!

JIM: Ha-ha!

LAURA: Oh, my goodness!

JIM: Ha-ha-ha! (*They suddenly bump into the table.* JIM *stops.*) What did we hit on?

LAURA: Table.

JIM: Did something fall off it? I think —

LAURA: Yes.

JIM: I hope that it wasn't the little glass horse with the horn!

LAURA: Yes.

JIM: Aw, aw, aw. Is it broken?

LAURA: Now it is just like all the other horses.

JIM: It's lost its —

LAURA: Horn! It doesn't matter. Maybe it's a blessing in disguise.

JIM: You'll never forgive me. I bet that that was your favorite piece of glass.

LAURA: I don't have favorites much. It's no tragedy, Freckles. Glass breaks so easily. No matter how careful you are. The traffic jars the shelves and things fall off them.

JIM: Still I'm awfully sorry that I was the cause.

LAURA (*smiling*): I'll just imagine he had an operation. The horn was removed to make him feel less — freakish! (*They both laugh.*) Now he will feel more at home with the other horses, the ones that don't have horns . . .

JIM: Ha-ha, that's very funny! (*Suddenly serious.*) I'm glad to see that you have a sense of humor. You know — you're — well — very different! Surprisingly different from anyone else I know! (*His voice becomes soft and hesitant with a genuine feeling.*) Do you mind me telling you that? (LAURA *is abashed beyond speech.*) I mean it in a nice way . . . (LAURA *nods shyly, looking away.*) You make me feel sort of — I don't know how to put it! I'm usually pretty good at expressing things, but — This is something that I don't know how to say! (LAURA *touches her throat and clears it — turns the broken uni-*

corn in her hands.) (*Even softer.*) Has anyone ever told you that you were pretty? (PAUSE: MUSIC.) (LAURA *looks up slowly, with wonder, and shakes her head.*) Well, you are! In a very different way from anyone else. And all the nicer because of the difference, too. (*His voice becomes low and husky.* LAURA *turns away, nearly faint with the novelty of her emotions.*) I wish that you were my sister. I'd teach you to have some confidence in yourself. The different people are not like other people, but being different is nothing to be ashamed of. Because other people are not such wonderful people. They're one hundred times one thousand. You're one times one! They walk all over the earth. You just stay here. They're common as — weeds, but — you — well, you're — *Blue Roses!*

(IMAGE ON SCREEN: BLUE ROSES.)

(MUSIC CHANGES.)

LAURA: But blue is wrong for — roses . . .
JIM: It's right for you — You're — pretty!
LAURA: In what respect am I pretty?
JIM: In all respects — believe me! Your eyes — your hair — are pretty! Your hands are pretty! (*He catches hold of her hand.*) You think I'm making this up because I'm invited to dinner and have to be nice. Oh, I could do that! I could put on an act for you, Laura, and say lots of things without being very sincere. But this time I am. I'm talking to you sincerely. I happened to notice you had this inferiority complex that keeps you from feeling comfortable with people. Somebody needs to build your confidence up and make you proud instead of shy and turning away and — blushing — Somebody ought to — Ought to — *kiss* you, Laura! (*His hand slips slowly up her arm to her shoulder.*) (MUSIC SWELLS TUMULTUOUSLY.) (*He suddenly turns her about and kisses her on the lips. When he releases her* LAURA *sinks on the sofa with a bright, dazed look.* JIM *backs away and fishes in his pocket for a cigarette.*) (LEGEND ON SCREEN: "SOUVENIR.") Stumble-john! (*He lights the cigarette, avoiding her look. There is a peal of girlish laughter from* AMANDA *in the kitchen.* LAURA *slowly raises and opens her hand. It still contains the little broken glass animal. She looks at it with a tender, bewildered expression.*) Stumble-john! I shouldn't have done that — That was way off the beam. You don't smoke, do you? (*She looks up, smiling, not hearing the question. He sits beside her a little gingerly. She looks at him speechlessly — waiting. He coughs decorously and moves a little farther aside as he considers the situation and senses her feelings, dimly, with perturbation. Gently.*) Would you —

care for a — mint? (*She doesn't seem to hear him but her look grows brighter even.*) Peppermint — Life Saver? My pocket's a regular drug store — wherever I go . . . (*He pops a mint in his mouth. Then gulps and decides to make a clean breast of it. He speaks slowly and gingerly.*) Laura, you know, if I had a sister like you, I'd do the same thing as Tom. I'd bring out fellows and — introduce her to them. The right type of boys of a type to — appreciate her. Only — well — he made a mistake about me. Maybe I've got no call to be saying this. That may not have been the idea in having me over. But what if it was? There's nothing wrong about that. The only trouble is that in my case — I'm not in a situation to — do the right thing. I can't take down your number and say I'll phone. I can't call up next week and — ask for a date. I thought I had better explain the situation in case you misunderstood it and — hurt your feelings. . . . (*Pause. Slowly, very slowly, LAURA's look changes, her eyes returning slowly from his to the ornament in her palm.*)

(AMANDA *utters another gay laugh in the kitchen.*)

LAURA (*faintly*): You — won't — call again?

JIM: No, Laura, I can't. (*He rises from the sofa.*) As I was just explaining, I've — got strings on me, Laura, I've — been going steady! I go out all the time with a girl named Betty. She's a home-girl like you, and Catholic, and Irish, and in a great many ways we — get along fine. I met her last summer on a moonlight boat trip up the river to Alton, on the *Majestic.* Well — right away from the start it was — love! (LEGEND: LOVE!) (LAURA *sways slightly forward and grips the arm of the sofa. He fails to notice, now enrapt in his own comfortable being.*) Being in love has made a new man of me! (*Leaning stiffly forward, clutching the arm of the sofa,* LAURA *struggles visibly with her storm. But* JIM *is oblivious, she is a long way off.*) The power of love is really pretty tremendous! Love is something that — changes the whole world, Laura! (*The storm abates a little and* LAURA *leans back. He notices her again.*) It happened that Betty's aunt took sick, she got a wire and had to go to Centralia. So Tom — when he asked me to dinner — I naturally just accepted the invitation, not knowing that you — that he — that I — (*He stops awkwardly.*) Huh — I'm a stumble-john! (*He flops back on the sofa. The holy candles in the altar of* LAURA's *face have been snuffed out. There is a look of almost infinite desolation.* JIM *glances at her uneasily.*) I wish that you would — say something. (*She bites her lip which was trembling and then bravely smiles. She opens her hand again on the broken glass ornament. Then she gently takes his hand and raises it level with her own. She carefully places the unicorn in the palm of his hand, then pushes his fingers closed upon it.*) What are you — doing that for? You want me to have him? — Laura? (*She nods.*) What for?

LAURA: A — souvenir . . .

(*She rises unsteadily and crouches beside the victrola to wind it up.*)

(LEGEND ON SCREEN: "THINGS HAVE A WAY OF TURNING OUT SO BADLY!")

(OR IMAGE: "GENTLEMAN CALLER WAVING GOODBYE! — GAILY.")

(*At this moment* AMANDA *rushes brightly back in the front room. She bears a pitcher of fruit punch in an old-fashioned cut-glass pitcher and a plate of macaroons. The plate has a gold border and poppies painted on it.*)

AMANDA: Well, well, well! Isn't the air delightful after the shower? I've made you children a little liquid refreshment. (*Turns gaily to the gentleman caller.*) Jim, do you know that song about lemonade?
"Lemonade, lemonade
        Made in the shade and stirred with a spade —
        Good enough for any old maid!"

JIM (*uneasily*): Ha-ha! No — I never heard it.

AMANDA: Why, Laura! You look so serious!

JIM: We were having a serious conversation.

AMANDA: Good! Now you're better acquainted!

JIM (*uncertainly*): Ha-ha! Yes.

AMANDA: You modern young people are much more serious-minded than my generation. I was so gay as a girl!

JIM: You haven't changed, Mrs. Wingfield.

AMANDA: Tonight I'm rejuvenated! The gaiety of the occasion, Mr. O'Connor! (*She tosses her head with a peal of laughter. Spills lemonade.*) Oooo! I'm baptizing myself!

JIM: Here — let me —

AMANDA (*setting the pitcher down*): There now. I discovered we had some maraschino cherries. I dumped them in, juice and all!

JIM: You shouldn't have gone to that trouble, Mrs. Wingfield.

AMANDA: Trouble, trouble? Why it was loads of fun! Didn't you hear me cutting up in the kitchen? I bet your ears were burning! I told Tom how outdone with him I was for keeping you to himself so long a time! He should have brought you over much, much sooner! Well, now that you've found your way, I want you to be a very frequent caller! Not just occasional but all the time. Oh, we're going to have a lot of gay times together! I see them coming! Mmm, just breathe that air! So fresh, and the moon's so pretty! I'll skip back out — I know where my place is when young folks are having a — serious conversation!

JIM: Oh, don't go out, Mrs. Wingfield. The fact of the matter is I've got to be going.

AMANDA: Going, now? You're joking! Why, it's only the shank of the evening, Mr. O'Connor!

JIM: Well, you know how it is.

AMANDA: You mean you're a young workingman and have to keep workingmen's hours. We'll let you off early tonight. But only on the condition that next time you stay later. What's the best night for you? Isn't Saturday night the best night for you workingmen?

JIM: I have a couple of time-clocks to punch, Mrs. Wingfield. One at morning, another one at night!

AMANDA: My, but you *are* ambitious! You work at night, too?

JIM: No, Ma'am, not work but — Betty! (*He crosses deliberately to pick up his hat. The band at the Paradise Dance Hall goes into a tender waltz.*)

AMANDA: Betty? Betty? Who's — Betty! (*There is an ominous cracking sound in the sky.*)

JIM: Oh, just a girl. The girl I go steady with! (*He smiles charmingly. The sky falls.*)

(LEGEND: "THE SKY FALLS.")

AMANDA (*a long-drawn exhalation*): Ohhhh . . . Is it a serious romance, Mr. O'Connor?

JIM: We're going to be married the second Sunday in June.

AMANDA: Ohhhh — how nice! Tom didn't mention that you were engaged to be married.

JIM: The cat's not out of the bag at the warehouse yet. You know how they are. They call you Romeo and stuff like that. (*He stops at the oval mirror to put on his hat. He carefully shapes the brim and the crown to give a discreetly dashing effect.*) It's been a wonderful evening, Mrs. Wingfield. I guess this is what they mean by Southern hospitality.

AMANDA: It really wasn't anything at all.

JIM: I hope it don't seem like I'm rushing off. But I promised Betty I'd pick her up at the Wabash depot, an' by the time I get my jalopy down there her train'll be in. Some women are pretty upset if you keep 'em waiting.

AMANDA: Yes, I know — The tyranny of women! (*Extends her hand.*) Good-bye, Mr. O'Connor. I wish you luck — and happiness — and success! All three of them, and so does Laura! — Don't you, Laura?

LAURA: Yes!

JIM (*taking her hand*): Good-bye, Laura. I'm certainly going to treasure that souvenir. And don't you forget the good advice I gave you. (*Rises his voice to a cheery shout.*) So long, Shakespeare! Thanks again, ladies — Good night!

(*He grins and ducks jauntily out.*)

(*Still bravely grimacing,* AMANDA *closes the door on the gentleman caller. Then she turns back to the room with a puzzled expression. She and* LAURA *don't dare to face each other.* LAURA *crouches beside the victrola to wind it.*)

AMANDA (*faintly*): Things have a way of turning out so badly. I don't believe that I would play the victrola. Well, well — well — Our gentleman caller was engaged to be married! Tom!

TOM (*from back*): Yes, Mother?

AMANDA: Come in here a minute. I want to tell you something awfully funny.

TOM (*enters with macaroon and a glass of the lemonade*): Has the gentleman caller gotten away already?

AMANDA: The gentleman caller has made an early departure. What a wonderful joke you played on us!

TOM: How do you mean?

AMANDA: You didn't mention that he was engaged to be married.

TOM: Jim? Engaged?

AMANDA: That's what he just informed us.

TOM: I'll be jiggered! I didn't know about that.

AMANDA: That seems very peculiar.

TOM: What's peculiar about it?

AMANDA: Didn't you call him your best friend down at the warehouse?

TOM: He is, but how did I know?

AMANDA: It seems extremely peculiar that you wouldn't know your best friend was going to be married!

TOM: The warehouse is where I work, not where I know things about people!

AMANDA: You don't know things anywhere! You live in a dream; you manufacture illusions! (*He crosses to door.*) Where are you going?

TOM: I'm going to the movies.

AMANDA: That's right, now that you've had us make such fools of ourselves. The effort, the preparations, all the expense! The new floor lamp, the rug, the clothes for Laura! All for what? To entertain some other girl's fiancé! Go to the movies, go! Don't think about us, a mother deserted, an unmarried sister who's crippled and has no job! Don't let anything interfere with your selfish pleasure! Just go, go, go — to the movies!

TOM: All right, I will! The more you shout about my selfishness to me the quicker I'll go, and I won't go to the movies!

AMANDA: Go, then! Then go to the moon — you selfish dreamer!

(TOM *smashes his glass on the floor. He plunges out on the fire-escape, slamming the door.* LAURA *screams — cut by door.*)

(*Dance-hall music up.* TOM *goes to the rail and grips it desperately, lifting his face in the chill white moonlight penetrating the narrow abyss of the alley.*)

(LEGEND ON SCREEN: "AND SO GOOD-BYE . . .")

(TOM's *closing speech is timed with the interior pantomime. The interior scene is played as though viewed through soundproof glass.* AMANDA *appears to be making a comforting speech to* LAURA *who is huddled upon the sofa. Now that we cannot hear the mother's speech, her silliness is gone and she has dignity and tragic beauty.* LAURA's *dark hair hides her face until at the end of the speech she lifts it to smile at her mother.* AMANDA's *gestures are slow and graceful, almost dancelike, as she comforts the daughter. At the end of her speech she glances a moment at the father's picture — then withdraws through the portieres. At close of* TOM's *speech,* LAURA *blows out the candles, ending the play.*)

TOM: I didn't go to the moon, I went much further — for time is the longest distance between two places — Not long after that I was fired for writing a poem on the lid of a shoe-box. I left Saint Louis. I descended the steps of this fire-escape for a last time and followed, from then on, in my father's footsteps, attempting to find in motion what was lost in space — I traveled around a great deal. The cities swept about me like dead leaves, leaves that were brightly colored but torn away from the branches. I would have stopped, but I was pursued by something. It always came upon me unawares, taking me altogether by surprise. Perhaps it was a familiar bit of music. Perhaps it was only a piece of transparent glass — Perhaps I am walking along a street at night, in some strange city, before I have found companions. I pass the lighted window of a shop where perfume is sold. The window is filled with pieces of colored glass, tiny transparent bottles in delicate colors, like bits of a shattered rainbow. Then all at once my sister touches my shoulder. I turn around and look into her eyes . . . Oh, Laura, Laura, I tried to leave you behind me, but I am more faithful than I intended to be! I reach for a cigarette, I cross the street, I run into the movies or a bar, I buy a drink, I speak to the nearest stranger — anything that can blow your candles out! (LAURA *bends over the candles.*) — for nowadays the world is lit by lightning! Blow out your candles, Laura — and so good-bye. . . .

(*She blows the candles out.*)

THE SCENE DISSOLVES

PRODUCTION NOTES

Being a "memory play," *The Glass Menagerie* can be presented with unusual freedom of convention. Because of its considerably delicate or tenuous material, atmospheric touches and subtleties of direction play a particularly important part. Expressionism and all other unconventional techniques in drama have only one valid aim, and that is a closer approach to truth. When a play employs unconventional techniques, it is not, or certainly shouldn't be, trying to escape its responsibility of dealing with reality, or interpreting experience, but is actually or should be attempting to find a closer approach, a more penetrating and vivid expression of things as they are. The straight realistic play with its genuine frigidaire and authentic ice-cubes, its characters that speak exactly as its audience speaks, corresponds to the academic landscape and has the same virtue of a photographic likeness. Everyone should know nowadays the unimportance of the photographic in art: that truth, life, or reality is an organic thing which the poetic imagination can represent or suggest, in essence, only through transformation, through changing into other forms than those which were merely present in appearance.

These remarks are not meant as comments only on this particular play. They have to do with a conception of a new, plastic theater which must take the place of the exhausted theater of realistic conventions if the theater is to resume vitality as a part of our culture.

THE SCREEN DEVICE

There is *only one important difference between the original and acting version of the play* and that is the *omission* in the latter of the device which I tentatively included in my *original* script. This device was the use of a screen on which were projected magic-lantern slides bearing images or titles. I do not regret the omission of this device from the . . . Broadway production. The extraordinary power of Miss Taylor's performance made it suitable to have the utmost simplicity in the physical production. But I think it may be interesting to some readers to see how this device was conceived. So I am putting it into the published manuscript. These images and legends, projected from behind, were cast on a section of wall between the front-room and dining-room areas, which should be indistinguishable from the rest when not in use.

The purpose of this will probably be apparent. It is to give accent to certain values in each scene. Each scene contains a particular point (or several) which is structurally the most important. In an episodic play, such as this, the basic structure or narrative line may be obscured from the audience; the effect may seem fragmentary rather than architectural. This may not be the fault of the play so much as a lack of attention in the audience. The legend or image upon the screen will strengthen the effect of what is merely allusion in the writing and allow the primary point to be made more simply and lightly than if the entire responsibility were on the spoken lines. Aside from this structural value, I think the screen will have a definite emotional appeal, less definable but just as important. An imaginative producer or director may invent many other uses for this device than those indicated in the present script. In fact the possibilities of the device seem much larger to me than the instance of this play can possibly utilize.

THE MUSIC

Another extra-literary accent in this play is provided by the use of music. A single recurring tune, "The Glass Menagerie," is used to give emotional emphasis to suitable passages. This tune is like circus music, not when you are on the grounds or in the immediate vicinity of the parade, but when you are at some distance and very likely thinking of something else. It seems under those circumstances to continue almost interminably and it weaves in and out of your preoccupied consciousness; then it is the lightest, most delicate music in the world and perhaps the saddest. It expresses the surface vivacity of life with the underlying strain of immutable and inexpressible sorrow. When you look at a piece of delicately spun glass you think of two things: how beautiful it is and how easily it can be broken. Both of those ideas should be woven into the recurring tune, which dips in and out of the play as if it were carried on a wind that changes. It serves as a thread of connection and allusion between the narrator with his separate point in time and space and the subject of his story. Between each episode it returns as reference to the emotion, nostalgia, which is the first condition of the play. It is primarily Laura's music and therefore comes out most clearly when the play focuses upon her and the lovely fragility of glass which is her image.

THE LIGHTING

The lighting in the play is not realistic. In keeping with the atmosphere of memory, the stage is dim. Shafts of light are focused on selected areas or actors, sometimes in contradistinction to what is the apparent center. For instance, in the quarrel scene between Tom and Amanda, in which Laura has no active part, the clearest pool of light is on her figure. This is also true of the supper scene, when her silent figure on the sofa should remain the visual center. The light upon Laura should be distinct from the others, having a peculiar pristine clarity such as light used in early religious portraits of female saints or madonnas. A certain correspondence to light in religious paintings, such as El Greco's, where the figures are radiant in atmosphere that is relatively dusky, could be effectively used throughout the play. (It will also permit a more effective use of the screen.) A free, imaginative use of light can be of enormous value in giving a mobile, plastic quality to plays of a more or less static nature.

T.W.

In RETROSPECT one sees that the appearance of *The Glass Menagerie* in 1945 marked the beginning (at any rate, the public beginning) of the most exciting dramatic career in post-war America. Williams' later plays, all dealing with love's failure in a world brutalized and perverse to the extent to which it betrays love, have not fulfilled the promise of quiet loveliness that *The Glass Menagerie* gave, but his imaginative use of the stage and the poetry of his realistic dialogue have hardly diminished in power. He argues no themes, is not a master of suspense, but he makes of the theater significant space for living characters. A dimension of meaning — wistfulness, tragicomedy — is (to take an example) added to the bittersweet drama of the Wingfields by the smiling face of the footloose father, the happy doughboy, that presides over the heartbreaks of his deserted family. The aliveness is harder to analyze. The effect of Amanda's speech, "Sticks and stones may break our bones, but the expression on Mr. Garfinkel's face won't harm us!" has something to do with the way the associations of the first half clash with the prosaism of rhythm and reference of the second. The child's jingle of studied unconcern at being spiritually hurt becomes a brittle defense against poverty and humiliation and does not quite cover the cruelty that poverty and humiliation entail: Laura's having to face Mr. Garfinkel. The speech is a sad, soft woman's effort to be gay and hard. Williams' plays are full of such speeches. They ring true; people seem to talk like that. The very idiosyncrasies of image, diction, and cadence amount to lifelikeness.

Williams' success as the realist of frustration and despair may at first seem to contradict the artistic theory he propounds in the "Production Notes" to *The Glass Menagerie*. Actually, the theory explains the success. "Everyone" (he says in the notes) "should know nowadays the unimportance of the photographic in art: that truth, life, or reality is an organic thing which the poetic imagination can represent or suggest, in essence, only through transformation, through changing into other forms than those which were merely present in appearance." The crucial words here are "in essence." Williams' characters get their faintly fantastic inner glow from being "essences." They are convincingly real *because* they are more than life-like prototypes. They are defined, assume shape and three dimensions, in terms of their obsessions, their mannerisms, their associations with certain objects. Amanda is fluttering gentility, forlorn Southern belle of vivacious humor long frayed by wear, puzzled and panicked because of her daughter's failure to attract a single specimen of the breed of males by which, in Amanda's set of values, a woman's success and happiness are measured. Laura is defined by her glass menagerie. The animals both symbolize her fragility and her quaint beauty and represent the world of lovely imagination into which she escapes from typing charts and speed tests. Tom writes poems on the lids of shoe boxes, and his emblems are the movies and the pirate ship, escapist symbols of glamorous adventure. Jim O'Connor chews gum and believes in Dale Carnegie and the future of television. These are portraits not in depth but in sharp focus. The method may represent Williams' limitation; he is neither a profound nor a versatile writer. But it makes his plays.

Williams' vignettes of the frustrations of ordinary people suggest Chekhov in their reliance on mood and atmosphere and in their near-plotlessness. No one who reads Chekhov right will find anything paradoxical in the fact that Williams also scorns dramatic photography. His attitude, of course, is quite orthodox among contemporary playwrights, who all have read their Strindberg and Pirandello. But in *The Glass Menagerie* Williams is not just following fashion; the break with realism can be justified on the intrinsic grounds that the play is a "memory play." Its premise is the subjectivity of modern relativism: reality, it implies, is not what happened but how you feel about what happened. Clearly, the solidities of naturalistic staging would have crushed Tom's delicate memories of mother and sister. The transparent apartment, the easy transitions from one point of time to another, the use of light and music to throw characters, objects, and events into relief — all this is a kind of poetry of the theater and psychologically true to the play's status as a record of inner experience. At the same time, the inner experience has been objectified by the theater medium. When Tom gulps his breakfast and quarrels with his mother he is simply another character, though the stage is his own mind. His double function in the play insures esthetic distance. The play is enclosed by the narrator-director-character's memory, the Shakespeare of the shipping room.

But the memory device has not made the play rigid nor us uncomfortable. Only the literal-minded would object to Tom's staging a scene at which he was not himself present — the climactic one between Laura and Jim. By the strict logic of Tom's being the rememberer, the scene is construction by inference or, possibly, by report by either one or both of the two principals. But merely to begin speculating and explaining along these lines shows up the irrelevance of the whole issue. The play works by a higher logic than mere consistency of decorum, just as it is also too subtle to need the projection of theme-focusing "legends" and "images" on a screen wall that Williams had planned originally. It makes its meaning without such obvious and heavy-handed new stagecraft devices.

In keeping with the memory-play premise the plot is slight. Much of the play is little more than a tenuously coherent sequence of scenes of people getting on each other's nerves when their dreams and longings clash and wound. What story there is begins late: Tom, giving in to his mother's nagging, provides a gentleman caller for his sister, and for a few moments there is a promise of happy ending as the princess almost comes out of the spell that shyness and lameness have cast upon her. But the prince of the magic kiss turns out to be very much engaged, and the music from the old victrola again takes over from the Paradise Dance Hall band. In these elusive, fleeting, pastel reminiscences of moods, the only element of intrigue — the coincidence that Tom's friend turns out to be Laura's secret high-school ideal — seems almost to belong to another, more mechanical, kind of playwriting.

Whose play is *The Glass Menagerie?* Not Tom's; he is not himself the main character of his memories. And Jim is even more than Tom primarily a means to an end: a nice young man caught in an awkward situation, decent enough to sense its pathos and half-educated enough to try to remedy it with newspaper column psychology, socially deft enough to get out without too much embarrassment. The end both he and Tom serve is one they share with most of Tennessee Williams' male characters: to reveal female lovelornness and broken illusions. The play is Laura's and Amanda's, mother's and daughter's both, not the one's more than the other's, although Amanda mainly exists in terms of Laura's situation. Laura's unfitness for social life — her scene with Jim is an almost tender parody of a home date — is her distinction. She is exquisite because she is different and rare — blue roses among red, unique as a unicorn. Like her unicorn, she is fragile. She would be less precious were she more robust. The unicorn loses its horn during the dance, and Laura — dancing, kissed — becomes for a moment like other girls. But as her mother's laughter tinkles in the kitchen the gentleman caller announces his unavailability, and her and her mother's dream shatters — not on human cruelty, for Jim is not cruel, but on the blind, casual cruelty of life itself: "Things have a way of turning out so badly." There is hardly the stuff of tragedy in middle-aged girlishness and pathetic shyness due to a physical defect, in frustration by coincidence. The play is squarely in the modern democratic tradition that assumes that serious drama can be made of the sufferings of small people and which proceeds to write such plays, foregoing claims to traditional tragic magnitude of destiny and language. But *The Glass Menagerie* is something more as well. In Tom's final memory image Amanda passes from exasperating silliness to a kind of tragic dignity as the eternal mother sorrowing for her sorrowing child. The child becomes the girl of candles in a world "lit by lightning."

The Glass Menagerie fittingly introduces the sequence of Williams' plays, for it anticipates important themes and motifs and images of his later, more violent critiques of the spiritual desolation of the modern world. The notion that the weakest, the most vulnerable, are the best because their weakness and vulnerability signify sensitivity and imagination has become almost a hallmark with Williams. Fragile objects have continued to be important symbols in his plays. And the moon rising over Garfinkel's delicatessen suggests the blend of romantic daydream and sordidness, of sentimentality and comic realism, that defines his dramatic world.

Eugène Ionesco

THE LESSON

Translated by Donald M. Allen

The Characters

> THE PROFESSOR, *aged 50 to 60*
> THE YOUNG PUPIL, *aged 18*
> THE MAID, *aged 45 to 50*

SCENE: *The office of the old professor, which also serves as a dining room. To the left, a door opens onto the apartment stairs; upstage, to the right, another door opens onto a corridor of the apartment. Upstage, a little left of center, a window, not very large, with plain curtains; on the outside sill of the window are ordinary potted plants. The low buildings with red roofs of a small town can be seen in the distance. The sky is grayish-blue. On the right stands a provincial buffet. The table doubles as a desk, it stands at stage center. There are three chairs around the table, and two more stand on each side of the window. Light-colored wallpaper, some shelves with books.*

(When the curtain rises the stage is empty, and it remains so for a few moments. Then we hear the doorbell ring.)

VOICE OF THE MAID *(from the corridor)*: Yes. I'm coming.

(THE MAID comes in, after having run down the stairs. She is stout, aged 45 to 50, red-faced, and wears a peasant woman's cap. She rushes in, slamming the door to the right behind her, and dries her hands on her apron as she runs towards the door on the left. Meanwhile we hear the doorbell ring again.)

Originally published by Grove Press, Inc., in *Four Plays* by Eugène Ionesco, translated by Donald M. Allen. Copyright © 1958, by Grove Press, Inc. Reprinted by permission.

MAID: Just a moment, I'm coming.

(*She opens the door. A* YOUNG PUPIL, *aged 18, enters. She is wearing a gray student's smock, a small white collar, and carries a student's satchel under her arm.*)

MAID: Good morning, miss.
PUPIL: Good morning, madam. Is the Professor at home?
MAID: Have you come for the lesson?
PUPIL: Yes, I have.
MAID: He's expecting you. Sit down for a moment. I'll tell him you're here.
PUPIL: Thank you.

(*She seats herself near the table, facing the audience; the hall door is to her left; her back is to the other door, through which* THE MAID *hurriedly exits, calling.*)

MAID: Professor, come down please, your pupil is here.
VOICE OF THE PROFESSOR (*rather reedy*): Thank you. I'm coming . . . in just a moment . . .

(THE MAID *exits;* THE PUPIL *draws in her legs, holds her satchel on her lap, and waits demurely. She casts a glance or two around the room, at the furniture, at the ceiling too. Then she takes a notebook out of her satchel, leafs through it, and stops to look at a page for a moment as though reviewing a lesson, as though taking a last look at her homework. She seems to be a well-brought-up girl, polite, but lively, gay, dynamic; a fresh smile is on her lips. During the course of the play she progressively loses the lively rhythm of her movement and her carriage, she becomes withdrawn. From gay and smiling she becomes progressively sad and morose; from very lively at the beginning, she becomes more and more fatigued and somnolent. Towards the end of the play her face must clearly express a nervous depression; her way of speaking shows the effects of this, her tongue becomes thick, words come to her memory with difficulty and emerge from her mouth with as much difficulty; she comes to have a manner vaguely paralyzed, the beginning of aphasia. Firm and determined at the beginning, so much so as to appear to be almost aggressive, she becomes more and more passive, until she is almost a mute and inert object, seemingly inanimate in* THE PROFESSOR'S *hands, to such an extent that when he makes his final gesture, she no longer reacts. Insensible, her reflexes deadened, only her eyes in*) *an expressionless face will show inexpressible astonishment and fear. The transition from one manner to the other must of course be made imperceptibly.*

THE PROFESSOR *enters. He is a little old man with a little white beard. He wears pince-nez, a black skull cap, a long black schoolmaster's coat, trousers and shoes of black, detachable white collar, a black tie. Excessively polite, very timid, his voice deadened by his timidity, very proper, very much the teacher. He rubs his hands together constantly; occasionally a lewd gleam comes into his eyes and is quickly repressed.*

During the course of the play his timidity will disappear progressively, imperceptibly; and the lewd gleams in his eyes will become a steady devouring flame in the end. From a manner that is inoffensive at the start, THE PROFESSOR *becomes more and more sure of himself, more and more nervous, aggressive, dominating, until he is able to do as he pleases with* THE PUPIL, *who has become, in his hands, a pitiful creature. Of course, the voice of* THE PROFESSOR *must change too, from thin and reedy, to stronger and stronger, until at the end it is extremely powerful, ringing, sonorous, while* THE PUPIL'S *voice changes from the very clear and ringing tones that she has at the beginning of the play until it is almost inaudible. In these first scenes* THE PROFESSOR *might stammer very slightly.*)

PROFESSOR: Good morning, young lady. You . . . I expect that you . . . that you are the new pupil?

PUPIL (*turns quickly with a lively and self-assured manner; she gets up, goes towards* THE PROFESSOR, *and gives him her hand*): Yes, Professor. Good morning, Professor. As you see, I'm on time. I didn't want to be late.

PROFESSOR: That's fine, miss. Thank you, you didn't really need to hurry. I am very sorry to have kept you waiting . . . I was just finishing up . . . well . . . I'm sorry . . . You will excuse me, won't you? . . .

PUPIL: Oh, certainly, Professor. It doesn't matter at all, Professor.

PROFESSOR: Please excuse me . . . Did you have any trouble finding the house?

PUPIL: No . . . Not at all. I just asked the way. Everybody knows you around here.

PROFESSOR: For thirty years I've lived in this town. You've not been here for long? How do you find it?

PUPIL: It's all right. The town is attractive and even agreeable, there's a nice park, a boarding school, a bishop, nice shops and streets . . .

PROFESSOR: That's very true, young lady. And yet, I'd just as soon live somewhere else. In Paris, or at least Bordeaux.

PUPIL: Do you like Bordeaux?

PROFESSOR: I don't know. I've never seen it.

PUPIL: But you know Paris?

PROFESSOR: No, I don't know it either, young lady, but if you'll permit me, can you tell me, Paris is the capital city of . . . miss?

PUPIL (*searching her memory for a moment, then, happily guessing*): Paris is the capital city of . . . France?

PROFESSOR: Yes, young lady, bravo, that's very good, that's perfect. My congratulations. You have your French geography at your finger tips. You know your chief cities.

PUPIL: Oh! I don't know them all yet, Professor, it's not quite that easy, I have trouble learning them.

PROFESSOR: Oh! it will come . . . you mustn't give up . . . young lady . . . I beg your pardon . . . have patience . . . little by little . . . You will see, it will come in time . . . What a nice day it is today . . . or rather, not so nice . . . Oh! but then yes it is nice. In short, it's not too bad a day, that's the main thing . . . ahem . . . ahem . . . it's not raining and it's not snowing either.

PUPIL: That would be most unusual, for it's summer now.

PROFESSOR: Excuse me. miss, I was just going to say so . . . but as you will learn, one must be ready for anything.

PUPIL: I guess so, Professor.

PROFESSOR: We can't be sure of anything, young lady, in this world.

PUPIL: The snow falls in the winter. Winter is one of the four seasons. The other three are . . . uh . . . spr . . .

PROFESSOR: Yes?

PUPIL: . . . ing, and then summer . . . and . . . uh . . .

PROFESSOR: It begins like "automobile," miss.

PUPIL: Ah, yes, autumn . . .

PROFESSOR: That's right, miss. That's a good answer, that's perfect. I am convinced that you will be a good pupil. You will make real progress. You are intelligent, you seem to me to be well informed, and you've a good memory.

PUPIL: I know my seasons, don't I, Professor?

PROFESSOR: Yes, indeed, miss . . . or almost. But it will come in time. In any case, you're coming along. Soon you'll know all the seasons, with your eyes closed. Just as I do.

PUPIL: It's hard.

PROFESSOR: Oh, no. All it takes is a little effort, a little good will, miss. You will see. It will come, you may be sure of that.

PUPIL: Oh, I do hope so, Professor. I have a great thirst for knowledge. My parents also want me to get an education. They want me to specialize. They consider a little general culture, even if it is solid, is no longer enough, in these times.

PROFESSOR: Your parents, miss, are perfectly right. You must go on with your studies. Forgive me for saying so, but it is very necessary. Our contemporary life has become most complex.

PUPIL: And so very complicated too . . . My parents are fairly rich, I'm lucky. They can help me in my work, help me in my very advanced studies.

PROFESSOR: And you wish to qualify for . . . ?

PUPIL: Just as soon as possible, for the first doctor's orals. They're in three weeks' time.

PROFESSOR: You already have your high school diploma, if you'll pardon the question?

PUPIL: Yes, Professor, I have my science diploma and my arts diploma, too.

PROFESSOR: Ah, you're very far advanced, even perhaps too advanced for your age. And which doctorate do you wish to qualify for? In the physical sciences or in moral philosophy?

PUPIL: My parents are very much hoping — if you think it will be possible in such a short time — they very much hope that I can qualify for the total doctorate.

PROFESSOR: The total doctorate? . . . You have great courage, young lady, I congratulate you sincerely. We will try, miss, to do our best. In any case, you already know quite a bit, and at so young an age too.

PUPIL: Oh, Professor.

PROFESSOR: Then, if you'll permit me, pardon me, please, I do think that we ought to get to work. We have scarcely any time to lose.

PUPIL: Oh, but certainly, Professor, I want to. I beg you to.

PROFESSOR: Then, may I ask you to sit down . . . there . . . Will you permit me, miss, that is if you have no objections, to sit down opposite you?

PUPIL: Oh, of course, Professor, please do.

PROFESSOR: Thank you very much, miss. (*They sit down facing each other at the table, their profiles to the audience.*) There we are. Now have you brought your books and notebooks?

PUPIL (*taking notebooks and books out of her satchel*): Yes, Professor. Certainly, I have brought all that we'll need.

PROFESSOR: Perfect, miss. This is perfect. Now, if this doesn't bore you . . . shall we begin?

PUPIL: Yes, indeed, Professor, I am at your disposal.

PROFESSOR: At my disposal? (*A gleam comes into his eyes and is quickly extinguished; he begins to make a gesture that he suppresses at once.*) Oh, miss, it is I who am at *your* disposal. I am only your humble servant.

PUPIL: Oh, Professor . . .

PROFESSOR: If you will . . . now . . . we . . . we . . . I . . . I will begin by making a brief examination of your knowledge, past and present, so that we may chart our future course . . . Good. How is your perception of plurality?

PUPIL: It's rather vague . . . confused.

PROFESSOR: Good. We shall see.

(*He rubs his hands together.* THE MAID *enters, and this appears to irritate* THE PROFESSOR. *She goes to the buffet and looks for something, lingering.*)

PROFESSOR: Now, miss, would you like to do a little arithmetic, that is if you want to . . .

PUPIL: Oh, yes, Professor. Certainly, I ask nothing better.

PROFESSOR: It is rather a new science, a modern science, properly speaking, it is more a method than a science . . . And it is also a therapy. (*To* THE MAID:) Have you finished, Marie?

MAID: Yes, Professor, I've found the plate. I'm just going . . .

PROFESSOR: Hurry up then. Please go along to the kitchen, if you will.

MAID: Yes, Professor, I'm going. (*She starts to go out.*) Excuse me, Professor, but take care, I urge you to remain calm.

PROFESSOR: You're being ridiculous, Marie. Now, don't worry.

MAID: That's what you always say.

PROFESSOR: I will not stand for your insinuations. I know perfectly well how to comport myself. I am old enough for that.

MAID: Precisely, Professor. You will do better not to start the young lady on arithmetic. Arithmetic is tiring, exhausting.

PROFESSOR: Not at my age. And anyhow, what business is it of yours? This is my concern. And I know what I'm doing. This is not your department.

MAID: Very well, Professor. But you can't say that I didn't warn you.

PROFESSOR: Marie, I can get along without your advice.

MAID: As you wish, Professor. (*She exits.*)

PROFESSOR: Miss, I hope you'll pardon this absurd interruption . . . Excuse this woman . . . She is always afraid that I'll tire myself. She fusses over my health.

PUPIL: Oh, that's quite all right, Professor. It shows that she's very devoted. She loves you very much. Good servants are rare.

PROFESSOR: She exaggerates. Her fears are stupid. But let's return to our arithmetical knitting.

PUPIL: I'm following you, Professor.

PROFESSOR (*wittily*): Without leaving your seat!

PUPIL (*appreciating his joke*): Like you, Professor.

PROFESSOR: Good. Let us arithmetize a little now.

PUPIL: Yes, gladly, Professor.

PROFESSOR: It wouldn't be too tiresome for you to tell me . . .

PUPIL: Not at all, Professor, go on.

PROFESSOR: How much are one and one?

PUPIL: One and one make two.

PROFESSOR (*marveling at* THE PUPIL's *knowledge*): Oh, but that's very good. You appear to me to be well along in your studies. You should easily achieve the total doctorate, miss.

PUPIL: I'm so glad. Especially to have someone like you tell me this.

PROFESSOR: Let's push on: how much are two and one?

PUPIL: Three.

PROFESSOR: Three and one?

PUPIL: Four.

PROFESSOR: Four and one?

PUPIL: Five.

PROFESSOR: Five and one?

PUPIL: Six.

PROFESSOR: Six and one?

PUPIL: Seven.

PROFESSOR: Seven and one?

PUPIL: Eight.

PROFESSOR: Seven and one?

PUPIL: Eight again.

PROFESSOR: Very well answered. Seven and one?

PUPIL: Eight once more.

PROFESSOR: Perfect. Excellent. Seven and one?

PUPIL: Eight again. And sometimes nine.

PROFESSOR: Magnificent. You are magnificent. You are exquisite. I congratulate you warmly, miss. There's scarcely any point in going on. At addition you are a past master. Now, let's look at subtraction. Tell me, if you are not exhausted, how many are four minus three?

PUPIL: Four minus three? . . . Four minus three?

PROFESSOR: Yes. I mean to say: subtract three from four.

PUPIL: That makes . . . seven?

PROFESSOR: I am sorry but I'm obliged to contradict you. Four minus three does not make seven. You are confused: four plus three makes seven, four minus three does not make seven . . . This is not addition anymore, we must subtract now.

PUPIL (*trying to understand*): Yes . . . yes . . .

PROFESSOR: Four minus three makes . . . How many? . . . How many?

PUPIL: Four?

PROFESSOR: No, miss, that's not it.

PUPIL: Three, then.

PROFESSOR: Not that either, miss . . . Pardon, I'm sorry . . . I ought to say, that's not it . . . excuse me.

PUPIL: Four minus three . . . Four minus three . . . Four minus three? . . . But now doesn't that make ten?

PROFESSOR: Oh, certainly not, miss. It's not a matter of guessing, you've got to think it out. Let's try to deduce it together. Would you like to count?

PUPIL: Yes, Professor. One . . . two . . . uh . . .

PROFESSOR: You know how to count? How far can you count up to?

PUPIL: I can count to . . . to infinity.

PROFESSOR: That's not possible, miss.

PUPIL: Well then, let's say to sixteen.

PROFESSOR: That is enough. One must know one's limits. Count then, if you will, please.

PUPIL: One . . . two . . . and after two, comes three . . . then four . . .

PROFESSOR: Stop there, miss. Which number is larger? Three or four?

PUPIL: Uh . . . three or four? Which is the larger? The larger of three or four? In what sense larger?

PROFESSOR: Some numbers are smaller and others are larger. In the larger numbers there are more units than in the smaller . . .

PUPIL: Than in the small numbers?

PROFESSOR: Unless the small ones have smaller units. If they are very small, then there might be more units in the small numbers than in the large . . . if it is a question of other units . . .

PUPIL: In that case, the small numbers can be larger than the large numbers?

PROFESSOR: Let's not go into that. That would take us much too far. You must realize simply that more than numbers are involved here . . . there are also magnitudes, totals, there are groups, there are heaps, heaps of such things as plums, trucks, geese, prune pits, etc. To facilitate our work, let's merely suppose that we have only equal numbers, then the bigger numbers will be those that have the most units.

PUPIL: The one that has the most is the biggest? Ah, I understand, Professor, you are identifying quality with quantity.

PROFESSOR: That is too theoretical, miss, too theoretical. You needn't concern yourself with that. Let us take an example and reason from a definite case. Let's leave the general conclusions for later. We have the number four and the number three, and each has always the same number of units. Which number will be larger, the smaller or the larger?

PUPIL: Excuse me, Professor . . . What do you mean by the larger number? Is it the one that is not so small as the other?

PROFESSOR: That's it, miss, perfect. You have understood me very well.

PUPIL: Then, it is four.

PROFESSOR: What is four — larger or smaller than three?

PUPIL: Smaller . . . no, larger.

PROFESSOR: Excellent answer. How many units are there between three and four? . . . Or between four and three, if you prefer?

PUPIL: There aren't any units, Professor, between three and four. Four comes immediately after three; there is nothing at all between three and four!

PROFESSOR: I haven't made myself very well understood. No doubt, it is my fault. I've not been sufficiently clear.

PUPIL: No, Professor, it's my fault.

PROFESSOR: Look here. Here are three matches. And here is another one, that makes four. Now watch carefully — we have four matches. I take one away, now how many are left?

(*We don't see the matches, nor any of the objects that are mentioned.* THE PROFESSOR *gets up from the table, writes on the imaginary blackboard with an imaginary piece of chalk, etc.*)

PUPIL: Five. If three and one make four, four and one make five.

PROFESSOR: That's not it. That's not it at all. You always have a tendency to add. But one must be able to subtract too. It's not enough to integrate, you must also disintegrate. That's the way life is. That's philosophy. That's science. That's progress, civilization.

PUPIL: Yes, Professor.

PROFESSOR: Let's return to our matches. I have four of them. You see, there are really four. I take one away, and there remain only . . .

PUPIL: I don't know, Professor.

PROFESSOR: Come now, think. It's not easy, I admit. Nevertheless, you've had enough training to make the intellectual effort required to arrive at an understanding. So?

PUPIL: I can't get it, Professor. I don't know, Professor.

PROFESSOR: Let us take a simpler example. If you had two noses, and I pulled one of them off . . . how many would you have left?

PUPIL: None.

PROFESSOR: What do you mean, none?

PUPIL: Yes, it's because you haven't pulled off any, that's why I have one now. If you had pulled it off, I wouldn't have it anymore.

PROFESSOR: You've not understood my example. Suppose that you have only one ear.

PUPIL: Yes, and then?

PROFESSOR: If I gave you another one, how many would you have then?

PUPIL: Two.

PROFESSOR: Good. And if I gave you still another ear. How many would you have then?

PUPIL: Three ears.

PROFESSOR: Now, I take one away . . . and there remain . . . how many ears?

PUPIL: Two.

PROFESSOR: Good. I take away still another one, how many do you have left?

PUPIL: Two.

PROFESSOR: No. You have two, I take one away, I eat one up, then how many do you have left?

PUPIL: Two.

PROFESSOR: I eat one of them . . . one.

PUPIL: Two.

PROFESSOR: One.

PUPIL: Two.

PROFESSOR: One!

PUPIL: Two!

PROFESSOR: One!!!

PUPIL: Two!!!

PROFESSOR: One!!!

PUPIL: Two!!!

PROFESSOR: One!!!

PUPIL: Two!!!

PROFFESSOR: No. No. That's not right. The example is not . . . it's not convincing. Listen to me.

PUPIL: Yes, Professor.

PROFESSOR: You've got . . . you've got . . . you've got . . .

PUPIL: Ten fingers!

PROFESSOR: If you wish. Perfect. Good. You have then ten fingers.

PUPIL: Yes, Professor.

PROFESSOR: How many would you have if you had only five of them?

PUPIL: Ten, Professor.

PROFESSOR: That's not right!

PUPIL: But it is, Professor.

PROFESSOR: I tell you it's not!

PUPIL: You just told me that I had ten . . .

PROFESSOR: I also said, immediately afterwards, that you had five!

PUPIL: I don't have five, I've got ten!

PROFESSOR: Let's try another approach . . . for purposes of subtraction let's limit ourselves to the numbers from one to five . . . Wait now, miss, you'll soon see. I'm going to make you understand.

(THE PROFESSOR *begins to write on the imaginary blackboard. He moves it closer to* THE PUPIL, *who turns around in order to see it.*)

PROFESSOR: Look here, miss . . . (*He pretends to draw a stick on the blackboard and the number 1 below the stick; then two sticks and the number 2 below, then three sticks and the number 3 below, then four sticks with the number 4 below.*) You see . . .

PUPIL: Yes, Professor.

PROFESSOR: These are sticks, miss, sticks. This is one stick, these are two sticks, and three sticks, then four sticks, then five sticks. One stick, two sticks, three sticks, four and five sticks, these are numbers. When we count the sticks, each stick is a unit, miss . . . What have I just said?

PUPIL: "A unit, miss! What have I just said?"

PROFESSOR: Or a figure! Or a number! One, two, three, four, five, these are the elements of numeration, miss.

PUPIL (*hesitant*): Yes, Professor. The elements, figures, which are sticks, units and numbers . . .

PROFESSOR: At the same time . . . that's to say, in short — the whole of arithmetic is there.

PUPIL: Yes, Professor. Good, Professor. Thanks, Professor.

PROFESSOR: Now, count, if you will please, using these elements . . . add and subtract . . .

PUPIL (*as though trying to impress them on her memory*): Sticks are really figures and numbers are units?

PROFESSOR: Hmm . . . so to speak. And then?

PUPIL: One could subtract two units from three units, but can one subtract two twos from three threes? And two figures from four numbers? And three numbers from one unit?

PROFESSOR: No, miss.

PUPIL: Why, Professor?

PROFESSOR: Because, miss.

PUPIL: Because why, Professor? Since one is the same as the other?

PROFESSOR: That's the way it is, miss. It can't be explained. This is only comprehensible through internal mathematical reasoning. Either you have it or you don't.

PUPIL: So much the worse for me.

PROFESSOR: Listen to me, miss, if you don't achieve a profound understanding of these principles, these arithmetical archetypes, you will never be able to perform correctly the functions of a polytechnician. Still less will you be able to teach a course in a polytechnical school . . . or the primary grades. I realize that this is not easy, it is very, very abstract . . . obviously . . . but unless you can comprehend the primary elements, how do you expect to be able to calculate mentally — and this is the least of the things that even an ordinary engineer must be able to do — how much, for example, are three billion seven hundred fifty-five million nine hundred ninety-eight thousand two hundred fifty-one, multiplied by five billion one hundred sixty-two million three hundred and three thousand five hundred and eight?

PUPIL (*very quickly*): That makes nineteen quintillion three hundred ninety quadrillion two trillion eight hundred forty-four billion two hundred nineteen million one hundred sixty-four thousand five hundred and eight . . .

PROFESSOR (*astonished*): No. I don't think so. That must make nineteen quintillion three hundred ninety quadrillion two trillion eight hundred forty-four billion two hundred nineteen million one hundred sixty-four thousand five hundred and nine . . .

PUPIL: . . . No . . . five hundred and eight . . .

PROFESSOR (*more and more astonished, calculating mentally*): Yes . . . you are right . . . the result is indeed . . . (*He mumbles unintelligibly:*) . . . quintillion, quadrillion, trillion, billion, million . . . (*Clearly:*) one hundred sixty-four thousand five hundred and eight . . . (*Stupefied:*) But how did you know that, if you don't know the principles of arithmetical reasoning?

PUPIL: It's easy. Not being able to rely on my reasoning, I've memorized all the products of all possible multiplications.

PROFESSOR: That's pretty good . . . However, permit me to confess to you that that doesn't satisfy me, miss, and I do not congratulate you: in mathematics and in arithmetic especially, the thing that counts — for in arithmetic it is always necessary to count — the thing that counts is, above all, understanding . . . It is by mathematical reasoning, simultaneously inductive and deductive, that you ought to arrive at this result — as well as at any other result. Mathematics is the sworn enemy of memory, which is excellent otherwise, but disastrous, arithmetically speaking! . . . That's why I'm not happy with this . . . this won't do, not at all . . .

PUPIL (*desolated*): No, Professor.

PROFESSOR: Let's leave it for the moment. Let's go on to another exercise . . .

PUPIL: Yes, Professor.

MAID (*entering*): Hmm, hmm, Professor . . .

PROFESSOR (*who doesn't hear her*): It is unfortunate, miss, that you aren't further along in specialized mathematics . . .

MAID (*taking him by the sleeve*): Professor! Professor!

PROFESSOR: I hear that you will not be able to qualify for the total doctor's orals . . .

PUPIL: Yes, Professor, it's too bad!

PROFESSOR: Unless you . . . (*To* THE MAID:) Let me be, Marie . . . Look here, why are you bothering me? Go back to the kitchen! To your pots and pans! Go away! Go away! (*To* THE PUPIL:) We will try to prepare you at least for the partial doctorate . . .

MAID: Professor! . . . Professor! . . . (*She pulls his sleeve.*)

PROFESSOR (*to* THE MAID): Now leave me alone! Let me be! What's the meaning of this? . . . (*To* THE PUPIL:) I must therefore teach you, if you really do insist on attempting the partial doctorate . . .

PUPIL: Yes, Professor.

PROFESSOR: . . . The elements of linguistics and of comparative philology . . .

MAID: No, Professor, no! . . . You mustn't do that! . . .

PROFESSOR: Marie, you're going too far!

MAID: Professor, especially not philology, philology leads to calamity . . .

PUPIL (*astonished*): To calamity? (*Smiling, a little stupidly.*) That's hard to believe.

PROFESSOR (*to* THE MAID): That's enough now! Get out of here!

MAID: All right, Professor, all right. But you can't say that I didn't warn you! Philology leads to calamity!

PROFESSOR: I'm an adult, Marie!

PUPIL: Yes, Professor.

MAID: As you wish. (*She exits.*)

PROFESSOR: Let's continue, miss.

PUPIL: Yes, Professor.

PROFESSOR: I want you to listen now with the greatest possible attention to a lecture I have prepared . . .

PUPIL: Yes, Professor!

PROFESSOR: . . . Thanks to which, in fifteen minutes' time, you will be able to acquire the fundamental principles of the linguistic and comparative philology of the neo-Spanish languages.

PUPIL: Yes, Professor, oh good! (*She claps her hands.*)

PROFESSOR (*with authority*): Quiet! What do you mean by that?

PUPIL: I'm sorry, Professor. (*Slowly, she replaces her hands on the table.*)

PROFESSOR: Quiet! (*He gets up, walks up and down the room, his hands behind his back; from time to time he stops at stage center or near* THE PUPIL, *and underlines his words with a gesture of his hand; he orates, but without being too emotional.* THE PUPIL *follows him with her eyes, occasionally with some difficulty, for she has to turn her head far around; once or twice, not more, she turns around completely.*) And now, miss, Spanish is truly the mother tongue which gave birth to all the neo-Spanish languages, of which Spanish, Latin, Italian, our own French, Portuguese, Romanian, Sardinian or Sardanapalian, Spanish and neo-Spanish — and also, in certain of its aspects, Turkish which is otherwise very close to Greek, which is only logical, since it is a fact that Turkey is a neighbor of Greece and Greece is even closer to Turkey than you are to me — this is only one more illustration of the very important linguistic law which states that geography and philology are twin sisters . . . You may take notes, miss.

PUPIL (*in a dull voice*): Yes, Professor!

PROFESSOR: That which distinguishes the neo-Spanish languages from each other and their idioms from the other linguistic groups, such as the group of languages called Austrian and neo-Austrian or Hapsburgian, as well as the Esperanto, Helvetian, Monacan, Swiss, Andorran, Basque, and jai alai groups, and also the groups of diplomatic and technical languages — that which distinguishes them, I repeat, is their striking resemblance which makes it so hard to distinguish them from each other — I'm speaking of the neo-Spanish languages which one is able to distinguish from each other, however, only thanks to their distinctive characteristics, absolutely indisputable proofs of their extraordinary resemblance, which renders indisputable their common origin, and which, at the same time, differentiates them profoundly — through the continuation of the distinctive traits which I've just cited.

PUPIL: Oooh! Ye-e-e-s-s-s, Professor!

PROFESSOR: But let's not linger over generalities . . .

PUPIL (*regretfully, but won over*): Oh, Professor . . .

PROFESSOR: This appears to interest you. All the better, all the better.

PUPIL: Oh, yes, Professor . . .

PROFESSOR: Don't worry, miss. We will come back to it later . . . That is if we come back to it at all. Who can say?

PUPIL (*enchanted in spite of everything*): Oh, yes, Professor.

PROFESSOR: Every tongue — you must know this, miss, and remember it *until the hour of your death* . . .

PUPIL: Oh! yes, Professor, until the hour of my death . . . Yes, Professor . . .

PROFESSOR: . . . And this, too, is a fundamental principle, every tongue is at bottom nothing but language, which necessarily implies that it is composed of sounds, or . . .

PUPIL: Phonemes . . .

PROFESSOR: Just what I was going to say. Don't parade your knowledge. You'd do better to listen.

PUPIL: All right, Professor. Yes, Professor.

PROFESSOR: The sounds, miss, must be seized on the wing as they fly so that they'll not fall on deaf ears. As a result, when you set out to articulate, it is recommended, insofar as possible, that you lift up your neck and chin very high, and rise up on the tips of your toes, you see, this way . . .

PUPIL: Yes, Professor.

PROFESSOR: Keep quiet. Remain seated, don't interrupt me . . . And project the sounds very loudly with all the force of your lungs in conjunction with that of your vocal cords. Like this, look: "Butterfly," "Eureka," "Trafalgar," "Papaya." This way, the sounds become filled with a warm air that is lighter than the surrounding air so that they can fly without danger of falling on deaf ears, which are veritable voids, tombs of sonorities. If you utter several sounds at an accelerated speed, they will automatically cling to each other, constituting thus syllables, words, even sentences, that is to say groupings of various importance, purely irrational assemblages of sounds, denuded of all sense, but for that very reason the more capable of maintaining themselves without danger at a high altitude in the air. By themselves, words charged with significance will fall, weighted down by their meaning, and in the end they always collapse, fall . . .

PUPIL: . . . On deaf ears.

PROFESSOR: That's it, but don't interrupt . . . and into the worst confusion . . . Or else burst like balloons. Therefore, miss . . . (THE PUPIL *suddenly appears to be unwell.*) What's the matter?

PUPIL: I've got a toothache, Professor.

PROFESSOR: That's not important. We're not going to stop for anything so trivial. Let us go on . . .

PUPIL (*appearing to be in more and more pain*): Yes, Professor.

PROFESSOR: I draw your attention in passing to the consonants that change their nature in combinations. In this case *f* becomes *v*, *d* becomes *t*, *g* becomes *k*, and vice versa, as in these examples that I will cite for you: "That's all right," "hens and chickens," "Welsh rabbit," "lots of nothing," "not at all." *

PUPIL: I've got a toothache.

PROFESSOR: Let's continue.

PUPIL: Yes.

PROFESSOR: To resume: it takes years and years to learn to pronounce. Thanks to science, we can achieve this in a few minutes. In order to project words, sounds and all the rest, you must realize that it is necessary to pitilessly expel air from the lungs, and make it pass delicately, caressingly, over the vocal cords, which, like harps or leaves in the wind, will suddenly shake, agitate, vibrate, vibrate, vibrate or uvulate, or fricate or jostle against each other, or sibilate, sibilate, placing everything in movement, the uvula, the tongue, the palate, the teeth . . .

PUPIL: I have a toothache.

PROFESSOR: . . . And the lips . . . Finally the words come out through the nose, the mouth, the ears, the pores, drawing along with them all the organs that we have named, torn up by the roots, in a powerful, majestic flight, which is none other than what is called, improperly, the voice, whether modulated in singing or transformed into a terrible symphonic storm with a whole procession . . . of garlands of all kinds of flowers, of sonorous artifices: labials, dentals, occlusives, palatals, and others, some caressing, some bitter or violent.

PUPIL: Yes, Professor, I've got a toothache.

PROFESSOR: Let's go on, go on. As for the neo-Spanish languages, they are closely related, so closely to each other, that they can be considered as true second cousins. Moreover, they have the same mother: Spanishe, with a mute *e*. That is why it is so difficult to distinguish them from one another. That is why it is so useful to pronounce carefully, and to avoid errors in pronunciation. Pronunciation itself is worth a whole language. A bad pronunciation can get you into trouble. In this connection, permit me, parenthetically, to share a personal experience with you. (*Slight pause.* THE PROFESSOR *goes over his memories for a moment; his features mellow, but he recovers at once.*) I was very young, little more than a child. It was during my military service. I had a friend in the regiment, a vicomte,

* All to be heavily elided. [Translator's note.]

who suffered from a rather serious defect in his pronunciation: he could not pronounce the letter *f*. Instead of *f*, he said *f*. Thus, instead of "Birds of a feather flock together," he said: "Birds of a feather flock together." He pronounced filly instead of filly, Firmin instead of Firmin, French bean instead of French bean, go frig yourself instead of go frig yourself, farrago instead of farrago, fee fi fo fum instead of fee fi fo fum, Philip instead of Philip, fictory instead of fictory, February instead of February, March-April instead of March-April, Gerard de Nerval and not as is correct — Gerard de Nerval, Mirabeau instead of Mirabeau, etc., instead of etc., and thus instead of etc., instead of etc., and thus and so forth. However, he managed to conceal his fault so effectively that, thanks to the hats he wore, no one ever noticed it.

PUPIL: Yes, I've got a toothache.

PROFESSOR (*abruptly changing his tone, his voice hardening*): Let's go on. We'll first consider the points of similarity in order the better to apprehend, later on, that which distinguishes all these languages from each other. The differences can scarcely be recognized by people who are not aware of them. Thus, all the words of all the languages . . .

PUPIL: Uh, yes? . . . I've got a toothache.

PROFESSOR: Let's continue . . . are always the same, just as all the suffixes, all the prefixes, all the terminations, all the roots . . .

PUPIL: Are the roots of words square?

PROFESSOR: Square or cube. That depends.

PUPIL: I've got a toothache.

PROFESSOR: Let's go on. Thus, to give you an example which is little more than an illustration, take the word "front" . . .

PUPIL: How do you want me to take it?

PROFESSOR: However you wish, so long as you take it, but above all do not interrupt.

PUPIL: I've got a toothache.

PROFESSOR: Let's continue . . . I said: Let's continue. Take now the word "front." Have you taken it?

PUPIL: Yes, yes, I've got it. My teeth, my teeth . . .

PROFESSOR: The word "front" is the root of "frontispiece." It is also to be found in "affronted." "Ispiece" is the suffix, and "af" the prefix. They are so called because they do not change. They don't want to.

PUPIL: I've got a toothache.

PROFESSOR: Let's go on. (*Rapidly:*) These prefixes are of Spanish origin. I hope you noticed that, did you?

PUPIL: Oh, how my tooth aches.

PROFESSOR: Let's continue. You've surely also noticed that they've not changed in French. And now, young lady, nothing has succeeded in changing them in Latin either, nor in Italian, nor in Portuguese, nor in Sardanapalian, nor in Sardanapali, nor in Romanian, nor in neo-Spanish, nor in Spanish, nor even in the Oriental: front, frontispiece, affronted, always the same word, invariably with the same root, the same suffix, the same prefix, in all the languages I have named. And it is always the same for all words.

PUPIL: In all languages, these words mean the same thing? I've got a toothache.

PROFESSOR: Absolutely. Moreover, it's more a notion than a word. In any case, you have always the same signification, the same composition, the same sound structure, not only for this word, but for all conceivable words, in all languages. For one single notion is expressed by one and the same word, and its synonyms, in all countries. Forget about your teeth.

PUPIL: I've got a toothache. Yes, yes, yes.

PROFESSOR: Good, let's go on. I tell you, let's go on . . . How would you say, for example, in French: the roses of my grandmother are as yellow as my grandfather who was Asiatic?

PUPIL: My teeth ache, ache, ache.

PROFESSOR: Let's go on, let's go on, go ahead and answer, anyway.

PUPIL: In French?

PROFESSOR: In French.

PUPIL: Uhh . . . I should say in French: the roses of my grandmother are . . . ?

PROFESSOR: As yellow as my grandfather who was Asiatic . . .

PUPIL: Oh well, one would say, in French, I believe, the roses . . . of my . . . how do you say "grandmother" in French?

PROFESSOR: In French? Grandmother.

PUPIL: The roses of my grandmother are as yellow — in French, is it "yellow"?

PROFESSOR: Yes, of course!

PUPIL: Are as yellow as my grandfather when he got angry.

PROFESSOR: No . . . who was A . . .

PUPIL: . . . siatic . . . I've got a toothache.

PROFESSOR: That's it.

PUPIL: I've got a tooth . . .

PROFESSOR: Ache . . . so what . . . let's continue! And now translate the same sentence into Spanish, then into neo-Spanish . . .

PUPIL: In Spanish . . . this would be: the roses of my grandmother are as yellow as my grandfather who was Asiatic.

PROFESSOR: No. That's wrong.

PUPIL: And in neo-Spanish: the roses of my grandmother are as yellow as my grandfather who was Asiatic.

PROFESSOR: That's wrong. That's wrong. That's wrong. You have inverted it, you've confused Spanish with neo-Spanish, and neo-Spanish with Spanish . . . Oh . . . no . . . it's the other way around . . .

PUPIL: I've got a toothache. You're getting mixed up.

PROFESSOR: You're the one who is mixing me up. Pay attention and take notes. I will say the sentence to you in Spanish, then in neo-Spanish, and finally, in Latin. You will repeat after me. Pay attention, for the resemblances are great. In fact, they are identical resemblances. Listen, follow carefully . . .

PUPIL: I've got a tooth . . .

PROFESSOR: . . . Ache.

PUPIL: Let us go on . . . Ah! . . .

PROFESSOR: . . . In Spanish: the roses of my grandmother are as yellow as my grandfather who was Asiatic; in Latin: the roses of my grandmother are as yellow as my grandfather who was Asiatic. Do you detect the differences? Translate this into . . . Romanian.

PUPIL: The . . . how do you say "roses" in Romanian?

PROFESSOR: But "roses," what else?

PUPIL: It's not "roses"? Oh, how my tooth aches!

PROFESSOR: Certainly not, certainly not, since "roses" is a translation in Oriental of the French word "roses," in Spanish "roses," do you get it? In Sardanapali, "roses" . . .

PUPIL: Excuse me, Professor, but . . . Oh, my toothache! . . . I don't get the difference.

PROFESSOR: But it's so simple! So simple! It's a matter of having a certain experience, a technical experience and practice in these diverse languages, which are so diverse in spite of the fact that they present wholly identical characteristics. I'm going to try to give you a key . . .

PUPIL: Toothache . . .

PROFESSOR: That which differentiates these languages, is neither the words, which are absolutely the same, nor the structure of the sentence which is everywhere the same, nor the intonation, which does not offer any differences, nor the rhythm of the language . . . that which differentiates them . . . are you listening?

PUPIL: I've got a toothache.

PROFESSOR: Are you listening to me, young lady? Aah! We're going to lose our temper.

PUPIL: You're bothering me, Professor. I've got a toothache.

PROFESSOR: Son of a cocker spaniel! Listen to me!

PUPIL: Oh well . . . yes . . . yes . . . go on . . .

PROFESSOR: That which distinguishes them from each other, on the one hand, and from their mother, Spanishe with its mute *e*, on the other hand . . . is . . .

PUPIL (*grimacing*): Is what?

PROFESSOR: Is an intangible thing. Something intangible that one is able to perceive only after very long study, with a great deal of trouble and after the broadest experience . . .

PUPIL: Ah?

PROFESSOR: Yes, young lady. I cannot give you any rule. One must have a feeling for it, and well, that's it. But in order to have it, one must study, study, and then study some more.

PUPIL: Toothache.

PROFESSOR: All the same, there are some specific cases where words differ from one language to another . . . but we cannot base our knowledge on these cases, which are, so to speak, exceptional.

PUPIL: Oh, yes? . . . Oh, Professor, I've got a toothache.

PROFESSOR: Don't interrupt! Don't make me lose my temper! I can't answer for what I'll do. I was saying, then . . . Ah, yes, the exceptional cases, the so-called easily distinguished . . . or facilely distinguished . . . or conveniently . . . if you prefer . . . I repeat, if you prefer, for I see that you're not listening to me . . .

PUPIL: I've got a toothache.

PROFESSOR: I say then: in certain expressions in current usage, certain words differ totally from one language to another, so much so that the language employed is, in this case, considerably easier to identify. I'll give you an example: the neo-Spanish expression, famous in Madrid: "My country is the new Spain," becomes in Italian: "My country is . . .

PUPIL: The new Spain.

PROFESSOR: No! "My country is Italy." Tell me now, by simple deduction, how do you say "Italy" in French?

PUPIL: I've got a toothache.

PROFESSOR: But it's so easy: for the word "Italy," in French we have the word "France," which is an exact translation of it. My country is France. And "France" in Oriental: "Orient!" My country is the Orient. And "Orient" in Portuguese: "Portugal!" The Oriental expression: My country is the Orient is translated then in the same fashion into Portuguese: My country is Portugal! And so on . . .

PUPIL: Oh, no more, no more. My teeth . . .

PROFESSOR: Ache! ache! ache! . . . I'm going to pull them out, I will! One more example. The word "capital" — it takes on, according to the language one speaks, a different meaning. That is to say that when a Spaniard says: "I reside in the capital," the word "capital" does not mean at all the same thing that a Portuguese means when he says: "I reside in the capital." All the more so in the case of a Frenchman, a neo-Spaniard, a Romanian, a Latin, a Sardanapali . . . Whenever you hear it, young lady — young lady, I'm saying this for you! Pooh! Whenever you hear the expression: "I reside in the capital," you will immediately and easily know whether this is Spanish or Spanish, neo-Spanish, French, Oriental, Romanian, or Latin, for it is enough to know which metropolis is referred to by the person who pronounces the sentence . . . at the very moment he pronounces it . . . But these are almost the only precise examples that I can give you . . .

PUPIL: Oh dear! My teeth . . .

PROFESSOR: Silence! Or I'll bash in your skull!

PUPIL: Just try to! Skulldugger!

(*The Professor seizes her wrist and twists it.*)

PUPIL: Oww!

PROFESSOR: Keep quiet now! Not a word!

PUPIL (*whimpering*): Toothache . . .

PROFESSOR: One thing that is the most . . . how shall I say it? . . . the most paradoxical . . . yes . . . that's the word . . . the most paradoxical thing, is that a lot of people who are completely illiterate speak these different languages . . . do you understand? What did I just say?

PUPIL: . . . "Speak these different languages! What did I just say?"

PROFESSOR: You were lucky that time! . . . The common people speak a Spanish full of neo-Spanish words that they are entirely unaware of, all the while believing that they are speaking Latin . . . or they speak Latin, full of Oriental words, all the while believing that they're speaking Romanian . . . or Spanish, full of neo-Spanish, all the while believing that they're speaking Sardanapali, or Spanish . . . Do you understand?

PUPIL: Yes! yes! yes! yes! What more do you want . . . ?

PROFESSOR: No insolence, my pet, or you'll be sorry . . . (*In a rage:*) But the worst of all, young lady, is that certain people, for example, in a Latin that they suppose is Spanish, say: "Both my kidneys are of the same kidney," in addressing themselves to a Frenchman who does not know a word of Spanish, but the latter understands it as if it were his own language. For that matter he thinks it is his own language. And the Frenchman will reply, in French: "Me too, sir, mine are too," and this will be perfectly comprehensible to a Spaniard, who will feel certain that the reply is in pure Spanish and that Spanish is being spoken . . . when, in reality, it was neither Spanish nor French, but Latin in the neo-Spanish dialect . . . Sit still, young lady, don't fidget, stop tapping your feet . . .

PUPIL: I've got a toothache.

PROFESSOR: How do you account for the fact that, in speaking without knowing which language they speak, or even while each of them believes that he is speaking another, the common people understand each other at all?

PUPIL: I wonder.

PROFESSOR: It is simply one of the inexplicable curiosities of the vulgar empiricism of the common people — not to be confused with experience! — a paradox, a non-sense, one of the aberrations of human nature, it is purely and simply instinct — to put it in a nutshell . . . That's what is involved here.

PUPIL: Hah! hah!

PROFESSOR: Instead of staring at the flies while I'm going to all this trouble . . . you would do much better to try to be more attentive . . . it is not I who is going to qualify for the partial doctor's orals . . . I passed mine a long time ago . . . and I've won my total doctorate, too . . . and my supertotal diploma . . . Don't you realize that what I'm saying is for your own good?

PUPIL: Toothache!

PROFESSOR: Ill-mannered . . . It can't go on like this, it won't do, it won't do, it won't do . . .

PUPIL: I'm . . . listening . . . to you . . .

PROFESSOR: Ahah! In order to learn to distinguish all the different languages, as I've told you, there is nothing better than practice . . . Let's take them up in order. I am going to try to teach you all the translations of the word "knife."

PUPIL: Well, all right . . . if you want . . .

PROFESSOR (*calling* THE MAID): Marie! Marie! She's not there . . . Marie! Marie! . . . Marie, where are you? (*He opens the door on the right.*) Marie! . . . (*He exits.*)

(THE PUPIL *remains alone several minutes, staring into space, wearing a stupefied expression.*)

PROFESSOR (*offstage, in a shrill voice*): Marie! What are you up to? Why don't you come! When I call you, you must come! (*He reenters, followed by* THE MAID.) It is I who gives the orders, do you hear? (*He points at* THE PUPIL:) She doesn't understand anything, that girl. She doesn't understand!

MAID: Don't get into such a state, sir, you know where it'll end! You're going to go too far, you're going to go too far.

PROFESSOR: I'll be able to stop in time.

MAID: That's what you always say. I only wish I could see it.

PUPIL: I've got a toothache.

MAID: You see, it's starting, that's the symptom!

PROFESSOR: What symptom? Explain yourself? What do you mean?

PUPIL (*in a spiritless voice*): Yes, what do you mean? I've got a toothache.

MAID: The final symptom! The chief symptom!

PROFESSOR: Stupid! stupid! stupid! (THE MAID *starts to exit.*) Don't go away like that! I called you to help me find the Spanish, neo-Spanish, Portuguese, French, Oriental, Romanian, Sardanapali, Latin and Spanish knives.

MAID (*severely*): Don't ask me. (*She exits.*)

PROFESSOR (*makes a gesture as though to protest, then refrains, a little helpless. Suddenly, he remembers*): Ah! (*He goes quickly to the drawer where he finds a big knife, invisible or real according to the preference of the director. He seizes it and brandishes it happily.*) Here is one, young lady, here is a knife. It's too bad that we only have this one, but we're going to try to make it serve for all the languages, anyway! It will be enough if you will pronounce the word "knife" in all the languages, while looking at the object, very closely, fixedly, and imagining that it is in the language that you are speaking.

PUPIL: I've got a toothache.

PROFESSOR (*almost singing, chanting*): Now, say "kni," like "kni," "fe," like "fe" . . . And look, look, look at it, watch it . . .

PUPIL: What is this one in? French, Italian or Spanish?

PROFESSOR: That doesn't matter now . . . That's not your concern. Say: "kni."

PUPIL: "Kni."

PROFESSOR: . . . "fe" . . . Look. (*He brandishes the knife under* THE PUPIL'S *eyes.*)

PUPIL: "fe" . . .

PROFESSOR: Again . . . Look at it.

PUPIL: Oh, no! My God! I've had enough. And besides, I've got a toothache, my feet hurt me, I've got a headache.

PROFESSOR (*abruptly*): Knife . . . look . . . knife . . . look . . . knife . . . look . . .

PUPIL: You're giving me an earache, too. Oh, your voice! It's so piercing!

PROFESSOR: Say: knife . . . kni . . . fe . . .

PUPIL: No! My ears hurt, I hurt all over . . .

PROFESSOR: I'm going to tear them off, your ears, that's what I'm going to do to you, and then they won't hurt you anymore, my pet.

PUPIL: Oh . . . you're hurting me, oh, you're hurting me . . .

PROFESSOR: Look, come on, quickly, repeat after me: "kni" . . .

PUPIL: Oh, since you insist . . . knife . . . knife . . . (*In a lucid moment, ironically:*) Is that neo-Spanish . . . ?

PROFESSOR: If you like, yes, it's neo-Spanish, but hurry up . . . we haven't got time . . . And then, what do you mean by that insidious question? What are you up to?

PUPIL (*becoming more and more exhausted, weeping, desperate, at the same time both exasperated and in a trance*): Ah!

PROFESSOR: Repeat, watch. (*He imitates a cuckoo:*) Knife, knife . . . knife, knife . . . knife, knife . . . knife, knife . . .

PUPIL: Oh, my head . . . aches . . . (*With her hand she caressingly touches the parts of her body as she names them:*) . . . My eyes . . .

PROFESSOR (*like a cuckoo*): Knife, knife . . . knife, knife . . .

(*They are both standing.* THE PROFESSOR *still brandishes his invisible knife, nearly beside himself, as he circles around her in a sort of scalp dance, but it is important that this not be exaggerated and that his dance steps be only suggested.* THE PUPIL *stands facing the audience, then recoils in the direction of the window, sickly, languid, victimized.*)

PROFESSOR: Repeat, repeat: knife . . . knife . . . knife . . .

PUPIL: I've got a pain . . . my throat, neck . . . oh, my shoulders . . . my breast . . . knife . . .

PROFESSOR: Knife . . . knife . . . knife . . .

PUPIL: My hips . . . knife . . . my thighs . . . kni . . .

PROFESSOR: Pronounce it carefully . . . knife . . . knife . . .

PUPIL: Knife . . . my throat . . .

PROFESSOR: Knife . . . knife . . .

PUPIL: Knife . . . my shoulders . . . my arms, my breast, my hips . . . knife . . . knife . . .

PROFESSOR: That's right . . . Now, you're pronouncing it well . . .

PUPIL: Knife . . . my breast . . . my stomach . . .

PROFESSOR (*changing his voice*): Pay attention . . . don't break my window . . . the knife kills . . .

PUPIL (*in a weak voice*): Yes, yes . . . the knife kills?

PROFESSOR (*striking* THE PUPIL *with a very spectacular blow of the knife*): Aaah! That'll teach you!

(THE PUPIL *also cries "Aaah!" then falls, flopping in an immodest position onto a chair which, as though by chance, is near the window. The murderer and his victim shout "Aaah!" at the same moment. After the first blow of the knife,* THE PUPIL *flops onto the chair, her legs spread wide and hanging over both sides of the chair.* THE PROFESSOR *remains standing in front of her, his back to the audience. After the first blow, he strikes her dead with a second slash of the knife, from bottom to top. After that blow a noticeable convulsion shakes his whole body.*)

PROFESSOR (*winded, mumbling*): Bitch . . . Oh, that's good, that does me good . . . Ah! Ah! I'm exhausted . . . I can scarcely breathe . . . Aah! (*He breathes with difficulty; he falls — fortunately a chair is there; he mops his brow, mumbles some incomprehensible words; his breathing becomes normal. He gets up, looks at the knife in his hand, looks at the young girl, then as though he were waking up, in a panic:*) What have I done! What's going to happen to me now! What's going to happen! Oh! dear! Oh dear, I'm in trouble! Young lady, young lady, get up! (*He is agitated, still holding onto the invisible knife, which he doesn't know what to do with.*) Come now, young lady, the lesson is over . . . you may go . . . you can pay another time . . . Oh! she is dead . . . dea-ead . . . And by my knife . . . She is dea-ead . . . It's terrible. (*He calls* THE MAID:) Marie! Marie! My good Marie, come here! Ah! ah! (*The door on the right opens a little and* THE MAID *appears.*) No . . . don't come in . . . I made a mistake . . . I don't need you, Marie . . . I don't need you anymore . . . do you understand? . . .

(THE MAID *enters wearing a stern expression, without saying a word. She sees the corpse.*)

PROFESSOR (*in a voice less and less assured*): I don't need you, Marie . . .

MAID (*sarcastic*): Then, you're satisfied with your pupil, she's profited by your lesson?

PROFESSOR (*holding the knife behind his back*): Yes, the lesson is finished . . . but . . . she . . . she's still there . . . she doesn't want to leave . . .

MAID (*very harshly*): Is that a fact? . . .

PROFESSOR (*trembling*): It wasn't I . . . it wasn't I . . . Marie . . . No . . . I assure you . . . it wasn't I, my little Marie . . .

MAID: And who was it? Who was it then? Me?

PROFESSOR: I don't know . . . maybe . . .

MAID: Or the cat?

PROFESSOR: That's possible . . . I don't know . . .

MAID: And today makes it the fortieth time! . . . And every day it's the same thing! Every day! You should be ashamed, at your age . . . and you're going to make yourself sick! You won't have any pupils left. That will serve you right.

PROFESSOR (*irritated*): It wasn't my fault! She didn't want to learn! She was disobedient! She was a bad pupil! She didn't want to learn!

MAID: Liar! . . .

PROFESSOR (*craftily approaching* THE MAID, *holding the knife behind his back*): It's none of your business! (*He tries to strike her with a blow of the knife;* THE MAID *seizes his wrist in mid-gesture and twists it;* THE PROFESSOR *lets the knife fall to the floor*): . . . I'm sorry!

MAID (*gives him two loud, strong slaps;* THE PROFESSOR *falls onto the floor, on his prat; he sobs*): Little murderer! bastard! You're disgusting! You wanted to do that to me? I'm not one of your pupils, not me! (*She pulls him up by the collar, picks up his skullcap and puts it on his head; he's afraid she'll slap him again and holds his arm up to protect his face, like a child.*) Put the knife back where it belongs, go on! (THE PROFESSOR *goes and puts it back in the drawer of the buffet, then comes back to her.*) Now didn't I warn you, just a little while ago: arithmetic leads to philology, and philology leads to crime . . .

PROFESSOR: You said "to calamity"!

MAID: It's the same thing.

PROFESSOR: I didn't understand you. I thought that "calamity" was a city and that you meant that philology leads to the city of Calamity . . .

MAID: Liar! Old fox! An intellectual like you is not going to make a mistake in the meanings of words. Don't try to pull the wool over my eyes.

PROFESSOR (*sobbing*): I didn't kill her on purpose!

MAID: Are you sorry at least?

PROFESSOR: Oh, yes, Marie, I swear it to you!

MAID: I can't help feeling sorry for you! Ah! you're a good boy in spite of everything! I'll try to fix this. But don't start it again . . . It could give you a heart attack . . .

PROFESSOR: Yes, Marie! What are we going to do, now?

MAID: We're going to bury her . . . along with the thirty-nine others . . . that will make forty coffins . . . I'll call the undertakers and my lover, Father Auguste . . . I'll order the wreaths . . .

PROFESSOR: Yes, Marie, thank you very much.

MAID: Well, that's that. And perhaps it won't be necessary to call Auguste, since you yourself are something of a priest at times, if one can believe the gossip.

PROFESSOR: In any case, don't spend too much on the wreaths. She didn't pay for her lesson.

MAID: Don't worry . . . The least you can do is cover her up with her smock, she's not decent that way. And then we'll carry her out . . .

PROFESSOR: Yes, Marie, yes. (*He covers up the body.*) There's a chance that we'll get pinched . . . with forty coffins . . . Don't you think . . . people will be surprised . . . Suppose they ask us what's inside them?

MAID: Don't worry so much. We'll say that they're empty. And besides, people won't ask questions, they're used to it.

PROFESSOR: Even so . . .

MAID (*she takes out an armband with an insignia, perhaps the Nazi swastika*): Wait, if you're afraid, wear this, then you won't have anything more to be afraid of. (*She puts the armband around his arm.*) . . . That's good politics.

PROFESSOR: Thanks, my little Marie. With this, I won't need to worry . . . You're a good girl, Marie . . . very loyal . . .

MAID: That's enough. Come on, sir. Are you all right?

PROFESSOR: Yes, my little Marie. (THE MAID *and* THE PROFESSOR *take the body of the young girl, one by the shoulders, the other by the legs, and move towards the door on the right.*) Be careful. We don't want to hurt her. (*They exit.*)

(*The stage remains empty for several moments. We hear the doorbell ring at the left.*)

VOICE OF THE MAID: Just a moment, I'm coming!

(*She appears as she was at the beginning of the play, and goes towards the door. The doorbell rings again.*)

MAID (*aside*): She's certainly in a hurry, this one! (*Aloud:*) Just a moment! (*She goes to the door on the left, and opens it.*) Good morning, miss! You are the new pupil? You have come for the lesson? The Professor is expecting you. I'll go tell him that you've come. He'll be right down. Come in, miss, come in!

⌒⌒⌒(THE LESSON, first performed in Paris in 1951, is the product of an age that can dispassionately contemplate its own wounds, derive a grim pleasure from philosophical nihilism, and produce literature that honestly seeks neither to please nor to instruct. Instead, it reflects reality in a shattered mirror — as bizarre and macabre and incoherent but sharply etched scenes of infinite suggestiveness — "open" parables that puzzle, tease, and elude interpretation. If one insists — it is hard to say how well or ill advised such an effort is — on relating a play like *The Lesson* to other areas of the contemporary intellectual scene, existentialism comes to mind, with its godless universe and its doctrine that man is what man does. But neither philosophy nor psychology nor any other rational discipline is likely to explain *The Lesson*. By the same token, one can have no argument with those who find its absurdities uninteresting or even offensive, or with the naive sophisticates who "refuse to be taken in" by something that is "obviously meant as a joke." But whether callous or gullible, one *can* try to record one's own unmistakable sense of dramatic power in the play.

It begins normally enough. Its stage picture and its opening action — the drab, professorial dining room-office, the small town glimpsed beyond the potted plants in the window, the red-faced maid rushing to answer the door — are the paraphernalia of straightforward, humdrum naturalism. The long stage direction near the beginning anticipates queerer developments to come as well as a patterned action,* but the Professor's and the Pupil's opening speeches seem to promise nothing more extraordinary than a satirical farce on timid pedantry and brash young ignorance. The satire grows more hilarious as the arithmetic lesson proceeds, but there is also Marie's ominous interruption, and we begin to be aware of speeches that touch on more than just the idiocies of the learning process:

PROFESSOR: . . . If they are very small, then there might be more units in the small numbers than in the large . . . if it is a question of other units . . .

PUPIL: In that case, the small numbers can be larger than the large numbers?

Still, what seems to be happening is that the lesson is turning into a clash of impeccable mathematical theory and common sense. The farce comes to a climax when the girl, earlier lavishly complimented

---

* Since the stage direction is not available to the theater audience, *reading The Lesson* — like reading a play by Shaw — clearly differs from *seeing* it in a way fundamentally different in kind from that in which reading and seeing any play can be said to differ. In the stage direction, Ionesco, as it were, tells all, and if he does not eliminate suspense, he substitutes one kind of suspense for another: we wonder not what will happen but how and why it happens and what the Professor's "final gesture" will be.

for knowing the name of the capital of France, suddenly proves to possess a brain like an electric computer in answering the Professor's preposterous problem in multiplication and the Professor sullenly rejects the answer — not because it is not correct (it is), but because it has not been arrived at by the proper method. And yet, there is an element of reasonableness in the Professor's attitude: the girl's triumph is due to rote learning, not to grasp of mathematics. On the other hand (the ironies flicker in all directions), *what* rote learning!

But we are also becoming aware of the two opposite movements announced in the long stage direction, and as the movements intersect and draw, respectively, toward frenzy and trance, we find it increasingly difficult to reduce their significance to a satirical allegory of how old teacher saps and absorbs young pupil's vitality until learning conquers and kills life. The double movement gives the play structure, but the allegory cannot contain its ending. It is both too ritualistic and too raw to be simply satirical. Satire does not account for the obvious sexual implications of the murder scene or for Marie's role as habitual accomplice. It does not answer the questions about the plot. What about the other thirty-nine victims? Where are the coffins? Why isn't the town alarmed, why are no inquiries made? Why the cyclical nature of the action? What about the nice young girl, all vivacity and thirst for knowledge, who is about to become still another victim of the total doctorate? For that matter, is there a sense in which the dead Pupil may be said to have reached her ambition?

Answers are not forthcoming. We may refuse to take the play seriously — but if we do, we have not come to terms with it; we have only refused to consider it worth bothering about. But the play remains — with the sharp solidity of its setting, the unambiguity of its events, its penetration of the rationalities with which we invest our experience of ourselves and our world. Even a prank — particularly a prank — has the power to embody Ionesco's conviction that "comic and tragic are merely two aspects of the same situation," that "there are no alternatives: if man is not tragic, he is ridiculous and painful, 'comic,' in fact" and that "by revealing his absurdity one can achieve a sort of tragedy."

APPENDIX

Biographical Notes and Suggested Reading

HENRIK IBSEN (1828-1906) was born in Skien, a small town in southern Norway. His father, a merchant, went bankrupt when the boy was eight. At sixteen he was apprenticed to a druggist. Two years later a maid in the household gave birth to his illegitimate child. These early events may have conditioned his later reticence and excessive outer propriety. Both financial ruin and bastardy are recurrent motifs in his plays. He wrote his first play in 1848, under the influence of the liberalism of the February revolution of that year. In the 1850's and early 1860's he held positions as salaried playwright and director at theaters in Bergen and Christiania (Oslo). Norway's failure to help Denmark in her war against Prussia in 1864 disillusioned him deeply (though he did not himself volunteer), and he and his wife and son left Norway for twenty-seven years of self-imposed exile in Italy and Germany. He died in Christiania after several years' illness.

Ibsen's iconoclasm, naturalistic symbolism, and novel and influential dramaturgy have earned him the label "father of modern drama." His canon, however, is more varied than the label suggests. His early plays dealt with saga and peasant subject matter. His first popular success was the philosophical dramatic poem *Brand* (1866), followed by the complementary, antithetical *Peer Gynt* (1867). His third period comprises the so-called social problem plays on which his world fame largely rests. The main ones are: *A Doll's House* (1879), *Ghosts* (1881), *An Enemy of the People* (1882), *Rosmersholm* (1886), and *Hedda Gabler* (1890), though the last two are only incidentally problem plays at all. His last plays are heavily symbolic and interiorized and partly of autobiographical import, such as *The Master Builder* (1892) and *When We Dead Awaken* (1899).

Suggested Reading

Downs, Brian W., A *Study of Six Plays by Ibsen*. Cambridge: Cambridge University Press, 1950.

McFarlane, James W., *Ibsen and the Temper of Norwegian Literature*. London: Oxford University Press, 1960.

Northam, John, *Ibsen's Dramatic Method*. London: Faber and Faber, 1953.

Tennant, P., *Ibsen's Dramatic Technique*. Cambridge: Bowes & Bowes, 1948.

Weigand, Hermann, *The Modern Ibsen*. New York: E. P. Dutton & Co., 1960 (first published in 1925).

(GEORGE) BERNARD SHAW (1856-1950) was born in Dublin of impoverished English parents. His formal education ended when he was fifteen. In 1876 he arrived in London, entered journalism, wrote five unsuccessful novels, and joined the Fabian Society, a group of radical socialist intellectuals. His political views, however, never became the orthodoxy of any ideological camp. Between 1886 and 1898 he wrote art, music, and drama criticism for leading periodicals. *The Quintessence of Ibsenism*, which he published in 1891, is enthusiastic propaganda for Ibsen as a playwright of liberal ideas, but it says perhaps more about Shaw himself than about Ibsen. The long series of his plays began in 1891 with *Widowers' Houses*, a play of social criticism, and ended only in 1947. Shaw's prefaces to his plays, in impeccably lucid, incisive prose, are often as good clues to his thought as the plays themselves. In 1905 he bought the house at Ayot St. Lawrence in Hertfordshire in which he lived till his death. He received the Nobel Prize in 1925. He was a life-long vegetarian and teetotaller, was against vivisection and vaccination, and willed the bulk of his fortune to a project for reforming English spelling.

Shaw's plays are drama of dialectics rather than of character — brilliant and caustic exposures of sham and nonsense, more serious than their flamboyant wit immediately suggests. The following are among his best and most representative: *Candida* (1894), *Caesar and Cleopatra* (1898), *Man and Superman* (1903), *Major Barbara* (1905), *The Doctor's Dilemma* (1906), *Pygmalion* (1912), *Heartbreak House* (1916), *Back to Methuselah* (1921), *Saint Joan* (1923).

Suggested Reading

Bentley, Eric, *Bernard Shaw*, rev. ed. New York: New Directions, 1957.

———, *The Playwright as Thinker*. New York: Meridian Books, 1957.

Henderson, Archibald, *George Bernard Shaw: Man of the Century*. New York: Appleton-Century-Crofts, 1956.

Kronenberger, Louis, ed., *George Bernard Shaw: A Critical Survey*. Cleveland: World Publishing Company, 1953.

Nethercot, Arthur H., *Men and Supermen*. Cambridge, Mass.: Harvard University Press, 1954.

Shaw, Bernard, *Shaw on Theatre*, ed. E. J. West. New York: Hill and Wang, 1958.

Anton Pavlovich Chekhov (1860-1904) was born in Taganrog on the Sea of Azov in southern Russia, the grandson of a serf. A harsh boyhood was followed by medical studies in Moscow. He received his degree in 1884, but he never practiced medicine regularly and during his last years not at all. While he was still a student he began to write — and to get published — small, comical sketches. In 1886 a successful collection of short stories, somewhat in the manner of de Maupassant, brought him acceptance in leading literary circles. His early plays failed on the stage, but in 1898 *The Seagull*, which had been a humiliating fiasco in St. Petersburg two years earlier, was a brilliant success in the newly opened Moscow Art Theater, under the direction of Konstantin Stanislavsky. *The Seagull* established Chekhov's reputation as playwright, the success of the "Stanislavsky method" of naturalistic acting, and the finances of the new theater. During the few remaining years of his life, Chekhov, already desperately ill with tuberculosis, spent his winters in Yalta on the Crimea. He wrote three additional plays for the Moscow Art Theater: *Uncle Vanya* (1899), *Three Sisters* (1901), and his greatest success, *The Cherry Orchard* (1904). In 1901 he married one of the Theater's leading actresses. He died at a sanatorium in southern Germany.

Suggested Reading

Magarshack, David, *Chekhov the Dramatist*. New York: Hill and Wang, 1960.

Toumanova, Princess Nina Andronikova, *Anton Chekhov: The Voice of Twilight Russia*. New York: Columbia University Press, 1960.

August Strindberg (1849-1912) was born in Stockholm, the son of a stolid, middle-class father and a working-class mother. The couple had children together before their marriage, but the future playwright was born in wedlock. Strindberg unsuccessfully tried for an advanced university degree and a career in acting. The eight years of his young manhood when he worked as a librarian, became a scholar of some note, and wrote his earliest plays and tales, may have been the happiest in his restless, tragic life. In 1877 he married for the first time. Two years later he made a name for himself with the satiric, realistic novel *The Red Room* and left Sweden to live by his pen abroad. In 1884 he was acquitted of a charge of blasphemy, but the affair strained his hypersensitive nerves. There followed a period of frenetic literary activity, partly in Sweden, partly on the Continent. His autobiographical writing from the 1880's and the naturalistic plays *The Father* (1887), *Miss Julie* (1888), and *Creditors* (1888) reflect the growth of the mysogyny which contributed to the dissolution of his marriage in 1891. Through most of the 1890's Strindberg suffered from a persecution complex attended by hallucinations, though authorities disagree as to whether he ever actually became what should be called insane. Between voluntary stays at mental hospitals he studied and wrote on botany and chemistry — but also alchemy, occultism, and demonology. A second marriage failed in 1894. The autobiographical narrative *Inferno* (1897) records the critical years of his psychopathy. From 1902 till his death Strindberg lived in Stockholm, indubitably sane though hardly serene. His third marriage ended in divorce in 1904, but his amazing literary creativity never again left him: novels, tales, short stories, historical writings, philological, anthropological, and political essays, and plays, poured from his pen. Among the last were religious dramas: *To Damascus* (1898); *Dance of Death* (1902), another play about married horrors; *The Dream Play* (1901), an early example of expressionism; a long series of plays with subjects from Swedish history; and, finally, a group of esoteric, often fantastic "chamber plays," performed at the Intimate Theater, Strindberg's own stage, managed by a younger friend. *The Storm* and *The Pelican* (like *The Ghost Sonata* written in 1907) are the most significant of these last plays.

Suggested Reading

Bentley, Eric, *The Playwright as Thinker*. New York: Meridian Books, 1957.

Dahlström, C. E. W. L., *Strindberg's Dramatic Expressionism*. Ann Arbor, Mich.: University of Michigan Press, 1930.

Mortensen, Brita M. E., and Brian W. Downs, *Strindberg: An Introduction to His Life and Work*. Cambridge: Cambridge University Press, 1949.

Sprigge, Elizabeth, *The Strange Life of August Strindberg*. London: Hamish Hamilton, 1949.

LUIGI PIRANDELLO (1867-1936) was the son of a rich owner of sulphur mines in the town of Agrigento on the south coast of Sicily. After studies at the University of Rome he went on to take his doctorate at the University of Bonn, Germany, on a philological study of his home dialect. His early literary production — composed for pleasure, not to make a living — included poems and prose fiction, mostly short stories. By family arrangement he married the daughter of his father's partner. Both families lost their money when the mines were flooded in 1904, and Pirandello was forced to make a living as instructor at a woman's teacher's college in Rome. Soon after, his wife's mind gave way. Too poor to put her in a private institution and too conscientious to put her in a public one, Pirandello endured life with a lunatic till her death in 1918. By then he had attained fame as playwright and could give up teaching. By the early twenties he was an international celebrity. In 1925 he founded his own art theater, which successfully toured some of the world's great stages. Pirandello's brooding, restless, cerebral inquiries into the nature of reality seem quite alien to the muscular aggressiveness of Mussolini's Italy, but Pirandello himself was not hostile to Fascism. "I am a Fascist because I am an Italian," he said once in an interview in New York. His acceptance of the Nobel Prize in Literature in 1934 was officially approved.

It does not seem unreasonable to assume a connection between his domestic tragedy and the philosophical nihilism of his plays. To the unhappy, the belief that all experience is illusory is not a remote solace. The titles of several of his best known plays suggest his paradoxical relativism: *It Is So! (If You Think So)* (1917), *Each In His Own Way* (1924), *As You Desire Me* and *Tonight We Improvise* (both 1930). Another famous and characteristic play is *Henry IV* (1922), along with *Six Characters* generally considered his best work.

Suggested Reading

Bentley, Eric, *In Search of Theater*. New York: Alfred A. Knopf, 1953.

————, *The Playwright as Thinker*. New York: Meridian Books, 1957.

Fergusson, Francis, *The Idea of a Theater*. Garden City, N.Y.: Doubleday & Company (Anchor Book), 1949.

Krutch, Joseph Wood, *"Modernism" in Modern Drama*. Ithaca, N.Y.: Cornell University Press, 1953.

MacClintock, Lander, *The Age of Pirandello*. Bloomington, Ind.: Indiana University Press, 1951.

Nelson, Robert J., *Play within a Play*. New Haven, Conn.: Yale University Press, 1958.

Starkie, Walter, *Luigi Pirandello: 1867-1936*, 2nd ed. New York: E. P. Dutton & Co., 1937.

Vittorini, Domenico, *The Drama of Luigi Pirandello*. Philadelphia: University of Pennsylvania Press, 1935.

WILLIAM BUTLER YEATS (1865-1939) was the son of a distinguished Dublin portrait painter, and he, too, for a time practiced painting. His childhood was divided between London and his mother's home in Sligo county in western Ireland, a country that influenced motif and imagery in his poetry. His early verse was in the contemporary manner of the pre-Raphaelites and their successors — sensuously romantic, rich, a little soft and vague. In 1899 he was one of the founders of the Irish Literary Theater and was for many years its leader. He dreamed of making it a center for the revival of a mystical, poetic theater, but though several of his own plays were performed there and he brought to the theater John Millington Synge, perhaps the greatest dramatic talent of the Irish literary renaissance, and though the Abbey Theater (as it came to be known) became one of modern Europe's great stages, Yeats never realized his dream of a poetic Irish theater. In the 1920's and '30's Yeats's poems gained in depth and in taut, sparse strength, but his growing reliance on a semi-private stock of metaphors and symbols derived from his reading in mysticism and occultism often made them difficult. For some years after 1922 he was a member of the Senate of the newly independent Irish republic, though many aspects of politics in a modern democracy were distasteful to his aristocratic, tradition-oriented, non-pragmatic loyalties. In 1923 he received the Nobel Prize.

Yeats's early, most popular plays are based on themes from Irish folklore: *The Countess Kathleen* (1889-1892), *The Land of Heart's Desire* (1894), *Cathleen ni Houlihan* (1902), *The Hour Glass* (1902). *At the Hawk's Well* (1914) and *The Death of Cuchulain* (1938-1939) are early and late examples of his later, terse and emblematic manner.

Suggested Reading

Ellis-Fermor, Una, *The Irish Dramatic Movement*. London: Methuen & Co., 1954.

Ellmann, Richard, *Yeats, the Man and the Masks*. New York: The Macmillan Co., 1948.

Wilson, F. A. C., *W. B. Yeats and Tradition*. London: Victor Gollancz, 1958.

BERTOLT BRECHT (1898-1956) was born in the south German town of Augsburg in Bavaria. He studied medicine, served in World War I, began writing plays and in the 1920's was part of a group of avant-garde and leftist poets, playwrights, actors, and artists in Berlin. He fled Germany when Hitler came to power, lived in Denmark during the late '30's and in California from 1941 to 1947. For a while he worked in Hollywood. For two years after his return to Europe after the war he wrote and produced plays for the National Theater in Zürich, Switzerland. He moved to East Berlin in 1949, where he worked with his own ensemble till his death, staunchly supporting the Communist régime. Some of his anti-war poems are modern classics in Germany, but abroad he is most famous for his dramas: *The Three-Penny Opera* (1928) with music by Kurt Weill (a modern version of the early eighteenth century *Beggar's Opera* by John Gay); *The Private Life of the Master Race* (1937), an anti-Nazi play; *Mother Courage* (1941); *Galileo* (1943, 1947); *The Caucasian Chalk Circle* (1948). Brecht has been influential not only as playwright and director but also as theorist of the theater.

Suggested Reading

Bentley, Eric, *The Playwright as Thinker*. New York: Meridian Books, 1957.

Esslin, Martin, *Brecht, the Man and His Work*. Garden City, N.Y.: Doubleday & Company, 1960.

Willett, John, *The Theatre of Bertolt Brecht*. London: Methuen & Co., 1959.

TENNESSEE WILLIAMS (1914-   ) was born in Columbus, Ohio. Of his family he has said that "there was a combination of Puritan and Cavalier strains in my blood which may be accountable for the conflicting impulses I often represent in the people I write about." The family's move to St. Louis in 1926 brought the boy a sense of loss of social class; it is the "feel" of his own home milieu (though not its particulars) that he sketches in *The Glass Menagerie*. His college career during the depression was interrupted by a job as clerk in the shoe company for which his father was a salesman. He received his B.A.

degree from Iowa in 1938. After a succession of odd jobs (including Hollywood scriptwriting) he won recognition as playwright with *The Glass Menagerie* in 1945. Early in his career he substituted "Tennessee" (in honor of the state of his pioneer forefathers) for his given name, Thomas Lanier. His early works include poetry and fiction. He has written one novel, *The Roman Spring of Mrs. Stone* (1950).

Noteworthy in a long series of plays are *A Streetcar Named Desire* (1947, awarded the Pulitzer Prize), *Summer and Smoke* (1948), *The Rose Tattoo* (1951), the expressionistic *Camino Real* (1953), *Cat on a Hot Tin Roof* (1955, awarded the Pulitzer Prize), *Sweet Bird of Youth* (1959), *The Night of the Iguana* (1961). Several of his plays have been made into successful motion pictures, most of them representative of Hollywood's "new trend" in the treatment of sex. Among them are *Twenty-Seven Wagons Full of Cotton* (1946, filmed as *Baby Doll*) and *Suddenly Last Summer* (1957). Many critics have found his recent plays "decadent" denials of all human values. In an autobiographical sketch some years ago he called his "politics" "humanitarian."

Suggested Reading

Downer, Alan S., *Fifty Years of American Drama*. Chicago: Henry Regnery, 1951.

Jones, Robert E., "Tennessee Williams' Early Heroines," *Modern Drama*, II (1959), 211-219.

Lumley, Frederick, *Trends in Twentieth Century Drama*. London: Rockliff, 1956.

Nelson, Benjamin, *Tennessee Williams*. New York: Ivan Obelensky, 1961.

Popkin, Henry, "The Plays of Tennessee Williams," *Tulane Drama Review*, IV (Spring, 1960), 45-64.

Tischler, Nancy M., *Tennessee Williams*. New York: The Citadel Press, 1961.

Vowles, Richard B., "Tennessee Williams: The World of His Imagery," *Tulane Drama Review*, III (Dec., 1958), 51-56.

EUGÈNE IONESCO (1912-   ), though Romanian by birth, has lived most of his life in France and writes in French. For a few years he taught French in Bucharest; later he worked in a Paris publishing house. He started writing plays, he says, because he disliked the theater. Whether this means that he hoped to improve upon an unsatisfactory dramatic repetory or is simply another Ionescian paradox is hard to say. During the 1950's he became one of the most publicized and controversial of contemporary playwrights. Like the Irishman Samuel Beckett, Ionesco represents the "absurd" theater, and like Beckett he is almost constantly preoccupied with the failure of human communication, specifically with the disjunction of speech and meaning. Critical opinion about him ranges from the charge that his plays are "hollow and pretentious fakery" to enthusiastic approval of his cultivation of "pure" theater and comparisons with such diverse figures as Molière, Lewis Carroll, and Strindberg. Besides *The Lesson*, his best known plays are *The Bald Soprano* (1950), *The Chairs* (1952), and *Rhinoceros* (1960).

Suggested Reading

Fowler, W., "New French Theater," *Sewanee Review*, LXVII (Autumn, 1959), 643-657.

Grossvogel, David I., *The Self-Conscious Stage in Modern French Drama*. New York: Columbia University Press, 1958.

Ionesco, Eugène, "The World of Ionesco," *Tulane Drama Review*, III (Oct., 1958), 45-47.

Watson, Donald, "The Plays of Ionesco," *Tulane Drama Review*, III (Oct., 1958), 48-53.

SUGGESTED GENERAL READING

Theory

Barnet, Sylvan, *et al.*, eds., *Aspects of the Drama: A Handbook*. Boston: Little, Brown and Company, 1962.

Brooks, Cleanth, and Robert B. Heilman, *Understanding Drama: Twelve Plays*. New York: Henry Holt and Company, 1948.

Butcher, S. H., *Aristotle's Theory of Poetry and Fine Art*. New York: Dover Publications, 1951.

Clark, Barrett H., ed., *European Theories of Drama, with a Supplement on the American Drama*. New York: Crown Publishers, 1947.

Downer, Alan S., *The Art of the Play: An Anthology of Nine Plays*. New York: Henry Holt and Company, 1955.

Drew, Elizabeth, *Discovering Drama*. New York: W. W. Norton & Co., 1937.

Eliot, T. S., *Poetry and Drama*. Cambridge, Mass.: Harvard University Press, 1951.

Fergusson, Francis, *The Idea of a Theater*. Garden City, N.Y.: Doubleday & Company (Anchor Book), 1949.

Nicoll, Allardyce, *The Theory of Drama*. London: G. G. Harrap & Company, 1937.

Peacock, Ronald, *The Art of Drama*. London: Routledge & Kegan Paul, 1957.
Sewall, Richard B., *The Vision of Tragedy*. New Haven, Conn.: Yale University Press, 1959.
Thompson, Alan R., *The Anatomy of Drama*, 2nd ed. Berkeley, Calif.: University of California Press, 1946.

History and Criticism

Bentley, Eric, *In Search of Theater*. New York: Alfred A. Knopf, 1953.
———, *The Playwright as Thinker*. New York: Meridian Books, 1957.
Gassner, John, *Form and Idea in Modern Theatre*. New York: Dryden Press, 1956.
———, *Masters of the Drama*, 3rd rev. ed. New York: Dover Publications, 1954.
———, *The Theatre in Our Times*. New York: Crown Publishers, 1954.
Nicoll, Allardyce, *World Drama from Aeschylus to Anouilh*. London: G. G. Harrap & Company, 1949.
Steiner, George, *The Death of Tragedy*. New York: Alfred A. Knopf, 1961.

Theater Arts

Cole, Toby, and Helen Krich Chinoy, eds., *Actors on Acting*. New York: Crown Publishers, 1949.
Gorelik, Mordecai, *New Theatres for Old*. New York: S. French, 1940.
Macgowan, Kenneth, and William Melnitz, *The Living Stage: A History of the World Theater*. New York: Prentice-Hall, Inc., 1955. (A shorter version is *The Golden Ages of the Theater*, 1959.)
Stanislavsky, Constantin, *An Actor Prepares*, tr. Elizabeth Reynolds Hapgood. New York: Theatre Arts Books, 1936.

Reference

Hartnoll, Phyllis, ed., *The Oxford Companion to the Theatre*, 2nd ed. London: Oxford University Press, 1957.

Some Useful Collections of Plays

Bentley, Eric, ed., *The Play: A Critical Anthology*. New York: Prentice-Hall, 1951.
———, *The Modern Theatre*, I-VI. Garden City, N.Y.: Doubleday & Company (Anchor Books), 1955-1960.
Block, Haskell, and Robert Shedd, eds., *Masters of Modern Drama*. New York: Random House, 1961.

Gassner, John, ed., *Treasury of the Theatre*, I-II. New York: Simon and Schuster, 1950-1951.

Grene, David, and Richmond Lattimore, eds., *The Complete Greek Tragedies*, I-IV. University of Chicago Press, 1959.

Ulanov, Barry, ed., *Makers of the Modern Theater*. New York: Mc-Graw-Hill Book Co., 1961.

Watson, E. Bradlee, and Benfield Pressey, eds., *Contemporary Drama, 11 Plays*. New York: Charles Scribner's Sons, 1956.

———, *Contemporary Drama, 15 Plays*. New York: Charles Scribner's Sons, 1959.